AFTER POSTSTRUCTURALISM

THE HISTORY OF CONTINENTAL PHILOSOPHY

General Editor: Alan D. Schrift

1. Kant, Kantianism, and Idealism: The Origins of Continental Philosophy
Edited by Thomas Nenon

2. Nineteenth-Century Philosophy:
Revolutionary Responses to the Existing Order
Edited by Alan D. Schrift and Daniel Conway

3. The New Century: Bergsonism, Phenomenology, and
Responses to Modern Science
Edited by Keith Ansell-Pearson and Alan D. Schrift

4. Phenomenology: Responses and Developments
Edited by Leonard Lawlor

5. Critical Theory to Structuralism: Philosophy, Politics,
and the Human Sciences
Edited by David Ingram

6. Poststructuralism and Critical Theory's Second Generation
Edited by Alan D. Schrift

7. After Poststructuralism: Transitions and Transformations
Edited by Rosi Braidotti

8. Emerging Trends in Continental Philosophy
Edited by Todd May

AFTER POSTSTRUCTURALISM
TRANSITIONS AND TRANSFORMATIONS

Edited by Rosi Braidotti

VOLUME 7
THE HISTORY OF CONTINENTAL PHILOSOPHY

General Editor: Alan D. Schrift

ACUMEN

First published in 2010 by Acumen
First published in paperback by Acumen in 2013

Acumen Publishing Limited
4 Saddler Street
Durham
DH1 3NP

www.acumenpublishing.com

ISBN: 978-1-84465-615-8 (paperback)
ISBN: 978-1-84465-668-4 (paperback 8-volume set)
ISBN: 978-1-84465-217-4 (hardcover)
ISBN: 978-1-84465-219-8 (hardcover 8-volume set)

British Library Cataloguing-in-Publication Data
A catalogue record for this book is available from the British Library.

Typeset in Minion Pro.
Printed and bound in the UK by CPI Group (UK) Ltd, Croydon, CR0 4YY.

CONTENTS

Series Preface   vii
Contributors   xiii

Introduction   1
ROSI BRAIDOTTI

1. Postmodernism   13
   SIMON MALPAS

2. German philosophy after 1980: themes out of school   33
   DIETER THOMÄ

3. The structuralist legacy   55
   PATRICE MANIGLIER

4. Italian philosophy between 1980 and 1995   83
   SILVIA BENSO AND BRIAN SCHROEDER

5. Continental philosophy in the Czech Republic   111
   JOSEF FULKA, JR.

6. Third generation critical theory: Benhabib, Fraser, and Honneth   129
   AMY ALLEN

7. French and Italian Spinozism   149
   SIMON DUFFY

8. Radical democracy   169
   LASSE THOMASSEN

9. Cultural and postcolonial studies   187
   IAIN CHAMBERS

10. The "ethical turn" in continental philosophy in the 1980s   203
    ROBERT EAGLESTONE

11. Feminist philosophy: coming of age   221
    ROSI BRAIDOTTI

12. Continental philosophy of religion   247
    BRUCE ELLIS BENSON

13. The performative turn and the emergence of post-analytic
    philosophy   275
    JOSÉ MEDINA

14. Out of bounds: philosophy in an age of transition   307
    JUDITH BUTLER AND ROSI BRAIDOTTI

    Chronology   337
    Bibliography   355
    Index   385

SERIES PREFACE

"Continental philosophy" is itself a contested concept. For some, it is understood to be any philosophy after 1780 originating on the European continent (Germany, France, Italy, etc.). Such an understanding would make Georg von Wright or Rudolf Carnap – respectively, a Finnish-born philosopher of language and a German-born logician who taught for many years in the US – a "continental philosopher," an interpretation neither they nor their followers would easily accept. For others, "continental philosophy" refers to a style of philosophizing, one more attentive to the world of experience and less focused on a rigorous analysis of concepts or linguistic usage. In this and the accompanying seven volumes in this series, "continental philosophy" will be understood *historically* as a tradition that has its roots in several different ways of approaching and responding to Immanuel Kant's critical philosophy, a tradition that takes its definitive form at the beginning of the twentieth century as the phenomenological tradition, with its modern roots in the work of Edmund Husserl. As such, continental philosophy emerges as a tradition distinct from the tradition that has identified itself as "analytic" or "Anglo-American," and that locates its own origins in the logical analyses and philosophy of language of Gottlob Frege. Whether or not there is in fact a sharp divergence between the work of Husserl and Frege is itself a contested question, but what cannot be contested is that two distinct historical traditions emerged early in the twentieth century from these traditions' respective interpretations of Husserl (and Heidegger) and Frege (and Russell). The aim of this history of continental philosophy is to trace the developments in one of these traditions from its roots in Kant and his contemporaries through to its most recent manifestations. Together, these volumes present a coherent and comprehensive account of the continental philosophical tradition that offers readers a unique resource for understanding this tradition's complex and interconnected history.

Because history does not unfold in a perfectly linear fashion, telling the history of continental philosophy cannot simply take the form of a chronologically organized series of "great thinker" essays. And because continental philosophy has not developed in a vacuum, telling its history must attend to the impact of figures and developments outside philosophy (in the sciences, social sciences, mathematics, art, politics, and culture more generally) as well as to the work of some philosophers not usually associated with continental philosophy. Such a series also must attend to significant philosophical movements and schools of thought and to the extended influence of certain philosophers within this history, either because their careers spanned a period during which they engaged with a range of different theorists and theoretical positions or because their work has been appropriated and reinterpreted by subsequent thinkers. For these reasons, the volumes have been organized with an eye toward chronological development but, in so far as the years covered in each volume overlap those covered in the subsequent volume, they have been organized as well with the aim of coordinating certain philosophical developments that intersect in a fashion that is not always strictly chronological.

Volume 1 begins with the origins of continental philosophy in Kant and the earliest responses to his critical philosophy, and presents an overview of German idealism, the major movement in philosophy from the late eighteenth to the middle of the nineteenth century. In addition to Kant, the period covered in the first volume was dominated by Fichte, Schelling, and Hegel, and together their work influenced not just philosophy, but also art, theology, and politics. This volume thus covers Kant's younger contemporary Herder, and his readers Schiller and Schlegel – who shaped much of the subsequent reception of Kant in art, literature, and aesthetics; the "Young Hegelians" – including Bruno Bauer, Ludwig Feuerbach, and David Friedrich Strauss – whose writings would influence Engels and Marx; and the tradition of French utopian thinking in such figures as Saint-Simon, Fourier, and Proudhon. In addition to Kant's early critics – Jacobi, Reinhold, and Maimon – significant attention is also paid to the later critic of German idealism Arthur Schopenhauer, whose appropriation and criticism of theories of cognition later had a decisive influence on Friedrich Nietzsche.

Volume 2 addresses the second half of the nineteenth century, in part as a response to the dominance of Hegelian philosophy. These years saw revolutionary developments in both European politics and philosophy, and five great critics dominated the European intellectual scene: Feuerbach, Marx, Søren Kierkegaard, Fyodor Dostoevsky, and Nietzsche. Responding in various ways to Hegelian philosophy and to the shifting political landscape of Europe and the United States, these thinkers brought to philosophy two guiding orientations – materialism and existentialism – that introduced themes that would continue to play out throughout the twentieth century. The second half of the nineteenth century also saw the emergence of new schools of thought and new disciplinary thinking, including the birth of sociology and the social sciences, the development of French spiritualism, the beginning of American pragmatism, radical developments in science and mathematics, and the development of hermeneutics beyond the domains of theology and philology into an approach to understanding all varieties of human endeavor.

Volume 3 covers the period between the 1890s and 1930s, a period that witnessed revolutions in the arts, science, and society that set the agenda for the twentieth century. In philosophy, these years saw the beginnings of what would grow into two distinct approaches to doing philosophy: analytic and continental. It also saw the emergence of phenomenology as a new rigorous science, the birth of Freudian psychoanalysis, and the maturing of the discipline of sociology. Volume 3 thus examines the most influential work of a remarkable series of thinkers who reviewed, evaluated, and transformed nineteenth-century thought, among them Henri Bergson, Émile Durkheim, Sigmund Freud, Martin Heidegger, Edmund Husserl, Karl Jaspers, Max Scheler, and Ludwig Wittgenstein. It also initiated an approach to philosophizing that saw philosophy move from the lecture hall or the private study into an active engagement with the world, an approach that would continue to mark continental philosophy's subsequent history.

The developments and responses to phenomenology after Husserl are the focus of the essays in Volume 4. An ambiguity inherent in phenomenology – between conscious experience and structural conditions – lent itself to a range of interpretations. While some existentialists focused on applying phenomenology to the concrete data of human experience, others developed phenomenology as conscious experience in order to analyze ethics and religion. Still other phenomenologists developed notions of structural conditions to explore questions of science, mathematics, and conceptualization. Volume 4 covers all the major innovators in phenomenology – notably Sartre, Merleau-Ponty, and the later Heidegger – as well as its extension into religion, ethics, aesthetics, hermeneutics, and science.

Volume 5 concentrates on philosophical developments in political theory and the social sciences between 1920 and 1968, as European thinkers responded to the difficult and world-transforming events of the time. While some of the significant figures and movements of this period drew on phenomenology, many went back further into the continental tradition, looking to Kant or Hegel, Marx or Nietzsche, for philosophical inspiration. Key figures and movements discussed in this volume include Adorno, Horkheimer, and the Frankfurt School,

Schmitt, Marcuse, Benjamin, Arendt, Bataille, black existentialism, French Marxism, Saussure, and structuralism. These individuals and schools of thought responded to the "crisis of modernity" in different ways, but largely focused on what they perceived to be liberal democracy's betrayal of its own rationalist ideals of freedom, equality, and fraternity. One other point about the period covered in this volume is worthy of note: it is during these years that we see the initial spread of continental philosophy beyond the European continent. This happens largely because of the emigration of European Jewish intellectuals to the US and UK in the 1930s and 1940s, be it the temporary emigration of figures such as Adorno, Horkheimer, Lévi-Strauss, and Jakobson or the permanent emigration of Marcuse, Arendt, and Gurwitsch. As the succeeding volumes will attest, this becomes a central feature of continental philosophy's subsequent history.

Volume 6 examines the major figures associated with poststructuralism and the second generation of critical theory, the two dominant movements that emerged in the 1960s, which together brought continental philosophy to the forefront of scholarship in a variety of humanities and social science disciplines and set the agenda for philosophical thought on the continent and elsewhere from the 1960s to the present. In addition to essays that discuss the work of such influential thinkers as Althusser, Foucault, Deleuze, Derrida, Lyotard, Irigaray, Habermas, Serres, Bourdieu, and Rorty, Volume 6 also includes thematic essays on issues including the Nietzschean legacy, the linguistic turn in continental thinking, the phenomenological inheritance of Gadamer and Ricoeur, the influence of psychoanalysis, the emergence of feminist thought and a philosophy of sexual difference, and the importation of continental philosophy into literary theory.

Before turning to Volume 7, a few words on the *institutional* history of continental philosophy in the United States are in order, in part because the developments addressed in Volumes 6–8 cannot be fully appreciated without recognizing some of the events that conditioned their North American and anglophone reception. As has been mentioned, phenomenologists such as Alfred Schutz and Aron Gurwitsch, and other European continental philosophers such as Herbert Marcuse and Hannah Arendt, began relocating to the United States in the 1930s and 1940s. Many of these philosophers began their work in the United States at the University in Exile, established in 1933 as a graduate division of the New School for Social Research for displaced European intellectuals. While some continental philosophy was taught elsewhere around the United States (at Harvard University, Yale University, the University at Buffalo, and elsewhere), and while the journal *Philosophy and Phenomenological Research* began publishing in 1939, continental philosophy first truly began to become an institutional presence in the United States in the 1960s. In 1961, John Wild (1902–72) left Harvard to become Chair of the Department of Philosophy at Northwestern University. With a commitment from the provost of the university and the Northwestern University Press to enable him to launch the Northwestern Series in Phenomenology and Existential Philosophy, Wild joined William Earle and James Edie, thus making Northwestern a center for the study of continental philosophy. Wild set up an organizational committee including himself, Earle, Edie, George Schrader of Yale, and Calvin Schrag (a former student of Wild's at Harvard, who was teaching at Northwestern and had recently accepted an appointment at Purdue University), to establish a professional society devoted to the examination of recent continental philosophy. That organization, the Society for Phenomenology and Existential Philosophy (SPEP), held its first meeting at Northwestern in 1962, with Wild and Gurwitsch as the dominant figures arguing for an existential phenomenology or a more strictly Husserlian phenomenology, respectively. Others attending the small meeting included Erwin Straus, as well as Northwestern graduate students Edward Casey and Robert Scharff, and today SPEP has grown into the second largest society of philosophers in the United States. Since those early days, many smaller societies (Heidegger Circle, Husserl Circle, Nietzsche Society, etc.) have formed and many journals and graduate programs devoted to continental philosophy have appeared. In addition, many of the important continental philosophers who first became known in the 1960s – including Gadamer, Ricoeur, Foucault, Derrida, Lyotard, and Habermas – came to hold continuing appointments at major American universities (although, it must be mentioned, not always housed in departments of philosophy) and, since the 1960s, much of the transmission of continental philosophy has come directly through teaching as well as through publications.

The transatlantic migration of continental philosophy plays a central role in Volume 7, which looks at developments in continental philosophy between 1980 and 1995, a time of great upheaval and profound social change that saw the fruits of the continental works of the 1960s beginning to shift the center of gravity of continental philosophizing from the European continent to the anglophone philosophical world and, in particular, to North America. During these years, the pace of translation into English of French and German philosophical works from the early twentieth century as well as the very recent past increased tremendously, and it was not uncommon to find essays or lectures from significant European philosophers appearing first in English and then subsequently being published in French or German. In addition, the period covered in this volume also saw the spread of continental philosophy beyond the confines of philosophy departments, as students and faculty in centers of humanities and departments of comparative literature, communication studies, rhetoric, and other interdisciplinary fields increasingly drew on the work of recent continental philosophers. Volume 7 ranges across several developments during these years – the birth of postmodernism, the differing philosophical traditions of France, Germany, and Italy, the third generation of critical theory, and the so-called "ethical turn" – while also examining the extension of philosophy into questions of radical democracy, postcolonial theory, feminism, religion, and the rise of performativity and post-analytic philosophy. Fueled by an intense ethical and political desire to reflect changing social and political conditions, the philosophical work of this period reveals how continental thinkers responded to the changing world and to the key issues of the time, notably globalization, technology, and ethnicity.

The eighth and final volume in this series attempts to chart the most recent trends in continental philosophy, which has now developed into an approach to thinking that is present throughout the world and engaged with classical philosophical problems as well as current concerns. The essays in this volume focus more on thematic developments than individual figures as they explore how contemporary philosophers are drawing on the resources of the traditions surveyed in the preceding seven volumes to address issues relating to gender, race, politics, art, the environment, science, citizenship, and globalization. While by no means claiming to have the last word, this volume makes clear the dynamic and engaged quality of continental philosophy as it confronts some of the most pressing issues of the contemporary world.

As a designation, "continental philosophy" can be traced back at least as far as John Stuart Mill's *On Bentham and Coleridge* (1840), where he uses it to distinguish the British empiricism of Bentham from a tradition on the continent in which he sees the influence of Kant. Since that time, and especially since the early twentieth century, the term has been used to designate philosophies from a particular geographical region, or with a particular style (poetic or dialectical, rather than logical or scientistic). For some, it has been appropriated as an honorific, while for others it has been used more pejoratively or dismissively. Rather than enter into these polemics, what the volumes in this series have sought to do is make clear that one way to understand "continental philosophy" is as an approach to philosophy that is deeply engaged in reflecting on its own history, and that, as a consequence, it is important to understand the *history* of continental philosophy.

While each of the volumes in this series was organized by its respective editor as a volume that could stand alone, the eight volumes have been coordinated in order to highlight various points of contact, influence, or debate across the historical period that they collectively survey. To facilitate these connections across the eight volumes, cross-referencing footnotes have been added to many of the essays by the General Editor. To distinguish these footnotes from those of the authors, they are indicated by an asterisk (*).

Alan D. Schrift, General Editor

CONTRIBUTORS

Amy Allen is the Parents Distinguished Research Professor in the Humanities and Professor of Philosophy at Dartmouth College. Her work is situated at the intersection of the Frankfurt School tradition in critical theory, Foucaultian poststructuralism, and feminist theory, and focuses on the concepts of power, subjectivity, and autonomy. She is the author of *The Power of Feminist Theory: Domination, Resistance, Solidarity* (1999) and *The Politics of Our Selves: Power, Autonomy, and Gender in Contemporary Critical Theory* (2008), coeditor of the journal *Constellations: An International Journal of Critical and Democratic Theory*, and the editor of the book series New Directions in Critical Theory.

Silvia Benso is Professor of Philosophy at Rochester Institute of Technology, where she works in the areas of contemporary European philosophy and ancient philosophy. She is the author of *Pensare dopo Auschwitz: Etica filosofica e teodicea ebraica* (1992) and *The Face of Things: A Different Side of Ethics* (2000). With Brian Schroeder she is the coeditor of *Contemporary Italian Philosophy: Crossing the Borders of Ethics, Politics, and Religion* (2007) and *Between Nihilism and Politics: The Hermeneutics of Gianni Vattimo* (2010), and cotranslator of Carlo Sini's *Ethics of Writing* (2009) and Ugo Perone's *The Possible Present* (forthcoming). With Brian Schroeder she also coedits the series Contemporary Italian Philosophy.

Bruce Ellis Benson is Professor of Philosophy at Wheaton College (IL). He is the author of *Graven Ideologies: Nietzsche, Derrida and Marion on Modern Idolatry* (2002) and *Pious Nietzsche: Decadence and Dionysian Faith* (2007). He is coeditor of *The Phenomenology of Prayer* (with Norman Wirzba; 2005),

Hermeneutics at the Crossroads (with Kevin J. Vanhoozer and James K. A. Smith; 2006) and *Transforming Philosophy and Religion: Love's Wisdom* (with Norman Wirzba; 2008). His areas of research include continental philosophy of religion, Nietzsche, and political theology.

Rosi Braidotti is Distinguished University Professor at Utrecht University in the Netherlands and founding Director of the Centre for the Humanities at Utrecht University. She was the founding Chair and Professor of Women's Studies in the Arts Faculty of Utrecht University (1988–2005), Scientific Director of the Netherlands Research School of Women's Studies (1995–2005), set up the Network of Interdisciplinary Women's Studies in Europe (NOI♀SE) within the Erasmus Programme in 1989, and has been elected to the Australian Academy of the Humanities. She has published extensively in feminist philosophy, epistemology, poststructuralism, and psychoanalysis, and is the author of several books, including *Patterns of Dissonance* (1991), *Nomadic Subjects: Embodiment and Sexual Difference in Contemporary Feminist Theory* (1994, 2011 [2nd ed.]), *Metamorphoses: Towards a Materialist Theory of Becoming* (2002), and *Transpositions: On Nomadic Ethics* (2006), and *Nomadic Theory: The Portable Rosi Braidotti* (2011).

Judith Butler is Maxine Elliot Professor in the Departments of Rhetoric and Comparative Literature at the University of California, Berkeley. She is the author of *Subjects of Desire: Hegelian Reflections in Twentieth-Century France* (1987), *Gender Trouble: Feminism and the Subversion of Identity* (1990), *Bodies That Matter: On the Discursive Limits of "Sex"* (1993), *Excitable Speech* (1997), *The Psychic Life of Power: Theories of Subjection* (1997), *Antigone's Claim: Kinship Between Life and Death* (2000), *Hegemony, Contingency, Universality* (with Ernesto Laclau and Slavoj Žižek; 2000), *Precarious Life: Powers of Violence and Mourning* (2004), *Undoing Gender* (2004), *Giving an Account of Oneself* (2005), and *Frames of War: When is Life Grievable* (2009). A recipient of the Mellon Distinguished Achievement in the Humanities award (2009–12), she continues to write on cultural and literary theory, philosophy, psychoanalysis, feminism, and sexuality and gender as well as the politics of human rights, and is currently working on essays pertaining to Jewish philosophy, focusing on pre-Zionist criticisms of state violence, notions of cohabitation and remembrance.

Iain Chambers is Professor of Sociology, and teaches cultural and postcolonial studies of the Mediterranean, at the University of Naples, "Orientale." A former graduate of the Centre for Contemporary Cultural Studies, Birmingham, he is the author of *Urban Rhythms: Pop Music and Popular Culture* (1985), *Popular Culture: The Metropolitan Experience* (1986), *Border Dialogues* (1990), *Migrancy,*

Culture, Identity (1993), *Culture after Humanism* (2001), and *Mediterranean Crossings: The Politics of an Interrupted Modernity* (2007), and editor of *Esercizi di potere: Gramsci, Said e il postcoloniale* (2006), and *The Postcolonial Question: Common Skies, Divided Horizons* (with Lidia Curti; 1995).

Simon Duffy is a Senior Lecturer at Yale-NUS College, Singapore. His research interests include early modern philosophy, European philosophy, the history and philosophy of science, and bioethics. He is the author of *The Logic of Expression* (2006), *Deleuze and the History of Mathematics* (2013), and translator of Albert Lautman's *Mathematics, Ideas and the Physical Real* (2011).

Robert Eaglestone is Professor of Contemporary Literature and Thought at Royal Holloway, University of London. He works on contemporary literature and philosophy, and literary theory, and on Holocaust and genocide studies. He is the author of *Ethical Criticism: Reading after Levinas* (1997), *Doing English* (1999, 3rd ed. 2009), *Postmodernism and Holocaust Denial* (2001), and *The Holocaust and the Postmodern* (2004), and the editor of several books, most recently *J. M. Coetzee in Theory and Practice* (2009), and the *Blackwell Encyclopaedia of Literary and Cultural Theory*, volume 2 (2010). He is the series editor of the book series Routledge Critical Thinkers.

Josef Fulka, Jr. teaches modern philosophy and literary theory at the Faculty of Humanities, Charles University, Prague. He is the author of *Zmeškané setkání: Denis Diderot a myšleni 20. stoleti* (The missed encounter: Denis Diderot and twentieth century thought; 2004), and *Psychoanalýza a francouzské myšleni* (Psychoanalysis and contemporary French thought; 2008), and coauthor of *Michel Foucault: politika a estetika* (Michel Foucault: politics and aesthetics; with Pavel Barša, 2005). He translates from French (Althusser, Barthes, Chion, Derrida, Foucault, Kristeva, and others). His areas of research include psychoanalysis, contemporary French philosophy, and literary theory.

Simon Malpas is a lecturer of English Literature at Edinburgh University. He is the author of *Jean-Francois Lyotard* (2003) and *The Postmodern* (2005), and has edited *Postmodern Debates* (2001), *The New Aestheticism* (with John Joughin; 2003), and *The Routledge Companion to Critical Theory* (with Paul Wake; 2006), and has published articles on literature and philosophy, aesthetics, postmodernism, and Romanticism.

Patrice Maniglier is Maître de Conférences at the University of Paris Ouest-Nanterre-La Défense. Before coming to Nanterre, he was Lecturer at the University of Essex (2007–2012) and taught in several institutions in France, including

Nanterre, Lille, the École Normale Supérieure-Ulm and Nice School of Arts. He is the author of *La Vie enigmatique des signes, Saussure et la naissance du structuralisme* (2006) and many articles on structuralism and postwar French philosophy, where he argues for a reinterpretation and reactualization of structuralism and of the semiotic tradition. He is currently working on a book on the metaphysical stakes of structural anthropology.

José Medina is Associate Professor of Philosophy at Vanderbilt University. He works in philosophy of language, social and political philosophy, and philosophy of race. Medina's publications include the books *The Unity of Wittgenstein's Philosophy* (2002), *Language* (2005), and *Speaking from Elsewhere* (2006). He has also published two edited volumes: *Truth: Engagements Across Philosophical Traditions* (with David Wood; 2005) and *Identity and Ethnicity* (*The Journal of Speculative Philosophy*, April 2004).

Brian Schroeder is Professor and Chair of Philosophy and Director of Religious Studies at Rochester Institute of Technology. With Silvia Benso, he is coeditor of the book series Contemporary Italian Philosophy. The author of *Altered Ground: Levinas, History and Violence* (1996), he is, with Silvia Benso, coauthor of *Pensare ambientalista: Tra filosofia e ecologia* (2000), with whom he has also coedited *Contemporary Italian Philosophy: Crossing the Borders of Ethics, Politics, and Religion* (2007), *Levinas and the Ancients* (2008), and *Between Nihilism and Politics: The Hermeneutics of Gianni Vattimo* (2010), and cotranslated Carlo Sini's *Ethics of Writing* (2009) and Ugo Perone's *The Possible Present* (forthcoming). Schroeder's other edited books include *Thinking Through the Death of God* (2004) and *Japanese and Continental Philosophy: Conversations with the Kyoto School* (2010).

Dieter Thomä is Professor of Philosophy at the University of St. Gallen in Switzerland. He works in social philosophy, ethics, phenomenology, and aesthetics, and is the author of seven books: *Die Zeit des Selbst und die Zeit danach: Zur Kritik der Textgeschichte Martin Heideggers 1910–1976* (1990), *Eltern: Kleine Philosophie einer riskanten Lebensform* (1992), *Väter: Eine moderne Heldengeschichte* (2008), *Erzähle dich selbst: Lebensgeschichte als philosophisches Problem* (1998/2007), *Unter Amerikanern: Eine Lebensart wird besichtigt* (2000), *Vom Glück in der Moderne* (2003), and *Totalität und Mitleid* (2006). He is also the editor of *Analytische Philosophie der Liebe* (2000) and *Heidegger Handbuch: Leben, Werk, Wirkung* (2003).

Lasse Thomassen is Senior Lecturer in the School of Politics and International Relations at Queen Mary, University of London. His research focuses on tolerance discourse, the relationship between Derrida and Habermas, and theories of radical democracy. He is the author of *Deconstructing Habermas* (2007) and *Habermas: A Guide for the Perplexed* (2010), the editor of *The Derrida–Habermas Reader* (2006) and the coeditor of *Radical Democracy: Politics between Abundance and Lack* (2005).

INTRODUCTION

Rosi Braidotti

I. AFTER THE WALL

If there ever was an age of historical and philosophical transition, it would have to be the 1980–95 period that is addressed in this volume. Let us play with a few significant dates to illustrate the point: In 1979, the high priest of the radical libertarian Left Herbert Marcuse dies, followed in 1980 by the cofounder of existentialism, Jean-Paul Sartre, and by Jacques Lacan in 1981. With the death of General Tito, also in 1980, many start mourning the crisis of Western European Marxism, while a greater portion of the world youth is far more affected by the assassination of John Lennon, in New York, which also took place in the year of (dis)grace 1980. "Lennon, not Lenin!" had been a cry of revolutionary youth throughout the previous decade and it acquires a more poignant meaning at the dawn of the 1980s, as the fallout from the previous radical decades comes to a new and sharper focus.

In her seminal text *The Summer of 1980*, the French writer Marguerite Duras, who was also a member of the communist anti-Nazi resistance in her youth, comments extensively on the political events taking place in the Gdansk shipyard in Poland. Under the leadership of Lech Walesa (future Nobel Peace Prize winner) and the trade union Solidarity, Soviet hegemony is being challenged to the core. It is the beginning of the end for Soviet-style communism, announces Duras with barely contained joy. Paris had provided the world forum for progressive and even left-wing critiques of Soviet communism since the 1970s, and for the elaboration of alternative forms of political radicalism. This positions French philosophy as a particularly important factor in the philosophical landscape of the period under review in this volume. Two examples: Nobel Peace

1

Prize winner Alexander Solzhenitsyn's *Gulag Archipelago*, written in secrecy in the USSR as the definitive account of Stalin's death camps, was published in three volumes in Paris between 1973 and 1978. It provides the background for many of the poststructuralist philosophers' critiques of the failed social experiments of Soviet socialism, as well as extra ammunition for the conservatives' opposition to Marxism. The second significant event: Ayatollah Khomeini, the spiritual leader and political inspiration behind the Iranian Islamist revolution of 1979 was in exile in Paris in the years preceding the fall of the Shah. The 1980s is in many ways a decade dominated by the cultural and political energies emanating from Paris.

Then comes the landmark year 1989, which signals the fall of the Berlin Wall, the events of Tiananmen Square, and the opening of a new geopolitical era under the aegis of American domination. The philosophical implications of the historical defeat of communism are enormous: both theoretically and politically, the end of the Cold War marks the official rejection of Marxism as a platform for thinking and political organizing. Nineteen eighty-nine also marks the Soviet withdrawal from Afghanistan and the buildup of Islamist opposition that will consolidate Osama Bin Laden's power base in the region. An era of perpetual warfare seems to open after 1989, both in the Balkans and in the Gulf area.

For an era that proudly announced itself as marking the "end of ideology," the 1980s and 1990s witnessed a series of conservative ideological onslaughts, starting with the election of Margaret Thatcher as prime minister in the UK in 1979 and of Ronald Reagan as president in the US in 1980. The Christian-driven American Right celebrates both the end of history (Fukuyama) and the triumph of advanced capitalism as the highest point of human evolution. This conservative political ontology centered on American hegemony is unquestionably one of the offshoots of the end of the Cold War, and although it meets with robust opposition, especially in France after the election of François Mitterrand as president in 1981, it sets the tone for the fast-growing globalization project. Alain Touraine describes it as "one-way thought," that is to say, a unilateral approach to geopolitical affairs and a monological idea of social progress. In this regard, 1989 marks simultaneously the end of communism and the birth of neo-Marxist resistance: both the resurgence of neoliberal economics and its betrayal by neoconservative Christian and, later, Muslim fundamentalists. How and to what extent these in turn result in the renegotiation of the groundings of philosophical practice in this period is a crucial point for discussion.

It is striking, as one looks back over this period, to what extent issues of cultural identity and ideological belonging, of imperial and postcolonial legacies, and of new modes of resistance come to the fore. The Berlin Wall, in fact, fell on both sides, which means that this event challenges binary identity definitions in the former West as well as in the former East, and that it restructures discursive power relations accordingly. Post-Cold War scholarship can now begin, as Gayatri Spivak announces in *Death of a Discipline*: the "postcommunist" era in the East is matched by a global "postcolonial" era in the West, that is to say, a dual displacement of the core of formerly unitary and oppositional identities. Continental philosophy cannot avoid confrontation with these shifting relations and terms. Historical events unfold alongside each other and shift the axis of philosophical reflection across the board: the election of Benazir Bhutto as the first woman leader of an Islamic nation takes place in 1988; the liberation of Nobel Peace Prize-winning Nelson Mandela in 1990; the Maastricht Treaty is signed in 1992, the same year as the signing of the North American Free Trade Agreement (NAFTA), while the World Trade Organization (WTO) is set up in 1995.

This speed of events introduces new levels of complexity into the discussion of what counts as the basic unit of continental philosophy: Is it Europe? Which idea of Europe would that entail? And what might be its conceptual, ethnic, and territorial border? What is the legacy of the colonial and fascist past in the present discursive relations engendered by the practice of this discipline? The self-perception of the former West shifts towards a more acute awareness of its colonial and postcolonial legacy. The impetus for this revision does not originate in philosophy, but the discipline cannot fail to be affected by it. The dislocation of eurocentrism becomes a central concern and is especially important to the discussions about the new cosmopolitanism and non-Western humanism. In this volume we dedicate a chapter to the rise of cultural and ethnic studies and their impact on philosophy. This chapter should be approached as a marker of the philosophical relevance and the lasting legacy of anticolonial philosophies and postcolonial theories. These concerns are also featured elsewhere in *The History of Continental Philosophy* and should therefore be approached as transversal and recurrent concerns.

These developments affect also the world-historical and political project that is the European Union (EU). The construction of the EU, through the enlargement process, is made both possible and necessary by the postcommunist/postcolonial conjunction. This issue unfortunately still remains largely unexamined in philosophy, but *The History of Continental Philosophy* does recognize the emergence of the EU as a philosophical question and addresses it accordingly (in Volume 8). For this volume, we try to come to terms with it by devoting special attention to what one could define as philosophical area studies: we have specific chapters on German, Italian, and Czech philosophies, which try to assess whether the changing political context in continental Europe actually affects the practice and the agenda of continental philosophy.

In other words, our understanding of "continental philosophy" has broadened since philosophy extricated itself from the Cold War in 1989, in that philosophy needs to be redefined in a transnational manner in the context of globalization, postcommunism, and postcolonialism. As a result, continental philosophy is caught, more than ever, in a dialogue with and excursions into its multiple "outsides," both geopolitically and conceptually. This means that the contributors to this volume resist any attempt to flatten out the diversity of political traditions and histories within former Central and Eastern but also former Western Europe. We neither assume nor support any common metanarrative of postcommunist philosophy or any consensus about a post-1989 neoliberal world order, let alone the place and role of philosophy within it.

Because the contributors to this volume come from a great diversity of geopolitical locations, and because of the large number of Europe-based authors we have been able to gather, more reflection is needed in order to account for this diversity of locations. The specificity of our respective location, in the sense of a sociocultural history as well as a geopolitical position, needs to be taken into account as a factor that shapes post-1989 continental philosophy and leads to the contemporary developments that will be mapped out in this and also the last volume of *The History of Continental Philosophy*.

II. THAT POSTMODERNISM WHICH WAS NOT ONE

In other disciplines, notably cultural and film studies and comparative literature, the 1980s may count as the era of "high" postmodernism. Jean-François Lyotard's seminal text *The Postmodern Condition* appears in 1979, Fredric Jameson's equally influential *Postmodernism, or, the Cultural Logic of Late Capitalism* appears in 1991. In this period, the discipline of philosophy experiences a great deal of interdisciplinary expansion, as Judith Butler and I argue in this volume. This interdisciplinary drift – which is likely to horrify the philosophical purists – is philosophy's way of coping with the staggering technological and cultural developments of this era.

Again, let us look at some dates: 1980 is the year that Cable News Network (CNN) begins to provide twenty-four-hour television news coverage, while the watershed debut of MTV occurs in 1981. Madonna's first agenda-setting album is released in 1981, while Michael Jackson's legendary *Thriller* comes out in 1982. *The Oprah Winfrey Show* debuts in 1986, while the World Wide Web becomes publicly available on the internet in 1991.

The convergence between advanced technologies in the field of communication and information on the one hand, and the bioscientific domain on the other, contributes to accelerate the social and intellectual changes. Nineteen eighty-four fails to live up to the apocalyptic, proto-totalitarian scenario dreamed up by George Orwell in the throes of the Cold War. "Big Brother" will soon become the title of a globally successful reality television program and 1984 goes down in history as the year of publication of William Gibson's *Neuromancer*, the book that launches a thousand links and provides the imaginary to code the emerging phenomenon that is the internet. Michel Foucault's death is mourned by many that year, but the masses are more concerned about the disastrous outcome of the miners' strike in the UK, which will mark a resolute political victory for the neoliberal forces that back Thatcher. The rise of digital culture and the demise of the old Left stand side by side as landmarks of the era and mirror images of each other. As Donna Haraway publishes her paradigm-shifting text "A Cyborg Manifesto" in 1985, J. G. Ballard's *Crash* – first published as a novel in 1973, but issued as a film in 1996 – casts a more pensive but also more decadent shadow over the ongoing cybernetic revolution. The process of biogenetical recoding of reproduction, which opens in 1978 with the birth of the first test-tube baby, Louise Brown, culminates in 1996 with the cloning of Dolly the sheep, while the Human Genome Project is officially launched in 1990.

The posthuman element of the postmodern condition comes to the fore with increasing insistence throughout the period covered in this volume, making it redundant to wonder whether we are or ever were postmodern. This age of transition is so intense and speedy as to question the very status of what counts as human. Reflections of humanism, posthumanism and antihumanism, Western and non-Western humanism, increase within philosophy, contributing to the so-called "ethical turn," but also overcoming it in the direction of transnational and postcolonial perspectives. Philosophy's unresolved relationship to technology proves quite an obstacle in the discipline's attempt to stay relevant in a technologically mediated and globalized world.

The fact that most of the material in this volume is very contemporary and concerns philosophers who are still alive and writing has also a number of important methodological implications. The first is that by virtue of the ongoing nature of many movements of thought outlined in this volume, the contributors honored their commitment to the social relevance of philosophy by working hard to engage productively with the contradictions, paradoxes, and injustices of their historical context. Furthermore, given that so much of the contemporary context has to do with complex transformations, social mutations, and technological change, they encourage philosophy to think about processes rather than concepts. This is neither a simple nor a particularly welcome task in the theoretical language and disciplinary conventions that have become the norm in philosophical practice. The fact that theoretical reason is concept-bound and fastened on essential notions makes it difficult to find adequate representations for processes, fluid in-between flows of data, experience, and information. They tend to get frozen in spatial, metaphorical modes of representation that itemize them as "problems." As Gilles Deleuze puts it, the task of philosophy in our times is not to know who we are, but rather what, at last, we are in the process of becoming. Methodologically speaking, transitions require cartographies that are closer to weather maps than to strict synoptic tables. The contributors to this volume had the unenviable task of trying to capture processes, not single events, and detect collectively enforced movements, not just the rise of proper-noun celebrities. This calls for inventiveness as well as rigor.

This takes us to the second methodological implication: the criteria for the selection of the main texts and authors out of the ongoing processes this volume attempts to account for. Our hope is that decisions about what texts to include from the recent past do not claim to, nor do they objectively have the power to, actually create a canon. The selection therefore reflects something other than the lasting philosophical importance of the works cited. It is rather the case that the works that are mentioned are there to help historically contextualize the overall narrative about the 1980–95 period, more than to acknowledge the appearance of canonical works. The chronology that appears at the end of the volume serves essentially the purpose to align chronologically cultural, historical, and philosophical events so that they can resonate with each other. It is an event-based timeline for the period under scrutiny, which aims at emphasizing processes of change.

Another side effect of this methodological choice is that in this volume chronological linearity is replaced by a more complex kind of temporality. There are two main reasons for this added historico-temporal complexity; first, it reflects the main hypothesis of this volume, namely, that in the 1980–95 period philosophy "explodes" outwards in a number of interdisciplinary thematic and theoretical developments that ignore the canonical periodization of the institutional practice. Second, it fulfills a genealogical purpose that, given the new interdisciplinary orientation, forces many of the authors to cover a broader temporal frame that often begins long before 1980. For instance, the essay on French and Italian Spinozism has to look back to the earlier parts of the twentieth century in order to set the context for what emerges in the 1980s. Similarly, the chapter on postcolonial theory has to extend the time frame of this volume in order to account for philosophical events that are central to it, but took root much earlier. And the essays that explore philosophical developments in the national contexts of France, Germany, Italy, and the Czech Republic must also examine the genealogy of these developments in the intellectual influences and formations of the philosophers discussed.

A third methodological implication of the contemporaneity of the topics discussed here is that the speed of the social and political transformations of the period covered in this volume is itself an important factor. By the start of the third millennium, the social context has changed considerably since the days when the poststructuralist philosophers discussed in Volume 6 of *The History of Continental Philosophy* first put "difference" on the theoretical and political agenda. The return of biological essentialism, under the cover of genetics, molecular biology, evolutionary theories, and the despotic authority of DNA has caused both inflation and a reification of the notion of "difference." As the US celebrates its first black president, in Europe today contemporary racism celebrates rather than denies differences. In this reactionary discourse, however, cultural and ethnic differences are essentialized and attached to firm beliefs about national, regional, provincial, or even town-based parameters. In this context, however, difference is a term indexed on a hierarchy of values that it governs by exclusions through binary oppositions.

This political context makes it all the more important to return the post-poststructuralist and other philosophies of difference to their original progressive and even radical potential. After thirty years of postmodernist debates for, against, or undecided on the issue of the "nonunitary," split, in-process, knotted, rhizomatic, transitional, nomadic subjects, issues of fragmentation, complexity, and multiplicity have become part of philosophical terminology and practice. The relative popularity of these notions, however, and the radical-chic appeal of the terminology, does not make for consensus about the issues at stake. It is therefore urgent to assess the implications for contemporary culture and politics of the critiques of the subject that have been developed throughout the 1980s and 1990s. Much disagreement and cross-purpose arguments have been voiced as to the ethical and political issues that the question of the subject raises in contemporary culture and politics. In other words, the "so what?" part of the discussion on philosophical subjectivity is more open than ever, while the contradictions and the paradoxes of our historical condition pile up around us. This volume accordingly gives ample space to the ethical turn, to issues of epistemology, and to the redefinition of the political. These mark major shifts of the categorical distinctions among different branches of philosophy and return to the basic questions about the values, norms, and criteria that philosophy can offer to a fast-changing world.

The volume has been organized according to a rhythmic sequence that groups the chapters in significant clusters. We open with Simon Malpas and the keynote concept of postmodernism, which is contextualized in the political context of advanced capitalism, marked by both fast social change and high levels of cultural anxiety. The unprecedented rate and type of technological developments led by advanced technologies results in critical questioning of the Enlightenment notions of the self-regulating and intrinsically liberating powers of scientific rationality, for instance in the work of Jean Baudrillard, Fredric Jameson, and Jean-François Lyotard. As advanced societies slide toward a culture of digital simulation and virtual reality, the social nexus that held together the Enlightenment project of European modernity slackens off. This requires new critical interventions on the part of philosophers.

There follows a cluster of essays that aim to outline relevant philosophical developments in the field in a number of different national contexts. In "German Philosophy after 1980: Themes Out of School," Dieter Thomä argues that a dissolution of boundaries takes place in this period not only between continental and analytic philosophy, but also within them. He points to the alliance between Habermas and Derrida, or to Honneth reading Levinas, as clear indication that the labels of the old philosophical "schools" lose much of their relevance in the period under scrutiny in this volume and require more creativity on our part. Writing from France about the lasting legacy of that generation, Patrice Maniglier addresses "The Structuralist Legacy." He emphasizes the importance of the theory of subjectivity that sustains the epistemological core of structuralism. By analyzing the agenda-setting journal *Cahiers pour l'analyse* and stressing the structuralists' interest in the ontological nature of the dynamic unity of subjectivity, Maniglier draws illuminating connections between Althusser, Lacan, Lévi-Strauss and contemporary developments by Badiou, Balibar, and Lecourt. "Italian Philosophy Between 1980 and 1995," by Silvia Benso and Brian Schroeder, explores a historical context marked by the rigid separation of three cultural domains: the Catholic area, the secularist, and the Marxist thinkers. These domains affect and frame the reception and local developments of wider movements of thought, resulting in three main strands: the crisis of reason and subjectivity, modernity and postmodernity, and hermeneutics and "weak thought." In his chapter on "Continental Philosophy in the Czech Republic," Josef Fulka, Jr. adds a much needed note from the eastern side of the former Berlin Wall. By focusing on political and theoretical development in the Czech Republic and especially the thought of Jan Patočka, Fulka traces also the intense and often informal networks of philosophical exchanges that connected East to West during the Cold War. He also highlights the important role played by French philosophy as a harbinger of democracy and freedom.

It is evident that the range of essays included in this section is not exhaustive but is at best a selective choice necessitated by the limitations of size and scope of the volume. The selection could have been expanded to include similar developments both within the European Union and elsewhere in the world. The case of Spain and of Spanish philosophy comes to mind as a particularly relevant one, considering the wealth and continuity of philosophical tradition it offers in the works of, for example, Eugenio Trías Sagnier (1942– ; considered by many the most important Spanish philosopher since Ortega y Gasset), ethical philosopher Fernando Fernández-Savater Martín (1947– ; who follows in the tradition of Nietzsche and Emil Cioran), and critical and postcolonial theorist Eduardo Subirats (1947–). Philosophical thought in Asia, notably the adaptation of phenomenology to traditions of thought in China, Korea, and, in particular, Japan should also have received more attention than we could grant them here.[1] However regrettable, such omissions are inevitable in a volume that aims not at exhaustiveness but rather at tracking the developments of the main traditions of continental German and French philosophies not only in their home countries but more especially in the diasporic mode that is central to the period covered in this volume. The central hypothesis that sustains the selection made here in fact is that continental philosophy after poststructuralism explodes outside the established institutional and disciplinary framework and goes nomadic. Tracking this diasporic move fully would require more space and resources than we could mobilize here. It might be more fitting therefore to read these essays on different national contexts as fulfilling an exemplary function. This is particularly true of the only essay that explicitly examines continental philosophical developments in Eastern Europe: the chapter on the Czech Republic should be approached as representative of the vitality of philosophy behind the Iron Curtain and of its expansion after 1989, rather than as a compre-

---

1. Nishida Kitaro (1870–1945), widely considered modern Japan's first original philosopher, introduced Husserl's work to Japan, thus beginning a long tradition of Japanese phenomenological and postphenomenological philosophy. Taking its point of departure from the thinking of Nishida, the "Kyoto School" – whose name was coined by Tosaka Jun (1900–1945) in 1932 – came into its own via Nishida's younger colleagues and successors Tanabe Hajime (1885–1962) and Nishitani Keiji (1900–1990), who, through their original contributions, helped shape and solidify the school's early identity by their association with contemporary European thinking of the day. Both Tanabe and Nishitani studied in Germany during the years between the First and Second World Wars (Tanabe in 1922–24, Nishitani in 1936–39). Tanabe, whose formation in Western philosophy was grounded in Kant and German idealism, had gone to Germany to explore the relation between Kant's transcendental logic, Bergson's vitalism, and Husserl's phenomenology, but encountered the work of the young Heidegger, who impressed him with his "phenomenology of life." On his return to Japan, Tanabe wrote the first article in the world on Heidegger's thought. Nishitani, who wrote a dissertation on Schelling and Bergson, returned from Germany to Japan where he became perhaps the most influential proponent of Heideggerian philosophy and an even stronger proponent of Nietzsche, with whose thought Heidegger was actively engaged at the time. Kuki Shūzō (1888–1941) also traveled to Germany, where he studied with Husserl, Heidegger, and Rickert before traveling to Paris in 1928, where he hired, as a French tutor, a young Jean-Paul Sartre, and it has been claimed that it was Kuki who first interested Sartre in Heidegger's philosophy (see Graham Parkes, *Heidegger and Asian Philosophy* [Honolulu, HI: University of Hawaii Press, 1990], 158). Kuki wrote the first book-length study of Heidegger (*The Philosophy of Heidegger*, 1933). Heidegger's *Sein und Zeit*, published in 1927, appeared in Japanese translation in 1939, while an English translation did not appear until 1962 and a complete French translation not until 1985. More recently, continental philosophical themes have appeared in the work of Kojin Karatani (1941– ; *Transcritique: On Kant and Marx* [2001], Sabu Kohso [trans.] [Cambridge, MA: MIT Press, 2003]), Akira Asada (1957–), and Kuniichi Uno (1948–). For a critical exploration of the relation between the Kyoto School and continental philosophers, see Bret W. Davis *et al.* (eds), *Japanese and Continental Philosophy: Conversations with the Kyoto School* (Bloomington, IN: University of Indiana Press, 2010).

hensive or definitive survey of the importation of continental philosophy into Eastern Europe after 1980.

The next cluster of essays addresses more directly issues in political philosophy. Amy Allen, in "Third Generation Critical Theory: Benhabib, Fraser, and Honneth," examines the work of Habermas's three most prolific students as they critically engage his reorientation of critical theory toward normative justifications, the pragmatics of language, and the discourse theory of morality, law, and politics. "French and Italian Spinozism," by Simon Duffy, on the other hand, traces the development of an alternative ethics inspired by French philosophers' innovative take on Spinoza. Spinozist materialism as the antidote to Hegelian idealism becomes one of the driving forces in poststructuralist innovations in thinking the political in the work of Étienne Balibar, Pierre Macherey, Gilles Deleuze, and Antonio Negri. This line is pursued and expanded by Lasse Thomassen in "Radical Democracy," which is presented as an antifoundationalist approach to democratic politics. Focusing on thinkers such as William E. Connolly, Ernesto Laclau, Chantal Mouffe, and Slavoj Žižek, Thomassen explores the longer-term political implications of poststructuralism.

A cluster on new normative approaches to philosophy opens with "Cultural and Postcolonial Studies" by Iain Chambers. He highlights the innovative force of the interdisciplinary field of race and postcolonial theory, mostly in the work of Stuart Hall, Paul Gilroy, and Gayatri Spivak. The innovation is both political and conceptual in that it highlights the critique of racialized power relations while rejecting black essentialism or any kind of essentialism. Chambers also bring out the wealth of philosophical texts generated by anticolonial politics and pleads for a reappraisal of their importance for a contemporary history of philosophical thought. "The 'Ethical Turn' in Continental Philosophy in the 1980s," by Robert Eaglestone, takes the influential figure of Levinas as the lead in sketching the phenomenon of a return to issues of norms and values in the period covered by this volume. Both in reaction to the structural injustices of globalization, and as the effect of poststructuralist critiques, ethics emerges as the main forum for debates about contemporary subjectivity. In my own essay "Feminist Philosophy: Coming of Age," I explore the explosion of scholarly work in this field after poststructuralism. I argue that an interdisciplinary impetus as well as radical politics drive the "intermediate" generation's work in developing the insights of "high" poststructuralism toward new understandings of what is the matter with materialism and the materiality of the sign. Bruce Ellis Benson's contribution, "Continental Philosophy of Religion," analyzes the theological turn, mostly in French philosophy, with special emphasis on Jean-Louis Chrétien, Jacques Derrida, Michel Henry, Emmanuel Levinas, Jean-Luc Marion, and Paul Ricoeur. The chapter traces its definition and development, as well as the ways in which theological and religious concerns affect not only philosophical discourse but also phenomenology's very structure as a theologically neutral discourse. "The Performative Turn and the Emergence of Post-Analytic Philosophy," by José Medina, follows the lead of the linguistic turn as a thread that runs through both analytic and continental philosophy. This achieves a double result: it develops new perspectives at the intersection of the great schools, but it also challenges the categorical distinctions between them. Again interdisciplinary in approach, post-analytic thought addresses issues of identity, knowledge, and values that reach well beyond the confines of academic philosophy.

This is precisely the theme addressed by the essay that closes this volume: "Out of Bounds: Philosophy in an Age of Transition," by Judith Butler and myself. The chapter documents the interdisciplinary explosion of the discipline in the 1980–95 period and the extent to which this extracurricular vitality challenges the traditional disciplinary constraints. The nonacademic energy of philosophy in this period is sustained by an intense political desire to reflect the changing historical and social conditions of a world that is rapidly becoming globally linked, technologically mediated, and ethnically mixed. That challenge continues and grows in quantity and quality in the following decades, decades that are addressed in the eighth and closing volume of *The History of Continental Philosophy*.

1

POSTMODERNISM

Simon Malpas

> Simplifying to the extreme, I define *postmodern* as incredulity
> toward metanarratives. ... To the obsolescence of the metanarra-
> tive apparatus of legitimation corresponds, most notably, the crisis
> of metaphysical philosophy and of the university institution which
> in the past relied on it. The narrative function is losing its functors,
> its great hero, its great dangers, its great voyages, its great goal.
>
> (Lyotard, *The Postmodern Condition*)[1]

Although by no means the first instance of the term "postmodern," this is
probably one of the most immediately recognizable. The publication in 1979
of Jean-François Lyotard's *La Condition postmoderne: Rapport sur le savoir* –
an investigation into "the condition of knowledge in the most highly developed societies"[2] commissioned by the Council of Universities of the Provincial
Government of Quebec – provides a useful moment at which to locate the beginning of a very rapid spread of postmodernism as a subject of theoretical and
philosophical discussion throughout a wide range of academic disciplines and,
beyond them, across the media and culture of the developed world. The worldview presented in Lyotard's book encapsulates the sense of change that was in
the air at the beginning of the period covered in this volume of *The History of
Continental Philosophy*, and anticipates what would become for people across
the globe some of the defining experiences of the final decades of the twentieth

---

1. Jean-François Lyotard, *The Postmodern Condition: A Report on Knowledge*, Geoff Bennington
   and Brian Massumi (trans.) (Minneapolis, MN: University of Minnesota Press, 1984), xxiv.
2. *Ibid.*, xxiii.

century. At the beginning of the 1980s, with the elections that brought Ronald Reagan's and Margaret Thatcher's new breeds of monetarist economics, market deregulation, and ideologies of aggressively anti-welfare-state individualism to the US and UK, Lyotard's invocation of the transformation of knowledge from an end in its own right into just one more product to be bought and sold in an international marketplace seemed to many to capture the spirit of the time. The "great goals" of Enlightenment philosophy – truth and emancipation – appeared to be replaced by new, less apparently noble objectives as knowledge became the quintessential commodity for a postmodern consumer society: "Knowledge is and will be produced in order to be sold," Lyotard declared, "it is and will be consumed in order to be valorized in a new production: in both cases, the goal is exchange."[3] In this sense, postmodernism located knowledge within the newly deregulated markets that came quickly to define the experience of economic life in the 1980s.

Alongside this commodification of knowledge, the period also saw radical innovations in communications media with the rapid development of the internet, the spread of digital telephony, and the ever-increasing numbers of radio and television channels catering to more specialized tastes, all of which created a sense of more and more complex and fragmented modes of production, interaction, and exchange. The collapse of the Berlin Wall in 1989 and the dissolution of the Soviet Union led some in the West to declare not just victory in the Cold War but, as the title of Francis Fukuyama's 1992 book put it, the "end of history" itself with the triumph of a US form of "free-market democracy" and what President George Bush (senior) was to call a "New World Order." It appeared for a time that economically, politically, socially, and culturally the global order was changing, and for many commentators the theories and arguments of those philosophies grouped beneath the banner of postmodernism best captured the opportunities and threats this new world might have to offer. Even if Lyotard's particular responses to this change have frequently been questioned and challenged, the general sense that the world was in the process of undergoing a profound transformation rapidly developed into a key topic for debate, and the term "postmodern" became increasingly ubiquitous as the designation of this new "condition."

There were moments in the 1980s and 1990s where it seemed that every new innovation, idea, and artifact had to be hailed or dismissed as "postmodern," where discussions of culture were obliged to invoke the term to identify anything even remotely contemporary, and its deployment by journalists, commentators, critics, and students was practically mandatory. For better or worse, by 1995 it had become clear to many that, although the meaning of the term was

---

3. *Ibid.*, 4.

anything but certain, Western culture and society had incontrovertibly become "postmodern." One consequence of this, and a key difficulty for any attempt to delineate precisely what the term designates, is that precise analytical definitions of the postmodern in such works as Lyotard's quickly became difficult to discern among the myriad mass-media and popular-cultural invocations. Some thinkers, faced with such confusion, explicitly renounced the term's association with their work: for example, both Derrida and Foucault reject the application of postmodernism as a label for their work, with Foucault going so far as to claim that he has no idea what it might mean.[4] Separating out a rigorously philosophical postmodernism from the significantly wider phenomenon that shaped many aspects of the cultural climate of Europe and North America during the 1980s and 1990s is no easy task.

This, though, is the aim here: to isolate and identify some of the key philosophical problems and arguments associated with postmodernism. Rather than attempting to encompass the countless different definitions provided by commentators from the whole range of humanities and social science disciplines, the objective is to explore postmodernism's engagement with some of the problems and ideas it inherits from the continental philosophical tradition. For the purposes of this essay, then, the focus will fall predominantly on the work of the three most central and influential postmodern philosophers of the period: Fredric Jameson, Jean Baudrillard, and Lyotard.[5] The aim is to outline the key tenets of their definitions of the postmodern, to produce a brief account of the philosophical contexts in which their work might be located, and to explore their influence on the broader thought and culture of the period.

Beginning with Jameson, the chapter will outline his arguments about the disruption of modern identity through the pastiche and schizophrenia generated in contemporary consumer society, and explore his critique of the idea of a loss of critical distance in postmodernist culture. The chapter will then introduce some of Baudrillard's attempts to reorient philosophy, including the moves from a representational to a simulation-focused epistemology, from a Marxist production-orientated analysis of society to one driven by a thinking of consumption, from ethics to seduction and – in what is perhaps his most controversial work on such topics as the Gulf War and international terrorism – from

---

4. See Jacques Derrida, "Some Statements and Truisms about Neologisms, Newisms, Postisms, Parasitisms, and Other Small Seismisms," in *The States of "Theory": History, Art, and Critical Discourse*, David Carroll (ed.) (New York: Columbia University Press, 1990), and Michel Foucault, "Critical Theory/Intellectual History," Jeremy Harding (trans.), in *Politics, Philosophy, Culture: Interviews and Other Writings, 1977–1984*, Lawrence D. Kritzman (ed.) (New York: Routledge, 1988), 34.

*5. For a discussion of Lyotard's philosophy more generally, see the essay by James Williams in *The History of Continental Philosophy: Volume 6*.

oppositional critique to the ironic detachment of "skeptical intelligence." Moving on to Lyotard's more robustly pro-postmodern formulations, it will then discuss his analyses of the breakdown of modernity's master narratives, his rethinking of Kantian reflective judgment, and his transformation of the category of the sublime, in order to facilitate explorations of the unpresentable, the differend, and the event.

I. THE DEATH OF THE SUBJECT IN LATE CAPITALISM

According to Jameson,[6] a key aspect of postmodernism is "the 'death' of the subject itself – the end of the bourgeois monad or ego or individual."[7] The Cartesian subject, the keystone of modern philosophy, politics, and social science, loses its purchase in a postmodern world, and with it go modernist conceptions of aesthetic form, representation, critique, and collective politics. For Jameson, the disruption of such categories is the most profound and troubling aspect of the move to postmodernism. The causes and consequences of the death of the subject are central to his influential definition of postmodernism as "the cultural logic of late capitalism" in his important essay "Postmodernism, or, the Cultural Logic of Late Capitalism," first published in the journal *New Left Review* in 1984, and expanded into a book with the same title in 1991. In these texts, Jameson develops an analysis of postmodernism that presents it as the cultural consequence of a transformation of capitalist economics in the second half of the twentieth century and seeks a means by which radical political critique might be able to continue in the contemporary world. He defines "late capitalism" as a "world capitalist system fundamentally distinct from the older imperialism"[8] in which the globalization of stock-market speculation, the movement of industrial production to developing countries by multinational business, increasing automation and computerization, and the disruption and dispersal of the proletariat of classical Marxism give rise to new forms of identity, experience, and culture that can be called "postmodern." The result of this,

---

6. Fredric Jameson (April 14, 1934– ; born in Cleveland, Ohio) received a BA from Haverford College (1954), and MA and PhD from Yale University (1956, 1959). His influences include Freud, Hegel, Lacan, Lukács, Mandel, Marx, and Sartre. He has held appointments at Harvard University (1961–67), in French and comparative literature at the University of California, San Diego (1967–76), in French at Yale University (1976–83), in literature and history of consciousness at the University of California, Santa Cruz (1983–85), and in comparative literature at Duke University (1986–).

7. Fredric Jameson, *Postmodernism, or, the Cultural Logic of Late Capitalism* (Durham, NC: Duke University Press, 1991), 15.

8. *Ibid.*, 3.

according to Jameson, is that "every position on postmodernism in culture ... is also at one and the same time, and *necessarily*, an implicitly or explicitly political stance on the nature of multinational capitalism today."[9] This is crucial: for Jameson, the innovation and experimentation of contemporary artistic and cultural production can be grasped only as an expression of the transformed conditions of modern society, politics, and economics.

On the basis of this account of postmodernism as the superstructural expression of the development of global capitalism, Jameson presents a historically materialist-inflected analysis of contemporary culture in terms of the commodification of aesthetic experience:

> Aesthetic production today has become integrated into commodity production generally: the frantic economic urgency of producing fresh waves of ever more novel-seeming goods (from clothing to aeroplanes), at ever greater rates of turnover, now assigns an increasingly essential structural function and position to aesthetic innovation and experimentation.[10]

This focus on the aesthetics of production and the consumption of aesthetic affect is crucial to his analysis of contemporary experience, identity, and politics. In a series of discussions of art, poetry, architecture, cinema, and television, Jameson traces the movement from what he identifies as the modernist idea of cultural practice as a vehicle that contests and parodically undermines bourgeois assumptions about the world to what he sees as the significantly less challenging postmodern notion of cultural production as having become just another aspect of commodity exchange and thereby lacking a critical edge. Modernist parody, he argues, has degenerated into little more than "blank pastiche" as art mixes and matches elements and fragments of everyday life without any sense of critical engagement or challenge, and in doing so has lost touch with the materiality of existence and community.

More generally, what is at stake in the commodification of aesthetic production is what Jameson sees as an increasing aestheticization of day-to-day identity: the key focus of production and consumption in late capitalism is the generation and marketing of images, lifestyles, and modes of being. The Western consumer purchases identities in the shape of everything from fashionable brands whose advertisements hold out the promise of spontaneous personal fulfillment as one joins the "smart set" to empty signifiers of identity such as trendy ringtones for mobile telephones that are designed less to inform

---

9. *Ibid.*
10. *Ibid.*, 4–5.

us that we have a call than to tell those around us how cool we are and which cultural clique we have bought our way into. "Postmodernism," Jameson asserts, "is the consumption of sheer commodification as a process."[11] Commodities are no longer simply objects; they are brands, identities, ways of forging personalities and communities in a world that, he claims, has lost touch with traditional senses of being in common.

Jameson illustrates this process by contrasting two works of art: Vincent Van Gogh's *A Pair of Boots* – which also formed the focus of Martin Heidegger's seminal essay "The Origin of the Work of Art"[12] and from which Jameson draws ideas – with Andy Warhol's *Diamond Dust Shoes*. Unlike the former, which presents "the whole object world of agricultural misery," the latter, he argues, "no longer speaks to us with any of the immediacy of Van Gogh" nor even provides "a minimal place for the viewer" in a work that simply embraces the "commodity fetishism" rather than offering any form of critique.[13] Shorn of context and history, Warhol's shoes are presented immediately as a random collection of desirable commodities without the depth of community or history.

This postmodern consumption of images has, in its turn, a profound effect on identity. Commodified and aestheticized by the ubiquitous and all-encompassing fashion and marketing industries, the world "comes before the subject with heightened intensity, bearing a mysterious charge of affect, here described in the negative terms of anxiety and loss of reality, but which one could just as well imagine in the positive terms of euphoria, a high, and intoxicatory or hallucinogenic intensity,"[14] which Jameson identifies with schizophrenia. Caught up in the infinite transformation and interchangeability of fashions and commodities, which are all the postmodern subject has to ground her or his sense of identity, the rapid alternations between anxiety and euphoria disable any potential for objective analysis or understanding of self or world. The consequences of contemporary culture's schizophrenic intensity are a destruction of subjective identity, a loss of a sense of history, and a disruption of the ability to engage with the real:

> Cultural production is thereby driven back inside a mental space which is no longer that of the old monadic subject but rather that of some degraded collective "objective spirit": it can no longer gaze directly on some putative real world, at some reconstruction of a

---

11. *Ibid.*, x.
*12. For a discussion of Heidegger's "The Origin of the Work of Art," see the essay by Galen A. Johnson in *The History of Continental Philosophy: Volume 4*.
13. Jameson, *Postmodernism*, 9.
14. *Ibid.*, 27–8.

past history which was once present; rather, as in Plato's cave, it must trace our mental images of that past upon its confining walls.[15]

Enclosed in the illusory world of the postmodern commodity, in the degraded objectivity of infinite financial exchange, the subject loses all sense of a real, all access to history and any ability to form or maintain firm distinctions between self, other, and world.

The loss of critical distance in the schizophrenic depthlessness of postmodern culture, Jameson argues, appears to disable modern forms of political critique and collective action. If an artistic or philosophical challenge to late capitalism is to be mounted and modern forms of political resistance and organization are to be re-enabled in the contemporary world, radical critique must begin with the rediscovery of the forms of identity and agency that stood at the core of the modern subject: "the practical reconquest of a sense of place and the construction or reconstruction of an articulated ensemble which can be retained in memory and which the individual can map and remap along the moments of mobile alternative trajectories."[16] In other words, Jameson calls for a process of critique that allows the subject to reorient herself or himself through a process of "cognitive mapping" that generates a "situational representation" from the mass of images and commodities that make up the experience of everyday life in order to make apparent the "vaster and properly unrepresentable totality which is the ensemble of society's structures as a whole."[17] A coherent political response to the postmodern superstructure of our late-capitalist world must, according to Jameson, begin with a reorientation of experience in order to ground the subject in a manner that allows the revivification of modern political categories. Whether postmodern culture is able to provide the resources for this, he argues, remains an open question.

II. SIMULATION, HYPERREALITY, AND THE "END OF HISTORY"

Just as it does for Jameson, the problem of a loss of critical distance plays a crucial role in the work of Baudrillard:[18] it is "the perfect crime" of postmodern

---

15. *Ibid.*, 25.

16. *Ibid.*, 51.

17. *Ibid.*

18. Jean Baudrillard (July 29, 1929–March 6, 2007; born in Rheims, France; died in Paris) received a PhD in sociology, and the habilitation, from the University of Paris X–Nanterre (1966, 1972). His influences include Bataille, Debord, Freud, Lefebvre, Marx, Mauss, McLuhan, and Nietzsche, and he held appointments at the University of Paris X–Nanterre (1966–86), and

culture, "the murder of reality."[19] If the former's analysis of the postmodern superstructure of late capitalism focuses on the problematic of subjective orientation, Baudrillard's diagnosis of the challenges of the postmodern world presents contemporary culture as a perverse "hyperreal" literalization of G. W. F. Hegel's assertion about the relation between the real and the rational in the Preface to *The Philosophy of Right* (1820):

> There is no longer any critical and speculative distance between the real and the rational. There is no longer really even any projection of models in the real … but an in-the-field, here-and-now transfiguration of the real into model. A fantastic short-circuit: the real is hyperrealized. Neither realized nor idealized: but hyperrealized. The hyperreal is the abolition of the real not by violent distinction, but by its assumption, elevation to the strength of the model.[20]

For Baudrillard, postmodernism marks the point at which the real has been entirely replaced and "transfigured" by rationalized models with the result that any possibility of a "critical and speculative distance" between them has collapsed. If, as Hegel argues, the movement of history can be understood in terms of a progressive transformation of rationality's grasp of reality by means of ideas, practices, and institutions that develop dialectically to overcome particular forms of impasse thrown up by the contradictions inherent in this movement, Baudrillard presents the postmodern as a moment at which this process has been bypassed in a "fantastic short-circuit" generated by the immediacy of a technological hyperreality in which the rational/actual "distinction" of modernity is simply abolished "by its assumption," "elevation," and "transfiguration" into the postmodern "model." Modern history, on this reading, has run its course, and the orientation it once offered to speculative dialectical philosophy has disappeared. The consequences of Baudrillard's discussion of the "end of history," however, are quite different from those presented in the readings of Hegel that see his work as aimed at the realization of universal freedom as well as from the so-called "good news" about the final triumph of North American free-market democracy over its various political alternatives that is announced in Fukuyama's *The End of History and the Last Man*. Instead, according to Baudrillard, this postmodern end of history marks the absolute annihilation of critical distance and the disruption rather than completion of modern political

---

at the Institut de Recherche et d'Information Socio-Économique (IRIS) at the University of Paris IX–Dauphine (1986–90).

19. Jean Baudrillard, *The Perfect Crime*, Chris Turner (trans.) (London: Verso, 1996), 1.
20. Jean Baudrillard, *Simulations*, Paul Foss *et al.* (trans.) (New York: Semiotext(e), 1983), 83–4.

thought: we can no longer use reason to map the real because, owing to the precision, complexity, and ubiquity of contemporary modelling systems, any resistance or difference that allowed the latter to remain distinct has vanished. What Baudrillard means by this is that with the advent of new sciences and technologies, the models that can be produced to understand the world have become more real, more sophisticated, and more accurate than reality itself. He depicts this process by evoking a telling inversion of the image of the "perfect" map from Jorge Luis Borges's short story "On Exactitude in Science":[21]

> The territory no longer precedes the map, nor survives it. Henceforth, it is the map that precedes the territory ... it is the map that engenders the territory and if we were to revive the fable today, it would be the territory whose shreds are slowly rotting across the map. ... *The desert of the real itself.*[22]

The breaking down of the distinction between rationality and actuality, and the insistence that in contemporary culture the map precedes the territory, marks a move Baudrillard makes from a philosophy founded on questions of representation to one that focuses on the concept of simulation. Simulation, which Baudrillard presents as the quintessence of postmodern culture, refuses to raise those questions of originality and referentiality that are central to representationalist philosophies. For him, images and objects function only as placeholders in a structural system in which all values are exchangeable: the postmodern subject exists within the framework of an "infinite code" to which no one has the key. Baudrillard develops this idea of the infinite code of images from a reading of the work of the Situationist theorist Guy Debord, who argued in his 1967 book *The Society of the Spectacle* that the "whole life of those societies in which modern conditions of production prevail presents itself as an immense accumulation of *spectacles*. All that was once lived has become mere representation" so that spectacle "epitomizes the prevailing model of social life," the "very heart of society's real unreality."[23] Working through the logic of Debord's arguments, Baudrillard removes from them any vestiges of representationalist philosophy to focus rigorously on postmodern simulation. Contemporary culture, he asserts, is not the producer of simulations, but their product: in postmodern simulation, meaning "implodes" as any last instance of a distinction between rational and

---

21. See Jorge Luis Borges, "On Exactitude in Science," in *Collected Fictions*, Andrew Hurley (trans.) (Harmondsworth: Penguin, 1998).
22. Baudrillard, *Simulations*, 1.
23. Guy Debord, *The Society of the Spectacle*, Donald Nicholson-Smith (trans.) (New York: Zone Books, 2002), 12–13.

actual is abolished and the world moves from the critical distance inherent in representational reality to the immediacy of the hyperreal.

"Hyperreality" is not, of course, simply "unreality." Baudrillard uses the term to identify a culture in which the fantastical creations of media, film, and computer technologies are more real, and interact more fundamentally with experience and desire, than the hitherto dominant "realities" of nature or spiritual life. The real, he argues in *Simulations*, is now "produced from miniaturized units, from matrices, memory banks and command models …. It is a hyperreal: the product of an irradiating synthesis of combinatory models in a hyperspace without atmosphere."[24] In an often-cited passage about Disneyland, Baudrillard produces a clear example of how simulation operates to generate hyperreality:

> Disneyland is there to conceal the fact that it is the "real" country, all of the "real" America, which *is* Disneyland …. Disneyland is presented as imaginary in order to make us believe that the rest is real, when in fact all of Los Angeles and the America surrounding it are no longer real, but of the order of the hyperreal and simulation. It is no longer a question of a false representation of reality (ideology), but of concealing the fact that the real is no longer real …[25]

Disneyland is not a fantastic space that makes the mundane reality of everyday American life more bearable, but is rather a means of masking the fantastical nature of that day-to-day existence: it is, he claims, "a deterrence machine set up in order to rejuvenate in reverse the fiction of the real."[26] The function of Disneyland is to appear fantastical so as to conceal the loss of everyday reality in postmodern simulation, to prevent the American public from recognizing the "fact that the real is no longer real."

As well as disguising the disconnection of representation and reality, Disneyland is a useful illustration of a key economic and political aspect of Baudrillard's postmodernism: the "deterrence"-effect of the seductive power of consumer culture. Like Jameson, Baudrillard's discussions of the postmodern focus explicitly on the structures of global capitalism. In *The Mirror of Production*, Baudrillard asserts that, today, "capitalism crosses the entire network of natural, social, sexual and cultural forces, all languages and codes."[27] It is ubiquitous, he argues, not simply present in the circulation of money and commodities in the financial marketplaces, but everywhere, infecting every aspect of experience:

24. Baudrillard, *Simulations*, 3.
25. *Ibid.*, 25.
26. *Ibid.*
27. Jean Baudrillard, *The Mirror of Production*, Mark Poster (trans.) (St. Louis, MO: Telos, 1975), 138.

The circulation, purchase, sale, appropriation of differentiated goods and signs/objects today constitute our language, our code, the code by which the entire society *communicates* and converses. Such is the structure of consumption, its language, by comparison with which individual needs and pleasures are merely speech effects.[28]

In *The Consumer Society*, Baudrillard equates the commodity with the sign and argues that as they collapse into one another, they generate the language or code that shapes postmodern identity. The postmodern consumer, he argues, "sets in place a whole array of sham objects, of characteristic signs of happiness, and then waits … for happiness to alight."[29] This passivity is the result of the "seduction" of the commodity: the unfulfillable desire to find happiness among the "array of sham objects" that make up modern life is produced by contemporary capitalism as the organizing force of experience and leads to the most central aspect of Baudrillard's postmodernity – the ubiquity of the messages produced by advertising in the communications media and the subsequent annihilation of reality, agency, and the possibility of critique.

The postmodern mass media present a "*dizzying whirl of reality*" that is not a reflection or representation of actuality, but rather the production of a simulated world in which "we live, sheltered by signs, in the denial of the real."[30] It is in terms of this account of the seductive apathy generated in a media-produced world of hyperreal simulation that Baudrillard's work has become most notorious. In a series of articles published in 1991, he argued that the Gulf War "will not," "is not," and "did not" take place. The central thrust of these polemical pieces is the argument that in an age of mass-media simulation and the commodification of the image, any coverage of the war is readable only in terms of promotion: "The media promote the war, the war promotes the media, and advertising competes with the war …. It allows us to turn the world and the violence of the world into a consumable substance."[31] In the ubiquity, immediacy, and self-referentiality of the blanket media coverage of the twenty-four-hour news channels, access to any "real war" behind the self-promotion, speculation, and manufactured dissension of the "fake and presumptive warriors, generals, experts and television presenters" that fill the screens is impossible. In the face of this infinite spiral of promotion, Baudrillard argues, the Western subject as a consumer of media images becomes incapable of making rational judgments about what is "really taking place": "uncertainty

---

28. Jean Baudrillard, *The Consumer Society: Myths and Structures*, Chris Turner (trans.) (London: Sage, 1998), 79–80.

29. *Ibid.*, 31.

30. *Ibid.*, 34.

31. Jean Baudrillard, *The Gulf War Did Not Take Place*, Paul Patton (trans.) (Bloomington, IN: Indiana University Press, 1995), 31.

invades our screens like a real oil slick, in the image of that blind sea bird stranded on a beach in the Gulf, which will remain the symbol-image of what we all are in front of our screens, in front of this sticky and unintelligible event."[32]

In the light of this, and on the basis of what he sees as the impossibility of breaking through the infinite code of simulation, Baudrillard despairs of any genuine engagement with the actuality of the war and calls instead for what he terms a "skeptical intelligence": "If we do not have practical intelligence about the war (and none among us has), at least let us have a skeptical intelligence towards it, without renouncing the pathetic feeling of absurdity."[33] What this skeptical intelligence might amount to as a mode of critical engagement with the contemporary world is something critics of Baudrillard have found difficult to pin down. To his detractors, Baudrillard's postmodernism offers nothing on which to base a politics of collective action and little more than sardonic detachment as means of resistance to contemporary culture. His work is attacked as a fashionable nihilism that is incapable of producing any call to action by such thinkers as Christopher Norris, who responds explicitly to the politics of Baudrillard's philosophy in *Uncritical Theory: Postmodernism, Intellectuals and the Gulf War*. Less negatively, Baudrillard has been presented as a diagnostician of the conflicts and tensions of today's world: a thinker whose arguments allow other postmodern theorists and political and social philosophers to identify crucial elements and effects of postmodernity even if he refuses to offer his own alternatives to the status quo.[34] His work is provocative, and this provocation is itself the point. In the most positive light, then, critics argue that the explicit irony of Baudrillard's skeptical writings generate a space in which the apparently totalizing seductive forces of contemporary mass-media simulation and capitalist commodification are shown to be finite, fragmentary, and anything but transparent, and therefore fit subjects for criticism.

III. REFLECTION, SUBLIMITY, AND THE DIFFEREND

If Jameson's analysis of postmodern culture results in a call for new modes of cognitive mapping as a means to renew modern political organization, and Baudrillard's explorations of hyperreality appear to reject oppositional politics in its entirety in favor of a detached mode of ironic skepticism, Lyotard's[35] work

---

32. *Ibid.*, 32.

33. *Ibid.*, 58.

34. See, for example, Paul Patton, "Introduction," in *The Gulf War Did Not Take Place*, or Rex Butler, *Jean Baudrillard: The Defence of the Real* (London: Sage, 1999).

35. Jean-François Lyotard (August 10, 1924–April 21, 1998; born in Versailles, France; died in Paris) was educated at the Lycée Buffon, Lycée Louis-le-Grand, and received his *agrégation de*

sets out to generate a resolutely postmodern political philosophy that seeks to engage with, critique, and disrupt the totalizing power structures of the contemporary world. The call issued in the well-known closing passage from his influential 1982 essay "Answering the Question: What is Postmodernism?" to "wage a war on totality," to "be witnesses to the unpresentable," and to "activate the differences [*différends*]"[36] is central to this work and forms the basis of his postmodern philosophy.

It is important not to read the account of the contemporary commodification of knowledge in *The Postmodern Condition* as a summation of Lyotard's entire engagement with postmodernism. Although his analyses of commodification in that book appear bleak and incapable of offering a coherent alternative to the status quo, the account there is a diagnosis of a condition rather than the active critique of totalizing and totalitarian systems of thought that much of his other work is concerned to develop. While it refuses to discard many of the arguments developed there, the focus of Lyotard's work changes to present the postmodern less a historical condition and more as a mode of critical intervention in the continuing development of modernity. Like Baudrillard, Lyotard is careful to distance his critique from the systematic philosophies of modernity that he discovers in the work of thinkers such as Hegel and Marx, and instead seeks to identify and activate the moments where such modern systems appear to fall into contradiction, and it is this idea of the postmodern as a disruptive force that offers the best way into his work.

Although beginning his career as a Marxist philosopher, activist, and member of the radical group Socialisme ou Barbarie[37] in the 1950s and 1960s, his 1974 book *Libidinal Economy* marks a violent rejection of systematic political organization. In what he was later to call his "evil book,"[38] Lyotard attacks Marxism as a political philosophy head on, challenging its pretension to systematically diagnose, oppose, and resolve the evils of capitalism. In a particularly notorious

---

philosophie in 1950 and his *doctorat d'état* from the University of Paris X–Nanterre in 1971. His influences included Deleuze, Derrida, Freud, Kant, Levinas, Marx, Nietzsche, Souyri, and Wittgenstein, and he held appointments at the Lycée de Constantine, Algeria (1952), the University of Paris (Sorbonne [1960–66]; Nanterre [1966–68]; and Vincennes [1970–87]), and CNRS (1968–70), and was visiting professor to Johns Hopkins University, the University of California-San Diego, in French and Italian at the University of California-Irvine (1987–94), and in French at Emory University (1994–98).

36. Jean-François Lyotard, "Answering the Question: What is Postmodernism?," Regis Durand (trans.), in *The Postmodern Condition: A Report on Knowledge*, Geoff Bennington and Brian Massumi (trans.) (Minneapolis, MN: University of Minnesota Press, 1984), 82.

*37. *Socialisme ou Barbarie* is discussed in more detail in the essay on French Marxism by William L. McBride in *The History of Continental Philosophy: Volume 5*.

38. Jean-François Lyotard, *Peregrinations: Law, Form, Event* (New York: Columbia University Press, 1988), 13.

passage, he launches his critique of Marxist thought by splitting the figure of Karl Marx into two characters, each of whom represents a different relation to capitalism found in Marx's texts: the first is the Moses-like figure of "Old Man Marx," who scientifically and systematically describes the ills of capitalism and provides sets of laws to determine its overthrow, and the second is the erotically fixated "Little Girl Marx," who is seduced by it and enters into a love affair with capitalism's perverse body, enjoying its violent destructive power.[39] In this way, Lyotard argues that Marxism exists in a paradoxical relationship with capitalism as it simultaneously condemns it and is captivated by it: Old Man Marx is the systematizer, the producer of Marxism's grand narrative that presses everything into its mold, whereas Little Girl Marx points toward what he identifies as the *jouissance* of capitalist culture: the necessary excess of speculative value that arises from commodity exchange as the engine to perpetuate desire and consumption in a manner that exceeds rational definition and constantly haunts Marx's systematic thought with desire and seduction.

Lyotard's conversion of Marx into a "strange bisexual assemblage"[40] was not simply done to offend his ex-colleagues in Socialisme ou Barbarie (although it certainly achieved this). Rather, it highlights the ways in which capitalism "exceeds the capacity of theoretical discourse" to explain its effects.[41] Owing to its love–hate relationship with capitalism, *Libidinal Economy* argues, Marxism's analyses remain complicit with the latter's conception of social change as a grand narrative of development, and in the end both are able to depict the people caught up in capitalism only as objects of this development, as "cattle who couldn't enter the future except backwards under a hail of blows."[42]

If Lyotard makes his final break with some of the key premises of modern political philosophy in *Libidinal Economy*, it is during his discussions of postmodernism in the 1980s and 1990s that he begins to formulate alternative bases for critique, most explicitly through a rereading of Immanuel Kant's analyses of reflective judgment and aesthetics in the *Critique of Judgment*. The question of aesthetics is crucial for Lyotard's analysis of the postmodern, just as it is for Jameson and Baudrillard. Unlike them, however, in "Answering the Question: What is Postmodernism?" Lyotard is careful to present postmodern aesthetics as a disruptive element within a continuing modernity rather than a new mode of representation that simply replaces the modern. In this essay, he defines and distinguishes between three forms of presentation: realism, modernism, and

---

39. Jean-François Lyotard, *Libidinal Economy*, Iain Hamilton Grant (trans.) (London: Athlone, 1993), 97.
40. *Ibid.*, 96.
41. *Ibid.*, 98.
42. Jean-François Lyotard, *Duchamp's TRANS/formers*, Ian McLeod (trans.) (Venice, CA: Lapis, 1990), 17.

postmodernism. These are not historical categories that succeed one another in time; rather, all exist simultaneously and are manifest in many different cultures and periods. In fact, throughout his work, Lyotard is careful always to demonstrate that modernism and postmodernism are irreducible to straightforward historical categories: so, for example, he identifies aspects of the work of thinkers as historically diverse as Aristotle, Augustine, Montaigne, and Kant as explicitly postmodern, and quite explicitly defines the thinking behind some recent developments in digital technology and culture as modernist or even realist.[43] Grasping what realism, modernism, and postmodernism are and how they are related will, then, take us right to the heart of Lyotard's postmodern philosophy.

Defining realism as the mainstream style of presentation in a culture, Lyotard sees its task as to "stabilize the referent, to arrange it according to a point of view which endows it with a recognizable meaning, to reproduce the syntax and vocabulary which enable the addressee to decipher images and sequences quickly" so that the viewers, auditors, or readers can "preserve [their] consciousnesses from doubt."[44] In other words, the aim of realism is to depict the world according to conventions with which the addressee is already familiar so that it can quickly and unproblematically be understood and consumed. Realism is not simply a reflection of a pregiven reality, but is, as Lyotard defines it in Postmodern Fables, "the art of making reality, of knowing reality and knowing how to make reality."[45] Like Baudrillard's hyperreality, realism is the presentation of the world as a comprehensible, mappable, and functional totality.

In contrast to this realism, Lyotard sets modernism and postmodernism, both of which he sees as potentially disruptive forms whose task is to "present the fact that the unpresentable exists. To make visible that there is something which can be conceived and which can neither be seen nor made visible: this is what is at stake."[46] Instead of realistically presenting a world that is immediately recognizable, modern and postmodern presentations disrupt recognition by alluding to what a particular culture represses or excludes from its normal means of communication. They are, in other words, deliberately difficult and disturbing: direct challenges to accepted realist practices of presentation and understanding. Lyotard, explicitly invoking Kant's aesthetics, calls the effect of

---

43. This noncontemporary sense of postmodernism is, for example, the basis of Lyotard's discussion in his last (unfinished) book, The Confession of Augustine. His analysis of the "realism" of new technologies is most explicit in the essay "Can Thought go on without a Body?" in The Inhuman: Reflections on Time, Geoffrey Bennington and Rachel Bowlby (trans.) (Cambridge: Polity, 1993), 8–23.

44. Lyotard, The Postmodern Condition, 74.

45. Jean-François Lyotard, Postmodern Fables, Georges Van Den Abeele (trans.) (Minneapolis, MN: University of Minnesota Press, 1997), 91.

46. Lyotard, The Postmodern Condition, 78.

this sort of presentation "sublime." In contrast to the beautiful, which is based on a feeling of harmony and attraction between the subject and the world, the sublime is a mixed feeling of pleasure and pain: simultaneous attraction and repulsion, awe and terror. De-emphasizing the traditional sense of a possible transcendence inherent in sublime presentation, Lyotard focuses on its capacity to "develop a conflict" between conception and presentation, and thereby upset the apparent seamlessness of a realist worldview.[47] This notion of the sublime as a disturbance of everyday sense-making activity is central to Lyotard's postmodern philosophy, whether he is discussing art and literature, history, technology, politics, or philosophy.

He differentiates between the modern and the postmodern sublime by arguing that in the former the unpresentable is "put forward only as the missing contents; but the form, because of its recognizable consistency, continues to offer to the reader or viewer matter for solace and pleasure," while the latter "puts forward the unpresentable in presentation itself."[48] In other words, modernism presents the fact that there is within the culture in which it exists something that eludes presentation, but does so in a form that remains familiar and assimilable. In contrast to this, postmodernism confronts the reader or viewer with a presentation that is challenging in terms of both form and content; it sets out deliberately to unsettle, seeking to generate "new presentations, not in order to enjoy them, but in order to impart a stronger sense of the unpresentable."[49] The postmodern sublime disturbs, disrupts, and challenges the subject to respond without providing the recognizable forms that make it possible to determine in advance what mode that response should take.

For Lyotard, then, modernism and postmodernism are modes of presentation that work to disrupt the realist conventions and expectations of a culture, and change as that culture is transformed and readers and spectators become used to, and no longer shocked by, their contents and methods. So, while for nineteenth-century European culture the quattrocento-style representational painting and triple-decker realist novel might have been the norm, the rapidly moving images of today's MTV music video and the self-referential parody of the viral advertising campaign are equally realist in Lyotard's sense of the term, as they are familiar, quickly decodable, and unproblematically assimilated by contemporary capitalism. In contrast to this, the modern and (especially) the postmodern are explicitly critical. For Lyotard, the role of postmodern presentation is to perform an immanent critique of the day-to-day structures of this realism; it operates within the realist context of a given culture to shatter its norms and challenge its

---

47. *Ibid.*, 77.
48. *Ibid.*, 81.
49. *Ibid.*

assumptions, not with a new set of criteria drawn from outside of that culture, but rather by showing the contradictions the culture contains, what it represses, refuses to recognize, or makes unpresentable.

While "Answering the Question" focuses its discussion predominantly on visual art, *The Differend: Phrases in Dispute*, which many see as Lyotard's most important book, develops this model much further to outline a postmodern mode of ethical and political engagement as well as discussing culture, history, and philosophy. Although employing a slightly different lexicon, the distinction between a realist mode of politics and a model that seeks to testify to the existence of the unpresentable and mobilize sublime feeling and reflective judgment remains central to the book.

Lyotard defines a differend as "the unstable state of language wherein something which must be able to be put into phrases cannot yet be."[50] A differend thus occurs as a feeling, a moment or event that agitates and dislocates experience as it is irreducible to the categories and conventions of the community – specifically, it happens as the presentation that there is something unpresentable. It is thus an interruption of the seamlessness of realism, a break in the flow of language, a moment where the "right words" will not come. And, for Lyotard, this lack of propriety is tied explicitly to the question of justice – in another definition, he presents a differend as:

> a case of conflict, between (at least) two parties, that cannot be resolved for lack of a rule of judgment applicable to both of the arguments. One side's legitimacy does not imply the other's lack of legitimacy. However, applying a single rule of judgment to both in order to settle their differend as though it were merely a litigation would wrong (at least) one of them (and both of them if neither side admits this rule).[51]

In this sense, a differend appears as an apparently intractable dispute: it marks a point of suffering where an injustice cannot find a space to articulate itself, where an injury is silenced or a mode of testimony rejected. Lyotard offers a series of examples in the book, ranging from the claims of Holocaust deniers to the idea of the unpublished masterpiece of literature, but in each case the focus falls on the question of how the occurrence of a wrong provokes ethical questions and how the victim of that wrong might be helped to find means of self-presentation.

---

50. Jean-François Lyotard, *The Differend: Phrases in Dispute*, Georges Van Den Abeele (trans.) (Minneapolis, MN: University of Minnesota Press, 1988), 13.
51. *Ibid.*, xi.

Differends are thus the point of departure for Lyotard's exploration of the politics and philosophy of language in *The Differend*. He argues that their existence places an obligation on thought to attempt to "find new rules for forming and linking phrases that are able to express the differend disclosed by the feeling [of injustice], unless one wants the differend to be smothered right away in a litigation and for the alarm sounded by the feeling to have been useless."[52] While the role of realism is, precisely, to "smother" any differend that occurs in order to "preserve consciousnesses from doubt,"[53] Lyotard argues that the ethical response to the feeling of the unpresentable differend must be to work actively to transform the context in which it occurs by seeking "new rules for forming and linking phrases" so as to "bear witness to differends by finding idioms for them."[54]

A differend is, in other words, an event. And for Lyotard, the thinking of the event in a manner that is open to its singularity and difference lies at the heart of the postmodern. In an article on the abstract expressionist painter Barnett Newman, Lyotard argues that the event is:

> what dismantles consciousness, what deposes consciousness, it is what consciousness cannot formulate, even what consciousness forgets in order to constitute itself. What we do not manage to formulate is that something happens .... An event, an occurrence – what Martin Heidegger called *ein Ereignis* – is infinitely simple, but this simplicity can only be approached through a state of privation. That which we call thought must be disarmed.[55]

This disarming of thought, the breaking open of the closed system of realism that would silence the event by assimilation into the grand narrative of a systematic philosophy, is the basis for Lyotard's construction of a postmodern politics. In a manner that differs from both Jameson and Baudrillard, he explicitly rejects the idea that the problems and categories of philosophical modernity have been or should be left behind, but seeks to mobilize events, to "activate the differends," in order to disrupt the closed systems of thought and presentation that shape our continuing modernity.

In keeping with this model, at the end of the 1980s Lyotard came to differentiate his work from the then ubiquitous popular-cultural definitions of postmodernism that celebrated the freedoms offered by new forms of communications

52. *Ibid.*, 13.
53. Lyotard, *The Postmodern Condition*, 74.
54. Lyotard, *The Differend*, 13.
55. Lyotard, "The Sublime and the Avant-Garde," in *The Inhuman*, 102.

technology. In an article that takes the phrase as its title, he does this by describing what is at stake in his work as "rewriting modernity":

> Rewriting clearly has nothing to do with what is called postmodernity or postmodernism on the market of contemporary ideologies .... Postmodernity is not a new age, but the rewriting of some of the features claimed by modernity, and first of all modernity's claim to ground its legitimacy on the project of liberating humanity as a whole through science and technology .... Rewriting means resisting the writing of that supposed [technological] postmodernity.[56]

In other words, the technological acceleration that is driven by contemporary capitalism, which Jameson and Baudrillard both identify as the essence of postmodernity, is for Lyotard the very realism that the postmodern rewriting of modernity sets out to disrupt. By paying attention to the sublime feeling produced by the unpresentable event of a differend, modernity's legitimizing claims can, he asserts, be questioned, challenged and opened to critique. This is what Lyotard sees as the central stake of a "war on totality."

This chapter has focused on three central accounts of the postmodern: Jameson's analysis of it as the "cultural logic of late capitalism"; Baudrillard's presentation of it as the culture that arises as a result of a movement from representation to simulation, seduction, and hyperreality; and Lyotard's discussion of a postmodern resistance within a continuing modernity that emerges from the events and differends that disturb and dislocate modern institutions by opening them up to their own unpresentable alterity. That these three versions of the postmodern are impossible to draw together to form a coherent definition is part of the point: throughout the 1980s and 1990s, postmodernism's challenge lay as much in its disruption of identity and definition as it did in any form of coherent philosophical or political alternative. Although there is no coherent postmodern philosophical or political program, its continuing interest lies in the development of a capacity to interrogate and challenge the everyday sense-making processes of the contemporary world.

---

56. Lyotard, "Rewriting Modernity," in *The Inhuman*, 34–5.

2

GERMAN PHILOSOPHY AFTER 1980:
THEMES OUT OF SCHOOL

Dieter Thomä

I. THE DISCONTENT WITH CONTINENTAL PHILOSOPHY

German philosophy is regarded by many as the epitome of "continental philosophy." This claim would gain credibility if French philosophy, the other main contender for this title, could be traced back to German origins as well, be it to the so-called three "H's" – Hegel, Husserl, and Heidegger – or to their counterparts Marx, Nietzsche, and Freud. (Vincent Descombes explored these two genealogies as early as 1979.)[1] Yet instead of indulging in any such philosophical imperialism, we should rather raise the question of whether the label "continental philosophy" suits recent German philosophy at all. Moreover, we should be aware of the conceptual problems that go along with this label. Addressing these problems will eventually provide us with a kind of "entry code" to the philosophical labyrinth that we are about to explore.

First, we should be aware of the fact that the term "continental" does not render any substantial information on how philosophers proceed and which problems they tackle. As the label "continental" is so vague, it tends to fuel the suspicion that a philosophy of this kind is in want of a clear focus. If we are to take "continental philosophy" seriously, we need to identify a set of questions that deserve to be called "philosophical," with no strings attached.

Second, we should not expect to discover some kind of common denominator, a unified self-image that German philosophers share by virtue of their

---

1. See Vincent Descombes, *Modern French Philosophy*, L. Scott-Fox and J. M. Harding (trans.) (New York: Cambridge University Press, 1980); originally published as *Le Même et l'autre* (Paris: Éditions de Minuit, 1979).

belonging to "continental" thought. Given the multitude of voices in recent German philosophy (and the controversies between and among them), the search for such a self-image is futile. In order to do justice to recent philosophical debates in Germany, we should take into account the plurality of partly incompatible traditions on which they are based.

We are thirdly invited to appreciate the attempts of German philosophers to build bridges to the "analytic" camp. The building blocks for bridges of this kind were laid when the cold war between analytic and continental philosophy was still raging: From the late 1970s on, authors from different camps published books that generously combined discussions of philosophers with wildly different affiliations. In his *Self-Consciousness and Self-Determination* (1979), Ernst Tugendhat referred to Heidegger on the one hand, Hector-Neri Castañeda and W. V. O. Quine on the other. In recent years, analytic philosophers have become more and more interested in the work of so-called continental thinkers and vice versa. As the label "continental" fades, its counterpart, the "analytic," is on the brink of being put out of service as well,[2] even though some representatives of these two camps confidently stick to what may be called their philosophical "identity politics."

In order to come to grips with the discontent with "continental philosophy," we need to engage in the three arguments described above. (i) We should identify the key issues addressed in recent debates in Germany and situate these debates in the philosophical framework at large (the "bigger picture"). Recent German philosophy should not be portrayed as being in a state of less than splendid isolation. (ii) Yet we are also obliged to reconstruct the specific philosophical traditions at work in major contributions from German philosophers in the past decades. This will prevent us from imposing an artificially unified research agenda; it will "teach us differences" (as Shakespeare would put it). (iii) We will also have to take into consideration how German philosophers seek to overcome the constraints set by these traditions and how they consciously and conscientiously combine insights from seemingly unrelated theoretical contexts. In the following, I will slightly alter the sequence of these questions: I will remind the reader of the major schools setting the scene for late-twentieth-century German philosophy (section II), and then identify four key issues (section III) that can be used for mapping the philosophical landscape of the day (sections IV–VII).

---

2. Cf. Peter Bieri, "Was bleibt von der analytischen Philosophie?" *Deutsche Zeitschrift für Philosophie* 55 (2007).

II. GERMAN PHILOSOPHY AFTER THE POSTWAR PERIOD

The year 1989 is to be regarded as the "closing bell," putting an end to the postwar period in German history: German reunification made disappear what had been the indirect, yet most obvious and obtrusive, consequence of the political and moral collapse of Germany in the Nazi period – the existence of two "Germanys." If we were to answer the question of when the postwar period in German philosophy came to a close, however, we would not want to identify one single emblematic event, nor would we choose a date as late as 1989. In the field of philosophy, the end of the postwar era can be linked to the death of the leading figures or founding fathers of the three most influential philosophical schools in Germany after the Second World War: Theodor W. Adorno and Max Horkheimer, the leading figures of the Frankfurt School,[3] died in 1969 and 1973 respectively; Heidegger, whose influence in postwar Germany was mainly mediated through Hans-Georg Gadamer's hermeneutics, died in 1976; and the so-called "Ritter School" lost its central figure with the death of Joachim Ritter in 1974.[4] This last name on the list may come as a surprise, as Ritter is not regarded as a major philosophical figure equal in rank to Adorno or Heidegger. But it is safe to say that his institutional influence exceeded that of the Frankfurt School; in fact, a recent debate circled around the question of whether Ritter's neo-Aristotelian approach and his theory of political and cultural institutions actually represented the philosophical core identity of the so-called "old," that is pre-1989, Federal Republic of Germany.[5]

It is important to note that the epochalization suggested above does not refer to a new beginning or breakthrough, but rather indicates that an era has come to an end. I do not mean to imply that the schools mentioned above disappeared from the scene for good in the 1970s; Habermas and other younger members of the Frankfurt School published some of their main works after that date, Gadamer had a lasting and even growing influence until his death in 2002, and so on. Yet it is safe to say that those schools have lost most of their identificatory, defining force in German philosophy since the mid-1970s. This loss could

---

*3. Adorno, Horkheimer, and other figures associated with the Frankfurt School are discussed in several essays in *The History of Continental Philosophy: Volume 5*.

4. Born in 1903, Joachim Ritter studied with Ernst Cassirer, to whom he submitted his thesis on Nicolas of Cusa in 1927. From 1946 until his retirement in 1968, he was Professor of Philosophy at the Westfälische Wilhelms-Universität in Münster. Among his most important works are *Metaphysik und Politik*; *Subjektivität*; and *Hegel and the French Revolution*. Ritter was the initiator and main editor of the comprehensive *Historisches Wörterbuch der Philosophie*, whose twelve volumes appeared between 1971 and 2005.

5. Jens Hacke, *Philosophie der Bürgerlichkeit* (Göttingen: Vandenhoeck & Ruprecht, 2006); Herbert Schnädelbach, "Die Verteidigung der Republik," *Deutsche Zeitschrift für Philosophie* 55 (2007).

also be regarded as a win of a kind: "Schools" tend to become scholastic, which does not coalesce particularly well with philosophical creativity. It should also be acknowledged that some of the main representatives of those schools were actively involved in the self-abolition of philosophical factions themselves. That this is particularly true for the Frankfurt School becomes clear when we think of Habermas eventually joining forces with Derrida, or of Honneth reading Levinas.[6] Here and elsewhere, we can observe a dissolution of boundaries.

If we want to understand how the philosophical debates have picked up new momentum in the more recent past, we need to briefly reflect on the legacy set by those three schools mentioned above. Their trajectories provide the framework for the more individual itineraries that have moved into uncharted territory in the last quarter of the twentieth century and up to the present. When going through these different legacies, we aim to switch back and forth between the focus on "schools" on the one hand, and the focus on "topics" on the other. Instead of merely reconstructing different scholarly traditions in a historical manner, we seek to establish patterns of themes in which we can locate German philosophy as it emerges after the end of the postwar period.

III. VARIETIES OF A THEORY OF MODERNITY

If there is such a thing as a common denominator shared by the Heideggerians, critical theorists, and the circle around Ritter, it is the search for a theory of modernity.

Heidegger

In Heidegger, this search is framed in his project of rewriting the "history of metaphysics." Cartesian subjectivity, Hegelian reason, Nietzschean will to power, and modern technology in general are described as variants of a dualist model that eventually leads back to Plato. In modern times, this dualism has become the standard device for dealing with the world and with ourselves: we have come to totally dominate nature and to turn ourselves into "rational animals." Heidegger's "destruction" of this dualism was first formulated in *Being and Time* (1927) in his attempt to redescribe human existence as "Being-in-the-world,"

---

6. See Giovanna Borradori, *Philosophy in a Time of Terror: Dialogues with Jürgen Habermas and Jacques Derrida* (Chicago, IL: University of Chicago Press, 2003); Axel Honneth, "The Other of Justice: Habermas and the Ethical Challenge of Postmodernism," in *The Cambridge Companion to Habermas*, Stephen White (ed.) (Cambridge: Cambridge University Press, 1995).

and later became part of his project of "overcoming metaphysics."[7] Although Heidegger's unique terminology tends to make him immune to external criticisms and makes it difficult to contextualize his approach, it is still legitimate to highlight certain topics that make his work appear to be a natural part of the philosophical debates of the day (be they analytic or continental). Two such themes deserve particular attention.

(i) *Being and Time*, as well as Heidegger's later texts on the "history of metaphysics," can be regarded as contributions to the debates on the concept of a *person* and to the theory of the *subject*. In his earlier work, he deals with the structure of "self-relation" and with issues of authenticity in a more constructive sense; his later work is dedicated to the "destruction" of the metaphysical "subject." Hans Blumenberg's account of self-preservation in the modern age, Dieter Henrich's work on subjectivity and selfhood, and Tugendhat's discussion of self-consciousness and self-relation have all been developed in critical reference to Heidegger, as will be seen in the extended discussion below. But it also should be said at the outset that the debates on the "subject" and the "person" are by no means limited to a Heideggerian framework.

(ii) Throughout his writings, Heidegger grapples with the problem of *language*. In *Being and Time*, Heidegger gives an outline of nonpropositional language, and discusses its reduction to idle talk on the one hand and its powers of "disclosure" on the other. Language becomes a battleground for the encounter between those who objectify the world, propagate a "worldview," and forget about the secret of "Being," and those who stress the insurmountable difference between what is and what is said. In this crisis of representation and referentiality, poetry and art in general gain particular relevance. It is obvious how and why discussions of Heidegger's early conception of language have drawn comparisons to Wittgenstein's theory of language games and life forms, or how and why Heidegger's later writings served as an inspiration for the deconstructivist critique of logocentrism.[8]

The Frankfurt School

It is safe to say that what Heidegger and the Frankfurt School had in common was their interest in the theory of modernity. In spite of Adorno's fierce critique

---

*7. Heidegger's work is discussed in detail in the essays by Miguel de Beistegui in *The History of Continental Philosophy: Volume 3*, and Dennis J. Schmidt in *The History of Continental Philosophy: Volume 4*.

8. Cf. Manfred Frank, *What is Neostructuralism?*, Sabine Wilke and Richard Gray (trans.) (Minneapolis, MN: University of Minnesota Press, 1989); Thomas Rentsch, *Heidegger und Wittgenstein* (Frankfurt: Suhrkamp, 1990).

of Heidegger's "jargon of authenticity" and Heidegger's unrelenting ignorance of critical theory,[9] there are striking similarities between Heidegger's and Adorno's accounts of the subject's striving for domination. This does not mean, however, that these accounts were compatible. The distinctive features of critical theory come to the fore when we once again turn to the "subject" and, second, to "society."

(i) Whereas Heidegger seeks to eventually overcome subjectivity as such and to outbid history by the "destiny of Being," the Frankfurt School describes the *subject* as being fully and inevitably immersed in the dynamics of history. They describe the dialectics of Enlightenment and the crisis of modernity as emerging from the internal logic of subjective empowerment and alienation. In this perspective, any "great escapes" to another way of thinking (or being) are deemed to be illusory or even ideological. The Hegelian legacy that comes to the fore here is still visible in more recent contributions of critical theorists to the fields of moral philosophy and aesthetics.[10] It is this Hegelian perspective that also enables critical theorists to engage in a fruitful dialogue with the contextualist or holistic approaches put forward by Charles Taylor or Robert Brandom.[11]

(ii) If the subject cannot escape from history, it cannot escape from *society* either. Critical theorists turn their attention to societal aspects of the functioning and formation of the individual. Some have stressed the oppressive nature of modern societies, while others have highlighted the constitutive role of intersubjectivity, interaction, reciprocity, and recognition for individual self-determination. In more recent years, this second group has become more and more influential, and this group has left its marks in the field of moral philosophy as well as in the theory of the subject.[12] The sharp critique of the modern "subject" that played a central role in the early classic *Dialectic of Enlightenment* (1944) has been superseded by less bleak theories of self-determination and by a reappraisal of social relations. Within critical theory and also on its margins, important contributions to the theory

---

9. See my "Verhältnis zur Ontologie: Adornos Denken des Unbegrifflichen," in *Theodor W. Adorno, Negative Dialektik*, Axel Honneth and Christoph Menke (eds) (Berlin: Akademie, 2006).

10. Christoph Menke, *Reflections of Equality*, Howard Rouse and Andrei Denejkine (trans.) (Stanford, CA: Stanford University Press, 2006); Albrecht Wellmer, *Ethik und Dialog* (Frankfurt: Suhrkamp, 1986).

11. See Jürgen Habermas, "Struggles for Recognition in the Democratic Constitutional State," Shierry Weber Nicholsen (trans.), in *Multiculturalism: Examining the Politics of Recognition*, Amy Gutmann (ed.) (Princeton, NJ: Princeton University Press, 1994). [*] For a discussion of Brandom, see the essay by John Fennell in *The History of Continental Philosophy: Volume 8*.

*12. See the essay by Amy Allen in this volume.

of intersubjectivity and sociality have been published in recent years (see section VI).

The Ritter School

When the members of the so-called "Ritter School" talk about modernity, they choose a Hegelian starting-point that is clearly distinguished from the approach chosen by the Frankfurt School. Instead of focusing on the dynamics of modern societies as they emerge from internal contradictions, they settle for Hegel's insight into the inevitability of "diremption" (*Entzweiung*) in modern societies.[13] Following this account, the differentiation of social spheres has led to a liberation of the individual that bears new risks and gives way to dissatisfaction and discontent. This theory of modernity is not so much concerned with an attempt to reconcile the individual and the universal or to sharply analyze the alienating effects of overpowering institutions, as with the *malaise* of the individual and its lack of orientation.

In a certain respect, Ritter has a more positive reading of modernity than the members of the Frankfurt School. Instead of tracing down the alienating effects of capitalism, he acknowledges the liberating effects of modern diremption. In another respect, however, Ritter is driven by a discontent with liberation. He claims that the individual will not find an answer to the old Socratic question of "how to live" without relying on institutions that compensate for the shortcomings of subjective orientation. As the Ritter School questions the historical malleability of human beings, it is called on to identify patterns of human life and of the "good life." This is why the Ritter School takes a step back from Hegel to Aristotle and moves on to questions of *anthropology*. As we will see in section VII, the reappraisal of classical "philosophical anthropology" (Arnold Gehlen, Helmuth Plessner, etc.) meanwhile goes far beyond the Ritter School itself.

Let me briefly recall the key concepts that have emerged in this short discussion of major philosophical schools in postwar Germany: our list consists of *subject*, *language*, *society*, and *anthropology*. In the following, I will leave the perspective of "schools" aside and focus on a number of philosophers whose contributions can be organized along the lines of these key concepts. But it should be made clear at the outset that if, in what follows, a certain philosopher, for example, is discussed under the label of "anthropology," this is not meant to imply that he is a member of the Ritter School, or that the Heideggerians are the only philosophical school concerned with "language."

---

13. Joachim Ritter, *Metaphysik und Politik* (Frankfurt: Suhrkamp, 1969), 213.

IV. THE THEORY OF THE SUBJECT AND THE CONCEPT OF
A PERSON: IMMEDIATE SELF-ACQUAINTANCE, SELF-RELATION,
AND SELF-APPROPRIATION

In the following, I will briefly discuss some contributions to the theory of the subject and to the concept of a person made by philosophers from extremely different backgrounds.

As early as 1955, Henrich[14] made clear that the theory of the subject – the topic that would be central to virtually all of his writings – would lead him back to classical German philosophy, primarily Kant and Fichte, and force him to engage critically with Heidegger's critique of the subject. In his 1955 review of Heidegger's *Kant and the Problem of Metaphysics*,[15] he combines a defense of Kant with an attack on Heidegger, in which he anticipates his later claim that the subject is anything but a stronghold of "unrestrained power." Instead of settling for a critique of such a subject, as Heidegger and Adorno had, Henrich explores the primordial structure of self-awareness as a form of "being-a-self" (*Selbstsein*) or of "conscious life" (*bewusstes Leben*).[16] The primacy of subjectivity is also defended against a scientific reductionism advocated by some representatives of the life sciences and against a linguistic reductionism that takes the subject to be an epiphenomenon generated by propositional, pronominal language or by autobiographical self-construction.[17] Henrich defends the immediacy or unmediatedness of self-awareness against the popular model of self-reflection that has always been charged with the problem that the object appearing in the mirror needs to be artificially and belatedly identified with the subject looking into the mirror. Following Henrich, the immediacy of self-awareness is to be distinguished from more elaborate forms of self-knowledge, as it is inextricably bound to consciousness of any kind.

Henrich's reading of subjectivity as immediate self-awareness has attracted objections from different camps, which, in turn, have prompted Henrich and his disciples to further refine their position and to raise counter-arguments. Two characteristics of these controversies are particularly interesting. First, they often cross the boundaries between analytic and continental philosophy; and second, they establish connections between the problem of subjectivity on the one hand,

---

14. Dieter Henrich (1927–) studied philosophy at the University of Heidelberg with Gadamer. He has taught at the Free University of Berlin (1960–65), University of Heidelberg (1965–81) and University of Munich (1981–).

15. Dieter Henrich, "Die Einheit der Subjektivität," *Philosophische Rundschau* 3 (1955).

16. Dieter Henrich, "Selbsterhaltung und Geschichtlichkeit," in *Subjektivität und Selbsterhaltung*, Hans Ebeling (ed.) (Frankfurt: Suhrkamp, 1976), 307; and *Denken und Selbstsein* (Frankfurt: Suhrkamp, 2007).

17. Dieter Henrich, *Bewußtes Leben* (Stuttgart: Reclam, 1999), 40, 43, 54–6.

and language and society on the other. The leading representative of a linguistic theory of subjectivity is Tugendhat, while Habermas is the leading theorist who focuses on the link between self and society.

Henrich claims that self-awareness or self-acquaintance is independent from references to objects or other persons. Self-awareness does not coincide with self-knowledge, as the latter is already based on a distinction between a knowledgeable person and the content of her knowledge. Self-awareness is regarded as being prior to language and society: if you talk about yourself, you already have to be familiar with yourself; if you are recognized by others, you need to be "you" in order to experience it. When Henrich and his disciples, first and foremost Manfred Frank,[18] discuss the immediacy of self-acquaintance, they painstakingly avoid any allusions to relatedness.[19] The fact that you are acquainted "with" yourself must still be clearly distinguishable from, say, being friendly "with" a neighbor. Henrich and Frank argue that you cannot think of yourself as *not* being acquainted with yourself.[20] Any linguistic or societal account of subjectivity based on human relatedness seems to be "running late." Any self-relation is to be founded on something that antecedes relation.

Tugendhat[21] actually sides with Henrich's critique of self-reflection and with his claim that it is impossible to think of myself as not being me.[22] Yet instead of explaining this phenomenon by going back to the immediacy of consciousness, he hints at the tautological character of propositions of the type "I know that I do *x*." It goes without saying that these two "I's" are identical: there is nothing mysterious about it. Following Tugendhat, self-relation is based on self-attributions: on a permanent process of describing me as doing *x* or being *y*. He also highlights the normative implications of such a process of self-attribution, as beyond their epistemic status they also allow for self-evaluations, that is, for appreciating or deprecating certain attitudes. This practical "taking stance" is part and parcel of a person's becoming herself or forming a character.[23] Tugendhat's model of practical self-relation is indebted to Aristotle and Heidegger; it is worth mentioning that his reference to "care" and to "being

---

18. Manfred Frank (1945–) studied philosophy at the University of Heidelberg with Gadamer, Karl Löwith, Tugendhat, and Henrich. He has taught at the University of Dusseldorf (1971–82), University of Geneva (1982–87), and University of Tübingen (1987–).

19. On self-acquaintance as being "totally irrelational," cf. Manfred Frank, *Die Unhintergehbarkeit von Individualität* (Frankfurt: Suhrkamp, 1986), 60.

20. Dieter Henrich, "Selbstbewußtsein, kritische Einleitung in eine Theorie," in *Hermeneutik und Dialektik*, Rüdiger Bubner *et al.* (eds) (Tübingen: Mohr/Siebeck, 1970), 266.

21. Ernst Tugendhat (1930–) studied philosophy at Stanford University and at the University of Freiburg with Heidegger. He has taught at the University of Heidelberg (1966–75), the Max Planck Institute in Starnberg (1975–80), and the Free University of Berlin (1980–).

22. Ernst Tugendhat, *Selbstbewußtsein und Selbstbestimmung* (Frankfurt: Suhrkamp, 1979), 68.

23. *Ibid.*, 182, 189.

related to oneself" puts the early Heidegger into play again, whereas Henrich is intent on dismissing Heidegger's later critique of subjective power. In his reply to Tugendhat and defense of Henrich's position, Frank claims that such an external, linguistic approach to self-consciousness barely grasps the individual experience of biographical coherence and continuity.[24] It is still unclear, though, why and how such a temporal process should be more accessible to those who rely on Henrich's abstract notion of consciousness and self-awareness.

It is important to note that Tugendhat, a student of Heidegger's and an analytically trained philosopher, has recently complemented his linguistic reflections on personal identity with considerations on mysticism. Even though Tugendhat does not refer to Henrich in his 2003 book *Egozentrizität und Mystik*, the implicit alternatives that are at stake between them are fairly evident, and their importance is considerable. In his most recent work, *Denken und Selbstsein* (Thinking and being-a-self; 2007), Henrich goes back to his old idea that the self can rely on an "internal foundation of its own possibility";[25] he now takes this foundational subject as a building block for a comprehensive model of epistemology and ethics that centers around a subject that, as Henrich puts it, "reaches out [to] the whole of a world."[26] Tugendhat takes issue with such a centralized subject in his latest writings. As he has objected to the primacy of self-awareness from very early on and has always thought of the subject as referring to something or being involved in something, he now discusses mysticism as an attempt to overcome self-centeredness and to make peace with the world.[27]

Whereas Tugendhat wants to prove that Henrich's position is untenable,[28] Habermas does not seem to see any need for such strong judgments. But, like Tugendhat,[29] he shies away from Henrich's "metaphysical" assumptions on a primordial subject. Given his record as a philosopher of communicative action, it does not come as a surprise that Habermas[30] is at odds with Henrich's claim that subjectivity is prior to intersubjectivity.[31] Habermas criticizes the "extra-mundane" status of Henrich's subject.[32] Their disagreement also resonates in their respective accounts of social norms and morality: Henrich chooses a fairly

---

24. Frank, *Die Unhintergehbarkeit von Individualität*, 100.
25. Dieter Henrich, "Die Grundstruktur der modernen Philosophie," in *Subjektivität und Selbsterhaltung*, Ebeling (ed.), 114.
26. Henrich, *Denken und Selbstsein*, 98, cf. 88–9, 101–2.
27. Ernst Tugendhat, *Egozentrizität und Mystik* (Munich: Beck, 2003), 29, 146, 149.
28. Tugendhat, *Selbstbewußtsein und Selbstbestimmung*, 57.
29. Ernst Tugendhat, *Anthropologie statt Metaphysik* (Munich: Beck, 2007).
30. Jürgen Habermas, *Nachmetaphysisches Denken* (Frankfurt: Suhrkamp, 1988), 23, 34.
31. Henrich, *Denken und Selbstsein*, 152–63.
32. Habermas, *Nachmetaphysisches Denken*, 272.

traditional Kantian approach based on the autonomy of the subject,[33] while Habermas takes the social dimension of moral justification into account.[34]

Henrich's and Frank's theory of immediate self-acquaintance and Tugendhat's concept of self-relation are based on different theoretical premises, but they both argue for what may be called a "thin" conception of the subject. In Henrich's case, the idealist core of the subject is the autonomy of the spirit; in Tugendhat's case, the self is identical with itself by being responsible for its practical instantiations. Neither Henrich nor Tugendhat are particularly concerned with what has become a major topic in the contemporary debates on the subject or the person. This topic is aptly characterized by the Nietzschean question of "how one becomes what one is."[35] By going beyond the formal analysis of self-acquaintance or self-relation, those contributing to this debate seek to describe the process of shaping qualitative identity, fostering commitments, and so on. This debate has drawn increasing attention in the light of recent controversies on the freedom of the will triggered by the neurosciences. Those who do not defend freedom by tracing it back to an intangible human spirit redescribe it as the capacity to know what you want and what you are. The concept of a person or a subject thus leads to a theory of self-formation. In an exemplary manner, this in turn is put into practice in the recent work of a former student of Henrich's who, in his earlier career, was one of the main mediators of analytic philosophy in Germany: Peter Bieri.[36]

In his 2001 book *Das Handwerk der Freiheit* (The craft of freedom), Bieri relies heavily on Harry Frankfurt's concepts of "care" and "commitment." These concepts obviously resonate with Heidegger's (and Foucault's) notion of "care," yet instead of exploring such correspondences between the analytic and the continental tradition, Bieri seeks to overcome his analytic past by engaging in a groundbreaking meditation on the freedom of the will. Bieri's answer to the question of "how we become who we are" culminates in a notion of freedom that is associated with internal consistency and relies on a process of "self-appropriation."[37] Bieri argues for a "thick" conception of subjectivity that circles

---

33. Henrich, *Denken und Selbstsein*, 93–105.
*34. For further discussion of Habermas's moral philosophy, see the essay by Christopher F. Zurn in *The History of Continental Philosophy: Volume 6.*
35. This is, of course, the subtitle of Nietzsche's final work, *Ecce Homo.*
36. Peter Bieri (ed.), *Analytische Philosophie des Geistes* (Königstein: Hain, 1981) and *Analytische Philosophie der Erkenntnis* (Frankfurt: Athenäum, 1987). Bieri (1944–) studied philosophy at the University of Heidelberg with Henrich and Tugendhat. He has taught philosophy at the University of Bielefeld (1983–90), the University of Marburg (1990–93), and the Free University of Berlin (1993–2007).
37. Peter Bieri, *Das Handwerk der Freiheit: Über die Entdeckung des eigenen Willens* (Munich: Hanser, 2001), 381–415.

around the question of how a person learns to know herself. The social sphere, however, is as secondary in his approach as it is in Henrich's.

Two other points should be mentioned before closing this section on the theory of the subject. First, Blumenberg also argues for a "thick" conception of subjectivity, but insofar as his account is as much indebted to the debate on philosophical anthropology as it is to the discourse on the subject, Blumenberg's position will be discussed in section VII. Second, although the critique of the subject put forward by early critical theory primarily focused on the subjective domination of external and internal nature, more recent contributions from members of the Frankfurt School have become increasingly interested in the process of self-formation in a social context. Some of these contributions will be discussed in section VI.

V. LANGUAGE: PERSPECTIVISM, INTERPRETATIONISM, AND AESTHETICIZATION

In Gadamer's hermeneutics, Heidegger's theory of language and understanding is transformed into a methodology of the humanities or *Geisteswissenschaften* in general.[38] Language appears as a fabric of meanings, as a kingdom of ideas. This approach misses out on the internal connection between discourse and power that plays a central role, for example in Foucault's adaptation of Heidegger and Nietzsche. That analytic philosophy became particularly appealing to young German philosophers in the 1980s and 1990s was, to a certain extent, owing to the fact that Gadamer had turned most of "philosophy" into "history of philosophy." Overcoming an old-fashioned historicism of this kind was also instrumental for rediscovering and reappropriating the best of so-called continental philosophy itself.

An important preparatory step on the way to this reappropriation was taken by Wolfgang Müller-Lauter[39] in his interpretation of Nietzsche's theory of the will. This interpretation was directed against Heidegger's influential Nietzsche lectures from the 1930s and 1940s and brings to the fore that Nietzsche talks about a plurality of the will as embodied in individuals. Müller-Lauter's anti-metaphysical reading of Nietzsche also leads to a reappraisal of perspectivism:[40]

---

*38. For a discussion of Gadamer's hermeneutics, see the essay on the legacy of phenomenology by Wayne J. Froman in *The History of Continental Philosophy: Volume 6*.

39. Wolfgang Müller-Lauter (1924–2001) studied philosophy at the Free University of Berlin with Wilhelm Weischedel. After having taught for many years at the Kirchlichen Hochschule in Berlin, he was professor emeritus at Humboldt University, Berlin from 1993 until his death.

40. See Martin Heidegger, *Nietzsche*, 2 vols (Pfullingen: Neske, 1961); Wolfgang Müller-Lauter, *Nietzsche-Interpretationen I–III* (Berlin: De Gruyter, 1999–2000).

the plurality of the will corresponds to a plurality of interpretations. Whereas a hermeneutical account focuses on meanings and their unstable reference to reality, a perspectivist reading turns to the conflict between interpretations and their respective claims to truth. It could be said that truth, in Nietzsche himself, appears to be reduced to a matter of power, but perspectivism in a broader sense also leads to a recontextualization and reappreciation of language in cultural, ethical, and even epistemological respects.

By intentionally using the rare, almost awkward plural form of "the wills to power," Günter Abel[41] stresses the inherent plurality of Nietzsche's perspectivism and draws a line from Nietzsche to Nelson Goodman's "ways of world-making."[42] In Abel's book *Interpretationswelten* (Worlds of interpretations), Nietzschean perspectivism, while rarely mentioned, is virtually omnipresent, hidden behind discussions of analytic controversies on realism and linguistic indeterminacy. His main interest lying in the context of epistemology, Abel seeks to respond to the relativist threat of perspectivism by introducing clearly distinguished levels of interpretations that go along with different validity claims.

With or without reference to Nietzsche, a number of other philosophers suggest that the philosophy of language should embrace cultural and symbolic patterns of human self-understanding. Nietzsche is very much present in contributions by Josef Simon (1930–) and Werner Stegmaier (1946–), who remain critical of universalistic claims founded in ahistorical reason and defend the ethical potential of perspectivism.[43] The leading phenomenological school in Germany – the group around Bernhard Waldenfels[44] – does not pay particular attention to Nietzsche's antidualist concept of the "body," but comes to similar conclusions by going back to Merleau-Ponty's philosophy of the "flesh" and his theory of "signs." The reinsertion of language in the context of life-worlds allows Waldenfels to widen the perspective and leads him from a hermeneutical account of the clash of interpretations to the task of approaching and acknowledging the "other," the "stranger," or the "alien": this task is central to what he calls "responsive phenomenology."[45]

---

41. Günter Abel (1947–) studied philosophy at the University of Marburg. He has taught philosophy at the Berlin Institute of Technology since 1987.

42. Günter Abel, *Nietzsche: Die Dynamik der Willen zur Macht und die ewige Wiederkehr* (Berlin: De Gruyter, 1984).

43. Josef Simon, *Philosophy of the Sign*, George Heffernan (trans.) (Albany, NY: SUNY Press, 1995); Werner Stegmaier, *Nietzsches "Genealogie der Moral"* (Darmstadt: WBG, 1994).

44. Bernhard Waldenfels (1934–) studied philosophy at the University of Bonn and the University of Munich. He has taught at the universities in Munich (1968–76) and Bochum (1976–).

45. Bernhard Waldenfels, *Der Stachel des Fremden* (Frankfurt: Suhrkamp, 1990), *Order in the Twilight*, David J. Parent (trans.) (Athens, OH: Ohio University Press, 1996), and *The Question of the Other* (Albany, NY: SUNY Press, 2007).

It is in line with Nietzschean perspectivism or the phenomenology of "life-worlds" that philosophy goes beyond the analysis of propositional language and takes the expressive and aesthetic qualities of language into account. The debate on aesthetics in recent German philosophy mainly circles around the question of whether artworks are defined by their trans- or antipolitical potential, or whether they contribute to the refinement of judgment and to the conversation of mankind, albeit in an indirect manner. Whereas Karl Heinz Bohrer (1932–) defends artistic transgression beyond any social or ethical concerns,[46] Wolfgang Welsch (1946–) combines a broad phenomenological account of Aristotelian *aisthesis* with an analysis of the cultural and social impact of postmodern aestheticization.[47]

In contributions from more recent critical theory, the account of the aesthetic revolves around an ambivalence that is central to the work of Adorno, who sees the work of art as a reminder of another possible world, yet warns against the collapse of aesthetic autonomy, which would be the price paid for turning life into a work of art. Whereas Martin Seel (1954–) explores potential convergences between aesthetics and the theory of the good life, Christoph Menke (1958–) insists on the rift between art and reality. He also uses Adorno's concept of the "nonidentical" as a springboard for building bridges to deconstructivist theories of language and politics.[48]

VI. SOCIETY: RECOGNITION, SELF-TRANSCENDENCE, SOCIAL SYSTEMS

Social philosophy has long been the domain of critical theory in Germany. As another chapter in this volume extensively discusses the more recent developments in this field, let me here complement the discussion of Honneth, Fraser, and Benhabib by hinting at the fact that critical theory has recently moved in two fairly different directions and, consequently, has entered fairly different philosophical debates.

When it comes to the normative grounds of social cooperation, Habermas's theory of communicative action and discourse ethics obviously has a lot in

---

46. Karl Heinz Bohrer, *Suddenness: On the Moment of Aesthetic Appearance*, Ruth Crowley (trans.) (New York: Columbia University Press, 1994), and *Ästhetische Negativität* (Munich: Hanser, 2002).
47. Wolfgang Welsch, *Aisthesis* (Stuttgart: Klett-Cotta, 1987), and *Undoing Aesthetics*, Andrew Inkpin (trans.) (Thousand Oaks, CA: Sage, 1997).
48. Christoph Menke, *The Sovereignty of Art: Aesthetic Negativity in Adorno and Derrida*, Neil Solomon (trans.) (Cambridge, MA: MIT Press, 1998); Martin Seel, *Aesthetics of Appearing*, John Farrell (trans.) (Stanford, CA: Stanford University Press, 2004).

common with liberal theories of justice and contractual theories: the anticipation of possible objections or disagreements inherent to rational discourse is, like Rawls's concept of the "veil of ignorance," indebted to the ideal of impartiality. With or against Habermas, a number of moral and political philosophers (Ursula Wolf, Wolfgang Kersting, Otfried Höffe, and others) have been involved in debates on sources of normativity and on justice and human rights; it would be a task of its own to put these debates in relation to the international debate on these matters, and I cannot address this here.[49]

Yet the task of social philosophy is not confined to a primarily normative approach, and the subject's social behavior is of interest philosophically even if it does not comply with the standards of universalized norms. This is where critical theory has taken a different turn. With Axel Honneth's refined theory of recognition, we learn to distinguish between different social spheres – reaching from the political sphere to civil society, or from the workplace to the family – and to relate them to different self-images and forms of self-esteem.[50] The formal distinction between different social roles gives rise to a more complex description of the subject or the social actor. Such an account is directed against minimalist accounts of the person as an agent maximizing benefits as well as against functionalist social theories that make the subject emerge from behavioral patterns and structural settings.

A younger generation of social philosophers and social theorists has grown suspicious of an unfettered defense of autonomy and seeks to reconstruct the social embeddedness of individuals by carefully analyzing the intertwinement of autonomy and self-abandonment (Seel[51]) or the dialectics between "self-determination" and "self-transcendence" (Hans Joas[52]). In a poignant synthesis of German social philosophy, communitarianism, and American pragmatism, Joas, in *The Genesis of Values*, argues that the involvement of a person in symbolic orders or social imaginaries is not just an obstacle to autonomy, but plays a constitutive role in the process of self-constitution, in the "genesis of

---

49. Cf. Otfried Höffe, *Democracy in an Age of Globalisation*, Dirk Haubrich and Michael Ludwig (trans.) (Dordrecht: Springer, 2007); Wolfgang Kersting, *Theorien der sozialen Gerechtigkeit* (Stuttgart: Metzler, 2000); Ursula Wolf, *Das Tier in der Moral* (Frankfurt: Klostermann, 1990).

50. Axel Honneth, *The Struggle for Recognition: The Moral Grammar of Social Conflicts,* Joel Anderson (trans.) (Cambridge, MA: MIT Press, 1995). The plurality of spheres has also been explored by Michael Walzer in *Spheres of Justice* (New York: Basic Books, 1983) and by Charles Taylor in his defense of cultural identity in "The Politics of Recognition," in *Multiculturalism,* Gutmann (ed.).

51. Martin Seel, *Versuch über die Form des Glücks* (Frankfurt: Suhrkamp, 1995).

52. Hans Joas (1948–) studied sociology at the Free University of Berlin. He has taught at the University of Erlangen-Nuremberg (1987–90), at the Free University of Berlin (1990–2002), at the University of Chicago (2000–) and the University of Erfurt (2002–2011).

values," or in what Charles Sanders Peirce called "the fixation of belief." This new approach has much in common with what may be called a social turn within phenomenology: Waldenfels (see section V), Hans Jonas (see section VII), Michael Theunissen,[53] Rainer Marten (1928–),[54] and others venture to think with and against Heidegger's "being-with" and seek to understand the relation to the Other without relying on either individualistic premises or on an all-embracing social framework.

The emphasis on the agent, a main feature of Habermas's Kantian transformation of early critical theory, paves the way to a reconsideration of the complex internal structure of the subject, but it also attracts criticisms from social theorists who dismiss any strong notion of agency and autonomy and turn to social structures instead. In the famous controversy on "theory of society or social technology," Niklas Luhmann's "systems theory" established itself, at least in Germany, as the main contender to Habermas's social philosophy.[55] From the late 1980s on, Luhmann[56] published a series of volumes that were dedicated to the analysis of different social spheres: the economy, education, art, politics, religion, and so on. In his groundbreaking work *Social Systems*, Luhmann describes "self-referential systems" and the "co-evolution" of societal structures on the one hand, psychological structures of individuals on the other.[57] Following Luhmann, the identity of individuals is emerging from an "autopoietical" process of social differentiation and is directly linked to socially generated meaning. Luhmann borrows this concept of meaning from Husserl's phenomenology, yet he does not allow for an account of subjective intentionality or for an analysis of individual agency from within.[58]

A discontent with the subject in a totally different context comes to the fore in the work of Peter Sloterdijk.[59] In his account of modern societies, he neither analyzes the premises of individual agency and commitment (as do Habermas, Joas, and others), nor promotes disillusionment in Luhmann's sense. It could be said that Sloterdijk is rather concerned with a reenchantment of the world, as he seeks to reorganize our modern worldview along the lines of fairly vague

---

53. Michael Theunissen, *Der Andere: Studien zur Sozialontologie der Gegenwart* (Berlin: De Gruyter, 1965), and *Selbstverwirklichung und Allgemeinheit* (Berlin: De Gruyter, 1982).
54. Rainer Marten, *Der menschliche Mensch* (Paderborn: Schöningh, 1988).
55. Jürgen Habermas and Niklas Luhmann, *Theorie der Gesellschaft oder Sozialtechnologie* (Frankfurt: Suhrkamp, 1971).
56. Niklas Luhmann (1927–98) studied law at the University of Freiburg. After numerous administrative positions, he taught sociology at the University of Bielefeld from 1968 to 1993.
57. Niklas Luhmann, *Soziale Systeme* (Frankfurt: Suhrkamp, 1984), 24, 92.
58. *Ibid.*, 60, 93.
59. Peter Sloterdijk (1947–) studied philosophy and literature at the University of Munich. He has taught at the University of Arts in Karlsruhe (1992–) and the Academy of Fine Arts in Vienna (1993–).

metaphors such as "globe," "bubble," "foam," and so on. His approach has much in common with Oswald Spengler's "morphology" in *The Decline of the West*, which was published shortly after the First World War.[60] As a member of the "New Age" generation who spent two years with Bhagwan Shree Rajneesh in India, and as a representative of what he calls the "Heideggerian Left," Sloterdijk criticizes the self-confidence of the "active subject."[61] His attempt to recreate a new shelter for the modern individual remains highly ambivalent though, as his discontent or weariness with the present age makes him susceptible to the temptation of overcoming the "human" and making use of modern genetics for creating or rearing a new mankind.[62]

VII. ANTHROPOLOGY: THE THEORY OF COMPENSATION, NEO-ARISTOTELIANISM, METAPHOROLOGY

The dissatisfaction with the master-narrative of individual emancipation has led not only to postmodernism, but also to a reappraisal of premodern traditions. As mentioned above (see section II), the Ritter School was centrally concerned with modern diremption in a Hegelian sense, yet instead of enrolling in a project of modernity that would eventually lead to the liberalization of lifestyles and to the self-organization of citizenry, the Ritter School said "farewell"[63] to theories of progress and to the Hegelian tradition of *Geschichtsphilosophie*. According to Ritter and his disciples Robert Spaemann[64] and Odo Marquard,[65] modern diremption cannot be healed or sublated in some kind of higher reconciliation. We can bear the burden of modernity only by relying on institutions that compensate for a blatant loss of orientation. Central to their account is the theory of "compensation"[66] that they borrow from one of the main representatives

---

60. Peter Sloterdijk, *Sphären I/II/III: Blasen/Globen/Schäume* (Frankfurt: Suhrkamp, 1998–2004).

61. Peter Sloterdijk, *Kritik der zynischen Vernunft* (Frankfurt: Suhrkamp, 1983), 395, 938–42; published in English as *Critique of Cynical Reason*, Michael Eldred (trans.) (Minneapolis, MN: University of Minnesota Press, 1987), 209, 537–40.

62. Peter Sloterdijk, "Regeln für den Menschenpark: Ein Antwortschreiben zu Heideggers Brief über den Humanismus," in *Nicht gerettet: Versuche nach Heidegger*, Peter Sloterdijk (ed.) (Frankfurt: Suhrkamp, 2001).

63. Odo Marquard, *Schwierigkeiten mit der Geschichtsphilosophie* (Frankfurt: Suhrkamp, 1973), 20.

64. Robert Spaemann (1927–) studied philosophy at the University of Münster with Ritter. He has taught at the universities in Stuttgart (1962–68), Heidelberg (1969–72), and Munich (1972–92).

65. Odo Marquard (1928–) studied philosophy at the University of Münster with Ritter and at the University of Freiburg with Max Müller. He has taught at the University of Giessen (1965–93).

66. Cf. Odo Marquard, "Kompensation: Überlegungen zu einer Verlaufsfigur geschichtlicher Prozesse," in *Aesthetica und Anaesthetica*, Odo Marquard (ed.) (Paderborn: Schöningh, 1989),

of philosophical anthropology in Germany, Arnold Gehlen.[67] This theory is guided by the idea that the shortcomings of individual self-regulation are to be compensated for by cultural, social, and political institutions. This account has an anthropological twist as it is based on the assumption that such compensation meets certain invariable, unalterable needs of human being as such.

The second generation of the Ritter School does not speak with one voice. For example, Marquard defends compensation in the light of a more negative, skeptical account of modern life, and his skepticism regarding social experiments leads him to a defense of traditions and to an affirmation of the status quo.[68] Spaemann's praise of institutions, in turn, is based on a more positive account of human existence and personal integrity. In a compelling critique of Luhmann's sociological functionalism, Spaemann turns away from the notion of the modern individual as a "man without qualities."[69] The fact that Spaemann discussed Luhmann's work in such detail stands as an impressive example of an intellectual exchange among German philosophers and social theorists that transcends methodological and ideological borders. Spaemann seeks to retrieve the "qualities" of the modern man by interpreting the human being as a "person" whose integrity deserves protection and entails moral obligations.[70] Following Spaemann, a person leading a life that aims at the "good life" cannot help but refer to and rely on values. A person does not generate them, but cannot do without them or even "owes" herself to them. Spaemann argues that a Nietzschean reevaluation of values runs against the human condition, as does a Kantian or Habermasian rational justification of values. Spaemann does not deny human freedom, but redefines it based on primordial commitments and convictions. In his critique of Frankfurt, Spaemann suggests that freedom consists in revising volitions rather than in determining them.[71] When we compare Spaemann's Aristotelian Catholicism to, for example, Martha Nussbaum's "Aristotelian social

---

and "Zukunft und Herkunft: Bemerkungen zu Joachim Ritters Philosophie der Entzweiung," in *Skepsis und Zustimmung* (Stuttgart: Reclam, 1994), 15–29.

67. Arnold Gehlen (1904–76) taught at universities in Leipzig, Königsberg, Vienna, Speyer, and Aachen. He was one of the founders of "philosophical anthropology." His major work *Der Mensch: Seine Natur und seine Stellung in der Welt* (*Man: His Nature and Place in the World*) appeared in 1940 and, in a "de-Nazified" version, in 1950.

68. Marquard, *Skepsis und Zustimmung*, 12–13.

69. Robert Spaemann, "Niklas Luhmanns Herausforderung der Philosophie: Laudatio anläßlich der Verleihung des Hegel-Preises 1989 an Niklas Luhmann," in Niklas Luhmann and Robert Spaemann, *Paradigm lost: Über die ethische Reflexion der Moral* (Frankfurt: Suhrkamp, 1990).

70. Robert Spaemann, *Personen: Versuche über den Unterschied zwischen "etwas" und "jemand"* (Stuttgart: Klett-Cotta, 1996), 84.

71. *Ibid.*, 233.

democracy,"[72] it becomes evident that Spaemann's anthropological account puts much more weight on substantial preconditions of the "good life" than does Nussbaum. In his view of education, for instance, he puts values first and allows for critical reconsiderations of any kind only after a set of firm convictions has already been established.[73]

It is safe to say that the issue of intergenerational relations presents a particular challenge to liberal moral philosophy. Spaemann detects this challenge in his claim that the ideal of autonomous decision-making cannot be applied to children and may even not be an ideal suitable to the human life form at all. Intergenerational relations could be regarded as a kind of showcase for the new fusion of anthropology and ethics in general. On display are the limits of emancipation as well as alternative justifications for moral duties. Thus Jonas[74] discovers a primal scene of morality in the anthropological bond between parent and child. In his work on *The Imperative of Responsibility*, he seeks to overcome the "is–ought" problem by claiming that the parental "being with the child" is insolubly linked to the immediate moral demand for protecting it, caring for it, and so on. In an ethical re-reading of Heidegger's "being-with," Jonas urges us to rely on this primordial source of morality and to extend it to a responsibility for a livable future on earth in general. Substantialist anthropologies of this kind are always prone to generalizing certain findings: in this case, the bond between parents and children. It is hard to make the case that this bond is not subject to historical change and cultural differences. Yet there is also a type of anthropology that evades criticisms from the side of historical relativists. For example, an anthropological account does not necessarily aim at substantial claims on the assets of human nature, but could also be concerned with structural descriptions of human behavior: Plessner's notion of the "eccentric positionality" of the person that accounts for individual embodiment as well as for reflective self-distancing may serve as an example in this respect. Plessner, who is much more cautious with references to biological findings than Gehlen, has also been a major inspiration for Hans-Peter Krüger's (1954–) innovative contributions to this area of research.[75]

---

72. Martha Nussbaum, "Aristotelian Social Democracy," in *Liberalism and the Good*, R. Bruce Douglass *et al.* (eds) (New York: Routledge, 1990).

73. Hermann Lübbe *et al.*, "Erklärung," in *Mut zur Erziehung*, Wilhelm Hahn *et al.* (eds) (Stuttgart: Klett-Cotta, 1979), 163–5. For a critique of Spaemann's view of education, see Ernst Tugendhat, *Ethik und Politik* (Frankfurt: Suhrkamp, 1992), 17–25.

74. Hans Jonas (1903–93) studied at the University of Freiburg and the University of Marburg with Heidegger and Bultmann. He emigrated to England in 1933, joined the British Army during the Second World War and also fought in the 1948 Arab–Israeli War. He later taught at the New School of Social Research in New York (1955–76).

75. Cf. Hans-Peter Krüger, *Zwischen Lachen und Weinen*, Vol. I: *Das Spektrum menschlicher Phänomene* (Berlin: Akademie, 1999), and *Zwischen Lachen und Weinen*, Vol. 2: *Der dritte*

While Spaemann's and Jonas's philosophical anthropology is pitched to the liberal consensus in recent moral philosophy, Blumenberg's[76] anthropology is pitched to the consensus that describes the modern age as a success story of full-fledged emancipation. Blumenberg's anthropological reflections go back to the beginning of the modern age, that is to the age of "secularization" and "self-assertion."[77] His reading of the modern subject is not based on a theory of self-acquaintance (as is Henrich's), but goes back to the concern with self-preservation that plays a central role in early modern philosophy. Compared to this tradition, however, Blumenberg's concept of self-preservation has its own distinctive features.

Blumenberg does not address self-preservation as it appears on the horizon of the individual and its interests (e.g. in Hobbes); instead, he asks the question of how self-preservation could be put on the modern agenda in the first place. He sees it as an outcome of a dramatic resurgence of human finitude, of earthly existence. According to Blumenberg, the modern age is humane in the specific sense that it is willing to finally acknowledge and to take charge of the finite existence of human beings. The "legitimacy" of the modern age in general and of technological progress in particular does not consist in Promethean emancipation,[78] but lies in the willingness to take the concerns of finite existence seriously. Blumenberg shares this interest in temporality with Theunissen,[79] who complements current theories of the good life by exploring various forms of pathologies linked to temporal experiences and by hinting at life forms that make temporality bearable or livable, guided by the question "Können wir in der Zeit glücklich sein?" (Is it possible to be happy under the reign of time?).[80]

With the focus on individual frailty, Blumenberg marks the greatest possible difference from the critique of the modern subject put forward by Heidegger on the one hand and Horkheimer/Adorno on the other hand (see above, section

---

Weg Philosophischer Anthropologie und die Geschlechterfrage (Berlin: Akademie, 2001); cf. Bernard G. Prusak, "The Science of Laughter: Helmuth Plessner's Laughing and Crying Revisited," *Continental Philosophy Review* 38(1–2) (2005).

76. Hans Blumenberg (1920–96) studied philosophy in Frankfurt, but later became a victim of racial persecution and had to hide from the Nazis. After the Second World War he continued his studies at the University of Hamburg and the University of Kiel with Ludwig Landgrebe. He taught at the universities in Hamburg (1958–60), Giessen (1960–65), Bochum (1965–70), and Münster (1970–85).

77. Hans Blumenberg, *The Legitimacy of the Modern Age*, Robert M. Wallace (trans.) (Cambridge, MA: MIT Press, 1983), 63, 125.

78. Cf. the comments on technology and against emancipation in Hans Blumenberg, *Wirklichkeiten, in denen wir leben* (Stuttgart: Reclam, 1981), 47, 49.

79. Michael Theunissen (1932–) studied philosophy at the University of Bonn and the University of Freiburg with Max Müller. He has taught at the universities in Berne (1967–71), Heidelberg (1971–80), and Berlin (1980–98).

80. Michael Theunissen, *Negative Theologie der Zeit* (Frankfurt: Suhrkamp, 1991), 37–86.

II). Given the contingency and frailty of human existence, self-preservation is concerned not only with bodily needs, but with individual vulnerability as such. A major challenge to the concern with individual self-preservation is the collapse of a cosmological order (or the "disembedding" of the individual, as it has been called in a totally different context[81]). Under modern conditions, the individual becomes more and more aware of the dramatic rift between its lifespan and the world as a whole.[82] The individual's place in the world is insecure; it is left alone with its sense of belonging.

Even though Blumenberg did not belong to the Ritter School, he was at least as impressed by Gehlen's theory of compensatory institutions[83] as were Marquard and others. Yet in his theory of compensation, Blumenberg proves to be aware of the limited reach of social institutions. His quest for an order that may provide orientation leads him to language, which itself is deemed to be fragile. We are not capable of scientifically reorganizing our world, hence we take refuge in metaphors that serve us as guidelines. As these metaphors are irreducible to any objective reality, they can only be "absolute metaphors."[84] This does not mean that they are useless, however. According to Blumenberg, human self-understanding cannot engage with "reality" in any direct, unmediated manner and relies on words lacking unequivocal referentiality.[85] When he uses the term "anthropology," he does not mean to refer to biological findings, but hints at the fact that the *conditio humana* is the condition of an "*animal symbolicum*," referring at this point directly to Ernst Cassirer's theory of symbolic forms.[86] Thus the debate on anthropology reaches out to the philosophical debate on language. If "being human" means relying on something that "is not," that is metaphors, we are invited to adopt a paradoxical self-image that leads from being to nonbeing and vice versa. It is striking to see how these considerations based on Blumenberg's metaphorology come close to debates that are familiar to theorists of deconstruction. Whoever wants to attack complacent self-identity finds the best possible witness in Michel de Montaigne, who is quoted by Blumenberg with the marvelous phrase: "The worst place we can take is in ourselves."[87]

---

81. Anthony Giddens, *The Consequences of Modernity* (Stanford, CA: Stanford University Press, 1990), 21–8.

82. Hans Blumenberg, *Lebenszeit und Weltzeit* (Frankfurt: Suhrkamp, 1986), 67.

83. Blumenberg, *Wirklichkeiten, in denen wir leben*, 115.

84. Hans Blumenberg, *Paradigmen zu einer Metaphorologie* (Frankfurt: Suhrkamp, 1998), 11.

85. Blumenberg, *Wirklichkeiten, in denen wir leben*, 115.

86. *Ibid.*, 114; cf. Ernst Cassirer, *An Essay on Man* (New York: Doubleday, 1956), 44. [*] For a discussion of Cassirer's theory of symbolic forms, see the essay by Sebastian Luft and Fabien Capeillères in *The History of Continental Philosophy: Volume 3*.

87. Blumenberg, *Wirklichkeiten, in denen wir leben*, 135.

VIII. CONCLUSION

Given the vast array of topics and traditions that we have encountered on our path through the labyrinth of recent German philosophy, any attempt to summarize these "themes out of school" would be futile. Let me instead conclude with three short remarks.

1. It goes without saying that this account of some recent developments in German philosophy is by no means exhaustive. This short overview could at best serve as an invitation to the reader to further engage in these debates and to explore what has been left aside or mentioned in passing only. Among the significant thinkers who, because of space constraints, have not been discussed are Rüdiger Bubner, Volker Gerhardt, Friedrich Kambartel, and Hermann Lübbe.[88]
2. It should have become clear that the most striking and promising contributions often seek to cross boundaries: be it that they cross the line between different scholarly traditions and think "outside the box," or that they seek to overcome any narrow account of the subject, language, society, or anthropology. It should be regarded as a philosophical achievement of a kind if, at the end of the day, these topical distinctions appear to be insufficient.
3. If the reader came to the conclusion that the label "continental" does not really fit the philosophical work that has been presented here, I would not disagree.

---

88. Rüdiger Bubner (1941–2007) taught at the universities in Frankfurt (1973–79), Tübingen (1979–96), and Heidelberg (1996–2007). His work is in the areas of hermeneutics, political philosophy, and aesthetics. A specialist on Kant and Nietzsche, Volker Gerhardt (1944–) taught at Münster, Cologne, and Halle, before becoming professor of philosophy at Humboldt-Universität in Berlin in 1992. Friedrich Kambartel (1935–), who taught at the universities in Constance (1966–93) and Frankfurt (1993–2000), is a specialist in philosophy of language, science, and mind. Hermann Lübbe (1926–) taught at a number of German universities before joining the faculty in Zurich, where he taught from 1971 to 1991. He published widely on topics in political philosophy.

3

THE STRUCTURALIST LEGACY

Patrice Maniglier

It may seem strange to publish an essay entitled "The Structuralist Legacy" in a volume devoted to 1980s and 1990s French philosophy. After all, was structuralism not dominant for only a brief period of time in the 1960s (and maybe only from 1966 to 1968[1])? And was it not both rapidly disavowed by its own leaders (some of them giving way to "post-structuralism"), and also questioned on the level of its very identity, both as it hesitates between philosophy and the human sciences, and as it is progressively evolved into many arguably incompatible individual projects, such as those of Lévi-Strauss, Lacan, Foucault, Althusser, Deleuze, or Derrida? Equally, from a scientific perspective, has it not been superseded by cognitivism as the new transversal paradigm for the social sciences? While this may be the common view, the conviction underlying this essay is that structuralism has been the fundamental matrix of twentieth-century postwar French philosophy, running right up until the end of the century – a matrix realized in a diverging constellation of answers to philosophical problems raised by the introduction of structural methods into the social sciences. But it needs to be said from the beginning that we will not understand structuralism here as a determinate set of affirmative propositions bearing a lumbering, dogmatic identity, but rather as a movement that presents a problematic unity.[2] This unity derives from methodological reforms in the various empirical sciences that made them realize, each in their own way, that they could not establish them-

---

1. In 1966, both Foucault's *Les Mots et les choses* and Lacan's *Écrits* were published, and were huge best-sellers.
2. See Étienne Balibar, "Structuralism: A Destitution of the Subject," *Differences: A Journal of Feminist Cultural Studies* 14(1) (Spring 2003).

selves without passing through philosophical reflections on the very strange ontological nature of new entities that had been introduced into the scientific domain, such as the purely differential and positional entities that Ferdinand de Saussure called signs.

I would like to argue here that some of the most important works of 1980s and 1990s French philosophy (those of Alain Badiou, Étienne Balibar, Dominique Lecourt, Jacques-Alain Miller, Jean-Claude Milner, Michel Pêcheux, and Jean Petitot) originate in the idea – first put forward by both Lacan and Althusser in misleadingly similar terms just before 1968 – that far from dismissing the notion of subjectivity, structuralism offers the scientific and philosophical framework to give an accurate account of the emergence of subjects in the world. Most of these philosophers began their intellectual career as contributors to a little-known journal, the *Cahiers pour l'analyse*, which seems retrospectively to have staged the problematic of the next decades. Created by students of Althusser who attended Lacan's seminar when it was relocated to the École Normale Supérieure, the *Cahiers pour l'analyse* aimed to inquire into the epistemological status of psychoanalysis in the context of structuralism.[3]

Structuralism, thus understood, appears as an attempt to overcome Kant's dilemma: either science is possible, but we cannot understand how any subject can appear in the very world that can be made an object of science (since the transcendental structure of this world leaves no room for a genuinely self-determined entity); or there *are* subjects in the world, but we have to accept that something in reality resists scientific objectification. In contradistinction to Kant, structuralism aimed to make science and subjectivity compatible. However, this scientifically objectified world in which subjectivity could appear was not *nature*, but rather *culture*, understood as a set of symbolic systems (as in Lévi-Strauss's definition).[4] Here, the term symbolic refers not so much to a certain function (that of communication), as to a certain type of being, the being of differential and positional entities whose identities depend on their oppositional relations and structural positions within a system. In other words, structuralism offered a chance to make objective science and subjective experience compatible because it offered, through the concept of the sign, a new tran-

---

3. Ten issues of the journal appeared between 1966 and 1969. They are now all available online thanks to the AHRC funded project at Middlesex University "Concept and Form: The *Cahiers pour l'analyse* and Contemporary French Thought," www.web.mdx.ac.uk/crmep/cahiers (accessed August 2010). I am grateful to Peter Hallward, Ray Brassier, and Christian Kerslake for having provided me with their English translations of the texts.

4. See the definition of culture by Lévi-Strauss: "Any culture can be considered as a combination of symbolic systems headed by language, the matrimonial rules, the economic relations, art, science, religion" (*Introduction to the Work of Marcel Mauss*, Felicity Baker [trans.] [London: Routledge & Kegan Paul, 1987], 16).

scendental "ontology." Structuralism claimed that given what a cultural system is in general, it is possible, perhaps even necessary, for subjects to arise within it. Thus, the guiding question became transcendental: What must the ontology of culture, that is, the ontology of signs, be, so that subjects can appear and operate within our world? In what follows, I would like to show that the relation between structure as an ontological concept and subjectivity as an effect has been the vexing question of one of the most significant parts of post-1968 French philosophy, and that it remains a fertile issue today.

I. FROM STRUCTURALISM TO HYPERSTRUCTURALISM: ONTOLOGY OF STRUCTURE AND SUBJECTIVITY AS AN EFFECT

The idea that structuralism, far from dismissing the notion of subjectivity, on the contrary allowed us to understand it in a truly Freudian sense, was at the core of Lacan's teaching in the 1960s.[5] Freud's second topography – dividing the psyche into the agencies of ego, id, and superego – was, according to Lacan, nothing but "a reworking of the analytic experience in accordance with a dialectic best defined as what structuralism has since allowed us to elaborate logically: namely, the subject – the subject caught up in a constituting division."[6] Lacan finds in "a very particular mode of the subject" – a mode in which "the subject is, at it were, internally excluded from its object" – "the crucially important mark of structuralism."[7] To explain this sentence would require much more space than this essay allows,[8] but it is nonetheless necessary to briefly answer two preliminary questions, since both psychoanalysis and structuralism are commonly deemed to have utterly dismissed the notion of subjectivity in the account of our life.

Following French Marxist philosopher Georges Politzer's 1928 breakthrough work *Critique des fondements de la psychologie*, Lacan was convinced that psychoanalysis could not function without a notion of truth. Furthermore, this truth could not be an objective and substantial one (as if behind the illusions of the ego reigned the positive and deterministic forces of the unconscious), but needed to be a truly subjective one. There are good arguments for such a claim. As Sartre put it, why would I feel concerned by those wishes that appear through the cure to be at the origin of my symptoms and dreams if they were nothing but

---

*5. Lacan is the focus of an essay by Ed Pluth in *The History of Continental Philosophy: Volume 5*.

6. Jacques Lacan, *Écrits* (Paris: Éditions du Seuil, 1966), 856; published in English as *Écrits: The First Complete Edition in English*, Bruce Fink (trans.) (New York: Norton, 2006), 727.

7. Lacan, *Écrits*, 861; *Écrits: The First Complete Edition in English*, 731.

8. For a detailed account of Lacan's theory of subjectivity, see Bruce Fink, *The Lacanian Subject: Between Language and Jouissance* (Princeton, NJ: Princeton University Press, 1995).

rough facts, simple data of the world, or if I refer to them in an intersubjective way or as "other"?[9] What reason do I have to consider them as "mine"? Why should I assume these wishes more than, say, the ones of the analyst? And if I do not assume them, can the cure still be efficient?

But if the subject is not a *thing*, nor is it a transparent, self-determined, and self-constituted capacity of action, as Kant suggested. To put it rather metaphorically, we could say that the subject is never contemporary or coincident with its own engendering (as it is for Kant, since it is strictly coextensive with the rationality of moral law). Instead, the subject is always behind itself, it finds itself as having-always-already-*decided*, constituting itself through this very delay even though this primary being-already-here does not enable it to record itself as a fact. To designate the paradoxical nature of the subject, Lacan famously coined the term "split subject," characterized as follows: "I am thinking where I am not, therefore I am where I am not thinking."[10] This does not mean, though, that I am somewhere else, but rather that I am *nothing other than this very displacement*. We may add that Lacan suggested that such a truth, which does not lie in the correspondence between a sign and a fact, can be found in *figures*, in the sense of rhetorical figures, where a sign functions not by referring to a thing, but as a displacement from one sign to another. The truth of a proposition such as "I want to kill my father" would be of the same kind as "We are such stuff as dreams are made on and our little life is rounded by a sleep."

Now, this definition of the subject may strike us as rather unoriginal. After all, a very long tradition running at least from Hegel to Sartre, passing via Kierkegaard and Heidegger, also defined the subject as a relation to oneself given by the impossibility of coinciding with oneself, whether this takes the form of an impossible being that is what it is not and is not what it is, or of one for whom identity and difference are identical, of one that is at the same time a given and a task, or of one that is eventually an ecstatic term that cannot stand (in) itself.

What is original, though, is the claim that this paradoxical element, far from being originary and only accessible through a philosophical *a priori* approach, is "best elaborated" by a scientific approach such as structuralism. So, already a second preliminary question arises: In what sense does structuralism have anything to say about subjectivity? Has Saussure not argued that meaning is

---

9. "I *am* the ego, but I *am not* the *id*. I hold no privileged position in relation to *my* unconscious psyche. … I stand, in relation to my 'id,' in the position of the *Other*" (Jean-Paul Sartre, *L'Être et le néant: Essai d'ontologie phénoménologique* [Paris: Gallimard, 1943], 50–51; published in English as *Being and Nothingness: An Essay on Phenomenological Ontology*, Hazel E. Barnes [trans.] [London: Routledge, 1956], 90).

10. Lacan, *Écrits*, 517; *Écrits: The First Complete Edition in English*, 430.

not found in subjective intentions, but in signs' respective oppositions?[11] Did Lévi-Strauss not accept the characterization of his philosophical position as a "Kantianism without a transcendental subject"?[12] Did Althusser not defend a Spinozist "process without subject"?

The best argument to show that structuralism *needed* a theory of subjectivity was given by Jacques-Alain Miller, at the time only twenty years old, who would later become the editor of the *Cahiers pour l'analyse* and eventually Lacan's son-in-law and legatee. This argument was given in "Action de la structure," an article that, I will argue, formulates the basic program of his generation. If structuralism does not provide a theory of subjectivity, he writes, its extension to all the domains of cultural sciences, and especially to anthropology, is invalid: "as long as the *alteration* brought about by the exclusion of the speaking subject is not annulled, the structures proper to linguistics are of no value beyond their region of origin."[13] Why so? First, while linguistics may study the abstract objects that Saussure called *langues*, anthropology studies man in his living totality, including the complete range of his actions (speaking, working, etc.), as Lévi-Strauss himself acknowledged, reminding his readers that the true meaning of Mauss's notion of "total social fact" is precisely to "reintegrate subjectivity in objectivity."[14] But second, if structuralism is unable to explain the emergence of a subject as one of its effects (this very subject who considers himself or herself to be, at least in principle, the *origin* of all meanings), it will have to leave the explanation of the real functioning of structures to the most classic philosophical anthropology. For, even if we accept that a linguistic performance is nothing but the actualization of a possibility predetermined in the linguistic system, how can we account for *this* particular possibility being actualized rather than another one? Must it not be because of a subject who "chooses" it? Everything that structuralism was deemed to undermine – subjectivity, context, reference, practice – will then come back at another level, the level of *use* or *speech*, as Ricoeur's work convincingly shows.[15]

---

*11. For a discussion of Saussure's linguistic theory, see the essay by Thomas F. Broden in *The History of Continental Philosophy: Volume 5*.

12. As characterized by Paul Ricoeur; see "Structure and Hermeneutics," in *The Conflict of Interpretation: Essays on Hermeneutics*, Don Ihde (trans.) (Evanston, IL: Northwestern University Press, 1974), 52.

13. Jacques-Alain Miller, "Action de la structure," in *Un début dans la vie* (Paris: Gallimard, 2002), 61. This text was written in September 1964 and signed also by Jean-Claude Milner and Yves Duroux, in order to introduce a "cartel" (defined by its interest in "discourse theory") and then join Lacan's new school; it was published four years later in volume 9 of the *Cahiers pour l'analyse*; for details see Miller, *Un début dans la vie*, 57.

14. Lévi-Strauss, *Introduction to the Work of Marcel Mauss*, 33.

15. See Ricoeur, "Structure, Word, Event," in *The Conflict of Interpretations*, 79–97.

"Action de la structure" therefore argues that structuralism needs to give way to a perfectly general concept of structure (which therefore belongs to what he calls a *logic*, a theory of the form of a symbolic system in general, which he will call the "logic of the signifier"), one that will also explain or formalize the implication of a subjective effect in the workings of every symbolic system. These two aspects – a strictly conceptual approach to structuralism and a causal theory of subjectivity – define what Jean-Claude Milner will later call "hyperstructuralism."[16]

But a last preliminary concern arises: Can structuralism actually function at such a general level? Is there any such thing as a general logic of structure? Is it not the task of each discipline, concerned with its particular domain of culture (be it language, fashion, kinship, ritual, or myths), to offer a specific account of the actual subjective effect of its symbolic structures? Is it not well known that all general concepts of structure are either too precise to encompass the variety of usage of structural terms in the various disciplines it has been imported into, or too broad to be truly significant?

The best argument in favor of such a "logical" approach to the relation between structure and subjectivity is to be found not in Miller's 1964 "Action de la structure," but in Milner's later book *Le Périple structural* (2002), which is both one of the few serious historical interpretations of this period in French and a major sign of the renewed interest in structuralism in contemporary French philosophy. Milner's argument, coming from a linguist, has the advantage of being grounded in a profound understanding of the philosophical issues raised by structural linguistics. He remarks that it is inaccurate to say that structural linguistics discovered a structural dimension in language; one should rather say that it has *defined* linguistic reality by this structural dimension. For, belonging to a system is not a *property* of signs; it is that which constitutes them in their existence and essence: "structural linguistics constitutes itself precisely by aiming at disregarding in language everything that would be specific to language and

---

16. See Jean-Claude Milner, *L'Œuvre claire: Lacan, la science, la philosophie* (Paris: Éditions du Seuil, 1995), 104–12, and *Le Périple structural: Figures et paradigmes* (Paris: Éditions du Seuil, 2002), 141–68. Milner was a founding contributor to the *Cahiers pour l'analyse* and among the authors of "Action de la structure." He later turned to linguistics, developing one of the most important works in French linguistics, which offers an original criticism of structuralism under the influence of Noam Chomsky, but is ultimately critical of generative grammar (see Milner, *Introduction à une science du langage* [Paris: Éditions du Seuil, 1989]). Also influenced by Lacan, he devoted a large part of his work to the confrontation of linguistics with psychoanalysis (see his *L'Amour de la langue* [Paris: Éditions du Seuil, 1978], published in English as *For the Love of Language*, Ann Banfield [trans.] [Basingstoke: Macmillan, 1990]), before coming back on a historical and conceptual basis to the history of structuralism in *Le Périple structural*.

would thus obscure the structural level as such."[17] Therefore structuralism is the extension of a linguistic model to all cultural phenomena only because it is first a reduction of language to structure as such. We can go even further and argue that the extension of the concept of the sign to various cultural phenomena is not grounded on the assumption of a common *function* (for instance, that of communicating, as Roman Jakobson argued), but on a common problematic *mode of existence*. If variants of myths can rightfully be called signs, it is not because they serve to communicate, but because they share the same ontological characteristics that Saussure first isolated in language: differentiality, duality, codetermination, and so on.[18] There must, therefore, be a general theory of structure that sustains each application of structure to a particular domain. If it appears that such a general theory is in fact impossible, this would be a decisive argument against structuralism. In short, structuralism must be hyperstructuralist.

This remark is also important because it clarifies, retrospectively, the nature of the "logic" Miller pointed toward in "Action de la structure": this "logic," in truth, turns out to be an ontology. The *Cahiers pour l'analyse* therefore represents the moment when structuralism realizes its own ontological dimension. This gives us a more vivid image of its main hypothesis: it is because we are sensitive to the strange entities that Saussure called signs that we are constituted as subjects. Of course, this means that there needs to be some sort of cognitive function that underlies the constitution of these objects; however, this could very well be a blind, automatic, data-processing function – the symbolic function. Subjectivity itself, far from being the origin of discourse or the function that precedes and supports the signs we produce, is something that occurs in an already given domain of objects, the domain of language or discourse.[19] To the familiar structuralist motto "It speaks [*ça parle*]," we should add that the way it speaks implies that "I speak."

However, Miller used another argument in "Action de la structure" in favor of a purely conceptual or logical approach. He invokes Georges Canguilhem's

---

17. Milner, *Le Périple structural*, 144. See also what Milner calls "minimalisme de l'objet": "One will know a linguistic system only by constraining oneself to consider in it nothing but the minimal properties that constitute it as a system, that can be analyzed into minimal elements" (*L'Œuvre claire*, 97).

18. See Milner about Saussure: "Taken in its extension, the program could apply to any species of reality, if it is admitted (strong structuralist assumption) that any reality can be considered only from the point of view of its systemic relations. Pushed to its extreme point, it led to a new type of ontology. One understands that it ended up affecting all parts of the culture, from psychoanalysis to philosophy" (*Le Périple structural*, 38). For a detailed argument, see my *La Vie énigmatique des signes: Saussure et la naissance du structuralisme* (Paris: Léo Scheer, 2006).

19. Foucault will give a powerful expression to these structuralist themes in particular in *The Discourse on Language*.

definition of concepts[20] (which will figure in the epigraph of every issue of the *Cahiers pour l'analyse*) as a tool for exporting ideas and methods from one theoretical domain to another. For Canguilhem, Bachelard had argued that science was worked through by a "dialectic" that recognizes the same problematic structure in two apparently dissimilar domains of knowledge; for example, the dialectic between the theory of electricity and the theory of movement gives way to modern physics.[21] In the same way, according to Miller, the theory of structure was deemed to uncover the deep identity of apparently dissimilar theoretical domains; for example, Marxism and psychoanalysis, or, rather, the respective reinterpretations of each of them offered by Althusser and Lacan. Just as Lacan argued that the unconscious is not a positive substance behind consciousness, Althusser argued that the "real" causal forces in history do not constitute another substantial level of determination behind those that we believe to be efficacious, but are on the contrary to be looked for at the surface of these different levels and in the way they relate to each other in a "complex articulated whole."[22] The cause, therefore, is not a *thing*, but the structure itself. From this it is arguable that Althusser and Lacan's works are connected through their belief that a certain concept of structure has genuine causal power without defining another level of reality. This leads to the theory of "structural causality," in which structure is not another being behind appearances but is rather the "absent cause": a cause that exists only through its interpretations/effects.

The nature of the problem can now be reformulated: we have to find the concept of a cause that operates through the very way it triggers chains of operations where it *does not* "seem" to operate, or rather – since we must obviously avoid intentional concepts – that is absent from the very operations it guides. Hence the concept of a "causality of the lack" (*causalité du manque*), where the absence of the cause is the principle of its efficaciousness. If we can successfully argue that in each and every symbolic system there is one term that is included by the very manner in which it is excluded, that is, by a possibility that at the same time is its own impossibility, then we would have shown that symbolic systems cannot constitute themselves without implying a subject in the Freudian sense. How so? Because we have seen that the authentic definition of the subject

---

20. "[T]o work on a concept is to vary its extension and comprehension, to generalize it by incorporating exceptional traits, exporting it beyond its original region, taking it for a model or inversely seeking a model for it, in brief, to progressively confer the function of a form by regulated transformations" (Georges Canguilhem, "Dialectique et philosophie du non chez Gaston Bachelard," in *Etudes d'histoire et de philosophie des sciences* [Paris: Vrin, 1970], 206).
21. Gaston Bachelard, *Le Rationalisme appliqué* (Paris: Presses Universitaires de France, 1949), 200–201.
*22. Althusser is the focus of an essay by Warren Montag in *The History of Continental Philosophy: Volume 6*.

is not as a positive entity, but rather as a term that exists only in the form of a *being displaced*, as the impossibility of coinciding with itself.

II. SUTURE AND THE LOGIC OF THE SIGNIFIER:
JACQUES-ALAIN MILLER

The construction of this "logic of the signifier" has known many different stages. The first attempt was in a very influential text by Jacques-Alain Miller published in the first issue of the *Cahiers pour l'analyse*: "La Suture."[23] "Suture" is the name Miller gives to the relation whereby causality operates via what is lacking. The argument, though, seems surprising. Miller does not start from signs in Saussure's sense, but rather from Frege's tentative reduction of arithmetic to logic in his *Foundations of Arithmetic*, as if to show that in logic itself one can find a trace of subjectivity, that is, of a term that has no substantial identity but only a displacing function. Miller isolates three steps in Frege's reasoning. First, number is defined as *the concept of an identity to a concept*; for instance, "children of Agamemnon and Cassandra" refers to Pelops and Teledamus, but the concept "identical to the concept 'children of Agamemnon and Cassandra'" refers to 2, Pelops and Teledamos having been deprived of all their qualities and reduced to pure marks. Second, Frege invokes the concept of an object that is "non-identical to itself." Its extension is null, but the extension of the concept "identical to the concept of 'non-identical to itself'" is not empty: it is precisely *zero*. Zero is an object, although it does not subsume any object. Third, we remark that the concept of "the sequence of all the numbers up to 3" subsumes *four* terms: 3, 2, 1, and 0. Therefore, zero introduces an imbalance in the relation between numbers and objects: there are always more numbers than objects. What appears as an absence on the side of things functions as an excess on the side of names. This very imbalance is enough to engender the entire series of natural numbers, as if it was because we can represent nothing by something that everything can be put in a serial univocal order. The lack that zero subsumes does not exist, but it is efficacious: it operates, and operates even more because it does not exist as such. Zero is nothing but the displacement that it imposes on every other term in the series.

Of course, Miller sees in zero the trace of the subject:

> The impossible object, which the discourse of logic summons as
> the not-identical with itself and then rejects as the pure negative,

---

23. "La Suture" was published before "Action de la structure," but written after it, as "Action de la structure" was first presented at Lacan's seminar on February 24, 1965.

which it summons and rejects *wanting to know nothing of it*, we name this object, in so far as it functions as the excess which operates in the series of numbers, the subject. Its exclusion from the discourse which internally it intimates is suture. If we now determine the trait as the signifier and ascribe to the number the position of signified, the relation of the lack to the trait should be considered as the logic of the signifier.[24]

Miller's idea seems to be that because traditional forms of logic cannot account for zero, this would require another logic, one that is not concerned with concepts and objects, but rather with lacks and marks, or rather with signifier and subject, with signifiers that signify (literally) nothing, but, precisely because of this, are signified in turn by another signifier, illustrating Lacan's definition of the signifier as that which signifies the subject (the impossible or contradictory term) for another signifier.

Miller's construction is also in line with Lacan's notorious phrase: "The subject of the unconscious is the subject of science."[25] But its status is unclear. Is it just an example of the way "suture" (*causa in absentia*) works? Is it a way of clarifying the nature of the operation through which the subject exists in every structural domain by appealing to an analogy? But this interpretation would fall prey to a sort of vicious circle since the "logic of the signifier" would be made clear by appealing to what it grounds. We must rather read this text as an attempt to make a stronger point: that even the most formal and apparently unequivocal form of thinking relies on our access to the symbolic, that is, on our capacity to apprehend the strange entities that structuralists called signifiers. These do not function through reference, but thanks to the ability of one of them to hold the place of nothing and to trigger an autonomous series where each sign is built on another one by means of the imbalance between the positivity of signs and the nothing that they mark. This is a way of saying that behind formal logic itself one should look for the most fundamental logic, as in the first pages of Lévi-Strauss's *The Savage Mind*, where symbolic thought is presented as the precondition of every thought; this assumes that we define signs by a relation between not concepts and objects, but lacks and marks. However, it is fair to say that this "logic" cannot yet be found in "La Suture."

To find it, we have to turn to Miller's 1975 text "Matrice." We will reconstruct somewhat freely its argument in order to show its relation to the ontology of signs. According to Saussure, signs are positional entities: they have no other

---

24. Jacques-Alain Miller, "*Suture* (Elements of the Logic of the Signifier)," Jacqueline Rose (trans.), *Screen* 18 (Winter 1978), 32.

25. See Lacan, *Écrits*, 858; *Écrits: The First Complete Edition in English*, 729.

reference than their own position. But what is a position other than what is left when everything of the mark itself is erased – hence nothing? Therefore, a positional entity is an entity that contains, *as part of itself*, its own absence. The very concept of a positional entity thus implies a splitting of the object between itself and itself-*plus*-its-own-absence.[26] This provides the matrix for the iteration Term → Lack → Term (= Term + Nothing) → Lack …. It is still possible to distinguish among these terms (T', T'', …), but only by considering two series: the series of the terms and the series of their absences. These series are not parallel, but lagged (*décalés*) and relate to one another thanks to this very lag (*décalage*). It is also possible to consider them as the iteration of only one impossible or split entity, an entity that is all of them without being able to be any of them, an impossible object that is distant from itself and can thus be rightly called the subject.

A similar and somewhat simpler argument has been offered by Milner in *Le Périple structural*, arguing on the basis of the *differential* nature of signs. First, says Milner, we must remember that signs are relational entities. This implies that they have no properties unless there is another term. For instance, the phoneme /p/ can be said to be "voiceless," because there exists a term from which it is distinct (in English) according to this feature, /b/. Rigorously, /p/ does not *have* any property, since it is impossible to separate it from them: there is no substance to which we attribute these properties since it is *defined* by its distinctive features as a purely differential term.[27] Second, there is one property that is common to all the terms of any symbolic system: their being differential. But there needs to be a term to which all of them refer in this regard (since there are no properties without terms). Now, this term must also relate to itself as being distinct from itself. The conclusion follows that this term is the impossible or paradoxical term that exists only by absenting itself from every occurrence – the *subject*, in accordance with the tradition that defines it by this noncoincidence to itself: "Allowing that any structural term as such is non-identical to oneself, the subject is the term of the chain which supports the 'not-identical to oneself' of any term of the chain."[28]

Many objections could be made to this argument, but here let me simply draw attention to its reliance on two disputable presuppositions. The first one is that the very idea of a "logic of the signifier" implies that this logic must be valid for every symbolic process, and therefore both for scientific and nonscientific discourses alike. The problem here is that this claim could be accused of erasing

---

26. While Miller's reconstruction of Saussure bears some resemblance to Derrida's account of the trace, I would suggest that while Derrida's concept of trace implies a notion of time, with a reference to Husserl and Heidegger, such a notion of time is absent in Miller's account.

27. See Milner, *Le Périple structural*, 160–65.

28. *Ibid.*, 165.

the distinction between science and ideology under a homogeneous theory of symbolic processes. The second objection is that these analyses make sense (if they do) only on condition that the structuralist approach to cultural phenomena as signs (and therefore as differential entities) is empirically grounded. But this very approach has been challenged by Noam Chomsky's generative grammar. These objections will give way to alternative forms of "hyperstructuralism," which construe differently both the concept of structure and the concept of the subject.

III. FROM FORMAL PRODUCTIVITY TO THE MATHEMATICS OF BEING: BADIOU AGAINST THE LOGIC OF THE SIGNIFIER

The first objection was advanced by one of the most important contemporary French philosophers, Badiou, in one of his first articles, "Marque et manque: À propos du zéro," published precisely in *Cahiers pour l'analyse*.[29] I will even argue that Badiou's entire philosophical undertaking is rooted in the issues discussed here. Jacques-Alain Miller's application of the "logic of the signifier" to formal logic relies on Frege's unquestioned claim that the constitution of arithmetic requires an appeal to a purely conceptual impossibility (the "non-identical with itself"), to some unthinkable. But in "Marque et manque," Badiou attempts to prove that logic does not need to appeal to this operation that Miller called "suture," and logic is therefore liberated from the constraints of semiotic thinking. In line with Althusser's Spinozist inspiration in the 1960s, Badiou defends the claim that science, as opposed to ideology, is a process without a subject, a process entirely contained in the immanent productivity of its formal apparatus, and that, in direct contradistinction to Lacan, "there is no subject of science."

The heart of the objection is quite simple: Frege's construction relies on a definition of meaning as referring to an object. But this is not, according to Badiou, the way logical symbols work. In accordance with the most formalist understanding of logic, Badiou emphasizes that logical symbols should be regarded as letters that define operations on other letters, and that they do not refer to anything other than what has been previously introduced as a letter (or a sequence of letters) through purely constructive procedures that have nothing to do with "suture."[30] Likewise, zero refers to something that has been previously

---

*29. For a detained discussion of Alain Badiou, see the essay by Bruno Bosteels in *The History of Continental Philosophy: Volume 8*.

30. "La relation … de dénotation … dissimule l'essence strictement fonctionnelle des renvois intérieurs au mécanisme logique" (Alain Badiou, "Marque et manque: À propos du zéro," *Cahiers pour l'analyse* 10 [1969], 156).

defined at another level or layer of the formal theory. For it is a characteristic of every formal system that it is stratified: new systems can be built by introducing new rules and symbols in the former one. Badiou provides in his article the formal demonstration that it is possible to deduce zero without making any appeal whatsoever to the Unthinkable, but instead by playing on these different layers, zero being introduced at one level, excluded at another one, and reintroduced in the last one. A lack, in a formal system, is always the lack of a mark: there is no mark of the lack as such.

From this we can conclude that there is at least one language in which we do not need to speak of a subject (as an impossible object marked by a "placeholder"). This language is logic itself, the language of "science," and the core of all mathematical thinking. Therefore, Lacan was wrong to say that "the subject of the unconscious is the subject of science." Science has no subject, and this is what defines it in opposition to "ideology" or symbolic thought, which are characterized precisely by the way they hide their own productive processes.[31]

This early text is all the more interesting because Badiou's mature work appears as a sort of rigorous redaction of this first position. In *Being and Event*, Badiou endorses a clear "hyperstructuralist" perspective. First, he explicitly renounces the logicist understanding of mathematics that underpinned his critique of Miller's argument.[32] Second, he defends the claim that the subject, far from being a function of *ideology*, is a function of *truth*,[33] and even more strikingly, he endorses Miller's question about the compatibility of such a theory of the subject with ontology.[34] Third, this ontology appears to be a general theory of structure, and of a structure that leaves room for the emergence of a subject, closely echoing Miller's attempt to "formalize" Lacan's concepts. In short, it seems that in his later work, Badiou endorses the hyperstructuralist program, although redefining both the concept of structure and the notion of subject. While I cannot here do justice to Badiou's highly articulated construction, it may be enough to say that the gist of the attempt to prove the compatibility between a structural ontology and a theory of the subject relies on the discrepancy between structure (here defined as a way of turning a pure multiplicity

---

31. "The suture thus is not a concept of the signifier in general, but the property characteristic of the signifying order that comes to bar a subject. By name, *ideology*. There is always a subject of ideology, and this is the mark by which it is recognizable" (*ibid.*, 162).

32. "I had been caught in the grip of a logicist thesis which holds that the necessity of logico-mathematical statements is formal due to their complete eradication of any effect of sense" (Alain Badiou, *Being and Event*, Oliver Feltham [trans.] [London: Continuum, 2005], 5).

33. See *ibid.*, meditation 35.

34. "But that the process-subject be compatible with what is pronounceable – or pronounced – of being, there is a serious difficulty for you, one, moreover, that I pointed out in the question posed directly to Lacan by Jacques-Alain Miller in 1964: 'What is your ontology?' Our wily master responded by an allusion to Non-Being, which was well judged, but brief" (*ibid.*, 4).

– which as such contains nothing but multiplicities, thereby making it impossible to *count* – into a multiplicity of *units*, i.e., of elements belonging to it, that can be distinguished and counted[35]), and what Badiou calls metastructure. This metastructure replicates the operation of structure on its own effects, no longer counting elements, but subsets, and thus *re-presenting* the units that were previously presented by the structure. Now, it is well known that there are always more subsets of elements of a set than there are elements in a set. Badiou makes use of an important theorem by Paul Cohen (published in 1963), which proved that for infinite sets this difference cannot even be measured, to situate what in Being (i.e. multiples or sets) allows for the appearance of a subject. For, in these infinite sets, there are subsets that can be proved to exist even though they cannot be constructed from inside the language of the original situation: they are said to be "indiscernible." Badiou's claim is that truths are such subsets that we cannot grant existence to on the basis of what we already know, but that can be "forced" to realization. Now, the subject is nothing other than the operation through which a set is reorganized according to the *hypothesis* of the existence of such an indiscernible subset. Subjects are not entities but rather operations through which the consequences of a truth unfold in a world in which, prior to the truth's unfolding, they cannot be grounded.[36] But it is clear that the condition of possibility of the emergence of a subject in the world is the essential tearing up of any structure. Therefore, for Badiou as for Miller or Milner, it is the structural construal of Being that accounts for the possibility of subjectivity.

Even so, *Being and Event* can be seen as still marked by the decisions taken in his early article, and if there is one thing that characterizes Badiou's original answer to the Lacanian question, it is its enduring skepticism toward the very program of the "logic of the signifier." First, in the same way that he does not believe in a deeper logic than formal logic, Badiou does not accept the idea of a *specific* ontology of signs.[37] He claims that ontology is a perfectly general, nonspe-

---

35. "This is the most general definition of a *structure*; it is what prescribes, for a presented multiple, the regime of its count-as-one" (*ibid.*, 24).

36. For a more detailed and remarkable analysis of Badiou's theory of subjectivity, see Peter Hallward, *Badiou: A Subject to Truth* (Minneapolis, MN: University of Minnesota Press, 2003); and for an excellent account of Badiou's early controversy with Miller's "logic of the signifier" and more generally of the entire philosophical context that is discussed here, see Bruno Bosteels, "Alain Badiou's Theory of the Subject: Part I. The Recommencement of Dialectical Materialism," *Pli* 12 (2001).

37. The only moment in which Badiou seemed to have taken seriously the idea of a specific "logic" or ontology is *Théorie du Sujet*. But Badiou will disavow this attempt in the introduction of *Being and Event*, as a pointless pursuit of a dialectics of nature (see *L'Être et l'événement* [Paris: Éditions du Seuil, 1988], 10). But it could be argued that the very idea of a "great logic," which is at the core of his last major book, *Logics of Worlds*, nuances the picture here sketched and complicates Badiou's stand toward the legacy of a specifically semiotic ontology (see Patrice

cific theory of what *is*, inasmuch as it *is*, and inasmuch as it is nothing in particular. This single ontology is as valid for nature as it is for culture, and Badiou does not wish to distinguish between them. In the same way that formal logic does not require any "other" logic to provide a symptomal analysis of the former (as Miller pretended to do with Frege), Badiou holds that mathematics constitutes a qualitatively distinctive regime of signs that is entirely self-sufficient and cannot gain anything by being understood from the point of view of a general capacity for speaking or the symbolic function (in other words: there is no semiotic of mathematics). Particularly decisive is the fact that, for Badiou, the subject is not a *condition* coextensive to the constitution of a structure, but is rather something that arises from the introduction of a *transgressive* element within the structure: the event, defined as a set that belongs to itself. In contrast with Miller and Milner, who thought that every structure required a paradoxical element, for Badiou structured sets can perfectly well exist without implying any paradoxical element. The question is not "What must Being be in order that subjects *necessarily* arise?" but rather "What must Being be so that subjects *may* arise?" It is, in other words, a question of compatibility, not of emergence.[38] This point is very important because it implies that, for Badiou, it is not enough to be able to speak to become a subject; becoming a subject requires access to truth, not merely to signifiers, and this access is by definition *rare*. Subjectivity is not a *given* dimension of our lives and, in opposition to Lacan, who he claims "supposed there were 'always' some truths and some subjects,"[39] Badiou holds that many speaking beings can perfectly well live their entire lives without becoming subjects.

IV. A THEORY OF IDEOLOGY: LECOURT, BALIBAR, PÊCHEUX

This impressive attempt to provide a theory of the subject from a different form of hyperstructural perspective, one that does not make any appeal to the "logic of the signifier," is nonetheless confronted by two lines of objections, defining two new topical positions on the map of late twentieth-century French philosophy we are trying to draw. The first one remains on the epistemological terrain that motivated Badiou's first objection. For in both his early articles and his late books, Badiou relies heavily on the main thesis of what has been called the

---

Maniglier and David Rabouin, "A quoi bon l'ontologie? Les Mondes selon Badiou," *Critique* 719 [April 2007]).

38. Meditation 15 of *Being and Event* criticizes Hegel for offering a "generative ontology," one that tries to make the One emerge from the multiple.

39. Badiou, *Being and Event*, 474.

French epistemological tradition[40] (which was being reinterpreted at that time by Althusser): the thesis that science is not about *finding* truths, as if such truths were out there waiting for an adequate intelligence to bring them to light, but about *creating* them. This *creation* does not imply any form of relativism; on the contrary, it grounds their universality (since they cannot be reduced to their own conditions of occurrence). Bachelard's concept of "epistemological break" was intended precisely to argue that science is not a continuous process of ever accumulating correct opinions about the world, but rather a discontinuous series of complete reframings of the very structure of thought, as if truths always created their own subjective conditions.[41] Truth is always revolutionary, changing at the same time both what can be held as objective and the subjective capabilities of thought.

But this sharp distinction between science and nonscience has been put in question within the Bachelardian tradition itself by several of Althusser's students. They claim that this distinction is a typical way of ideologizing science, one that hypostasizes (not to say totemizes) it by taking it away from the history of human beings. It thus remains always in danger of losing Bachelard's main breakthrough: that there is no such thing as science in general, only *effects* of historical disruption.

Dominique Lecourt, whose later work in philosophy and history of science would prove to be very attentive to the images that guide our concept of science and their political implications,[42] pointed out very early in his career that "it is clear what is designated, but not thought, by Bachelard: the necessity, in order to build the concept of a history of science, to refer it to a theory of ideologies and to their history."[43] This translation into the vocabulary of ideology aimed to overcome the main disadvantage of Bachelard's concept of *imagination*: its absolutely nonhistorical character. Imagination, for Bachelard, is the

---

*40. For a discussion of this tradition, see the essay by Pierre Cassou-Noguès in *The History of Continental Philosophy: Volume 4*.

41. This idea would lead to the program of a historicization of transcendental philosophy that Foucault makes fully explicit in *The Archaeology of Knowledge*. About Foucault, see Béatrice Han, *Foucault's Critical Project: Between the Transcendental and the Historical*, Edward Pile (trans.) (Stanford, CA: Stanford University Press, 2002); and about this peculiar link between truth and history, which is characteristic of the French epistemological tradition, see Enrico Castelli Gattinara, *Les Inquiétudes de la raison: Épistémologie et histoire en France dans l'entre-deux-guerres* (Paris: Vrin, 1998).

42. See Dominique Lecourt, *Lyssenko: Histoire réelle d'une "science prolétarienne"* (Paris: François Maspéro, 1976), *Prométhée, Faust, Frankenstein: Fondements imaginaires de l'éthique* (Le Plessis-Robinson: Institut Synthélabo, 1996), and *Déclarer la philosophie* (Paris: Presses Universitaires de France, 1997).

43. Dominique Lecourt, *Marxism and Epistemology: Bachelard, Canguilhem and Foucault*, Ben Brewster (trans.) (London: New Left Books, 1975), 141.

function that produces the evident perceptions through which we make sense of our everyday world and that constitutes obstacles to scientific knowledge. But Lecourt rightfully remarks that this concept undermines Bachelard's own breakthrough – the rejection of any general philosophy of knowledge (science, being a historical process continually tumbling over its own conditions, ruins in advance all attempt to specify them *a priori*) – since imagination is nothing but the timeless condition of science, with Bachelard's "poetics" as the equivalent of a transcendental theory of knowledge. Ideology, on the contrary, designates the historical apparatuses that *produce* these evident perceptions. Since this formulation, Lecourt has provided many practical examples of a history of science that refuses to sever itself from cultural history.

Étienne Balibar, who is best known for his contributions to political philosophy,[44] defended the same arguments on a more conceptual basis in a series of articles about Althusser (*Écrits pour Althusser*) and a short book entitled *Lieux et noms de la vérité*. Drawing on Canguilhem's paradoxical concept of "scientific ideology,"[45] he undertook to show, through the example of mechanism, that ideology is not only a negative condition from which we have to depart, but that it is also a positive factor that contributes to history. Even though the metaphysical (viz. "ideological") debates about the possible interpretations (substantialist or positivist) of the concepts of force, absolute space, and time, function as "epistemological obstacles" in light of Einstein's revolutionary transformation of physics, they also make explicit the internal contradictions of Newton's classical mechanics, thus preparing its crisis: "[Mechanism's] role of epistemological obstacle is not turned solely toward the past. On the contrary, it dialectically contributes to carry science toward its future, thus towards its crisis."[46] Therefore the relation of "science" and "ideology," far from being one of only asymmetrical breaking-up, is more dialectical: the reideologization of science contributes to its history. This means that truths can never break so completely from the general history of mankind that they could be said to be "eternal" (in the sense that they would create their own conditions of intelligibility): they cannot function outside their own ideological context. As a consequence, the history of science can neither be separated from cultural history nor reduced to it. Truths are local processes, and even though they cannot be reduced to mere symptoms of a worldview or to social contradictions, they must nonetheless be defined by what they *do* to the symbolic or ideological systems they contribute

---

*44. Balibar's work in political philosophy is discussed in this volume in the essay on Spinozism by Simon Duffy, and in the essay by Rosi Braidotti in *The History of Continental Philosophy: Volume 8*.

45. Georges Canguilhem, "Qu'est-ce qu'une idéologie scientifique?," in *Idéologie et rationalité dans l'histoire des sciences de la vie* (Paris: Vrin, 1977).

46. Étienne Balibar, *Lieux et noms de la vérité* (La Tour-d'Aigues: Édition de l'Aube, 1994), 146.

to transforming. Saying this does not open the door to relativism, but escapes the very opposition between relativism and universalism.[47] The entire question becomes one of the transfer of scientific events into the world they bring about in order that they maintain their revolutionary power.[48] While Badiou wants to guarantee that truths will always have the same persisting power (once a truth, forever a truth), Balibar and Lecourt argue that, even if it is right to say that science escapes from time,[49] it is truer to say that it never ceases tearing itself away from it.[50] Truth is a process or, even better, an *activity*, rather than an event separating two entirely distinct regimes of thought.[51]

This has far-reaching consequences for the problems at stake in this essay, since the concept of the subject can no longer be derived from a radical break from the ordinary circumstances of symbolic life. However, we also cannot reduce scientific discourses to any general symbolic logic, since there *are* ruptures: the subject of science *is not* the subject of the unconscious. Instead of trying to explain subjectivity within a univocal logic either of the signifier or of truth, we should rather pay attention to the variety of regimes of subjectification at work in different types of discourses, and to the different forms of subjectification at work within each regime. The theory of subjectivity is now understood as the theory of the techniques through which historically resulting forms of thought erase their own production in order to appear as obvious, intuitive, and deprived of any historical conditions. Epistemological breaks become *displacements* of already given intuitions and, therefore, processes of *desubjectivization* and *resubjectivization*.[52] In other words, as Althusser argued in his late work, the theory of subjectivity is nothing but the theory of ideology – and vice versa.[53]

---

47. "One could even say, negatively, that a general definition of the break consists of this: scientific knowledge is only thinkable insofar as it produces an effect of truth, *neither as 'absolute,' nor as 'relative'*" (*ibid.*, 158, my translation).

48. The characteristic of a scientific concept, such as the concept of relativity, is that it "can be carried out in contradictory research programs which follow one another indefinitely" (*ibid.*, 155, my translation).

49. "Science escapes from 'general time' (the time of the world, of humanity, of universal history, in which the idea of progress, or relative truth, would like on the contrary to bring it back, as if science and history were the mirror of each other)" (*ibid.*, 161, my translation).

50. "[L]a science ne cesse jamais de s'en extraire" (*ibid.*).

51. It is fair to say that Badiou's last book, *Logics of Worlds*, offers a powerful answer to this criticism, since it defines the eternity of truth as a capacity of being transported from the world in which it occurs to any other world it contributes to bring about. See our discussion of Badiou on this point in Maniglier and Rabouin, "A quoi bon l'ontologie?"

52. "Any science is as such, not the knowledge of a pure 'object,' but science of *something of the formal determinations of a subject*" (Balibar, *Lieux et noms de la vérité*, 130, my translation).

53. "[T]here is no ideology except by the subject and for subjects" (Louis Althusser, "Ideology and Ideological State Apparatuses," in *Lenin and Philosophy and Other Essays*, Ben Brewster [trans.] [London: New Left Books, 1971], 170).

However, the most complete formulation of such a theory is not to be found in Balibar's or Lecourt's contributions, but in the work of another student of Althusser and contributor to the *Cahiers pour l'analyse* (under the pseudonym Thomas Herbert[54]), Michel Pêcheux.[55] In his unfortunately little-known work, he is among the few philosophers to have tried to draw the consequences for an empirical theory of language of Lacan's and Althusser's questions about the relation between structure and subjectivity. In his main book, *Les Vérités de la palice*, Pêcheux sets for himself the ambitious project of producing a theory of the subject as an effect of a symbolic process, a process that is exactly coextensive with the production of *meaning*. This is the theory of a mechanism that produces *as a result* something that does not seem to be produced at all, a thing that functions as a *cause of itself*.[56]

Pêcheux first criticizes the idea that meaning could possibly be an immanent property of linguistic signs belonging to the linguistic *system* itself. He argues that meaning is always ascribed from a position within an enunciative context; the meaning of the same words can vary according to the position taken by the speaker. There is no meaning, therefore, without somebody being constituted as a subject of discourse. The first part of his book is devoted to proving that referentialist theories of meaning (Frege and Russell in particular) necessarily imply an appeal to an enunciative context, expressed through words such as "this," "here," and "now," which obviously only makes sense along with "I."

However, instead of considering the situation where "I see this thing, here and now" is the real originary source of meaning, Pêcheux argues for a truly materialist theory of both meaning and subjectivity. He appeals to Althusser's theory of interpellation, according to which the subject is produced, but produced as that which does not need to be produced, as that which is "always-already there." Althusser illustrated the concept of interpellation with the famous little dialogue: "Hey, you there!" "Yes, here I am!" In this, the "I" does not precede the answer, but is rather constituted by recognizing itself in the one that is addressed. This

---

54. See Thomas Herbert, "Réflexions sur la situation théorique des sciences sociales et, spécialement, de la psychologie sociale," *Cahiers pour l'analyse* 2 (February 1966), and "Pour une théorie générale des idéologies," *Cahiers pour l'analyse* 9 (Summer 1968).

55. Michel Pêcheux (1938–83) sought to contribute to a general theory of ideology in the line of Althusser, and he imagined very early that real discursive machines, that is computers, could contribute to discourse analysis (Michel Pêcheux, *Analyse automatique du discours* [Paris: Dunod, 1969]). His originality is to have pulled together a Marxist theory of ideology and a computer-simulated theory of discourse.

56. "[I]t treats of *the subject as process (of representation) inside the non-subject constituted by the network of signifier, in Lacan's sense: the subject is 'caught' in this network* – 'common nouns' and 'proper names,' 'shifting' effects, syntactic constructions, etc. – *such that he results as a 'cause of himself,'* in Spinoza's sense of the phrase" (Michel Pêcheux, *Language, Semantics and Ideology*, Harbans Nagpal [trans.] [Basingstoke: Macmillan, 1982], 108, my translation).

recognition, therefore, is not simple; it functions through a retroactive effect via which the subject appears to have always-already been here to answer the appeal.

Pêcheux then tries to uncover the linguistic conditions for such a paradoxical self-erasing process. This can be summarized in a few theses. First, language is not homogeneous but is constituted by a multiplicity of heterogeneous discursive formations, where the meaning of each term is defined through paraphrases and reformulations (such as "Kepler" = "the one who discovered the elliptical form of planetary orbits"). Second, the syntactic mechanisms of language make it possible to inscribe, in one and the same discursive process, terms that belong to each other, that is, terms that evoke things as *having been said* elsewhere. He calls this insertion the "preconstruct effect." Therefore, speaking is not only about actualizing possibilities defined *within* a discursive formation (i.e. to choose within a paradigmatic set of options), but also about articulating discourses that are external to one another in the same syntagmatic series; we say what we say by evoking what has been said and therefore what does not need to be said again. Through this, Pêcheux suggests a new method for interpreting relative sentences in sentences such as "Whoever discovered the elliptic form of the planetary orbits died in misery," which Frege famously claimed was not a real proposition. Instead of interpreting this sentence, as Frege did, as denoting an object (and not a thought or a truth value) and therefore judging it the illusion of a proposition, one that reveals the imperfections of natural language, Pêcheux argues we should see it as an appeal to something said elsewhere, something that does not need to be constructed as such.

The consequence is that the same term can appear both as being constructed in a discursive process and as having "always-already" been constructed. This duplication appears in paradoxes and witticisms such as "Is this the place where the Duke of Wellington spoke his famous words? – Yes, this is the place, but he never spoke those words," or "There are no cannibals anymore in this country, we ate the last one yesterday," or "He who saved the world by dying on the cross never existed." In all these cases, the same term appears twice in the same discursive act: once as part of what is actually said here and now and once with some distance maintained from the enunciation. Thanks to this mechanism (and a few others), linguistic terms "duplicate and divide to act on themselves as other than themselves."[57]

This mechanism sustains the production of subjectivity: "it is possible to regard *the effect of the preconstructed as the discursive modality of the discrepancy by which the individual is interpellated as subject … while still being 'always-already a subject.'*"[58] The subject is precisely what is constituted by the very way

---

57. *Ibid.*
58. *Ibid.*, 107.

it identifies as that which does not need to be constituted because it is always-already there. In the expression "Here I am," I both *say something* and say it as that which *does not need to be said*. In other words, the preconstruction mechanism allows us to think of a relation to oneself as being behind oneself (an identity requiring lag), constituted in the very way it resists every constitution, which was, as was said earlier, one of the definitions of subjectivity.[59]

This short sketch does not do justice to Pêcheux's rich empirical and speculative work, and will certainly raise many objections. However, it is hopefully sufficient to indicate yet another path that the radicalization of structuralism that Milner called hyperstructuralism has taken, a path where the theory of the subject as an effect is grounded on a theory of discourse sustained by a theory of ideology, and which allows precise empirical analyses of real discourses. It will find its acknowledged development in what has since become, on the other side of the English Channel and under the influence of Ernesto Laclau, discourse theory.

V. AN ONTOLOGY OF SIGNS: JEAN PETITOT

However, there is yet another reply to Badiou's objection to the very idea of the "logic of the signifier," one that reactivates the problematic of an ontology of signs. For the paradox of Badiou's solution is to have provided an ontology that *cannot* apply to signs in Saussure's sense. The very definition of the identity of a mathematical set is fundamentally incompatible with Saussurean signs because set-identity depends on the contents of the set: it is extensional and internal (i.e. indifferent to what exists elsewhere). Saussure's signs, on the other hand, have no positive identity; a sign is everything the other signs are not, it can be radically changed by a movement in them, and its identity is therefore relational and external.[60] Therefore, even if we accept Badiou's solution as a convincing ontological framework for *a* theory of subjectivity, in what sense can it be valid *for us* as agents enmeshed in semiotic networks? The kind of beings that we require a theory of constitution for is not the being of mathematical structures, but the being of languages, mythological systems, and political discourses. In the face

---

59. The paradox of subjectivity appears in typical mistakes that children make when they say, for example, "I have three brothers, Mike, Henry and me," which Lacan relished quoting because it illustrates well that the subject replicates himself in what is said about him.

60. "The change which has occurred ... would tell us nothing if our explanation of it centered on the form itself. Its only source is in the *comparable forms ... as always in morphology, movement comes from the sides*" (Ferdinand de Saussure, *Writings in General Linguistics*, Carol Sanders and Matthew Pires [trans.] [Oxford: Oxford University Press, 2006], 129). See my *La Vie énigmatique des signes*, 180–85, for a detailed commentary on this idea.

of this demand, Badiou's attempt to use the language of mathematics to speak about our "situation" may seem at best metaphorical.

Now, the positional and differential ontology in which Jacques-Alain Miller and Jean-Claude Milner argued for a theory of subjectivity as effect can make sense only if structuralists, following Saussure, are right to assume that cultural phenomena can be best scientifically objectified by methods that treat them as systems of differential and positional entities. In other words, the ontological deduction of subjectivity relies on empirical claims. However, at the very time that the idea of the "logic of the signifier" was evoked, the empirical kernel of structural linguistics was forcibly challenged by the successes of generative grammar. Milner himself was one of those who clearly saw that generative grammar ruled out the ontological claims that followed from structural linguistics.[61] For, as Chomsky himself made clear in his critique of Saussure, it implied a substitution of the conception of "*langue*" as a set of codetermined elements endowed with a differential and positional identity with a conception of "*langue*" as a system of rules generating valid or invalid *judgments* of grammaticality, displacing the philosophical question to that of the status of the mental.[62] Milner therefore holds that structuralism as a scientific research program has been superseded by generative grammar, in the sense that the latter has proved more successful than the former.[63] While he still tries to defend the interests of hyperstructuralism from a purely philosophical standpoint, it remains a fact that the interest of structuralism lay precisely in the intricate articulation between philosophy and empirical science it represented. Therefore, the very philosophical context that we have tried to reconstruct would be definitively over if Chomsky's objections to structuralism cannot be answered.

One author, who did not belong to the group of the *Cahiers pour l'analyse*, but who, as we will see, shared their interests, undertook a reply to Chomsky in favor of a reactivation of structuralism. In his 1985 book *Morphogenèse du sens*, Petitot unambiguously endorses the claim that beyond both poststructuralist and neorationalist critiques, structuralism is still more alive than ever: "far from becoming obsolete as the incurable instigators of fashion would like to make it believe, structuralism is on the contrary discovering the mathematical Idea conforms to its concept."[64] He too sees in structuralism an ontological chal-

---

61. "[T]hey return to a definition of linguistic objects by a positive matter and not only by a negative form" (Milner, *Le Périple structural*, 39); and see Milner, *L'Amour de la langue*, 61–5; *For the Love of Language*, 89–92.

62. See Noam Chomsky, *Current Issues in Linguistic Theory* (The Hague: Mouton, 1964), 11–23. For a detailed confrontation between the taxonomic and transformational models, see my *La Vie énigmatique des signes*, 131–212.

63. See Milner, *Introduction à une science du langage*.

64. Jean Petitot, *Morphogenesis of Meaning* (Berne: Peter Lang, 2003), 19.

lenge raised by the introduction in the empirical sciences of new objects (such as phonemes). Moreover, Petitot finds, as did Miller, that this challenge bears on the notion of a positional entity, an entity that cannot be said to occupy a position but *is* its own position. Interestingly enough, he praises Deleuze for having formulated this question better than anyone in his famous article "How do we Recognize Structuralism?" Petitot's originality is first to explicitly conceive of ontology as a transcendental reconstruction of our categorical apparatus (in a Kantian sense) on the basis of ever new forms of scientific positivity, and second to argue that such an ontology requires adequate mathematical models to provide the *schematization* of the categories without which they cannot be related to the positive phenomena produced by empirical sciences.

But Petitot is aware that no philosophical and mathematical construal of the concept of structure will make sense unless the empirical objections raised by generative grammar are answered. As Chomsky made clear in his criticism of Saussure, the debate is between a rule-based model – for which speaking is about generating an indefinite number of well-formed utterances through a hierarchy of formal rules applied to basic mental representations processed from one module (system of rules) to another one – and a taxonomic one – for which speaking is nothing other than the identification of a possibility globally defined through its contrast with other possibilities. There are two arguments in favor of the latter. The first is that generativism cannot provide an answer to the problem that motivated the original introduction of structural methods in linguistics, that is, the relation between the self-identical units of language that we actually perceive and the physical or phonetic signals we observe. For example, it is a scientific fact that it is impossible to define a phoneme via a set of positive phonetic features that would be instantiated in all and only the occurrences in which native speakers do perceive them. The signals appear to be continuous and scattered, whereas the phonemes are perceived as discontinuous and invariant units. This is the reason Saussure made the hypothesis that phonemes should not be defined by any positive features (such as phonetic properties), but rather as strictly relational and positional entities interdefined in an abstract system.

The second objection to Chomsky concerns the fact – which became more and more inescapable with the growth of generative grammar and eventually brought it to a crisis demanding its complete reconstruction[65] – that the various modules (and the rules inside each module) are not applied in a simple sequential order: that it may be necessary, for instance, to have some semantic

---

65. This paradigm shift is known as the passage from a rule-based model to the approach called "Principles and Parameters"; see Noam Chomsky, *Some Concepts and Consequences of the Theory of Government and Binding* (Cambridge, MA: MIT Press, 1982).

information in order to know which syntactic rule should be applied. Far from mental representations undergoing a series of rewrites through sequentially related modules (or systems of rules), we would require a multidimensional responsive system to identify a single linguistic possibility.[66] As a consequence, not only do Chomsky's arguments against the taxonomic model seem to have been refuted by the progress of the very discipline he established, but also his inaugural dismissal of meaning in linguistics, along with his dismissal of the sign as the nature of linguistic objects,[67] would need to be reconsidered.

Therefore, Petitot is able to reformulate the theoretical and philosophical program of structuralism as an open research project.[68] Structuralism must not only philosophically and mathematically construe the concept of positional entities; it must also explain the passage from continuous and variable substrata to relatively substance-independent positional systems. His claim is that the mathematical formalization that structuralism requires can be found in René Thom's catastrophe theory. It is impossible within the confines of this essay to do more than provide a suggestive account of his demonstration. Petitot's claim relies on a rigorous analogy between the phonological categorization of phonetic spaces and the phenomena of physical transitions between material phases, such as the passage from water to ice that occurs at a precise temperature and is modeled by catastrophe theory. In the same way that, in the case of water, the parameter (temperature) is continuous but the morphological effect is discontinuous (from liquid to solid), phonemes (and semiological entities) are discreet morphological "catastrophes" on a continuous phonetic substratum. Transition phases can be geometrized by ascribing to the substratum a certain type of dynamics, far from equilibrium but without becoming chaotic, which results in abrupt changes in a small number of forms precisely theorized by catastrophe theory. A phonological system would be the result of a morphogenetic process grounded in the dynamics of phonetic substances.

But these catastrophic schemes not only capture the passage from substance to form, but also allow us to formulate what Miller called the *action* of the structure, since they "become the generative devices of actantial relations,"[69] that is,

---

66. See Ronald W. Langacker, *Foundations of Cognitive Grammar, Vol. I: Theoretical Prerequisites* (Stanford, CA: Stanford University Press, 1987), and Bernard Laks, *Langage et cognition: L'Approche connexionniste* (Paris: Hermès, 1996) for precise arguments about this.

67. "[W]e are studying language as an instrument or a tool, attempting to describe its structure with no explicit reference to the way in which this instrument is put in use" (Noam Chomsky, *Syntactic Structures* [New York: de Gruyter, 2002], 103).

68. For a more introductory presentation of Petitot's reading of structuralism, see Jean Petitot, "Structure," in *Encyclopedic Dictionary of Semiotics, Vol. 2,* Thomas A. Sebeok (ed.) (New York: de Gruyter, 1986).

69. Petitot, *Morphogenesis of Meaning*, 193.

relations in which the terms do not relate to each other as alternative categories (this phonetic signal is *either* /p/ *or* /b/), but functional connections (expressed in relations such as: "after /p/ you cannot figure /b/"). Exactly as Miller wanted to construe the "virtual" system in such a way that it implies its actualization in symbolic "chains," Petitot claims that catastrophic formalization allows us to understand not only why systems of discreet categories (what structuralists called "paradigms") emerge from the substratum, but also the serial orders in which these categories actualize (what Saussure called "syntagms"). In other words, it would be possible to deduce from the very nature of the paradigmatic units the syntagmatic chains in which they are actualized. Refusing the separation between formal syntax and semantic interpretation, he draws on A. J. Greimas's actantial model to explain what he calls "conversion": the projection of the paradigmatic systems into syntagmatic chains. This projection shows the intrinsically *discursive* nature of symbolic systems: it is as if we cannot divide the real into alternative identities as is the basis of traditional structuralism without triggering narrative formats.[70] Interestingly enough, subjects are no longer paradoxical entities belonging to systems only by absenting themselves from them; instead they are actants corresponding to different positions in the serial succession of symbolic terms. The ontological paradox is not on the side of the subject anymore, but on the side of *values*, that is, of these objects that, according to Lévi-Strauss, have to be exchanged and circulate in the actual working of a symbolic system. Subjectivity is an effect of the fact that symbolic objects never present themselves as real things: they are always divided into partial and complementary perspectives.[71]

Therefore, the two main problems of structuralism – the passage from "substances" (such as phonetic substrata) to "forms" (systems of interdefined positional entities), and the passage from paradigmatic systems to syntagmatic series defining subjective positions – are both answered at once. It is apparent that after this move we are now very close to satisfying Milner's demands for the hyperstructuralist program. But we must remark that this new solution requires, apart from a new understanding of subjectivity, a major displacement.

---

70. "The contents deep semantics articulates (Life/Death, Nature/Culture, Man/Woman, Divine/Human, etc.) do not have a reference in the objective world. They are some sort of psychical drives or ideals that 'give meaning to life,' *a meaning that cannot be grasped as such but only experienced via its conversion into actantial structures*" (*ibid.*, 49). See also *ibid.*, 193–248.

71. "Only the circulation of such objects of value can allow them to be subjectivized; in other words, they can become part of the subject only through experiences and actions" (*ibid.*, 49). Contemporary anthropology (Marilyn Strathern, Eduardo Viveiros de Castro, Roy Wagner) provides solid empirical grounds for this hypothesis and a renewed form of structuralism (see Eduardo Viveiros de Castro, "Intensive Filiation and Demonic Alliance," in *Deleuzian Intersections in Science, Technology, and Anthropology*, Casper Bruun Jensen and Kjetil Rödje [eds] [Oxford: Berghan Books, 2009]).

The symbolic systems appear now as *emerging* forms, and the real processes underlying these forms are not to be found at the same level on which they operate. The processes are in the specific dynamic of the substratum, and the morphological semiotic distribution simply emerges from it in the same way a Kanizsa triangle emerges from three incomplete disks. The ontology of signs would then have to be answered from an emergentist perspective. Following a suggestion made more than once by Lévi-Strauss and drawing on models of cognitive simulation other than the classic Turing Machine (such as connectionist models[72]), Petitot in his later work tries to find in the nature of the brain the physiological realization of such mechanisms. Of course, this peculiar form of "hyperstructuralism," with its strong links to mainstream cognitivism, is no more safe from objections than the other ones discussed above. However, our discussion does prove that questions raised forty years ago about the articulation between a formal and ontological construal of the concept of structure and the theory of subjectivity as effect are still relevant in the most contemporary scientific and philosophical debates.

We therefore have good reasons to think that, beyond the main two opposing directions taken after (and against) structuralism by theoretical and philosophical thought, namely cognitivism and poststructuralism, contemporary French philosophy has been worked through, until the end of the century, by the question of a conceptual and formal (viz. ontological and mathematical) construal of the concept of structure valid for every symbolic domain, one that at the same time could offer an account of subjectivity itself as a necessary effect. But, rather than defining the "present moment" in contemporary French philosophy through a positive common feature or collective insight, the ambition of this essay was to define it (one may remark, in a truly structuralist way) as a *problem*: one that produces many alternative paths that some of the most important contemporary philosophers have pursued. In the process, four answers to the question of the theory of subjectivity articulated through a theory of structure have been distinguished: the "logic of the signifier" pretends to deduce a subject effect as a paradoxical term necessarily belonging to systems of positional and differential entities (Miller and Milner); another path refuses the specificity of the symbolic and grounds the theory of subjectivity on a set-theoretical ontology that leaves room for truth as a creation of unconstructible sets (Badiou); a third option tries to associate a theory of ideology with a theory of discourse construed as the set of mechanisms that produces the subject as *that which does not need to be produced* (Balibar, Lecourt, and Pêcheux); while the fourth suggestion argues for a morphodynamic interpretation of structuralism where

---

72. See Jean Petitot, "Why Connectionism is such a Good Thing: A Criticism of Fodor's and Pylyshyn's Criticism of Smolensky," *Philosophica* 47(1) (1991).

symbolic systems emerge from a certain type of dynamic process, distributing complementary perspectives in a symbolic exchange (Petitot). Four ways are thus traced of construing the concept of structure (signifier, matheme, discourse, and morphologies), to which corresponds four concepts of the subject (as a figurative displacement, as a consequent bet, as a preconstructed term, as an actant). It would not now be difficult to distribute in this chart other important contemporary thinkers such as: Miller's former student, Slavoj Žižek; the founding figure of the British School of discourse analysis, Ernesto Laclau; or the post-Althusserian theorist of subjectivity, Judith Butler, among many others.[73] Therefore, we have a strong basis for thinking that, far from having been outdated by developments in cultural science or philosophy, structuralism, at least as a problematic space, is still a major though secret matrix of contemporary philosophy. Answers, of course, remain to be assessed or enriched, and, even better, to be discovered. However, such discovery requires that we are at least not oblivious to their history.[74]

---

*73. The work of Žižek, Laclau, and Butler are all addressed in essays in *The History of Continental Philosophy: Volume 8*.

74. I wish to thank Tim Secret for his excellent job editing the text in English, Alan Schrift for his helpful comments and generous editing work, Yves Duroux for having introduced me to this literature and discussing with me some of these issues, Étienne Balibar for being at the origin of this work, and, finally, Rosi Braidotti for having asked it of me and for her patience waiting for its completion.

4

ITALIAN PHILOSOPHY BETWEEN
1980 AND 1995

Silvia Benso and Brian Schroeder

I. THE GENERAL ITALIAN LANDSCAPE

Italian philosophy is characterized in the period immediately following the Second World War by the somewhat rigid distinction among three main cultural domains: religious (principally Catholic), laicist (*laica*), and Marxist.[1] This distinction mirrors the political laceration within the country, split between the religious inspiration of the Christian Democratic Party (DC) and the liberal, secular tradition derived from the *Risorgimento*[2] that often includes, although laterally, the Socialist Party (PSI), with the strong constituency of the Communist Party (PCI) rigorously excluded from all government coalitions.[3]

The religious philosophical domain is marked in general by a strong interest in metaphysical themes having to do with foundational issues such as the problem of the absolute, the possibility of metaphysical reason, and the universality of

---

1. For a discussion on these themes, see Maurizio Pagano, "Contemporary Italian Philosophy: The Confrontation between Religious and Secular Thought," in *Contemporary Italian Philosophy: Crossing the Borders of Ethics, Politics, and Religion*, Silvia Benso and Brian Schroeder (eds), Silvia Benso (trans.) (Albany, NY: SUNY Press, 2007).

    Where indicated, published English translations are cited in the text and notes; all other English translations are those of the authors. Where two publication dates are given in parentheses, the one in brackets is the Italian publication date, and the other is the publication date of the English translation.

2. This is the period of Italian history that, through a series of independence wars, led to the political unification of most of the Italian peninsula, and eventually to the establishment of the kingdom of Italy in 1861 and to the annexation of Rome in 1870.

3. This occurred from 1948 to 1976 and then again from 1979 to 1991, while during the period 1977–79 the PCI granted external support to the government.

morality. These issues are often discussed in light of the problem of the relation between Christianity and philosophy, and between faith and reason. The great metaphysical themes led to a renewed interest in Aristotle and Aquinas in a number of neoclassical, neoscholastic, and neo-Thomist thinkers, for example: Agostino Gemelli (1878–1959), the founder in 1921 of the Università Cattolica del Sacro Cuore in Milan, the center of Italian neoscholasticism; Francesco Olgiati (1886–1962), the founder of the Centro di Studi Filosofici Cristiani di Gallarate (Gallarate Center of Christian Philosophical Studies), for whom philosophy's starting-point is not knowledge but metaphysics; Carlo Giacon (1900–1984), a historian of scholasticism; Gustavo Bontadini (1903–90), a firm supporter of classical metaphysics; Cornelio Fabro (1911–95), who is also a scholar of existentialism and a translator of Kierkegaard; Marino Gentile (1906–91), who embraces an Aristotelian-influenced metaphysics marked by problematizing (*problematicità*) and historicity; and Umberto Padovani (1894–1968), for whom the philosophy of religion must justify religion.

Opposed to this array of thinkers is the variegated, less-unitary group of Christian spiritualist thinkers who, being more receptive of the neoidealist tradition of Benedetto Croce and Giovanni Gentile,[4] accentuate the dimension of

---

4. Benedetto Croce (1866–1952) was educated at the school of Francesco De Sanctis (who was the major literary critic and historian of literature in nineteenth-century Italy and was formed in the legacy of Vico), and Antonio Labriola (an Italian philosopher with strong interests in Marxism). His encounter with Hegel's philosophy confronted him with the idea of Spirit as the dialectical principle of reality born out of ever-new contradictions. Unlike Hegel, Croce neglected the role of the realm of nature (and hence the role of science) in the development of Spirit (this neglect remained as a legacy in much subsequent Italian philosophy and education), and developed instead an absolute historicism based on the idea that all reality is Spirit, but Spirit manifests itself only in history and human activities. From here derives Croce's emphasis on the cultural (especially his influential work on aesthetics) and historico-political world (Croce was a theorist and defender of liberalism during the fascist regime, and actively participated in the political life of the Italian state). His works include *Historical Materialism and the Economics of Karl Marx* ([1900] 2008), *The Aesthetic as the Science of Expression and of the Linguistic in General* ([1902] 1992), *Philosophy of the Practical: Economic and Ethic* ([1909] 2004), and *History as the Story of Liberty* ([1938] 2000). [*] For a discussion of Croce's aesthetic theory, see the essay by Gary Shapiro in *The History of Continental Philosophy: Volume 2*.

Giovanni Gentile (1875–1944) taught philosophy at the universities of Palermo, Pisa, and then Rome. He was deeply influenced by Hegelian philosopher Donato Jaja (1839–1914) during his studies at the Scuola Normale Superiore in Pisa. Taking up Hegel's idealism, Gentile accentuates the position and role of consciousness as self-consciousness as ground of reality, and considers the act of thinking, that is, the "pure act," as the principle and form of becoming. Hence, his philosophy is known as "*attualismo*" (actualism). Gentile was also a pedagogue and took part in several political, cultural, and educational initiatives during the fascist era (resulting in Croce's severing of their relationship). Among his works are *La riforma della dialettica hegeliana* (The reform of Hegelian dialectics; 1913), *The Theory of Mind as Pure Act* ([1916] 2007), *The Reform of Education* ([1920] 2007), and *Origins and Doctrine of Fascism* ([1929] 2004).

self-consciousness in the Absolute. Among them, albeit on differentiated positions, are Armando Carlini (1878–1959) and Augusto Guzzo (1894–1986), both students of Gentile and dedicated to a retrieval of the motifs of interiority, spiritual life, and religious transcendence, and Michele Federico Sciacca (1908–75), who denies the sharp opposition between neo-Thomism and spiritualism characterizing the debate of the period. An original proposal that links together metaphysics and personalism is the "theological personalism" of Carlo Arata, for whom the Person – understood as first person (*ego sum qui sum*: I am the one who I am) – constitutes the coherent radicalization of Aquinas's *actus essendi*.

The secular culture is split between a properly laicist tradition (*laicismo*) of liberal descent (including also some nondogmatic Catholic or Marxist thinkers) that claims the reciprocal autonomy of all human activities in the name of the values of pluralism, freedom, and tolerance, and a Marxist current inspired and revitalized in its traditionally Marxist principles by the philosophy of Antonio Gramsci (1891–1937),[5] whose *Quaderni dal carcere* (*Prison Notebooks*) were published immediately after the Second World War. In general, the laicist domain, whose main centers are at the universities of Turin, Milan, and Florence, seeks a critical and nondogmatic (that is, non-Catholic and non-Marxist) employment of reason, and also moves against the idealist tradition of Croce and Gentile, even when it engages in explicitly historiographic inquiries. Moreover, this area searches for and encourages contacts with the most advanced forms of recent international philosophical trends, such as phenomenology and existentialism, but also American pragmatism. A strong interest in the sciences and scientific methodology should also be noted. Two major tendencies can be retraced within the laicist tradition. The first has a clearly theoretical attitude with neo-Enlightenment positions inspired by the appeal to reason, the struggle against metaphysics, and the rediscovery of experience. The second is marked more by a historicist attitude that leads to important historiographic activities. The leading thinkers in this laicist area are Nicola Abbagnano (1901–90) and his students Pietro Rossi, Pietro Chiodi, and Carlo Augusto Viano, and also Norberto Bobbio, Ludovico Geymonat, Enzo Paci, Giulio Preti, Mario Dal Pra, Eugenio Garin, and Paolo Rossi.

Within the Italian Marxist philosophical tradition of this period and up to the crisis of Marxism that starts in the early 1970s, two fundamental trends can be identified. The first, supported by the cultural politics of the Italian Communist Party, combines Marxism with the idealist, humanist, and historicist tradition of Crocian descent associated with the mainly bourgeois culture, and focuses on the relation between human being and society, on Marx's humanism, and on

---

*5. Gramsci is discussed in an essay by Chris Thornhill in *The History of Continental Philosophy: Volume 5*.

historical materialism. This line of interpretation, which affects also the reading of Gramsci's own texts as promoted by the PCI leader Palmiro Togliatti, was predominant in Italy up to the 1960s – that is, up to the crisis that followed Khrushchev's report on Stalin's crimes, the Hungarian Revolution, and the parallel capitalist economic boom of the early 1960s. Representatives of this trend are, among others, Valentino Gerratana (1919–2000) and Nicola Badaloni (1925–2005). Opposed to this is the trend that focuses on the relation between human being and nature found in dialectical materialism, and therefore centers on the problem of scientific knowledge understood in terms of a nondogmatic materialism attentive to contemporary epistemological debate. A major representative of this current is Geymonat and his Milan school. Other Marxist thinkers who move outside the division delineated above and who deserve special mention because of their influence on future philosophers are Galvano Della Volpe (1895–1968) and Cesare Luporini (1909–93). Della Volpe develops a "Galileian" Marxism opposed to the Hegelian–Marxian line of interpretation, to Gramscian historicism, and to Soviet dogmatism; Della Volpe finds in Marx a historico-experimental (Galileian) logic articulated in the circle "concrete–abstract–concrete," according to which experimental verification is needed to integrate the historico-material data from which any inquiry starts and the abstract rational hypothesis, that is, to integrate matter and rationality. Close to Louis Althusser's position of an "epistemological break" in the development of Marx's thought, Luporini stresses the importance of the conditioning power of structures, but also insists on the fact that structures are for Marx functional to the individuals, and not vice versa.

The cultural–ideological division mapped above contributes greatly toward shaping the longstanding Italian tradition of schools of thought, which gravitate toward single philosophical personalities or approaches and significantly complicate the map of Italian philosophy. Thus, the same philosophical figures and themes can be developed in completely different directions. Specific interpretations depend in fact on whether the interpreting scholars are situated in the neoscholastic, metaphysical tradition of the Milan Catholic Università del Sacro Cuore, which, in addition to openings to (especially German) phenomenology, develops metaphysical themes by relying on Aristotle read through Aquinas, or whether they are located in the Padua tradition that, despite its mainly Catholic legacy, bypasses scholasticism and studies Aristotle through a less religious lens, thus elaborating a different metaphysical and political approach; whether they are part of the Milan tradition of the Università Statale, in which existentialism and phenomenology are often coupled with Marxism[6] and Anglo-American

---

6. See Andrzej Nowicki, "Marxism and Phenomenology in Contemporary Italian Philosophy," *Dialectics and Humanism* 2 (1975).

pragmatism, or whether they partake of the Florentine school of thought, in which Marxism is paired with critical theory, especially as developed by the Frankfurt School, and in general with an interest in social and cultural critique, and thus in history. The historical approach of the Florentine school, which shares many elements with the approach associated with the University of Pisa with its additional focus on the history and philosophy of science, is very different, however, from the idealist–historicist attitude of the University of Naples, in which the neo-Hegelian influence of Croce and Gentile is still alive together with a purely historic-oriented tradition that goes back to Vico.[7] Other schools of thought possessing a specific identity can be found at the University of Turin, divided into a secular, neo-Enlightenment, even neopositivist varia-tion focused on the privileging of reason and history and a spiritualist variant open to French and German existentialism and personalism, and later accepting the results of a properly hermeneutic position; and the Venice school, in part born out of a secession from the Catholic Università del Sacro Cuore in Milan, in which metaphysics, nihilism, and religious considerations of various nature intersect.

From being almost nonexistent in the period following the Second World War, conversations among the three cultural areas of philosophy and the schools of thought that develop in parallel connection grow increasingly common from the mid-1950s up to the late 1970s, and an array of cultural and philosoph-ical orientations more or less loosely inspired by Marxist and Christian prin-ciples flourish. During this period, interesting hybrids are produced such as the nearing of: Marxism and Christianity (in Italo Mancini [1925–93]); Christian existentialism and hermeneutics (in Luigi Pareyson [1918–91]); Marxism, exis-tentialism, and phenomenology (in Enzo Paci [1911–76]), religious experience, hermeneutics, and nihilism (in Alberto Caracciolo [1918–90]), neopositivism and Marxism (in Geymonat and Preti), and neoscholasticism and phenomen-ology (in Sofia Vanni Rovighi [1908–90]).[8]

The physiognomy of the philosophical debate takes up new forms in the late 1970s, and the old ideological–cultural distinction in the three areas begins to lose its relevance. The novel panorama occurs in part because of the crisis of

---

7. For an overview of Hegel's influence on Italian philosophy, see Angelica Nuzzo, "An Outline of Italian Hegelianism (1832–1998)," *Owl of Minerva* 29(2) (1998).

8. For overviews of Italian philosophy in general up to the late 1970s, see Adriano Bausola *et al.* (eds), *La filosofia italiana dal dopoguerra a oggi* [Italian philosophy from the postwar to today] (Rome-Bari: Laterza, 1985); Giovanna Borradori (ed.), *Recoding Metaphysics: The New Italian Philosophy* (Evanston, IL: Northwestern University Press, 1988); Pietro Rossi and Carlo A. Viano (eds), *Filosofia italiana e filosofie straniere neldopoguerra* [Italian philosophy and other philosophies after the war] (Bologna: Il Mulino, 1991).

Marxism,[9] many forms of which circulate in Italy, such as Geymonat's dialectical materialism, Preti's pragmatism, Paci's Husserlianism, Augusto Del Noce's atheism, and Emanuele Severino's nihilism. The interest in Lukács, present in the late 1950s and 1960s, is replaced in the 1970s with an interest in heterodox Marxist thinkers such as Horkheimer, Adorno, Marcuse, Luxemburg, Benjamin, Bloch, and Korsch, and then with French inspired Marxism as developed by Sartre, Althusser, and Foucault.[10] The varieties of Marxism and their inspirations in fact provoke a fading of the separation between Christian thought and secular culture. The reconfiguration of the areas and terms of the philosophical debate also occurs, however, in part because of the new and somewhat sudden interest across the three traditional cultural areas for authors of the so-called "irrationalist" trend of the nineteenth and twentieth centuries, namely Nietzsche, Heidegger, and Wittgenstein during his Vienna period (then a very different thinker from the one appropriated by the analytic tradition). Additional recent authors who exercise a deep influence on Italian philosophers of the 1980s are Ricoeur, Gadamer, and Derrida, who join thinkers such as Benjamin, Adorno, Rosenzweig, and other philosophers already present in the Italian discussion such as Hegel, Marx, Husserl, and some American pragmatists, especially Dewey but also Peirce. An increased interest in authors such as Apel and Habermas, and in German practical philosophy in general is also to be recorded in these years.

A traditional, idealist legacy[11] mandates that in Italy the learning of the history of philosophy is a basic requirement for all *licei* (that is, for the nontechnical high schools that constitute the preferred access to a university education), and that the high-school teacher of philosophy – which is always understood as history of philosophy[12] – is also the history teacher. Because of this tight intersection (that finds its roots already in the Italian liberal tradition of the *Risorgimento*) between (history of) philosophy and history in the formation of most Italian intellectuals in addition to the Marxian emphasis on the funda-

---

9. An exemplary case of a Marxist intellectual whose very own itinerary of thought represents the ascent and crisis of Italian Marxism is Lucio Colletti (1924–2001), a student of Della Volpe who, in the late 1970s, after having been one of the most renowned theoreticians of the Marxist doctrine for almost twenty years, became a resolute critic of the Marxist ideology.

*10. For a discussion of some of these figures, see the essays by Chris Thornhill, John Abromeit, Deborah Cook, and William L. McBride in *The History of Continental Philosophy: Volume 5*.

11. This legacy was formalized in the so-called *Riforma Gentile* carried out by the neo-idealist philosopher Giovanni Gentile during his tenure as Minister of Education during the fascist regime.

12. This coincidence gives to the historiographic, historicist tradition in Italy a legitimacy that goes beyond purely philological interest. In this sense, one could refer to the continuous flourishing and health of historiographic schools such as those of Abbagnano, Dal Pra, Garin, Geymonat, Giovanni Reale, Pietro Rossi, Viano, and others.

mental role of the intellectuals – an emphasis acknowledged by Marxist and leftist thinkers and accentuated by Gramsci's theory of the "organic intellectual"[13] – Italian philosophy is characterized by a strong civic commitment and engagement in history and public life, which in turn has affected the configuration of Italian philosophy. This influence occurs parallel to external theoretical stimuli and resonances certainly coming from the broader international philosophical debate.

The Italian philosophical scene between the years 1980 and 1995 is framed by two sets of historico-political events.[14] The period opens with the kidnapping and subsequent murder of the leader of the Christian Democratic Party Aldo Moro, allegedly by the Red Brigades (*Brigate Rosse*), in 1978.[15] Gianni Vattimo's *pensiero debole* (weak thought), arguably the most original and renowned expression of Italian philosophy during this time, develops "as a response to the terrorist interpretation of the Italian democratic left during the 1970s, as a recognition of the unacceptability of the Red Brigades' violence."[16] Terrorism, the use of force, and the widespread killings (the so-called *stragismo*) of the early 1980s spur, for example, many of the reflections on violence, law, justice, rights, and the state of Bobbio, one of Italy's leading political philosophers, scholar of

---

13. See Antonio Gramsci, *Gli intellettuali e l'organizzazione della cultura* [The intellectuals and the organization of culture] (Turin: Einaudi, 1949). According to this theory, the intellectuals are both product and consciousness of a specific sociopolitical group.

14. Such events, on which a completely clear light has yet to be cast, are two attacks carried out, albeit by forces of an entirely different nature and origin, against the legitimacy of the democratically constituted political regime. Thus, they both represent a direct attack against the rationality of the political subject and its power.

15. Moro, who had been Professor of Philosophy of Law at the University of Bari, was the political leader and statesman who, as president of the DC, favored the dialogue (the so-called *compromesso storico*, or historical compromise) between the Democrazia Cristiana (Christian Democrats) and the PCI led by Enrico Berlinguer to avoid the political and institutional dangers of what some perceived as the possibility of a "Chilean crisis" (that is, a *coup d'état* by the conservative forces) in Italy. The Red Brigades is the name of a terrorist organization founded on radical Marxist–Leninist principles. It became operative in Italy in the early 1970s with the intention of destroying the state and replacing it with a popular democracy. The murder of Moro occurred just before the parliamentary vote that marked, for the first time since 1947, the entry of the Communist Party (PCI) in the ruling majority. Moro's murder, which also brought to a climax the *strategia della tensione* (stress strategy) enacted by terrorist groups during the so-called *anni di piombo* (years of lead; with a clear reference to the heavy atmosphere characterizing all aspects of Italian life but also to the material of which bullets are made), raised major issues, also of a philosophical nature, by radically calling into question the use of force and violence, on all sides, in the political life of a democratic state. While fascinating, the complexities of this political period of turmoil, which among other events sees the presence of terrorist activities of opposite extremes, are too complex to be taken up here.

16. Santiago Zabala, "Gianni Vattimo and Weak Philosophy," in *Weakening Philosophy: Essays in Honour of Gianni Vattimo*, Santiago Zabala (ed.) (Montreal: McGill-Queen's University Press, 2007), 13.

rights, and activist, who is for several days in 1992 a presidential candidate for the Italian Republic.[17]

In the context of the social, political, and institutional turmoil and instability leading to and following the murder of Moro, mention should also be made of Antonio (Toni) Negri, a Padua philosopher and Professor of Theory of the State.[18] Negri was the founder with Mario Tronti[19] of various journals of Marxist

---

17. Norberto Bobbio (1909–2004) was a student of jurist Gioele Solari and of philosopher Annibale Pastore (1868–1956) in Turin. Inspired by Hobbes and Kelsen, he reread the history of philosophy (Kant, Locke, Hegel, Marx) in their light. Defender of a procedural concept of democracy, that is, a democracy based on the minimal principle of consensus and thus opposed to any authoritarian imposition of truth, Bobbio argued against the confusion of ethics and right. With Abbagnano, Geymonat, and other philosophers of the Turin school he shared a form of neo-Enlightenment geared toward a retrieval of the legacy of eighteenth-century rationalism to promote a concept of philosophy closer to science and to the Anglo-Saxon line of reflection on the philosophy of language. A strenuous defender of the republic, Bobbio represented the secular, liberal, anti-fascist but also anti-Marxist-orthodoxy soul of the Italian republic, and deeply engaged in the public debate, especially when of an ethical nature.

18. Antonio Negri (1933–) was educated at the University of Padua under the guidance of Umberto Padovani. Negri was Professor of Theory of the State, a peculiarly Italian field of studies concerned with juridical and constitutional law, at the same university from 1967 to 1979, during which time he was also a visiting lecturer at the École Normale Supérieure in Paris. Negri was arrested in 1979 with, among other charges, the accusation (dropped after a few months) of being the ideologue of the Red Brigades and the moral mastermind of the Moro kidnapping. He was ultimately convicted in a long, complex, controversial, and highly politicized case for the "constitution of armed group and subversive association" (a verdict confirmed in 1988). Negri escaped part of the punishment through an equally controversial fourteen-year exile in France. He expiated the remainder of the sentence after his voluntary return to Italy in 1997. During his sojourn in France (1983–97), he taught at the University of Paris VIII–St. Denis, Collège International de Philosophie, and at the Collège de France. Among his works are *Stato e politica* (State and politics; 1970), *Marx Beyond Marx: Lessons on the* Grundrisse ([1979] 1991), and, with Michael Hardt, *Labor of Dionysus: A Critique of the State-Form* (1994 [1995]), and the important trilogy *Empire* (2000), *Multitude: War and Democracy in the Age of Empire* (2004), and *Commonwealth* (2009).

19. Mario Tronti (1931–) was Professor of Moral Philosophy and then of Political Philosophy at the University of Siena. A militant in the PCI in the 1950s and then a supporter of Berlinguer, he was one of the major theoreticians of *operaismo* (workers' movement), a political position that challenges the traditional workers' organizations such as the party and the trade unions in favor of the direct connection with the working class, and considers the factories as the site of the class struggle. Under the influence of Marxist philosopher Della Volpe and in an anti-Gramscian interpretation, he elaborated a philosophical position geared toward reopening the revolutionary chance of Marxism in Western societies as attested in his fundamental 1966 work *Operai e capitale* (Workers and capital), a very influential book for the subsequent period of youth contestation and political mobilizing. Abandoning the position of *operaismo* (he broke with Negri in 1967–68), Tronti focused on the notion of the "autonomy of the political" based on an original mixing of Marx and Carl Schmitt. He is the author of *Hegel politico* (The political Hegel; 1975), *Sull'autonomia del politico* (On the autonomy of the political; 1977), and *La politica al tramonto* (Politics at its decline; 1998).

inspiration (albeit deeply critical of the reformist turn taken by the PCI through its theorization of a "national way," that is, "an Italian way to socialism") such as *Quaderni Rossi* (Red notebooks) in 1961 and *Classe operaia* (Workers' Class) in 1964; he was also an exponent of the extraparliamentary revolutionary organization *Potere operaio* (Workers' Power), which included in its ranks some of Negri's students and also the younger Rome philosopher Paolo Virno.[20] After its dissolution in 1973, *Potere operaio* evolved into *Autonomia operaia* (Workers' Autonomy), a movement whose connections with the Red Brigades are too complicated and still unclear to be taken up here. Both the journals and the political organizations of which Negri was part, in opposition to the organized moments of workers' affirmation such as trade unions and parties, exalted the centrality of the workers' class and its spontaneity, and the role of factories as privileged places of the class struggle.

The latter years of the period 1980–95 in Italy are marked, more than by the fall of the Berlin Wall,[21] by the series of events that follow the car bombing at Capaci, near Palermo, orchestrated by the Mafia, in which the anti-Mafia high commissioner and judge Giovanni Falcone was killed on May 23, 1992.[22]

---

20. Paolo Virno (1952–) graduated in philosophy from the University of Rome "La Sapienza" in 1977 with a dissertation on the concept of work and the theory of consciousness in Adorno. A member of *Potere operaio* and later of the journal *Metropoli*, he was placed in preventive custody, accused of belonging to the Red Brigades (although his participation was never proved), and convicted for "subversive activities and constitution of armed groups," a conviction eventually overturned in 1987. During his years in prison, he developed a materialistic conception of language centered on the notion of thought as work and on the historical and linguistic feature of all political categories. The Spinozist concept of "multitude" lies at the core of his most recent reflections. He has published *Convenzione e materialismo* (Convention and materialism; 1986), *Parole con parole: Poteri e limiti del linguaggio* (Words with words: Powers and limits of language; 1995), and *Il ricordo del presente: Saggio sul tempo storico* (The memory of the present: Essay on historical time; 1999).

21. In Italy, the crisis of Marxism and of the dialectical reason inspiring it had already been consumed during the 1980s. The degeneration of terrorism further contributed to the calling into question of Marxist ideology and the spreading of a different *Stimmung*. As Lucio Colletti remarks, "the publishing houses of the extreme left, which are often the most sensitive seismographers … have moved from Rosa Luxembourg to Lou Salomé. From Marx to Nietzsche. And if they have not gotten hold of Heidegger, it is only because in this case they have been preceded by the Catholic publishers" (*Tramonto dell'ideologia* [Decline of ideology] [Rome-Bari: Laterza, 1980], 80). This situation of general crisis of Marxist ideology culminated in the decision by the PCI led by Achille Occhetto on February 3, 1991, to dissolve the Party and promote the constitution of the Partito Democratico della Sinistra (PDS, Democratic Party of the Left), in which the name change was meant to underline the accentuated democratic component of the newly named party. A number of delegates who did not accept the name change convened in the formation of the Partito di Rifondazione Comunista (PRC, Party for a Communist Refoundation).

22. Judge Falcone lost his life, as did his wife and entire escort, in a killing that upset the whole country at various levels.

This killing starts a process eventually leading to the electoral victory in 1994 of Silvio Berlusconi.[23] The success of Berlusconi's coalition marks the role of media technology and its owners on the configuration of political power, and *de facto* radically alters the concepts of democracy, political representation, subjectivity and power, and even civic and political commitment and responsibility.[24] It is not by chance, then, that on a strictly philosophical level the main debate of this period originates in conversation with authors such as Nietzsche, Heidegger, Wittgenstein, Foucault, Gadamer, Ricoeur, Derrida, and Rorty, who have radically called into question the concepts of subjectivity, reason, history, foundations, power, technology, and other metaphysically fixed entities such as ground and being. And it is also not by chance that – perhaps as a consequence of, or in response to, Berlusconi's ascent to power, orchestrated mainly through the channels of mass media public appearance – several philosophers revive the traditional Italian idea of civic and political engagement[25] by intensifying in turn their own media appearances as public figures, and by explicitly engaging in various reflections on the nature and role of technology, especially the mass media. On this front, the position of Mario Perniola[26] seems particularly relevant. Perniola collapses the traditional metaphysical distinction between being and appear-

---

23. The killing of Falcone was followed by the murder of another anti-Mafia magistrate, Paolo Borsellino, a few days later; then by a series of alleged Mafia attacks against various targets in Florence, Rome, Milan, and Sicily; and finally, by the success and then progressive stalling of the so-called *Tangentopoli* (bribe-city) trial carried out by the magistrates of the Milan-based pool "*Mani pulite*" (clean hands), who were investigating and letting surface the connections between briberies (possibly of a mafia kind) and existing traditional political party powers. Taken together, these were all episodes that greatly contributed to the dissolution of the traditional political parties and to the revolution on the political scene culminating in the electoral victory, on March 27, 1994, of the coalition led by former cruise ship entertainer, entrepreneur, business man, and media owner Silvio Berlusconi, a nontraditional figure of a politician, who was himself formally charged with corruption in 1994 while presiding over a world conference on crime organized by the United Nations in Naples.

24. The election of Berlusconi ended the tradition of the so-called First Republic, formally already defunct through the passage (in 1993) from the proportional to the majoritarian form of government based on the personal charismatic power – almost always built through a connivance of economic and technological ownership – of individual political leaders.

25. On the intersection between political events in Italy and the positions that philosophy has taken up ethically, that is, on the relation between facts and ideas in Italy from 1943 up to the late 1990s, see Remo Bodei, *We, the Divided: Ethos, Politics and Culture in Post-War Italy, 1943–2006*, Jeremy Parzen and Aaron Thomas (trans.) (New York: Agincourt Press, 2006). See also Robert Caponigri, "Italian Philosophy, 1943–1950," *Philosophy and Phenomenological Research* 11 (1951); and Michele F. Sciacca, "Chronicle I: Present-Day Italian Philosophy," *New Scholasticism* 39 (1965): 69–83.

26. Mario Perniola (1941–) is Professor of Aesthetics at the University of Rome "Tor Vergata." He was educated in Turin under Luigi Pareyson, and then developed an interest for the avant-garde, meta-literature, and situationism, especially as developed by Guy Debord. Among his works are: *La società dei simulacri* (The society of simulacra; 1980), *Transiti: Come si va dallo*

ance, and reduces all being to appearance construed as mere semblance. In this sense, Perniola writes of *simulacra*: that is, images, or copies without the original, "that impose their own effectiveness on the subjects dissolving their reality."[27] The cultural societal forms such as parties, educational institutions, and especially the mass media are not mirrors of reality, then, but simply *simulacra* that act as conditions of social experience. In this condition of heightened public performance, many philosophers seem to resurrect the Platonic model of the philosopher-king by renewing the traditional Italian civic commitment to and involvement in various political activities.[28]

In this context and from a purely theoretical perspective, Salvatore Veca (1943–) is, as Remo Bodei recognizes, "the political philosopher who has translated into the language of 'public ethics' the demands for social justice previously advanced by Marxism, and who, together with Bobbio, keeps alive, in other ways, the traditional civic vocation of Italian philosophy."[29] Raised in Paci's phenomenological school, Veca moved from the study of Kant's epistemology and Marx's scientific economic program to the "contractualist" variant of Anglo-American political philosophy, especially Rawls's theory of justice. Considering the idea of global justice as the major challenge for contemporary normative political theory, Veca is interested in determining how the maximum level of common good may be reached in societies marked by the ideals of pluralism and individualism.[30]

During the years 1980–95 various parallel conversations and interest develop, such as the concern with analytic philosophy of language in Andrea Bonomi (1940–), Marco Santambrogio (1946–), and Diego Marconi (1947–). Santambrogio, in particular, has become known for "institutionalizing" the

---

stesso allo stesso (Transits: How to go from the same to the same; 1985), *Del sentire* (Of sensing; 1991), and *Il sex-appeal dell'inorganico* (*The Sex Appeal of the Inorganic*; 1994).

27. Mario Perniola, *La società dei simulacra* (Bologna: Cappelli, 1980), 65. Perniola and Jean Baudrillard, both of whom published in the journal *Traverses*, are on similar ground regarding the analysis of simulacra as mechanically reproducible in the mediatic context (see *ibid.*, 121–2, 127–8). Baudrillard refers to Perniola's book in *Simulacra and Simulations*, Sheila Faria Glaser (trans.) (Ann Arbor, MI: University of Michigan Press, 1991), 40.

28. Most famously, Massimo Cacciari became mayor of Venice in 1996; Marcello Pera became senator for the Berlusconi's party in 1996 and then president of the senate in 2001; Aldo Masullo was involved in the government of Naples and became senator for two legislatures in 1994; Ugo Perone, a Turin philosopher of the Pareyson school, held several positions in the Turin administration before being appointed director of the Italian Cultural Institute in Berlin in 2001; and Gianni Vattimo started a political career that led him to winning a seat in the European Parliament in 1999.

29. Remo Bodei, *Il noi diviso: Ethos e idee dell'Italia repubblicana* (Turin: Einaudi, 1988), 135.

30. Salvatore Veca is currently Professor of Philosophy of Politics at the University of Pavia. Among his publications are: *La società giusta* (The just society; 1982), *Cittadinanza: Riflessioni filosofiche sull'idea di emancipazione* (Citizenship: Philosophical reflections on the idea of emancipation; 1990), and *La filosofia politica* (Political philosophy; 1998).

Italian interest for analytic philosophy of language through the publication in 1992 of the edited volume *Introduzione alla filosofia analitica del linguaggio* (Introduction to the analytic philosophy of language). There also emerges an interest for various forms of applied ethics and for the theories of justice, for example in Eugenio Lecaldano (1940–), Maurizio Mori (1946–) and Sebastiano Maffettone (1948–). A concern with philosophy of science and epistemology in general is found in the thinking of Francesco Barone (1923–2001) and Paolo Parrini (1943–), who develop neopositivist studies and positions, in Sergio Moravia (1940–), who defines himself as a "neo-pragmatist" and an "applied epistemologist," and in Evandro Agazzi (1934–), Giulio Giorello (1945–), Marcello Pera (1943–), and Dario Antiseri (1940–), with the latter two contributing significantly to the diffusion of Karl Popper's philosophy in Italy. The main general reflection of this period gravitates, however, around three major themes of debate, within which individual philosophical thinkers whose contribution to the conversation is particularly (although not exclusively)[31] relevant will be indicated in what follows. The three topics of debate, which are in many ways deeply intertwined, are the crisis of reason and subjectivity; the concepts of modernity, postmodernity, and their relation; and hermeneutics as philosophical *koine* and the notion of "weak thought."

II. THE CRISIS OF REASON AND SUBJECTIVITY

In 1979, Aldo Gargani edited a famous collection titled *Crisi della ragione* (Crisis of reason), to which many renowned Italian philosophers contributed.[32] Gargani

---

31. It should be noted that most Italian philosophers in one way or another entered the discussion of the three main themes.

32. Educated in the Pisan environment of analytic philosophy by the philosopher of science Francesco Barone, Gargani (1933–2009) has studied various areas of thought (from the history of modern philosophy, especially Descartes, Bacon, Hobbes and Locke, through the epistemology of physical and mathematical sciences, and psychoanalysis, to early-twentieth-century middle-European culture). He has also explored the logical-theoretical issues developed in analytic philosophy, especially in logical neopositivism. Gargani is currently Professor of History of Contemporary Philosophy at the University of Pisa. Among his publications are: *Lo stupore e il caso* (Astonishment and chance; 1986), *Sguardo e destino* (Gaze and destiny; 1988), and *L'altra storia* (The other history; 1990). On the place of philosophy of science and neopositivism in recent Italian philosophy, see Luigi Barrotta, "Contemporary Philosophy of Science in Italy: An Overview," *Journal for General Philosophy of Science* 29 (1998); also, Paolo Parrini, "Neo-Positivism and Italian Philosophy," *Vienna Circle Institute Yearbook* 6 (1998).
     Among the philosophers who contribute to *Crisi della ragione* are Bodei, Veca, and Viano. See Aldo Gargani (ed.), *Crisi della ragione: Nuovi modelli nel rapporto tra sapere e attività umane* [Crisis of reason: New models in the relation between knowledge and human activities] (Turin: Einaudi, 1979).

had already challenged the foundational solidity of sciences in an earlier work, *Il sapere senza fondamenti* (Knowledge without foundations; 1975). According to him, reason, which he names not without equivocation "classical reason," is incapable of reflecting adequately the laws and forms of reality first of all because reality is not an objective world that can be grasped; rather, reality is itself the consequence of a series of choices, values, interests, and myths constituting a specific civilization. The traditional, rationalistic image of reason inspired by a desire for omnipotence should be denounced and renounced, he argues, whereas philosophy should no longer aim at producing foundations or logical argumentations, and should stop competing for status with the hard sciences. Furthermore, philosophy should, as Gargani himself does, unfold into "narrated thought," which intertwines reflection and narration, development of ideas and personal experiences, philosophy and literature. With no preconstituted certainties to move from, one should learn to transform chance into advantage and benefit, in the recognition that truth is neither possession nor goal but simply a matter of "influential images directing our lives."[33] The idea of a self-centered subject is only "a theater," a "great exorcism carried out against reality."[34] The task is that of accepting the existential challenge and acquiring "the courage to be" always different from oneself in the unforeseeable encounters to which one is constantly exposed.[35]

The idea of *Krisis*, which somehow sustains Gargani's position, is explicitly thematized in the philosophy of Massimo Cacciari, who had already devoted to this topic his books *Krisis: Saggio sulla crisi del pensiero negativo da Nietzsche a Wittgenstein* (*Krisis*: An essay on the crisis of negative thought from Nietzsche to Wittgenstein; 1976) and *Pensiero negativo e razionalizzazione* (Negative thought and rationalization; 1977).[36] Cacciari opposes to the soteriological, conciliatory, continuous images of reason and history, especially of a dialectical

33. Aldo Gargani, "La verità come immagine influente" [Truth as influential image], in *Il destino dell'uomo nella società post-industriale* [The destiny of humanity in postindustrial society], Aldo Gargani (ed.) (Rome-Bari: Laterza, 1987), 10.

34. Aldo Gargani, "L'attrito del pensiero" [The friction of thought], in *Filosofia '86*, Gianni Vattimo (ed.) (Rome-Bari: Laterza, 1987), 11, 22.

35. Aldo Gargani, *Il coraggio di essere: Saggio sulla cultura mitteleuropea* [The courage to be: Essay on middle-European culture] (Rome-Bari: Laterza, 1992).

36. Massimo Cacciari (1944–) was three times the mayor of Venice, after being a member of the Italian Parliament, the European Parliament, and the regional government of Veneto. Cacciari studied philosophy at the University of Padua with a dissertation on Kant's *Critique of Judgment*; he became Professor of Aesthetics at the University of Venice and later Professor of Philosophy at the Vita-Salute San Raffaele University in Milan. He has been among the founders of some of the most important philosophical and cultural journals in Italy: *Angelus Novus* (1964–74), *Contropiano* (1968–71), *Laboratorio Politico* (1980–85), *Il Centauro* (1980–85), and *Paradosso*, started in 1992 and codirected with Sergio Givone, Carlo Sini, and Vincenzo Vitiello.

(Hegelian–Marxian as well as Lukácsian) kind, the idea of *Krisis* as the permanent emergency in which thinking and being are situated. In this situation of antidialectical "negative thought," which is exemplified in the "decadent" figures of Nietzsche and the early-twentieth-century Austrian thinkers Freud, Hoffmannstahl, Rilke, Roth, Schönberg, Trakl, and Wittgenstein, no salvation is ever granted or assured, and there is no possibility for a dogmatic uniqueness of the truth, not even the truth of subjectivity. In *Icone della legge* (Icons of the law; 1985), the symbol of the enigmatic ambiguity of existence bordering on tragedy, that is, of the *Krisis* of *nomos*, becomes the Kafkan and Rosenzweigian metaphor of the door, which can be understood both as a barrier that could have been destroyed and as an opening at the end of any apparently closed life path. The contemporary subject is placed in the situation of constantly having to make choices on behalf of a law and a goal the meanings of which are no longer clear – they are obfuscated or lost. Contemporary subjectivity is completely autonomous, but in the sense of its being entirely uprooted from all grounds, and thus standing on a precarious nothing. This is the deepest sense of the nihilism that Cacciari reaches also through a meditation on Heidegger's *Nietzsche*. The contemporary individual is placed in a situation of nomadism similar to that of the children of Israel. At this point, and especially in some later works, Cacciari's philosophical approach intertwines with more theological themes, as becomes explicit in his books *The Necessary Angel* ([1986] 1994), an allegory for the infinite tension between the human limited ability of representation and the nonrepresentable, and *Dell'inizio* (On the beginning; 1990), which explores the traditional philosophical theme of the beginning as the proper philosophical problem, whereas all other disciplines start from an already constituted object. Cacciari's itinerary leads him to reconsider the entire history of metaphysics according to a different line of interpretation than the one suggested by Heidegger. His "negative thought" in fact rereads the history of philosophy according to a different line of origin or beginning, which goes from Proclus to Damascius to Scotus Eriugena to Meister Eckhardt to Cusanus to Schelling and which intersects, once again, philosophy and theology to produce a new "double" heresy. In his works from the mid-1990s, *Geo-filosofia dell'Europa* (Geo-philosophy of Europe; 1994) and *L'arcipelago* (The archipelago; 1997), Cacciari's philosophical sensitivity to those differences that "negative thought" does not want to unify and reconcile manifests itself through an exploration of the irreducible plurality of cultural roots present in the European landscape.

The idea of a crisis of reason with its tragic and nihilistic implications[37] is parallel to the theme of a crisis of the monolithic subject sustaining such

---

37. The theme of tragedy becomes explicit in Luigi Pareyson's later work on Dostoevsky, Schelling, and Heidegger (see note 48), and finds its utmost conceptualization in his *Ontologia della*

rationality. The themes of the subject and subjectivity in their genesis and as structuring Western modern individuals are powerfully present in the philosophy of Bodei, starting with his work *Scomposizioni: Forme dell'individuo moderno* (Decompositions: Forms of the modern individual; 1987), which in many senses is an inaugural text with respect to later reflections on subjectivity, multiplicity, and the "multiverse."[38] Moving from the consideration of a fragment by Hegel in which individuality is structured in a pyramidal manner, Bodei understands history, and the individual, neither as a continuum according to the historicist model nor as eternal history *à la* Vico, but rather as a *metamorphosis*, a stratification, a layering, and a passage of forms according to the suggestions of Gestalt psychology. *Scomposizioni* is the first volume in a series including *Geometria delle passioni: Paura, speranza e felicità: filosofia e uso politico* (Geometry of passions: Fear, hope and happiness – philosophy and political use; 1991), *Ordo amoris: Conflitti terreni e felicità celeste* (The order of love: Earthly conflicts and celestial happiness; 1991), and *Logics of Delusion* ([2002] 2007), all devoted to exploring forms of logics different from the one displayed by theoretical rationality, through an extensive conversation with Descartes, Hobbes, and Spinoza, but also Augustine, Foucault, and psychiatric theory. Bodei's theoretical project aims at the elaboration of a logical-interpretative structure capable of thinking conceptual and historical tensions and conflicts as a form of antagonistic complicity, that is, of a *logos* intrinsically connected but also foreign to *polemos*. He thus extends the sphere of intelligibility to notions such as passion,

---

libertà: Il male e la sofferenza (Ontology of freedom: evil and suffering; 1995). The concept of the tragic is present also in the considerations of Sergio Givone (1944–), a student of Pareyson in Turin and currently Professor of Aesthetics at the University of Florence. For Givone, the tragic, explored in its Romantic and not only Nietzschean implications, constitutes the hermeneutic model capable of confronting the current historical epoch hanging over the abyss of nihilism. Among Givone's publications are *Ermeneutica e romanticismo* (Hermeneutics and Romanticism; 1983), *Disincanto del mondo e pensiero tragico* (Disenchantment of the world and tragic thought; 1988), and *Storia del nulla* (History of nothingness; 1996).

38. Remo Bodei (1938–) studied at the University of Pisa. He was then awarded various fellowships at the universities of Tübingen and Freiburg, where he attended lectures by Ernst Bloch and Eugen Fink, and at the University of Heidelberg, where he attended lectures by Karl Löwith and Dieter Henrich. In 1971 he was appointed Professor of History of Philosophy at the University of Pisa. After being granted a Humboldt fellowship at the Ruhr University in Bochum (1977–79), he became visiting professor at King's College, Cambridge (1980), and later at Ottawa University (1983). He taught for many years (1969–93) at the Scuola Normale Superiore in Pisa. He has also taught on several occasions at New York University, and more recently at the University of California, Los Angeles. His books have been translated into many languages. Among his publications are *Sistema ed epoca in Hegel* (System and epoch in Hegel; 1975), *Multiversum: Tempo e storia in Ernst Bloch* (Multiversum: Time and history in Ernst Bloch; 1979), and *Le forme del bello* (The forms of the beautiful; 1995).

delusion, history, and beauty while preserving their alterity by not submitting them to a form of rationality that searches for absolute exactness and certainty.

The theme of subjectivity is central also to Aldo Masullo, a Neapolitan philosopher educated under the guidance of Antonio Aliotta (1881–1964) and Cleto Carbonara (1896–1976) in the tradition of a historicism of a liberal nature, which is deeply aware of the insufficiencies in which the idealistic historicism *à la* Giovanni Gentile had fallen.[39] Following Croce's teaching, Masullo neither abandons the field of history nor understands the humanistic ideal of freedom as spiritual freedom that translates into cultural works and political institutions. Sharing with Gargani and Bodei a deeply antimetaphysical sentiment, Masullo exercises a radical criticism of the foundational pretension of philosophy and of its substantialized concepts. His reflection gravitates toward the notion of subjectivity no longer understood as pure and disembodied activity as in the rationalist or transcendental subject. Rather, Masullo construes subjectivity in terms of passivity, and thus of intersubjectivity. The individual is an intimacy on which time and experience carve deep marks, and leave traces constituting the individual as he or she is. The individual is time, which also means that subjectivity is finite, that is, exposed. This is the dimension of affectivity, or pathic character of the subject, which is not a subject unless it is in a relation of intersubjectivity, that is of dialogue and communication with others. Far from an ingenuous exaltation of the individual and the power of the will and rationality, Masullo's philosophy borders on some of the themes of nihilism in the awareness of the unstable and vulnerable nature of subjectivity and the unhappiness of reason, doomed to search for a foundation it can never achieve. Masullo's project is to elaborate "an active ethics of salvation" understood in a nonreligious register as the ability to recognize the intersubjective connection linking all individuals and as the availability to work within history without closure to the novelty history may bring unexpectedly.

The theme of ethics as the proper field of activities in which contemporary subjectivity can confront and care for its own finitude is present also in Salvatore Natoli, a student of Severino (see below) at Milan Catholic University.[40] Through a meditation on Nietzsche, Heidegger, and Foucault, Natoli elaborates an ethics

---

39. Aldo Masullo (1923–) is the author of *Il senso del fondamento* (The sense of ground; 1967), *Anti-metafisica del fondamento* (Antimetaphysics of ground; 1971), and *Filosofie del soggetto e diritto del senso* (Philosophies of the subject and the law of sense; 1990).

40. Salvatore Natoli (1942–) is Professor of Theoretical Philosophy at the University of Milan-Bicocca. His publications include *Vita buona, vita felice: Scritti di etica e di politica* (Good life, happy life: Essays in ethics and politics; 1990), *L'esperienza del dolore: Le forme del patire nella cultura occidentale* (The experience of pain: Forms of suffering in Western culture; 1995), and *Soggetto e fondamento: Il sapere dell'origine e la scientificità della filosofia* (Subject and ground: Knowledge of the origin and the scientific character of philosophy; 1996).

of finitude capable of including passions, affections, happiness, the dimension of corporeality, and, in Natoli's later writings, also the sacred. These dimensions have all been underestimated and marginalized by classical rationalism and contribute to a different configuration of subjectivity. Natoli proposes a form of neopaganism made possible by modernity and secularization. Such paganism abandons Christianity insofar as Natoli's proposal relies on finitude in its natural and unrevealed dimension: that is, it is centered on an ethos of self-sufficient finitude. It also differs from ancient and modern paganism insofar as Natoli's neopaganism is void of the tragic aspect characterizing ancient paganism, and it is not anti-Christian (like modern paganism) but rather post-Christian. The measure of finitude is death, which does not open up to nothingness but rather to a sense of mystery. Natoli's project is therefore not nihilist. Whereas it utters a need for the salvation of the finite, it does not find such salvation in the redemption of the finite but rather in its *ethos*, in the dwelling in it as self-sufficient as long as it lasts.

A reflection on subjectivity interpreted under the rubric of "person" is carried out by Enrico Berti, who intertwines historical, theoretical, and ethical analyses with the study of Aristotle, an area in which Berti is a world-renowned scholar.[41] Berti, who belongs to a neoclassical and neo-Aristotelian tradition, also engages in a confutation of the absoluteness of experience, which for him always refers to the transcendence of the Principle: that is, to the recognition of the necessity of a transcendent absolute. Such a Principle, or Infinite, is independent of any dogmatic or confessional religious belief, and its necessity, although not its nature, is knowable by finite reason. A supporter of ethical personalism, Berti is especially interested in practical philosophy, a theme privileged also by his student Franco Volpi (1952–2009), a scholar of Heidegger and of Aristotle's presence in Heidegger's thought.

In this general climate of a rethinking of the role and nature of reason and subjectivity, an interesting experience occurs that, however, remains marginal and unnoticed to the broader philosophical and even academic community.[42] It is the creation by a group of women philosophers of *Diotima*, a philosophical women's community based at the University of Verona and finding its major

---

41. A student of the neoclassical philosopher Marino Gentile, Berti (1935–) is Professor of Philosophy at the University of Padua. Among his works are *Contraddizione e dialettica negli antichi e nei moderni* (Contradiction and dialectic in the ancients and the moderns; 1987), *Analitica e dialettica nel pensiero antico* (Analytics and dialectics in ancient thought; 1989), and *Soggetti di responsabilità* (Subjects of responsibility; 1993).

42. Despite the history of political activism and success of the women's liberation movements in Italy, to this day there are no departments of women's studies in Italian universities where feminist theorists can be housed and develop a "thought of sexual difference" in all its aspects and implications.

representatives in Adriana Cavarero (1947–), Luisa Muraro (1940–), and Chiara Zamboni (1954–). Their philosophical activity is inspired by the thought of Luce Irigaray[43] and the cultural–political debate of women's movements, especially the so-called feminism of difference. They engage in a rereading of the history of philosophy and culture, and a reconfiguration of subjectivity according to women's lines of thought (*pensiero al femminile*). By reconfiguring subjectivity according to sexual difference, they challenge the universality and neutrality of the philosophical discourse and its concepts, which are in fact revealed as the historical and symbolic expression of male subjects. More specifically, they thematize the issues of women's authority, the symbolic order of the mother, the concept of mother tongue, and the idea of philosophical practice as a starting-from-oneself.

Through the discussion on the crisis of reason and subjectivity, Italian philosophers acknowledge that there is no unifying history providing a single meaning to the world, no unitary knowledge capable of systematizing the various fields of experience, no overarching rationality penetrating and adequately mirroring the complexity of reality, and no monolithic subject supporting all this. During the 1980s and 1990s, the world of modernity and its optimism seems to have come to an end.

III. MODERNITY AND POSTMODERNITY

The second topic of debate that occupies Italian philosophers of the period contemplates precisely the status of the current condition of a general loss of unitary meaning, what has been called "the postmodern condition," in relation to the previous condition of modernity.[44] This debate, which often assumes the tones of an open, harsh, and in the end sterile polemic, and which prolongs itself for almost a decade, finds major representatives in Gianni Vattimo, Paolo Rossi (1923–2012), and Carlo Augusto Viano (1929–), with the last two taking an explicit position in favor of modernity against any postmodern configuration. Fundamental works engaging the debate are Vattimo's *The Adventure of Difference: Philosophy After Nietzsche and Heidegger* ([1980] 1993), *The End of Modernity: Nihilism and Hermeneutics in Postmodern Culture* ([1985] 1992), and the reactions to the postmodern position delineated by Vattimo and others (such as Gargani, Cacciari, Eco, and many of the thinkers analyzed in the present

---

*43. For a discussion of Luce Irigaray, see the essay by Mary Beth Mader in *The History of Continental Philosophy: Volume 6*.

44. See Hugh Silverman, "Postmodernism and Contemporary Italian Philosophy," *Man and World* 27(4) (1994).

essay) as discussed in Viano's numerous journal articles in the *Rivista di Filosofia* and in *Va' pensiero: Il carattere della filosofia italiana contemporanea* (Onward, thought: The character of contemporary Italian philosophy; 1985), and in Paolo Rossi's *Paragone degli ingegni moderni e postmoderni* (Comparison between modern and postmodern minds; 1989). The debate between the two positions, which originated in the Turin school but ended up dividing the Italian philosophical world, is documented in Giovanni Mari's edited volume *Moderno Postmoderno* (Modern postmodern; 1987) and in Berti's *Le vie della ragione* (The ways of reason; 1987).

Since, in general, postmodernism appears as an evaluation of history and metaphysics that reconfigures them (when they are not abandoned) in terms of break and discontinuity, the debate on modernity and postmodernity takes up the features of a discussion on the historical and metaphysical categories guiding modernity. The defenders of modernity support neo-Enlightenment, neorationalist, and secular theses considered to be bearers of reform projects and reconfigurations of knowledge in close proximity to science. Among them are Abbagnano's Turin students, such as Pietro Rossi and Viano, who devote themselves to a historiographic production accompanied by a theoretical commitment against irrationalistic positions. Historiography, which in Italy enjoys a long tradition going back at least to Vico, finds additional representatives in Milan with Dal Pra and his students, and in Florence with the school of Garin. Both schools are geared toward an anti-idealist understanding of the development of history, which is grounded in the empirical historicity of various human beings and philosophers. Among the opponents of postmodernism are also some historians and intellectuals formed in the Marxist tradition such as Lucio Colletti, concerned by the postmodern abandonment of the idea of critical and scientific rationality and the escape into antiscientist positions.

Among the secular scholars, particularly vocal in the debate against postmodernism are Viano and Paolo Rossi. In *Va' pensiero*, Viano links postmodernism and its Italian specific variation, Vattimo's weak thought, to an anti-Enlightenment, antireformist, and traditionalist tendency. This trend, widespread in Italy and internationally, is contrary to science and the industrial society in general, which it counters with tradition and edifying literature. Similarly, Paolo Rossi criticizes and confutes on historical grounds the postmodern discourse of a unified, homogeneous, totalizing "classical rationality" geared toward unity and dominating the philosophical scene up to the twentieth century, when it would finally come to an end. Through the study of major representatives of so-called classical reason such as Bacon, Hobbes, Diderot, and Comte, Rossi shows how the postmodern theses, which unfold out of a Heideggerianism radically different from the one that inspired many Marxist thinkers during the 1960s and 1970s, are an undocumented, superficial construct geared toward attributing prophetic legitimacy to its supporters in an anti-Enlightenment move. It should be noted that while quite vehement in their tone, the positions outlined above defending modernity represent a minority perspective in Italian philosophy, as they do not seem capable of counteracting the widespread affirmation of the various postmodern attitudes against metaphysics.

An interesting thinker to be considered within the range of this debate because in fact he radically jumps over the terms of the discussion is Emanuele Severino,[45] who, taking recourse to Nietzsche's concept of the eternal recurrence and Heidegger's analysis of technology and the contemporary world, argues for the return to a pre-Greek, premodern form of thinking as exemplified by Parmenides. Severino was educated at the University of Pavia under the guidance of classical metaphysician Bontadini, with whom he clamorously broke relations while they were teaching together at the Milan Catholic University of the Sacred Heart in 1970. This break, which originated in a dispute regarding Bontadini's analysis of becoming and prompted Severino's move to the University of Venice, marked the beginning of the development of Severino's own original thinking, which has been named "neo-Parmenideanism." According to Severino, whose philosophical position develops in sustained conversation with Nietzsche, Heidegger, and Marx, the Western world is dominated by a nihilistic will to power, domination, abuse, and the devastation of nature, which is the consequence of the folly of placing trust in the notion of becoming. The will to power, ultimately displayed in the technological attitude and in capitalism but also guiding scientific behavior, is in fact based on the conviction that things and humans are destructible, modifiable, and manipulable because they are exposed to the nullification due to the process of becoming. Against the "folly of becoming" with its dominating and violent charge, Severino suggests a return to Parmenides that does not deny the multiplicity of beings, but rather asserts, *contra* Heidegger, the immutability of Being and the eternity of all beings because becoming is the appearing and disappearing of the eternal. Through his original Parmenidean ontology, which configures itself as an "ontology of necessity" against much "ontology of freedom" (as in Pareyson's case, discussed below), Severino reads the entire history of metaphysics as the alteration and forgetfulness of the authentic meaning of being. Thus, his postmetaphysical invi-

---

45. Emanuele Severino (1929–) graduated at the University of Pavia in 1950 under the guidance of Gustavo Bontadini with a dissertation on Heidegger and metaphysics. After teaching at the Catholic University of the Sacred Heart in Milan, he became Professor of Theoretical Philosophy at the University of Venice. He is a member of the Italian National Academy (Accademia Nazionale dei Lincei), and writes regularly for the Italian daily newspaper *Corriere della Sera*. His publications include *Essenza del nichilismo* (Essence of nihilism; 1972), *Techne: Le radici della violenza* (*Techne*: The roots of violence; 1979), *Destino della necessità* (Fate of necessity; 1980), and *L'anello del ritorno* (The ring of the return; 1999).

tation is the return to a premetaphysical, premodern place of thinking that *de facto* ignores the controversy between modernity and postmodernity.

A postmetaphysical position that tries to keep together the results of modernity, especially in its Kantian, transcendental legacy, and the insights of existentialism and hermeneutics, is the one developed by Virgilio Melchiorre.[46] Melchiorre's thought develops within the tradition of classical metaphysics, but he subjects it to a double verification, stemming from phenomenology and hermeneutics, respectively. In the mode of French phenomenology and especially Ricoeur, he considers the concreteness of history and human beings as the center of philosophical discourse, and thus develops an interest in the themes of the body, space, and time. Within these themes, however, Melchiorre finds the experience of something that cannot be dismissed as simple becoming (which is, for him, a concept as abstract as that of pure being). From this experience, one is called to interpret reality, which is better understood in terms of finitude and precariousness rather than becoming. The interpretation leads to a move to the transcendental level in the quest for the conditions of possibility of the finite being that phenomenology and hermeneutics describe. For Melchiorre, the path is thus from consciousness and its concrete historicity to an "ultimately unconditioned," which is in itself unsayable, but which transpires in the individual perspectives. The analogical path (*via analogica*) becomes the way through which, within the horizon of finitude, the structures of being as unconditioned are revealed; reason necessarily requires such structures not simply as its goal but also as the immanent horizon of sense that is implied in every specific meaning. Melchiorre's long analogical path preoccupies itself with ethical questions, with issues in the philosophy of history, with the topic of symbolism as various ways to indicate a direction toward the unconditioned, which is simultaneously the most sayable (because always implied) and the least determinable (because always escaping speech and communication).

IV. HERMENEUTICS AS PHILOSOPHICAL *KOINE* AND WEAK THOUGHT

The third theme that occupies Italian philosophers, especially in the second part of the 1980s, is *il pensiero debole*, a term that indicates, even before Vattimo's

---

46. Virgilio Melchiorre (1931–) taught moral philosophy at the University of Venice. Later, he became Professor of Moral Philosophy at the Catholic University of the Sacred Heart in Milan, where he had previously taught the philosophy of history since 1961. In 2000, he became Professor of Theoretical Philosophy at the same university, where he also directed the School of Specialization in Social Communications. His publications include *Essere e parola: Idee per una antropologia metafisica* (Being and word: Ideas for a metaphysical anthropology; 1982), *Corpo e persona* (Body and person; 1987), and *La via analogica* (The analogical way; 1996).

own specific position, a constellation of positions geared toward a rethinking in "weak" terms of traditional metaphysical categories. In parallel with weak thought and in many senses as a premise for the possibility of the development of weak thought, there emerge various attempts at a reconfiguration of reason, which has undergone a crisis in its techno–scientific–rationalistic as well as Hegelian–Marxist–dialectical variations, both a legacy of modernity. The reconfiguration occurs in terms of the complexity of a hermeneutic reason open to discourse and confrontation with alterities. Thus, a variety of philosophical positions not necessarily associated with weak thought yet more or less loosely affiliated with a properly hermeneutic stance develop. This justifies Vattimo's recognition of hermeneutics as the contemporary cultural *koine*.

Vattimo's weak thought could not have been accomplished without the fundamental influence of Luigi Pareyson, who in Europe is often considered the third hermeneutic variant beside Gadamer and Ricoeur.[47] Pareyson's philosophical itinerary begins in Turin under the guidance of spiritualist and personalist philosophers Guzzo and Carlini, and moves from existentialism, which Pareyson first introduced into Italy and which appears in him not only in its German variations (Jaspers, Barth, Heidegger, Kierkegaard), but also in its French interpretations (especially Marcel and Lavelle, but also Maritain, and, later, Pascal, although he is not canonically an existentialist). He develops a rereading of the history of German Romanticism and classical idealism that releases its representatives (most notably Fichte and later Schelling, but also Schiller and Novalis) from their subservience to Hegel. Pareyson also manifests an interest in aesthetics through the elaboration of the notion of "formativity" that opens up the path to a conception of art (and thus of myth and religion) as a place of interpretation of the truth, and thus as a hermeneutic site.[48] In 1971, Pareyson published his highly original and innovative book, *Verità e interpretazione* (Truth and interpretation), which is arguably the most important essay in Italian hermeneutics. Truth is here understood as something not ineffable (as in Heidegger, who thus walks down the "dead end" of an ontology of the ineffable, or a "negative ontology"), but rather inexhaustible (*inesauribile*). Quoting Pareyson's most famous claim, made against any objectivistic and thereby scientist notion of truth, "of the truth there can only be interpretations; and any interpretation can only be of

---

*47. For a discussion of the hermeneutic theories of Gadamer and Ricoeur, see the essay by Wayne J. Froman in *The History of Continental Philosophy: Volume 6*.

48. Among Pareyson's other works are *Esistenza e persona* (Existence and person; 1950), *Estetica: Teoria della formatività* (Aesthetics: Theory of formativity; 1954), and *Dostoevskij: Filosofia, romanzo ed esperienza religiosa* (Dostoevsky: Philosophy, fiction and religious experience; 1993). For an overview of Pareyson's philosophy, see Silvia Benso, "On Luigi Pareyson: A Master of Italian Hermeneutics," *Philosophy Today* 49(4–5) (2005).

the truth,"[49] which because of its inexhaustibility constantly spurs new interpretations, that is, new relations to itself. Since any interpretation is, ultimately, a matter of a historical and personal decision in favor of a faithfulness to truth and being or a betrayal of them both (and thus any interpretation involves a risk), the theme of interpretation develops, in Pareyson's final years, in the direction of an "ontology of freedom." The ontology of freedom not only locates the possibility for human freedom but also, through a reading of Schelling and Dostoevsky, it situates freedom, as both beginning and choice, in God. This is not the God of metaphysics but rather the biblical God, the God of Christianity who is abandoned by God and dies on the cross, God against God, a tragic God who does not explain but rather assumes on himself death, doubt, anguish, and atheism. For Pareyson, the heart of reality is thus freedom and ambiguity, suffering, pain, and evil, as the title of his final, posthumously published volume, *Essere libertà ambiguità* (Being freedom ambiguity; 1998), suggests and as a philosophical hermeneutics of Christian religious experience reveals.

In 1983, Vattimo and Pier Aldo Rovatti published their important and influential coedited volume *Il pensiero debole* (Weak thought), which, besides their own contributions, also contains essays by Leonardo Amoroso, Gianni Carchia, Filippo Costa, Franco Crespi, Alessandro Dal Lago, Umberto Eco, Maurizio Ferraris, and Diego Marconi. Vattimo and Rovatti are the two major representatives of this widespread, precise (although with indefinite margins) philosophical position known as *pensiero debole* ("metaphor," as it is qualified in their preface to the volume, which Vattimo now prefers to replace with the less demanding term "ontology of decline"), although Vattimo is now its principal proponent.[50]

As evidenced in *Al di là del soggetto* (Beyond the subject; 1981), and *The End of Modernity: Nihilism and Hermeneutics in Postmodern Culture* ([1985] 1991), Vattimo's thought emerges from the realization (which he has matured through association with his teachers Pareyson, Gadamer, and Löwith and his readings of Barth, Benjamin, Bloch, Croce, Heidegger, Lukács, Marcuse, and Nietzsche) of the current impossibility of any fixed structure of being. Such impossibility has been completed through the philosophies of Nietzsche and Heidegger.

---

49. Luigi Pareyson, *Verità e interpretazione* (Milan: Mursia, 1971), 53.
50. Gianni Vattimo (1936–) was a student of Pareyson, under whose guidance he graduated in 1959 in Turin with a dissertation on Aristotle. He studied in Heidelberg with Karl Löwith and Hans-Georg Gadamer, whose thought he introduced in Italy. After teaching aesthetics at the University of Turin, he later became Professor of Theoretical Philosophy there. He has been a visiting professor at various universities in the United States. Recently he was an elected member of the European Parliament in Brussels. Among his publications are *Il soggetto e la maschera: Nietzsche e il problema della liberazione* (The subject and the mask: Nietzsche and the problem of liberation; 1974), *The Transparent Society* ([1989] 1992), and *Beyond Interpretation: The Meaning of Hermeneutics for Philosophy* ([1994] 1997).

The experience of the oblivion of being and of the death of God,[51] however, are not carried far enough by the widespread discourses on the crisis of reason and "negative thought" because of their fundamental nostalgic attitude toward metaphysics. Weak thought aims at completing the process initiated by the two German thinkers by weakening or disempowering the strong metaphysical structures and entities (such as reason, truth, absolute values, and so on) that have constituted modernity. Vattimo thus wishes for an overcoming of metaphysics that results in an ethics of interpretation insofar as the truth is resolved into its continuous interpretations. Playing on the meaning of *Überwindung* (overcoming) as *Verwindung* (distortion or twisting), Vattimo considers metaphysical "immutables" as traces that are no longer practicable as absolutes and yet are unrenounceable as the provenance from which the postmodern subject comes. Truth becomes for Vattimo the transmission of a linguistic and historical legacy orienting one's own understanding of reality. Toward such a legacy, one can only exercise a form of *pietas* and, as far as the present and the future are concerned, concentrate on an "ontology of actuality" (the term is borrowed from Foucault) focused on the elaboration of a nonunitary, multifaceted subject open to freedom, tolerance, building of consensus, and relations with other cultures. Emancipation for Vattimo is not a matter of a progressive liberation from prejudices toward the goal of a clear, objective truth, but rather the freedom from strong metaphysical structures that hermeneutic reason achieves through the realization that all truths are a matter of interpretation.

The ethical implications of weak thought are taken up by Pier Aldo Rovatti.[52] Although he shares with Vattimo many philosophical presuppositions, Rovatti is a phenomenologist and does not recognize himself in the general landscape of hermeneutics. Especially in his book *L'elogio del pudore: Per un pensiero debole* (In praise of modesty: Toward a weak thought; 1989), written with Dal Lago, and in conversation with Freud, Heidegger, Husserl, Levinas, and Vattimo, Rovatti introduces the metaphor of modesty (and elsewhere the dimension of silence, as in *L'esercizio del silenzio* [The exercise of silence; 1992]) as a way to respond ethically to the weakening of philosophy attested in Vattimo's philosophical hypoth-

---

51. On these themes as they relate to Vattimo, see Brian Schroeder, "Theological Nihilism and Italian Philosophy," *Philosophy Today* 49(4–5) (Winter 2005).

52. Pier Aldo Rovatti (1942–) completed his studies in theoretical philosophy with a dissertation on Whitehead at Milan State University under the guidance of Enzo Paci and Ludovico Geymonat. After working as a theater critic for the daily newspaper *L'Avanti*, he taught at Milan State University and later at the University of Trieste, where he is currently Professor of Theoretical Philosophy. Among his publications are *La posta in gioco* (What is at stake; 1987), *Le trasformazioni del soggetto: Un itinerario filosofico* (The transformation of the subject: A philosophical itinerary; 1992), and *Abitare la distanza: Per un'etica del linguaggio* (Inhabiting distance: Toward an ethics of language; 1994).

esis. Modesty is defined by Rovatti as a movement of withdrawal of thought from things and events so as to allow the emergence of a "shadow zone" that remains invisible and ineffable, a zone of renunciation of the claims advanced by traditional philosophy to be able to grasp its objects. The contemporary weakening of philosophy thus entails an ethical aspect, which can be identified with the modesty, discretion, and lack of violence of a universe of thought deprived of its dimension of will to power. Rovatti's invitation is to an "ethics of diminution," that is, an ethics of dwelling in the distance, from oneself and from others.

Interesting philosophical perspectives that unfold with hermeneutics on their background and accentuate various different components of the contemporary debate are those of Umberto Eco, Carlo Sini, Vincenzo Vitiello, and Mario Ruggenini. Among the four, the thinker who is most clearly influenced by hermeneutics is Ruggenini, who, in conversation with Heidegger, develops hermeneutics on the grounds of a general evaluation of the crisis of metaphysics inherited from his teacher Severino.[53] Starting with a hermeneutic retrieval of phenomenological themes (Husserl and Heidegger), Ruggenini's overall philosophy develops the theme of the finitude of existence in relation to the problem of alterity, so as to replace the metaphysics of meaning and sufficient reason with a different experience of the truth – an experience of truth that occurs in human speech and in the conversation with others in which the world opens up. In general, three themes recur in Ruggenini's philosophy: a rethinking of ontological issues in a hermeneutic-phenomenological register; a new hermeneutics of the I or self that is made possible out of the relation with the other and constitutes the I neither as substance nor as self-certainty, but rather as responsibility for the other; and the appeal of the other as opening to the dimension of the sacred. The sacred is here understood not as the god of presence and ontotheology, but rather as the god of absence, which entails for human beings faithfulness to the earth and a retrieval of the religious sense of philosophical questioning. The entire Western tradition is for Ruggenini marked by an immanent nihilism, which is deepened through the Christian idea of creation from nothingness, since such *creatio ex nihilo* constantly exposes the world to the

---

53. Mario Ruggenini (1940–) is Professor of Theoretical Philosophy at the University of Venice. A student of Emanuele Severino first at the University of the Sacred Heart in Milan, Ruggenini then followed Severino to Venice after the latter's break with his master and then colleague Bontadini. He has spent periods of study and research in Cambridge and Oxford, and has lectured on questions of phenomenology and hermeneutics in various universities in Europe and elsewhere. Among his publications are *Volontà e interpretazione: Le forme della fine della filosofia* (Will and interpretation: The forms of the end of philosophy; 1984), *I fenomeni e le parole: La verità finita dell'ermeneutica* (Phenomena and speech: The finite truth of hermeneutics; 1991), and *Il discorso dell'altro: Ermeneutica della differenza* (Discourse of the other: Hermeneutics of difference; 1996).

risk of a renewed fall into the nothingness from which it comes. The only way out of such nihilism is through a radically and genuinely hermeneutic attitude. The fall into nothingness is strictly related to the violent domination by a single truth; nothingness can be defeated only with the recognition that the truth is multiple and cannot be owned or possessed. Rather, truth gives itself in the changing and rich intertwining of multiple discourses. As Ruggenini repeats on the wave of Hölderlin, "we are a discourse," since our finite being is always and already in a relation in which we are, first and foremost, listeners and interlocutors. Ruggenini's perspective is thus that of a hermeneutic philosophy that has abandoned all forms of transcendence since transcendence is implicitly considered an (albeit unintentional) generator of nihilism. Such a perspective opens up to a dimension of sacredness that is clearly identified with the finitude of human existence, which is always conversation.

The philosophy of Vitiello is also deeply engaged with a hermeneutic of Christian thought, which he rereads in a direction that eliminates all perspectives of redemption while emphasizing finitude.[54] A scholar of German classical idealism, Nietzsche, Heidegger, and the Christian and Neoplatonist traditions (especially Plotinus and Augustine), Vitiello has focused his research on some crucial theoretical questions such as the interpretation of time, the concept of difference, and the relation between dialectic and hermeneutics, arriving at his own hermeneutic theory – which he names "topology" – founded on a reinterpretation of the notion of space. The recognition of the multiplicity of the truth does not lead him to nihilism or relativism; rather, it solicits the retrieval of a conceptual site or *topos* capable of constituting the true possibility of the concept. He explores a "topology of the modern," that is, a possible and always questionable identity constituting the truth of the modern. The concept of possibility extends also to divine being, which Vitiello interprets in the sense of omnipossibility, that is, of complete possibility of everything, at all times – of creation as well as "de-creation." The Christian experience of the cross becomes the experience of a God that does not save, opening up the dimensions of restlessness, of anguish, of *Angst*. The cross marks the limit of human beings. The notion of the redeeming God, who denies such dimensions in the victory of salvation, is replaced with the concept of the *deus absconditus*, which in turn relies on a radical faithfulness to finitude.

---

54. Vincenzo Vitiello (1935–) studied at the University of Naples Federico II, where he wrote on the topic of "Freedom and Justice in the Thought of Benedetto Croce." He has taught aesthetics, the history of modern and contemporary philosophy, and currently is Professor of Theoretical Philosophy at the University of Salerno. He has also taught in several German and Spanish universities, and at the University of Chapingo in Mexico. Among his publications are *Utopia del nichilismo* (Utopia of nihilism; 1983), *Topologia del moderno* (Topology of the modern; 1992), and *Cristianesimo senza redenzione* (Christianity without redemption; 1995).

The themes of hermeneutics as philosophy of interpretation are taken in a different direction by Umberto Eco, a student of Pareyson who interlaces hermeneutics and semiotic interests in his own original way.[55] The hermeneutic theme of an infinity of interpretations, filtered through Peirce's notion of unlimited semiosis, is taken up by Eco with the suggestion of the construction of "encyclopedia-like semantics," which, unlike and in opposition to "dictionary semantics," because of their rhizomatic and labyrinthine structure insert the reader into an open, potentially infinite, at least indefinite, even if perhaps contradictory plot of interdisciplinary references proper to intertextuality. The theory of an interpretative cooperation of various narrative texts extends to the reader, who is also caught in an interpretative game to become the model reader for each particular text. Against many deconstructionist positions, especially in their American variations, Eco nevertheless asserts the limits of interpretation when claiming that, if it is not possible to legitimate good interpretations, it is always possible to invalidate bad ones. The open multiplicity of interpretations is always confronted with the already given and already said, which thus work as the limits of any interpretative freedom. In his philosophy of language, Eco embraces a "contractualist" position not only in reference to signifieds but also to signifiers, which are the result of valid agreements made correctly to mean certain expressions; in other words, their validity is entirely practical.

Linguistic themes, especially the notion of sign, are at the center of the philosophy of Carlo Sini, who is deeply influenced by Peirce's semiotics, which he intertwines with suggestions coming from Heidegger, phenomenology, the hermeneutic tradition, and Derrida.[56] Although Sini is not exactly a hermeneutic philosopher, strong motifs coming from hermeneutic theory play a fundamental role in his position. For Sini, signs are not things but rather relations referring on the one side to the object, and on the other to the interpreter. Objects subsist only as indicated by a sign, and never in themselves. Analogously, interpreters are neither metaphysical subjects nor empirical figures; rather, they are formed within and by virtue of interpretations that are themselves situated within a process of unlimited semiosis understood as event and not as fact. An originary

---

55. Umberto Eco (1932–) is Professor of Semiotics at the University of Bologna. In addition to various novels, he is the author of *A Theory of Semiotics* ([1975] 1976), *The Role of the Reader: Explorations in the Semiotics of Texts* ([1979] 1979), *Interpretation and Overinterpretation* ([1995] 1992), and *The Limits of Interpretation* ([1990] 1990).

56. Carlo Sini (1933–) was educated in the tradition of the Milan State University, where he studied under the guidance of Enzo Paci. Sini is Professor of Theoretical Philosophy at the Milan State University. His publications include *Passare il segno* (Passing the sign; 1981), *Il silenzio e la parola: Luoghi e confine del sapere per un uomo planetario* (Silence and speech: Places and boundary of knowledge for a planetary human; 1989), and *Etica della scrittura* (Ethics of writing; 1992). [*] For a discussion of Peirce, see the essay by Douglas R. Anderson in *The History of Continental Philosophy: Volume 2*.

form of the eventuation of signs is writing, which for Sini is more than a purely mechanical activity. Writing is in fact a practice characterized, as we know it, by the alphabet. This specific alphabetic practice, itself inserted in various other practices based on bodies, voices, writing tools, and material support such as stone, paper, computer screen, and so on, defines the specific way of being of Western civilization with its values and concepts gravitating around logic and scientific rationality. Truth is here inserted in a universe of practices that themselves conform to other social practices while founding new ones. Thus, practices, and the specific practice of writing constituting philosophy, are linked to ethics understood simply as being or dwelling in the world. Following Husserl, Sini is convinced that all theories are in fact the practices through which we inhabit our time. Whereas Husserl's phenomenology aimed at a rigorous form of knowledge, Sini's encyclopedic phenomenology retraces various practices that have more or less meaning, but that can never claim for themselves the status of absolute truth. Thus, Husserl's phenomenology is reinterpreted in the sense of a "phenomenography" geared toward translating truth into signs. This is a commitment, or an *ethos*, each individual takes upon himself or herself, thereby becoming the figure and not the foundation of a continuously different practice. For Sini, then, the confrontation (made possible by the awareness that Western theory as the outcome of the alphabetic practice is one practice among many, one way of inhabiting the truth among many) among diverse concrete practices of life, discourses, and forms of writing would lead to a profitable reconsideration of various forms of knowledge in the richness of their differences – which cannot be reduced to the alphabetic practice of writing and its will to power.

The three areas of reflection discussed above – the crisis of reason and subjectivity, modernity and postmodernity, and hermeneutics and weak thought – certainly do not exhaust the varied and multiple interests of the Italian philosophical panorama during the years 1980–95. Nevertheless, by challenging and rethinking traditional metaphysical concepts, especially those of subjectivity and the role and nature of philosophy, the Italian philosophers of this period prepare the way for the ethical, political, and religious reflection that shapes much of the philosophical discourse that follows.

5

CONTINENTAL PHILOSOPHY IN
THE CZECH REPUBLIC

Josef Fulka, Jr.

The end of the 1970s is marked by the "adventures" of the Charter 77 and by the death of Jan Patočka (1907–77), a former student of Husserl and Heidegger and the most prominent Czech philosopher of the second half of the twentieth century. It is not an exaggeration to say that most of what happened in the following decade is delimited by various efforts to prolong and develop Patočka's specific version of phenomenology and philosophy of history, even though these interpretations very often took unexpected and peculiar forms of personal "philosophies" of particular authors, for whom Patočka's own ideas represent a pretext for the development of their own specific positions.

A lot has been said about the "underground" character of philosophical activity during the 1970s and 1980s. One of the very few fields of study that seem to have been spared the general persecution of non-Marxist philosophy was German idealism, considered as a precursor of Marxism. For example, remarkable and subtle interpretative work was accomplished by Milan Sobotka (1927–), a specialist on Hegel and author of several books on classical German philosophy (the most important being probably *Člověk, práce a sebevědomí* [Man and work in German philosophy], published in 1964). Sobotka wrote, coauthored with Ladislav Major (1935–), a clear and concise introduction to Hegel, published in 1979. In 1993, his texts on Hegel (results of seminars on *Phenomenology of Spirit* and Hegel's philosophy of law) were published under the title *Stati k Hegelově Fenomenologii a filosofii práva* (Studies in Hegel's phenomenology and philosophy of law). Sobotka's interpretation is concerned with the relation between Hegelianism and the philosophy of antiquity, and with Hegel's criticism of Kant and the development of post-Hegelian left-oriented philosophy and its Marxist results. Another example is Jiří Pešek (1929–2003), who produced interesting and nondogmatic interpretations of the notion of "division of labor" in Marxism. Pešek wrote an important work entitled *Dialektika dělby práce* (The dialectics of the division of labor) in 1966, and his later interests in the problem of temporality led to his work *Active Man and Time* in 1986. Both Sobotka and Pešek helped form a new generation of students, many of whom became university teachers after 1989 (Milan Znoj, Ladislav Benyovszky, and others).

Nonetheless, the most powerful current of Czech non-Marxist philosophy remained a matter of private teaching. The tradition of Patočka's private seminars and courses – held during the 1970s with a group of students founded by Ivan Chvatík – has been continued on various levels and in different contexts. Daniel Kroupa, Julius Tomin, Petr Rezek, Zdeněk Neubauer, Ladislav Hejdánek, and Radim Palouš[1] were among the most active organizers of lectures and seminars dealing more or less loosely with philosophical matters. On the other hand, this does not mean that Czech philosophy was condemned to remain in complete isolation: a very intense collaboration between the Czech and "Western" philosophers began in the late 1970s, thanks especially to Kathy Wilkes, who came to give a lecture on Aristotle in Tomin's seminar as early as in 1979. Afterwards, many other thinkers followed: Roger Scruton (who lectured on Wittgenstein in 1979), Alan Montefiore, Anthony Kenny (whose seminar on Aristotle was interrupted by the secret police), Christopher Kirwan (who lectures on Augustine in Hejdánek's seminar), and others. These visits soon became systematically organized: the Jan Hus Association was founded in 1980 to facilitate the intellectual exchanges between Anglo-Saxon and Czech philosophers and to provide material aid (books, research fellowships) to isolated Czech intellectuals. This project soon included the French intellectual scene as well. Jean-Pierre Vernant became the president of the French section of the Jan Hus Association (he remained in this position until his death in 2007, when the presidency was taken over by Étienne Balibar), and Jacques Derrida accepted the role of vice-president. This moment marked the beginning of regular visits of French philosophers in unofficial Czech seminars – the first being Paul Ricoeur in 1980. In 1984, Derrida came to Prague to give a lecture on Descartes in Hejdánek's seminar, after which a bizarre and well-known incident occurred: he was arrested by the police, accused of drug smuggling, and released only after the intervention of the French government. This curious event, however, did not dissuade others from coming, and Jean-Claude Eslin, Balibar, Richard Rorty, Jürgen Habermas, and Ernst Tugendhat were among the other lecturers who took part in the Czech

---

1. Daniel Kroupa (1949–) became a deputy in the Czech parliament in 1996. He also teaches political philosophy at the University of Plzeň. Radim Palouš (1924–) worked as a rector of the Charles University from 1990–94. In his theoretical work, he concentrates on the philosophy of education and his approach is inspired especially by Patočka and Levinas. Julius Tomin (1938–) studied philosophy and psychology. He works especially on Descartes and Plato.

"underground university." The publication policy reflected this rather unusual situation. Very few philosophers managed to write (and to publish) a full book: most of what happened in Czech philosophy is concentrated in articles that were published in *samizdat* editions – Hejdánek directed the publishing house OIKOYMENH, which became official after 1989 and is now a leading publisher of philosophical literature in the Czech Republic. Karel Palek, a philologist and author of a book on the relation between totalitarianism and language,[2] founded a *samizdat* review entitled *Kritický sborník* (Critical review). This review played a particularly important role in the Czech underground intellectual scene in the 1980s and started to be published officially in the 1990s. Apart from original works, several translations were produced, mainly as a result of the work in the seminars: these include Nietzsche's *Untimely Meditations*, Heidegger's *Being and Time*, and works by Levinas, Popper, and others.

From this tumultuous atmosphere an unusual image of Czech philosophy emerges: a sort of *bricolage*, an unusual mixture of penetrating insights and curious conceptions, high ambitions and abandoned projects that often remained in the form of unfinished sketches, plans and proclamations. There are, however, at least two lines of thought that are specific to Czech philosophy and represent an original achievement. The first consists in reinterpreting and developing Patočka's phenomenology; the second in connecting the legacy of the Czech structuralism (particularly the thought of Jan Mukařovský) with French poststructuralism and deconstruction. In what follows, it is those two domains that we will briefly examine.

I. PATOČKA AND HIS SHADOW

In his philosophical project, Patočka outlined several domains of reflection that remain "open" for future interpreters. As early as the 1950s, he developed his conception of negative Platonism, which is an original reinterpretation of the notion of idea in Plato's philosophy. Although Patočka's essay on negative Platonism deals specifically with Plato, the question involved concerns Western metaphysics in general and the problem of ideality in particular. As a starting-point, Patočka takes the Platonic notion of *khorismos* (the dividing line between the sphere of ideality and the material world) and reinterprets it in a negative way: *khorismos* is not a border between two realms, an ideal one and a material one, but rather an expression of the separation itself, a negativity that makes it impossible to hypostatize the ideality as a "second positivity" based on the model

---

2. Karel Palek, *Jazyk a moc* [Language and power] (Munich: K. Jadrný, 1983); Published in French as *L'Esprit post-totalitaire*, Erica Abrams (trans.) (Paris: B. Grasset, 1986).

of a material object. Human freedom and indeterminacy (living "on the edge," we might say) is a correlate of this negative experience of separation that is a basic structure of human existence.

Another important project, formulated in a series of articles written in German,[3] consists in predicting the possibility of what Patočka calls "asubjective phenomenology." Asubjective phenomenology is not a phenomenology without subject; such a claim would be ridiculous. Rather, it is a phenomenological project in which the subject loses the status of transcendental guarantee of the phenomenal field (Patočka's criticism of Husserl's alleged subjectivism goes precisely in this direction) and becomes a part of the structure of appearance (i.e. the world). In other words, the subject becomes implied in the world and ceases to be an abstract instance to which the world appears (certain parallels here between Patočka and late Merleau-Ponty are obvious). As a consequence, Patočka proposes to understand the subject as a corporeal entity whose existence in the world is conceived in terms of *movement* (one of the most important notions in Patočka's later philosophy, which originated in his interpretation and radicalization of Aristotle), which represents the most fundamental dimension of being-in-the-world; hence Patočka's renewed interest in the Husserlian concept of *Lebenswelt*, which became a key notion for many of his Czech interpreters.

Last but not least, it is Patočka's philosophy of history that has attracted considerable attention. Patočka's considerations on history are expressed – in its most consistent form – in his last great work, *Heretical Essays in the Philosophy of History*.[4] This book was heavily influenced by Heidegger; especially the final essay entitled "Wars of the Twentieth Century and the Twentieth Century as War." In this essay, Patočka stressed the ecstatic, "nocturnal" experience of the war front, but in a way that leaves the reader both fascinated and perplexed, as it reminds one more of Georges Bataille than phenomenology.

In the Czech context, all of the motives mentioned above were taken over and developed, enabling the Czech philosophers, for whom Patočka was the major point of reference, to delimit their own positions.

---

3. Jan Patočka, "Der Subjektivismus der Husserlschen und die Forderung einer asubjektive Phänomenologie," *Sborník prací filosofické fakulty brněnské univerzity* [The yearbook of the Faculty of Arts of Brno University] 19–20 (1971), "Der Subjektivismus der Husserlschen und die Möglichkeit einer asubjektive Phänomenologie," in *Philosophische Perspektiven, ein Jahrbuch*, vol. 2, R. Berlinger and E. Fink (eds) (Frankfurt: V. Klostermann, 1970), and "Epoché und Reduktion: Einige Bemerkungen," in *Bewußt Sein: Gerhard Funke zu eigen*, A. J. Bucher *et al.* (eds) (Bonn: Bonnier Verlag H. Grundmann, 1975).

4. Jan Patočka, *Kacířské eseje o filosofii dějin* (Prague: Academia, 1990); published in English as *Heretical Essays in the Philosophy of History*, Erazim Kohák (trans.) (La Salle, IL: Open Court, 1996).

Ladislav Hejdánek (1927–) studied philosophy in the late 1940s and early 1950s, worked as a manual laborer and librarian in the 1950s and became, for a short period in the late 1960s (1968–71) a researcher at the Academy of Science. He signed the Charter 77 and during the 1970s and 1980s, he became one of the most efficient organizers of the underground intellectual life. In his own philosophy – developed in a series of essays – Patočka's influence, although it is not the only one, is undeniable and is overtly acknowledged in the preface to one of his most important books.[5] The notion of negative Platonism led Hejdánek to specify the two key notions of his own philosophical project: nonobjective thought and meontology.[6] Roughly speaking, the idea of *nonobjectivity* or rather *nonobjectiveness* (partly inspired by the Patočkian interpretation of the *khorismos*[7]) led Hejdánek to criticize the stiff model of the subject–object relation, as well as the correlative notion of the subject as a non-object, and to propose a model of thought that is based on meontological (from the Greek *me ontos*) premises, according to which non-being is more originary than positivity. In this perspective, the subject is no longer considered as a stable constitutive entity but rather as an *event* whose concrete form is unforeseeable and cannot be subjected to calculable laws. It is in theology and in religious experiences that Hejdánek finds a model for such unforeseeable and nonobjectifiable events – a conclusion that seems to resonate, for example, with Jean-Luc Marion's conception of the saturated phenomenon. Even what Hejdánek calls "the loss of subject" in contemporary philosophy is interpreted in the same vein: as a crisis of the objectifying thought for which the positive delimitation of the subject is "an unthinkable and untenable concept."[8] The problems of such a philosophical perspective are obvious enough: it may present itself as an impressive philosophy of invention, unforeseeability, and event, but the fact remains that the all-embracing notion of nonobjectivity remains vague (unlike Patočka's very precise reinterpretation of Plato). Moreover, Hejdánek's essays often take the form of programmatic

---

5. See Ladislav Hejdánek, *Nepředmětnost v myšlení a ve skutečnosti* [Non-objectiveness in thought and in reality] (Prague: OIKOYMENH, 1997), 16. Even though the book in question was published in 1997, it is composed mainly of essays written in the 1980s.

6. The adjective "non-objective" is a clumsy translation of the Czech word "*nepředmětný*," which could equally be translated "insubstantial." "*Nepředmětný*" does not mean a lack of objectivity, but rather a distance taken toward the notion of object and toward the objectifying tendency of thought. Hejdánek's "self-made" and highly personal terminology makes him very often exceedingly difficult to translate.

7. In an article on Patočka's negative Platonism, Hejdánek speaks explicitly about "a problem of non-objective 'reality' that cannot be conceived of as a 'thing.'" See Hejdánek, "Nicota a odpovědnost: problém negativního platonismu v Patočkově filosofii" [Nothingness and responsibility: the problem of negative Platonism in Patočka's philosophy], *Filosofický časopis* [The philosophical review] 39(1) (1991), 37.

8. Hejdánek, *Nepředmětnost v myšlení a ve skutečnosti*, 156.

proclamations rather than of a concise and consistently developed philosophical analysis. Recently, Hejdánek has been heavily criticized for inconsistencies and his generalizing tendencies of thought, and criticisms of his very specific terminology often verge on irony.[9]

Zdeněk Neubauer (1942–) is a former biologist who turned to philosophy and tried to connect phenomenological perspectives with scientific thought in the strict sense of the word. Neubauer criticizes the traditional conception of scientific objectivity (drawing often on thinkers such as Prigogine, Kuhn, and others) and defends the essentially subjective nature of experience. The notion of the natural world (*Lebenswelt*) becomes a key feature of this critique. According to Neubauer, the task of philosophy is "to take care of the natural world, of its sense and unity."[10]

It is, nonetheless, the work of Petr Rezek and Miroslav Petříček that might be seen as the most remarkable accomplishments of Czech phenomenological philosophy in the 1980s. Rezek (1948–), an important but also a very controversial figure, has acquired the reputation of an *enfant terrible* of Czech philosophy. A psychologist by profession, he studied under Patočka's guidance in the 1970s, and his private seminar, which he led during the 1980s, was one of the most popular and productive ones. His interests range from philosophy to visual arts, music, and psychopathology. His most original contribution consists in drawing a link between phenomenology and aesthetics, which he elaborated in a series of articles, later gathered in volumes entitled *Jan Patočka a věc fenomenologie* (Jan Patočka and the problem of phenomenology; 1993), and *Tělo, věc a skutečnost v současném umění* (Body, thing and reality in contemporary art; 1983). In 1991, he published *Filosofie a politika kýče* (Philosophy and politics of Kitsch), a violent attack on several Czech philosophers (including Neubauer and Hejdánek) whom he accuses – in a very straightforward and ironic manner – of incompetence and lack of rigor.

In his interpretations of Patočka, Rezek concentrates – unlike his colleagues – on the originality of Patočka's position within the frame of phenomenology itself. By abandoning the idea of the transcendental subject as a substratum of apparition, Patočka is forced to come up with a new conception of the relation between the subject and the world. This relation, as we have already mentioned, takes form in movement; it is, therefore, no longer treated in terms of contemplation or objectifying intentionality (as in early Husserl) but rather in terms of

---

9. Lenka Karfíková, "Továrna na budoucno," *Reflexe* 32 (2007). The translation of the title is quite eloquent: "The Factory of the Future" is a hint at the title of a science fiction novel, *The Factory of the Absolute* by Karel Čapek.

10. Zdeněk Neubauer, "O povaze bytí" [On the nature of being] (1985), in *Smysl a svět* [Sense and world] (Prague: Moravia Press, 2001), 38.

the active engagement of the subject in the world.[11] Therefore, the corporeality of the subject, which acquires an "ontological status,"[12] becomes a key issue in this version of phenomenology, albeit in a different sense from, for example, Merleau-Ponty, who speaks about the intertwining of the body and the world. Where Merleau-Ponty transforms this into his famous concept of the flesh of the world, Patočka treats the relation in question on the level of the subject's corporeal capacity to move. In Rezek's view, the very notion of the world is deeply affected by this change of perspective. The world is not an intentional correlate of a transcendental consciousness, but rather a *milieu* or a system of places. With the shift from transcendental ego to movement, the subject becomes situated – placed in the world. The theory of movement "is not a theory of absolute subjectivity, but rather a *topology* of the natural world."[13] The notion of the *Lebenswelt* as topology enables Rezek to grasp the radicalism of the transformation Patočka has brought about, as well as to stress the undeniable fact that this version of phenomenology verges on a kind of cosmology because the capacity to move is not specific to the human subject. Another inevitable consequence is that the relation of the subject to his milieu is less transparent than in classical phenomenology: Patočka discovers, according to Rezek, the dark side of human existence, which can never be clarified and which finds its paroxysmal expression in the last of the *Heretical Essays*.

In his essays on aesthetics, Rezek tries to apply Patočkian phenomenology to modern visual arts. In the Czech context, it is one of the rare attempts to elaborate an interdisciplinary approach based on phenomenology. As Rezek clearly states in the introduction of *Tělo, věc a skutečnost v současném umění* (Body, thing and reality in contemporary art), phenomenology is not "a vision of the visible, but rather a search for the vision itself."[14] This basic principle is the starting-point of analyses of pop art, body art, conceptual art, or modern sculpture. Even if some of Rezek's formulations remind us of Merleau-Ponty's interpretation of Cézanne,[15] in other essays, he attempts a more original approach. Thus, modern sculpture, interpreted from the point of view of a (potential) haptic contact, is envisaged through the prism of Patočka's theory of movement

---

11. It is not by chance that Patočka was, toward the end of his life, fascinated by the work of Hannah Arendt, whose influence is obvious, especially in *Heretical Essays in the Philosophy of History*.

12. See Paul Ricoeur, "Pocta Janu Patočkovi" [Tribute to Jan Patočka], Marcela Sedláčková (trans.), *Filosofický časopis* 39(1) (1991), 7.

13. Petr Rezek, *Jan Patočka a věc fenomenologie* (Prague: OIKOYMENH, 1993), 109.

14. Petr Rezek, *Tělo, věc a skutečnost v současném umění* (Prague: Jazzová sekce, 1982), 11.

15. "The painter treats the phenomenality of phenomena in such a way as to show their corporeal manifestation in the painting" (*ibid.*, 184). [*] Merleau-Ponty's essay on Cezanne is discussed extensively in the essay by Mauro Carbone in *The History of Continental Philosophy: Volume 4*.

and the corporeal character of the subject: sculpture is an "invitation to move-ment" and "our corporeal life in the mode of an 'ability to move' finds its counter-weight in modern sculpture."[16] In some of these texts, Rezek seems to anticipate the phenomenological conception of ontological desire, proposed recently by Renaud Barbaras,[17] as well as the attempts to enrich strictly phenomenological thought (like Merleau-Ponty before him) with references to Kurt Goldstein and Gestalt psychology.

Miroslav Petříček (1951–), who studied under Patočka from 1972 to 1977, spent the 1980s working in the Czech Meteorological Institute. Equipped with an impressive knowledge of phenomenology and German idealism (he translated Schelling together with Patočka), he soon took interest in contemporary French philosophy. After 1989, while he worked as a researcher at the Czech Academy of Science and as a teacher at the Central European University in Prague, he became one of the most active promoters on the Czech intellectual scene – both as a translator and original philosopher – of French thought. In 1993, he published an excellent volume of translations of Derrida's works, including *Speech and Phenomena* and a selection of essays from *Margins of Philosophy*, *Writing and Difference*, and *Positions*, that was accompanied by a long preface in which a comprehensive introduction to Derrida's thought is combined with a very specific interpretation of the deconstruction that seems to have set the tone of Petříček's own thought in the years to come (we will deal with this text in the next section). His other translations include Deleuze's *Qu'est-ce que la philosophie?* Levinas's *Totalité et infini*, a selection of Lyotard's essays from *Des dispositifs pulsionnels*, *L'Inhumain*, and *Moralités postmodernes*, Ricoeur's *Temps et récit*, Merleau-Ponty's *Le Visible et l'invisible*, Barthes's *La Chambre claire,* and many others. In 1991, he published *Úvod do (současné) filosofie* (An intro-duction to (contemporary) philosophy), a book based on introductory lectures on twentieth-century philosophy. Dealing with authors as diverse as Bergson, Husserl, Levinas, Camus, Foucault, or Derrida, Petříček's introduction still remains one of the most popular textbooks of modern philosophy. Later, in 2000, his reflections resulted in *The Majesty of Law*, an unusual philosophical interpretation of detective stories (by Raymond Chandler in particular) based implicitly on Derrida (who is hardly mentioned but constantly present), but also Montaigne, Adorno, and others.

As far as the strictly phenomenological line of Petříček's reflection is concerned, he stresses, like Rezek, the fecund notion of movement, which "refers to human corporeality as a basis for realizing human possibilities and enables

---

16. Rezek, *Tělo, věc a skutečnost v současném umění*, 196.
17. See Renaud Barbaras, *Le Désir et la distance* (Paris: Vrin, 1998) and *Le Mouvement de l'existence* (Paris: Éditions de la transparence, 2007).

the understanding of human life as a possibility that comes into existence in the relation of man and world, of which we are both actors and witnesses."[18] On the other hand, he interprets Patočka's break with classical phenomenology as a philosophical move that brings Patočka closer to French thinkers, and to poststructuralism. This interpretation is outlined notably in an extensive essay entitled "Jan Patočka a myšlenka přirozeného světa" (Jan Patočka and the idea of the natural world), published in 1990, even though the first version of the text originates from 1987. If we understand human existence as movement, there is no longer a place for the invariant structures in the sense of Husserl's eidetics. The natural world is a world of praxis and of active participation with the things that surround us. Petříček does not stress the motif of language, which is considered in Patočka's later works, as an objectifying instrument but as an *element* that pervades perception itself. In this sense, "in the development of Patočka's formulations concerning the natural world, it is easy to find a parallel to the development of structuralism."[19] If, as Patočka's most fundamental innovations proposed, static eidetic structures are replaced by the dynamism of the natural world and the constitutive transcendental ego steps aside in order to make a place for the possibility of an asubjective phenomenology, where the *epochē* concerns not only the phenomena themselves but also the very status of the subject to whom they appear, a possibility is opened for a new dialogue between phenomenology and structuralism. This new version of phenomenology examines the process behind the structure rather than the structure itself, and the birth of subjectivity rather than the stable intentional substratum: *l'engendrement de la signification*, as Petříček puts it. Therefore, it is not illogical to find an indirect link between this dynamic phenomenology and, for example, Derrida's *différance* or Foucault's epistemic foundation of subject and knowledge. This perspective seems rather refreshing, given the fact that even in France (with a few exceptions, such as Ricoeur's attempt to reconcile structuralism and phenomenologically inspired hermeneutics or Derrida's early interpretations of Husserl), phenomenology and structuralism have developed more or less separately. Even Patočka's negative Platonism, considered as an experience of separation that is not a separation between two symmetrical domains (which might make us think of the notion of "difference," reinvented by Deleuze and other French thinkers), may be reinterpreted in the same spirit. Petříček speaks

---

18. Miroslav Petříček, "Patočkův filosofický projekt" [Patočka's philosophical project], in Jan Patočka, *Přirozený svět jako filosofický problém* [The natural world as a philosophical problem] (Prague: Československý spisovatel, 1992), 279.

19. Miroslav Petříček, "Jan Patočka a myšlenka přirozeného světa" [Jan Patočka and the idea of the natural world], *Filosofický časopis* 38(1–2) (1990), 38.

about Patočka's philosophy as "heterology" (a term taken over from Bataille), an experience of radical alterity that ties Patočka closely to Levinas or Derrida.[20]

These few names do not form an exhaustive list. Among other scholars who were involved in the interpretation of Patočka's philosophy are Pavel Kouba, working especially on Nietzsche and Arendt (his interpretation of Nietzsche will be discussed below) and Ivan Chvatík (1941–), publisher of Patočka's collected papers (twenty-seven volumes published until 1989) and founder of Patočka's Archive in Prague in 1990; Jiří Němec (1932–2001), a clinical psychologist, who was also associated with Patočka's group; Jiří Michálek (1941–), who considers himself a pupil of Patočka, and whose special interests are Heidegger and the philosophy of education; and Ivan Dubský (1926–), who works in the domain of both philosophy and literature and who wrote a book on Patočka in 1991.[21] Václav Bělohradský (1944–), a philosopher teaching in Italy since the early 1970s, transposes Patočka's reflection into the realm of political philosophy: the title of his most important book, *Přirozený svět jako politický problém* (The natural world as a political problem), is a clear allusion to Patočka's early work *Přirozený svět jako filosofický problém* (The natural world as a philosophical problem). Inspired by the Husserlian notion of the crisis of the European sciences, by Patočka's return to the natural world, and by Arendt's notion of the banality of evil (and possibly by the Heideggerian concept of *Gestell*), Bělohradský criticizes the classical Western conception of universalism as an overcoming of "the personal consciousness," as he puts it, and attempts to "look for universality in what has been up to now stigmatized as unreal and illusionary: in the natural world given in the first person and in personal consciousness."[22] This attempt permits us to grasp "the ethical aspect of phenomenology," in the sense that "phenomenology is a radical critique of European reason insofar as it refuses the legitimacy of any claim to rationality, if it is not founded … in the reflection on the contents of the personal consciousness."[23] Thus, phenomenology represents a counterpoint of an alleged impersonality of ideology and totalitarianism, because in the phenomenological view, "personal consciousness" is not considered as "merely" private, but constitutes the most essential starting-point of philosophical reflection. The natural world becomes a political problem not in the sense of a "subjectivization" of the political (a sort of political "anything goes"), but in the sense that the political subject cannot be reduced to an impersonal entity devoid of affective states and personal experiences.

---

20. See Miroslav Petříček, "Mýtus v Patočkově filosofii" [Myth in Patočka's philosophy], *Reflexe* 5–6 (1992).
21. Ivan Dubský, *Filosof Jan Patočka* [Jan Patočka, philosopher] (Prague: OIKOYMENH, 1997).
22. Václav Bělohradský, *Přirozený svět jako politický problém* [The natural world as a political problem] (Prague: Československý spisovatel, 1991), 100–101.
23. *Ibid.*, 110.

Erazim Kohák (1933–), who lived in the United States until 1990 and whose work concerns especially the philosophy of nature, translated some of Patočka's texts into English (*Heretic Essays*; *Body, Community, Language, World*; *Introduction to Husserl's Phenomenology*) and wrote an introductory book *Jan Patočka: Philosophy and Selected Writings*. After 1989, he returned to Prague and lectured especially on ethics and phenomenology.

Even nowadays, the interest in Patočka's philosophy is considerable. Thanks to the activity of the Patočka Archive and Center for Theoretical Studies, the Czech school of phenomenology has gained something of a reputation abroad. Patočka's work became known especially in France: brilliant translations of Patočka into French (by Erica Abrams) enabled the French phenomenologists (namely Renaud Barbaras, Marc Richir, and Françoise Dastur, not to mention the well-known essay on Patočka by Jacques Derrida[24]) to incorporate his theory of movement, asubjective phenomenology and natural world into their own reflection.

II. OPENING THE STRUCTURES

Apart from the Patočkian heritage, there is another important current of reflection, inaugurated by the tradition of Czech structuralism, that has been connected with the activity of the famous Prague Linguistic Circle in the 1920s and 1930s. (Roman Jakobson lived in Prague from 1920 to 1939 and had intense relations with both Czech poets and linguists.[25]) Prague structuralism found its most considerable achievement in the work of Jan Mukařovský (1891–1975). His multifaceted *oeuvre* includes erudite studies on Czech poetry (the Czech romantic poet Mácha in particular) as well as a general theory of aesthetics that is based on the notion of the aesthetic function.[26] In this line of reasoning, the aesthetic character of any part of reality (the aesthetic function is not limited to an intentionally created work of art) is the basis of the aesthetic function that any object might possibly acquire and opens a way for introducing more subtle analytical criteria than those dictated by the rigid notion of structure. Structural aesthetics is replaced by functional aesthetics within a domain where

---

24. See Jacques Derrida, *Donner la mort* (Paris: Éditions Galilée, 1999).

*25. For a discussion of Jakobson and the Prague School, see the essay by Thomas F. Broden in *The History of Continental Philosophy: Volume 5*.

26. See Jan Mukařovský, "Estetická funkce, norma a hodnota jako sociální fakty," in *Studie z estetiky* [Studies in aesthetics] (Prague: Odeon, 1966); published in English as *Aesthetic Function, Norm, and Value as Social Facts*, M. E. Suino (trans.) (Ann Arbor, MI: University of Michigan Press, 1970).

new realities may enter that have hitherto been ignored or left unexplained by classical structuralism.

It is clear that the thought inspired by structuralism constantly oscillated between literary theory and philosophy in the proper sense of the word. In this respect, we must mention at least the name of Josef Zumr (1928–), who – apart from strictly philosophical work – has always manifested a deep interest in literature, especially in the work of Bohumil Hrabal; and Ladislav Klíma (1878 –1928), a Czech philosopher and writer known for his slightly bizarre novels and short stories, as well as for his highly personal reinterpretation of Nietzsche and Schopenhauer. Květoslav Chvatík (1930–2012) has done important work introducing the Czech school of structuralism to the German-speaking world in two books: *Tschekoslowakischer Strukturalismus: Theorie und Geschichte* (Czechoslovak structuralism: Theory and history; 1981) and *Mensch und Struktur* (Man and structure; 1987). *Tschekoslowakischer Strukturalismus* deals with the history of the Czech structuralist movement and with its philosophical bases, while *Mensch und Struktur* (1987) is a collection of essays on more particular topics. Oleg Sus (1924–82) and Felix Vodička (1909–74) have added their personal insights to structuralist perspectives. Theorists such as Miroslav Červenka (1932–2005), the editor of Jakobson's selected paper and author of a monograph *Styl a význam* (Style and meaning; 1991), developed the incentives of structuralism in the field of poetics. Last, but certainly not least, is Robert Kalivoda (1923–89) who in the late 1960s had already attempted to find a bridge between Marxist dialectics and structuralism.[27]

In a series of texts inaugurated in the late 1960s, literary theorist Milan Jankovič (1929–) has elaborated his own version of structuralism that often incorporates philosophical elements. His most important text, "Dílo jako dění smyslu" (The work as a process of meaning), takes off from Mukařovský's concept of "semantic gesture." Semantic gesture is:

> an organizing principle of the semantic construction of the work, which nevertheless cannot be identified with a noetic relation that the author entertains with reality and which appears, in an analysis of the work, rather as a principle of its formal construction, as an author's particular technique.[28]

---

27. See Jan Kalivoda, "Dialektika strukturalismu a dialektika estetiky" [The dialectic of structuralism and the dialectics of aesthetics], in *Moderní duchovní skutečnost a marxismus* [Modern spiritual reality and Marxism] (Prague: Československý spisovatel, 1968).

28. Milan Jankovič, "Dílo jako dění smyslu" [The work as a process of meaning], in *Cesty za smyslem literárního díla* [Pathways toward the meaning of literary work] (Prague: Karolinum, 2005), 59.

The construction of a literary work, for Jankovič, has an essentially dynamic character: speaking about literary meaning in terms of process means, of course, getting away from classical, static structuralism. Mukařovský's conception of the aesthetic function enables Jankovič to abandon the static structuralist frame and to conceive the literary work as a movement rather than a fixed state. The very notion of semantic *gesture* suggests the idea of dynamism rather than that of stable structural relations. It is therefore not surprising that Jankovič studies the literary work from the point of view of its "corporeal energy,"[29] rather than that of authorial intention or ideality.

Despite these innovations, Jankovič is a devoted follower of Mukařovský and remains more or less resistant to French poststructuralism and deconstruction. In his work, Roland Barthes's semiology is mentioned with sympathy: the vision of literary work as an active interplay of signifiers may get very close to the dynamism of semantic gesture. On the other hand, Jankovič believes that Barthes's weakness is due to his refusal to study this play of signifiers on the level of particular texts, to pass from *langue* to *parole*, as he himself puts it, to move "from the linguistic conception of the system of *literature* to the aesthetic theory of the *work*."[30] Even though one might object that in *S/Z* or *Sade, Fourier, Loyola*, Barthes does precisely what Jankovič misses in him, that is, he passes from the *langue* of literature to the *parole* of individual writers, the fact remains that Jankovič's book is one of the texts that prepares the way for the reception of poststructuralist thinkers in the Czech Republic.

In 1991, Petříček published an article on "Mukařovský and Deconstruction," in which the potentialities of the passage from the closed to the open structures are outlined in a very clear manner. This perspective is brought to more radical conclusions in Petříček's long preface to his translation of Derrida in 1993. Petříček speaks about an "elementary phenomenology of border, limit, and dividing line."[31] This project puts forward the question of limit not as an outer limitation, but as an internal element and foundation of any structure or system. The limit thus conceived does not divide the inside from the outside, but becomes an internal and constitutive element of any structure – because the structure is founded by its own limit. The Derridian inspiration of such a view is obvious. It needs to be added that in Petříček's view, the key issue in deconstructive thought is not transcendence but transgression. Once we adopt the deconstructive approach, the problem is "not a transcendental interrogation, but the

---

29. *Ibid.*, 88.
30. *Ibid.*, 91.
31. Miroslav Petříček, "Předmluva, která nechce být návodem ke čtení" [A preface that is not supposed to be a reader's guide], in Jacques Derrida, *Texty k dekonstrukci* [On deconstruction], Miroslav Petříček (trans.) (Bratislava: Archa, 1993), 21.

transgression of limits."[32] This leads Petříček to meditate on the concept of pure difference, which he develops not only in the preface we are dealing with here, but also in many texts on thinkers as different as Barthes, Levinas, or Foucault. If the object of deconstructive transgression is the difference between the inside and the outside itself, any structure becomes essentially open and infinite. It might seem that such a view leads to an exclusion of otherness: if the structure is infinite, no "outside" is possible and the famous Derridian adage according to which "There is nothing outside the text" takes slightly negative connotations, as it may be understood as a neutralization of alterity, event, or encounter. Petříček, however, does not share this interpretative approach and tries to coin a concept of alterity that would not fall under the simple dichotomy inside/outside. Deconstruction and the concept of pure difference, according to him, offer a certain possibility to think of an "otherness different from metaphysical alterity."[33] It is not surprising that Levinas becomes a key reference in this effort, regardless of the criticism Derrida addressed to him.[34]

In a monograph *Nietzsche: Filosofická interpretace* (Nietzsche: A philosophical interpretation), published in 1995, Kouba (1953–), a specialist on hermeneutics, Patočka, and Arendt, takes a different view of deconstructive philosophy. His *Nietzsche* is the fruit of many years of research and it still remains one of the most interesting books that appeared after 1989. French Nietzscheanism[35] is not dealt with directly – Deleuze is mentioned only once and Klossowski not at all – but one chapter is devoted to the central motif that French continental philosophy has undoubtedly inherited from Nietzsche, namely what Kouba calls "perspectivism." By perspectivism, which is considered to be an emblematic character of contemporary (French) thought, Kouba understands the stress put on "the rhetorical and narrative nature of knowledge and on the literary character of philosophy itself."[36] The conditioned character of knowledge, which can no longer be based on the classical model of *theoria*, does not lead to nihilism and this version of perspectivism abandons precisely the notion of perspective as a *mere* perspective. If contemporary French thought – and deconstruction in particular – adopts this idea of an impossibility of

---

32. *Ibid.*, 23.
33. *Ibid.*, 25.
34. See Miroslav Petříček, "Derrida a Lévinas" [Derrida and Levinas], *Česká mysl* [Czech mind] 1–2 (1992), where Petříček stresses the "out-of-joint" nature of philosophical concepts that both Derrida and Levinas bring to philosophy.
*35. For a discussion of French Nietzscheanism, see the essay by Alan D. Schrift in *The History of Continental Philosophy: Volume 5*. Nietzsche is the focus of an essay by Daniel Conway in *The History of Continental Philosophy: Volume 2*.
36. Pavel Kouba, *Nietzsche: Filosofická interpretace* (Prague: OIKOYMENH, 2006), 203.

"any recourse to pre-linguistic evidence,"[37] the problem remains – at least for Kouba – that the Derridian reformulation of Nietzsche's starting-point implies a misunderstanding, as far as the original Nietzschean view itself is concerned: imposing "the autonomy of the signifier" leads to a situation in which "we are left among the perspectives that – given the absence of a regulative idea and the ever escaping character of *différance* – always remain, in a sense, the same."[38] The question Kouba asks is the following: how does a clash – or at least a dialogue – among those perspectives, none of which aspires to be a true one, become possible? What is abandoned is not a philosophical (or metaphysical) naivety that counts on the existence of objective fact, but the very difference between truth and untruth that Nietzsche himself has never given up. The Nietzschean innovation consists in dynamizing the truth–untruth distinction, not in abandoning it altogether: "Nietzsche destroys the metaphysical foundation of the truth/untruth dichotomy, but insists on a *situated* persistence of this distinction in a dynamized form," as well as on our capacity of distinguishing the truth and untruth *from our perspective*.[39] For Kouba, deconstruction is, in fact, a neutralization of alterity rather than its affirmation in a nonmetaphysical form: a uniform slippage of the signifiers (or perspectives) always oscillating between presence and nonpresence and characterized by the *sameness* of this oscillation. Here, the elusive and omnipresent specter of the *différance* itself is what precisely excludes alterity from this movement.

Apart from these very different interpretations of deconstruction, the question of alterity or "becoming other," to be more precise, is a central problem in the first monograph on Foucault written by a Slovak philosopher: Miroslav Marcelli (1947–).[40] The title of the book itself is quite eloquent: *Michal Foucault alebo stať sa iným* (Michel Foucault or how to become other). The question of otherness is treated on two different levels: first, as a fantasy of Foucault himself, leading him to change constantly his theoretical positions and to undermine any stable identity he might have acquired. This does not mean that the book in question would make any attempt to "psychoanalyze" Foucault. Rather, the idea of becoming other is understood as an impetus inherent to the movement of Foucault's work itself. In Marcelli's own words: "I attempt to determine the starting points that did not allow Foucault to remain attached to the positions he has elaborated and led him to constantly change. I am convinced that such an impetus of his theoretical and practical activity was an effort to become other."[41]

---

37. *Ibid.*, 211.
38. *Ibid.*, 220.
39. *Ibid.*, 222.
40. Marcelli is well known for his fine translation of *The Order of Things*, one of the rare translations from modern French philosophy published officially before 1989.
41. Miroslav Marcelli, *Michal Foucault alebo stať sa iným* (Bratislava: Archa, 1995), 19.

Becoming other thus develops into a concept enabling Marcelli to envisage Foucault's work as a "syntax of space," which he systematically explores. The second level on which the otherness is analyzed is more concrete: the experience of otherness is very often an explicit subject of Foucault's analyses, be it the otherness of madness in *Madness and Civilization* (the debate between Foucault and Derrida concerning Descartes is interpreted in this manner: what is at stake here is the question whether the otherness is or is not internal to *cogito*), the "death of the author," or even the late Foucault whose work on Greek and Roman thought "opens a perspective of individual existence: there is the possibility of becoming other and making of one's life a work of art."[42]

Marcelli's book, despite its relative shortness, is a remarkable achievement insofar as it – together with Petříček's translations and writings – inaugurated an interest in French thought at a time when Czech continental philosophy was still dominated (almost exclusively) by phenomenology and hermeneutics. Since then, an impressive number of translations of Foucault, Derrida, Barthes, and Lyotard appeared, making their philosophy accessible to a larger audience. A very unusual and amusing example of this interest is a book by Ladislav Šerý (1958–), himself a translator of Bataille, Artaud, Jean Genet, and others, entitled *První knížka o tom, že řád je chaos* (The first book on the fact that order is actually chaos; 1997) and written provocatively in nonacademic, colloquial Czech. Drawing on Bataille, Foucault, Pierre Clastres, but also the early Rousseau, the author develops a concept of subversion that echoes Bataille's transgression, and attacks Patočka's authority by mocking his "monumental" conception of European history.

The same interest shows in numerous books by Jiří Pechar (1929–), a well-known translator who first translated literature (including Proust's *Remembrance of Things Past* or Huysmans's *Against the Grain*), but later turned to philosophy, with translations of Wittgenstein's *Philosophical Investigations*, Lyotard's *Postmodern Condition*, and other works. His studies provide good and concise information on the topics he chooses, although they rarely go beyond mere summary. However, it needs to be mentioned that Pechar has filled a considerable gap by writing a book on psychoanalysis, overcoming at least partly the absence of interest in this domain that Czech philosophers have generally manifested.[43]

---

42. *Ibid.*, 133.

43. Jiří Pechar, *Prostor imaginace* [The space of imagination] (Prague: Psychoanalytické nakladatelství, 1992).

III. AFTER 1989

Even with nearly twenty years of hindsight, it is not easy to sum up the development that Czech philosophy has undergone after the major political change in 1989. It would be, of course, naive to believe that everything changed all at once and that a fully developed philosophical culture has emerged out of nowhere. A long and often painful reorganization of philosophy departments was needed, which lasted for many years and was not often devoid of personal conflicts. People like Sobotka or Pešek became highly respected experts on German idealism (Pešek died in 2003 and Sobotka still teaches at Charles University in Prague). Rezek started to teach at the philosophy department at the Faculty of Arts in Prague, but not content with the level on which philosophy was taught, he left in the mid-1990s and founded his own publishing house, which specializes in ancient philosophy (Plotinus, Aristotle, and others). Petříček and Kouba have worked in the same department and at the Center for Phenomenological Research in Prague since the early 1990s and are still its most active members. Zdeněk Pinc (1945–), a former student of Patočka, and Jan Sokol (1936–), Patočka's son-in-law, a former minister of education and the presidential candidate of the Social Democratic party in 2003, founded the Faculty of Humanities at Charles University, conceived as a more liberal counterpoint of the Faculty of Humanities. Philosophy was an integral part of the curriculum and, as time progressed, a specific group of philosophers emerged at the Faculty of Arts, constituting a philosophical school oriented mainly toward Hegel and Heidegger.

It is obvious that a domain in which Czech philosophy was lacking was translation. Officially published translations from modern continental philosophy were extremely rare before 1989. There were only three books by Husserl (*Cartesian Meditations, The Crisis* and *The Lectures on Internal Time Consciousness*, all published in a relatively liberal period in the late 1960s), a rather poor translation of a selection of essays by Merleau-Ponty (*Eye and Mind and Other Essays*), some works by Sartre, Max Scheler, Walter Benjamin, Claude Lévi-Strauss and a few others (*The Second Sex* by Simone de Beauvoir, for example). Even though the efforts to translate contemporary philosophy have been considerable since the beginning of the 1990s (we have already mentioned Petříček's translation of Derrida and others, and Pechar's translation of Lyotard and Wittgenstein), it was not until the second half of the decade that twentieth-century philosophy was systematically introduced. Even today, the state of things is far from satisfactory, given the limited number of translators capable of translating difficult philosophical texts. Nonetheless, very few important modern European thinkers remain who have not been translated at all into Czech. OIKOYMENH, the publishing house mentioned in the introduction, became an official enterprise and has played a considerable role in this respect, as well as *Filosofický časopis* (The philosophical review), which abandoned its former Marxist orientation and became the most important review publishing both translations and original contributions. Among other publishers, there was a publishing house – Herrmann a synové – oriented especially toward French thought (Foucault, Deleuze, Bataille, Blanchot, and others), and FILOSOFIA, publishing both phenomenology and analytic philosophy.

The time period between 1989 and 1995 may be considered a transitory one, dominated by a general feeling that there is much to be done and by intense, although sometimes a little chaotic, efforts to catch up on what had been missed during the communist era. The early 1990s also marks the advent of a new generation of younger philosophers, often trained abroad and equipped with a remarkable technical knowledge of the history of philosophy. Filip Karfík (1963–), a former classical philologist, works on both Patočka and ancient philosophy. Lenka Karfíková (1963–) became a professor of theology and is an expert on medieval thought. Karel Thein (1961–) studied in Paris under Derrida in the early 1990s and wrote his thesis on Plato in French. His interests range from Plato and the Stoics to Foucault and Benjamin, literature, and film studies. Karel Novotný (1964–) started working on Kant and Fichte, but later turned to Patočka and French phenomenology (Merleau-Ponty, Levinas, and Marion). Jindřich Karásek (1963–) is an accomplished Kant expert. Sobotka's student Milan Znoj (1952–) became an authority in the field of political philosophy, and Ladislav Benyovszky (1958–), who studied under Pešek, continues his work on Heidegger and German idealism. It is also thanks to them – and many others – that Czech philosophy has overcome its fragmentary and dispersed character and become a disciplined area of research in the realms of both the history of philosophy and systematic philosophy.

6

THIRD GENERATION CRITICAL THEORY:
BENHABIB, FRASER, AND HONNETH

Amy Allen

The second generation of Frankfurt School critical theory was largely defined by one towering figure – Jürgen Habermas – and his reorientation of critical theory around issues of normative justification, the pragmatics of language use, and, more recently, the discourse theory of morality, law, and politics.[1] It is perhaps no surprise, then, that members of the third generation of critical theory have devoted a good deal of time and attention to developing criticisms of Habermas's work. As valuable and important as such critical perspectives are, the third generation has not rested content with this project. Rather, they have used these critiques as a springboard for the development of their own, original work in critical theory. This essay offers an overview of the main themes of three major third generation critical theorists – Seyla Benhabib, Nancy Fraser, and Axel Honneth[2] – in each case, situating their work *vis-à-vis* their critical engagements with Habermas and with each other.

---

*1. For a discussion of Habermas and other members of the second generation of Frankfurt School critical theorists, see the essays by Christopher F. Zurn and James Swindal in *The History of Continental Philosophy: Volume 6*.

2. Seyla Benhabib (September 9, 1950– ; born in Istanbul, Turkey) received a BA from the American College for Girls, Istanbul (1970), a BA in philosophy from Brandeis University (1972), and a PhD in philosophy from Yale University (1977). Her influences include Arendt, Habermas, Hegel, and Horkheimer, and she has held appointments in philosophy at Boston University (1981–85), in government at Harvard University (1987–89, 1993–2001), in philosophy and women's studies at SUNY Stony Brook (1989–91), in political science and philosophy at the New School (1991–93), and in political science and philosophy at Yale (2001–).

  Nancy Fraser (May 20, 1947– ; born in Baltimore, Maryland) received a BA in philosophy from Bryn Mawr College (1969) and a PhD in philosophy from the City University in New York (1980). Her influences include Arendt, Foucault, Habermas, and Marx, and she has held

A distinctive feature of the critical theory tradition is its dual emphasis on the project of critiquing actually existing societies (in contrast to analytic political philosophy, which concentrates on the project of ideal theory) and on the location of progressive, context-transcending potentials for change within the existing societies it aims to critique (a point that is often thought to set it at odds with the major figures of poststructuralism, although this point is debatable). In light of this dual emphasis, it is especially important to understand the project of third generation critical theory in terms of how it is shaped by and responds to its social, political, cultural, and historical context. The figures under consideration here were born in the middle of the twentieth century, which means that they came of age as intellectuals against the backdrop of the massive social and cultural upheaval that began in May 1968. As a result, their work has been profoundly shaped by the so-called new social movements of the 1970s.[3] More recently, they have faced the fall of soviet communism and the resulting exhaustion of left-wing utopian energies, the accelerating pace of globalization, and the continual damage wrought by capitalism in its contemporary, neoliberal, globalized form. True to the critical theory tradition, these thinkers are not only shaped by these historical developments, but they continually reflect explicitly on such developments, and strive to develop critical-theoretical tools that can illuminate both the chief dangers of the present moment and the immanent potentials for progressive transformation of it.

There is an inherent difficulty in any attempt to identify a "generation" of thinkers.[4] Moreover, it may be surprising to some readers that two of the three figures identified here as representative of the third generation are not German

---

appointments at the University of Georgia (1980–82), Northwestern University (1982–95), and the New School (1995–).

Axel Honneth (July 18, 1949– ; born in Essen, Federal Republic of Germany) studied philosophy, sociology, and German literature at the Universities of Bonn and Bochum (1969–74), Promotion (~PhD) from the Free University Berlin (1982); and habilitation from the JW Goethe University, Frankfurt (1990). His influences include Adorno, Foucault, Habermas, Hegel, Horkheimer, and George Herbert Mead, and he has held appointments at the Free University of Berlin (1992–96), JW Goethe University, Frankfurt (1996–), and as Director at the University of Frankfurt Institute for Social Research (2001–).

3. For Fraser's comments on the relationship between her activism and her philosophical work, see her *Unruly Practices: Power, Discourse, and Gender in Contemporary Social Theory* (Minneapolis, MN: University of Minnesota Press, 1989), 1–13. For Benhabib's views on her work in relation to the new social movements, see the interview with her at: http://globetrotter.berkeley.edu/people4/Benhabib/benhabib-con0.html (accessed May 2010).

4. On this point, see Joel Anderson's fine essay "The 'Third Generation' of the Frankfurt School," *Intellectual History Newsletter* 22 (2000); online at www.phil.uu.nl/~joel/research/publications/3rdGeneration.htm (accessed May 2010). Anderson confines the bulk of his discussion to Honneth, whose work he rightly takes to be representative of the third generation in Germany.

(although both Benhabib and Fraser certainly do situate their work with respect to the German critical theory tradition). To be sure, there are many important third generation critical theorists from both sides of the Atlantic whose work could arguably also be included here.[5] Nevertheless, one could, I think, make a strong case that the work of Benhabib, Fraser, and Honneth is both more original and systematic than that of many of their contemporaries and also is the most familiar to the English-speaking philosophical audience for a volume such as this one. This, in turn, would allow one to make the observation that with the rise of the third generation the center of gravity of critical theory is no longer exclusively in Frankfurt. Critical theory is now thriving at least as much outside Germany as within it.

Because these theorists have developed their ideas largely in and through conversation with one another, I have chosen to organize this discussion thematically, rather than by individual thinker. I begin in the first two sections by discussing two strands of the third generation's critique of Habermas and the ways in which these criticisms have served as the basis for the development of the third generation's own distinctive version of critical theory. The first section focuses on Hegelian themes, in particular on Benhabib's and Honneth's efforts to contextualize and historicize the insights of Habermas's communicative action paradigm. The second section focuses on the Foucaultian theme of the role of power in the lifeworld, articulated primarily by Honneth but also by Fraser, and also considers the third generation's encounter with Foucaultian poststructuralism more broadly. Subsequent sections take up the third generation's conceptualizations of subjectivity and selfhood and their attempts to rethink the postsocialist condition around the notions of recognition and redistribution. By way of a conclusion, in the final section I consider an emerging trend in third generation critical theory by briefly discussing Benhabib and Fraser's recent work on cosmopolitanism and global justice.

I. CRITICAL ENGAGEMENTS WITH HABERMAS: HEGELIAN THEMES

Although each of the thinkers considered here has his or her own specific and detailed critique of Habermas, at least two common themes emerge from these critical engagements. The first set of criticisms, which I discuss in this section, concerns the overly rational, procedural, and formal character of his understanding of ethics and morality. The second set, which I turn to in the next section, concerns his inadequate conceptualization of power, particularly as it

---

5. For a comprehensive list of both German and American third generation critical theorists, see Anderson, "The 'Third Generation' of the Frankfurt School."

functions in the lifeworld. In articulating these criticisms, the third generation relies on certain Hegelian and Foucaultian themes that Habermas's work arguably represses.

Benhabib's critical appropriation of Habermas, for instance, is explicitly grounded in a resuscitation of Hegel's critique of Kant's ethics.[6] Although Benhabib does not go so far as to argue for a Hegelian or Aristotelian alternative to discourse ethics, she does advance a more Hegelian version of discourse ethics, one that stresses the contextual, the ethical, the particular, and the concrete as crucial aspects of moral-political deliberation. In so doing, Benhabib develops an interactive version of universalism that is more attentive than is Habermas to the ineliminable role of particularity in our ethical and political lives.

Benhabib's central criticism of Habermas, articulated in her first book, *Critique, Norm, and Utopia*, is that, notwithstanding Habermas's attempts to avoid the empty formalism of Kant's moral theory, his theory of communicative action and his communicative ethics remain excessively and problematically rationalist. The general thrust of Benhabib's critical engagement with Habermas and of her own critical theory is the development of a more contextualized and concretized version of critical theory.[7] More specifically, Benhabib criticizes the status of the idealizations that form the normative core of Habermas's moral-political universalism. Indeed, Benhabib maintains that Habermas's "program of a strong justification of communicative ethics cannot succeed" (CNU 263). As she puts it:

> the constituents of communicative rationality like decentration, reflexivity, and the differentiation of value spheres can be said to have "universal significance and validity" only in a weak sense. One cannot claim that they are "quasi-transcendental," only that they are the outcome of contingent learning processes whose internal evolution we can cogently reconstruct: what was once learned for good reasons, cannot be unlearned at will. Furthermore, the "epistemological reflexivity" of modern belief systems gives rise to a hermeneutical circle which we cannot overcome or escape. Finally, these structures

---

6. See Seyla Benhabib, *Critique, Norm, and Utopia: A Study of the Foundations of Critical Theory* (New York: Columbia University Press, 1986), ix–xi. Hereafter cited as CNU followed by the page number.

7. In this respect, her project is similar to that of Thomas McCarthy, who has also developed a more contextualized and pragmatic version of Habermasian critical theory in works such as *Ideals and Illusions: On Deconstruction and Reconstruction in Contemporary Critical Theory*; and (with David Hoy) *Critical Theory*. I discuss McCarthy's work in more detail in my *The Politics of Our Selves: Power, Autonomy, and Gender in Contemporary Critical Theory* (New York: Columbia University Press, 2008), ch. 6.

are "irreversible" in that the future we would like to see can only be realized by fulfilling their still unexhausted potential.   (CNU 279)

In addition to this critique of the status of Habermas's normative idealizations, Benhabib is also critical of his notion of autonomy. Here, once again, the central point is that Habermas falls into "a certain rationalistic fallacy of the Kantian sort, in that it ignores the contingent, historical, and affective circumstances which made individuals adopt a universalist-ethical standpoint in the first place" (CNU 298). In other words, Habermas's allegedly purely formal accounts of universal pragmatics and of the postconventional self necessarily have "a cultural-historical content built into them" (CNU 306). This does not mean that Benhabib thinks we should give them up. On the contrary, Benhabib is quite clear that she shares the normative presuppositions of universal respect and egalitarian reciprocity that she claims are implicit in Habermas's idealizations.[8] But she does think we should advance more modest claims about their status than does Habermas. As Benhabib puts it, our commitment to such norms "is not a consequence of conceptual analysis alone; rather, it reflects the commitments of a moral philosophy as practiced by individuals who are themselves members of a culture that cherishes universalism" (CNU 306).

This critique of Habermas leads Benhabib, in *Situating the Self* (1992), to attempt to develop a "post-Enlightenment defense of universalism," one that is "interactive not legislative, cognizant of gender difference not gender blind, contextually sensitive and not situation indifferent" (STS 3). Benhabib delineates three steps that are involved in developing such an interactive universalism. First, following Habermas and Karl-Otto Apel, Benhabib offers a discursive and communicative, rather than substantive, conception of rationality. Second, she understands subjects of reason as "finite, embodied and fragile creatures, and not disembodied cogitos or abstract unities of transcendental apperception to which may belong one or more bodies" (STS 5). Third, because she regards reason itself as "the contingent achievement of linguistically socialized, finite and embodied creatures," Benhabib reformulates the moral point of view as "the contingent achievement of an interactive form of rationality rather than as the timeless standpoint of a legislative reason" (STS 6). Even as the first aspect of Benhabib's post-Enlightenment defense of universalism draws on Habermas for inspiration, her second and third points push beyond his discourse-ethical framework. Indeed, Benhabib claims that her aim is "to save discourse ethics from the excesses of its own rationalistic Enlightenment legacy" (STS 8). This

---

8. See Seyla Benhabib, *Situating the Self: Gender, Community and Postmodernism in Contemporary Ethics* (New York: Routledge, 1992), 29–33. Hereafter cited as STS followed by the page number.

involves developing the insights of communicative ethics in a more historically self-conscious way. Thus, for instance, Benhabib emphasizes that the normative principles of universal respect and egalitarian reciprocity:

> are our philosophical clarification of the constituents of the moral point of view from *within* the normative hermeneutic horizon of modernity. These principles are neither the *only allowable* interpretation of the formal constituents of the competency of postconventional moral actors nor are they unequivocal transcendental presuppositions which every rational agent, upon deep reflection, must concede to.   (STS 30)

Benhabib's universalism is not only historically self-conscious but also interactive, in that the goal of her communicative ethics is not consensus (even as a counterfactual ideal) but instead "the idea of an ongoing moral conversation" (STS 38). Thus, in her version of communicative ethics, "the emphasis now is less on *rational agreement*, but more on sustaining those normative practices and moral relationships within which reasoned agreement *as a way of life* can flourish and continue" (STS 38). Benhabib's interactive universalism presupposes a completely open-ended model of discourse, one in which "even the presuppositions of discourse can themselves be challenged, called into question and debated" (STS 74).

In addition to offering a more historically self-conscious, interactive, and open-ended version of communicative ethics, Benhabib also aims to articulate a specifically feminist version of Habermasian critical theory. This aim is already evident in *Critique, Norm, and Utopia*, when she asks: "can the theory of communicative action really explain the emergence of one of the most significant social movements of our times, namely, the women's movement?" (CNU 252). In *Situating the Self*, Benhabib further clarifies her feminist engagement with Habermas, arguing that one of her aims is to "'engender' the subject of moral reasoning, not in order to relativize moral claims to fit gender differences but to make them gender sensitive and cognizant of gender difference" (STS 8). This is part and parcel of her broader goal, which is "to situate reason and the moral self more decisively in contexts of gender and community, while insisting upon the discursive power of individuals to challenge such situatedness in the name of universalistic principles, future identities and as yet undiscovered communities" (STS 8).

A related criticism of Habermas's excessive formal and concomitant contextualizing impulse can be found in Honneth's work on recognition. As Honneth argues in his 1993 inaugural lecture at the Free University of Berlin, the central problematic of critical theory and what makes it distinctive as a mode of social critique is "its attempt (which still has not been abandoned) to give the standards of critique an objective foothold in pre-theoretical praxis."[9] Whereas first-generation theorists[10] located this foothold in the point of view of the proletariat, subsequent critiques of the notion of a working-class subject have rendered this strategy unworkable. As Honneth sees it, however, Habermas completely sidesteps this issue when he attempts to ground the normative demands of critical theory in a pragmatic account of language use. As Honneth puts it,

> the emancipatory process in which Habermas socially anchors the normative perspective of his Critical Theory in no way appears as an emancipatory process in the moral experiences of the subjects involved. They experience an impairment of what we can call their moral experiences, i.e., their "moral point of view," not as a restriction of intuitively mastered rules of language, but as a violation of identity claims acquired in socialization.[11]

Honneth's way out of this problem is to "follow Habermas's communication paradigm more in the direction of its intersubjective, indeed sociological, presuppositions."[12] The central intersubjective presupposition of the communication paradigm is, according to Honneth, the acquisition of social recognition, which "constitutes the normative expectations connected with our entering into communicative relationships."[13]

In his 1992 *Habilitationsschrift*, *Kampf um Anerkennung*, published in English as *The Struggle for Recognition*, Honneth locates the foothold for critique within the subjective experience of injustice that arises when one's legitimate expectations for recognition are violated. Drawing on the writings of Hegel's Jena period and on George Herbert Mead's social psychology, Honneth develops a tripartite conception of social recognition. Following Hegel, Honneth delineates three primary forms of mutual recognition: love in primary (particularly familial) relationships, legal rights, and communal solidarity. Following Mead, Honneth connects these forms of mutual recognition to a social psychological account of the intersubjective development of three primary forms of

---

9. Axel Honneth, "The Social Dynamics of Disrespect: On the Legacy of Critical Theory Today," in *Disrespect: The Normative Foundations of Critical Theory*, Joseph Ganahl (trans.) (Cambridge: Polity, 2007), 66.

*10. The first generation of Frankfurt School theorists are discussed in several essays in *The History of Continental Philosophy: Volume 5*.

11. Honneth, "The Social Dynamics of Disrespect," 70.

12. *Ibid.*

13. *Ibid.*, 71.

practical self-relation: basic self-confidence, self-respect, and self-esteem.[14] As Joel Anderson points out, "these three modes of relating practically to oneself can be acquired and maintained only intersubjectively, through relationships of mutual recognition."[15] Basic self-confidence is dependent on intact mutual recognition in loving, familial relations; self-respect is rooted in legal recognition; and self-esteem is grounded in the mutual recognition afforded by membership in a community of value. Together, these three forms of practical self-relation are constitutive of the possibility of individual autonomy. Honneth also connects these three forms of recognition and of practical self-relation to forms of disrespect: abuse and rape, which undermine basic self-confidence; denial of rights or legal exclusion, which undermine self-respect; and the denigration of culturally specific ways of life, which undermines self-esteem.[16] These forms of disrespect generate subjective feelings of humiliation and injustice that can, under the right sorts of social conditions, generate social struggles for the expansion of recognition and that serve, in Honneth's theory, as the pretheoretical foothold for critical theory in social praxis.

In the final chapter of *The Struggle for Recognition*, Honneth develops these insights in the direction of a formal conception of the good life that further signals his departure from Habermasian proceduralism.[17] Unlike Habermas, who attempts to develop his normative perspective independently of an ethical-existential conception of the good life, Honneth maintains that a normatively oriented critical theory must appeal at least hypothetically to a provisional conception of the good life. Indeed, Honneth's teleological account of the progressive expansion of the three forms of recognition through the vehicle of social struggle necessitates such a move. Unlike communitarians, such as Charles Taylor, however, Honneth does not conceive of the good life "as the expression of substantive values that constitute the *ethos* of a concrete tradition-based community."[18] Rather, in an attempt to split the difference between proceduralism and communitarianism, Honneth conceives of the good life formally, in terms of "structural elements of ethical life" or "necessary conditions for individual self-realization."[19] These necessary conditions are the three forms of practical relation to self – self-confidence, self-respect and self-esteem – that emerge

---

14. See Axel Honneth, *The Struggle for Recognition: The Moral Grammar of Social Conflicts*, Joel Anderson (trans.) (Cambridge, MA: MIT Press, 1995), ch. 5.

15. Anderson, "The 'Third Generation' of the Frankfurt School," 8.

16. See Honneth, *The Struggle for Recognition*, ch. 6.

17. For critical discussion of this aspect of Honneth's work, see Christopher Zurn, "Anthropology and Normativity: A Critique of Axel Honneth's 'Formal Conception of Ethical Life,'" *Philosophy and Social Criticism* 26(1) (2000).

18. Honneth, *The Struggle for Recognition*, 172.

19. *Ibid.*, 172, 173–4.

only as a result of intact mutual recognition in the forms of love, rights, and solidarity. By rooting his normative perspective in a theory of the good life, albeit a formal one, Honneth has placed much greater emphasis on the ethical notion of self-realization than does Habermas, whose Kantianism has compelled him to endorse a razor-sharp distinction between the right and the good.[20]

II. CRITICAL ENGAGEMENTS WITH HABERMAS:
FOUCAULTIAN THEMES

The relationship between third generation critical theory and Foucaultian poststructuralism is complex and multifaceted.[21] All three of the thinkers considered here have offered trenchant – although not always fully convincing – critiques of poststructuralism. Nevertheless, Honneth and Fraser have also drawn productively – although sometimes only implicitly – on Foucaultian themes both in their critical engagements with Habermas and in the articulation of their own critical theories. Indeed, in general, the third generation distinguishes itself from Habermas by its degree of openness to the insights generated by Foucaultian poststructuralism, particularly when it comes to his analysis of power. In this section, I will start by briefly laying out the criticisms of Foucault (and the related critique of Judith Butler's early feminist-Foucaultian work) offered by the third generation. I will then go on to consider how Honneth in particular mobilizes Foucaultian themes in his critical engagements with Habermas and in the articulation of his own critical theory.

In a series of essays originally published in the early 1980s and subsequently reprinted as the first three chapters of her first book, *Unruly Practices*, Nancy Fraser initiated the third generation's critical encounter with Foucault.[22] Fraser presents two main criticisms of Foucault, the first focusing on his conception of power, the second, on his critique of humanism. First, in her extremely influential essay "Foucault on Modern Power: Empirical Insights and Normative Confusions," Fraser argues that Foucault offers a rich and useful empirical

---

20. On this point, see Jürgen Habermas, *Moral Consciousness and Communicative Action*, Christian Lenhardt and Shierry Weber Nicholsen (trans.) (Cambridge, MA: MIT Press, 1990), and *Justification and Application: Remarks on Discourse Ethics*, Ciaran Cronin (trans.) (Cambridge, MA: MIT Press, 1993).

*21. For a discussion of Foucault, see the essay by Timothy O'Leary in *The History of Continental Philosophy: Volume 6*. Foucault's Nietzscheanism is also discussed by Alan D. Schrift in *Volume 6*.

22. Indeed, in something of a generational inversion, Fraser's critique of Foucault was also highly influential for Habermas's critical engagement with Foucault in *The Philosophical Discourse of Modernity*. Thus, Fraser's work shaped both the third and second generation's encounters with Foucault.

account of micropractices of power but remains "normatively confused" inasmuch as his work lacks "normative criteria for distinguishing acceptable from unacceptable forms of power."[23] Second, in her essays "Michel Foucault: A Young Conservative?" and "Foucault's Body Language: A Posthumanist Political Rhetoric?," Fraser argues that Foucault's critique of humanism is unviable both because it commits the genetic fallacy and because Foucault fails to articulate a plausible alternative conception of human freedom.[24]

In her well-known debate with Butler,[25] Benhabib echoes some similar themes, while also bringing a new issue into focus: the problem of the subject. Although Benhabib's initial critique of what she calls "postmodernism" ranges over a number of issues, including the postmodern critique of grand metanarratives of historical progress and Enlightenment notions of transcendent reason,[26] it is the issue of the so-called "death of man" that takes center stage in the debate. Although Benhabib sees no problem with a weak version of the "death of man" thesis, according to which the subject is always situated in various social and linguistic practices, she rejects the strong version, which dissolves the subject into just another position in language/discourse, on the grounds that this thesis is "not compatible with the goals of feminism."[27] Speaking of Butler's Nietzschean and Foucaultian inspired notion of the gendered self, Benhabib asks:

> If we are no more than the sum total of the gendered expressions we perform, is there ever any chance to stop the performance for a while, to pull the curtain down, and let it rise only if one can have a say in the production of the play itself? Isn't this what the struggle over gender is all about?[28]

In general, Benhabib diagnoses the feminist alliance with postmodernism as symptomatic of a broader "retreat from utopia" in feminist thinking.[29]

---

23. Fraser, *Unruly Practices*, 31, 33. In a more recent essay, Fraser has substantially weakened the empirical insightfulness claim, arguing that Foucault's account of power is more suited for the Fordist world of the 1970s than it is for the post-Fordist, globalized, flexibilized world of the early twenty-first century. See Nancy Fraser, "From Discipline to Flexibilization: Rereading Foucault in the Shadow of Globalization," in her *Scales of Justice: Reframing Justice in a Globalizing World* (Cambridge: Polity, 2008).
24. See Fraser, *Unruly Practices*, chs 2, 3.
*25. Butler's work is the focus of an essay by Gayle Salamon in *The History of Continental Philosophy: Volume 8.*
26. See Seyla Benhabib *et al.*, *Feminist Contentions: A Philosophical Exchange*, Linda Nicholson (ed.) (New York: Routledge, 1995), ch. 1; and Benhabib, *Situating the Self*, ch. 7.
27. Benhabib *et al.*, *Feminist Contentions*, 20.
28. *Ibid.*, 21.
29. *Ibid.*, 29–30.

In her response, Butler scoffs at Benhabib's overly simplistic characterization of postmodernism, but defends a central insight of Foucaultian poststructuralism, namely, that the subject can be both constituted by power relations and still capable of agency and resistance. Indeed, as Butler puts it, "the constituted character of the subject is the very precondition of its agency. For what is it that enables a purposive and significant reconfiguration of cultural and political relations, if not a relation that can be turned against itself, reworked, resisted?"[30] Fraser, in her reply to this exchange, echoes and affirms Butler's point: *pace* Benhabib, "nothing in principle precludes that subjects are *both* culturally constructed *and* capable of critique."[31] What feminists need, according to Fraser, is "an alternative conceptualization of the subject, one that integrates Butler's poststructuralist emphasis on construction with Benhabib's critical-theoretical stress on critique."[32]

Although Benhabib has more recently shown a greater appreciation for Butler's work on the subject,[33] and although she has incorporated some Derridean themes in her recent work on cosmopolitanism,[34] Benhabib has remained more steadfastly critical of poststructuralism than has either Fraser or Honneth. In this respect, Benhabib is perhaps closer to Habermas than her fellow third generation critical theorists. Honneth, by contrast, despite his critique of what he calls Foucault's "systems-theoretical solution to the *Dialectic of Enlightenment*,"[35] also relies on Foucaultian themes in his critical engagement with Habermas. In *The Critique of Power*, Honneth criticizes Habermas's social-theoretical distinction between system and lifeworld on the grounds that it presents a problematically norm-free system and a problematically power-free lifeworld.[36] In the "Afterword" to the second German edition of *The Critique of Power*, Honneth claims that a central question for critical social theory is "the question of how the conceptual framework of an analysis has to be laid out so that it is able to comprehend both the structures of social domination *and* the

---

30. *Ibid.*, 46.
31. *Ibid.*, 67.
32. *Ibid.*, 69.
33. See Seyla Benhabib, "Sexual Difference and Collective Identities: The New Global Constellation," *Signs: Journal of Women in Culture and Society* 24(2) (1999).
34. See her discussion of democratic iterations in Seyla Benhabib, *The Rights of Others: Aliens, Residents, and Citizens* (Cambridge: Cambridge University Press, 2004), 176–83, and *Another Cosmopolitanism* (Oxford: Oxford University Press, 2006), 47–51.
35. Axel Honneth, *The Critique of Power: Reflective Stages in a Critical Social Theory*, Kenneth Baynes (trans.) (Cambridge, MA: MIT Press, 1991), 201; the argument for this reading of Foucault is the topic of chs 4, 5, and 6.
36. Fraser develops a similar critique of Habermas in her essay "What's Critical About Critical Theory: The Case of Habermas and Gender," although without any explicit reference to Foucault. See Fraser, *Unruly Practices*, ch. 6.

social resources for its practical overcoming."[37] Honneth's central critique of Habermas here is that, as a result of his distinction between system and life-world and his insufficient attention to the role that power plays in the latter, he is incapable of fully illuminating both sides of this duality. As Honneth puts it: "the dynamic that arises in the historical development of social orders can be fully explained only by extending the sphere of communicative action to include the negative dimension of struggle."[38] To be sure, Honneth is likewise critical of Foucault for the inverse reason. He maintains that whereas Foucault help-fully theorizes the negative moment of social domination, he does not give an account – indeed, perhaps even denies the possibility of – the positive moment that enables the practical overcoming of domination.[39] Still, Honneth empha-sizes that the systematic aim of including Foucault in his study was "to show that the dimension of social conflict that Foucault makes central can only be invoked at the level of a social theory if it is grasped as the negative moment of a comprehensive process in the formation of social consensus."[40]

It is Honneth's interest in bringing out this "negative moment" empha-sized in Foucault's theory of power that leads to his emphasis on social strug-gles for recognition within the lifeworld. As he puts it in the "Introduction" to *The Struggle for Recognition*, his account of recognition is motivated by his conclusion in *The Critique of Power* that "any attempt to integrate the social-theoretical insights of Foucault's historical work within the framework of a theory of communicative action has to rely on the concept of morally motivated struggle."[41] Hence, despite his criticisms of Foucault, Honneth's critical engage-ment with Habermasian social theory and his own recognition-theoretical contribution to critical theory draw a great deal of inspiration from Foucault's analysis of power.[42]

---

37. Honneth, *The Critique of Power*, xiv.
38. *Ibid*., xxviii.
39. On this point, see *ibid*., xxii–xxviii.
40. *Ibid*., xxii.
41. Honneth, *The Struggle for Recognition*, 1.
42. Similarly, Fraser, both in her intervention in the Benhabib–Butler debate and in essays such as "Social Criticism Without Philosophy" (coauthored with Linda Nicholson) and "A Genealogy of Dependency" (coauthored with Linda Gordon), indicates a much greater open-ness to the insights of poststructuralism than does Habermas, while still remaining crit-ical of what she takes to be its normative deficits. See Nancy Fraser and Linda Nicholson, "Social Criticism without Philosophy," in *Feminism/Postmodernism*, Linda Nicholson (ed.) (New York: Routledge, 1990), 19–38; and Nancy Fraser and Linda Gordon, "A Genealogy of Dependency: Tracing a Keyword of the US Welfare State," in Fraser, *Justice Interruptus: Critical Reflections on the "Postsocialist" Condition* (New York: Routledge, 1997), 121–49.

III. RECONCEPTUALIZING THE SUBJECT

The problem of the subject is an important theme not only in the debate between Butlerian poststructuralism and Benhabibian critical theory, but also in much third generation critical theory, just as it is in twentieth-century continental philosophy as a whole. It surfaces particularly in the work of Benhabib, which articulates a narrative conception of the self, and of Honneth, whose account of recognition entails an intersubjectivist account of the subject.

Elements of Benhabib's narrative conception of the self are evident already in her classic essay on the Gilligan–Kohlberg debate, in which she criticizes the social contract tradition for failing to realize that "the self is not a thing, a substrate, but the protagonist of a life's tale" (STS 162), and in her critique of Butler, in which she argues that "a subjectivity that would not be structured by language, by narrative and by the symbolic structures of narrative available in a culture is unthinkable. We tell of who we are, of the 'I' that we are by means of a narrative."[43] Similarly, in her book on Hannah Arendt, Benhabib argues that one of Arendt's most important contributions to twentieth-century philosophy is her idea of the web of relationships and narratives as forming the space of human appearance.[44] In her recent work, Benhabib expands on these earlier insights and develops them more systematically. In *The Claims of Culture*, she argues that "to be and to become a self is to insert oneself into webs of interlocution; it is to know how to answer when one is addressed and to know how to address others."[45] As Benhabib notes, we are all thrown, in the Heideggerian sense, into various webs of interlocution or narrative – familial narratives, gender narratives, narratives of ethnic, racial, religious, national identity, and so forth – and "we become who we are by learning to be a conversation partner in these narratives."[46] Moreover, although we are thrown into these ongoing narratives and thus are not in a position to choose them or our interlocutors, "our agency consists in our capacity to weave out of those narratives and fragments of narratives a life story that makes sense for us, as unique individual selves."[47] We are, in other words, not just the protagonists but also the authors of our own stories.

---

43. Benhabib *et al.*, *Feminist Contentions*, 20.
44. Seyla Benhabib, *The Reluctant Modernism of Hannah Arendt* (London, Sage, 1996). In this book, Benhabib stakes out a provocative middle-ground reading of Arendt according to which she is neither a Heideggerian or Nietzschean antimodernist nor a Derridean postmodernist but instead a reluctant modernist who therefore has more in common with the Habermasian discourse ethical tradition than most commentators have assumed.
45. Seyla Benhabib, *The Claims of Culture: Equality and Diversity in the Global Era* (Princeton, NJ: Princeton University Press, 2002), 15.
46. Benhabib, "Sexual Difference and Collective Identities," 344.
47. *Ibid.*

In contrast to Taylor, from whom Benhabib borrows the idea of webs of inter-locution, Benhabib emphasizes the anti-essentialism of her narrative conception of the self. Because Benhabib insists that the core of the self consists not in any substantive commitments but in an ability or capacity to make sense of our lives by fitting our experiences into a coherent narrative, Benhabib arguably salvages coherence for the self without essentializing it. Moreover, Benhabib insists that she makes no strong claims about the mastery of the narrative self. We are never in complete control of our own narratives, as they must attain some degree of fit with the continually unfolding narratives of those others with whom our own life stories are inextricably intertwined.[48]

Honneth's intersubjectivist account of the self emerges out of his analysis of the struggle for recognition. As I discussed above, the three practical relations to self – self-confidence, self-respect, and self-esteem – that are made possible by intact mutual recognition – in the forms of love, rights, and solidarity – are condi-tions for the possibility of individual self-realization and autonomy. Honneth's intersubjectivist account of the self both overlaps with Habermas's – which also draws its inspiration from Mead[49] – and departs from it, by offering a thicker and richer conception of self-realization. Honneth also departs from Habermas (and aligns himself more with first generation critical theory) by drawing extensively on the insights of psychoanalysis, in particular, the object-relations psychoana-lytic theory of Donald Winnicott.[50] Honneth's greater appreciation for psycho-analysis goes hand in hand with what Anderson calls a greater appreciation for the Other of Reason; as such it is conceptually related to his greater openness to the insights generated by Foucault's analysis of power.[51] In his inaugural lecture at the Free University of Berlin, Honneth makes clear his dissatisfaction with the narrow focus on rationality in Habermas's work. As he puts it:

> As soon as the communication paradigm is grasped not in the sense of a conception of rational understanding, but as a conception of the conditions of recognition, the critical diagnosis of the times may no longer be pressed into the narrow scheme of a theory of rationality.[52]

---

48. Benhabib also questions the mastery of the narrative self on the grounds of the psychoanalytic insight that the I is not the master of its own house. See *ibid.*, 349.
49. For Habermas's Meadian account, see Jürgen Habermas, "Individuation through Socialization: On George Herbert Mead's Theory of Subjectivity," in *Postmetaphysical Thinking: Philosophical Essays*, William Mark Hohengarten (trans.) (Cambridge, MA: MIT Press, 1992).
50. For Honneth's discussion of Winnicott, see Honneth, *The Struggle for Recognition*, 98–106. For some remarks on the differences between Honneth and Habermas's uses of psychoanalysis, see Honneth, *The Critique of Power*, xxx–xxxi.
51. See Anderson, "The 'Third Generation' of the Frankfurt School."
52. Honneth, "The Social Dynamics of Disrespect," 74.

For Honneth, a truly critical diagnosis of the times needs to be rooted in a fuller conception of subjectivity, one that pays greater attention to the affective and recognitional aspects of our selves.

IV. RECOGNITION AND/OR REDISTRIBUTION?

The issue of how best to understand the problematic of recognition – as part of an intersubjectivist theory of the self and of the necessary conditions for ethical self-realization or as part of a broader conception of injustice that construes recognition on the model of the Weberian notion of status – is a central one in the debate between Fraser and Honneth. This debate arose out of Fraser's 1996 Tanner Lectures, for which Honneth served as a commentator, and which grew into their coauthored book, *Redistribution or Recognition? A Political-Philosophical Exchange*. However, also at stake here is the much broader question of how best to renew the tradition of critical theory in a post-Habermasian vein. As they write in their introduction, Fraser and Honneth both "believe that critique achieves both its theoretical warrant and its practical efficacy only by deploying normative concepts that are also informed by a structural understanding of contemporary society, one that can diagnose the tensions and contextualize the struggles of the present."[53]

In her Tanner Lectures and in her 1997 book, *Justice Interruptus*, Fraser is critical of the one-sidedness of the philosophical focus on the cultural politics of recognition, and she situates this critique in the context of what she calls the "postsocialist condition." In the wake of the fall of communism, Fraser argues, the political and cultural landscape is characterized by an exhaustion of left-wing utopianism, a lack of clear alternatives to the present social order, a rise in recognition-based cultural politics to the relative eclipse of an economic politics of redistribution, and a resurgence of economic neoliberalism.[54] Even worse, social and political theorists reflecting on the current landscape have taken the economic politics of redistribution and the cultural politics of recognition to represent an either/or choice, generating what Fraser argues is a false antithesis. Failing to call this false antithesis into question amounts to evading what Fraser takes to be:

> the crucial "postsocialist" tasks: first, interrogating the distinction between culture and economy; second, understanding how both

---

53. Nancy Fraser and Axel Honneth, *Redistribution or Recognition? A Political-Philosophical Exchange* (London: Verso, 2003), 4. For an astute appraisal of the exchange, see Thomas McCarthy's review of *Redistribution or Recognition?* in *Ethics: An International Journal of Social, Political and Legal Philosophy* 113(2) (January 2005).

54. See Fraser, *Justice Interruptus*, "Introduction."

work together to produce injustices; and third, figuring out how, as a prerequisite for remedying injustices, claims for recognition can be integrated with claims for redistribution in a comprehensive political project.[55]

Indeed, the guiding assumption of Fraser's work of the mid- to late 1990s is "that the cultural politics of recognition ought not simply to supplant the social politics of redistribution. Rather, the two need to be integrated with one another."[56] Fraser proposes to integrate these two conceptions of politics into a two-dimensional conception of justice that encompasses redistribution and recognition. *Contra* Honneth, who seeks to ground the entire normative framework of critical theory in the notion of recognition, Fraser argues that we cannot fully understand the predicaments of certain oppressed groups without utilizing both of these analytical frameworks; thus, we need to combine them into a single framework of justice. Also *contra* Honneth, who maintains that misrecognition is unjust because it is an impediment to full individual self-realization, Fraser construes the wrong of misrecognition as being a function of its impeding some individuals from participating as a peer with others in social life. Hence, she proposes a status model of recognition according to which misrecognition is unjust because through it certain individuals or groups "are denied the status of full partners in social interaction simply as a consequence of institutionalized patterns of cultural value in whose construction they have not equally participated and which disparage their distinctive characteristics or the distinctive characteristics assigned to them."[57] Fraser's conception of justice is perspectivally dualist, encompassing both misrecognition and maldistribution as analytically distinct but practically entwined forms of injustice,[58] and normatively monistic, inasmuch as it brings both types of injustice under the measure of a single normative standard. This standard, which Fraser labels the principle of parity of participation, she defines as follows: "according to this norm, justice requires social arrangements that permit all (adult) members of society to interact with one another as peers."[59]

In his reply to Fraser, Honneth underscores three aims of his recognition-based approach to critical theory. First, his approach roots critical theory in a phenomenology of the experience of injustice, as opposed to tying it to the aims and self-understandings of social movements, as does Fraser.[60] Second,

---

55. *Ibid.*, 3.
56. *Ibid.*, 6.
57. Fraser and Honneth, *Redistribution or Recognition?*, 29.
58. See *ibid.*, 63.
59. *Ibid.*, 36.
60. Fraser defines critical theory, following Marx, as "the self-clarification of the struggles and wishes of the age" (*Unruly Practices*, 113), struggles that she sees articulated through the

contra Fraser, Honneth maintains that his recognition theory can do justice to distributional injustices, for even these "must be understood as the institutional expression of social disrespect."[61] On Honneth's view, then, "distribution conflicts" are understood as "a specific kind of struggle for recognition in which the appropriate evaluation of the social contributions of individuals or groups is contested."[62] Third, and finally, Honneth sees the major conceptual issue as how to normatively ground critical theoretical demands for justice. Whereas Fraser attempts to ground these deontologically in her principle of parity of participation,[63] Honneth insists that they must be grounded teleologically in a (formal) conception of the good life.

Hence, the Fraser–Honneth debate raises but leaves unresolved a number of serious questions for critical theory.[64] What is the best pretheoretical reference point for critical theory: social movements or the subjective experience of injustice?[65] Which is better, a dualistic or monistic framework for conceptualizing injustice?[66] Finally, in an echo of Hegel's critique of Kant, which should critical theory take to be prior, the right or the good? Third and subsequent generations of critical theorists continue to grapple with these and related issues in an attempt to make sense of the social, cultural and political landscape of the early twenty-first century.

V. EMERGING TRENDS IN CRITICAL THEORY: COSMOPOLITANISM AND GLOBAL JUSTICE

However, as Fraser has argued in her more recent work, the categories of recognition and redistribution may well be insufficient to conceptualize the political conditions of an increasingly globalized, post-Westphalian world. Picking up

---

demands of social movements. For further comment on the role of social movements in Fraser's critical theory, see Fraser and Honneth, *Redistribution or Recognition?*, 11–16.

61. *Ibid.*, 114.

62. *Ibid.*, 171.

63. For Fraser's argument to this effect, see *ibid.*, 26–48.

64. For insightful discussion of these and other sticking points in the debate, see McCarthy's review of *Redistribution or Recognition?*, and Christopher Zurn, "Identity or Status? Struggles over 'Recognition' in Fraser, Honneth, and Taylor," *Constellations* 10(4) (2003).

65. For Fraser's critique of Honneth on this point, see Fraser and Honneth, *Redistribution or Recognition?*, 201–11. For Honneth's reply, see *ibid.*, 238–47. For further discussion of Honneth's views on this issue, see also "The Social Dynamics of Disrespect," 77.

66. In her more recent work, Fraser has argued in favor of expanding her framework even further, to encompass the specifically political question of representation alongside issues of recognition and redistribution. She indicates that this move may be necessary in Fraser and Honneth, *Redistribution or Recognition?*, 68. Actually achieving an expansion of this framework is the chief aim of Fraser, *Scales of Justice*.

where her work on recognition and redistribution left off, Fraser's recent work expands her formerly two-dimensional framework of justice into a multidimensional one that can accommodate the specifically *political* dimension of justice (as opposed to the economic or cultural dimensions highlighted by redistribution and recognition, respectively). Fraser's focus now is on the issue of political representation, specifically, on the metapolitical issues of *who* counts as a subject of justice and *how* questions of the frame of justice get decided now that it no longer goes without saying that the bounded nation-state is the proper frame for matters of justice. Her framework now combines "a multidimensional social ontology with normative monism,"[67] still relying on the norm of parity of participation, now construed in both substantive and procedural terms.[68] Staking out a distinctive ground in the vast literature on global justice, Fraser argues for a democratization of the process by which the boundaries of political questions – issues of *who* is a subject of justice – are determined.

In a similar vein, Benhabib has also turned in her recent work to focus on the issue of cosmopolitan justice. As she argues in her 2004 Tanner Lectures, we are in a period of world history marked by a transition from international to cosmopolitan norms of justice. The former are binding on states or their authorized agents and only as a function of treaties or agreements between states, whereas the latter "accrue to individuals as moral and legal persons in a worldwide civil society."[69] This situation generates what Benhabib calls the paradox of democratic legitimacy, a paradox that arises at two levels: first, at the level of the intersection between the political sovereignty of bounded territorial states and moral universality of human rights, and second, at a level internal to democracies themselves, given that they "cannot choose the boundaries of their own membership democratically."[70] Benhabib attempts not to resolve but to mediate or negotiate these paradoxes through her concept of democratic iterations. Drawing inspiration from Derrida's notion of iterability, Benhabib defines democratic iterations as "linguistic, legal, cultural and political repetitions-in-transformation, invocations that are also revocations. They not only change established understandings but also transform what passes as the valid or established view of an authoritative precedent."[71] In her recent work, Benhabib analyzes recent clashes over culture (including the French *affaire du foulard*) and citizenship (including recent debates over German citizenship) and shows how, in these cases, the force of democratic iterations have pushed polities in

---

67. Fraser, *Scales of Justice*, 58.
68. *Ibid.*, ch. 2.
69. Benhabib, *Another Cosmopolitanism*, 16.
70. *Ibid.*, 35.
71. *Ibid.*, 48.

the direction of expanding the *demos*.[72] She also argues, *contra* communitarians, liberal nationalists, and some advocates of cosmopolitanism, for "moral universalism and cosmopolitan federalism."[73]

These and related issues of cosmopolitanism and global justice will no doubt be on the agenda of critical theorists for some time to come. The challenge facing critical theorists of the third and subsequent generations is to continue to craft theoretical perspectives that are capable of illuminating the main dangers and possibilities for change in the world that we now inhabit and to do so without relying for normative support on questionable notions such as the working-class subject or the allegedly context-transcendent ideals of the pragmatic presuppositions of discourse. Each of the third generation theorists discussed here has offered a unique and provocative set of answers to this challenge. Whether they are ultimately successful or not will be for future critical theorists to judge, in light of as yet unforeseen and unforeseeable developments of world history.

MAJOR WORKS

Seyla Benhabib

Critique, Norm, and Utopia: A Study of the Foundations of Critical Theory. New York: Columbia University Press, 1986.

Situating the Self: Gender, Community and Postmodernism in Contemporary Ethics. New York: Routledge, 1992.

Feminist Contentions: A Philosophical Exchange (with Judith Butler, Drucilla Cornell, and Nancy Fraser). Edited by Linda Nicholson. New York: Routledge, 1995.

The Reluctant Modernism of Hannah Arendt. London, Sage, 1996.

The Claims of Culture: Equality and Diversity in the Global Era. Princeton, NJ: Princeton University Press, 2002.

The Rights of Others: Aliens, Residents, and Citizens. Cambridge: Cambridge University Press, 2004.

Another Cosmopolitanism. Oxford: Oxford University Press, 2006.

Dignity in Adversity: Human Rights in Troubled Times. Cambridge: Polity, 2011.

Nancy Fraser

Unruly Practices: Power, Discourse, and Gender in Contemporary Social Theory. Minneapolis, MN: University of Minnesota Press, 1989.

Justice Interruptus: Critical Reflections on the "Postsocialist" Condition. New York: Routledge, 1997.

Scales of Justice: Reframing Justice in a Globalizing World. Cambridge: Polity, 2008.

With Axel Honneth. *Redistribution or Recognition? A Political-Philosophical Exchange*. London: Verso, 2003.

---

72. See Benhabib, *The Rights of Others*, ch. 5, and *Another Cosmopolitanism*, lecture 2.

73. Benhabib, *The Rights of Others*, 220–21.

Axel Honneth

Kritik der Macht: Reflexionsstufen einer kritischen Gesellschaftstheorie. Frankfurt: Suhrkamp, 1985. Published in English as *The Critique of Power: Reflective Stages in a Critical Social Theory*, translated by Kenneth Baynes. Cambridge, MA: MIT Press, 1991.

Kampf um Anerkennung: Zur moralischen Grammatik sozialer Konflikte. Frankfurt: Suhrkamp, 1992. Published in English as *The Struggle for Recognition: The Moral Grammar of Social Conflicts*, translated by Joel Anderson. Cambridge, MA: MIT Press, 1995.

Das Andere der Gerechtigkeit: Aufsätze zur praktischen Philosophie. Frankfurt: Suhrkamp 2000. Published in English as *Disrespect: The Normative Foundations of Critical Theory*, translated by Joseph Ganahl. Cambridge: Polity Press, 2007.

Patholgien der Vernunft: Geschichte und Gegenwart der kritischen Theorie. Frankfurt: Suhrkamp, 2007. Published in English as *Pathologies of Reason: On the Legacy of Critical Theory*, translated by James Ingram. New York: Columbia University Press, 2009.

Das Recht der Freiheit. Berlin: Suhrkamp, 2011.

7

FRENCH AND ITALIAN SPINOZISM

Simon Duffy

A renaissance in Spinoza studies took place in France at the end of the 1960s, which gave new impetus to the study of Spinoza's work and continues to have a marked effect on the direction of research in the field today. The effect of this renewed interest and direction did not remain isolated to France but quickly spread across the continent. Although certain of the figures involved in this event have become rather well known in some academic circles, and their work widely read, the details of these developments and the specific texts that contributed to and sustained this new direction in research have remained largely unknown in the English-speaking world. The aim of this essay, therefore, is to provide a survey of this event, to review the background to these developments, to introduce the main protagonists – along with some of the lesser known but equally important figures – and to single out and assess the key texts, their specific focus and their contribution to the new direction in research.

One of the peculiarities of Spinoza's philosophy is that the history of its reception has passed through a number of phases, from its predominantly "materialist" reception in the seventeenth century, when Spinozism was reputed to be a form of atheism, to its "pantheist" instantiation during the greater part of the nineteenth century, due predominantly to the Spinozism of German Romanticism. After the polemics and condemnations of the nineteenth century, a number of sympathetic engagements with Spinoza's work began to emerge at the turn of the twentieth century in France that were intent on its explication and on promoting its comprehension. These works, however, developed only selected aspects of Spinoza's thought, and when examining the Spinozist system as a whole, there was a propensity to revert to traditional criticisms essentially characterized by the Spinozism of German Romanticism and the substantialist metaphysics that

Hegel ascribed to Spinoza. There was, in other words, no attempt to provide a coherent and consistent account of Spinoza's thought as a whole. After a number of years of inactivity, the 1950s–1960s witnessed a resurgence of interest in Spinoza scholarship, with research developing in several quite different directions. To begin with, there were the seminars and then the publications of both Martial Guéroult (1891–1976) and Ferdinand Alquié (1906–85),[1] each with rather different methods and conclusions that were somewhat opposed.

Guéroult's rigorous and systematic engagement with the *Ethics* – in his two-volume study *Spinoza I: Dieu* (1968) and *Spinoza II: L'Âme* (1974) – perfected the philological reading of Spinoza. In these works, which were devoted to studying the logical *order of reasons* that structured the system of the *Ethics*, Guéroult undertakes to demonstrate the unity and coherence of Spinoza's work that earlier readings had missed by systematically explicating Spinoza's arguments and reconstructing the structure or system internal to the *Ethics*. In the first volume, which discussed part I of the *Ethics*, Guéroult demonstrates the objective nature of the relation between the attributes, that is, that the attributes are really distinct from one another and yet unified as attributes of the one substance. In the second volume, which discussed part II, he explicates the deduction that necessarily proceeds from the adequate knowledge of the formal essence of the attributes to the adequate knowledge of the essence of things and thereby realizes the third kind of knowledge as it will be later defined in the *Ethics*. The critical analysis of parts I and II only touch on the broader themes of Spinoza's metaphysics, physics, and theory of knowledge, because Guéroult is primarily concerned with examining the foundations of the *Ethics*. These themes, which are developed in the three other parts of the *Ethics*, were to be the object of a projected third and final volume on parts III–V of the *Ethics*, but Guéroult died shortly after beginning work on it.

In *Le Rationalisme de Spinoza*, Alquié examines the genesis of the system of Spinoza's *Ethics*. His main objective is to determine whether or not Spinoza's system lives up to its ambitions to found and justify a rationalism that is absolute. Alquié methodically demonstrates that the concepts of most importance to Spinoza are "effectively unthinkable."[2] One of the limitations of Alquié's work is that his examination of Spinozist concepts is conducted from the point of view of Cartesian ideas, but this was not a limitation that Spinoza accepted. Alquié's work therefore raises the question of how or from what point of view can Spinoza be read such that Spinozist ideas are rendered "thinkable." It is

---

1. Alquié's lectures on Spinoza at the Sorbonne during the years 1958–59 have recently been published; see Ferdinand Alquié, *Leçons sur Spinoza* (Paris: La Table ronde, 2003).
2. Ferdinand Alquié, *Le Rationalisme de Spinoza* (Paris: Presses Universitaires de France, 1981), 14.

this problematic that will orient future research in Spinoza studies, and this is exemplified by the marked departure by the next generation of scholars from the Cartesian reading of Spinoza exemplified by Alquié, as they draw inspiration instead from the work of Guéroult.

Another important source of inspiration that contributed to enrich this renewal in Spinoza studies were the seminars and the work of Louis Althusser (1918–90).[3] Althusser's work, marked by a form of structuralism that can be compared to Guéroult, valued the importance of political thought in philosophy. In *Essays in Self-Criticism*, Althusser notes that his Spinozism was often mistaken for a form of structuralism. Although Althusser actually cites the importance of Spinoza to his own project in political philosophy and repeatedly draws attention to the importance of Spinoza's philosophy for Marxism, he himself wrote very little on Spinoza. When he did, Spinoza was cast as an important figure in Althusser's project of freeing Marxism from Hegelian idealism. The recourse to Spinoza made possible a radical critique of historicism, including Hegelianism. However this did not amount to a critique of Hegelianism *per se*. In France, from the 1960s on, it is from this perspective of an anti-Hegelianism, more or less generalized, that Spinoza is first brought on to the scene.

The generation of thinkers that followed Althusser, despite their own developments leading them in directions not entirely compatible with his thought, adopted the imperative of valuing political thought. One of the main characteristics that distinguishes the resurgence of interest in Spinoza in the 1960s is the attention that is given to Spinoza's political works – the *Tractatus Theologico-Politicus* and *Tractatus Politicus*.[4] As a result of the influence of Althusser, Spinoza's political texts became another means of addressing some of the issues of coherence and consistency that had troubled commentator's working on Spinoza's metaphysics.

The main figures of this renewal in Spinoza scholarship include Alexandre Matheron, Gilles Deleuze, Pierre Macherey, Antonio Negri, Étienne Balibar and Pierre-François Moreau. Each provides a highly original attempt to think through the work and thought of Spinoza focusing on the problem of the relation between Spinoza's metaphysical and political works. In doing so, these scholars have together irrevocably altered the direction of Spinoza scholarship today. The first generation of scholars, Matheron and Deleuze, independently developed a new ontological interpretation of Spinoza. Matheron's work, which examines parts III–V of the *Ethics*, can be seen to complement Guéroult's

---

*3. For a discussion of Louis Althusser, see the essay by Warren Montag in *The History of Continental Philosophy: Volume 6*.

4. Benedict Spinoza, *Tractatus Theologico-Politicus*, in *Spinoza: Complete Works*, Michael L. Morgan (ed.), Samuel Shirley (trans.) (Indianapolis, IN: Hackett, 2002) (hereafter cited as TTP), and *Tractatus Politicus*, in *Spinoza: Complete Works* (hereafter cited as TP).

unfinished project and to extend it to Spinoza's political work. Deleuze, on the other hand, develops this ontological interpretation into a new philosophy of power (*potentia*). The second generation, which includes Balibar, Macherey, and Moreau in France, poses the problem of the movement of immanence, and the fundamental theme of their work is the experience of being. There is also Negri in Italy, who sees in Spinozism the concept of a constitutive thought. Negri makes it his project to develop the political implications of such a thought. The influence of Marxism in these new readings of Spinoza is by no means universal; for example Deleuze's work on Spinoza is not assimilable to Marxism in any direct way, and nor is Moreau's more historiographical engagement with Spinoza. There is, however, a consensus about the close relationship between Spinoza's metaphysics, epistemology, ethics, and political philosophy: so much so that his works themselves are considered to exhibit a remarkable consistency. A new image of Spinoza is thus affirmed in the wake of the interpretive innovation of Matheron and Deleuze. These texts opened the way to a new set of readings that continued to share a concern to demonstrate the architectonic unity of his major works. The originality of a philosophy of power (*potentia*) and of its variations has allowed the development of a reading of Spinoza that is no longer solely post-Cartesian, neo-Stoic, or Hegelian. Spinoza now presents a philosophical position articulated between a positive ontology of immanence, a constitutive logic of the imagination, and an affirmative ethics of power (*potentia*).

In order to further explicate this new image of Spinozism, let us turn to the texts of those responsible for it, beginning with the texts of the first generation of Spinoza scholars in France: Matheron's *Individu et communauté chez Spinoza*, published in 1969, and Deleuze's *Spinoza et le problème de l'expression*, published in 1968 (although not actually made available until early 1969). Both Matheron and Deleuze cite Guéroult as a major influence on their work. Deleuze argues that:

> Guéroult renewed the history of philosophy through a structural-genetic method, which he had developed well before structuralism became fashionable in other disciplines. In Guéroult's method, a structure is defined by an *order of reasons*. Reasons are the differential and generative elements of the corresponding system; they are genuine philosophemes that exist only in relation to one another.[5]

---

5. Gilles Deleuze, "Gueroult's General Method for Spinoza," in *Desert Islands and Other Texts (1953–1974)*, David Lapoujade (ed.), Mike Taormina (trans.) (New York: Semiotext(e), 2004), 146.

Deleuze hailed Guéroult's work on Spinoza as having made possible for the first time a "genuinely scientific study of Spinozism."[6]

I. MATHERON

From the methodological point of view, Guéroult's structural genetic method, particularly as employed in his book on Descartes, also functioned as an ideal model for Matheron. He had initially considered studying Spinoza because of his merit as being a precursor to Marx,[7] but quickly came to realize that it was rather "Marx who has the great merit of being one of the successors of Spinoza in certain fields."[8] Matheron is one of the first to explore the conjuncture between Spinoza's metaphysics and his politics, as was suggested by Althusser. He takes Spinoza's politics seriously, by providing close readings of Spinoza's political texts, the *Tractatus Theologico-Politicus* and *Tractatus Politicus*.

Individu et communauté opens with a definition of *conatus*, and the recognition of its foundational role in Spinoza's ethics *and* politics. For Matheron, the *conatus*, or the effort by which an individual strives to persevere in its existence, is the formal element of *any* individual that unifies its material elements and is equated with its power to act.[9] Matheron begins the first chapter with the presentation of the idea of substance as pure activity. Rather than speaking about substance as having an attribute, Matheron speaks about substance as considered from the point of view of an attribute, in order to account for the method followed by Spinoza in the first proposals of the *Ethics*. What follows is that rather than the productivity being a property unfolding from an *a priori* essence of God, Spinoza considers the existence of God, and consequently also his essence, to be genesis and productivity and nothing else. This understanding is supported by both Deleuze and Negri.

In the first part of *Individu et communauté*, Matheron outlines an analogy between the constitution of human individuality and a form of contract characteristic of political systems that he calls the "physical contract."[10] Drawing on

---

6. *Ibid.*, 155.

7. Althusser regards "Spinoza as Marx's only direct ancestor, from the philosophical standpoint" (Louis Althusser and Étienne Balibar, *Reading Capital*, Ben Brewster [trans.] [New York: Pantheon, 1970], 102).

8. Alexandre Matheron, "A propos de Spinoza: Entretien réalisé par Laurent Bove et Pierre-François Moreau," *Multitudes* (2000). http://multitudes.samizdat.net/A-propos-de-Spinoza.html (accessed May 2010).

9. Alexandre Matheron, *Individu et communauté chez Spinoza* (Paris: Éditions de Minuit, 1969), 38–43.

10. *Ibid.*, 37–8.

Spinoza's concept of the *conatus*, Matheron characterizes this analogy according to a principle of self-regulation. For Spinoza, insofar as we act, we preserve our being, and anything that produces effects consequently preserves its being, since the effects that it produces cannot contradict its nature. For example, the free human being, who lives according to reason, endeavors to produce all the effects that follow from their nature as a free human being, and because of this, they tend to preserve their nature as a free human being.

Matheron also considers political systems to be self-regulating systems. The various models of self-regulation are based on the various ways that a mode strives for its preservation. There is a static self-preservation where the identical is reproduced, and there is a dynamic self-preservation where reproduction is achieved each time by rising to a higher level or degree of power (*potentia*). It is the same for individuals: there are those individuals who are preserved in a strict sense, in an identical way, and others who are preserved while developing and by increasing their productivity. Once adequate ideas start to play a predominant role in our mind, it is this second form of self-regulation that is put into play. As far as political systems are concerned, the Hebrew State would be a model of the former (static identity), and the States of the *Tractatus Politicus* – monarchy, aristocracy, democracy – a model of the latter (dynamic identity).

Matheron maintains that the whole domain of ethics could therefore be determined independently of the question of the preservation of identities, and instead in relation to the increase and decrease of the different degrees of an individual's power (*potentia*) to exist and act that result from their encounters. From the concept of the individual, the central concept that produces creative effects is the principle of the imitation of affects. It belongs to the essence of the human individual to be capable of the imitation of affects and thus of living in interaction with others. It is by means of this imitation of others that human individuals can together form a political individual. The question of the passions, from the point of view of their political productivity, is therefore central to Matheron's work.

On the basis of the logic of the imitation of affects, Matheron talks about the political productivity of indignation. The subjects of a corrupt sovereign or tyrant would gather against him under the influence of indignation. This would follow a process similar to that of the social contract; however, it would be determined rather by a "physical contract." Matheron draws on the *Tractatus Politicus* to reconstitute the theoretical genesis of political society independently of a social contract and the rational calculation of utility. Matheron considers the operation of the physical contract by means of the passion of indignation to be possible because, in a hypothetical state of nature, and insofar as men are able to experience indignation, there would never simply be one human being fighting to dominate another, or to steal their possessions. There would always be others who to some extent would intervene or "meddle in what doesn't concern them." According to the logic of the imitation of the affects, they take sides and experience indignation against the adversary. Matheron maintains that ultimately, without any calculation or social contract, an embryonic political society will be formed.

It is, however, necessary not to confuse the affect of indignation and that to which it eventually leads, if the final result is positive. Such a result, which is never guaranteed, always comes from something other than indignation. What is required are positive affects such as enthusiasm for freedom and justice, along with favorable historical and institutional conditions, together with much reflection.[11]

Once deployed, indignation cannot be extinguished in a society. Matheron characterizes it as a kind of original defect or flaw of political society – the original sin of the state – that can only be neutralized in varying degrees. The constitutions of the *Tractatus Politicus* attempt to motivate their citizens by positive feelings that limit indignation to the smallest possible role in society. This is achieved by transforming it into an abstracted indignation, directed no longer against specific people, but rather against those who deserve to be punished "in general," whoever they may be.

Matheron's reading of Spinoza remains today one of the major references for researchers in Spinoza studies in France. Although those who have recently published works on Spinoza all have rather different theses, they are always within the framework that has been defined by Matheron's work.

II. DELEUZE

According to the reading of Spinoza that Deleuze[12] presents in *Expressionism in Philosophy: Spinoza*, Spinoza's philosophy should not be represented as a moment that can be simply subsumed and sublated within the dialectical progression of the history of philosophy, as it is figured by Hegel in the *Science of Logic*, but rather should be considered as providing an alternative point of view for the development of a philosophy that overcomes Hegelian idealism.[13] Indeed, Deleuze demonstrates, by means of Spinoza, that a more complex philosophy antedates Hegel's, which cannot be supplanted by it. Spinoza therefore becomes a significant figure in Deleuze's project of renewing the history of philosophy by

---

11. See *ibid.*, 505–15.
*12. For a detailed discussion of Deleuze's philosophy, see the essay by Daniel W. Smith in *The History of Continental Philosophy: Volume 6*.
13. For a further explication of Hegel's reading of Spinoza, see the following section on Macherey.

tracing an alternative lineage that challenges the Hegelian concept of the history of philosophy determined by the dialectical logic, and that culminates in the construction of a philosophy of difference.[14] The problem that orients Deleuze's reading of Spinoza is the concept of expression. The first occurrence of the form of the verb *exprimere* that appears in the *Ethics* is in EID6:[15] "By God I understand a being absolutely infinite, that is, a substance consisting of an infinity of attributes, of which each one expresses an eternal and infinite essence." Deleuze argues that, rather than being a definition of substance, Spinoza here begins by characterizing the act of expressing or of being expressed. Deleuze considers Spinoza to have understood and explained expression in terms of the dynamic constitution and production of being, which is what actually constitutes reality.

The strategy of reading the *Ethics* as determined according to the logic of expression marks not only the originality of Deleuze's interpretation of Spinoza, but also one of the points where Deleuze can be considered to depart from the Hegelian and Cartesian Spinoza familiar to Spinoza studies. Rather than reading the philosophy of Spinoza either solely in relation to Descartes, or simply as one stage in the dialectical progression of the history of philosophy, Deleuze traces an alternative lineage in the history of philosophy that expresses the convergence between Spinoza's ontology, the mathematics of Leibniz, specifically his differential calculus,[16] and the metaphysics of Duns Scotus, in particular the concepts of formal distinction, the univocity of being, and individuality. Deleuze does not read Spinoza as a Scotist, but rather, by reading Scotus alongside Spinoza, he examines Spinoza's reformulation of these Scotist concepts in order to develop those aspects of Spinoza's philosophy that are specifically anti-Cartesian.[17] This anti-Cartesian reading of Spinoza provides the framework for the development of a reading of Spinoza that challenges the Hegelian concept of the dialectical progression of the history of philosophy.

Deleuze considers Spinoza's *Ethics* to have given expression to the concept of individuality, whose themes can be found scattered among several other

---

14. See Simon Duffy, *The Logic of Expression: Quality, Quantity and Intensity in Spinoza, Hegel and Deleuze* (Aldershot: Ashgate, 2006), 11–42.

15. Spinoza, *Ethics*, I, Definition 6. The following conventional abbreviated notation will be used when referring to Spinoza's *Ethics*: EI for *Ethics*, Part I (roman numerals refer to the parts of the *Ethics*); A for axiom; C for corollary; D for demonstration (or definition if followed by an Arabic numeral); L for lemma; Post. for postulate; P for proposition; S for scholium (Arabic numerals denote the lemma, proposition or scholium number); and, Ap for appendix. Thus EIP8S2 or *Ethics*, I, P8S2 refer to *Ethics*, Part I, Proposition 8, Scholium 2. Citations from the *Ethics* are quoted from *The Collected Works of Spinoza, Volume I*, Edwin M. Curley (trans.) (Princeton, NJ: Princeton University Press, 1985).

16. See Simon Duffy, "The Differential Point of View of the Infinitesimal Calculus in Spinoza, Leibniz and Deleuze," *Journal of the British Society for Phenomenology* 37(3) (2006).

17. See Duffy, *The Logic of Expression*, 95–119.

authors of the seventeenth century, most notably Duns Scotus. In relation to the concept of individuality, the Hegelian categories of quantity, quality, and relation, which articulate differences in the distances or dimensions of things (quantity), in their nature (quality), and in their order (relation), are considered by Deleuze to be antedated by the three different dimensions of the individual as presented by Spinoza, namely relation, power (quantity), and mode (quality). The individual is characterized as relation insofar as there is a composition of individuals in relation to one another, or among themselves. Deleuze maintains that it is the highest exercise of the imagination, the point where it inspires understanding, to have bodies or individuals meet according to composable relationships: both the physical composition of bodies and the political consti-tution of humans. Thus the importance of Spinoza's theory of common notions, which Deleuze considers to be a cornerstone of the *Ethics*. Deleuze maintains that for Spinoza, to think adequate ideas is not a natural faculty: it is rather a discovery, the product of an encounter. The form of the truth is therefore not given, but is rather obtained by experimentation. It is by means of developing common notions that we gain knowledge. In practice, this involves the experi-mental organization of ethical encounters: those encounters that allow us to understand the conditions of our knowledge, of our immanent thought. The object of this immanent thought is the body, understood as the product of its engagements with other bodies, ethical or adequate engagements that are expe-rienced as affects, and are expressed by the individual's power (*potentia*) to act.[18]

The characterization of the individual as power (*potentia*) indicates the indi-vidual's capacity to compose new relations with other individuals. The concept of *potentia* – translated by the concept of power as force or capacity – is different from that of *potestas* – translated by power in the juridico-political sense of the term[19] – insofar as it expresses that which an individual body can do, and which is verified by joy. Composition therefore refers not only to the charac-teristic relations between individuals, but also to the capacity or potential to create these kinds of relations. With the aid of chapter XVI of Spinoza's *Tractatus*

---

18. See François Zourabichvili, "Deleuze et Spinoza," in *Spinoza au XXe siècle*, Olivier Bloch (ed.) (Paris: Presses Universitaires de France, 1993), 243.

19. Guéroult is one of the first to demonstrate the importance of this distinction between *potentia* and *potestas* in Spinoza's *Ethics*; see Martial Guéroult, *Spinoza I: Dieu (Éthique, I)* (Paris: Aubier-Montaigne, 1968), 387–9. It is later taken up by Antonio Negri, who offers a thorough examination of the social and political implications of this distinction in relation to Spinoza's work as a whole. I have followed Michael Hardt's suggestion in the "Translator's Preface" to Negri's *The Savage Anomaly: The Power of Spinoza's Metaphysics and Politics* (Minneapolis, MN: University of Minnesota Press, 1991) to "make the distinction nominally through capi-talization, rendering *potestas* as 'Power' and *potentia* as 'power' and including the Latin terms in brackets where there might be confusion" (*ibid.*, xii).

Theologico-Politicus, Deleuze describes an ethical world where differences in power (*potentia*) are the sole principle of discrimination.

III. MACHEREY

Pierre Macherey's *Hegel ou Spinoza*, which appeared in 1979, is regarded as the definitive text that sets the record straight in regard to Hegel's reading of Spinoza as presented in *The History of Philosophy* and *The Science of Logic*. Macherey maintains that the position that Spinoza is given in the process of the development of philosophical thought by Hegel conditions the very interpretation that Hegel provides of his work.[20]

The question of whether or not one can find a dialectic operating in the *Ethics* is one of the defining problematics that Macherey brings to bear on Hegel's reading of Spinoza. He argues that Hegel transposes the *Ethics* by using the notions of opposition and contradiction, which are evidently not those of Spinoza, "implicitly making the dialectic, in the Hegelian sense, intervene" in the Spinozist system.[21] The simple negation that Hegel locates in the *Ethics* in this way serves to position the philosophy of Spinoza as one moment in the linear progression of the history of philosophy that is determined according to the Hegelian dialectical logic.[22] Macherey considers such a logic to be "manifestly absent" from Spinoza's work; he suggests rather that "it is Spinoza who constitutes the real alternative to the Hegelian philosophy."[23] What Macherey proposes is "to rethink the dialectic, starting with Spinoza";[24] such a project would require responding to the question of whether or not a concept of historical contradiction free from dialectical negativity is able to be determined in relation to Spinoza.

Hegel argues in *The History of Philosophy* that, in carrying the Cartesian system to its "furthest logical conclusions," Spinoza actually sets aside the dualism inherent in that system.[25] However, by reducing the attributes to external forms of reflection, of which only two are perceived, Hegel reinstalls in substance "a hidden duality." "The unity of substance is," for Hegel, "both resolved and

---

20. Pierre Macherey, *Avec Spinoza: Études sur la doctrine et l'histoire du spinozisme* (Paris: Presses Universitaires de France, 1992), 188.
21. Pierre Macherey, *Hegel ou Spinoza* (Paris: Presses Universitaires de France, 1979), 136.
22. See Georg W. F. Hegel, *Hegel's Science of Logic*, A. V. Miller (trans.) (London: George Allen & Unwin, 1969), 580.
23. Macherey, *Hegel ou Spinoza*, 12.
24. *Ibid.*
25. G. W. F. Hegel, *Hegel's Lectures on the History of Philosophy*, vol. 3, Elizabeth S. Haldane and Francis Simson (trans.) (London: Routledge & Kegan Paul, 1955), 252.

undone in the distinction of thought and extension." This allows Hegel "to redis-
cover Descartes in Spinoza." Hegel considers Spinoza to remain constrained by
"the same problem of the relation of two distinct entities, between which it is
necessary to establish the conditions of an agreement." "In this sense, Hegel can
say that Spinozism is a failed effort to go beyond the limits of Cartesianism."[26]
Insofar as Hegel's reading of Spinoza set the tenor of the reception of Spinoza
in the shadow of Descartes, it has thereby become one of the most influential
interpretations of Spinoza.

This controversy between Hegel and Spinoza turns around the question of
whether the attribute, as defined by Spinoza (EID4), is "attributed" to substance
by an intellect as a subjective representation, or whether it should rather be
considered as belonging to the objective reality of substance.[27] In book two of
the *Science of Logic*, Hegel offers a subjectivist interpretation of EID4. He argues
that despite his conception of a unitary absolute substance to which thought is
immanent, Spinoza still implicitly appeals to a form of thought that is opposed
to any conceivable form of thought found within substance.

Macherey develops an alternative to this Hegelian interpretation, according to
which the attributes are understood to be really distinct and the form of understanding implied in this definition, which Hegel construes as an abstract external
intellect, can be conceived as an understanding that is immanent to substance.
Hegel's error, Macherey contends, consists in having posed the distinction of
the attributes in a relation of opposition. The Spinozist thesis of "an infinity
of attributes" (EID6) allows this Hegelian complication to be avoided. Hegel
excludes this thesis by retaining only two opposing attributes. The reciprocal
irreducibility of the infinite number of infinite attributes, which is the positive
expression of infinite substance, is, according to Macherey, "perfectly coherent
with their [unity] in substance."[28] According to Macherey, the attribute belongs
to the objective reality of substance, as a positive expression, and therefore as a
constitutive form, of substance.

Spinozist thought represents "the positive sign of an anticipated resistance"[29]
to the idealism of the Hegelian dialectic. The "true question" that frames *Hegel ou
Spinoza* for Macherey then becomes "what is the limit which separates an idealist
dialectic from a materialist dialectic?"[30] Is a Spinozist corrective to the Marxist
dialectic, which would consist of a Marxism purged of all Hegelian elements,
conceivable? By examining Hegel's problematic reading of Spinoza, Macherey

---

26. Macherey, *Hegel ou Spinoza*, 106.
27. Pierre Macherey, *Introduction à l'Ethique de Spinoza* (Paris: Presses Universitaires de France, 1994–8), vol. I, 39.
28. Macherey, *Hegel ou Spinoza*, 136.
29. *Ibid.*
30. *Ibid.*

demonstrates that Spinoza eludes the grasp of the dialectical progression of the history of philosophy and thereby restores to the history of philosophy, and also to Marxism, what is valuable in Spinoza as an alternative to Hegel.

IV. NEGRI

The publication of Antonio Negri's *The Savage Anomaly* in 1981, and of the French translation, which appeared the following year with no less than three separate prefaces by the leading figures in French Spinoza scholarship (Deleuze, Macherey, and Matheron), provoked vigorous debate in Spinozist circles. Negri moves beyond the textual analysis that characterizes the French Spinozists to a consideration of the historical and political context of Spinoza's philosophical and political writing. Indeed, Negri, more so than his French counterparts, can be seen to pursue the concerns raised by Althusser by developing his hypotheses above all on the terrain of politics.

Negri considers the rediscovery of Spinoza at the end of the 1960s to open a series of fundamental problems associated with the definition of contemporary materialism, which relate to ontology, ethics, and politics. Negri proposes Spinoza as the philosopher of materialism, and by materialism he means the radical operation that allows the analysis of the world according to the real constitution of its power (*potentia*).

In political philosophy, Spinoza is often presented as belonging to the traditional legal lineage, the sovereign line that runs from Hobbes via Rousseau and Kant to Hegel, who give the state a specific dignity and legitimacy by contrasting it with society. This is not the case according to Negri, who recasts Spinoza as representing the linchpin of an antilegalist tradition that begins with Machiavelli and leads to Marx, and is opposed to the hegemony of the tradition of modern political thought. Negri's thesis is that Spinoza's theory of state and law is based on the ontological productivity of the multitude as the very agent of politics.

The force of Negri's work lies in his identification of Spinoza as the first philosopher to see society as "constituted" by the power of the masses or the multitude (*multitudo*). "The *multitudo* is now no longer a negative condition but the positive premise of the self-constitution of right."[31] Negri maintains that the *multitudo*, a term that rarely appears in the *Tractatus Theologico-Politicus* and only once in the *Ethics*, is absolutely central to Spinoza's *Tractatus Politicus*. Negri proposes a reading of Spinoza that pits a politics of the multitude against state domination. This culminates in a radically constitutive conception of democracy, which is the expression of the multitude without representation.

---

31. Negri, *The Savage Anomaly*, 194.

Negri argues that Spinoza founds his new concept of human existence on the dynamic of desire, as an expression of *potentia*, or natural power, which escapes the mediation imposed by the artificial order of *potestas*, which is a Power in the juridico-political sense of the term. He takes the philological distinction between *potestas* and *potentia* for granted and considers the problem instead as a philosophical and political issue that affords a new perspective on Spinoza's work. Negri seeks to demonstrate how such a Spinozist perspective would afford a richer understanding of the nature of power (*potentia*) and thereby provide new possibilities for contemporary political theory and practice.[32]

Negri argues that Spinoza's philosophy can be divided into two parts or periods, which he calls the first and the second foundations of Spinoza's metaphysics. The "first foundation," which culminates in the first two parts of the *Ethics* (I–II), attempts to synthesize the pantheism of the Spinoza circle, what Negri characterizes as the milieu in which Spinoza's early work was produced, by developing a substantialist ontology to its extreme limit. Negri maintains that this largely conforms to the neo-Platonic utopian idealism that had dominated much of the Renaissance. He argues that it is owing to the limits of utopian thought that the problems of substantial constitution characteristic of Spinoza's first foundation cannot be resolved, except by resorting to idealism and asceticism.

The break from the first foundation is effected by the *Tractatus Theologico-Politicus*, which Negri considers to play an extraordinarily important role in the history of the development of Spinoza's thought. Spinoza interrupted the composition of the *Ethics* in 1665, and began work on the *Theologico-Political Treatise* (1670) before returning to complete the *Ethics* between 1670 and 1675. The *Tractatus Theologico-Politicus* exhibits a tension between a juridical ideology of the social contract and a recognition of the power (*potentia*) (and simultaneously the right) of the multitude. Negri maintains that in the final chapters of the *Tractatus Theologico-Politicus*, Spinoza makes the decisive move in rejecting the utopia of ideal and substantial constitution and abandoning the problem of the dialectical mediation of the social contract, in order to reorient his work towards a conception of ontological "constitution" or of a physical and dynamic "composition." This move in Spinoza's work completely renews the question of the relation between the individual and the community.

The structural feature of the system of the *Ethics* that Negri identifies as determining the separation of the first two parts of the *Ethics* (I–II) from the last three parts (III–V), and therefore of the first from the second foundation, is the role of the attributes in Spinoza's thought. Negri makes the same interpretation of the attributes as Hegel. However, in doing so, they each come to opposing

---

32. *Ibid.*, xii.

conclusions about the role of the attributes in Spinoza's thought. Rather than concluding that this amounts to the insufficiency of the Spinozist point of view of philosophy, as Hegel does, Negri identifies the doctrine of the attributes with the first foundation, and argues that the tensions in the *Tractatus Theologico-Politicus* led to the necessity of overcoming this point of view. He maintains that the attributes start to resemble simple irrelevant contours within the framework of Spinoza's ontology. Negri dismisses the real, objective explication of the notion of attribute, and opts instead for their removal from the system entirely. By doing so, Negri splits the Spinozist perspective in two: into a purely intellectual, ascetic project (corresponding to the first foundation) on the one hand, and a materialist project (corresponding to the second foundation) on the other. Dividing Spinoza's major work in two in this way is considered to be a highly controversial move among scholars working in the field of Spinoza studies.[33] This hypothesis, however, is necessary in order for Negri to be able to characterize Spinoza as a materialist. In several later essays, Negri acknowledges that the distinction between the first and second foundations of Spinoza's metaphysics in the *Savage Anomaly* was overstated, but he nevertheless maintains it as an operative distinction in his own work.[34]

The philosophical tensions in the *Tractatus Theologico-Politicus* – the problem of mediation, both in the doctrine of the attributes and of the contract – find their resolution in the materialism of the mature Spinoza (parts III–V of the *Ethics*, together with the unfinished *Tractatus Politicus*), which Negri considers to be a revolutionary materialism based on the constitutive power of the multitude. Negri characterizes the metaphysics of Spinoza's second foundation as a dynamic transformative ontology, which is "founded on the spontaneity of needs and organized by the collective imagination."[35]

With these arguments Negri hopes to have demonstrated the central role of politics in Spinoza's philosophy. Indeed he maintains that Spinoza's thought is an example of how politics intervenes "in" philosophy, that is, from the interior, as distinct from "on" philosophy, from the outside. The enduring point that Negri picks up from the French Spinozists and develops to its logical extreme is that the *Ethics*, despite its manifest content, is already inhabited by a political preoccupation, even if this remains relatively unspoken. This preoccupation, he maintains, allows it to overcome the limits imposed by its initial problematic.

---

33. See Macherey, *Avec Spinoza*, 245–70; Alexandre Matheron, "*L'Anomalie sauvage* d'Antonio Negri," *Cahiers Spinoza* 4 (1982–83).
34. See Antonio Negri, *Subversive Spinoza*, Timothy S. Murphy (ed.) (Manchester: Manchester University Press, 2004), 101.
35. Negri, *The Savage Anomaly*, xxii.

V. BALIBAR

In *Spinoza and Politics*, Balibar continues the line of investigation established by his recent colleagues in French Spinoza studies, advocating the inseparability of Spinoza's metaphysics from his politics. However, Balibar begins with Spinoza's political works and from this starting-point aims to produce a coherent account of Spinoza's work as a whole. The result is a more rigorous engagement with the Althusserian problematic of the conjuncture between Spinoza's metaphysics and his politics. Like Negri, he maintains that each of Spinoza's texts should be understood as engagements with specific historical, political, and philosophical developments. However, Balibar investigates in far greater detail than earlier commentators the political and historical developments of the Dutch Republic in the latter half of the seventeenth century. He characterizes Spinoza's political works as a working through of the conflicts constitutive of liberal political theory. He argues that "the TTP could be seen as one great negative argument, a *reductio ad absurdum*."[36] In the *Tractatus Theologico-Politicus*, Spinoza announces that right is coextensive with power (*potentia*), and that "if the rights-powers of individuals do not combine harmoniously, civil society will be destroyed."[37] Balibar argues that this is "why men most often establish and respect rules by which their individual powers are combined."[38]

The most effective rule is that specified in the *Tractatus Theologico-Politicus*, which advocates the total freedom of expression, limited only (but rigorously) by the need to guarantee obedience to the law (TTP: XX). The problem of the *Tractatus Theologico-Politicus* is how to establish a state that can take advantage of the whole active potential of all its citizens, while at the same time securing their freedom of thought, the only one of their rights that Spinoza considers to be inalienable.

For Balibar, as a result of the political developments in the Netherlands after 1672, Spinoza's interest in the problem of freedom in the *Tractatus Theologico-Politicus* is attenuated in favor of the problem of security in the *Tractatus Politicus*. Balibar argues that this is reflected in the latter parts of the *Ethics*, by the tension between the affective, or passional, and the rational grounds for "sociability" (EIVP37D). As Balibar argues, reason, for Spinoza, does not need to master or transcend the affects or emotions in order to be effective. Instead, the traditional opposition between reason and the emotions is displaced by Spinoza with the difference between active and passive affects. While active affects increase the power of the body to act and simultaneously the power of

---

36. Étienne Balibar, *Spinoza and Politics*, Peter Snowdon (trans.) (London: Verso, 1998), 117.
37. *Ibid.*
38. *Ibid.*

the mind to think, passive affects or passions diminish our power to think and to act. The struggle to increase our power to act, "far from pitting us against [other] individuals, as if power were a possession to be fought over, leads us to unite with them to increase our power."[39] This marks the emergence of the multitude or mass on the political stage. It is in the *Tractatus Politicus* that Spinoza takes his postulates concerning power in the *Tractatus Theologico-Politicus* to their logical conclusions. In the *Tractatus Politicus*, the idea of a social contract is no longer one of the foundations of the state. In its place Spinoza offers a description of the process by which individuals with their natural right, that is, their power (*potentia*), come together to create "a *collective individual*, that is, the State as an individual of individuals."[40] Balibar maintains that "this collective individual has a 'body,' which is produced by the combination of the bodies of each and every one" of the individuals of which it is composed. And, in conformity with Spinoza's metaphysics, he insists the there is an *idea* of this body. This idea is the representation of the body either in the imagination, as "the expression of the collective passions," or in reason, as "the condition of effective decision (that is, government)."[41]

The inquiry into the conditions of freedom in *Tractatus Theologico-Politicus* is extended in the *Tractatus Politicus* to the question of how it can be guaranteed under different types of political regime. The security of the citizens of a state from internal conflict, which Spinoza considers to be the greatest threat to the body politic, is guaranteed only "when it is able to constitute itself as a stable individuality."[42] If these conditions are met, then the state can be characterized as "the collective author of every individual action that is in conformity with the law."[43]

Unlike Negri, who focuses on the positive, affirmative aspects of the multitude, Balibar insists on the aporetic character of Spinoza's reflections on the multitude, which he describes as a "mass":

> How can consensus be produced since the matter of politics is not constituted of isolated individuals but of a *mass*, whose most frequent passion is fear, and to whom everyone belongs, rulers and ruled alike? For a mass, in this sense is a fearful thing, not only to those who govern, but even to itself.[44]

---

39. *Ibid.*, xix.
40. *Ibid.*, 116.
41. *Ibid.*
42. *Ibid.*, 117.
43. *Ibid.*, 118.
44. *Ibid.*, 119.

Balibar emphasizes that there is a despairing gap between a mass ideally free and reasonable, and a really ignorant and "terrible crowd, when without fear" (TP: VII, 27). The point for Balibar is that the mass does not have an atemporal essence in Spinoza; it rather is a variable power (*potentia multitudinis*), an always unfinished process. Balibar also maintains that the mass behaves as a crowd within a precise institutional framework. The collective response to natural affects that are not easily avoidable are determined by social structures or institutions that use it to establish their own operations of Power (*potestas*).

For Balibar, then, the political question in Spinoza's work is: which institutions reduce men to being only masses, crowds? The response is that, in theory, every type of regime can have this effect. While Spinoza does assert that an effective democracy would be "the most stable" state, that is, would combine the greatest possible freedom and equality with the greatest possible security, he fails to demonstrate this assertion, because the *Tractatus Politicus* remains unfinished. Balibar maintains that rather than attempting to complete Spinoza's theory of democracy, the conclusion that we should draw from the state of the unfinished *Tractatus Politicus* should rather be that Spinoza has provided a "theory of *democratization* that is valid for every regime."[45]

VI. MOREAU

Moreau also considers Spinoza's works to exhibit a remarkable consistency, and in *Spinoza: L'Expérience et l'éternité*, he aims to demonstrate the systematic unity of Spinoza's thought. However, rather than beginning with Spinoza's political work, Moreau turns to the enigmatic fifth part of the *Ethics*. Moreau constructs his reading of Spinoza around the scholium of EVP23, where Spinoza claims that "we feel and know by experience that we are eternal." Moreau considers this claim to bring together all the difficulties of interpretation of the fifth part of the *Ethics*, and to be the key to the relation between the *Ethics* and *all* of Spinoza's other work. Moreau claims that this scholium, and a similar passage from Spinoza's correspondence with Simon de Vries, indicates that experience has an essential role to play in Spinoza's thought. Moreau maintains that this notion of experience has been neglected by scholars working in the field of Spinoza studies, as a result of it either being reduced to scientific experimentation, or marginalized along with, and as a necessary component of, imagination and error. Habitually, the logic of Spinoza's absolute rationalism is reduced to the geometrical method, which is solely represented as a deductive demonstration.

---

45. *Ibid.*, 121.

In *Spinoza: L'Expérience et l'éternité*, Moreau proposes to reevaluate the status of experience in Spinoza's thought.

Experientia is not opposed to reason; it is rather the mode of intervention of reason in the fields where reason does not have direct access. It is one of the principle forms of accounting for reality. It is also an essential means for understanding Spinoza's reflections on language, "our relation to words and to texts, to the passions, to the figure of the State, to circumstantial events, and to the historical destiny of the unforeseen or unexpected."[46] It is experience that provides the basis for our relations with others and the imitation of affects, and it allows what cannot yet be known of another mode to be accumulated. We have experience of what eludes the grasp of reason, and of how reason can neutralize inadequation and the partiality associated with the common life. Indeed Moreau engages with the often neglected problem of Spinoza's epistemology, that is, the problem of conceptualizing inadequate, or, as Spinoza also describes them, partial ideas, and the role they play in the development of adequate ideas of reason. Experience is thus not foreign or extrinsic to Spinoza's rationalism, but informs our relationship with the world, albeit under the guidance of reason.

One of the concepts that Moreau develops in his analysis is that of the *ingenium*, which is the collective term for the complex of passions of an individual. Each individual is dominated by a particular passion which is determined by its biographical and environmental context, and is therefore different for each individual. It accounts for why, despite all individual human beings being equal, they have diverse capacities both for knowledge and for practical activity. Moreau applies this criterion of the *ingenium* not only at the level of the individual, but also at the collective level. He considers the *ingenium* to mark the point of difference between a singular individual and a community. *Ingenia* vary not only from one individual to another, but also from one society to another, and throughout history. Moreau maintains that it is possible to think the individuality of a people in order to understand the form taken by its legislation. The laws of each state are adapted to the *ingenium* of its people. The *ingenium* therefore contributes to define the proper figure of the state.

While Spinoza does not develop a theory of the *ingenium*, he does mention in passing the traits characteristic of the *ingenium* of the Romans, the Greeks, and the ancient nations, including the Hebrews, Egyptians, and Babylonians respectively. By attributing an *ingenium* to each people, Moreau follows the suggestion of the *Tractatus Theologico-Politicus* and provides a history of the constitution of different legislations by analyzing the relations between the *ingenia* of each people and their systems of law.

---

46. Pierre-François Moreau, *Spinoza: L'Expérience et l'éternité* (Paris: Presses Universitaires de France, 1994), 522.

***

Since 1968, Guéroult's philological renewal of the history of philosophy, together with the renewed importance of Spinoza's political thought, have simultaneously contributed to enrich the resurgence of interest and productivity in Spinoza studies. The Spinoza that is engaged with in the field of Spinoza studies today is no longer solely post-Cartesian, Hegelian, or that of the German Romantics, but also the new ontological interpretation of Spinoza instigated by Matheron and Deleuze. All Spinozist research, in its great diversity, has developed since then in the wake of this interpretive innovation, particularly in France and Italy, but also in Germany and the United States. Spinoza's metaphysics, which had traditionally been the major focus of Spinoza studies, while not being relinquished, has since been displaced by interest in Spinoza's ethics and politics, and by attempts to provide systematic readings of Spinoza's work as a whole, including his political work. This new work on Spinoza's political philosophy is testament to the ongoing resonance of French Spinozism and continues to provide new possibilities for engaging with debates in ethical and political philosophy, both from the point of view of the history of philosophy, and from the point of view of contributing to contemporary ethical and political thought.[47]

MAJOR WORKS

Alquié, Ferdinand. *Le Rationalisme de Spinoza*. Paris: Presses Universitaires de France, 1981.

Alquié, Ferdinand. *Leçons sur Spinoza*. Paris: La Table ronde, 2003.

---

47. See, for example, the work of Moira Gatens, Warren Montag, and François Zourabichvili. In *Collective Imaginings: Spinoza, Past and Present* (London: Routledge, 1999), Gatens and Genevieve Lloyd reconsider the role of the imagination, as developed in the *Ethics*, both historically and from a contemporary political point of view. The book demonstrates how an appreciation of Spinoza's philosophy can form the basis of a constructive but critical engagement with contemporary concerns. See also Gatens, *Imaginary Bodies: Ethics, Power and Corporeality* (New York: Routledge, 1996). In *Bodies, Masses, Power: Spinoza and his Contemporaries* (New York: Verso, 1999), Montag makes a contribution to the ongoing discussion of radical democracy by drawing on Althusser's remarks about the connection between the theory of ideology and Spinoza's philosophy, as well as the work on Spinoza by Negri, Balibar, and Macherey, to formulate the core problem of his analysis: that there can be no liberation of the mind without a liberation of the body, and, therefore, that there can be no liberation of the individual without collective liberation. Montag thereby extends Spinoza's materialism in an attempt to characterize the affect of joy as a force of action that leads toward individual liberation. In *Le Conservatisme paradoxal de Spinoza: Enfance et royauté* (Paris: Presses Universitaires de France, 2002), Zourabichvili undertakes a systematic explication of Spinoza's theory of relations, centered on the much-debated question of the transformation of modes; and in *Spinoza, une physique de la pensée* (Paris: Presses Universitaires de France, 2002), he undertakes to analyze a "physics of thought" in the philosophy of Spinoza by determining the features of the laws of thought which are the correlates of the laws of bodies.

Balibar, Étienne. *Spinoza et la politique*. Paris: Presses Universitaires de France, 1985. Published in English as *Spinoza and Politics*, translated by Peter Snowdon. London: Verso, 1998.

Deleuze, Gilles. *Spinoza et le problème de l'expression*. Paris: Éditions de Minuit, 1968. Published in English as *Expressionism in Philosophy, Spinoza*, translated by Martin Joughin. New York: Zone Books, 1992.

Deleuze, Gilles. *Spinoza, philosophie pratique*. Paris: Éditions de Minuit, 1981. Published in English as *Spinoza, Practical Philosophy*, translated by Robert Hurley. San Francisco: City Lights Books, 1988.

Guéroult, Martial. *Spinoza I: Dieu (Éthique, I)*. Paris: Aubier-Montaigne, 1968.

Guéroult, Martial. *Spinoza II: L'Âme (Éthique, II)*. Paris: Aubier-Montaigne, 1974.

Macherey, Pierre. *Hegel ou Spinoza*. Paris: Presses Universitaires de France, 1979. Published in English as *Hegel or Spinoza*, translated by Susan M. Ruddick. Minneapolis, MN: University of Minnesota Press, 2011.

Macherey, Pierre. *Avec Spinoza: Études sur la doctrine et l'histoire du spinozisme*. Paris: Presses Universitaires de France, 1992.

Macherey, Pierre. *Introduction à l'Ethique de Spinoza*, vols I–V. Paris: Presses Universitaires de France, 1994–8.

Matheron, Alexandre. *Individu et communauté chez Spinoza*. Paris: Éditions de Minuit, 1969.

Matheron, Alexandre. *Le Christ et le salut des ignorants chez Spinoza*. Paris: Aubier-Montaigne, 1971.

Moreau, Pierre-François. *Spinoza: L'Expérience et l'éternité*. Paris: Presses Universitaires de France, 1994.

Negri, Antonio. *L'anomalia selvaggia: Saggio su potere e potenza in Baruch Spinoza*. Milan: Feltrinelli, 1981. Published in French as *L'Anomalie sauvage: Puissance et pouvoir chez Spinoza*, translated by François Matheron. Paris: Presses Universitaires de France, 1982. Published in English as *The Savage Anomaly: The Power of Spinoza's Metaphysics and Politics*, translated by Michael Hardt. Minneapolis, MN: University of Minnesota Press, 1991.

Negri, Antonio. *Subversive Spinoza*. Edited by Timothy S. Murphy. Manchester: Manchester University Press, 2004.

8

RADICAL DEMOCRACY

Lasse Thomassen

The term "radical democracy" refers to new ways of thinking about democratic politics beyond essentialist foundations. Radical democrats question not only existing liberal democratic institutions, but also the idea of essential universal foundations on which democracy could be based. Inspired by poststructuralist theories of language and identity, and by poststructuralists such as Michel Foucault, Jacques Derrida, and Jacques Lacan, a number of thinkers have attempted to rethink democracy along radical lines from about 1980 onward. These radical democrats include, among others, Ernesto Laclau, Chantal Mouffe, William E. Connolly, and Slavoj Žižek. Inspired by poststructuralist theories of language and identity, these authors have sought to rethink what radical politics means after poststructuralism.[1]

What, then, is radical democracy, and what is *radical* about it? We can think of the "radical" of radical democracy in two related ways. First, we may note the etymological root of the word, namely the Latin *"radix,"* root. The radical, then, pertains to the root, to what is fundamental. If we are to think of radical democracy as aiming at the roots and the foundations of democracy, the idea is not to provide a new foundation for democracy, for instance by showing that past and present foundations (natural rights, utility, species being, and so on)

---

1. For a good introduction to radical democracy, see Aletta J. Norval, "Radical Democracy," in *Encyclopedia of Democratic Thought*, P. Barry Clarke and Joe Foweraker (eds) (London: Routledge, 2001). See also the contributions to the following edited volumes: Chantal Mouffe (ed.), *Dimensions of Radical Democracy: Pluralism and Citizenship* (London: Verso, 1992); Lars Tønder and Lasse Thomassen (eds), *Radical Democracy: Politics between Abundance and Lack* (Manchester: Manchester University Press, 2005); and David Trend (ed.), *Radical Democracy: Identity, Citizenship and the State* (London: Routledge, 1996).

are inadequate and need to be substituted with a new and better foundation (say, rational discourse). That is, the aim is not to root democracy more firmly. Rather, the radical of radical democracy refers to the questioning of foundations. Thus, the question becomes what democracy looks like without foundations, without being rooted in something universal and ahistorical. If radical today also has the connotation of extreme, then the extremism of radical democracy is to push beyond any foundation. If this is how we understand the radical of radical democracy, then the question "What *is* radical democracy?" cannot be answered with reference to a foundation, root, or essence. This does not mean that there are no roots, only that those roots are contingent and, thus, contestable. Contestation of roots and foundations is central to radical democracy, but these contestations will always be partial and local.

There is a second, related sense of radical. When talking about politics or democracy, radical often implies transcending the present state of imperfectness of democracy. Thus radical politics becomes associated with a revolutionary politics that will take us to the other side, to a perfect democracy and society, as for instance in certain Marxist accounts of the communist revolution and society. Here radicalism would be the solution – once and for all – to the problems of democracy today (alienation, inequality, and so on). The radical of radical democracy does not imply this, however. This does not mean that we should accept the present state of things, or that only incremental changes are possible, changes that do not interfere with the very framework governing contemporary capitalist and liberal societies. That framework is also at stake with radical democracy, but transcending that framework will not necessarily have the form of a revolution, and radical democracy cannot guarantee that all alienation, inequality, and disagreement will disappear.

On the contrary, radical democrats hold that these issues will not simply disappear with the introduction of radical democracy. Radical democracy will itself involve exclusions and inequalities of various sorts. More fundamentally, we can think of radical democracy with a Derridean phrase as only possible as impossible. This means that radical democracy is not a regime with a set of institutions, procedures, and practices that can be realized. It cannot – with another phrase from Jacques Derrida – be present, even as a future present. It is, and will remain, "to come."[2] Radical democracy is not possible in the sense that it can be known or realized; it is only possible as impossible, that is, as incomplete and imperfect – in short, as "to come."

We can link this back to the first sense of radical as having no foundation. The question "What is radical democracy?" is an essential part of radical democracy.

---

2. Jacques Derrida, *Specters of Marx: The State of the Debt, the Work of Mourning, & the New International*, Peggy Kamuf (trans.) (London: Routledge, 1994), 64–5.

Not only are there *de facto* theoretical and empirical disputes over what radical democracy means and implies, but radical democracy is constituted by dispute and disagreement. If "What is radical democracy?" is part of the essence of radical democracy, then answers to the question "What is radical democracy?" can be only partial and provisional and can never be exhaustive. Thus, we can never rest content that now we know what it is, or now we have implemented it or even with the thought that we will someday realize radical democracy or know what it is. It is in this sense that radical democracy is possible only as impossible, as never present but always "to come." Thus, radical democracy is difficult – even impossible – to define, even if this is also what I have just tried to do. This difficulty is reflected in the problems others have with radical democracy: it appears elusive, and it is not always clear what is radical about it.[3]

In the following, I shed more light on radical democracy, first by situating radical democracy in relation to poststructuralism and then in relation to competing approaches within contemporary political philosophy. Subsequently I look at two representatives of radical democratic thought –Laclau and Connolly – and I try to tease out some of the differences between different theorists of radical democracy. I conclude with some remarks on the future of radical democratic thought.

I. POSTSTRUCTURALIST THEORIES OF RADICAL DEMOCRACY AND EARLIER RADICAL APPROACHES TO DEMOCRACY

The points raised above about the nature of the radicalism of radical democracy helps us to understand the differences between poststructuralist approaches to radical democracy (the topic of this chapter) and earlier approaches to radical democracy. In the eighteenth century, Jean-Jacques Rousseau criticized representative democracy – a critique echoed by republicans – in the name of an ideal of direct democracy, where the General Will rules. While radical democrats are sympathetic to the Rousseauian critique of liberal democracy for not addressing deeper issues of inequality and for the lack of a theory of community in liberal theory, they nonetheless have problems with Rousseau's account of democracy.

They object, first, to the ideal of a pure or perfect democracy with no division and to the ideal of a self-transparent and self-identical demos; these ideals, which are summed up in the Rousseauian General Will, are potentially dangerous, they argue. Second, they object to the very possibility that a new citizen and a new form of citizenship will solve the problems of modern society

---

3. See, for instance, Andrew Knops, "Agonism as Deliberation – On Mouffe's Theory of Democracy," *Journal of Political Philosophy* 15(1) (2007).

once and for all. Together these two points can be expressed as an objection to what Derrida calls the metaphysics of presence: for Rousseau, the people is identical to itself when (literally) coming together and speaking in the name of itself. The will of the people is present, and the people is One. This is why Derrida and Laclau have argued that representation, rather than the presence of the people, is constitutive.[4]

Similarly, poststructuralist radical democrats distinguish themselves from another earlier radical democrat: Karl Marx. Marx criticized the superficiality of liberal citizenship rights as well as the liberal idea of the disembedded, property-owning individual who stands opposed to other, similar individuals. This critique was carried out in the name of a critical ideal of species being and in the name of a teleological conception of history, of which the communist society was supposed to be the end point realizing human emancipation.

Radical democrats are equally critical of a certain superficiality of liberal democracy, especially the ways in which liberal citizenship abstracts from socio-economic inequalities and from gender, ethnicity, and so on, while at the same time reproducing inequalities and relations of domination. What is problematic in Marxism, however, is the view that all alienation and inequality can be overcome through a revolution of the present. In addition, radical democrats are skeptical of the foundation of the Marxist argument in a conception of human essence, in a teleological History and in the reduction of identity, consciousness, ideology, and the state to economic and class relations. Thus, radical democrats are critical of the radicalism of Marxist radical democracy in the two senses delineated above: the search for new foundations and the view that alienation and inequality can be transcended. Laclau and Mouffe sum up this part of their radical democratic and post-Marxist objection to Marxism in the following way:

> What is now in crisis is a whole conception of socialism, which rests upon the ontological centrality of the working class, upon the role of Revolution, with a capital "r", as the founding moment in the transition from one type of society to another, and upon the illusory prospect of a perfectly unitary and homogeneous collective that will render pointless the moment of politics.[5]

Finally, radical democrats are critical of the Marxist view of politics and democracy as superficial, that is, as merely secondary to and derived from the

---

4. Jacques Derrida, *Of Grammatology*, Gayatri Chakravorty Spivak (trans.), 2nd ed. (Baltimore, MD: Johns Hopkins Press, 1997), pt II, ch. 4; and Ernesto Laclau, *Emancipation(s)* (London: Verso, 1996), ch. 6.
5. Ernesto Laclau and Chantal Mouffe, *Hegemony and Socialist Strategy: Towards a Radical Democratic Politics*, 2nd ed. (London: Verso, 2001), 2.

economic base. For radical democrats, politics and democracy are important in their own right. Indeed, they argue that politics is constitutive, and they think of politics not as a regional category (as opposed to the economy, for instance), but as the very moment of the institution of the social (including the economy and what we usually refer to as politics: political institutions, identities, and behavior). It is in this sense that we can also say that representation is constitutive. That is, for radical democrats, politics is not a reflection of something more fundamental (and present); rather, the political refers to the moments in which sociopolitical institutions and practices are instituted or challenged. If there are roots, they are not prior to politics, but instituted – and challenged – by politics.

II. THE HISTORICAL BACKGROUND TO THE EMERGENCE OF RADICAL DEMOCRACY

The radical democratic critique of earlier radical approaches must also be seen against the background of events and developments at the end of the twentieth century. From the 1960s onwards, new social movements and struggles over identity gained increasing importance within mainstream politics. The civil rights movement, the student protests and the protests against the Vietnam War as well as the women's movement, the environmental movement, and the antinuclear protests all challenged the Marxist emphasis on class as the organizing principle of revolutionary consciousness and emancipatory struggles. Class gradually lost its empirical importance as well as its theoretical centrality to the diagnosis of, and solution to, the problems of contemporary capitalist society. In this light, the question became how to think emancipation without tying it to class. This is another sense in which poststructuralist radical democrats are also often post-Marxists.

Another problem faced by Marxists at the end of the twentieth century was the nonappearance of the revolution despite the developed character of capitalism in the West. In fact, the late 1970s and the 1980s saw the emergent hegemony of neoliberalism personified by Ronald Reagan and Margaret Thatcher. Again, radicals were faced by the question of strategy in the face of neoliberal hegemony and the inadequacy of Marxist analyses and strategies.

Finally, the fall of the Soviet bloc and "real existing socialism" reflected the hegemony of capitalism and liberal democracy and a general sense of "the end of history."[6] Again, this was no doubt an important event in terms of rethinking the strategy of the Left, although it must be remembered that most of the Left

---

6. See Derrida's critique of Francis Fukuyama's thesis of "the end of history" in *Specters of Marx*, ch. 2.

had already broken with Soviet-style communism after Stalinism and the Soviet invasions of Hungary and Czechoslovakia in 1956 and 1968 respectively. The fall of Soviet communism was, of course, not the end of history, but instead introduced a new period with new challenges that required both theoretical and political responses: the emergence of nationalism and xenophobia in Europe and beyond, the rise of religious fundamentalism, the question of the European Union, globalization and the alter-globalization movements, and so on. As Laclau and Mouffe write: "To reread Marxist theory in the light of contemporary problems necessarily involves deconstructing the central categories of that theory."[7]

III. THE POSTSTRUCTURALIST INFLUENCE: IDENTITY, LANGUAGE, AND UNIVERSALITY

The poststructuralist conceptions of language, meaning, and identity have been central to the development of new theories of radical democracy. Given the radical democratic critique of the status and centrality of class as a category, this is a useful starting-point for explaining the poststructuralist influence on radical democracy.

For radical democrats, identity is not the reflection of an essence, for instance one's class position. Class is not a transcendental signified that holds together a set of otherwise disparate identities that can be anchored in an analysis of their class position within the relations of production. Here we can think of identity in terms of the Saussurean sign and the poststructuralist deconstruction of it. Meaning and identity are constituted through relations of difference between signs (or rather, signifiers). That is, we should understand identities not as self-contained, but as relational and constituted through relations to others rather than reflections of an underlying essence or structure.

Identity is constituted within the web of signification, and as such we might think of identity as the effect of the system of differences. However, this comes with the important (*post*-structuralist) qualification that the structure of the differential relations is never closed or sutured; rather, it is inherently unstable and open to change through the de- and resignification of the signifiers. In other words, the system of differences is marked by some undecidability. For instance, if identity is constituted through relations of difference, we may ask how the system of differences as a whole and the limits of the system are constituted. The answer to that question is undecidable because the whole and its limits would have to be signified by something at once the whole and part of the whole, and

---

7. Laclau and Mouffe, *Hegemony and Socialist Strategy*, ix.

at once inside and outside the system. Given that the whole is involved in the signification of each part, every particular identity is marked by this undecidability. Hence, any identity is partly fluid.

Theorists of radical democracy think of identity and the subject in nonessentialist terms. Identities are inherently unstable, although they may have become more or less naturalized. Indeed, we may think about identity not as identity – that is, as something stable and achieved – but as continuous identifications that "fail" in the sense that they never become stable and self-contained.

We do not have simple pluralism in the sense of dispersed identities, nor do we have a simple plurality of identities as if each one of us were the aggregate of more than one identity. This pluralism is a fact of social life, but there is more to identity than this. No identity – even as the aggregate of different identities – is ever One. Identity is always subverted, for instance by a lack (Lacan and Laclau) or by the fact that they are constituted in flows of materiality that cannot be arrested (Deleuze and Connolly).

As a result, radical democrats focus on processes of identification and subjectivation: Which subjects are formed and how? How do these subjects relate to other subjects? What are the implications for citizenship of the ways in which subjects are formed? And so forth. A good example is Connolly's work on pluralism. Connolly talks about processes of pluralization – rather than simple pluralism – to refer to the ways in which identities are constantly being created and undone, processes Connolly believes that we must actively encourage through, among other things, agonistic respect.[8]

At this point, it is useful to return to the very beginning of the essay. I argued that one aspect of the radicalism of radical democracy is that it does not claim that radical democracy has an essence. That is, the question "What is radical democracy?" is part and parcel of radical democracy, and this will subvert any definition of it from within. We can connect this to the poststructuralist conception of meaning. Radical democracy – what it "is" and means – is not the reflection of some underlying structure of history or essence of man. Rather, radical democracy must be seen in relation to other forms of democracy and other regimes, and it is not one thing at all times; it is an essential part of radical democracy that it can be contested and resignified.

Poststructuralists talk a lot about language, and poststructuralism is part of the linguistic turn in philosophy.[9] However, it is important to make two points here with implications for radical democracy. First, structures are never

---

8. William E. Connolly, *The Ethos of Pluralization* (Minneapolis, MN: University of Minnesota Press, 1995), chs 1 and 6.

*9. For a discussion of the "linguistic turn" in continental philosophy, see the essay by Claire Colebrook in *The History of Continental Philosophy: Volume 6*.

entirely open and undetermined. We can talk of partly sedimented structures or discourses. Identities, for instance, can be de- and resignified, but they must be partly determined and fixed in order for us to be able to talk about identities in the first place. Similarly with meaning and society: complete plasticity is impossible, and there must be some fixation of meaning and of structures, for instance a partial determination of what citizenship means. The important questions are, then, what determinations dominate, and how we relate to them. Second, it is important to note that poststructuralists and radical democrats are not idealists. Rather, they treat the social as consisting of meaningful practices (texts in Derrida's terminology and discourses in Laclau's terminology). Radical democracy, then, also concerns what we usually think of as "material," especially the economic sphere, and it is not limited to the creation of new forms of identities (which of course have their own materiality).

On the basis of poststructuralist arguments, radical democrats eschew any form of essentialism and foundationalism. We may add that they are skeptical of grand narratives, to use Jean-François Lyotard's phrase.[10] For instance, radical democrats are skeptical of the Marxist grand narrative of emancipation and its links to essentialism and teleology; and they are skeptical of the Enlightenment grand narrative of Man, for instance the way it is expressed in the notion of human rights based on human nature. However, this does not stop radical democrats from talking about emancipation, human rights, and other "universals," although they have a different understanding of these. For instance, they think of emancipation – like democracy – as possible only as impossible. That is, we never achieve full emancipation (and autonomy, nonalienation, and so on), and emancipation is not a critical ideal, not even a counterfactual ideal. Rather, we have continuous emancipation*s* in the plural as continual processes of becoming rather than fixed states of being.[11]

With Judith Butler and Laclau, we can say that, for radical democrats, universals such as emancipation are the result of contingent significations.[12] They are not ahistorical or simply handed down to us as given, and therefore the task is to do genealogies of their conditions of emergence and to resignify them in new ways. For radical democrats, this resignification of universals must of course take place without founding them again in a new essence, teleology, and so on – in short, a new *radix*, root. Importantly, while radical democrats argue

---

10. Jean-François Lyotard, *The Postmodern Condition: A Report on Knowledge*, Geoff Bennington and Brian Massumi (trans.) (Minneapolis, MN: University of Minnesota Press, 1984), 37–41.

11. Laclau, *Emancipation(s)*, ch. 1.

12. See the exchanges between Butler and Laclau in "The Uses of Equality," *Diacritics* 27(1) (1997); and Judith Butler *et al.*, *Contingency, Hegemony, Universality: Contemporary Dialogues on the Left* (London: Verso, 2000).

that universals are open to resignification, there is no guarantee that it will be a progressive, leftist resignification that will be the dominant one.

IV. RADICAL DEMOCRACY AND CONTEMPORARY DEMOCRATIC THEORY

Radical democrats often distinguish their position through a critique of contemporary liberalism, for instance John Rawls's political liberalism. Like Marxists and republicans, radical democrats are critical of the liberal notion of the subject and, by implication, the liberal conception of the citizen.[13]

For radical democrats, one of the problems with the liberal subject is that it is a disembedded and disembodied individual, a kind of abstract individual outside historical and socioeconomic context and without a (gendered, racial, etc.) body. Liberals thereby overlook the ways in which subjects are constituted in the first place. In addition, they reify a certain kind of subject because the liberal subject is not just something shared by all subjects, abstracting from their particularities (as a thin notion of human nature, for instance); rather, the liberal subject is a particular kind of subject, historically associated with certain experiences and constituencies (the property-owning male, for instance).

Another criticism of the liberal subject concerns the rationality of the subject. First of all, radical democrats point out that the liberal subject is endowed with a certain kind of rationality, which is linked to the individual nature of the subject. It is the rationality of an individual standing apart from and facing the physical and social world in a relation of instrumental reason. Theorists of radical democracy are critical of rationality more generally, and especially of the grand narrative of Enlightenment reason. This is not just because we are facing a complex world and cannot have knowledge about everything; more fundamentally, on the basis of the poststructuralist critique of the subject and universals, radical democrats argue that reason is unable to establish its own foundations.

These criticisms of the liberal subject can be drawn together as a critique of autonomy understood as rational self-legislation. Radical democrats do not necessarily reject autonomy as a value, but they are critical of a liberal conception of autonomy centered on the atomistic individual. In addition, as is the case with emancipation, we must think of autonomy as possible only as impossible, that is, as always implicated with some heteronomy because it cannot establish

---

13. For good examples, see William E. Connolly, *Identity/Difference: Democratic Negotiations of Political Paradox* (Ithaca, NY: Cornell University Press, 1991), ch. 3, and *Why I Am Not a Secularist* (Minneapolis, MN: University of Minnesota Press, 1999), 62–70; Chantal Mouffe, *The Return of the Political* (London: Verso, 1993), chs 2 and 3.

its own foundations and conditions of possibility. Again we see how the rejection of foundationalism leads to a rethinking of modern ideals – in this case, autonomy – as something that must be renegotiated again and again without ever being fully achieved.

The radical democratic critique of the liberal subject is reflected in the critique of the liberal notion of citizenship centered as it is on the individual, self-interested bearer of rights. Rights, radical democrats argue, do not exhaust the political. Rather, we must also look at how subjects are constituted, and especially how new subjects are constituted, subjects that may challenge existing rights categories. Again, radical democrats do not simply reject rights or citizenship, but argue that a profound rethinking of these is necessary.

More generally, radical democrats do not simply reject liberal institutions (the rule of law, separation of powers, and so on). Those institutions have their value; for radical democrats, this is especially so in the light of the experiences with twentieth-century totalitarianism. Therefore we cannot reject liberal institutions as meaningless and inconsequential. Yet radical democrats insist on the need to be able to contest the liberal institutional framework of rights, citizenship, the rule of law, and so on. Among other things, this is in order to open up the possibility that new and hitherto excluded and marginalized constituencies gain a place within society on a par with the (so far) normal subjects. Thus, radical democracy is also an exercise in denaturalizing and denormalizing what we take as given, including our conceptions of the subject and of citizenship.[14]

To sum up, radical democrats want to radicalize liberal values and institutions in two different ways. They want, first, to deepen and extend those values and institutions (for instance, to extend equality to ever more areas in society); and, second, they want to rethink those values and institutions without foundations. They see these values and institutions not as natural or ahistorical, but as political all the way down, and in this way they stress their contestability. In short, theorists of radical democracy seek to repoliticize what has been depoliticized.

Deliberative democrats, such as Jürgen Habermas,[15] share some of the criticisms of liberalism raised by radical democrats. Thus, deliberative democrats believe that identity and interests are not given to the political process but constituted in it, and they also believe that the subject is not reducible to the self-interested and atomistic individual. Nonetheless, radical democrats are critical of deliberative democracy for some of the same reasons that they are critical of liberalism. First, radical democrats object to the emphasis on rationality and autonomy, even if these are understood by deliberative democrats in inter-

---

14. See especially Connolly, *The Ethos of Pluralization*, ch. 3.
*15. For a discussion of Jürgen Habermas, see the essay by Christopher F. Zurn in *The History of Continental Philosophy: Volume 6*.

subjectivist terms. For instance, theorists of radical democracy have criticized Habermas's idea of the forceless force of the good argument. Radical democrats have also objected to the emphasis on procedures because they believe that deliberative democrats thereby risk reducing politics to a matter of the right procedure.

In general terms, radical democrats are skeptical of the deliberative democratic conception of dialogue and deliberation. For radical democrats, communication is never transparent, but always marked by relations of power and asymmetry. For instance, some subjects are marked in advance as more rational than others, and some reasons as more reasonable than others. Therefore we need to examine the ways in which the space of dialogue and deliberation is constituted in the first place and what kind of practices and subjects have been excluded.

Similarly, radical democrats are skeptical of any consensus, even if it is the outcome of an allegedly rational discourse. This is not to say that radical democrats are necessarily against *any* consensus. For instance, Mouffe talks about a consensus on the principles of liberal democracy, namely liberty and equality for all. But, for her, this is a "conflictual" and temporary consensus, and there is no consensus without exclusion: a consensus is always a particular consensus linked to a particular "we" and, hence, to the exclusion of "them."[16]

Likewise, with regard to consensus, Connolly writes that it is "impossible to participate in discourse without projecting the counterfactual possibility of consensus; but … each attempt to interpret the actual import of that counterfactuality in any concrete setting is also problematical and contestable."[17] Connolly links this to contestability: "if a pluralizing ethos presupposes a 'consensus,' it is mobilized above all around reciprocal appreciation of the contestability of contending presumptions about the fundamental character of being. It is an ironic consensus."[18] As an ironic consensus, it reflects on its own contingency and the exclusions it implies. The alternative is to think of the relation to the other and of the public sphere in agonistic terms, as suggested by Connolly and Mouffe. This, they argue, will make us more attuned to subjects and constituencies that cannot at present be heard within the public sphere, and it underlines the contestability of the rules that constitute the public sphere.[19]

---

16. Chantal Mouffe, *The Democratic Paradox* (London: Verso, 2000), 48.

17. Connolly, *Why I Am Not a Secularist*, 38.

18. Connolly, *The Ethos of Pluralization*, 104. On radical democracy and consensus, see also Adrian Little, "Between Disagreement and Consensus: Unraveling the Democratic Paradox," *Australian Journal of Political Science* 42(1) (2007).

19. See, for instance, Chantal Mouffe, "For an Agonistic Public Sphere," in *Radical Democracy: Politics between Abundance and Lack*, Tønder and Thomassen (eds).

Finally, theorists of radical democracy share the communitarian critique of the liberal disembedded subject and the communitarian emphasis on questions of community and identity as one finds it in Michael Sandel, for instance. However, they have a very different conception of community and identity because they believe that division and disagreement are constitutive. In short, no community is a self-contained whole with clear limits.[20] This is the problem with communitarianism: it risks reifying existing (and past) communal identities. Inspired by poststructuralism, radical democrats do not see communities as closed or self-contained wholes; rather, identities are fluid and situated at the intersection of more than one communal identity.

We can sum up these points against liberal, deliberative, and communitarian approaches in the following way: for theorists of radical democracy, these alternative approaches all in one way or another depoliticize the subject, citizenship, consensus, and communal identities. Radical democracy, then, consists in repoliticizing what has been depoliticized, in showing that what appears to us as natural and ahistorical is in fact contingent, constructed, and contestable.

V. RADICAL DEMOCRACY BETWEEN ABUNDANCE AND LACK

So far, I have focused on poststructuralist radical democratic theory as a whole and distinguished it from earlier radical democratic theory and from competing contemporary approaches. I would now like to focus on debates *within* radical democratic theory. There are different ways to think about the differences between the various radical democratic theorists, although none of the ways of dividing the field entirely exhausts it.

Giorgio Agamben has suggested a distinction between immanence and transcendence as a way to make sense of the differences among contemporary French philosophers.[21] If we apply this distinction to radical democracy, Connolly, Michael Hardt and Antonio Negri (drawing on Spinoza and Deleuze) would represent the immanence side and Laclau and Mouffe (drawing on Derrida and

---

20. Connolly, *The Ethos of Pluralization*, 142–9; Alan Keenan, *Democracy in Question: Democratic Openness in a Time of Political Closure* (Stanford, CA: Stanford University Press, 2003), ch. 4; Mouffe, *The Return of the Political*, ch. 2. On radical democracy and the question of community more generally, see Adrian Little, "Community and Radical Democracy," *Journal of Political Ideologies* 7(3) (2002).

21. Giorgio Agamben, *Potentialities: Collected Essays in Philosophy*, Daniel Heller-Roazen (ed. and trans.) (Stanford, CA: Stanford University Press, 1999). See also William E. Connolly, "Immanence, Abundance, Democracy," in *Radical Democracy: Politics between Abundance and Lack*, Tønder and Thomassen (eds).

Lacan) would represent the transcendence side.[22] Here I will take Hardt and Negri and Laclau as representatives of the two sides.

The difference between Hardt and Negri and Laclau concerns whether an alternative to the present liberal-capitalist order will emerge immanently or requires a moment of transcendence. For Laclau, we need a moment of transcendence, albeit a "failed" transcendence. He understands this transcendence in terms of hegemony where a particular element comes to stand in for the whole, thus coalescing a hegemonic consensus around it, a hegemonic consensus that can oppose and dissolve the current hegemony. Hardt and Negri, on the other hand, believe that countering one hegemony with another reproduces a form of politics historically associated with Lenin and the vanguard (the Communist Party, taking over – but ultimately leaving intact – the state, and so on). For them, change must arise from below, from the multitude, and they find hope in, among other things, the alter-globalization movements. Thus, the immanence/transcendence distinction is not merely philosophical, but has important implications for political strategy.[23]

Another way of making sense of debates within poststructuralist radical democratic thought is through a distinction between abundance and lack.[24] This distinction is not unrelated to the immanence/abundance distinction, and Hardt and Negri (abundance) and Laclau (lack) would fall on opposite sides of the abundance/lack distinction. Here I will use the abundance/lack distinction heuristically to present two particular, but important, views of radical democracy, namely those of Connolly and Laclau and Mouffe.[25] The aim is to identify some of the theoretical and political choices facing radical democracy.

Central to Laclau and Mouffe's work is the category of hegemony, which they rework against its reception within Marxist thought and especially Antonio Gramsci's theory of hegemony.[26] For Laclau and Mouffe, hegemony

---

22. See Michael Hardt and Antonio Negri, *Empire* (Cambridge, MA: Harvard University Press, 2000). See Laclau's critique of Hardt and Negri in Ernesto Laclau, *On Populist Reason* (London: Verso, 2005), 239–44.

23. For an alternative application of Laclau's theory of hegemony to the alter-globalization movement, see Saul Newman, *Unstable Universalities: Poststructuralism and Radical Politics* (Manchester: Manchester University Press, 2007).

24. See Lars Tønder and Lasse Thomassen, "Introduction: Rethinking Radical Democracy Between Abundance and Lack," in *Radical Democracy: Politics between Abundance and Lack*, Tønder and Thomassen (eds), 1–13.

25. For discussions of the works of Connolly and Laclau, see David Campbell and Morton Schoolman (eds), *The New Pluralism: William Connolly and the Contemporary Global Condition* (Durham, NC: Duke University Press, 2008); and Simon Critchley and Oliver Marchart (eds), *Laclau: A Critical Reader* (London: Routledge, 2004).

26. For the theory of hegemony, see Butler *et al.*, *Contingency, Hegemony, Universality*; Ernesto Laclau, *New Reflections on the Revolution of Our Time* (London: Verso, 1990), ch. 1, *Emancipation(s)*, ch. 3, and *On Populist Reason*, chs 4–5; Laclau and Mouffe, *Hegemony and*

is essentially an operation whereby signifiers or demands are articulated into a chain of equivalence with other signifiers or demands. The chain of equivalence is organized around what Laclau calls an empty signifier, which fulfills the central role of keeping together otherwise disparate elements. In other words, the empty signifier represents what is otherwise absent or lacking, namely the community as a whole. There is thus a lacking fullness or being of the community, which could be a national community, a counter-hegemonic project, and so on. Hegemony consists in "filling" this lack. However, the filling of the lack always ultimately fails, and the lack always returns.

Any communal identity is marked by a lack, which it may try to project onto an external enemy (the figure of the Jew or the Islamic terrorist, for example). Similarly, any identity is marked by a lack, which sets in motion identifications with objects – a football club, a national symbol, and so on – that are supposed to fill the lack. Yet, even though this is how my identity is constituted, those identifications always ultimately fail. It follows that any identity is precarious and constantly renegotiated. It should be clear by now how Laclau thinks of hegemony in terms of lack, an idea he takes from Lacanian psychoanalysis.

Radical democracy is one hegemonic project among others. Specifically it consists in radicalizing the principles of liberal democracy, namely, equality and liberty. For Laclau and Mouffe, this radicalization implies deepening and extending equality and liberty and doing so without new foundations. In her work, Mouffe has focused on radical democracy and what she calls agonistic democracy.[27] Mouffe is interested in how the democratic "we" is established. For her, the democratic "we" is established hegemonically, for instance as a radical democratic "we," but importantly the "we" is not a closed whole because it is marked by internal division and differences. It is, thus, a "we" that is always unstable and in the process of being renegotiated. Although the "we" does involve limits and exclusions, these are contestable.

Agonistic democracy refers to the space within which different hegemonic projects – radical democracy being one of them – compete for hegemony. This space will be marked by differences and divisions (among "adversaries"), and it will be established through an exclusion of "enemies." The latter do not accept

---

Socialist Strategy. For a fuller explanation of the theory of hegemony in light of Laclau's most recent work, see Lasse Thomassen, "Discourse Analytical Strategies: Antagonism, Hegemony and Ideology after Heterogeneity," *Journal of Political Ideologies* 10(3) (2005). [*] For a discussion of Gramsci, see the essay by Chris Thornhill in *The History of Continental Philosophy: Volume 5*.

27. Mouffe, *The Return of the Political*, and *The Democratic Paradox*. For a good introduction to and discussion of Laclau and Mouffe's radical democracy, see Keenan, *Democracy in Question*, ch. 3. On the differences between Laclau and Mouffe, see Mark A. Wenman, "Laclau or Mouffe? Splitting the Difference," *Philosophy & Social Criticism* 29(5) (2003).

the principles of equality and liberty, as opposed to adversaries who do, even if adversaries interpret the principles in different ways. Here Mouffe draws on Carl Schmitt to argue for the ineradicability of exclusion and antagonism from politics.

Laclau and Mouffe are interested in the possibility of leftist hegemonic projects after foundationalism, and Mouffe is particularly interested in the way the democratic "we" and the framework for democratic disputes are established. Connolly, too, is interested in how political spaces and relations to others are constituted, but he takes a different approach. For Connolly, it is a question of how existing norms and institutions can be contested and thereby opened up. His focus is on how certain subjects and constituencies are excluded and marginalized, and on how we can relate to these in new ways, thereby giving them a place in the political space. In the process, our own identities and understandings will be put into question, so the process is also one of self-contestation. In other words, it is a matter of pluralization: contesting communal and individual selves and creating new selves.

Politics, for Connolly, concerns the ways in which our identities and our relations to others are articulated: "how an identity is experienced and how it defines itself with respect to different identities."[28] This is what Connolly has in mind when he talks about "agonistic respect," "critical responsiveness," and a "generous ethos of engagement": an agonistic relation to the other that engages with the identity of the other as well as with my own identity. Hence, for Connolly, we should avoid representing others as antagonistic others (as threats, enemies, and so on). In contrast with the respectful and responsive agonistic contests between citizens that are necessary for radical democratic politics, Connolly thinks of antagonism in terms of Nietzschean *ressentiment* where the self projects its own fragility onto an other, who is then rendered a threat. This is the source of fundamentalism:

> [W]hile every doctrine, culture, faith, identity, theory, and perspective rests upon fundamentals more or less protected from internal interrogation, fundamental*ism* is a set of political strategies to protect these fundamentals by defining every carrier of critique or destabilization as an enemy marked by exactly those defects, weaknesses, corruptions, and naïvetés you are under an absolute imperative to eliminate.[29]

---

28. Connolly, *Identity/Difference*, 9.
29. Connolly, *The Ethos of Pluralization*, 105–6.

We should instead constantly engage with the other – including the "fundamentalist" other – in order to engage with ourselves and with what appears most fundamental and natural to us.

Although Connolly's views bear many resemblances with Mouffe's position, he believes that there is something missing from Mouffe's account of agonistic and radical democracy.[30] While Mouffe rightly focuses on the agonistic relations among adversaries, she does not say much about the nature of these agonistic relations. In addition, Connolly believes that we must extend agonistic respect to the excluded others, for instance, the fundamentalist. For Connolly, then, Mouffe too readily accepts that exclusion is constitutive, and thereby she risks taking particular exclusions as given as well as taking the hegemonic way of organizing politics as given. Connolly's radical democracy is organized as a rhizome, as a network that connects and reconnects in new ways all the time; and he opposes this to a politics that takes the trunk as its model, for instance a hegemonic politics where a "we" is established in the center.[31]

Whereas Laclau and Mouffe draw inspiration from Derrida and Lacan, Connolly gets the image of rhizome and trunk from Deleuze, and in addition he draws on Foucault and Nietzsche. From these thinkers, he gets the view of identity as fluid and the view of the self as constituted in flows that prevent any self – whether an "I" or a "we" – from fully stabilizing. Identity is not to be thought of as something lacking, which would suggest a negation that risks reproducing what is negated. Rather, we should think of identity and of politics in terms of abundance – flows of energy, networks of materiality, processes of becoming, and so on – an abundance that is affirmed as a positive source of a politics of contestation.

VI. CONCLUSION

In conclusion, poststructuralist radical democratic theory is not radical in the sense of providing us with a new and better foundation for radical politics, but rather in the sense of asking what radical politics looks like without foundations. Linked to this, radical democrats do not promise to transcend alienation, inequality, and exclusion, and radical democracy is not an end state that could be reached in practice or even in theory.

---

30. William E. Connolly, "The Twilight of Idols," *Philosophy and Social Criticism* 21(3) (1995). For a comparison between Connolly and Mouffe, see Mark A. Wenman, "Agonistic Pluralism and Three Archetypal Forms of Politics," *Contemporary Political Theory* 2(2) (2003).
31. Connolly, *The Ethos of Pluralization*, 94–6.

This distinguishes poststructuralist radical democrats from earlier radical democrats such as Rousseau and Marx, and radical democracy also differs from alternative contemporary approaches to democracy. The work involved in defining radical democracy does not stop at distinguishing the radical democratic position from other positions, however. One must also examine debates within radical democratic theory – for instance, between theorists of abundance and theorists of lack – as well as the implications of these debates for radical politics.

Where does radical democracy go from here? I would like to suggest two points where theorists of radical democracy have to pay particular attention in the future. First, more empirical work must be done, analyzing and criticizing institutions and practices. Radical democratic theory has tended to be just that – theory; and debates among radical democrats have tended to focus on theoretical issues.[32] Second, radical democratic theory must pay attention to what we usually call the economic sphere. This is not an attempt to argue for the priority of the economic, but merely to highlight the fact that so far radical democrats have said relatively little about capitalism and the economic sphere.[33]

A final point concerns the present and future debates about radical democratic theory. Recently there has been a challenge to radical democracy from theorists such as Hardt and Negri, Agamben, Alain Badiou, and Slavoj Žižek, who all promise a more radical analysis of and break with contemporary liberal and capitalist society.[34] Whether this new radicalism can in fact be cashed in without giving up on the radicalism of radical democracy in the sense identified above is one of the questions of dispute between, for instance, Laclau and Žižek.[35] Žižek argues that Laclau and Mouffe's radical democracy ultimately

---

32. Exceptions here include the uses made of Laclau's theory of hegemony to analyze historical and contemporary discourses. See the contributions in David Howarth *et al.* (eds), *Discourse Theory and Political Analysis: Identities, Hegemonies and Social Change* (Manchester: Manchester University Press, 2000); and Francisco Panizza (ed.), *Populism and the Mirror of Democracy* (London: Verso, 2005).

33. For exceptions, see William E. Connolly, *Capitalism and Christianity, American Style* (Durham, NC: Duke University Press, 2008); and J. K. Gibson-Graham, *The End of Capitalism (as We Knew It): A Feminist Critique of Political Economy*, 2nd ed. (Minneapolis, MN: University of Minnesota Press, 2006).

*34. For a discussion of some of these theorists, see the essay by Emily Zakin in *The History of Continental Philosophy: Volume 8*.

35. See Butler *et al.*, *Contingency, Hegemony, Universality*; Laclau, *On Populist Reason*, 232–9, and "Why Constructing a People is the Main Task of Radical Politics," *Critical Inquiry* 32 (2006); Slavoj Žižek, "Against the Populist Temptation," *Critical Inquiry* 32 (2006), and "*Schlagend, aber nicht Treffend!*," *Critical Inquiry* 33 (2006). Žižek now rejects "radical democracy" as a label for his position. On the debates among theorists of radical democracy inspired by Lacan (Badiou, Laclau, Žižek, and Cornelius Castoriadis), see Yannis Stavrakakis, *The Lacanian Left* (Edinburgh: Edinburgh University Press, 2007).

buys into a liberal-capitalist ideology because it is too superficial and does not address what really matters according to Žižek, namely the capitalist mode of production. Laclau, on the other hand, retorts that Žižek remains trapped in old essentialist and foundationalist categories such as class, while never actually providing us with a way out of the existing order. Thus, the current debates about radical democracy still turn on the correct understanding of the "radicalism" of radical democracy, that is, whether democracy must be rooted in something more fundamental.[36]

---

36. I would like to thank Rosi Braidotti, Saul Newman, Alan D. Schrift, Lars Tønder, and the anonymous reviewer for their comments on earlier drafts of this chapter.

9

CULTURAL AND POSTCOLONIAL STUDIES

Iain Chambers

In an essay published in 1988 entitled "New Ethnicities," Stuart Hall announced the end of innocence for the "essential black subject."[1] Learning from the complex geography of black identity formations within occidental modernity, it is perhaps also possible to insist even more incisively on the end of innocence for the hegemonic "white subject." This would evoke a critical constellation in which the very idea of a "Black Atlantic," as proposed by Paul Gilroy, becomes a philosophical challenge to the assumed neutral, hence universal, coordinates for comprehending modernity.[2] In such a situation, voices that apparently reach us today from the peripheral margins of a once dying colonialism and a seemingly now distant imperial past, acquire an unsuspected centrality in the reformulation of a philosophical and critical agenda seeking to respond to the complexities of a worldly inheritance that is not only ours to explain and direct. The work of Aimé Césaire, Frantz Fanon, Édouard Glissant, Ranajit Guha, and the continuing elaborations of Hall, among others, insist in their critical challenge to contemporary thought and cultural analysis (Spivak, Bhabha, Gilroy), interrogating a world yet to come. A discursive formation – European philosophy – seemingly directly inherited from a tradition that was inaugurated on the shores of the Mediterranean by the Greeks, is here interrupted. It is neither cancelled, ignored, nor simply subverted; rather, it is forced to travel in an altogether more extensive space. A *continuity* that is nurtured and guaranteed by

---

1. Stuart Hall, "New Ethnicities," in *Stuart Hall: Critical Dialogues in Cultural Studies*, David Morley and Kuan-Hsing Chen (eds) (London: Routledge, 1996).
2. See Paul Gilroy, *The Black Atlantic: Modernity and Double Consciousness* (Cambridge, MA: Harvard University Press, 1992).

questions apparently generated from *within* the autonomous realm of thought is potentially disrupted and dispersed.

Precisely one of the ways to think the philosophical and cultural impact of cultural and postcolonial studies in the anglophone world would be to consider the life and career of the fundamental figure of Stuart Hall.[3] Having moved from the Caribbean to Europe, he represents an entwining of a critical and biographical figure, that leads, after empire, to thinking "without guarantees," now viewed through the supplementary lenses of race, gender, and ethnicity. This is a worldly location that cannot be ignored or simply separated from critical statements. To be a "black" male, and the "subject" of a "sound colonial education" (Derek Walcott), is by no means merely an individual trait. It is precisely this dimension – the biopolitical location of the voice in a critical cartography profoundly characterized by asymmetrical powers – that ignites what has probably acquired the most prominence in the field of cultural and postcolonial studies and its potential impact on contemporary philosophical configurations: the question of identity. To what degree the insistence of a body located, marked, and constructed by historical, political, cultural, and economic forces is allowed to intervene in the configuration of "philosophy" is by no means clear. Its ambiguous status disseminates a disturbance, an interrogation.

It is this slightly unruly, even irreverent, appropriation that induces a critical disposition whereby the "external" and the unrecognized, or "non-philosophical," irrupts into the field. In this scenario, the postcolonial body – historically marked and culturally located – is not so much a figure that seeks to establish an identity; he or she, as Fanon pointed out many decades ago, has already been thoroughly subjected to one: "Look, a Negro!"[4] He or she is rather a figure that *reveals* identity: its mechanisms, its disciplining, its ideologies. In this critical exposure the procedures and protocols of identity are disturbed and defamiliarized. Here, thinking the very grounds of thought, unpacking the imposed "burden of representation" (Kobena Mercer), and refusing to "be" what was previously ordained, leads into what can be considered a critical multiculturalism.[5] The very question of identity (for whom? where, when, and how?)

---

3. Stuart Hall was born on February 3, 1932, in Kingston, Jamaica. Educated at Oxford, and influenced by the work of Althusser, Foucault, Gramsci, and Marx, he served as Director for the Centre for Contemporary Cultural Studies, University of Birmingham (1968–79), and taught at the Open University (1979–97). Among his most important works are *Encoding and Decoding in the Television Discourse*; *Resistance Through Rituals: Youth Subcultures in Postwar Britain*; *Policing the Crisis*; and *Questions of Cultural Identity*.

4. Frantz Fanon, *Black Skin, White Masks*, Charles Lam Markmann (trans.) (London: Pluto, 1986), 109; originally published as *Peau noire, masques blancs* (Paris: Éditions de Seuil, 1952).

5. Kobena Mercer, *Welcome to the Jungle: New Positions in Black Cultural Studies* (New York: Routledge, 1994).

becomes problematic for *all*, and not merely for those previously located in the designated marginality and subaltern positions of black, native, indigenous, and other: everything that disturbs the colorless universality of whiteness. Here Paul Ricoeur's meditations on "oneself as another," Julia Kristeva's "strangers to ourselves," and Jacques Derrida's suggestive exploration of a "monolingualism," are declined into the rougher intercultural grammar of a quotidian becoming that consistently frustrates philosophical finitude.[6]

There is also the need here to acknowledge the overspill, interaction, and heterogeneous gestation of thought emerging between developments in continental philosophy, associated with "Paris," but actually coming out of a far wider configuration that includes anticolonialism and, in particular, the Algerian war, and the nascent British discourse of cultural studies. In the latter case, a post-imperial island is injected with the socially suggestive rigor of structuralism and a reconfigured Marxism sustained by the critical and problematic import of language itself. While the structuralist "dissolving" of man – from Lévi-Strauss and Althusser to Foucault and Derrida – will also come to be read in terms of the restrictive geography implicitly referenced in the humanist and existential Marxism – the "white mythologies" – that dominated post-1945 critical European thought and philosophy.[7]

This suggests a conjunctural analysis of the coming together and shaping of a critical constellation in the 1960s and 1970s, in which empire, colonialism, and their subsequent cultural and historical fall-out in diverse national formations, in particular those of Britain and France, intertwine in a critical constellation in which the weakness of Anglo-American empirical thought, already under pressure from student disavowal and the cultural secession of youth, is intersected by radical, systematic perspectives (in both the political and epistemological sense) coming from France. Accompanying and fertilizing these developments is the elaboration of British cultural studies through its "break" with a native literary tradition and, subsequently, with the existing modalities of the profoundly limited empiricism of the social sciences. This latter move is to be read less as simply settling accounts with the disciplinary inheritance of "English literature," "sociology," or "history," and rather more in terms of crossing these,

---

6. Paul Ricoeur, *Soi-même comme un autre* (Paris: Éditions de Seuil, 1990), published in English as *Oneself as Another*, Kathleen Blamey (trans.) (Chicago, IL: University of Chicago Press, 1992); Julia Kristeva, *Étrangers à nous-mêmes* (Paris: Flammarion, 1991), published in English as *Strangers to Ourselves*, Leon S. Roudiez (trans.) (New York: Columbia University Press, 1994); Jacques Derrida, *Le Monolinguisme de l'autre, ou, La prothèse d'origine* (Paris: Éditions Galilée, 1996), published in English as *Monolingualism of the Other; or, The Prosthesis of Origin*, Patrick Mensah (trans.) (Stanford, CA: University of Stanford Press, 1998).

7. Robert Young, *White Mythologies: Writing History and the West* (London: Routledge, 1990).

and other, disciplinary paths, in the critical appropriation of such problematic concepts as "culture," the "social," the "political," and the "historical."

Essential to this overall constellation was not merely the production of inter-disciplinary and intercultural spaces, but also a pronounced irritation with the self-serving institutionalization of "knowledge" as an autonomous academic pursuit. Nineteen sixty-eight, of course, but also, and as a consequence of that initial rebellion, the emergence of the critical excavation and evaluation of the archive of occidental modernity understood as a systematic network of power and associated knowledge "affects." Here, a Marxist inheritance eventually came to be interrogated by what it historically often ignored: the "peripheral" and "subaltern" voices of empire, colonialism, and gender. If feminism was a common thread, although diversely accented, between Paris and London, the attention to race and ethnicity was altogether more acutely considered in Britain. In this critical undoing of culture, now considered as a historical process and a shifting, consensual arrangement of power, there is also the significant reprise of the complex historical and political understanding of cultural formations elabo-rated in the 1930s by the Sardinian intellectual Antonio Gramsci, who is touched on in Althusser, persistently evoked by Hall at the Centre for Contemporary Cultural Studies in Birmingham, and extensively explored by Ranajit Guha[8] and the Subaltern Studies Group in India.

I. THE REFUSAL TO BE THE OTHER

It is at this point that it becomes legitimate to ask whether, for example, Fanon's *Les Damnés de la terre* (*The Wretched of the Earth*; 1961) is to be considered a philosophical text.[9] The very question poses a potential reconfiguration of the philosophical if we are to include it or, conversely, an institutional restriction if we exclude it. Fanon's writings most certainly invade and interrupt any thinking that considers itself to be universal and the epitome of humanity. In his preface to the text, Sartre famously defines Fanon as carrying out a "strip-tease of our

---

8. Ranajit Guha (1922–) is an Indian historian, influenced by the work of Antonio Gramsci, and most noted for his critical reconfiguration of historical studies with the Subaltern Studies Group.

9. Frantz Fanon (July 20, 1925–December 6, 1961; born in Martinique; died in Bethesda, Maryland, USA) studied medicine at the University of Lyon (1947–51). Among his influ-ences are Césaire, Sartre, and Senghor. He served as Chef de service at the psychiatric hospital of Blida-Joinville, Algeria (1953–56) and on the editorial board of the Algerian liberation movement (Front de Libération Nationale, or FLN) newspaper *El Moudjahid*. Among his important works not cited elsewhere in this essay is *L'An V de la révolution algérienne* (*A Dying Colonialism*) and *Pour la révolution africaine* (*Towards the African Revolution*).

humanism."[10] It was from such a universalism that the chilling certainty of a racist legislation descended on the planet.

In the cultural codification of difference, only the European is a moral subject capable of proposing universal values. History in the colonial world is hence exclusively the history of the colonizer and an extension of the European metropolis. The colonized is immobilized, fixed in her subaltern status, and stabilized in the repetition of a cultural identity that is not permitted to disturb the teleological movement of the colonizer's "progress." This is a complex constellation that while obviously theoretical is not always obviously philosophical *per se*; or, rather, it evokes a philosophical insistence that is continually bent to a cultural and political will. Against theoretical and scholarly rigor, attention is paid to the performative instance of critical thought. There is the enunciation of a volatile location destined to irritate inherited categories of understanding with an ambivalence that insists on the complexity and opaqueness of the world that thought seeks to discipline and render transparent. To insist on what sticks out in language is, as the Indian historian Ranajit Guha forcefully argues in *History at the Limit of World-History*, to deviate and subvert a linearity that anticipates its conclusions; it is to snap the chains of *that* history which considers itself to be the unique reason of the world. It is precisely to reintroduce what *that* language has avoided and negated.

As an *interdisciplinary* approach to the analyses of contemporary culture, cultural studies has historically posed some forceful epistemological objections to the social sciences and accompanying critical configurations. This has been accompanied by the significant analytical contamination of previously distinct popular and elite cultures. Shifting the aesthetic concerns of literary studies and art history into the critical conundrum of culture as a "whole way of life" (Raymond Williams), has led to thinking critically with other languages and texts rather than simply those inherited from a "Great Tradition" (F. R. Leavis) and its endorsement in the nation's literary canon, educational programs, museums, and libraries. In this sense, Bob Marley and reggae music can appear as critically suggestive as Goethe contemplating the possibilities of *Weltliteratur* or Heidegger considering the question of technology.

At this point there exists no external space. Everything presses in on the center in a political and cultural geography that renders disciplinary distinctions and unilateral perspectives problematic in the proximity of immediate complexities. We are encouraged to undertake what Edward Said calls a "contrapuntal reading" of the situation.[11] There is now no "native," "other," or "slave" to

---

10. Jean-Paul Sartre, "Foreword," in Frantz Fanon, *The Wretched of the Earth*, Richard Philcox (trans.) (New York: Grove Press, 2004), lvii.

11. Edward Said (November 1, 1935–September 25, 2003; born in Jerusalem, British Palestine; died in New York) received a BA from Princeton University (1957) and a PhD from Harvard University (1964). Influenced by Auerbach, Foucault, Gramsci, and Vico, Said spent his career,

legitimize the "progress" of a Hegelian logic or maintain a differential distance, only negated figures and repressed partners in the shared historical realization of modernity. In the complex and uneven act of framing, occidental modernity, rendered in its planetary transit susceptible to postcolonial criticism, loses unique possession of its languages.

To return to Fanon: for this French educated Martiniquan, Europe is not about the fulfillment of humanity, but historically represents the mystification and blocking of its realization. The West holds humanity in hostage, and humanism is transformed into a hypocrisy that consistently evades a "humanisme à la mesure du monde [humanism that is the measure of the world]."[12] Similarly, "underdevelopment" is not the sign of European superiority but rather an insulting term whose genesis reveals the cruel centrality of colonialism in the making of the modern world: "*L'Europe est littéralement la création du Tiers-Monde* [Europe is literally the creation of the Third World]."[13] The planet remains in the historical vice forged by Europe, "which never stops talking of man yet massacres him at every one of its street corners, at every corner of the world."[14] In *Peaux noires, masques blancs* (1952), Fanon is the doctor of a colonial hospital – caught between a Sartrean dialectic of two single subject positions sustained in antagonism and the split Lacanian subject unable to confirm him or herself – who describes psychic relationships sustained in the murderous embrace between the colonizer and the colonized. He is also the critical voice who announces the refusal to be the other.

Object of the exception – "Look, a Negro!" – the subaltern is (mis)recognized and has no other choice than that of shattering the mirror, refusing an imposed alterity. As the mute and immobile object of Western history, she has no alternative but to violate that which frames her or him as object in order to appropriate the right to narrate (Said, Bhabha). To insist on the right to disrupt an imposed and inherited history is not to evoke a philosophy of violence, but is rather to reply to the structures that sustain and disseminate violence; *in primis*, the reign of terror, as Michael Taussig describes it, that constitutes the space

---

beginning in 1963, in the Department of English and Comparative Literature at Columbia University. Among his more than twenty-five books are: *Orientalism*; *Covering Islam: How the Media and the Experts Determine How We See the Rest of the World*; *Musical Elaborations*; *Culture and Imperialism*; and *Reflections on Exile*. [*] Said's work, along with that of Spivak and Bhabha, is discussed in detail in the essay by Eduardo Mendieta in *The History of Continental Philosophy: Volume 8*.

12. Aimé Césaire, *Discours sur le colonialisme* (Paris: Éditions Réclame, 1950), 68; published in English as *Discourse on Colonialism*, Joan Pinkham (trans.) (New York: Monthly Review Press, 2001), 56, translation modified.

13. Frantz Fanon, *Les Damnés de la terre* (Paris: Maspero, 1961), 76; *The Wretched of the Earth*, 102.

14. Fanon, *Les Damnés de la terre*, 239; *The Wretched of the Earth*, 235.

of European colonialism and its mission of imposing its "self" on the rest of the world.[15] Here we are brought into the "heart of darkness" to confront the structures of violence, the violence of the structures, that cage the colonial and subaltern within modernity itself: nothing is separate, all is coeval as Johannes Fabian points out.[16]

We are here excavating the archive of modernity, where conditions of thought are inextricably woven into the making of a world designed to mirror, sanction, and extend that very same thought. Even those most directly affected by the rhetoric of the "progress" of the rule of reason – slaves waging war for their freedom on an eighteenth-century island in the French Caribbean – continue to be excluded from the historical, political, cultural and philosophical account: "I met History once, but he ain't recognize me."[17] The historically excluded, the cultural other, the racially abnegated, cannot be absorbed without inducing a sea change in the cartographies of thought (and power). We here return to Fanon's insistence on the necessity to escape the clutches of a hegemonic history – that of the colonizer who continues to narrate the metropolis on the colonial soil that he is stealing – which leads to sabotaging his historio-graphy and geo-graphy, that is, his specific elaboration of time and space.

It was another Martiniquan, the poet Aimé Césaire,[18] who drew out the terrible equivalence between colonialism and Nazism. Once again Fanon reminds his readers of this disturbing vicinity: "It was my philosophy professor, a native of the Antilles, who recalled the fact to me one day: 'Whenever you hear anyone abuse the Jews, pay attention, because he is talking about you.'"[19] The real "scandal" of the Nazi exercise of power consisted precisely in introducing directly into the heartlands of Europe the colonial discipline and discrimination of its internal populations. These were not distant crimes perpetuated against "native" and "savage" Arabs, Africans, Indians, and other non-Europeans, but were rather directly exercised on the bodies and lives of white, "civilized"

15. Michael Taussig, *Shamanism, Colonialism and the Wild Man: A Study in Terror and Healing* (Chicago, IL: University of Chicago Press, 1991).
16. Johannes Fabian, *Time and the Other: How Anthropology Makes its Object* (New York: Columbia University Press, 1983).
17. Derek Walcott, "The Schooner 'Flight,'" in *Collected Poems, 1948–1984* (New York: Farrar, Straus & Giroux, 1987).
18. Aimé Césaire (June 25, 1913–April 17, 2000; born in Martinique; died in Fort-de-France, Martinique) travelled to Paris supported by a scholarship, and was educated at the Lycée Louis-le-Grand and the École Normale Supérieure. Poet, politician, and one of the founders of the *Négritude* movement, Césaire returned to Martinique in 1939, where he taught at the Lycée Schoelcher, and was a powerful influence on Frantz Fanon. His political career began in 1945, when he was elected mayor of Fort-de-France, and he served for many years as Martinique's *député* to the French National Assembly.
19. Fanon, *Black Skin, White Masks*, 122.

Europeans, now selected and segregated according to racialized hierarchies that had been perpetuated for centuries overseas. Here the Shoah, and the exceptional concentration of an industrialized genocide, enters another genealogy: that of the long history of colonial terror now exercised on European soil. Auschwitz becomes the extreme, shocking realization of the debt of European modernity to colonial reason.[20] As a commentator has recently suggested, "Césaire takes the camp – to the degree that its exceptional status permits the comprehension of the concentrated colonial universe – as symbolizing, to paraphrase Giorgio Agamben's formula, the biopolitical *nomos* of colonialism."[21] We are brought to Albert Memmi's noted affirmation that, in its inescapable structural inequality, every colonial system is a form of fascism.[22]

II. COLONIAL CARTOGRAPHIES

Philosophy as an institutional practice, as a discursive field, was historically dependent as a part of the very formation of modern Europe, on the persistent distance and differing of the metropolitan center from the colonial periphery that permitted the (violent) maintenance of the illusory and hierarchical distinction between separate worlds. Yet this framing is consistently betrayed by the political and cultural economy that establishes and identifies "center" and "periphery," "First" and "Third" World, "developed" and "underdeveloped," within a common cartography of differentiated powers. For the very sense of "Europe," its authority and reason, is dependent, as the Congolese philosopher Valentin Y. Mudimbe has carefully argued, on the existence and invention of "Africa," "Asia," "Oceania," and the "Americas."[23]

"In the 1950s, Octave Mannoni, Frantz Fanon, and Albert Memmi transformed the paradigm of colonial studies."[24] To this apt observation by Françoise Vergès, it would surely be no exaggeration to argue that such voices have grown

---

20. Césaire, *Discours sur le colonialisme; Discourse on Colonialism*.

21. Dino Costantini, *Una malattia europea* (Pisa: Edizioni Plus, 2006), 218.

22. Albert Memmi, *Portrait du colonisé: Portrait du colonisateur* (Paris: Buchet-Chastel, 1957); published in English as *The Colonizer and the Colonized*, Howard Greenfield (trans.) (New York: Orion, 1965).

23. Valentin Y. Mudimbe, *The Invention of Africa: Gnosis, Philosophy and the Order of Knowledge* (Bloomington, IN: Indiana University Press, 1988).

24. Françoise Vergès, *Monsters and Revolutionaries: Colonial Family Romance and Métissage* (Durham, NC: Duke University Press, 1999), 11. Octave Mannoni (1899–1989) was a psychoanalyst who spent more than two decades in the French colony of Madagascar. On returning to France, he was much influenced by the work of Jacques Lacan. He is most widely known for his book *Prospero and Caliban: The Psychology of Colonization* (1950). Albert Memmi (1920–), whose mother tongue was Arabic, is of Jewish origin and was brought up in French

in volume in the radical reconstitution of critical thought throughout the developed world since that decade. Breaking the "implacable dependence" (Memmi) between the colonizer and the colonized, it has subsequently become impossible to ignore a fracture destined to vibrate throughout the body of occidental thought, its abstract purity now stained by the contingent disruptions of unruly histories, negated bodies, and the brutal inscriptions of power. Here the repressed colonial archive, and hence the secret histories of the historical and cultural making of modernity and its overall political economy, can no longer be evaded or marginalized.

At this point, we can ask, with Gayatri Chakravorty Spivak, who is the "we" of philosophy?[25] In her extended discussion of the anthropological moment of Kantian reason in the context of *The Critique of Reason*, the Bengali critic points to the Kantian evocation of the non-European native as the limit case of reason: "He is only a *casual* object of thought, not a paradigmatic example. He is not only not the subject as such; he also does not quite make it as an example of the thing or its species as natural product."[26] In other words, the presence of the native of Tierra del Fuego is not required, need not even exist, for the passage of philosophy to occur. Such "natives" sustain a narrative – anthropological, exotic, instances of the sublime – that does not yet bear the European signature of history. As the author of *A Critique of Postcolonial Reason* (the very title announces a doubling and dispersal of the inherited imposition of a Kantian logic) concludes: "We find here the axiomatics of imperialism as a natural argument to indicate the limits of the cognition of (cultural) man … The subject as such in Kant is geopolitically differentiated" (CPR 26–7).

The reply at this point is most certainly not about how to appropriate the "native informant" in order to mend and ultimately reconfirm a reconfigured discourse – yet a further imperial invocation – but precisely to leave the gaps, the holes, in critical language open, ambiguous, susceptible to eventual suturing into another place, another language, another subject-hood.

---

colonial Tunisia. He is known as both a novelist and for his critical work *The Colonizer and the Colonized* (1957).

25. Gayatri Chakravorty Spivak (February 24, 1942– ; born in Calcutta, India) received a BA in English from Calcutta University (1959), and a PhD in comparative literature from Cornell University (1967). Influenced by Derrida, Guha, and Said, she has taught at the University of Pittsburgh and, since 1991, Columbia University, where she is now a university professor and Director of the Center for Comparative Literature and Society. Among her most important works are: her "Translator's Preface" to Derrida's *Of Grammatology*; *In Other Worlds: Essays in Cultural Politics*; *The Post-Colonial Critic*; and *A Critique of Postcolonial Reason: Towards a History of the Vanishing Present*.

26. Gayatri C. Spivak, *A Critique of Postcolonial Reason: Towards a History of the Vanishing Present* (Cambridge, MA: Harvard University Press, 1999), 26. Hereafter cited as CPR followed by the page number.

Two centuries after Kant, such objections can still be moved against those who are apparently among the most radical expression of contemporary critical thought: Michel Foucault and Gilles Deleuze. In some densely argued pages in *A Critique of Postcolonial Reason*, Spivak deconstructs the unsuspected architecture of an ingenuous homogeneity in the Parisian referencing of subaltern struggles in both the First and the Third World. Via an intellectually staged ventriloquism, she argues, the rest of the world is still reduced to the rules of representation that render transparent the philosopher's will. Subjected to totalizing maps of *power* and *desire*, to the *vertreten* and *darstellen* of political and ideological representation, there is a simultaneous disavowal of the asymmetrical, inconclusive, and lived complexities of other, worldly subjects. As Spivak puts it, referring to Foucault and Deleuze, the "Third World can enter the resistance program of an alliance politics directed against a '*unified* repression' only when it is confined to the third-world groups that are directly accessible to the First World" (CPR 277). This is to forget the important advice of Assia Djebar: "Don't claim to 'speak for' or worse, to 'speak on,' barely speaking next to, and if possible *very close to* ...."[27]

There is, as Spivak notes, no space for a "counterhegemonic ideological production" (CPR 255). In this "empirical register of resistance talk," intellectual radicalism ends up playing witness to "capitalist colonialism" and its "positivist empiricism" (CPR 254–5). With the abstract concepts of *the* working class, *the* subaltern, and *the* multitude, political and ideological representation is reduced to the purity of an abstract plane, however folded and multiplied, that provokes the lines of flight, or relay, of theory itself, confirming the philosopher's desired will to revolt, while it paradoxically "restores the category of the sovereign subject within the theory that seems most to question it" (CPR 261).

The provenance of the pronouncement continues to configure the analytical constellation in a "topographical reinscription of imperialism" that invariably, even in its most radical formulations, exposes First World concerns (CPR 279). The failure and refusal to track discontinuity – geographical, economical, social, and cultural – in the differentiated but entwined complexity of what is clearly now a planetary mode of production and being ensures the sovereignty of the occidental subject as *the* subject of history. In such a manner, Foucault's clinic, asylum, and prison, like "deterritorialization" in Deleuze and Guattari, "seem to be screen-allegories that foreclose a reading of the broader narratives of imperialism" (CPR 279):

---

27. Assia Djebar, *Women of Algiers in their Apartments*, Marjolina de Jager (trans.) (Charlottesville, VA: University Press of Virginia, 1992), 2; originally published as *Femmes d'Alger dans leur appartement* (Paris: Albin Michel, 1980).

> This reintroduces the constitutive subject on at least two levels: the Subject of desire and power as an irreducible methodological presupposition; and the self-proximate, if not identical, subject of the oppressed. Further, the intellectuals, who are neither of these S/ subjects, become transparent in the relay race, for they merely report on the nonrepresented subject and analyze (without analyzing) the workings of (the unnamed Subject irreducibly proposed by) power and desire.   (CPR 264-5)

Beyond the troubling unconscious and the disturbance of ambiguity, all is dispersed into mobile vectors where dynamic monads form dualisms but avoid contaminating contradictions and the potential locations of critique: a machine "without organs." The subaltern is not allowed to invest in her itinerary, for she is already produced and spoken for in a logic overdetermined by economical, political, and cultural powers that are also theoretical. This particular subject – subaltern, oppressed, in resistance, and in revolt – belongs, as Spivak bluntly puts it, "to the exploiters side of the international division of labor. It is impossible for contemporary French intellectuals to imagine the kind of Power and Desire that would inhabit the unnamed subject of the Other of Europe" (CPR 265). I think we can safely substitute *occidental* for "French" on this point. The eventual hole, rent, and discontinuity in this discursive tissue challenges the sanctioned ignorance of a simulated identification with the "other," which is always about some form of self-investment. It registers precisely what exceeds and escapes "my" world as an insistent irreducibility: a perpetual interrogation and interruption of my "self" and its associated languages of meaning and managing the world.

This is not, of course, to suggest that such critical languages are unable to travel fruitfully elsewhere. However, it is precisely the fact of their being "othered" in the elsewhere that proves pertinent. Europe, once systemized in the Caribbean, for example, proposes a radical reassessment: from Fanon's stern insistence on taking the limits of European humanism seriously to Glissant's fluid, Deleuzian-influenced, explorations of the political and poetical conditions of *créolité*.[28] Here a continual *metissage* of languages, histories and cultures propose a profoundly Caribbean critical perspective in which Europe, Africa,

---

28. Édouard Glissant (1928–2011; born in Martinique) is a poet and writer, critically renowned for promoting a Caribbean and postcolonial understanding of critical creolization that produces a complex archipelago of shared difference. He draws inspiration from Deleuze and Guattari's work on rhizomatic becoming and "minor" literatures. Glissant's most important critical writings in English are *Caribbean Discourse: Selected Essays*, and *Poetics of Relation*. [*] For further discussion of Glissant, see the essay by Rosi Braidotti in *The History of Continental Philosophy: Volume 8*.

and the Americas are critically conjoined in earshot of the terrifying rhythms of slavery and its racist aftermath. Here, where the so-called "periphery" radically reassess the "center," the teleology of occidental "progress" is dispersed in an altogether more complex, unfinished, and rhizomatic becoming.

III. THE VIOLENCE OF IDENTITY

The historical sovereignty of this discourse, its position, its power, is founded, as Foucault himself insisted in *L'Archeologie du savoir* (1969), on the organizing principles of the occidental *ratio* in its relationship with all other societies. The elsewhere is always a product, an extension, and an "invention" of that cultural and historical order: a European mandate on the rest of the planet. The violence of the ensuing dichotomies is the violence of thinking the world in a manner that only mirrors your "self." As Mudimbe, following Foucault, points out, this is precisely the "epistemological possibility" of the discourse in question: the possibility and subsequent disciplining of thought that produces anthropology, comparative linguistics, geography, sociology, history, and the social sciences in general, as part of a precise historical and cultural, hence epistemic, formation.

The power and violence of language is evidenced in the success of conceptual systems able to take possession of the world in such a manner that they are universally recognized. To be recognized implies inhabiting this syntax. The structural violence of thought is enacted precisely in becoming a "subject." As Judith Butler argues, the subject must first be subjected, that is, subordinated and disciplined by the languages that permit her or him to appear and to act as a recognizable agent; that is, as a "subject."[29] Here we can register in the discursive formation of an "Orient," an "Africa," "underdevelopment," the "South," the "subaltern," an "other," the power of language that is simultaneously the language of power inscribed in the categorization of the world: the objectification of a precise subjectivity.

What is being entertained here is the undoing and dispersal – *not the cancellation* – of that configuration of knowledge, leading, in turn, to the unwinding of the legislative authority of the West as the unique subject of history. This is to push thinking into uncharted territory, for, to borrow a metaphor from urban geography, it suggests a vast and indefinite area – like the sprawling urban slums and shanty towns peopled by a complex, anonymous, marginalized underclass that is neither recognized as urban nor rural – that lies between disciplinary definitions and other modalities of knowledge (or gnosis, as Mudimbe puts

---

29. Judith Butler, *The Psychic Life of Power: Theories in Subjection* (Stanford, CA: Stanford University Press, 1997).

it). If the former presents themselves in terms of an epistemic and rigorous configuration of knowledge that pretends to impose itself universally and hence unilaterally, the latter, as a heterogeneous and unsystematic interrogation of that configuration, sets a limit, proposing an insistent border that provokes a transit, a translation, an elsewhere.

The occidental institution of philosophy rarely recognizes the full significance of this critical challenge. When there is seemingly a direct response – Deleuze, Negri, and Hardt – it remains locked within the confirmation of its own discursive horizon. As Spivak rightly points out, the other, as subaltern, multitude, immigrant, sustains, rather than shatters, the authority of the critical paradigm. It is precisely here that the deconstructive turn within occidental reasoning becomes most suggestive and subversive: as the internal "outsider," as the voice that speaks the "West" without being fully reducible to the law of its *logos*: thinking on the threshold of metaphysical certainties. If less direct, interesting symptoms have also emerged in the Italian proposal of "weak thought" (Gianni Vattimo and Pier Aldo Rovatti)[30] and the necessary recognition of the undoing of the metaphysical will. More recently there have been the precise considerations of Giorgio Agamben on the critical limits of representation and the authorization of its reason confronted with the incommensurable instance of genocide, the death camp, and the essential violence on which the liberal state establishes and, ultimately, propagates its legitimacy.[31]

To return to Butler's observations on our subjection in the languages in which we appear, act, and become "subjects," the complex traffic between occidental thought and the seemingly external space of the nonoccidental has now to be located in the coeval coordinates of a shared planetary spatiotemporality. The distance sought by a discipline is ontologically shrunk to a disturbing proximity, and the precise ethnoscape (Appadurai[32]) and location (Bhabha) of a discursive formation that declares itself universal looms into view.

If the West has worlded the world, if modernity has become the syntax of historical, cultural, and economic exchange, then Fabian's crucial idea of a shared or coeval time undermines an occidental epistemology intent on constructing, cataloguing, and distancing "objects" of study, polity, and rule.[33] It is precisely here, as Bhabha argues, that the mimicry, repetition, and dissemination of

---

*30. "Weak thought" is discussed in this volume in the essay by Silvia Benso and Brian Schroeder.

31. Gianni Vattimo and Pier A. Rovatti (eds), *Il pensiero debole* (Milan: Feltrinelli, 1983); Giorgio Agamben, *Homo sacer: Il potere sovrano e la nuda vita* (Turin: Einaudi, 1998); published in English as *Homo Sacer: Sovereign Power and Bare Life*, Daniel Heller-Roazen (trans.) (Stanford, CA: Stanford University Press, 1998).

32. See Arjun Appadurai, *Modernity at Large: Cultural Dimensions of Globalization* (Minneapolis, MN: University of Minnesota Press).

33. Fabian, *Time and the Other*.

modernity leads to the performative realizations of everyday hybridization, creolization, and *métissage*, leads to the emerging critical problematic of *translation*: historical, cultural, and poetical.[34] If this is by now a well-rehearsed debate in anthropology and postcolonial literary and cultural studies, it continues to propose a radical, but largely unsuspected, reconfiguration of the social and human sciences *tout court*. It is in this profound sense that the practices of the disciplines, and their scriptural economies of facts, documents, texts, and testimonies, always remain instances of interpretation, sites of ambivalence: are always historical and political acts. Philosophy is neither immune nor able to secede from this constellation.

Against this expansion of critical horizons we can conclude this journey by returning to Stuart Hall. Hall's earlier important work on the seemingly local configurations of television and the media in contemporary British culture was motivated by attention to the construction and articulation of a social, political, and cultural consensus. It was subsequently refined in his highly influential elaborations of the interactive construction of race in the positioning and defining of the racialized subject in the unfolding narration of the nation. This critical work rendered the performative affects of a language deeply political. It also rendered highly problematic the assumed neutrality and accompanying authority of the disciplinary voice (from sociology and social history to political and media commentary) that is analyzing, explaining, and defining the actors involved. Increasingly in Hall's more recent work, it has been in the altogether less-guaranteed spaces provided and provoked by the languages of the visual arts that such arguments have found an increasing resonance.[35] The turn to these languages, and a seemingly aesthetic discourse, has paradoxically provided the means to probe, provoke, and propagate a wider sense of the "political." In the 1980s and the Thatcherite epoch characterized by riots and resentment against racialized policing, and the tightening definitions of nation and citizenship, the radical insistence on being both black and British challenged a narrowing of social and cultural perspectives. This spilled over, not only into the streets, but also into an avantgardist black arts movement. The photographic, film and visual

---

34. Homi K. Bhabha (November 1, 1949– ; born in Mumbai, India) received a BA from the University of Mumbai and a PhD in English literature from Christ Church, Oxford University. Among his influences are Derrida, Foucault, Lacan, and Said. He has taught in the English Department at the University of Sussex (1978–94), in Humanities at the University of Chicago (1996–2000), and as Professor of English and American Literature and Language at Harvard University (2001–), where he also is Director of the Humanities Center. His best-known work is *The Location of Culture*.

35. Apart from many articles and talks on the argument, the culmination of Hall's direct involvement in these critical artistic processes has been his promotion and overseeing of the realization of the new location of the Institute of International Visual Arts (Iniva) and Autograph ABP at Rivington Place that opened in London in 2007.

work of young black artists such as Isaac Julien, Mona Hartoum, Keith Piper, Sonia Boyce, Eddie Chambers, and Sutapa Biswas, along with many others, opened up an important series of interventionary spaces in Britain. Through challenging more conservative understandings, the simultaneous occupation of aesthetic and ethical discourses (art and philosophy) achieved the conjunctural realization of a new critical constellation. Here, in the interdisciplinary and intercultural spaces registered and explored in the visual frame, inherited understandings of identity, language, and art were effectively reconfigured.

In this hybridizing space, sustained in the ambivalence between poetics and philosophy, critical distinctions between institutional and discursive competence (for example, between cultural and postcolonial studies) become increasingly difficult to maintain in a differentiated but shared planetary mesh. Critically attuned to the complex orchestration of location, the very idea of maintaining historical, cultural, disciplinary, ethnic, and religious autonomies sharply signals the rhetorical limits of "globalization." It is surely against this inherited positioning of authority and "knowledge" that occidental philosophy is required to measure itself. Its very identity, as with all identities, is perhaps less to be defended and rather to be disturbed and dissipated in order that other possibilities, other horizons, other hopes can acquire cultural shape and historical force.

201

10

THE "ETHICAL TURN" IN CONTINENTAL PHILOSOPHY IN THE 1980S

Robert Eaglestone

There is a general consensus that the late 1970s and 1980s saw an "ethical turn" in continental philosophy. Yet, like all generalizations about moments and movements in the history of philosophy, this overstatement has some truth about it. On the one hand, there was a change in the tenor of discussions; on the other, it is unclear if this was a wider "turn" or an "excavation" of a layer of thought brought to the surface by intellectual, cultural, and social events or the sudden elevation of one philosophical and theoretical conversation over others. The aim of this chapter is to explore this moment, its origins, and its significance. However, the nature of the subject matter makes this discussion much more complex.

Philosophizing about ethics is hard, especially in the continental tradition, because "ethics" is never just one topic among others; it is not what Heidegger calls "a classroom matter."[1] Faced properly, questions of ethics are interwoven with the most demanding questions that can be asked. Theodor Adorno finds a line in Sartre's *Morts sans Sépulture* that expresses this:

> [It] is said by a young resistance fighter who is subjected to torture, who asks whether one should live in a world in which one is beaten until one's bones are smashed. Since it concerns the possibility of the affirmation of life, this question cannot be evaded. And I would think that any thought which is not measured by this standard, which does not assimilate it theoretically, simply pushes aside at the

---

1. Martin Heidegger, "Letter on Humanism," in *Basic Writings*, David Farrell Krell (ed.) (New York: Harper & Row, 1977), 197.

outset that which thought should address – so that it cannot really be called thought at all.[2]

Ethics as a field of inquiry should not only challenge us, as it were, intellectually. It also overwhelms the disciplines and structures that try to analyze, describe, or encapsulate it, and so to attend to ethics – to the standard Adorno rightly demands here – is not just to attend to a narrow philosophical subject but to attend to an almost-infinite series of demands and questions across a huge range of discourses: technological, ontological, juridical, historical, cultural, social, and aesthetic.

Moreover, as the citation from Adorno suggests, there is a key sense in which the continental and analytic/Anglo-American traditions of ethical inquiry differ. Where the analytic/Anglo-American tradition of ethical inquiry can often appear etiolated, inquiring either into the meaning of ethical language or into the "professional ethics" of, say, doctors, the continental tradition is profoundly and self-consciously interwoven with history, both the history of philosophy and what one might call (hoping to encapsulate both considerations of the "history of being" and the micro-histories of the political) the histories of the world. This is to say that while the analytic/Anglo-American tradition often allies itself to law and legalistic frameworks, the continental tradition finds resources in the political, the historical, the literary, and the religious.

It is with these two ideas in mind – the sense that ethics is not simply one discourse among others, and the sense of its inextricable interweaving with history in the continental tradition – that the "ethical turn" of the 1980s has to be located. As I have suggested, like most "turns" in the history of philosophy, the shift in interest in relation to ethics was not so much a "turn," or even a "return," but more a twist in a continually changing and developing path. It represented a change both in thought and in the historical and cultural context of that thinking, but it did not generate a revolution. Its origins can be traced through two paths: through the historical conditions and intellectual questions that led to it and through the surge of interest in the major figure in this turn, Emmanuel Levinas.

I. HISTORICAL AND CULTURAL CONTEXT

The late 1970s and early 1980s were disorienting times for continental philosophy. First, and perhaps most urgently, a huge array of interlinked issues that

---

2. Theodor Adorno, *Metaphysics: Concepts and Problems*, Rolf Tiedemann (ed.), Edmund Jephcott (trans.) (Cambridge: Polity, 2000), 111.

stemmed from the nature and history of modernity were making an impact on intellectual life and work. The broad scope of issues included: feminism and other questions of gender relations and sexuality; questions about race, racism, and of the postcolonial settlement, about migration and state power; the relation between indigenous and migrant traditions and collective memories ("multiculturalism"); increasing flexibility of capital and global markets; contrasts between secular and religious frameworks; the changing nature of the industrial base in the West and the onset of the "digital age" – indeed, many of the complex cluster of issues that have come to be located in the early twenty-first century under the banner of "globalization." In addition, the rapid rise of technology raised questions from the fields of medicine and science about the nature of humanity in relation to bodily life and to consciousness. Finally, the environmental movement began to gather momentum in the late 1970s and early 1980s, and began to raise philosophical and ethical questions. While some of these issues and positions for inquiry found themselves in allegiance, others found themselves competing for intellectual space. All investigate the limitations of ethics as an intellectual location and questioned ethical frameworks from their particular standpoint.[3]

Second, many of the fundamental questions put to Western thought by, for example, Nietzsche and Freud, two "masters of suspicion," and in a more technically philosophical way by Husserl and by Heidegger, seemed to reemerge, as if generations had awoken from the nightmare of the Second World War and the happy dream of the 1960s. The great questions of the late nineteenth century that pertained to ethics in this broader sense – questions of nihilism, of science, of post-theological humanity – and the reemergence of questions that had begun to circulate at the beginning of the twentieth century – of order, of subjectivity, of what the human might be, of technology – seemed to rearticulate themselves and demand new answers. In addition, the experience of the Holocaust and other genocides, of vicious colonial wars and of voices previously unheard by the mainstream philosophical traditions became added to this complex mélange. Institutionally, too, there were changes. Thinkers from the canon of European thought – such as Husserl and Heidegger, but others, too – had been sidelined by other, principally analytic but also sociological and psychological ways of approaching issues and problems. In the US, these philosophers were isolated even within philosophy departments because they were seen to be engaged with "the history of philosophy" and were rarely taken seriously, except in departments that explored the philosophy of religion. However, intellectual changes,

---

*3. Many of the issues mentioned here – including gender and sexuality, postcolonialism, citizenship, environmentalism, and globalization – are discussed in essays in *The History of Continental Philosophy: Volume 8.*

often stemming from literature departments, created a new interest in the thinkers from this canon, and this itself led to a renewed interest in ethics.

Third, and perhaps most importantly, the political realm was radically changing: a generation earlier, the crimes of Stalinism and the events of the Hungarian uprising of 1956 led some intellectuals either into a wholesale reevaluation of their ethical and political commitments, or they engaged in arguments that often became farcical defenses of communism and Stalinism or of an exhausted and corrupt leftist tradition. By the 1970s, the failure of Marxism had become clear: the collapse of the "events" of 1968 in Paris (in which, of course, many French intellectuals had been involved), the crushing of the Prague "Spring," and the realization of the horrors of Mao's "Cultural Revolution" were all part of this, which coincided with the rise of an intellectually aggressive new Right, of which the apotheosis was the presidency of Ronald Reagan and premiership of Margaret Thatcher. The withering away of a broadly Marxist intellectual framework, which had generated either sufficient answers or, at the very least, provided a *marxisant* discourse for intellectual inquiry, meant that in the late 1980s and early 1990s, Marxism no longer offered convincing answers to questions of justice, especially social justice. Indeed, none of the previously established systems, either extant or ideal, could answer the political and social questions put to them.

In one way, all three of these areas – the changing status of political ideologies, rapid historical and social change, and the return of the most demanding intellectual questions – were often, and sometimes clumsily, summed up in the term "postmodernism." In this light, the question arose as to the "ethics of postmodernism," meaning the ethical response to all these complex interrelated issues and, in turn, what they meant for more traditional conceptions of ethics.

However, in a more profound way, these issues were bound up with a changing conception of – to speak very broadly – "otherness," and it is this concept that underlies much of the renewed interest in ethics. Of course, the term "otherness" is in one sense banal and too general, and led, naturally, to all sorts of banalities and generalities that amounted to little more than exhortations to "be good" or "play nicely." However, "otherness" also points to a complex series of interactions between the world and systems of thought. It can mean both a concrete living other, a person, persons, or categories of traditions that are different from the accepted conventions or general consensus. It can also be understood to mean that which is outside, an indefinable thing outside the system that indicates that the system is not closed. This second sense of "otherness," for example, underlies much of Derrida's work. Deconstruction, he says, is:

> a search for, but itself the consequence of, the fact that the system is impossible; it often consists … in making appear – in each alleged

system, in each self-interpretation of and by a system – a force of dislocation, a limit in the totalization ... it consists ... in remarking ... that what has made it possible for philosophers to effect a system is nothing other than a ... certain incapacity to close the system.[4]

It consists, in other words, of encountering the outside through an analysis that is other to the dominant discourse. And it is Derrida's work – itself and its influence – that played a crucial role in the "ethical turn." However, Derrida's own thinking, especially in relation to otherness, was shaped in turn by his encounter with the work of Levinas, a figure whose philosophical considerations of the other are unparalleled. Indeed, it is fair to say that, perhaps led by Derrida, the major influence in the turn toward ethics in the 1980s was the surge of interest – in France and in the anglophone world – in Levinas. As Alain Badiou writes, in a backhanded compliment, it is to Levinas "that we owe, long before the current fashion, a kind of ethical radicalism."[5]

II. LEVINAS'S LIFE AND WORK

Unlike many philosophers, who, in Heidegger's dictum, were born, thought, and died, Levinas's life was involved with the major events of Europe in the twentieth century and his biography is a useful way of situating his philosophical and ethical work and its relationship to history. Born in 1906 (or, in the then Russian Calendar, December 1905), in Kovno in Lithuania, his family was part of the large Jewish community there. Fleeing the German occupation in 1915, Levinas's family moved to Ukraine, and returned to Lithuania in 1920. In 1923, he went to study philosophy in France, and then in 1928, he traveled to Germany, to further explore Husserl's work. While in Germany, however, he was exposed to the work of Heidegger. In 1930, he married, became a French citizen, did military service and took a job teaching for the Alliance Israélite Universelle in Paris. Drafted into the army in 1939, he was captured by the Germans in 1940 and imprisoned in a camp for Jewish prisoners of war. His status as a French solider protected him from being murdered in the Holocaust. However, while his wife and daughter were hidden in France, the rest of his family in Lithuania were murdered by the Nazis or by Lithuanian nationalists.

After the war, Levinas returned to France and became director of the École Normale Israélite Orientale. Mixing in philosophical circles in Paris, Levinas

---

4. Jacques Derrida and Maurizio Ferraris, *A Taste for the Secret*, Giacomo Donis and David Webb (eds), Giacomo Donis (trans.) (Cambridge: Polity, 2001), 4.

5. Alain Badiou, *Ethics*, Peter Hallward (trans.) (London: Verso, 2001), 18.

published papers on a number of themes connected to ethics. He also began a study of Talmud with an enigmatic but influential master, Monsieur Chouchani,[6] Levinas became actively involved in Jewish intellectual life and became a major figure in the Jewish community, often giving radio talks and speaking at events. His first book, *Existence and Existents*, was published in 1947. However, the first of his two most important books, *Totality and Infinity*, was not published until 1961. Levinas taught at three well-known universities in Paris: in 1964, he was appointed Professor of Philosophy at Poitiers, in 1967 at Paris-Nanterre, and in 1973 at the Sorbonne. His second major book, *Otherwise than Being, or, Beyond Essence*, was published in 1974. Although he retired in 1976, he continued teaching and writing. In the 1980s and 1990s, many conferences were organized to discuss him and his works. In 1996 Levinas died after a long illness.

Levinas's work is rooted in the phenomenological tradition and interwoven with a concern for Judaism and religion, and with the impact of the Shoah on European Jews. Hence, his work draws on the prominent intellectuals of the European canon and is intimately interwoven with the Holocaust, an event that has led to more ethical questioning than any other in Europe. There is not space here to fully do his work justice, but only to explain why his work became of interest.

Levinas's work is centrally, almost exclusively, concerned with ethics. However, he proffers a number of meanings to the conceptualization of "ethics": ethics refers to the traditional philosophical discipline; it refers to his own philosophical discourse; and it refers to one's own relation to the other. As I have suggested, his work is both phenomenological and oriented by a tradition of phenomenology, drawn from Husserl and principally, although he was sometimes evasive about this, from Heidegger. The agonistic relationship between Levinas and Heidegger has prompted a significant amount of critical commentary that frequently begins with Levinas's remark that there was a "profound need to leave the climate" of Heidegger's philosophy that is linked with his "conviction that we cannot leave it for a philosophy that would be pre-Heideggerian."[7] Again, in a 1981 interview, Levinas said that "I think that one cannot seriously philosophize today without traversing the Heideggerian path in some form or other."[8] He also

---

6. "Monsieur Chouchani" was the pseudonym of a mysterious Jewish teacher who in post-Second World War Paris and elsewhere mentored a small number of distinguished students, including Levinas and Elie Wiesel. His gravestone in Montevideo, Uruguay, where he died in 1968, bears the epigraph written by Wiesel, "The wise Rabbi Chouchani of blessed memory. His birth and his life are sealed in enigma."
7. Emmanuel Levinas, *Existence and Existents*, Alphonso Lingis (trans.) (The Hague: Martinus Nijhoff, 1978), 19.
8. Richard Kearney, *Dialogues with Contemporary Continental Thinkers: The Phenomenological Heritage* (Manchester: Manchester University Press, 1984), 51.

speaks of the "debt" that every contemporary philosopher owes to Heidegger, "a debt that he often owes to his regret."[9] Stupefied and disappointed by Heidegger's active Nazism in 1933, Levinas continued utterly to despise Heidegger and his Nazi sympathies while admiring *Being and Time* as one the greatest works of philosophy. Even so, he asks if we can "be assured … that there was never any Echo of Evil in it?"[10] Still, as Levinas says, "Mont Blanc is Mont Blanc," meaning that however he feels, the influence is there.[11]

Levinas's crucial development of Heidegger's thought, which reveals a great deal about Levinas's work and about the ethical turn, can be seen by considering where each locates the "origin" of philosophy. If, for Heidegger, the experience of philosophy, of Dasein's being an issue for itself, begins with being-toward-death, and the associated phenomena of anxiety and care, it becomes the task of fundamental ontology to uncover these. In contrast, Levinas finds another, and for him, more important and "pre-ontological" starting-point: the encounter with the other. For Levinas, "ethics is first philosophy," by which he means that it is the actual concrete encounter with the other, with the "face" of the other, that underlies our sense of self and identity, and this in turn is the beginning of Levinas's understanding of what philosophy is. Philosophy begins, as it were, with the other. For Heidegger, death has mine-only-ness (*Jemeiningkeit*): "dying … is essentially mine in such a way that no one can be my representative" and it is through this angst that Dasein comes to its authenticity and individuality.[12] For Levinas, on the other hand, what generates crucial awareness, and self-understanding, is revealed in the underpinnings of existence – what it means to be other. He writes: "'Me' is not an inimitable nuance of *Jemeiningkeit* that would be added on to a being belonging to the genus 'soul' or 'man' or 'individual,' and would thus be common to several souls, men and individuals."[13] In other words, one's sense of subjectivity is not a category in a philosophical anthropology or a defining character of what it is to be "human." Rather, it is the basis of any such definition in the first place: "it is I, I and no one else, who am a hostage for the others. … The self in a being is exactly the not-being-able-to-slip-away-from an assignation" (OTB 26–7). The experience of ethics is that which underlies the self and is inescapable. Because ethics is not solipsistic but

---

9. Emmanuel Levinas, *God, Death and Time*, Bettina Bergo (trans.) (Stanford, CA Stanford University Press, 2000), 8.
10. Emmanuel Levinas, "As If Consenting to Horror," Paula Wissing (trans.), *Critical Inquiry* 15 (Winter 1989), 488.
11. Levinas, *God, Death and Time*, 158.
12. Martin Heidegger, *Being and Time*, John Macquarrie and Edward Robinson (trans.) (New York: Harper & Row, 1962), 297, 299.
13. Emmanuel Levinas, *Otherwise than Being, or, Beyond Essence*, Alphonso Lingis (trans.) (The Hague: Martinus Nijhoff, 1981), 126. Hereafter cited as OTB followed by the page number.

is (not just "comes from," but *is*) the experience of the other or, as Levinas calls it, "proximity," ethics is experienced as "obsession" (OTB 101): "responsibility justified by no prior commitment" (OTB 102); being "summoned as someone irreplaceable" (OTB 114); "being-in-one's-skin, having-the-other-in-one's skin" (OTB 115); the "unconditionality of being hostage" (OTB 117); "an accusation which I cannot answer, but for which I cannot decline responsibility" (OTB 127). One way of saying this, although using Heideggerian language, is to say that, where Heidegger states that Dasein and Mitsein are equiprimordial, for Levinas, Mitsein, being-with, is prior to Dasein.

A crucial passage in *Otherwise than Being* illuminates this. He asks: "[Why] does the other concern me? What is Hecuba to me? Am I my brother's keeper?" His answer is that these questions:

> have meaning only if one has already supposed the ego is concerned only with itself, is only a concern for itself. In this hypothesis, it indeed remains incomprehensible that the absolute outside-of-me, the other, would concern me. But in the "pre-history" of the ego posited for itself speaks a responsibility, the self is through and through a hostage, older than the ego, prior to principles.
>
> (OTB 117)

He is suggesting that before we think of ourselves as ourselves, we must consider our relationship to others because we are already responsible for the others who people the world. We are, to use one of his many terms for the experience of obligation, their hostages, and their very otherness – rather than some shared quality, such as national identity – imposes this burden on us. One of his key terms for this experience of the ethical both stems from and is named "the face." By this he means that when we face someone, before we decide how to respond (to give or not to give a beggar money, to wish someone "good morning" or to turn away), we are already put into a relationship with them. This unconditional responsibility is not something we take on or a rule by which we agree to be bound; instead, it exists before us and we are "thrown" into it, without any choice.

Levinas's work, then, is not aiming to offer a new moral or ethical system or provide a regulated moral standard; rather, it is an attempt to understand how our obligations to others arise, and this means that it is a form of metaethics. This aspect of Levinas's thought has caused some confusion. With the exception of some of his radio talks, Levinas's own philosophical work is not exhortative to an ethical life or a moral or political code. Rather, it is descriptive of the grounds of possibility of such codes – and indeed of all human interaction – in the first place. Levinas is not demanding that we become aware of the other, but is instead arguing phenomenologically that we always already are aware of the other. For example, in one of the most complex passages in *Totality and Infinity*, Levinas argues that murder already acknowledges the ethical relationship. He suggests that murder is not the domination or use of someone, the turning of another person from an end to a use. Instead, it is to recognize them as Other, as beyond one's power: the "Other is the sole being I can wish to kill."[14] One does not speak of killing a chair, or of murdering a cup of coffee. (One might speak of murdering – rather than butchering – a cow, which would raise the question, if, for Levinas or post-Levinasian thought, animals can be "other" in this ethical sense). The importance of Levinas's work, however, lies not only with the work itself; it also lies with its influence and reception, with how it became the fulcrum for the "ethical turn."

III. LEVINAS'S THOUGHT AND THE "ETHICAL TURN"

Levinas's thought is often understood as deeply interwoven with that of his friend and philosophical colleague, the critic and novelist Maurice Blanchot. Levinas and Blanchot met as students, and throughout their lives, their works responded to each other. Blanchot's thought is varied and complex, and in general focused on but not limited to the aesthetic, broadly defined. In this ethical context, there are three key elements that intertwine with Levinas (and are an influence on Derrida). The first is his unswerving thinking of singularity: in relation to literature, for example, he writes that:

> the essence of literature is precisely to evade any essential character-
> ization, any affirmation which would stabilize or even realize it: it is
> never already there, it is always to be rediscovered or reinvented. It
> is never even certain that the words "literature" or "art" correspond
> to anything real, anything possible, or anything important.[15]

That is to say, the categories of "art" and "literature" already overcode or cover up the singular event of the literary text: to properly encounter a work of litera-ture we cannot look for a "core" of the literary, a generic marker that all literary texts share. This is even more the case with the event of a human: like Levinas, Blanchot believes there is no "genus" of man. Each is a singularity and this

---

14. Emmanuel Levinas, *Totality and Infinity: An Essay on Exteriority*, Alphonso Lingis (trans.) (Pittsburgh, PA: Duquesne University Press, 1969), 198.
15. Maurice Blanchot, "The Disappearance of Literature," in *The Blanchot Reader*, Michael Holland (ed.) (Oxford: Blackwell, 1995), 141.

creates "the infinite relation of one person to another" which "obligates beyond any obligation."[16] In turn, this leads to the importance of the idea of "witnessing" to Blanchot. This is not "witnessing" in the sense of reporting back an event, but, in the language he develops from Levinas, a "saying," a witnessing of the event of the human. One consequence of this is what he sees – in a book mainly if implicitly about Levinas, *The Infinite Conversation* – as the impossibility of ever "having done" with questioning. Finally, and again in protracted literary dialogue with Levinas – and with his own right-wing views from the 1930s – Blanchot is centrally concerned with the Holocaust. His poetic/philosophical fragmentary meditation, *The Writing of the Disaster* is in no small part about this.

There are also congruencies between Levinas's work and the thought of Vladimir Jankélévitch, a thinker very little known outside France, as Levinas's short account of him in *Outside the Subject* illustrates. Like Levinas, Jankélévitch was influenced by Bergson, and sought to develop an ethics – like Levinas – as "first philosophy" that both underlies and is not delimited to declarations of principles. He is perhaps best known for his discussion about the relationship between forgiveness and the genocide of the European Jews. Here, often with the blackest humor, he argued against the possibility of forgiveness for the Nazi crimes:

> Today when the sophists recommend forgetfulness, we will force-fully mark our mute and impotent horror before the dogs of hate; we will think hard about the agony of the deportees without sepulchers and of the little children who did not come back. Because this agony will last until the end of the world.[17]

Here, both his sense of ethics and his division of "scientific" time and duration, developed from Bergson, bring to the fore the inexhaustibility of the Shoah.[18]

This way of conceptualizing ethics – as interwoven with metaphysics, as first philosophy – that is common to Levinas, Blanchot, and Jankélévitch, and was taken up by others, as I will suggest below, is strikingly different from some others and is the core of the "ethical turn." In contrast, for example, Foucault's late work is sometimes discussed or named as ethics. In a way, this has some purchase; however, his work focused more on the "technics of the self" – that is, the historical, political and cultural matrices that form subjectivity and the

---

16. Maurice Blanchot, *The Writing of the Disaster*, Ann Smock (trans.) (Lincoln, NE: University of Nebraska Press, 1986), 109.
17. Vladimir Jankélévitch, "Should We Pardon Them?" Ann Hobart (trans.), *Critical Inquiry* 22 (Spring 1996), 572.
18. Derrida's essay "On Forgiveness" also addresses Jankélévitch's work.

possibility of resistance to them or action within them – than on ethics *per se*, even as he attempted to develop ways of thinking about "how to live" in the contemporary situation of modernity.

IV. THE RECEPTION OF LEVINAS'S WORK AND THE "ETHICAL TURN"

During the 1960s and 1970s, Levinas's philosophy – his early essays and his two major books *Totality and Infinity* and *Otherwise than Being* – remained fairly obscure and seemed to have a limited effect outside of a very narrow philosophical and Jewish intellectual circle. In the Anglo-American world, too, this was the case. Translations of his work were published in an untimely manner and very little critical commentary was produced.[19] Even so, Levinas's work made an impact in a number of significant places. As I have suggested, his lifelong friend Blanchot was greatly influenced by Levinas's work and wrote both of and on him. Jean-François Lyotard, too, was greatly influenced by Levinas and discussed his work at length in his most important book, *The Differend* (1986).

In the philosophy of religion, Levinas's work made an impact and attracted commentary from, among others, leading theologian Jean-Luc Marion and Pope John Paul II. While Levinas argued that he articulated "a clear distinction, in what I write, between philosophical and confessional texts," he could not "deny that they ultimately have a common source of inspiration."[20] If philosophy and religion "happen to be in harmony … it is probably because every philosophical thought rests on pre-philosophical experiences."[21] Whether Levinas was, at heart, a religious thinker, or one who analyzes some of the phenomenological experiences of religion that are widely shared, is a matter for debate. One must note, however, that the influence of religion in his work has been of interest to theologians. Equally noteworthy, his work does play a large role in Dominique Janicaud's polemic about phenomenology and religion in French philosophy.[22]

Another major thinker, influenced in some part by Levinas's work, was Paul Ricoeur.[23] Ricoeur is a significant figure in European thought, and his work is

---

19. The first book on his work was Edith Wyschogrod's *Emmanuel Levinas: The Problem of Ethical Metaphysics* (The Hague: Martinus Nijhoff, 1974).

20. Kearney, *Dialogues with Contemporary Continental Thinkers*, 54.

21. Emmanuel Levinas, *Ethics and Infinity: Conversations with Philippe Nemo*, Richard A. Cohen (trans.) (Pittsburgh, PA: Duquesne University Press, 1985), 24.

22. Dominique Janicaud, *The Theological Turn of French Phenomenology*, Bernard G. Prusak (trans.), in Dominique Janicaud *et al.*, *Phenomenology and the "Theological Turn": The French Debate* (New York: Fordham University Press, 2000). Levinas's influence on French philosophy of religion and Janicaud's work is discussed by Bruce Ellis Benson in this volume.

*23. For a more extensive discussion of Ricoeur's philosophy, see the essay by Wayne J. Froman in *The History of Continental Philosophy: Volume 6*.

characterized by a desire to synthesize differing traditions, both within European philosophy and, especially in his work most centrally concerned with ethics, *Soi-même comme un autre* (*Oneself as Another*; 1990), European and analytic traditions. His work on ethics drew on the conceptions of "virtue ethics" developed by, among others, Alasdair MacIntyre, with whom he had worked closely. Ricoeur's work had long been concerned with the nature of narrative: in relation to the ethical, he argued that the *ipse*, the self-consistency of a self, is constructed in and understood through, and as, a narrative. Our identifications with our own narratives (which shape our habits, and our ways of seeing ourselves) lead us to moral behavior – preeminently exemplified, for Ricoeur, in keeping one's word. Perhaps the main consequence of this view is that it becomes impossible for us to see ourselves in isolation from others: instead, this view leads us to understand ourselves as constantly accountable to and responsible for others.

However, central to the "ethical turn" and to the reception and development of Levinas's work was the influence it had on the work and the thought of Jacques Derrida. *Totality and Infinity* was the subject of a long essay by Derrida, written in 1964, entitled "Violence and Metaphysics." This wide-ranging and complex essay is, as Robert Bernasconi suggests, not simply a critique by Derrida of Levinas, but one of the earliest of Derrida's deconstructive readings; indeed, it is "a key document both in Derrida's development of deconstruction and in the reception of Levinas's own ethical thinking."[24] In this essay, Derrida's chief argument is that in *Totality and Infinity* what is fundamental is not ethics *per se* but rather Levinas's phenomenological method of "uncovering" ethics. Derrida argues that this means that "ethics finds within phenomenology its own meaning, its freedom and its radicality."[25] For Levinas, Derrida suggests, it is the way in which ethics is represented by phenomenological thought that reduces ethics to representation; the "meaning of the non-theoretical as such (for example, ethics or the metaphysical in Levinas's sense)" is only made clear by "theoretical knowledge."[26] Ethics, then, is not "first philosophy." Rather, the representation of the ethical by phenomenological thought becomes first philosophy: the nontheoretical, the "true representation" of the face, is understood only through the theoretical, in this case, through the methodology of phenomenology.

---

24. Robert Bernasconi, "Deconstruction and the Possibility of Ethics," in *Deconstruction and Philosophy*, John Sallis (ed.) (Chicago, IL: University of Chicago Press, 1987), 124.
25. Jacques Derrida, "Violence and Metaphysics: An Essay on the Thought of Emmanuel Levinas," in *Writing and Difference*, Alan Bass (trans.) (Chicago, IL: University of Chicago Press, 1978), 121.
26. *Ibid.*, 122.

Derrida has returned to Levinas and recognizably Levinasian themes throughout his work.[27] However, many of Levinas's ideas – the idea of the trace, for example – were taken up and transformed by Derrida. In fact, it is possible to see Levinas's own work after "Violence and Metaphysics," including *Otherwise than Being*, as a response to Derrida's intervention. It is through Derrida's work that a generation of philosophers associated with him and with deconstruction were influenced by Levinas. Indeed, much of the "ethical turn" can be seen as a response to Derrida's own Levinas-influenced shift of emphasis over his prolific career from linguistic and epistemological questions (broadly understood) to ethical and political ones.

Like Derrida, Levinas's influence on the philosopher Jean-Luc Nancy can also be seen, although he engages more directly with political and communal concerns. In *The Inoperative Community* (1982), Nancy seeks to develop an idea of community beyond the traditional understanding of Western philosophy, which posits a shared characteristic communality – a "communitarian essence"[28] – that makes up a community. Instead, he posits a community of those who have nothing in common, a community made up precisely because they share having nothing in common save their finitude. Indeed, a community is thought out precisely "on the basis of a shared mortality which cannot be subsumed into any communal project or collective identity … the exposure of each singular existence, its being-outside-of-itself, to a death which is reveled in and through the death of others."[29] What creates the thought of a community is what exceeds it. In this, like Levinas, he prioritizes Mitsein, being-with, over Dasein. He continues to develop this theme – that our commonality lies not in any quality, but in our very experience of finitude and estrangement – in *Being Singular Plural* (1996), where he puts forward the idea that it is each of our being as singular that marks our communality.

V. PROBLEMS WITH LEVINAS AND THE "ETHICAL TURN"

There are two sorts of problems that are raised by the ethical turn within the history of contemporary philosophy. The first concerns the possible religious element of the turn in general, and in particular in Levinas's thought; the second concerns the relationship between the ethics espoused in this turn and the political.

---

27. See, for example, Jacques Derrida, *Adieu to Emmanuel Levinas*, Pascale-Anne Brault and Michael Naas (trans.) (Stanford, CA: Stanford University Press, 1999).
28. Jean-Luc Nancy, *The Inoperative Community*, Peter Connor (ed.), Peter Connor *et al.* (trans.). (Minneapolis, MN: University of Minnesota Press, 1991), 22.
29. *Ibid.*, 185.

Levinas's apparent religious commitments – whether or not they structure his more rigorous philosophical thought – have raised a range of questions. Indeed, one early and critical account by Gillian Rose argues that Levinas simply presents "Judaic theologico-political prophecy or ethics in philosophical terms as the end of philosophy."[30] It is unclear if the very idea of "the other" is not simply a cover for the "divine other." This is central to a number of critiques of Levinas's thought by leading contemporary thinkers. Badiou, for example, is highly critical of Levinas. While – rightly – he dismisses much vague talk of "the ethics of difference" that Levinas's work has inspired as "strikingly different from Levinas's actual conception of things," he argues that Levinas is at base a religious thinker.[31] Badiou goes further, and more interestingly, he states that "the ethical primacy of the Other over the Same" (what he takes to be the core of Levinas's thought) requires "that the experience of alterity be ontologically 'guaranteed' as the experience of a distance, or of an essential non-identity, the traversal of which is the ethical experience itself. But nothing in the simple phenomenon of the other contains such a guarantee."

In order for Levinas's ethics to function, then, Badiou asserts that it needs an axiom, that "ethics requires that the Other in some sense be carried by a principle of alterity which transcends mere finite experience." Badiou contends that Levinas calls this principle the "Altogether-other" and "it is quite obviously the ethical name for God." Badiou continues by arguing that this means that Levinas's philosophy is "annulled by theology" and that "every effort to turn ethics into a principle of thought and action is essentially religious … ethics is a category of pious discourse." In his book *After Finitude* (2006), Quentin Meillassoux makes a similar charge, accusing a whole tradition of phenomeno-logical thought of "fideism." While it is true that Levinas himself was a religious man, and his work is influenced by religious thought, and that uncovering the implicit workings of a reliance on the divine is a valid task for philosophers, there is much in these critiques that is open to question. Badiou bases his claim on an issue in Levinas's work – the fact that the alterity of the other cannot be guaranteed, or may not "occur" – that is present as an issue in *Totality and Infinity*, but that is explicitly addressed in *Otherwise than Being*. There, the "said" – the concretization of the other in a way that prevents its work as a rupture – overgrows the "saying" – the rupture caused by otherness. Moreover, Levinas never claims in his philosophical work that the "altogether-other" is Divine, and it need not be for his work to function as a description of the moment of ethics. Finally, while for Badiou the operation of axioms is crucial for philosophy, for

30. Gillian Rose, *Judaism and Modernity* (Oxford: Blackwell, 1993), 42.
31. Badiou, *Ethics*, 22. All citations in this paragraph appear on pages 22–3.

Levinas, axiomatic thought is only one part of philosophical work more widely understood.

Slavoj Žižek, too, shares some of these reservations, especially about the possible role of the Divine. Moreover, he finds the stress on the Face, in *Totality and Infinity* – which is changed in *Otherwise than Being* – too strong, even fetishist. Further, and again, without apparently having read *Otherwise than Being*, where Levinas addresses the question of social justice and the "third," Žižek questions how an asymmetrical ethics – one in which the "I" is responsible to the Other – can form a communal justice.

Žižek's concerns point to the second array of questions, about the nature of the ethical turn and the political. And it is in Derrida's use of Levinas that we see this issue in the "ethical turn" being addressed. This relationship is complex: it is not simply a matter of an "exhortative" gesture; after all, one does not need philosophy for preaching, or for trying to live the good life. Rather, the ethical turn, taking its cue from Levinas and from the phenomenological tradition, was not at first a political philosophy but rather a painstaking reflection on thought and on the traditions and canons of European thought itself that were aware of the exclusion or (often murderous) transformation of otherness. Hannah Arendt – like Levinas, a student of Heidegger – wrote, in *The Origins of Totalitarianism*, that we:

> can no longer afford to take that which was good in the past and simply call it our heritage, to disregard the bad and simply think of it as a dead load which by itself time will bury in oblivion. The subterranean stream of western history has finally come to the surface and usurped the dignity of our tradition. This is the reality in which we live. And this is why all the efforts to escape from the grimness of the present into nostalgia for a still intact past, or into the anticipated oblivion of a better future, are vain.[32]

The ethical turn was focused, then, on this "subterranean stream," which had "come to the surface" (after all, "Nazism was not born in a desert," Derrida writes).[33] It was the sense that Western thought was, as Levinas described it, an "Omnivorous philosophy" in which "'I think' comes down to 'I can' – to an appropriation of what is, to an exploitation of reality."[34] That is, the ethical turn can be seen as an attempt to disrupt the metaphysics of comprehension, the

---

32. Hannah Arendt, *The Origins of Totalitarianism* (London: Harcourt Brace, 1973), lx.
33. Jacques Derrida, *Of Spirit: Heidegger and the Question*, Geoffrey Bennington and Rachel Bowlby (trans.) (Chicago, IL: University of Chicago Press, 1989), 109.
34. Levinas, *Totality and Infinity*, 46.

gesture that characterizes Western thought. But this is not a rejection of Western thought or of politics. Levinas argued, instead, that this moment of engagement with the other, this:

> putting into question of the same by the Other … is, beyond knowledge, the condition of philosophy … not only attested by the articulations of Husserlian thought … but also appears at the summits of philosophies: it is the beyond-being of Plato, it is the entry through the door of the agent intellect in Aristotle; it is the idea of God in us, surpassing our capacity as finite beings; it is the exaltation of theoretical reasoning in Kant's practical reason; it is the study of the recognition by the Other in Hegel himself; it is the renewal of duration in Bergson; it is the sobering of lucid reason in Heidegger.[35]

The other is both the foundation and the demarcation of the limits of Western thought. However, this putting into question or thinking the limits can happen only in the conceptual language that is available: the language shaped and characterized by the Greek *logos*. For the West, no other conceptual language is easily available. Yet from this, thinkers have begun to develop and structure senses of political commitment. Of course, Levinas's work has offered a way of discussing ethics that was outside traditional *marxisant* models and drier, more analytic forms of ethical inquiry. That is, his work simply offered a way to discuss ethics and politics when no others were available or convincing. More than this, as I have suggested, it also brought the reflective critique of thought (traditions of thought inherited from Heidegger and strands of phenomenology) into an ethical arena. Even though Levinas's own politics were conservative, and sometimes, as Howard Caygill has argued, open to question even in light of his own philosophical commitments, the discussion of ethics began to make a bridge between philosophical and political commitments.[36]

Indeed, in "Violence and Metaphysics," Derrida proleptically suggests that this sort of approach to ethics is an "ethics without law and without concept, which maintains its non-violent purity only before being determined as concepts and laws."[37] That is, this understanding of otherness could not become a dictate of a series of moral axioms: it is beyond, although foundational for, law and politics. This might suggest its inapplicability to the political in any sense. Indeed, much in the "ethical turn" reflects an intellectual response to

---

35. Emmanuel Levinas, "Philosophy and Awakening," Mary Quaintance (trans.), in *Who Comes after the Subject?*, Eduardo Cadava *et al.* (eds) (New York: Routledge, 1991), 215.

36. See Howard Caygill, *Levinas and the Political* (London: Routledge, 2002).

37. Derrida, "Violence and Metaphysics," 111.

the Cold War: not by (*pace* Arendt in the 1950s) contrasting communism with democratic liberalism, but rather by revealing that any system itself (liberal, socialist) is a totalizing one. Evaluating systems in this way, in a globalized era, might be seen as enabling a new world order or it could, more sinisterly, be seen as an abdication of political responsibility. It is precisely this suggestion that one of the leading thinkers of the "ethical turn," Simon Critchley, has sought to address. Critchley's first book, *The Ethics of Deconstruction*, aimed to uncover the role that Levinas's thought played in Derrida's work and to argue that deconstruction was ethical in Levinas's sense. His recent work continues to develop this line of thought and to explore the impact of the ethical turn on current political thought. Critchley argues that "ethics without politics is empty ... politics without ethics are blind ... we need ethics in order to see what to do in a political situation."[38] He argues that the problem with much traditional thinking about politics is that it is "archic: it is obsessed with the moment of foundation, origination, declaration, or institution that is linked to the act of government, of sovereignty, of establishment of a state" (128). In contrast, the form of politics that he develops, from the ethical turn, is what he describes as "anarchical meta-politics." By this, and following up Levinas's suggestions, Critchley is not suggesting that anarchy should be a new "arche" – another political category – but that it should be the "negation of a totality and not the affirmation of a new totality ... a radical disturbance of the state, a disruption of the state's attempt to set itself up or erect itself into a whole" (122). "We might say," he continues, "that ethical anarchy is the experience of the multiple singularities of the encounter with others that defines the experience of sociality" (123). This means that politics, while guided by ethics, cannot respond to "systemic or structural laws" (132), or overarching principles, but requires "subjective invention, imagination and endurance, not to mention tenacity and cunning" (132). The result of the ethical turn in philosophy is to "construct political subjectivities that are not arbitrary or relativistic, but that are articulations of an ethical demand whose scope is universal and whose evidence is faced in a concrete situation. This is dirty, local, practical and largely unthrilling work" (132).

In a similar vein, Judith Butler's recent work circles around Levinasian themes and responses to political questions. Like Critchley, she seeks to link the ethical and political realms through a consideration of the Levinasian face, through issues of vulnerability. She writes that if:

> the humanities has a future as cultural criticism, and cultural criticism has a task at the present moment, it is no doubt to return us to

---

38. Simon Critchley, *Infinitely Demanding: Ethics of Commitment, Politics of Resistance* (London: Verso, 2007), 120. Subsequent references to this text are cited parenthetically by page number.

the human where we do not expect to find it, in its frailty and at the limit of its capacity to make sense. We would have to investigate the human at the limits of what we can know, what we can hear, what we can see, what we can sense.[39]

Critchley, Butler, and others are seeking philosophically informed ethical/political responses from outside the conventional Left/Right positions and are a part of the continuing legacy of the "ethical turn."

VI. CONCLUSION

I have argued that the transformation in continental philosophy in the 1980s, resulting in the "ethical turn," was a response to political, cultural, and historical events. The growing number of new areas of philosophical interest and a return to older questions that analyze, both practically and intellectually, the Marxist tradition led to a reconsideration of the category of "otherness." While Jacques Derrida was perhaps the central, and most well known, figure in this, the primary influence was Emmanuel Levinas, and much of the "ethical turn" can be seen as an exploration and development of themes in his philosophy.

Rooted agonistically in the phenomenological tradition and in a philosophical consideration of the darkest moments of twentieth-century European history, Levinas argued that "ethics was first philosophy": that is, that our ethical commitments originate in the concrete experience of our encounter with the other and that this "precedes" ontology and subjectivity, that "the self is through and through a hostage, older than the ego, prior to principles" (OTB 117). Until the 1970s and 1980s, this work had a narrow but significant influence. Over time it has become a major force in the theorization of ethics. Although the Levinasian approach – and the "ethical turn" in general – has been criticized for being apolitical and religious, its influence and legacy remains in the work of many recent thinkers who have countered these claims by developing further these Levinasian insights.

---

39. Judith Butler, *Precarious Life: The Power of Mourning and Violence* (London: Verso, 2004), 151.

11

FEMINIST PHILOSOPHY: COMING OF AGE

Rosi Braidotti

I. THE MULTIPLE TEMPORALITIES OF FEMINIST THOUGHT

Around 1981, as Jane Gallop put it in her homonymous book, the second feminist wave enters officially into the academic curriculum of American universities. The baby-boomers, whose restlessness and egalitarian aspirations shaped the politics and the cultural revolution of the 1970s, come of academic age in the 1980s and go knocking on the doors of academia, demanding reforms of the canonical curriculum that will reflect the concerns and anxieties of their generation. The disciplinary area that is most receptive to the theoretical insights, the political passions and the innovative style of the radical epistemologies of the social movements of the 1960s and 1970s is not, predictably enough, philosophy. The academic, institutional practice of philosophy is still quite conservative at the dawn of the 1980s, as argued in this volume by Judith Butler and Braidotti. It tends to resist against the swelling tide of radical philosophies and the social and political turmoil of the period. A crucial element of this hostility is related to the "Franco-American disconnection,"[1] and it underscores the extent to which French poststructuralist thought actually shaped the theoretical concerns of the rebellious generation who entered US academia at the end of the 1970s and was thus well placed to shape the agenda throughout the 1980s.

---

1. The term was coined by Domna Stanton in 1980 in "Language and Revolution: The Franco-American Dis-connection," in *The Future of Difference*, Hester Eisenstein and Alice Jardine (eds) (Boston, MA: G. K. Hall, 1980).

This is not to say, however, that the impact of French thought was uncontroversial, or that other traditions within continental philosophy did not impact positively on the development of feminist philosophies through the 1980s.

For instance, the German critical theory school continues to exert a productive influence on feminism, in the astute commentaries provided by a new generation of scholars,[2] but also in original elaborations. For example, Seyla Benhabib and Nancy Fraser provide new insights into democratic analyses of societal institutions and social movements.[3] Drucilla Cornell pursues a different route to radical democracy by combining the methods of deconstruction and psychoanalytic theory to the analysis of social phenomena.[4]

The legacy of phenomenology also endures and grows,[5] for example through Iris Marion Young's illuminating analyses of public policy, race politics, and democratic practices.[6] The phenomenology of race is enriched by the original gender perspectives introduced by Linda Alcoff, while Christine Battersby engages in productive dialogue with both phenomenology and poststructuralism.[7] One of the areas of phenomenology that grows exponentially in the period is the field of "Beauvoir studies," especially after the death of the grand lady in 1986.[8] Deirdre Bair publishes Simone de Beauvoir's official biography in 1990,[9] while critical overviews of Beauvoir's impact on contemporary feminism begin to appear.[10] This field of study will intensify at the end of the century and the start of the new millennium.

2. See, for example, the essays collected in Johanna Meehan (ed.), *Feminists read Habermas: Gendering the Subject of Discourse* (New York: Routledge, 1995).

3. See Seyla Benhabib, *Critique, Norm and Utopia: A Study of the Foundations of Critical Theory* (New York: Columbia University Press, 1986); Seyla Benhabib and Drucilla Cornell (eds), *Feminism as Critique: On the Politics of Gender* (Minneapolis, MN: University of Minnesota Press, 1987); Nancy Fraser, *Unruly Practices: Power, Discourse, and Gender in Contemporary Social Theory* (Minneapolis, MN: University of Minnesota Press, 1989).

4. See Drucilla Cornell, *Beyond Accommodation: Ethical Feminism, Deconstruction and the Law* (New York: Routledge, 1991), and *The Imaginary Domain: Abortion, Pornography and Sexual Difference* (New York: Routledge, 1995).

5. For a useful introduction, see Linda Fisher and Lester Embree (eds), *Feminism and Phenomenology* (Dordrecht: Kluwer, 1996).

6. See Iris M. Young, *Throwing Like a Girl and Other Essays in Feminist Philosophy and Social Theory* (Bloomington, IN: Indiana University Press, 1990), and *Justice and the Politics of Difference* (Princeton, NJ: Princeton University Press, 1990).

7. See for instance Christine Battersby, *The Phenomenal Woman: Feminist Metaphysics and the Patterns of Identity* (Cambridge: Polity, 1998).

8. Nineteen eight-six was the year that *Yale French Studies* devoted a special issue to "Simone de Beauvoir: Witness to a Century."

9. See Deirdre Bair, *Simone de Beauvoir: A Biography* (New York: Summit Books, 1990).

10. See especially Toril Moi, *Feminist Theory and Simone de Beauvoir* (Oxford: Blackwell, 1990); Margaret A. Simons (ed.) *Feminist Interpretations of Simone de Beauvoir* (University Park, PA: Pennsylvania State University Press, 1995). For an overview see Karen Vintges, *Philosophy*

Another field that grows fast in these years is feminist moral philosophy, which reaches greater heights with the theory of an "ethics of care" proposed by the social psychologist Carol Gilligan and developed into a new social theory of citizenship by Joan Tronto.[11] One of the most eminent feminist moral philosophers is Virginia Held, who combines the radical insights of feminist activism with broader ethical concerns.[12] Of great significance is also the work of Martha Nussbaum, who applies universal but situated ethical principles to public policy and urgent global social issues.[13] Analytic philosophy was itself not immune from the contagious creativity of the era.[14] The pace and quality of these new developments is such that it blurs the boundaries between established schools of thought and national traditions.

Nonetheless, French philosophy was clearly the inspirational force that propelled the most innovative theoretical developments for the feminist philosophers of the period throughout Europe and elsewhere.[15] Even the more skeptical-minded feminist philosophers have to come to terms with the challenges of difference.[16] French thought is thus the hidden agenda that makes

---

as Passion: *The Thinking of Simone de Beauvoir* (Bloomington, IN: Indiana University Press, 1996).

11. See, for example, Joan C. Tronto, *Moral Boundaries: A Political Argument for an Ethic of Care* (New York: Routledge, 1993).

12. See Virginia Held, *Feminist Morality: Transforming Culture, Society, Politics* (Chicago, IL: Chicago University Press, 1993), and *Justice and Care: Essential Readings in Feminist Ethics* (Boulder, CO: Westview Press, 1995).

13. See, for example, Martha Nussbaum, *The Fragility of Goodness* (Cambridge: Cambridge University Press, 1986), and *Cultivating Humanity: A Classical Defense of Reform in Liberal Education* (Cambridge, MA: Harvard University Press, 1999).

14. The main feminist contributions of the analytic feminist philosophers come much later and is best exemplified by Miranda Fricker and Jennifer Hornsby (eds), *The Cambridge Companion to Feminism in Philosophy* (Cambridge: Cambridge University Press, 2000). See also Lynn H. Nelson, *Who Knows: From Quine to a Feminist Empiricism* (Philadelphia, PA: Temple University Press, 1990).

15. The most significant works in this tradition are the Milan Women's Bookstore Collective's elaboration of *Sexual Difference: A Theory of Social-Symbolic Practice* (Bloomington, IN: Indiana University Press, 1990). This was developed into an original critique of the history of philosophy by Adriana Cavarero in *In Spite of Plato*. In German, the significant contributions are Herta Nagl-Docekal and Herlinde Pauer-Studer's edited collection *Denken der Geschlechterdifferenz: Neuen Fragen und Perspektiven des feministische Philosophie*, and Andrea Maihofer's *Geschlecht als Existenzweise: Macht, Moral, Recht und Geschlechterdifferenz*. In Spanish, the pioneering work is done by Celia Amorós in *Hacia una critica de la razón patriarchal* and by Maria Santa Cruz, Marie-Luisa Femenias, and Anna-Maria Bach on *Mujeres y filosofia* in Latin America.

16. This school, initiated by Janet Radcliffe Richards's *The Skeptical Feminist: A Philosophical Enquiry*, is pursued by Mary Hawksworth's "Knowers, Knowing, Known: Feminist Theory and Claims to Truth," which is a critical assessment of feminist postmodernism. Susan Hekman's *Gender and Knowledge: Elements of Postmodern Feminism* makes important progress on

traditional philosophers cringe with irritation and mistrust at the sight of new philosophical questions, supported by unfamiliar and foreign sounding terminology: subjectivity, discourse, materiality, and power as restrictive or negative (*potestas*), but also as positive and empowering (*potentia*). The impact of French poststructuralism on feminist theory is an epistemological upheaval: the French imports are clearly the fallout of what could be called "high" poststructuralism, namely the work of Lacan, Foucault, Derrida, Deleuze and their feminist counterparts Kristeva, Cixous, Kofman, Irigaray, and others.[17] This process of theoretical marketing, however, is not even: some texts – notably those of Foucault, Derrida, and Kristeva – enter rapidly into what Edward Said aptly labeled as the "travelling theories" mode, while others, notably those of Deleuze and Irigaray, had to wait much longer before being "discovered." The different rhythms of translation of these texts had a significant impact on the influence they exercised on Anglo-American feminism.

The effect of French poststructuralism was nonetheless instant and significant.[18] In the mid-1980s, as American feminism plunges into the "sex-wars" that will divide its radical wing,[19] the notion and the politics of difference move

---

materialism, while Anne Phillips's *Democracy and Difference* attempts an interesting dialogue between continental feminism and the British liberal tradition.

17. For a discussion of the work of many of these figures, see the essays in *The History of Continental Philosophy: Volume 6*. The French feminism phenomenon was analyzed lucidly by Claire Duchen in *Feminism in France: From May '68 to Mitterrand*, and it reads as a textbook case of cultural branding on the part of major English-language publishers. I analyzed the cultural marketing exercise with Jane Weistock in "Herstory as Recourse," in *Hecate*.

18. This movement is led by the linguistically oriented school, inspired by Jacques Lacan, Jacques Derrida, and Roland Barthes, that was centered in the Yale School of literary theory (for a discussion of the Yale School, see the essay by Jeffrey T. Nealon in *The History of Continental Philosophy: Volume 6*). The main feminist figures of this movement had a lot of influence on feminist philosophy, notably Barbara Johnson in *The Critical Difference* and *The Feminist Difference: Literature, Psychoanalysis, Race and Gender*. Shoshana Felman combined psychoanalysis and semiotics in inspiring ways in *What Does a Woman Want? Reading and Sexual Difference*, whereas Marjorie Garber adapted them both to cultural studies in *Vested Interests: Cross-dressing and Cultural Anxiety*. The pioneer of French feminist theory in the US was Domna Stanton, who worked on *The Female Autograph: Theory and Practice of Autobiography from the Tenth to the Twentieth Century*, a women-centered literary canon. Nancy Miller in *The Poetics of Gender*; Alice Jardine with *Gynesis*; Naomi Schor in "Dreaming Dissymmetry"; and Catharina Stimpson in *Where the Meanings Are*, developed radical perspectives on the specificity of the feminist approach to textual criticism. An inspiring deconstructivist like Gayatri Spivak also bases her interventions on the postpsychoanalytic and Derridian understanding of the ontological value of subjectivity and the primacy of the power relations that structure it.

19. The core argument of the "sex wars" was the campaign against pornography, which soon developed into a larger dispute about sexual politics and the understanding of sexual freedom. The influence of Andrea Dworkin and Catharine McKinnon resulted in a prohibitionist approach to sexual practices, which produced both an alliance with the Christian Right and a violent reaction by radical feminists and sexual liberationists. French philosophy provided

center stage.[20] The epicenter of the new philosophical developments stays in Paris, but a widespread diaspora of poststructuralist ideas takes place through the institutional basis for this movement of thought in the US, such as literary theory, comparative literature, cultural studies, and film theory. Philosophy departments place themselves at a clear and explicit distance from these fashionable trends and close ranks. This hostility will continue to grow throughout the 1980s as the "theory wars" rage through American universities under the combined effect of Reaganomics, neoconservatism, and the rise of the religious Christian Right. Poststructuralism did not fare much better on its home turf, especially after the presidential election of Mitterrand in 1981, when a wave of "new philosophers" (André Glucksmann, Bernard-Henri Lévy, etc.), turned its back on the philosophical giants of the previous generation.[21]

By 1995, the game will be over and the counter-offensive against poststructuralism will have won the day. Gayatri Spivak, looking back over this period in 2003, speaks of the death of a discipline to indicate the decline and fall of poststructuralist-driven literary theory and comparative literature in the US academy. Nonetheless, the hegemonic hold that high poststructuralist thought had over the most critical and creative minds of that academic generation endures. Spivak's analysis covers the external pressures of a fast-changing world driven by globalization, technological mediation, cultural hybridization, and the rising economic power of the global South. Spivak also stresses, however, the internal flaws of what she considers an incurably Eurocentric system of thought.[22] Gallop herself, writing in 1997[23] about a controversial lawsuit instigated by her lesbian students, spells out in unequivocal terms the political debacles generated by the rise of identity politics and the extent to which they absorbed the best energies of poststructuralism.

Narrating the course of feminist philosophies in the 1980–95 period means having to take into account this complex political and institutional history. The impact of high poststructuralism is in some ways a specifically American phenomenon, but it is connected to the French and European scene not only historically, but also through conceptual and personal ties: a whole generation of

---

a welcome alternative to this narrow and punitive reading of sexuality. For a comprehensive account of this phenomenon, see Carol Vance, *Pleasure and Danger: Exploring Female Sexuality* (London: Routledge & Kegan Paul, 1984).

20. See for instance the influential collection *The Future of Difference*, Hester Eisenstein and Alice Jardine (eds) (Boston, MA: G. K. Hall, 1983). For a philosophical defense see Marilyn Frye, "The Necessity of Differences: Constructing a Positive Category of Women," *Signs: Journal of Women in Culture & Society* 21(4) (1996).

21. See also my essay in *The History of Continental Philosophy: Volume 8*.

22. See, in this regard, the essay by Iain Chambers in this volume.

23. See Jane Gallop, *Feminist Accused of Sexual Harassment* (Durham, NC: Duke University Press, 1997).

graduate students and junior academics actually studied in Paris or read French theories as part of their often independently chosen curriculum. I was one of them and this personal involvement does not simplify my task in this chapter and increases my accountability accordingly. Because of the diasporic nature of poststructuralist philosophies of difference and subjectivity, however, and as a result of their enormous generative force, feminist philosophies in the 1980–95 period simply explode in an outburst of creativity. So much so that it is daunting to even attempt to account for the successful social and intellectual revolution that marks the coming of age of an entirely new generation of feminist philosophers who grew up with and after high poststructuralism.

The changing historical context also plays its hand in rendering feminist philosophy especially complex in this period. The twin phenomena of the fall of the Berlin Wall in 1989 and the enlargement of the European Union,[24] as well as the new wave of wars that emerge in the period (the first Gulf War, the Falklands War, and the Yugoslav and Balkans War), have major impact on the development of continental and transnational feminism.[25] The single most important development, however, is the expansion of feminism both east and west of the former border. In the former West, the institutional growth and consolidation of the field results in the creation of new PhD programs in women's studies. On the other side of the border, feminist philosophical voices from former Eastern Europe can now get a wider audience. This phenomenon is so vast and rich that it deserves a fuller treatment than I can grant it here. Suffice it to stress the importance of original political thinkers trained in philosophy, such as Zarana Papic, whose work on nationalism and subjectivity remains fundamental. Dasa Duhacek provides important analytical insights into Eastern European radical feminism as a critique of the patriarchal aspects of the Yugoslav communist state. Rada Iveković challenges narratives that assume the centrality of a Western philosophical perspective by adopting a broadened, antinationalist and postcolonial perspective.

As a consequence of these historical upheavals and intellectual developments, this chapter could not adopt a chronological structure, let alone a linear one. Nonlinearity has been a distinctive trait of feminist theory since the 1980s. In her seminal essay on women's time, also published in 1981, Julia Kristeva

---

24. See my "On Becoming Europeans," in *Women Migrants from East to West: Gender, Mobility, and Belonging in Contemporary Europe*, Luisa Passerini *et al.* (eds) (New York: Berghahn Books, 2007), 23–45.

25. Already at the beginning of the 1990s, feminist theory provides the basis for innovative critiques of globalization. Influential pioneers in this field are the political theorist Cynthia Enloe in *The Morning After: Sexual Politics at the End of the Cold War*, and the work of Inderpal Grewal and Caren Kaplan on transnational feminism in *Scattered Hegemonies: Postmodernity and Transnational Feminist Practices*.

stresses the cyclical, circular nature of female temporality, which she connects both to the specific rhythms of female embodiment and to the social division of labor that assigns women to the most repetitive and unappreciated tasks. Genealogical returns, not chronological continuity, fix the beat of feminist discursive production. The multiple temporalities of feminist philosophy spell patterns of becoming that challenge academic habits of linearity. I will attempt to account for these complex phenomena by drawing a cartography based on a generously broad, yet selective, bibliography of the main sources.

II. THE "INTERMEDIATE" GENERATION

The feminist philosophers who came after poststructuralism were too young to be real baby-boomers, but at the same time old enough to be eye-witnesses to the world-changing events of the 1970s and 1980s. I call the generation of feminist philosophers between 1981 and 1995 the "intermediate" generation, although what exactly it is intermediate between is open for discussion. At the start, it clearly follows "high poststructuralism," but what succeeds it – be it the third wave or a feminism yet to come – is still an open question. Truly poststructuralist in their desire to apply the great theoretical insights of the previous generation to a variety of social and discursive practices, feminists of the intermediate generation simultaneously pursue the aims of the second feminist wave and lay the foundations for future developments. They are the agents of the "long march through the institutions," which brings an entire new intellectual generation into academic positions, and with it a new theoretical and political agenda for the institutional practice of philosophy.

Although they are the real heiresses of high poststructuralist thought, there is no official testament to ensure the transmission of ideas, and not all of them had direct contact, either as students or colleagues, with the French master-thinkers who shaped that philosophical movement. They function in English and not all of them can read the French texts in the original, but this diasporic mode of thinking in translation, far from being a problem, turns into the strength of this particular generation of thinkers. Within the English language, many of the feminist philosophers of this period are not from the USA: for instance, the great pioneer of feminist philosophy Lorraine Code[26] is based in Canada, whereas under the influence of Genevieve Lloyd,[27] Australian feminist theory blossoms

---

26. See, for instance, Lorraine Code, *Epistemic Responsibility* (Hanover, NH: University Press of New England for Brown University Press, 1987), and *What Can She Know? Feminist Theory and the Constitution of Knowledge* (Ithaca, NY: Cornell University Press, 1991).

27. Genevieve Lloyd (1941–) studied philosophy at the University of Sydney and then at Somerville College, Oxford. Her DPhil, awarded in 1973, was on time and tense. From 1967

and spreads worldwide.[28] In the US, while many are products of philosophy departments, they tend to gather in interdisciplinary fields – as is the case for Butler, Cornell, and Elizabeth Grosz – although some manage jobs in continental philosophy, like Fraser and Alcoff.

In its diasporic and transnational mode, the intermediate generation of feminist philosophers embraces the concept of difference, but with the explicit aim of making it function differently. They recast feminist theory along a complex line of interrogation that includes race, sexual orientation, and age, and will target the main tenets of equality-minded feminism and question the view of the subject that is implicit in the political program of traditional emancipation in Europe and the liberal feminist politics of equal opportunities in the Anglo-American world. Irigaray's question "Equal to whom?"[29] could be taken as the war cry for the following generation, which refused to take equality as homologation or reduction to Sameness. The crucial idea is that difference functions as a multilayered concept not only between binaries, but also among diverse groups and more especially within each category. The "difference within" instills a constitutive distance between each concept and the metaphysical illusion of presence. It is a hiatus between the signifier and the signified in which the solidity of all meanings oscillates, stumbles, stutters, and falters. The positivity of difference, that is to say, the potential for radical transformation that is carried by subjects who are both socially and symbolically described as "others," becomes the focal point for both the political struggles and the theoretical debates.[30]

---

to 1987 she lectured at the Australian National University, and it was during this period that she developed her most influential ideas and wrote *The Man of Reason: "Male" and "Female" in Western Philosophy*, which was published in 1984. In 1987 she was appointed to the Chair of Philosophy at the University of New South Wales and was the first female professor of philosophy appointed in Australia. She was appointed Emeritus Professor on her retirement. Among her other important publications are *Being in Time: Selves and Narrators in Philosophy and Literature* (1993); *Part of Nature: Self-Knowledge in Spinoza's Ethics* (1994); and, with Gatens, *Collective Imaginings: Spinoza, Past and Present* (1999).

28. The Australian phenomenon is worthy of special note for the high quality and the overwhelming quantity of feminist philosophy it produces. Starting from Lloyd's critique of the masculinity of the history of philosophy in *The Man of Reason*, a whole generation is raised in this tradition. I am proud to be one of Lloyd's students. Carol Pateman develops important aspects of feminist political theory, and Elizabeth Grosz very early develops French philosophical insights, as will Moira Gatens. The trend will continue in a more diasporic vein after the period covered in this volume with Penelope Deutscher and Claire Colebrook, both of whom now teach in the US.

29. Luce Irigaray, "Egales à qui?," *Critique: Revue générale des publications Françaises et étrangères* 43(480) (1987); published in English as "Equal to Whom?," *Differences: A Journal of Feminist Cultural Studies* 1(2) (1988).

30. See also my "Sexual Difference Theory," in *A Companion to Feminist Philosophy*, Alison M. Jaggar and Iris M. Young (eds) (Oxford: Blackwell, 1998).

In terms of the philosophical agenda, the focus shifts accordingly from the humanist individualism of the liberal tradition in the US and the residual humanism of the Marxist traditions in Europe and Latin America to different figurations for the nonunitary structure of subjectivity. Humanist thought assumed a unitary and rational subject in charge of his/her historical endeavors; with the "death of Man" announced by Foucault and the subsequent "death of Woman" predicated by the high poststructuralist feminists, however, this unity is replaced by open structures and an emphasis on processes of subject formation rather than substances. As a consequence, high feminist poststructuralism was antihumanist in that it critiqued from within all the unitary identities because they assumed phallo-logocentric, Eurocentric, white supremacist, anthropocentric, and standardized views of what constitutes the humanist ideal of "Man." This militant antihumanism intersects productively with postcolonial and race perspectives, which critique humanism for its racist connotations and racialized bias and propose instead the critique of universalist white supremacy,[31] and non-Western forms of radical neohumanism.[32]

For all feminists inspired by poststructuralism, "difference," or more specifically, the notion of "otherness," functions through dualistic oppositions that confirm the dominant vision of the subject. In other words, the dominant apparatus of subjectivity is organized along a hierarchical scale that rewards "sameness" by defining the sovereign subject as the zero-degree of difference. By extension it also posits subcategories of difference – through processes of sexualization, racialization, and naturalization – and distributes them along a scale of asymmetrical power relations. Deleuze calls it "the Majority subject" or the Molar center of being, Derrida labels it "phallo-logocentrism," Irigaray calls it "the Same," or the hyper-inflated, falsely universal "He," whereas Hill Collins calls to accountability the white and Eurocentric bias of the subject of humanistic knowledge. The lessons of race and postcolonial theories[33] are of the greatest

---

31. See, for instance, bell hooks' influential *Yearning* (Toronto: Between the Lines, 1990).
32. See, for instance, Uma Narayan, "The Project of Feminist Epistemology: Perspectives from a Non-Western Feminist," in *Gender/Body/Knowledge: Feminist Reconstructions of Being and Knowing*, Alison M. Jaggar and Susan Bordo (eds) (New Brunswick, NJ: Rutgers University Press, 1989); Patricia Hill Collins, *Black Feminist Thought: Knowledge, Consciousness, and the Politics of Empowerment* (New York: Routledge, 1991); Vandana Shiva, *Bio-piracy: The Plunder of Nature and Knowledge* (Boston, MA: South End Press, 1997).
33. See Benedict Anderson, *Imagined Communities* (London: Verso, 1983); Stuart Hall, "What is This 'Black' in Black Popular Culture?," in *Black Popular Culture*, Gina Dent (ed.) (Seattle, WA: Boy Press, 1992); Gayatri C. Spivak, *A Critique of Postcolonial Reason: Towards a History of the Vanishing Present* (Cambridge, MA: Harvard University Press, 1999); Vron Ware, *Beyond the Pale: White Women, Racism and History* (London: Verso, 1992); and Robert Young, *White Mythologies: Writing History and the West* (London: Routledge, 1990).

importance to add a political inflection as well as higher degrees of complexity to this philosophical understanding of difference.

Whereas the generation that came of age philosophically with Beauvoir stressed transcendence and rationality, the difference thinkers stress immanence and a nonessentialist brand of embodiment. From Lacanian psychoanalysis they borrow the notion of the materiality of the linguistic sign and from deconstruction the critique of phallo-logocentrism. But over and above all borrowing, this "intermediate" generation of feminist philosophy rises to the challenge of great theoretical creativity and innovates both on categories of thought and on methods. They progress from the critique of classical dualistic notions of difference to the affirmation of diversity, and from the classical opposition transcendence–immanence to new epistemological schemes that allow more complex understandings of what exactly is the "matter" that poststructuralist materialism or deconstructive materiality are all about. However influenced by poststructuralism, the generation that is operational in the 1980–95 period thinks across borders and in an interdisciplinary manner that actually consolidates the entire field of feminist philosophy in powerful new ways.

III. GENDERING THE MASTER'S VOICE

The generation of feminists situated between 1980 and 1995 was the first to enjoy the institutional presence of supportive and talented women teachers and supervisors, many of whom were feminists themselves. The effects of the actual, physical presence of women lecturers in philosophy departments starting from the 1970s and 1980s cannot be stressed enough, and the influence of these teachers on the generation of radicalized younger women philosophers emerging from feminism was enormous.

The philosophical underpinnings of feminist teaching became a matter of great concern for the generation that pioneered feminist and women's studies in academic institutions. The premises rest on a number of notions derived from classical historical materialism but enriched by a gender perspective. In this respect, feminist philosophy has much in common with other critical epistemologies such as the radical pedagogy of Paulo Freire, liberation theology, and postcolonial and race theories. The main philosophical premises are the following: first, that the aim of a philosophical education is to cultivate the multifaceted aspects of the common humanity we share. This humanism stands in stark opposition to more utilitarian definitions of higher education, let alone the narrower functionalism that will spread throughout the 1990s as an effect of neoliberal economics and its academic managers.

Second, the basic unit of reference for a philosophical education is not liberal individualism but a social constructivist notion of the subject as a sociopolitical entity defined by material forces and relations. For feminism, these material social relations are linked to both production and reproduction and thus can be said to be embedded and embodied. This vision of the subject supports the humanist ideal described above in believing that education is a collective civic endeavor whose ultimate aims are freedom and equality of chances through socially enacted networks of solidarity.

Third, the neutrality of scientific knowledge, which follows from the idea of the self-regulating structure of rationality, and the method of dispassionate objective observation are challenged. The grounds for contestation are the same social constructivist notions defined above. The universalistic pretensions of the subject are debunked by an epistemic approach based on Adrienne Rich's idea of "the politics of location."[34] This is both a method and a strategy that makes sense of diversity among women. The category of sexual difference is not only understood as the binary opposite of the dominant phallo-logocentric subject, but also as the virtual potential for multiple differences.

The strategy of the politics of location is coupled with epistemological and political accountability. This is understood as the practice that consists in acknowledging and unveiling the power locations that one inevitably inhabits as the site of one's identity. Because a "location" is not a self-appointed and self-designed subject-position, but rather a collectively shared and constructed space, it refers to a process of consciousness-raising through the intervention of others. "Politics of locations" produce cartographies of power that rest on a form of self-criticism, a critical, genealogical self-narrative, that is relational and outward-bound. It then follows that feminist knowledge is an embodied, inter-active process that brings forth complex aspects of our existence, especially our own implication with power. Thus, black women's texts and experiences make white women see the limitations of their locations, truths and discourses. In Deleuzian language, it "de-territorializes" us, that is, it estranges us from the familiar, the intimate, the known, and casts an external light on it. The strategy of estrangement or defamiliarization transforms our knowledge of ourselves and others. This entails a critique of science and a thorough examination of the networks of power that constitute and sustain science as a social practice. In this respect, feminist epistemology shares a great deal with the radical thought of Feyerabend, Kuhn, and Foucault.

Last but not least, feminist genealogies come into operation by adopting the strategy of "thinking back through the women" to draw inspiration from the past. For Virginia Woolf this tactic was also a style of writing and a practice

---

34. The chapter is in Adrienne Rich, *Blood, Bread and Poetry* (New York: Norton, 1985).

of citation. Women-centered approaches are highly recommended to all the women who aspire to have a mind of their own and to reconnect with the deeper sources of their creativity. This is a groundbreaking development in itself and it becomes even more striking when read in a historical perspective. The previous generation of feminist philosophers – those who came of age in Europe in the 1950s and 1960s – settled into an ambiguous relationship to the actual institutional practice of philosophy. Beauvoir herself was not allowed to teach in the Grandes Écoles that train the French elites. Others, such as Françoise Collin,[35] were pioneer feminist philosophers who deliberately chose to function in self-run collectives or marginal organizations. Owing to the historical context, that generation continued to engage in dialogue more readily with the great male philosophers of the continental tradition than with any living women, let alone cross-referring to their own peer group. The high poststructuralist generation did not fare much better, although they did acknowledge some of the great, dead women intellectuals of the past.[36]

Michèle Le Doeuff,[37] in her work on the philosophical imaginary, was one of the first to raise the question of what she aptly named the Heloïse complex: women being devoted head and body to great philosophical masters who tend to take advantage of their love in every possible way. The second feminist wave was to change all this, but the effects on the pedagogical front were slower than the speed of social transformation.

Furthermore, if footnotes and bibliographies are the manifestation of democracy and belonging in a text, there is no question as to the undemocratic and often self-referential nature of a great deal of the feminist texts produced in France in the 1980s by the generation of high poststructuralism, starting from the holy trinity of French feminism itself: Irigaray, Cixous, and Kristeva. Almost in reaction to it, the intermediate generation made a point of using the scholarly

---

35. Françoise Collin is not well known enough in the anglophone world, although she is a pioneer on feminist philosophy in the francophone world. Belgian-born, and a classmate of Luce Irigaray and Jacques Taminiaux at the University of Louvain, she founded the feminist journal *Les Cahiers du Grif* in 1973 and moved the editorial office to Paris in 1981. She wrote a widely acclaimed study of Blanchot, *Maurice Blanchot et la question de l'écriture*, in 1971 (reprinted in 1986), and was the first to write on Hannah Arendt in France. She also coedited the best French anthology on feminist philosophy, *Les Femmes de Platon à Derrida: Anthologie critique* (2000).

36. Julia Kristeva will evolve in this direction with her trilogy on *Female Genius: Hannah Arendt*, Ross Guberman (trans.) (New York: Columbia University Press, 2001); *Melanie Klein*, Ross Guberman (trans.) (New York: Columbia University Press, 2000); and *Colette*, Jane Marie Todd (trans.) (New York: Columbia University Press, 2004).

37. See Michèle Le Doeuff, *The Philosophical Imaginary*, Colin Gordon (trans.) (Stanford, CA: Stanford University Press, 1989), and *Hipparchia's Choice: An Essay Concerning Women, Philosophy etc.*, Trista Selous (trans.) (Oxford: Blackwell, 1991).

apparatus of notes as a genealogical tool. They also took great pedagogical care to empower the critical independence of mind of younger generations of thinkers. This position can be summed up as a healthy disregard of the wholly male lineage in the history of philosophy on the one hand, and a passionate commitment to thinking through female feminist genealogies on the other. The latter implies an explicit recognition of the collective character of most knowledge claims and discursive production as well as the acknowledgment that the politics of citation are textual means by which alternative discursive communities can be constructed and radical democracy implemented.

The new forms of institutionalization also had methodological consequences: footnotes and bibliographies become all important and move to the center of the debates. Cartographies, collections, anthologies, and, after a while, encyclopedias, glossaries, and reference manuals in feminist theory are brought into existence and come into operation. The creation of new journals forms an integral part of these efforts to consolidate and expand the insights of modern-day feminism into philosophy: *Hypatia: A Journal of Feminist Philosophy* was founded in 1986 and remains a reference title in the field. Jane Flax[38] argues that a meta-methodological turn takes place in feminist philosophy at this time, which marks the beginning of a shift of paradigm. This is due to the sheer quantitative expansion of feminist practitioners of philosophy, but also to a qualitative leap in thinking: key concepts, accepted methods, and conventional procedures are questioned and redefined in original ways.

Let me illustrate it with some examples. In 1983, Alison Jaggar produced one of the very first taxonomies of feminist philosophy, *Feminist Politics and Human Nature*. It rests on a system of political classification of the different feminist schools of thought (socialist, Marxist, liberal, and radical). The influence of Marxism is then at its apex, as shown by the works of Angela Davis and Ti-Grace Atkinson.[39] A few years later in 1986, the epistemologist Sandra Harding and the philosopher Jean Grimshaw[40] were already in a position to adopt more specific and original categories of thought to do justice to the theoretical creativity of the feminist movement.[41] Of special significance among them is "standpoint

---

38. See Jane Flax, *Thinking Fragments: Psychoanalysis, Feminism, and Postmodernism in the Contemporary West* (New York: Routledge, 1990).
39. See Ti-Grace Atkinson, *Amazon Odyssey* (New York: Link Books, 1974); Angela Davis, *Women, Race, Class* (London: Women's Press, 1981).
40. See Jean Grimshaw, *Philosophy and Feminist Thinking* (Minneapolis, MN: University of Minnesota Press, 1986).
41. This was also the case for Hester Eisenstein's *Contemporary Feminist Thought*, the first comprehensive account of feminist theory.

feminist theory,"[42] which covers the full range of feminist philosophies of difference by privileging the epistemological insights of marginal subjects. Standpoint theory is also one of the feminist branches that intersect most productively with antiracist thought and links gender issues to race and postcolonial considerations.[43] By 1995, Jaggar and Iris Young had so much original feminist philosophical material at hand that they could edit a fully fledged companion to feminist philosophy, covering every major school and tradition of philosophical thought, all monotheistic and a few other religions, and the different constituencies within feminism itself. This shift and expansion of perspective took barely a decade.[44]

The politics change accordingly. Again, it may be useful to look at the publications to prove the point. In the 1980s very few collections on women and philosophy were available in the academic market. Carol Gould and Marx Wartofsky's *Women and Philosophy: Toward a Theory of Liberation* (1976) and Mary Vetterling-Braggin, Frederick Elliston, and Jane English's *Feminism and Philosophy* (1977) are among the first, followed closely by Marilyn Frye's *The Politics of Reality: Essays in Feminist Theory* in 1983. Although they make a claim to difference, these early works are in the spirit of equality-minded or emancipatory feminism in that they are focused on the under-representation of women both in philosophy departments and in the male domination of the actual curriculum of the history of philosophy. This is typically the "women and/ in philosophy" phase, which inserted women as an additive to existing philosophical and disciplinary categories, as evidenced by the leading publications of those days.[45]

Adding women to philosophy, however, could not leave the rules of the disciplinary game unchanged. It resulted instead in a frontal attack on the male domination of the philosophical canon and a concerted effort to dislodge the masculine subject from its falsely universal sovereign position. Lloyd's *The Man of Reason*, published in 1984, is the seminal text in this tradition. The feminist revisions of the history of philosophy pursued by Nancy Tuana in a

---

42. For a useful introduction see Sandra Harding, *The Science Question in Feminism* (Buckingham: Open University Press, 1986); Nancy C. M. Hartsock, "The Feminist Standpoint: Developing the Ground for a Specifically Feminist Historical Materialism," in *Discovering Reality*, Sandra Harding and Merrill B. Hintikka (eds) (Dordrecht: Reidel, 1983).

43. See Sandra Harding, *The "Racial" Economy of Science* (Bloomington, IN: Indiana University Press, 1983).

44. Tina Chanter, writing in *Ethics of Eros* in 1995, could legitimately speak of a feminist rewriting of the philosophers.

45. See, for instance, Jean Elshtain on social and political thought, Eva Kittay and Diana Meyers on moral theory, Ellen Kennedy and Susan Mendus on political philosophy, Andrea Nye on humanist thought, and Katharina Bartlett and Rosanne Kennedy on legal theory.

series of appraisals of key thinkers also contribute significantly to rethinking the canon.[46]

High poststructuralism challenged equality and highlighted the difference that feminist philosophers can make to the actual practice of philosophy. The generation that followed radicalized the concepts and methods and developed entire institutional, pedagogical, and methodological structures that brought the full potential of difference into concrete materialization and actual operation. This was not a flat application of pre-established principles, but rather the active creation of new ways of thinking. In so doing the post-poststructuralists of the intermediate generation ended up altering the very theoretical premises from which they had started, innovating on content and concepts. They also established a firm corpus of feminist scholarship that institutionalized the idea of collective teamwork as a key feminist method.

IV. THE INTERDISCIPLINARY FACTOR

The institutionalization process, combined with the emphasis on the positivity of difference, produced a high degree of interdisciplinarity in the philosophical works of this period. Thus, a collection such as Linda Nicholson's *Feminism/ Postmodernism*, although not strictly philosophical in itself, was influential across a broad academic field and affected the philosophical debates of the times. Considering the fact that many of the feminist philosophers of the poststructuralist generation found jobs outside academic philosophy, an accurate cartography of the period should therefore exceed the institutional boundaries of the discipline and include an interdisciplinary range of contributions.

Comparative literature, cultural, and film studies are of great importance, as I indicated above, especially volumes such as Teresa de Lauretis's *Technologies of Gender* and Sarah Franklin, Celia Lury, and Jackie Stacey's *Off-centre: Feminism and Cultural Studies*. Once again the impact of race and postcolonial theory is of crucial philosophical importance, with texts such as Spivak's *In Other Worlds*, Hill Collins's seminal *Black Feminist Thought*, and the growing influence of Chandra Mohanty.[47] Feminist legal theory provides new insights especially

---

46. Also significant in this vein are the writings of Linda Zerilli on high liberalism, Robin Schott on Kantianism, and especially Susan Bordo on Descartes. In France see Sarah Kofman, *Le Respect des femmes* (Paris: Éditions Galilée, 1982); Cathérine Chalier, *Figures du féminin: Lecture d'Emmanuel Levinas* (Paris: La nuit surveillée, 1982); Elisabeth de Fontenay, *Diderot ou le matérialisme enchanté* (Paris: Grasset, 1981).

47. See for instance, Chandra Mohanty et al. (eds), *Third World Women and the Politics of Feminism* (Bloomington, IN: Indiana University Press, 1991); and Chandra Mohanty, "Under Western Eyes: Feminist Scholarship and Colonial Discourse," *Boundary 2* 12(3)/13(1) (1984).

through the invention of the method of intersectionality[48] and the poststructuralist critical theory of the law of Drucilla Cornell. Ecofeminism also comes of philosophical age with the early Donna Haraway and the pioneer work of Val Plumwood.[49]

The interdisciplinary approach provides new themes for feminist philosophy. Lesbian theory, diversified by the impact of postmodernism, evolves through two spearheads: one is Rich's theory of the lesbian continuum, which locates the lesbian experience within a continuum of female sexuality defined in terms of constant woman bonding. As a result of this nondisruptive positioning of lesbian desire, Rich can defend lesbian motherhood in the key text *Of Woman Born*. Rich then goes on to develop woman-centered perspectives in art, culture, and science in seminal texts such as *Of Lies, Secrets and Silence* and *Blood, Bread and Poetry*. The other spearhead is Monique Wittig, who takes the antithetical viewpoint that a lesbian is not a woman, but a "third sex" who escapes the gender dichotomy and refuses to be defined by it. This will prove influential for queer theory throughout the 1990s.

An inspiring discipline for philosophy was feminist theology, which, with towering figures such as Mary Daly[50] leading a new movement of thought as well as practice, challenges Christian monotheistic logocentrism, just as Muslim feminists such as Fatima Mernissi[51] question Islam. Interest in mystical thinkers of previous generations such as Simone Weil[52] intensifies and the vast cluster of feminist spirituality will grow throughout the 1990s, producing what will become known as a postsecular turn in feminist theory.[53]

Psychoanalysis and film theory exercise huge influence, in spite of great feminist resistances to the idea of the unconscious as a principle of nonclosure of the subject. Key figures such as Jane Flax straddle the shaky ground between philosophy and the discourse of the unconscious by being practicing psychoanalysts. While Irigaray and Kristeva evolve respectively into the left wing and right wing of post-Lacanian psychoanalysis, Juliet Mitchell[54] is by far the most

48. See Kimberle W. Crenshaw *et al.* (eds), *Critical Race Theory: The Key Writings that Formed the Movement* (New York: New Press, 1995).

49. See especially Val Plumwood, *Feminism and the Mastery of Nature* (New York: Routledge, 1993).

50. See Mary Daly, *Gyn/Ecology: The Meta-Ethics of Radical Feminism* (Boston, MA: Beacon Press, 1978).

51. See Fatima Mernissi, *Beyond the Veil: Male–Female Dynamics in Modern Muslim Society* (London: AlSaqi Books, 1985).

52. See Simone Weil, *La Pésenteur et la grâce* (Paris: Gallimard, 1947).

53. See on this issue my "In Spite of the Times: The Postsecular Turn in Feminism," *Theory, Culture & Society* 25 (2008).

54. See Juliet Mitchell, *Psychoanalysis and Feminism: Freud, Reich, Laing and Women* (New York: Pantheon Press, 1974).

important influence in psychoanalytic thinking for an entire generation of English-speaking Lacanians. Teresa Brennan[55] is heiress to this tradition and pursues it in an original manner, while Jessica Benjamin[56] brilliantly bridges the gap between Lacanian and object-relation psychoanalytic theory.

The single most significant interdisciplinary coalition of the 1980s, however, is the new galaxy formed by women, gender, and feminist studies departments and programs, which grow from self-run classes into a strong academic movement that aims at reforming the curriculum and forces a revision of what counts as scientifically acceptable knowledge. The leading journal in feminist theory, *Signs: a Journal of Women in Culture and Society*, was founded in 1975. In Europe, the institutional rise of women's studies occurs later, as argued by Griffin and myself in *Thinking Differently*, but the theoretical creativity of feminist philosophies is strong from the start. Feminism in Europe draws inspiration from a political genealogy that takes the great women philosophers of European history as major points of reference and claims them as political leaders of the movement. Thus, a pedigree is created that runs from Mary Wollstonecraft to Simone de Beauvoir, to Rosa Luxemburg, and Hannah Arendt, with the historical event that is the women's movement as a central junction. From the 1960s on, this genealogy diversifies into a number of branches, all of which confirm the discursive privilege and prestige accorded by the feminist movement to its key women philosophers – to their critical skills as well as their visionary spirit. What is especially innovative about feminist philosophy, in fact, is the courage with which it turns critique into affirmation. As Joan Kelly argued,[57] feminism carries a double-edged vision that combines oppositional consciousness with deep empowering creativity. The affirmative element within the feminist recomposition of knowledge is one of this generation's most lasting theoretical legacies.

Women's studies, and gender and feminist studies, bring a necessary dose of supplementary knowledge to the academic practice of the discipline of philosophy. It is no coincidence that so much focus falls, in this period, on epistemological studies of the power structures that affect scientific knowledge production.[58] Discourse as power is such a foundational idea in the 1980s that feminist theory

---

55. See, for instance, Teresa Brennan (ed.), *Between Feminism and Psychoanalysis* (New York: Routledge, 1989), and *History after Lacan* (New York: Routledge, 1993).
56. See Jessica Benjamin, *The Bonds of Love* (New York: Pantheon, 1988).
57. See Joan Kelly, "The Double-edged Vision of Feminist Theory," *Feminist Studies* 5(1) (1979).
58. See Kathleen Lennon and Margaret Whitford (eds), *Knowing the Difference: Feminist Perspectives in Epistemology* (New York: Routledge, 1994); Alison M. Jaggar and Susan Bordo (eds), *Gender/Body/Knowledge: Feminist Reconstructions of Being and Knowing* (New Brunswick, NJ: Rutgers University Press, 1989).

is almost equated with the critique of epistemology. Sandra Harding[59] provides a canonical classification system of feminist thought, whereas feminists with a scientific background, notably Evelyn Fox Keller, Donna Haraway and Elizabeth Spelman, play a key role in this first wave of feminist epistemology.[60] Isabelle Stengers strikes a singular note of her own, pleading for a more systematic conceptual dialogue between feminism and science.[61] Linda Alcoff produces systematically the best cartographies of feminist philosophy and epistemology.[62]

The main epistemological debate of this era takes place between Harding and Haraway on the issue of the alleged relativism of postmodernist feminism. Harding privileges the claims to difference made by standpoint theory and is initially dismissive of poststructuralist critiques of reason. Haraway provides a strong rebuke of this position in 1988 in her seminal essay "Situated Knowledges: The Science Question in Feminism and the Privilege of Partial Perspectives." By the early 1990s a new consensus is forged in the feminist epistemic community on the need for a revised but "robust" notion of objectivity that avoids both universalism and relativism in the pursuit of alternative ways of grounding feminist knowledge claims.

V. FROM CORPO-REALITY TO MATTER-REALISM

Looking back over the intellectual development of the generation of feminist philosophers within and after poststructuralism, what strikes me is the original brand of embodiment and bodily materialism they developed, in a variety of different but interrelated conceptual ways. This materialist line of thought is different from the more linguistically oriented branch of poststructuralism mentioned (see note 18). They develop together, not so much in opposition as alongside each other, in constant dialogue and often in loving antagonism.[63]

In the last section of this essay, I will consequently concentrate on the concept of bodily materialism and how it developed throughout the 1990s. Feminist

---

59. See Sandra Harding, *The Science Question in Feminism*, and *Whose Science? Whose Knowledge?* (Ithaca, NY: Cornell University Press, 1991).

60. See Evelyn Fox Keller, *Reflections on Gender and Science* (New Haven, CT: Yale University Press, 1985), and *A Feeling for the Organism* (New York: Freeman, 1985); Elizabeth Spelman, *Inessential Woman: Problems of Exclusion in Feminist Thought* (Boston, MA: Beacon Press, 1988).

61. See Isabelle Stengers, *D'une science à l'autre: Des concepts nomades* (Paris: Éditions du Seuil, 1987), and *Power and Invention: Situating Science*, Paul Bains (trans.) (Minneapolis, MN: University of Minnesota Press, 1997).

62. See, for instance, Linda M. Alcoff and Elizabeth Potter (eds), *Feminist Epistemologies* (New York: Routledge, 1993).

63. I am grateful to Judy Butler for this felicitous formulation.

philosophy in this period combines in innovative ways phenomenological theories of embodiment with Marxist and psychoanalytic elaborations of the complex social and symbolic interaction between bodies and power. This approach grants an ontological value to the embodied roots of the subject, while resisting essentialism,[64] and hence it also upgrades the issues of subjectivity and of sexuality to a greater degree of complexity than the high poststructuralist generation itself. The notion of the body is transformed from a substance dualistically opposed to the mind, to a dynamic process of embodied interactions: relationality becomes a keyword. The intermediate generation coins the term "corpo-reality" to designate the form of dynamic bodily neomaterialism that they read back into high poststructuralism.

What is characteristic of the thinkers of this generation is that, inspired by Spinoza's monistic political ontology, they adopt a different political ontology from the Hegelian–Marxist generations that preceded them. They differ, in other words, from social constructivist oppositions between selves and society, because they either do not assume or openly challenge an exterior and prior grid of codification of meanings or master-signifiers that would somehow imprint social codes on the embodied subjects. They are, so to speak, less structuralist than the poststructuralists. In the work of Grosz, Gatens, Butler, or myself, one finds attempts to account for bodies as material and symbolic formations that are always already immersed in strategic conditions and relations of power. Because power, after Foucault, is not only or necessarily conceived in negative terms, however, its effects are perceived as multiple, contradictory, and productive. Power produces, among others, forms of active resistance to the very conditions it engenders.

Thus, the scheme of dialectical opposition is abandoned in favor of more complexity in accounting for the codes and the sociosymbolic processes that constitute the subject as a bounded field of relations to multiple others. The emphasis falls on relational processes of transformation and also on the contradictory power effects that constitute embodied subjects. The political ideal is as transformative as the ethics that sustains it: how to actualize empowering alternative technologies of self–other relations by experimenting with new ways of relating to a multiplicity of others. A sort of neoasceticism will emerge from this,[65] although reformulations of political agency in the period include also, alternatively or in combination: transnational feminist forms of micropolitical action on a global scale; a radical adaptation of Foucaultian politics of resistance;

---

64. The best discussion on poststructuralism and essentialism is in Diane Fuss, *Essentially Speaking: Feminism, Nature and Difference* (New York: Routledge, 1989).

65. For further commentary on this point see my *Transpositions: On Nomadic Ethics* (Cambridge: Polity, 2006); Benjamin Noys, "The End of the Monarchy of Sex: Sexuality and Contemporary Nihilism," *Theory, Culture & Society* 25(5) (2008).

the politics of melancholia and the politics of affirmation. This is the neomaterialist punch of feminist politics after high poststructuralism.

The materialist corpo-reality branch of feminist philosophy is sociopolitical in orientation and draws inspiration from Foucault and Deleuze, although they are equally attentive to Derrida and the material effects of language on the world. It emphasizes the crucial notion that sexuality is an integral part of the embodied structure of the subject: one is always already sexed. Sexuality is conceptualized, especially in Romance languages like French,[66] as a general life force that cannot be adequately contained within the dichotomous view of gender defined as the social construction of differences between the sexes. Social constructivism meets its limitations when confronted by the ontological shift to sexuality as life itself. Whereas high poststructuralist feminist theory is solidly ensconced in social constructivist methods and political strategies, thinkers of the next generation affirm and explore the ontological aspects of sexuality and sexual difference, and not only its constructed elements.

As a consequence, it is not so much the case that sexuality is caught in the sex-gender binary, but rather that it enjoys more transversal, structural, and vital connotations. Sexuality as life-force provides a nonessentialist ontological structure for the organization of human affectivity and desire. This notion clearly opposes the position of the linguistic mediation school, which argues that the discursive structure of gender functions as a coercive grid that constructs social relations and identities. The counterargument is that sexuality is a constitutive force that is always already present and hence prior to gender, although it intersects with it in constructing functional subjects in the social regime of biopolitical governmentality.

The early work of Foucault stresses the central importance of sexuality as a constitutive force that is targeted by social technologies of control, discipline, and punishment. The feminist commentators on Foucault[67] are aware of the specific brand of bodily materialism that is at stake here. Butler's appropriation of Foucault for queer theory in *Gender Trouble* is especially significant as it acquires a paradigmatic status especially in US feminism. All these thinkers

---

66. For more details on this issue see my "The Uses and Abuses of the Sex/Gender Distinction in European Feminist Practices," in *Thinking Differently: A Reader in European Women's Studies*, Gabriele Griffin and Rosi Braidotti (eds) (London: Zed Books, 2002).

67. See my *Patterns of Dissonance: A Study of Women in Contemporary Philosophy* (Cambridge: Polity, 1991); Irene Diamond and Lee Quinby (eds), *Feminism and Foucault: Reflections on Resistance* (Boston, MA: Northeastern University Press, 1988); Moira Gatens, *Feminism and Philosophy: Perspectives on Difference and Equality* (Bloomington, IN: Indiana University Press, 1991); Elizabeth A. Grosz, *Sexual Subversions: Three French Feminists* (Sydney: Allen & Unwin, 1989); Lois McNay, *Foucault and Feminism: Power, Gender and the Self* (Cambridge: Polity, 1992).

deal with corpo-reality and provide different answers to the question of how to disengage sexuality from the dominant masculinist, logocentric, ethnocentric, heterosexist, and anthropocentric codes of representation. The latter is taken in the double sense of cultural mediation and political intervention, as Spivak argues in her seminal essay "Can the Subaltern Speak?" As a result, how to disentangle sexuality from identity politics and the formulation of flat countersexual identities – even within feminism – is more than ever the question.

Deleuze-inspired feminists advocate a vision of the body as a sexually preconstituted, dynamic bundle of relations that is especially interesting. In opposition to the linguistic school – whose leading feminist thinkers opposed Deleuze's vitalist materialism vigorously[68] – Deleuzian feminists develop the notion of the materialist roots of embodied subjectivity and explore the transformative potential of a different concept of the political. They stress that the political advantage of this monistic and vital approach is that it provides a more adequate understanding of the fluid and complex workings of power in advanced capitalism and hence can devise more suitable forms of resistance.[69]

The long-term result of these explorations of corpo-reality or embedded and embodied materialism is a serious reconsideration of what counts as the "matter" for materialist feminist thought. Radical emphasis on a Spinozist monistic ontology results in overcoming the classical opposition "materialism/ idealism" and move towards a dynamic, nonessentialist and relational brand of materialist vitalism. "Matter-realism" designates the contemporary form of radical neomaterialism that emerges from corpo-reality and will also become known as vital politics or posthuman feminism.[70]

By the early 1990s, the biogenetic and information technologies revolution provide the historical backdrop for some significant shifts. The change of

---

68. This is especially the case for Alice Jardine in *Gynesis* and Judith Butler in *Subjects of Desire*.

69. See, for instance, my *Nomadic Subjects: Embodiment and Sexual Difference in Contemporary Feminist Theory* (New York: Columbia University Press, 1994); Moira Gatens, *Imaginary Bodies: Ethics, Power and Corporeality* (New York: Routledge, 1996); Elizabeth Grosz, *Volatile Bodies: Toward a Corporeal Feminism* (Bloomington, IN: Indiana University Press, 1994); Dorothea Olkowski, *Gilles Deleuze and the Ruin of Representation* (Berkeley, CA: University of California Press, 1999).

70. On "vital politics," see, for instance, Mariam Fraser *et al. Inventive Life: Approaches to the New Vitalism* (London: Sage, 2005). On "posthuman feminism," see, for instance, Anne Balsamo, *Technologies of the Gendered Body: Reading Cyborg Women* (Durham, NC: Duke University Press, 1996); Judith Halberstam and Ira Livingston, *Posthuman Bodies* (Bloomington, IN: Indiana University Press, 1995); Donna Haraway, *Modest_Witness@Second_Millennium. FemaleMan©_Meets_Oncomouse™: Feminism and Technoscience* (New York: Routledge, 1997); Katherine N. Hayles, *How we Became Posthuman: Virtual Bodies in Cybernetics, Literature, and Informatics* (Chicago, IL: University of Chicago Press, 1999).

focus is deliberate and comes in response to fast-shifting global changes[71] and technological innovations. Mostly thanks to Haraway's agenda-setting work on cyborg-feminism,[72] a younger generation of scholars gets inspired by an empiricist form of matter-realism, which combines realism with a twenty-first-century understanding of "matter" as a self-organizing principle. This generation of philosophers drops the endless critiques of representation that had become the trademark of high poststructuralism in the linguistic branch, to turn with renewed interest to ontological and epistemological questions. Claire Colebrook[73] is a notable example: resting on Deleuzian premises, she explores the potential of vitalist thought and argues for feminist reappraisals of contemporary technoscientific culture in a nondeterministic frame. What matters about this matter-realism, in other words, is the concept of "matter" itself: the switch to a monistic political ontology stresses processes, vital politics and nondeterministic evolutionary theories[74] as exemplified by Karen Barad's work on "agential realism."[75] Feminist epistemology and science studies replace cultural studies as priority research areas and comparative literature ceases to be the main arena for these debates, as Spivak noted in *Death of a Discipline*.

One of the main implications of this shift of perspective is that matter-realist feminists return again to sexuality, rather than the sex–gender distinction, to explore more specifically the notion of sexuality beyond gender. The polymorphous perversity of sexuality as an ontological force is emphasized, in opposition to a majoritarian or dominant line that privileges heterosexual reproductive sex. An important question that can be raised – after the making of Dolly the sheep in 1996 and the poststructuralist critiques of phallo-logocentrism – is: what happens to gender if sexuality is not based on oppositional terms? What

---

71. For a more detailed analysis, see my "A Critical Cartography of Feminist Post-postmodernism," *Australian Feminist Studies* 20(47) (July 2005).

72. Donna J. Haraway (1944–) is an American feminist and professor in the History of Consciousness Program at the University of California, Santa Cruz. She earned a degree in zoology and philosophy at Colorado College and received her PhD in the Department of Biology at Yale in 1972. She wrote her dissertation on the functions of metaphor in shaping research in developmental biology in the twentieth century. She writes on biology, techno-science and feminism. Among her main texts are *Primate Visions: Gender, Race, and Nature in the World of Modern Science* (1989), *Simians, Cyborgs, and Women: The Reinvention of Nature* (1991), and *Modest Witness@Second Millenium. FemaleMan©_Meets_Oncomouse™: Feminism and Technoscience* (1997).

73. The work of Claire Colebrook on Deleuze's philosophy of immanence is of great importance here. See for instance *Deleuze and Feminist Theory* (coedited with Ian Buchanan [Edinburgh: Edinburgh University Press, 2000]) and "Postmodernism is a Humanism: Deleuze and Equivocity," *Women: A Cultural Review* 15 (2004).

74. Indicative of this trend is Elizabeth Grosz's *Becomings: Explorations in Time, Memory and Futures*.

75. See Karen Barad, *Meeting the Universe Half Way* (Durham, NC: Duke University Press, 2007).

happens when there is sexuality without the possibility of either heterosexual or homosexual union? Patricia MacCormack[76] rests on Deleuze and Guattari's idea of radical empiricism and on Irigaray's emphasis on the sensible transcendental, to stress that corporeal becoming or transformations are open-ended and not necessarily contained by sociosymbolic forms, such as phallo-logocentrism or established categories. The ethics of becoming is rather an ethology of the forces that propel the subject to become by overcoming both forms and categories, deterritorializing all identity formations. By extension, this means that sexuality is a force, or constitutive element, that is capable of destabilizing gender identity and institutions: sexuality beyond gender. Another example of the same tendency is Luciana Parisi's innovative adaptation of Guattari and Lynn Margulis[77] to produce a schizo-genesis of sexual difference and of endosymbiosis as an organic variable of autopoesis.[78] The new matter-realism stresses the self-organizational capacity of matter, which results in questioning any ontological foundation for difference while avoiding social constructivism. Sexuality beyond gender is the epistemological but also political side of contemporary vitalist matter-realism. It consolidates a philosophical genealogy that includes creative deterritorializations, intensive and hybrid crossfertilizations and generative encounters with multiple and nonhuman others.

VI. CONCLUSION

A cartographic account cannot be concluded, but it must end. In this essay I have tried to steer a collective-minded course among a multiplicity of productive, innovative, radical developments in feminist philosophy that were inspired by French poststructuralist theories but thrived mostly in exile and in the diaspora. I have tried to show that the multiple temporalities of feminist theory and the essentially nonlinear character of feminist philosophy came to a greater degree of critical focus after high poststructuralism. The degree and quality of the scholarship produced in the period under review is such as to warrant the claim of a genuine "coming of age" of feminist philosophy. Central to the success of what I also referred to as the "intermediate" generation is the loyalty it shows to feminist theoretical and political genealogies. This non-oedipal and hence productive relationship to preceding generations of women philosophers

---

76. See Patricia MacCormack, *Cinesexuality* (Aldershot: Ashgate, 2008).
77. See Lynn Margulis and Dorion Sagan, *What is Life?* (Berkeley, CA: University of California Press, 1995).
78. See Luciana Parisi, *Abstract Sex: Philosophy, Bio-Technology and the Mutations of Desire* (London: Continuum, 2004), and the strong influence of Humberto Maturana and Francisco Varela, *Autopoesis and Cognition: The Realization of the Living* (Dordrecht: Reidel, 1972).

is strengthened by the fact that many of these were the actual teachers of this generation of scholars, and so they are connected by ties of gratitude and respect. This certainly describes my own position as both a member of this generation and the cartographer of this chapter, a position for which I hold myself accountable by making both my own and my colleagues' work visible for inspection as explicitly as possible.

If one keeps in mind furthermore that one of the main effects of the fast-growing process of institutionalization of feminist knowledge initiated by my generation was to produce a higher level of continuity in feminist thinking than we are historically used to, it follows that the question of the temporalities of feminist thought becomes even more complex as both a concept and as a practice. It results, for instance, in an acceleration of consciousness that produces a more acute sense of feminist intergenerational justice toward the future generations who will inherit and hopefully pursue this great tradition of scholarship. The so-called feminist third wave[79] is closely linked to the "intermediate" generation that built on the legacy of high poststructuralism and moved beyond.

A cartographer is no prophet. The impressive scholarship produced in feminist philosophy in this period is still very much ongoing and in the making and there is no telling which new directions it will take. I have tried, wherever possible, to indicate the points of convergence and divergence both within this generation and between this and the high poststructuralist generation that preceded it, especially on questions of difference, sexuality, embodiment, and materialism. At present one of the most promising lines of development is the one that challenges the deeply seated anthropocentrism that lurks beneath even the most self-assured feminist antihumanism inherited from high poststructuralism.[80] The nonhuman – animal, technological, ecological, and planetary – "others" are raising new questions that may trace new interconnections between feminism and animal rights, technology studies, disability, and ecological issues in the frame of the complex political economy of the globally connected world we now inhabit. Feminist philosophers confront the third millennium of Western philosophical history fully aware that they are historically relative newcomers in this discipline and have only just started to play an active role in it. They have also learned from postcolonial and race studies the need to decenter Western hegemony and look beyond ethnocentric boundaries, in a transnational perspective that refuses to equate continental philosophy with the continent of

---

79. See Astrid Henry, *Not My Mother's Sister: Generational Conflict and Third-Wave Feminism* (Bloomington, IN: Indiana University Press, 2004).
80. Beside the work of Donna Haraway see also Elisabeth de Fontenay, *Le Silence des bêtes: La Philosophie à l'épreuve de l'animalité* (Paris: Fayard, 1999).

Europe. Feminist philosophers pursue this critical line of inquiry, more sharply than ever, with acquired maturity and renewed vitality and inspiration.

MAJOR WORKS

Having noted the importance of bibliographies and the citation of sources, it is incumbent on me to include some of the major feminist texts that played a significant role in the period 1980–95.

Benhabib, Seyla, and Drucilla Cornell, eds. *Feminism as Critique: On the Politics of Gender.* Minneapolis, MN: University of Minnesota Press, 1987.

Bordo, Susan R. *The Flight to Objectivity: Essays on Cartesianism and Culture.* Albany, NY: SUNY Press, 1987.

Braidotti, Rosi. *Nomadic Subjects: Embodiment and Sexual Difference in Contemporary Feminist Theory.* New York: Columbia University Press, 1994.

Butler, Judith P. *Gender Trouble: Feminism and the Subversion of Identity.* New York: Routledge, 1990.

Brennan, Teresa, ed. *Between Feminism and Psychoanalysis.* New York: Routledge, 1989.

Cornell, Drucilla. *Beyond Accommodation: Ethical Feminism, Deconstruction and the Law.* New York: Routledge, 1991.

Crenshaw, Kimberle W., N. Gotanda, G. Peller, and K. Thomas, eds. *Critical Race Theory: The Key Writings that Formed the Movement.* New York: New Press, 1995.

Flax, Jane. *Thinking Fragments: Psychoanalysis, Feminism, and Postmodernism in the Contemporary West.* New York: Routledge, 1990.

Fraser, Nancy. *Unruly Practices: Power, Discourse, and Gender in Contemporary Social Theory.* Minneapolis, MN: University of Minnesota Press, 1989.

Gatens, Moira. *Imaginary Bodies: Ethics, Power and Corporeality.* New York: Routledge, 1996.

Grosz, Elizabeth. *Volatile Bodies: Toward a Corporeal Feminism.* Bloomington, IN: Indiana University Press, 1994.

Haraway, Donna. *Simians, Cyborgs and Women: The Reinvention of Nature.* London: Free Association Books, 1991.

Harding, Sandra. *The Science Question in Feminism.* Buckingham: Open University Press, 1986.

Held, Virginia. *Feminist Morality: Transforming Culture, Society, Politics.* Chicago, IL: Chicago University Press, 1993.

Hill Collins, Patricia. *Black Feminist Thought: Knowledge, Consciousness, and the Politics of Empowerment.* New York: Routledge, 1991.

Lloyd, Genevieve. *The Man of Reason: "Male" and "Female" in Western Philosophy.* London: Methuen, 1984.

Nicholson, Linda J., ed. *Feminism/Postmodernism.* New York: Routledge, 1990.

Nussbaum, Martha. *The Fragility of Goodness.* Cambridge: Cambridge University Press, 1986.

Rich, Adrienne. *Of Woman Born.* New York: Norton, 1977.

Spivak, Gayatri Chakravorty. *In Other Worlds: Essays in Cultural Politics.* New York: Methuen, 1987.

Young, Iris M. *Throwing Like a Girl and Other Essays in Feminist Philosophy and Social Theory.* Bloomington, IN: Indiana University Press, 1990.

12

CONTINENTAL PHILOSOPHY OF RELIGION

Bruce Ellis Benson

In his official report to the French government in 1991 regarding the state of philosophy in France – titled *The Theological Turn of French Phenomenology* – Dominique Janicaud claims that philosophy (in particular phenomenology, the dominant mode of French philosophy today) has been overtaken by theology.[1] In effect, he accuses Emmanuel Levinas and Jean-Luc Marion, along with Michel Henry and Jean-Louis Chrétien, of having appropriated phenomenology for distinctly "theological" concerns. Given both that Janicaud's report covers the years 1975–90 (roughly the same period as this volume) and that the theological turn (which in many ways coincides with the so-called "return to religion" in Europe) is surely the most important development in continental philosophy of religion during those years, the concerns of that report and the theological turn in general are the focus of this essay. Since that theological turn is largely distinct to French philosophy, this essay primarily traces its definition and development, as well as the ways in which theological and religious concerns affect not only

---

1. Dominique Janicaud, *The Theological Turn of French Phenomenology*, Bernard G. Prusak (trans.), in Dominique Janicaud *et al.*, *Phenomenology and the "Theological Turn": The French Debate* (New York: Fordham University Press, 2000); originally published as *Le Tournant théologique de la phénoménologie française* (Paris: Éditions de L'éclat, 1991). It should be pointed out that, in addition to Janicaud's text, there is a much earlier one that takes up this debate: Mikel Dufrenne, "Pour une philosophie non-théologique" [In defense of a nontheological philosophy], in *Le Poétique*, 2nd ed. (Paris: Presses Universitaires de France, 1973). There he argues that Derrida, Maurice Blanchot (1907–2003), Gilles Deleuze (1925–95), and others resort to negative theology in their philosophies of difference and absence. As we will see, Derrida explicitly denies this charge. Further, Dufrenne's charge is much less strong and has proved considerably less influential than that of Janicaud.

247

philosophical discourse but also phenomenology's very structure.[2] Foremost at issue are the questions of (i) the relation between faith and reason (or knowledge), (ii) how God relates to human beings and whether God can be properly addressed, and (iii) whether phenomenology is properly theologically neutral. As will become clear, these questions cannot be answered without considering how the introduction of "revelation" into phenomenology threatens to reverse the very structure of the intentionality that is at the heart of phenomenology.

Of course, one cannot begin to speak about more recent French philosophy of religion without tracing at least a basic outline of the German philosophy that heavily influences it. French philosophy's recent development is particularly indebted to five German figures: Immanuel Kant, G. W. F. Hegel, Friedrich Nietzsche, Edmund Husserl, and Martin Heidegger. Less directly, it is also connected to the French philosopher Paul Ricoeur. A short word regarding each is in order.

I. PHILOSOPHICAL BACKGROUND

First, in the *Critique of Pure Reason* (1781), Immanuel Kant (1724–1804) claimed that he "had to deny *knowledge* in order to make room for *faith*."[3] Here it might seem that faith is given the upper hand. Yet in *Religion Within the Boundaries of Mere Reason* (1793), it becomes clear that these roles have been reversed.[4] The very fact that Kant insists on religion being limited by reason means that anything religious that does not pass the rigorous test of reason must be either reinterpreted or jettisoned. Although Kant is hardly the first to pit reason against faith, the pattern of reason's hegemony that he sets up becomes paradigmatic for the subsequent development of continental philosophy of religion. It is a pattern to which recent philosophers (such as Levinas and Marion) have responded

---

2. Although the theological turn comes about amid an intense engagement with German philosophy, it is truly a French phenomenon without a German counterpart. Interestingly enough, when the Dutch philosopher Hent de Vries writes his text *Philosophy and the Turn to Religion*, his examples are exclusively *French*. It is worth noting that other figures could be included here – for example, Blanchot, Stanislas Breton (1912–2005), Jean-François Courtine (1944–), and Jean Greisch (1942–) – but the limits of a brief chapter like this make hard decisions necessary.

3. Immanuel Kant, *Critique of Pure Reason*, Paul Guyer and Allen W. Wood (eds and trans.) (Cambridge: Cambridge University Press, 1998), B xxx; originally published as *Kritik der reinen Vernunft* (Riga: Hartknoch, 1781).

4. Immanuel Kant, *Religion Within the Boundaries of Mere Reason*, in *Religion and Rational Theology*, Allen W. Wood and George Di Giovanni (eds and trans.) (Cambridge: Cambridge University Press, 1996); originally published as *Die Religion innerhalb der Grenzen der blossen Vernunft* (Königsberg: Friedrich Nicolovius, 1793).

quite vehemently. Moreover, it also raises the question of what counts as "faith" and what as "reason." That it is also one's *own* reason that judges faith is clear from Kant's 1784 essay "What is Enlightenment?" As he puts it there: "Have courage to make use of your *own* understanding!"[5]

Second, although G. W. F. Hegel (1770–1831) wrote a great deal on religion, it was his *Phenomenology of Spirit* that proved particularly influential for French philosophy. Surprisingly, even though the text had been published in 1806, Hegel's great work only arrived in France when Alexandre Kojève lectured on it in the 1930s.[6] Many of those who would become prominent philosophers in France either heard him lecture or else read Jean Hyppolite's translation of the text (published in two parts in 1939 and 1941) and his influential commentary on it that appeared in 1946.[7] Because Kojève's reading of the *Phenomenology* was particularly dominated by Hegel's famed master–slave dialectic, much of subsequent French philosophy became obsessed with Hegel's dialectical system that was, on the one hand, all encompassing and thus seemingly inescapable and, on the other hand, dependent on negation and so inherently violent. Whether one can escape this totality and the negation of violence prove to be central concerns of recent French philosophy.

Third, Nietzsche contends that the notion of absolute knowledge or any kind of totality is simply the product of human conceit. Moreover, he claims that the very project of adequation of thought to the thing it thinks is misguided and thus the correspondence theory of truth is highly problematic. Moreover, Nietzsche thinks that violence and suffering are irredeemably tragic, whatever "meaning" we may (vainly) attempt to give them. In (in)famously proclaiming that "God is dead,"[8] Nietzsche announces the end of Christianity as any kind of moral grounds for Western culture.[9] Yet he also declares the death of any metaphysical or even any totalizing project.[10] Strangely enough, while Nietzsche had

---

5. Immanuel Kant, "What is Enlightenment?," in *Practical Philosophy*, Mary J. Gregory (ed. and trans.) (Cambridge: Cambridge University Press, 1996), 17; originally published as "Beantwortung der Frage: Was ist Aufklärung?" In *Berlinische Monatschrift* 4 (1784). [*] Kant's philosophy of religion is also discussed in the essay on Kant by Thomas Nenon in *The History of Continental Philosophy: Volume 1*.

*6. For a discussion of Kojève's interpretation of Hegel, see the essay by John Russon in *The History of Continental Philosophy: Volume 4*.

7. Jean Hyppolite, *Genèse et structure de la "Phénoménologie de l'esprit" de Hegel* (Paris: Aubier, 1946); published in English as *Genesis and Structure of Hegel's Phenomenology of Spirit*, Samuel Cherniak and John Heckman (trans.) (Evanston, IL: Northwestern University Press, 1974).

*8. For a discussion of the "death of God," see the essay by Daniel Conway in *The History of Continental Philosophy: Volume 2*.

9. For Nietzsche's famous pronouncement, see *The Gay Science* (1882), §125.

10. For an influential interpretation of that pronouncement, see Martin Heidegger, "Nietzsche's Word: 'God is Dead,'" in *Off the Beaten Track*, Julian Young and Kenneth Haynes (eds and trans.) (Cambridge: Cambridge University Press, 2002).

arrived in France before the turn of the nineteenth century (well before Hegel),[11] his influence on French philosophy becomes particularly widespread and strong beginning in the 1960s and 1970s.[12] Precisely in light of Nietzsche the question arises of what it could mean to move from a totality in which everything can be recouped to one of fragmentation, loss, and tragedy.

Fourth, only a few years before Hegel's *Phenomenology* reached France, Edmund Husserl (1859–1938) had visited Paris. Although the reception of his lectures, delivered in 1929 and substantially revised, expanded, and published posthumously as the *Cartesian Meditations* (1950), was initially largely negative, interest in Husserl's phenomenological method eventually became widespread. For Husserl, the motto of phenomenology is "to the things themselves [*zu der Sachen selbst*]." Thus, the concern in phenomenology is to arrive at an "*adaequatio intellectus et rei*," literally, an adequation of the intellect and the thing. Husserl works this out in terms of intentionality, intuition, and immanence. We "intend" an object by way of consciousness and it is thus "intuited." While there are degrees to which an object can be fully intended (or made present to consciousness), the goal is a kind of "adequation," in which the intended object is fully immanent to consciousness and so "itself there," "immediately intuited."[13] Put in phenomenological terms, the act of thinking (*noesis*) becomes the exact equivalent to its object (*noema*). Husserl explains this by way of what he calls "the principle of all principles" in which "*everything originarily ... offered to us in 'intuition' is to be accepted simply as what it is presented as being, but also only within the limits in which it is presented there.*"[14] While this principle would seem to call for a strict phenomenological neutrality, in which the object sets the conditions for its appearance, both Levinas and Marion will argue that the "limits" of which Husserl speaks place the *subject* in control of the object. This problem becomes all the more acute in Husserl's later philosophy in which the transcendental ego becomes central: "*The world of transcendent 'res' is entirely referred to consciousness and, more particularly, not to some logically conceived consciousness but to actual consciousness.*"[15] If the world is ultimately dependent

---

11. For the story of Nietzsche's early reception in France, see Eric Hollingsworth Deudon, *Nietzsche en France: L'Antichristianisme et la critique, 1891–1915* (Washington, DC: University Press of America, 1982).

*12. For a discussion of Nietzsche's influence on French philosophy in the 1960s–1970s, see the essay "French Nietzscheanism" by Alan D. Schrift in *The History of Continental Philosophy: Volume 6*.

13. Edmund Husserl, *Cartesian Meditations*, Dorian Cairns (trans.), 5th ed. (The Hague: Martinus Nijhoff, 1974), 57.

14. Edmund Husserl, *Ideas Pertaining to a Pure Phenomenology and a Phenomenological Philosophy. Book I: General Introduction to a Pure Phenomenology*, Fred Kersten (trans.) (The Hague: Martinus Nijhoff, 1982), 44.

15. *Ibid.*, 110.

on my consciousness, then am I not the ground of that world? And, if so, how can there be an "otherness"? Does one not lose exactly the sense of the particularity of the object or the other? Such was a problem that Husserl certainly recognized, and it is addressed at length by Levinas.

Fifth, this question of how the "other" appears to me also concerned Heidegger (1889–1976), although he provides more than one answer. On the one hand, in *Being and Time* (1927) Heidegger speaks of the true phenomenon as "the showing-itself-in-itself [*das Sich-an-ihm-selbst-zeigen*]."[16] On the other hand, Heidegger speaks of the necessity of *logos* (one might say the "logy" in phenomenology) that not only "lets something be seen" but also is a "letting [something] be seen *as* something."[17] This latter aspect Heidegger terms the "as-structure [*als-Struktur*]" of perception and knowledge. (or, simply put, the "as such"). Thus, Heidegger's conception of how a phenomenon appears encounters the same difficulties as Husserl's principle of principles: ostensibly, the object appears just as it is, but then the process of interpretation – whether in the guise of Heidegger's "as" or Husserl's "limits" of the horizon of consciousness – itself appears. Heidegger seems to realize the problems with his earlier position and speaks differently in his "Letter on Humanism" (1947). There he speaks of language as beyond human control. In contrast to "language" and "thought," both of which imply the possibility of control or mastery, Heidegger juxtaposes "saying" and "thinking." To quote him: "thinking … lets itself be claimed by being so that it can say the truth of being"[18] To think or to say is an attempt to understand *without* claiming mastery. However, now the divine is situated within being, since "only from the truth of being can the essence of the holy be thought," and "only in the light of the essence of divinity can it be thought or said what the word 'God' is to signify."[19] Finally, though, in "The Onto-theo-logical Constitution of Metaphysics" (1957), Heidegger acknowledges that the *logos* of philosophy has dominated theology. "Metaphysics is a theology, a statement about God, because the deity enters into philosophy." Yet "the deity can come into philosophy only insofar as philosophy, of its own accord and by its own nature, requires and determines that and how the deity enters into it."[20] Such is not the God of Abraham, Isaac, and Jacob, but one that has been called "the god of the philosophers." Heidegger reminds us that "man can neither pray nor

---

16. Martin Heidegger, *Being and Time*, John Macquarrie and Edward Robinson (trans.) (New York: Harper & Row, 1962), 54.

17. *Ibid.*, 56.

18. Martin Heidegger, "Letter on Humanism," Frank A. Capuzzi (trans.), in *Pathmarks*, William McNeill (ed.) (Cambridge: Cambridge University Press, 1998), 239.

19. *Ibid.*, 267.

20. Martin Heidegger, "The Onto-theo-logical Constitution of Metaphysics," in *Identity and Difference*, Joan Stambaugh (trans.) (Chicago, IL: University of Chicago Press, 2002), 55, 56.

sacrifice" nor "fall to his knees in awe nor can he play music and dance before this god."[21] In effect, "God" has been reduced to the fundamental principle of metaphysics.

Sixth, while the French philosopher Paul Ricoeur[22] does not have quite the influence on those implicated in the theological turn as do the preceding philosophers, he does demonstrate the complexity of introducing theological concerns into the realm of phenomenology.

II. PAUL RICOEUR

Although there were a number of prominent French thinkers in the twentieth century who were working from an explicitly Christian perspective – for example – the medievalist Étienne Gilson (1884–1978) and the existentialist Gabriel Marcel (1889–1973) – Paul Ricoeur – a devout Protestant from the Alsace – was a pioneer in bringing theological concerns together with the phenomenological method.[23] Much like Levinas and then Marion, Ricoeur sought to keep his philosophical and theological writings separate, being particularly unwilling to use any theological authority in a text of philosophy.[24] Yet the influence of theological concerns and even theological concepts are to be found in all of his work, which effectively meant that he was kept outside the major Parisian intellectual circle (a situation that changed substantially with the publication of *Time and Narrative* in the 1980s). Largely sympathetic to the existential project of Marcel, Ricoeur took Husserl's eidetic reduction to be a more rigorous way to describe the embodied self.[25] Yet he likewise concludes that Husserl's reductions are too essentialistic and thus not concrete enough. The result is Ricoeur's

---

21. *Ibid.*, 72.

*22. For a more extensive discussion of Ricoeur's philosophy, see the essay by Wayne J. Froman in *The History of Continental Philosophy: Volume 6*.

23. Paul Ricoeur (February 27, 1913–May 20, 2005; born in Valence, France; died in Chatenay Malabry) was educated at the University of Rennes (1933), the Sorbonne (1934–35), and received a *doctorat ès lettres* from the Sorbonne in 1950. His influences included Arendt, Gadamer, Heidegger, Husserl, Jaspers, Kant, and Levinas, and he held appointments at the University of Strasbourg (1948–56), Sorbonne (1956–66), University of Nanterre (1966–80), University of Louvain (1970–73), and University of Chicago (1967–92). [*] For a discussion of Marcel, see the essays by Felix Ó Murchadha and Andreas Grossmann in *The History of Continental Philosophy: Volume 4*.

24. In an interview, Ricoeur says "I am very committed to the autonomy of philosophy and I think that in none of my works do I use any arguments borrowed from the domain of Jewish or Christian biblical writings." See Charles E. Reagan, *Paul Ricoeur: His Life and His Work* (Chicago, IL: University of Chicago Press, 1998), 125.

25. Paul Ricoeur, "Intellectual Autobiography," in *The Philosophy of Paul Ricoeur*, Lewis Edwin Hahn (ed.), Library of Living Philosophers (La Salle, IL: Open Court, 1995), 12.

"hermeneutical phenomenology" that first turns to analyses of the voluntary and involuntary aspects of human action in *Freedom and Nature*. In *Fallible Man*, Ricoeur's phenomenological analysis comes to the conclusion that evil is made possible precisely because, although human beings are finite, they tend to expect to achieve a level of infinitude (whether in respect to perception or knowledge or simply in terms of everyday practice). It is precisely in not seeing the whole of this equation that evil occurs. In the companion volume to *Fallible Man* – *The Symbolism of Evil* – Ricoeur sets his analysis in a hermeneutical context of religious symbols and myths. In effect, we can understand ourselves only in the context of myth and theology rather than in some sense of pure phenomenological neutrality. Ricoeur's thought subsequently turned to questions of hermeneutics more generally and his primary contributions to philosophy are these hermeneutical texts, rather than more explicit theological ones. All along, however, he continued to write shorter texts on theology, philosophy of religion, and biblical exegesis – and those theological concerns continued to be in the background of his more explicitly philosophical texts. We will see a similar pattern in both Levinas and Marion.

III. THE RADICALLY TRANSCENDENTAL OTHER: EMMANUEL LEVINAS

Somewhat like Hegel, Emmanuel Levinas[26] is another interesting case of delayed reception. Although he published his first book (on Husserl[27]) in 1930 and played a major role in introducing both Husserlian and Heideggerian phenomenology to France, only with the publication in 1961 of *Totality and Infinity* does he begin to gain significant recognition. Yet, by the 1980s, his thought had become highly influential in French philosophy, which is why Janicaud singles him out as having so radically affected phenomenology.[28] While Levinas reacts to both Husserl and Heidegger, he reads all of modern thought and the entire history

---

26. Emmanuel Levinas (January 12, 1906–December 25, 1995; born in Kaunas, Lithuania; died in Paris, France) was educated at the universities of Strasbourg (1923–30) and Freiburg (1928–29), and received a *doctorat d'université* from the University of Strasbourg (1930) and a *doctorat d'état* from the Sorbonne (1961). His influences included Buber, Heidegger, Husserl, Marcel, Rosenzweig, and Wahl, and he held appointments at the Alliance Israélite Universelle (1934–39), École Normale Israélite Orientale (1946–79), University of Poitiers (1964–67), University of Paris X–Nanterre (1967–73), and University of Paris IV–Sorbonne (1973–76).

27. Emmanuel Levinas, *Théorie de l'intuition dans la phénoménologie de Husserl* (1930); published in English as *The Theory of Intuition in Husserl's Phenomenology*, André Orianne (trans.) (Evanston, IL: Northwestern University Press, 1973).

28. Janicaud notes the, in his view, unfortunate coincidence of Levinas's *Totality and Infinity* appearing the same year – 1961 – as the death of the leading atheistic phenomenologist – Maurice Merleau-Ponty.

of Western metaphysics as an attempt to arrive at a mastery of all "otherness" in order to achieve a totality precisely by way of adequation in which there is "the rigorous coincidence between the thought" and the object "which this thought thinks."[29] When he goes on to say that this places everything – including God – within the "gesture or movement of being [*gest d'être*]," he is clearly criticizing both Heidegger and the entire tradition of metaphysics. One could say that the impossibility of an adequation is a problem of metaphysics or epistemology. Yet Levinas takes this in a different direction, declaring this to be primarily an *ethical* problem, so that ethics becomes "first philosophy." Thus, although what Levinas writes has deep metaphysical and epistemological implications, the implications of his thought are first and foremost ethical and religious.

If Levinas is right, then this requires rethinking the very structure of philosophy. Whereas Kant had extolled the virtue of thinking for oneself – what he calls "autonomy" – Levinas claims that only acting "heteronomously," in which the Other[30] curbs my freedom, is truly ethical. It becomes clear that Levinas is presenting us with a markedly different notion of freedom when he writes that "the presence of the Other, a privileged heteronomy, does not clash with freedom but invests it."[31] In effect, I am only really free when I serve the Other. Who exactly, though, is this "Other"? As it turns out, this question concerns not just ethics but also epistemology and metaphysics, for Levinas cannot specify who this Other is. To do so would make a claim of knowledge of the Other that neither Levinas nor any of us can (epistemologically) make precisely because the Other – in her very Otherness – always escapes our grasp (metaphysically and epistemologically). Any claims to truly know the Other are, further, unethical in that they do violence to whomever they presume to describe. So an absolute givenness (*donation*) or knowledge (in the sense of adequation) of the Other is out of the question. Instead, the Other appears to us as a "face" that "is present in its refusal to be contained."[32] Given Levinas's religious perspective, the paradigmatic figures for the Other are the powerless, or those whose power paradoxically comes from being destituted: "The Other who dominates me in his transcendence is thus the stranger, the widow, and the orphan, to whom I am

---

29. Emmanuel Levinas, "God and Philosophy," in *Of God Who Comes to Mind*, Bettina Bergo (trans.) (Stanford, CA: Stanford University Press, 1998), 55.
30. Whether or not to be consistent in capitalizing "Other" is a complicated question for commentators on Levinas. For a discussion of this issue, see Adriaan Peperzak's introduction to Levinas's *Basic Philosophical Writings*, Adriaan T. Peperzak *et al.* (eds) (Bloomington, IN: Indiana University Press, 1996), xiv–xv.
31. Emmanuel Levinas, *Totality and Infinity: An Essay on Exteriority*, Alphonso Lingis (trans.) (Pittsburgh, PA: Duquesne University Press, 1969), 88.
32. *Ibid.*, 194.

obligated."[33] Moreover, according to Levinas, the face breaks into my world and leaves me traumatized.[34] Naked and destitute, the face still commands my respect.

Obviously, Levinasian ethics are of a most rigorous sort. Yet he is not giving us merely an ethics but also a philosophy of religion, in which the two are closely intertwined. In effect, we encounter God by way of the human Other, who "is indispensable for my relation with God. ... The Other is not the incarnation of God, but precisely by his face, in which he is disincarnate, is the manifestation of the height in which God is revealed."[35] In the very midst of our relation to the Other, God is revealed.[36] Thus, the relation to the Other constitutes "religion" for Levinas. Of course, in making the Other so very much a part of our relation to God, Levinas further complexifies what – given his concept of the Other – is already complicated. How, exactly, are we to differentiate between the human and the divine Other? Levinas's early writings provide relatively little guidance on such a question. Yet, in "God and Philosophy" (1975), he addresses this explicitly:

> God is not simply the "first other," the other *par excellence*, or the "absolutely other," but other than the other, other otherwise, other with an alterity prior to the alterity of the other, prior to the ethical obligation to the other and different from every neighbor, transcendent to the point of absence, to the point of his possible confusion with the agitation of the *there is* [*il y a*].[37]

If the human Other cannot be truly known or mastered, it must be all the much more so for the ultimate Other.

Here it is helpful to consider Derrida's respectful although incisive critique of Levinas. While he shares Levinas's concerns, he criticizes Levinas for providing such a hyperbolic conception of Otherness and attempting to go beyond traditional metaphysical categories. First, Derrida points out that precisely the ability to identify the Other as another ego is what makes it possible to

---

33. *Ibid.*, 215.

34. Emmanuel Levinas, *Otherwise than Being, or, Beyond Essence*, Alphonso Lingis (trans.) (The Hague: Martinus Nijhoff, 1981), 111.

35. Levinas, *Totality and Infinity*, 78–9.

36. In a later text, Levinas puts this even more strongly: "In the other, there is a real presence of God. In my relation to the other, I hear the Word of God. It is not a metaphor; it is not only extremely important, it is literally true. I'm not saying that the other is God, but that in his or her Face I hear the Word of God" (*Entre Nous: On Thinking-of-the-Other*, Michael B. Smith and Barbara Harshav [trans.] [New York: Columbia University Press, 1998], 110).

37. Levinas, "God and Philosophy," 69.

perceive the human Other as "Other, and not a stone."[38] Derrida makes the point that recognizing the dissymmetry of the Other first requires recognizing the symmetry. While Levinas is attempting to get beyond a conception of the Other found in Husserl in which the Other is analogous to the self, the danger is that the Other becomes so undifferentiated that it loses the features that make the human Other worthy of being treated *as* human. Second, Derrida insists that it is the very tradition of Greek philosophy that Levinas criticizes that makes his own venture possible. "One still has to philosophize (to say it and think it)," writes Derrida quoting an ancient Greek. Further, one cannot (and here Derrida quotes Levinas himself) "arrest philosophical discourse without philosophizing." As hard as it might be for some to imagine Derrida insisting on the need for the classical concepts of metaphysics, such is how he responds to Levinas.

However, Levinas resists any dominance by a philosophy that "compels every other discourse to justify itself" and opines that "rational theology accepts this vassalage."[39] He refuses to move to something like "faith," insisting that the very dichotomy of faith and reason has been set up by philosophy so as to make reason superior to faith. In a defiant tone, he responds to Derrida by saying: "*Not to philosophize would not be still to philosophize.*"[40] However, one of the complexities of Levinas's thought is that he actually borrows from a variety of philosophers. The idea of the Good as "beyond being [*epekina tes ousias*]" he takes from Plato and applies to God. Here the idea is that God cannot be thought of in terms that would apply to being (an idea also found in Plotinus). Levinas finds an ally in Descartes, in one sense, when Descartes speaks of his idea of an infinite, perfect being that he discovers in his mind. In the same way that Descartes concludes that he – a finite, imperfect being – could never have conjured up an idea of such a radically different being, Levinas sees this as an example of God "breaking into" human consciousness. However, a problem emerges at this point. While Descartes seems to think that this idea of infinite perfection is an idea that all would have, many of Descartes's readers have pointed out that it is much more likely owing to the Christian culture in which he lived. In the same way, it would seem that Levinas's God is distinctly theological – and, specifically, *Jewish*. Levinas himself speaks of "the revealed God of our Judeo-Christian spirituality" who "shows himself only by his trace, as is said in Exodus 33."[41]

---

38. Jacques Derrida, "Violence and Metaphysics: An Essay on the Thought of Emmanuel Levinas," in *Writing and Difference*, Alan Bass (trans.) (Chicago, IL: University of Chicago Press, 1978), 125.

39. Levinas, "God and Philosophy," 55.

40. *Ibid.*, 77.

41. Emmanuel Levinas, "The Trace of the Other," Alphonso Lingis (trans.), in *Deconstruction in Context: Literature and Philosophy*, Mark C. Taylor (ed.) (Chicago, IL: University of Chicago Press, 1986), 359.

The problem that Levinas faces is twofold: On the one hand, if this trace is identifiable with God, then how can one speak "adequately" of God who is so unidentifiable? This is simply a divine version of the problem of relating to the human Other that Levinas also raises. Would a religious believer not want to be able to make at least limited suppositions about God's identity and character in order to have something to believe? On the other hand, one could argue that Levinas has simply imported a specifically Judeo-Christian idea of God and acted as if this were a purely "philosophical" move. It is not surprising that Janicaud contends that in Levinas "phenomenology has been taken hostage by a theology that does not want to say its name."[42] On Janicaud's reading, Levinas is simply doing a kind of theology, all the while claiming to do straight philosophy. But here Janicaud is claiming something Derrida had already said nearly three decades before. Speaking of *Totality and Infinity*, Derrida asks (rhetorically) "independent of its 'theological context' (an expression that Levinas would most likely reject) does not this entire discourse collapse?"[43] Of course, Levinas often claims that his philosophy and his theological writings are separate, pointing out that he had separate publishers for his philosophical and theological writings.[44] As true as that may be, what Janicaud – and much milder critics or even some friends – assert is that his theological commitments make their way into his philosophy. Janicaud puts it rather bluntly: "*Totality and Infinity* is the first major work of French philosophy in which this theological turn is not only discernible, but explicitly taken up within a phenomenological inspiration."[45] Certainly, it would be hard to see Levinas as anything but a theological thinker who appropriates philosophical language for a distinctly theological cause, one that – in a rather different way from Kant – makes room for faith. But of course, the question might be asked: What is so wrong with that? Are philosophers not allowed to bring their metaphysical or ethical commitments into their writing?

Yet here we come to the very heart of the phenomenological project. For Husserl, the goal of phenomenology is to leave what he calls "the natural standpoint" and move to a kind of theoretical neutrality. On this point, Husserl sounds remarkably Kantian: to be a person "who thinks for himself [*Selbstdenker*]" one

---

42. Janicaud, *The Theological Turn of French Phenomenology*, 43.
43. Derrida, "Violence and Metaphysics," 103.
44. In an interview, Levinas insists that he keeps "separate very clearly these two types of work [Talmudic commentary and philosophy]. I even have two publishers; the one publishes my confessional texts, the other my texts which are called purely philosophical." See Emmanuel Levinas, "Interview with François Poirié," in *Is It Righteous to Be? Interviews with Emmanuel Lévinas*, Jill Robbins (ed.) (Stanford, CA: Stanford University Press, 2001), 62.
45. Janicaud, *The Theological Turn of French Phenomenology*, 36.

must first be freed from "all prejudices."[46] Husserl explicitly insists that – as part of the phenomenological method – one must "bracket" anything other than the phenomenon itself. According to phenomenological orthodoxy, one concentrates only on the object as it is immanently given to consciousness. But, of course, it is the object *as* constituted by the *ego*. Thus, the phenomenological *I* is central. In contrast, Levinas reverses this phenomenological structure (a reversal found also in Henry, Marion, and Chrétien): whereas the subject had in effect been in control of the object, the subject is now "subject" to the object. For Levinas, the principle "object" that reverses the gaze (so that it is not the gaze of the subject looking at the object but the other way around) is the (face of the) Other, epitomized for him by those traditionally counted as among the "least." In effect, the organizing that was previously delegated solely to the intentionality of consciousness is now being more directed by the other.

Understandably, then, Janicaud can speak of Levinas having "shattered" the phenomenological order.[47] But here it must be asked as to exactly *who* is being more true to phenomenology. Husserl's "principle of principles" can be read as either privileging the object or the subject, depending on which phrase of it one emphasizes – either "*accepted simply as what it is presented as being*" or "*only within the limits in which it is presented there.*" Although one can argue that Levinas provides a distorted phenomenology – one that moves from a more active to a more passive subject and from phenomenological immanence to transcendence – that move could also be viewed as simply establishing the privilege of the object (*noema*) over the subject (ego). What is all the more remarkable about this move is that it is done in the name of *ethics*. Levinas would argue that the privileging of the self has been the guiding form philosophy has taken since its beginnings, whether in phenomenology or simply philosophy in general, and to do "ethics as first philosophy" requires privileging the Other and not the self.[48]

---

46. Edmund Husserl, *The Crisis of European Sciences and Transcendental Phenomenology: An Introduction to Phenomenological Philosophy*, David Carr (trans.) (Evanston, IL: Northwestern University Press, 1970), 72.

47. Janicaud published an additional "report" on French philosophy in 1998 titled *La Phénoménologie éclatée* (*Phenomenology "Wide Open": After the French Debate*). The term "*éclatée*" means "to rupture" or "to shatter." Thus, "phenomenology shattered" would be an alternative translation. In any case, that Janicaud would use such strong language gives an idea of what he think is at stake and how fundamentally he thinks Levinas disrupts phenomenology's structure.

*48. Levinas is also discussed in detail in the essay by S. K. Keltner and Samuel J. Julian in *The History of Continental Philosophy: Volume 4*, and by Robert Eaglestone in his essay in this volume.

IV. PHENOMENOLOGY *AS* REVELATION: MICHEL HENRY

Although Michel Henry's[49] principal works on Christianity and phenomenology come *after* 1995 – the time frame of this volume – a brief word on his work is appropriate, if for no other reason than that Janicaud includes Henry as part of the theological turn. Although *The Essence of Manifestation* is ostensibly a phenomenological text, there is every reason for Janicaud to detect in it a turn toward the theological insofar as Henry makes the reversal similar to that found in Levinas (and, as we will see, also in Marion). By critiquing the privileging of the subject in both Husserl and Heidegger, Henry clearly champions the phenomenality of the phenomenon. Henry's focus is the very phenomenon of "manifestation," which, in effect, is revelation, as he will come to term it in his later work. For Henry, manifestation is fully immanent, so much so that *"there is nothing transcendent."*[50] But then the question is: manifestation of *what*? Ultimately, the answer turns out to be manifestation of manifestation itself, which turns out to be God. It is no accident that Meister Eckhart makes more than a short appearance in *The Essence of Manifestation*, nor that the search for the absolute leads us to a version of God that is inspired by Eckhart.[51]

However, Henry goes beyond Eckhart, for God is life itself and, because we are alive, God is fully present to us. It is in his later writings that this theme of God as life is developed. There, Henry works out what it means to say that "living is possible only outside the world, where another Truth reigns."[52] Within Christianity, Henry claims, the very meaning of the word "truth" means something quite different than it does within the realm of empirical sciences. Whereas scientific truth alienates,[53] Christianity provides a radical phenomenology that reveals the ultimate. The result, though, is not *theology* but *phenomenology*. Henry's conception of God is considerably different from that of Levinas or Marion, who would emphasize the transcendence or "otherness" of God. Henry,

---

49. Michel Henry (January 10, 1922–July 2, 2002; born in Haiphong, French Indochina (now Vietnam); died in Albi, France) was educated at the Lycée Henri IV, and the University of Lille (1941–45), where he also received a *doctorat du troisième cycle* (1960). His influences included Heidegger, Husserl, Hyppolite, Kandinsky, Marx, Ricoeur, Sartre, and Wahl, and he held appointments at the Centre National de la Recherche Scientifique (1956–60), the University Paul-Valéry Montpellier (1960–82), and visiting appointments at the École Normale Supérieure, Sorbonne, Louvain, University of Washington (Seattle), and the University of Tokyo.

50. Michel Henry, *The Essence of Manifestation*, Girard Etzkorn (trans.) (The Hague: Martinus Nijhoff, 1973), 283.

51. See, for example, *ibid.*, 309–35, 683.

52. Michel Henry, *I am the Truth: Toward a Philosophy of Christianity*, Susan Emanuel (trans.) (Stanford, CA: Stanford University Press, 2003), 30.

53. Michel Henry, *Incarnation: Une Philosophie de la chair* (Paris: Éditions du Seuil, 2000), 143.

in contrast, stresses God's immanence to us. But in making God and revelation central to phenomenology, Henry remains nevertheless strongly linked with Levinas and Marion. We return here (and will do so again in what follows) to the question of just who is being most faithful to Husserl's "principle of principles." Like Levinas, Henry would consider himself to be one of the "true" phenomenologists. Yet, while Henry accepts most of the basic principles of Husserlian phenomenology, he reverses intentionality. In effect, intentionality is suspended in order to allow the object to be manifest in total immanence. What Henry thus explains is the very givenness of the phenomenological appearance. In this regard, it is no accident that Marion clearly acknowledges his indebtedness to Henry for the latter's earlier work on givenness.[54]

In his later work, Henry makes a claim that is very similar to that of Chrétien: that the structure of Christianity ultimately teaches us about the structure of phenomenology. It is the question of whether phenomenology is most itself when it is thoroughly secular and naturalistic or whether it is only truly phenomenological when placed into a decidedly Christian context. Janicaud, of course, is going to side with the former option. It is also significant that Henry gives us an account of suffering and violence that turns out to be much more like that of Chrétien than Derrida. Life, according to Henry, is constituted by a comingling of suffering and joy. They are our basic *Stimmungen* (moods) and they are joined in such a way that they cannot be separated. Henry goes so far as to speak of "*suffering and joy together and without distinction.*"[55] In seeing them as so close and without clear distinction, Henry sounds very much like Chrétien, as will become readily apparent.

V. THE PROBLEM OF IDOLATRY AND THE NATURE OF GIVENNESS: JEAN-LUC MARION

The central concerns of Levinas are certainly those of Jean-Luc Marion,[56] although Marion's interest in avoiding violence to the other and in reversing

---

54. Jean-Luc Marion, *Being Given: Toward a Phenomenology of Givenness*, Jeffrey L. Kosky (trans.) (Stanford, CA: Stanford University Press, 2002), 330 n.14. There Marion makes clear his indebtedness to Henry's *Phénoménologie matérielle*. That indebtedness is also expressed in the preface to Marion's *Reduction and Givenness: Investigations of Husserl, Heidegger, and Phenomenology*, Thomas A. Carlson (trans.) (Evanston, IL: Northwestern University Press, 1998), xi.

55. Henry, *The Essence of Manifestation*, 661.

56. Jean-Luc Marion (July 3, 1946– ; born in Meudon, France) was educated at the Lycée Condorcet (1964–67), École Normale Supérieure (1967–70), and University of Paris IV–Sorbonne (1970–74), and received from the Sorbonne a *doctorat du troisième cycle* in 1974 and a *doctorat d'état* in 1981. His influences include Alquié, Balthasar, Derrida, Descartes,

the structure of phenomenology are very much motivated by his Roman Catholicism. Like Ricoeur and Levinas, Marion tries to keep separate his more "philosophical" from his more "theological" works.[57] Yet, as with Levinas, both critics and supporters have argued that the separation is not quite so clear as Marion maintains. Much of Marion's work is developed in relation to the themes of idolatry and what he terms the "saturated phenomenon." As early as *The Idol and Distance* (1977), Marion had proclaimed Nietzsche's idea of the "death of God" to be no more than the death of a god who rightly should die, the god of the philosophers – an idol that "does not have any right to claim, even when it is alive, to be 'God.'"[58] According to Marion, such idols have taken the form of Plato's form of the Good, Aristotle's "thought thinking itself," Plotinus's One, Kant's "moral founder," and Hegel's *Geist*. To Heidegger's rhetorical question "will Christian theology one day resolve to take seriously the word of the apostle and thus also the conception of philosophy as foolishness?"[59] Marion responds: "To take seriously that philosophy is a folly means, for us, first (although not exclusively) taking seriously that the 'God' of onto-theology is rigorously equivalent to an idol."[60]

At the heart of *God Without Being* is the discussion of idols and icons. The idol is like a mirror, in which we see our own reflection. In contrast, the icon is like a window through which we look to something beyond. Whereas the idol satisfies the gaze, "the icon summons sight in letting the visible … be saturated little by little with the invisible."[61] Given that Paul speaks of Christ as the "icon" of God (Col. 1:15), Marion thinks of Christ as the model for icons, all of which are what he would term "saturated phenomena." Whereas according to Husserl's "principle of principles," the object of consciousness appears "within the limits" of consciousness, Marion contends that some phenomena simply "exceed" those limits, so that intuition is overwhelmed by that which is given. It is the *subject*,

---

Heidegger, Henry, Husserl, Levinas, Nietzsche, and Wittgenstein, and he has held appointments at the University of Paris IV–Sorbonne (1973–81), University of Poitiers (1981–88), University of Paris X–Nanterre (1988–95), University of Paris IV–Sorbonne (1995–), and University of Chicago (1994–).

57. Marion's "philosophical" reputation is first and foremost as a Descartes scholar. His works on Descartes include: *Descartes's Grey Ontology: Cartesian Science and Aristotelian Thought in the Regulae* (1975); *Sur la théologie blanche de Descartes: Analogie, creation de vérités éternelles et fondement* (1981); *On Descartes' Metaphysical Prism: The Constitution and the Limits of Onto-theo-logy in Cartesian Thought*; and *Cartesian Questions: Method and Metaphysics* (1991).

58. Jean-Luc Marion, *The Idol and Distance*, Thomas A. Carlson (trans.) (New York: Fordham University Press, 2001), 1.

59. Martin Heidegger, "Introduction to 'What is Metaphysics?,'" Walter Kaufmann (trans.), in *Pathmarks*, William McNeill (ed.) (Cambridge: Cambridge University Press, 1998), 288.

60. Marion, *The Idol and Distance*, 18.

61. Jean-Luc Marion, *God Without Being: Hors-Texte*, Thomas A. Carlson (trans.) (Chicago, IL: University of Chicago Press, 1991), 17.

then, that makes for a lack of *adaequatio*. While saturated phenomena come in a variety of types, it is revelation that particularly concerns Marion. In effect, the saturated phenomenon is a reworking of Kant's "aesthetic idea," which "furnishes much to think," so that "no determinate thought, or concept, can be adequate" to it.[62] Marion likens such an experience to that of one who comes out of Plato's cave and into the light of the sun. The experience is one of bedazzlement, in which the intuition of intentionality is simply overwhelmed by sheer excess. "Something is experienced as unbearable to the gaze because it weighs too much upon that gaze. … What weighs here is not unhappiness, nor pain, nor lack, but indeed glory, joy, excess."[63] The revelatory force of the saturated phenomenon unseats the ego, which loses control of its object (to which it, in effect, becomes subject).

Marion identifies two sorts of idolatry. The first is that of onto-theology and what he says in this regard resonates with Heidegger's critique. However, Marion accuses Heidegger of holding God captive to "Being," a move we noted earlier in Heidegger's "Letter on Humanism": "Beyond the idolatry proper to metaphysics, there functions *another* idolatry, proper to the thought of Being as such."[64] To counter this move, Marion attempts "to think God without any conditions, not even that of Being."[65] Here one is reminded of Levinas and his desire to think "otherwise." In place of a God "within" Being, Marion speaks of a God "without being," a God who is *agápē*, who appears to us as *gift* and thus cannot be mastered by intuition. As we will shortly see, Marion later develops this theme of givenness (Heidegger's *es gibt*, Levinas's *il y a*), extending it to all of phenomenology and claiming that "the phenomenon therefore manifests itself insofar as it gives itself."[66]

Strongly influenced by negative theology – *apophasis* or the "*via negativa*," which (simply put) is a way of speaking about God by saying what God is *not* – Marion insists that "predication must yield to praise," so that "faith neither speaks nor states."[67] Yet Marion is unwilling simply to accept the alternatives of assertion and negation. Instead, he postulates a "third way," in a manner similar to Levinas's "otherwise." As Marion asserts, "the language of praise plays its own game."[68] In effect, Marion envisions a "language" that is beyond the true and false logic of predication. He further insists that negative theology – or at least *his* version of negative theology – "does not aim to reestablish a 'superessentiality',

62. Jean-Luc Marion, "The Saturated Phenomenon," Thomas A. Carlson (trans.), in Dominique Janicaud *et al. Phenomenology and the "Theological Turn": The French Debate*, 196.

63. *Ibid.*

64. Marion, *God Without Being*, 41.

65. *Ibid.*, 45.

66. Marion, *Being Given,* 248.

67. Marion, *God Without Being*, 106, 183.

68. Marion, *The Idol and Distance*, 193.

since it aims neither at predication nor at Being."[69] It is unclear whether Marion can successfully assert the possibility of a "third way" and, regarding this claim, Derrida has been one of his sharpest critics (as we will see shortly).

In the end, the question of exactly what Marion is attempting to accomplish can be answered in more than one way. On the one hand, in such texts as *God Without Being*, Marion can be said to be doing philosophical theology in a phenomenological mode. There he makes very explicit theological claims, for instance that "*only the bishop merits, in the full sense, the title of theologian*," and that theology only properly takes place in the moment of the Eucharist.[70] There, and in other such theological texts, Marion's faith commitments are in full force and his attempt to move beyond metaphysics is distinctly *theological* in nature. On the other hand, his phenomenological trilogy (*Reduction and Givenness, Being Given*, and *In Excess*) attempts to move beyond metaphysics *phenomenologically*, as well as to open up a phenomenological space for nonimmanent (that is, transcendent) phenomena (which would include, although not be limited to, specifically religious phenomena). Thus, these phenomenological texts have very important theological implications, even though they are not theological *per se*. As Marion himself notes, *Being Given* works out the nature of saturated phenomena (including that of revelation) in a way that *God Without Being* could only do "bluntly" and by "direct recourse to theology."[71]

To move beyond metaphysics phenomenologically, Marion moves from focusing on either intentionality and intuition (Husserl) or being (Heidegger) to givenness. He makes this move by concentrating on what he takes to be even more primordial than Husserl's "principle of principles": "so much reduction, so much givenness" (or "the more reduction, the more givenness"), a principle that Marion invokes from Husserl's *The Idea of Phenomenology*.[72] According to this principle, the phenomenon must be (i) given intrinsically (purely from itself), (ii) irrevocably (essentially given), and (iii) radically (so that at heart it is characterized by givenness).[73] Since phenomenological givenness is prior to consciousness, it cannot be controlled by consciousness. Instead, the I – which Marion terms the "*interloqué*" – is compelled to answer to the phenomenon. "Deposed from autarchy and taken by surprise," the I experiences a reversal in that its *logos* is no longer in control and this "prohibits the *interloqué* from comprehending" in the sense of complete adequation.[74] In effect, Marion (again, like Levinas and Henry) turns the usual phenomenological stance around. The

---

69. *Ibid.*, 230 n.14.
70. Marion, *God Without Being*, 153.
71. Jean-Luc Marion, "Preface to the American Edition," in *Being Given*, ix.
72. Marion, *Being Given*, 14–15.
73. *Ibid.*, 119–21.
74. Marion, *Reduction and Givenness*, 201.

autonomous subject becomes the one who is interrogated – *l'interloqué* (the interrogated one) – whom eventually Marion comes to term *l'adonné* (the gifted one). The one who is gifted is in effect called – and thus must respond.[75]

Although *Being Given* is ostensibly about phenomenology's structure, it is telling that when Marion discusses the call, he turns to the classic call of God to Samuel, in which Samuel's response is "here I am." For *Being Given* tells the story not just of all objects that are given to us but likewise the story of the ultimate given: revelation. This raises the question of the "as such" or the hermeneutics that Marion employs. We noted earlier that Heidegger insists that phenomena must be interpreted "as" something. But Marion's conception of the saturated phenomenon in effect derails the "as such" aspect of intuition. As he puts it, "the claim to the 'as such' has no right to be made." To this claim Derrida responds: "Then would you dissociate what you call phenomenology from the authority of the as such? If you do that, it would be the first heresy in phenomenology. Phenomenology without the as such." Marion responds by quoting Levinas: "'Without horizon [i.e. the as such] there is no phenomenology.' [To which Marion adds:] And I boldly assume he was wrong."[76] Hermeneutics is effectively pushed aside, becoming a moment not of the first or initial appearance but of later reflection. The question, however, is whether Marion is justified in so doing, on two different levels. On the one hand, does Marion's account remain truer to the things themselves than the standard phenomenological "orthodoxy"? On the other hand, does the claim that the saturated phenomenon appears without any conditions being imposed by consciousness prove more truly "orthodox" phenomenologically? Not surprisingly, Janicaud thinks that Marion *has* a horizon, namely one imported from theology. The result is that, "despite all the denials, phenomenological neutrality has been abandoned."[77] But, again, precisely the question of whether such "neutrality" is either *possible or desirable* is what is at issue.

VI. THE QUESTION OF THE MESSIANIC: JACQUES DERRIDA

One can argue that the question of negative theology – or something very much like it – can be found throughout the thought of Jacques Derrida.[78] Not only

---

75. Marion makes explicit reference to Jean-Louis Chrétien's *The Call and the Response* (discussed below). See *Being Given*, 287.

76. Jacques Derrida *et al.*, "On the Gift: A Discussion Between Jacques Derrida and Jean-Luc Marion," in *God, the Gift, and Postmodernism*, John D. Caputo and Michael J. Scanlon (eds) (Bloomington, IN: Indiana University Press, 1999), 66.

77. Janicaud, *The Theological Turn of French Phenomenology*, 68.

78. Jacques Derrida (July 15, 1930–October 8, 2004; born in El-Biar, near Algiers, French Algeria; died in Paris, France) was educated at the Lycée Louis-le-Grand, École Normale

does he explicitly address the notion, but even the idea of the "messianic" in his late philosophy clearly has something like the structure of negative theology. As early as the essay "Différance" (1968), Derrida recognizes that his thought might seem almost "indistinguishable from negative theology." However, he goes on to point out that both *différance* – which encompasses both "to differ" and "to defer" – and deconstruction concern the possibility of presence to consciousness and thus thought and language *in general*, whereas negative theology has to do with both theological thought and language that claim a "superessentiality beyond the finite categories of essence and existence."[79] Derrida returns to the logic of negative theology in "How to Avoid Speaking: Denials" (1987), particularly the denial by negative theologians that Derrida argues can be read only as being an assertion. In this respect, negative theology repeats the logic of Plato's "beyond being." Just like Plato, Dionysius actually "asserts" that "God is the Good that transcends the Good and the Being that transcends Being."[80] Yet Derrida accuses this "logic" of "going further than is reasonably permitted. That is one of the essential traits of all negative theology: passing to the limit, then crossing a frontier." On the other hand, negative theology does not just go beyond what is permitted: it likewise proves to be kenotic. "Negative theology empties itself by definition, by vocation, of all intuitive plenitude," becoming in effect "*kenōsis* of discourse." One might say that negative theology proves to be exactly the opposite of Husserl's *adaequatio*: not a "full intuition" but "an empty or symbolic intending" or "inadequation."[81] As to the question of Marion's "third way," Derrida responds: "Even if it is not a predicative affirmation of the current type, the encomium [i.e. praise] preserves the style and the structure of a predicative affirmation."[82] Whereas Derrida thinks that prayer might have no particular person to whom it is addressed, he insists that praise always assumes some attributes of the being or thing praised, and so it is never directionless.

Supérieure (1952–56), and received from the Sorbonne *doctorat de troisième cycle* in 1967 and a *doctorat d'état* in 1980. His influences included Blanchot, Freud, Hegel, Heidegger, Husserl, Levinas, Nietzsche, and Rousseau, and he held appointments at the Lycée Le Mans (1959–60), Sorbonne (1960–64), École Normale Supérieure (1964–83), Collège Internationale de Philosophie (1982–84), École des Hautes Études en Sciences Sociales (1983–2004), Yale (1975–86), and the University of California, Irvine (1986–2003). [*] For a broader discussion and more complete list of "Major Works" of Derrida, see the essay by Samir Haddad in *The History of Continental Philosophy: Volume 6*.

79. Jacques Derrida, "Différance," in *Margins of Philosophy*, Alan Bass (trans.) (Chicago, IL: University of Chicago Press, 1982), 6.

80. Jacques Derrida, "How to Avoid Speaking: Denials," Ken Frieden (trans.), in *Derrida and Negative Theology*, Harold Coward and Toby Foshay (eds) (Albany, NY: SUNY Press, 1992), 113.

81. Jacques Derrida, "*Sauf le nom (Post-Scriptum)*," in *On the Name*, Thomas Dutoit (ed.), David Wood *et al.* (trans.) (Stanford, CA: Stanford University Press, 1995), 36, 50.

82. Derrida, "How to Avoid Speaking: Denials," 137.

Despite their differences regarding the possibility of a "third way," Derrida in effect creates his own "third way" in the concepts of *différance* and the messianic. For *différance* is neither pure sameness nor otherness and the messianic partakes of no particular messianism – Christian, Jewish, Muslim, or otherwise – but is a pure structure that has no need of any particular revelation. Although the concept of the messianic is one that Derrida adopts only in his later philosophy, he sees deconstruction as messianic in that it is always pointing us to the future – *l'avenir* – a future that is unforeseeable and thus unpredictable, and therefore never arrives. For this reason, Derrida claims that "*deconstruction is justice*," in the sense that deconstruction is always trying to bring about justice but justice is always on the way and never present.[83] "Deconstruction" is an elusive term to describe, although Derrida insists that it is not a "method." Instead, it is the questioning, modifying, and reformulating of all formulas and beliefs that naturally takes place precisely because all beliefs and formulas are always open to question and rethinking. Deconstruction serves justice by asking whether particular laws serve justice. Since laws can never perfectly embody justice, Derrida thinks we must always be vigilant.

Yet Derrida's concern for justice is not just ethical but also religious in nature. *The Gift of Death* brings together these two concerns. Beginning with Jan Patočka's claim that hidden within the responsibility of Christian ethics are the secrecy and mystery of the cultic, Derrida argues that Christianity has a fundamental mystery at its heart. The problem arises in that ethical responsibility is neither simply to the singular other nor to some universal rule. Reinterpreting the French euphemism for suicide – *donner la mort*, literally, "to give death" – Derrida maintains that ethics is always a sacrificing of oneself for another. Christianity promotes such a sacrifice, but it must be done in secret. Borrowing heavily from Kierkegaard's account of the near-sacrifice of Isaac by Abraham, Derrida emphasizes that Abraham cannot give a rational or ethical account for his action, which means he must act in secret. It is this secrecy that, for Derrida, applies to all ethical actions. If one were to explain one's actions, then one "loses the possibility of deciding or the right to decide. Thus every decision would, fundamentally, remain at the same time solitary, secret, and silent."[84] There is an essentially aporetic quality to responsibility, then, since it is neither simply an accounting for one's action (by recourse to the universal) nor a nonaccounting for one's action. Further, while God does ultimately reward Abraham, there is no "payback." Precisely the willingness to offer his son as a sacrifice without having

---

83. Jacques Derrida, "Force of Law: The 'Mystical Foundation' of Authority," Mary Quaintance (trans.), in *Acts of Religion,* Gil Anidjar (ed.) (New York: Routledge, 2002), 243.

84. Jacques Derrida, *The Gift of Death,* David Wills (trans.) (Chicago, IL: University of Chicago Press, 1995), 60.

any expectation of reward is the reason he receives a reward. Neither morality nor faith, for Derrida, partakes in economic exchange. Instead, the logic is that of the gift – a true sacrifice – in which there is no calculation or expectation. Yet such a "gift" is not merely difficult but represents for Derrida "*the* impossible," "the very figure of the impossible."[85] Christianity – in its very structure of morality and faith – exemplifies this logic. Or else, and this would be Nietzsche's view, it merely *appears* to do so. *The Gift of Death* ends with a question: when Jesus instructs his disciples to give in secret (Matthew 6), are they truly giving a gift or partaking in an even more calculating way in economic exchange?

As much as Derrida at times valorizes Christian morality, he speaks of his own religious beliefs by saying "I quite rightly pass for an atheist," although he also says "I pray, as I have never stopped doing."[86] Derrida wrestles with the question with which Augustine wrestled: "What do I love when I love my God?" The result is an interesting way of combining Kant's making room for faith and his demand that religion remain within the bounds of reason. Admitting that reason is always interlaced with faith, Derrida is critical of "dogmatic faith" that "claims to know" and thus "ignores the difference between faith and knowledge."[87] It would seem that, again like Kant, Derrida's faith is primarily moral in nature. Derrida is uncomfortable with any concrete "messianism," for he sees them as inherently violent and too sure of themselves. Instead, he speaks of the "messianic" in general, which is "the opening to the future or to the coming of the other" who arrives as an "absolute surprise."[88] For Derrida, such a general messianicity is possible by way of a "nondogmatic doublet of dogma ... a *thinking* that 'repeats' the possibility of religion without religion."[89]

However, Derrida can be questioned in a number of respects. Certainly one danger is that Derrida's "undecidability" could simply lead to indecision. Derrida insists that it *ought* not, but Derrida's own lack of decision (regarding, say, messianism and the messianic) demonstrates this tendency. Further, a general messianicity that is derived from singular beliefs seems at odds with Derrida's concern to protect singularity. For is messianicity not *necessarily* connected to some concrete messianism? Yet perhaps the most troubling aspect of Derrida's thought is that requirements for both justice and faith seem so high that they

---

85. Jacques Derrida, *Given Time I: Counterfeit Money*, Peggy Kamuf (trans.) (Chicago, IL: University of Chicago Press, 1992), 7.
86. Geoffrey Bennington and Jacques Derrida, "*Circumfession*," in *Jacques Derrida*, Geoffrey Bennington (trans.) (Chicago, IL: University of Chicago Press, 1993), 154–5, 56.
87. Jacques Derrida, "Faith and Knowledge: The Two Sources of 'Religion' at the Limits of Reason Alone," Samuel Weber (trans.), in *Acts of Religion*, Gil Anidjar (ed.) (New York: Routledge, 2002), 49.
88. *Ibid.*, 57.
89. Derrida, *The Gift of Death*, 49.

could never be properly instantiated. Both are always *avenir* (to come) and thus (seemingly) can never arrive.

VII. THE VOICE OF THE CALL: JEAN-LOUIS CHRÉTIEN

Jean-Louis Chrétien's "phenomenology" is difficult to characterize.[90] That he subtitles one of his books "Phenomenology of the Promise" might lead one to the conclusion that his thought is linked to Derrida's *l'avenir*. But Chrétien maintains that "the promise always already surrounds us."[91] The promise is both to come and yet already here. That kind of paradoxical formulation is at the heart of Chrétien's philosophy, which often evokes that Heideggerian phrase "always already [*immer schon*]." Although Janicaud admits that Chrétien writes with care and nuance, he insists that Chrétien is writing against the theological backdrop of Christ's incarnation.[92] Of course, Chrétien does nothing to hide his influences: he cites both philosophers and theologians abundantly and frequently centers his meditations around passages from both Hebrew and Christian scriptures. Thus, although he writes on such topics as the body, the presence of the voice, and testimony, his take on them is distinctly theological, which leads Janicaud to wonder how they could be *phenomenological*. Indeed, that Chrétien would have essays titled "The Obliqueness of the Human and the Obliqueness of the Divine in the *Christian Conversations* of Malebranche" and "The I and Sin according to Kierkegaard" – in which Chrétien takes seriously the implications of sin for the constitution of the self – would only seem to strengthen Janicaud's claim.[93] Yet, whereas Marion would insist that his phenomenology of the "givenness" of the saturated phenomenon is "strictly phenomenological" (even though, strangely enough, it leads to a "theophany"), Chrétien would say that including theological voices actually *illuminates* the phenomena, resulting

---

90. Jean-Louis Chrétien (July 24, 1952– ; born in Paris, France) was educated at the Lycée Henri-IV (1969–71), École Normale Supérieure (1971–75), and Fondation Thiers (1977–80), and received a *doctorat de troisième cycle* from the University of Paris IV–Sorbonne (1983) and *habilitation à diriger des recherches* from the University of Paris IV–Sorbonne (2004). His influences include Aristotle, Augustine, Claudel, Heidegger, Levinas, Philo of Alexandria, Plato, Plotinus, and Porphyry, and he has held appointments at the University of Paris XII–Créteil (1981–88), University of Paris IV–Sorbonne (1988–).

91. Jean-Louis Chrétien, *La Voix nue: Phénoménologie de la promesse* (Paris: Éditions de Minuit, 1990), 60.

92. Janicaud, *The Theological Turn of French Phenomenology*, 67.

93. Jean-Louis Chrétien, "L'Obliquité humaine et l'obliquité divine dans les *Conversations chrétiennes* de Malebranche" and "Le Moi et le péché selon Kierkegaard," in *La Voix nue*.

in what he insists is something that is "rigorously phenomenological."[94] The result is a clash between a minimal, naturalistic phenomenology and a radical phenomenology that is either somewhat secretly or quite explicitly motivated by religious concerns.

Although Chrétien writes on a wide variety of topics, the theme of a call that "wounds" is one that appears in multiple texts and can be considered a dominant motif in his thought. One might even argue that it is the heart of the theological turn not just in Chrétien but French phenomenology in general. For Chrétien insists that the call that comes to us always already precedes us and also has the effect of decentering us and constituting us. It is yet another example of the usual phenomenological paradigm being turned on its head. "We speak only for having been called," says Chrétien, who also claims "we are entangled in speech as soon as we exist."[95] In place of a privileged, autonomous subject, Chrétien sees us as intersubjectively constituted, so that our voice is never really our own. As such, we are part of an ongoing conversation and an ever-evolving hybridity of both speech and self. Indeed, Chrétien pushes this intersubjectivity to a point where the idea of the "self" as discrete is seriously challenged. And that challenge is clearly presented within a theological context.

In that regard, when Chrétien says that "each new encounter shatters us and reconfigures us,"[96] it is not incidental that the phrase appears in an essay on prayer. Yet what is remarkable about that essay is how Chrétien uses prayer – a specifically religious phenomenon – to illuminate speech and conversation in general. Whether in prayer or in conversation with a human other, one is both touched by the other and touches in return. This movement is further complicated by Chrétien's claim that any response to a call "also calls out in turn and appeals to other calls."[97] So the structure of the call is not merely two-way but multidirectional. Speech comes to us *as* gift and so we both give back and give away. For Chrétien, the problem of the gift (and thus economic exchange) simply is not a "problem" for him (as it is for Derrida) precisely because of a fundamental "inequality" of gifts. As he puts it, "no response will ever correspond. The perfection of the answer will lie forever in its deficiency, since what calls us in the call is from the start its very lack of measure, its incommensurability."[98] Is there a problem, though, with this logic? That gifts cannot be measured means

---

94. Marion, "The Saturated Phenomenon," 215; Chrétien, *The Call and the Response*, 33. Although Chrétien is particularly speaking here of "human sight" and even poses this as a rhetorical question, he undoubtedly sees himself as doing rigorous phenomenology.

95. Chrétien· *The Call and the Response*, 1, 28.

96. Jean-Louis Chrétien, "The Wounded Word," Jeffrey L. Kosky (trans.), in *Phenomenology and the "Theological Turn,"* Dominique Janicaud *et al.*, 156.

97. Chrétien, *The Call and the Response*, 24.

98. *Ibid.*, 23.

that there can be no reciprocity involving measurement (no "even exchange"). Yet, if the response is always deficient, then is there not some kind of measuring that must have already taken place insofar as the response is deemed to have not measured up? Chrétien does not really answer this question, although his claims about "nothingness" function as a way of at least addressing it. He claims that we possess "nothing" and so, when the gift comes to us, we cannot really possess (let alone measure) it but respond only by passing it on. Chrétien's argument would seem to be that since none of us can possess the gift and all of us possess only nothingness, we are always exceeded by the gift.

All of this exchange is deeply connected to wounding. It is not just that anyone who speaks "opens himself to more than himself and to others," but that every "opening up" is like a kind of wound. Chrétien is speaking particularly of prayer when he writes that it "exposes [the one praying] in every sense of the word *expose* and with nothing held back."[99] Prayer in particular is "always agonic" for it opens us up to God and even the act of prayer is a kind of "suffering." Here it is helpful to remember that many encounters with God in the Hebrew Bible are ones in which the one called by God is opened up. For example, in one of the earliest, Moses hears God speaking to him from the burning bush and replies: "Here I am," which signifies that he is willing to be at God's disposal. When we think of "suffering," we tend to forget that its original meaning – and its French equivalent "*suffrir*" – is "to submit to." Although Chrétien also has in mind the idea of being in pain, that notion of submitting is first and foremost. We become a "subject" before God, since "all prayer confesses God as giver by dispossessing us of our egocentrism."[100] So the same reversal that we found in Levinas and Marion is likewise found in Chrétien. But this is a *painful* reversal and decentering, precisely because we so want to be in the center. It should be no surprise, then, that Chrétien sees prayer as an agonic struggle and Jacob's wrestling with the man or angel or God in the book of Genesis as paradigmatic. What takes place is a *violent* and prolonged encounter in which there is *both* a wound (Jacob's hip is displaced) *and* a blessing (Jacob becomes Israel). Although not all such encounters with God (or with human others, for that matter) are so agonic in nature, Chrétien sees at least something agonic in prayer itself, since even the act of submitting to God is a struggle.

Unlike Levinas – and particularly unlike Derrida – Chrétien does not simply want to eliminate all violence or suffering (although here he is quite close to Henry, who, as we noted, sees suffering and joy as inextricably linked). So he

---

99. Chrétien, "The Wounded Word," 150.
100. *Ibid.*, 153. Chrétien clearly has this idea of the "Here I am" in mind for, elsewhere, he speaks of "the gift to which one is opened without recourse, about being the only one who can say *Me voici*, here I am," in Jean-Louis Chrétien, *The Unforgettable and the Unhoped For*, Jeffrey Bloechl (trans.) (New York: Fordham University Press, 2002), 120.

has a very different response to the problem of violence as posed by Hegel. In one sense, Chrétien can be viewed as simply more realistic than either Levinas or Derrida, for he thinks that struggles in which there is suffering or violence simply describe the human condition. Although some might be willing to level the charge of falling into an all too easy justification of evil, Chrétien has a highly nuanced account of suffering and violence in which he maintains that "the benediction can wound."[101] Here the reference is again to Jacob's struggle. Chrétien points out that it is hard to see in the narrative who is the victor or vanquished. Any simple interpretation of who "wins" here would be naive. So Chrétien does not provide a theodicy but a *phenomenology* that attempts to think "loss, wound, and passivity, as well as forgetting and fatigue" from the point of view in which "there is no philosophical *parousia*."[102] Precisely *because* there is no such *parousia*, thinking of loss, wound, and suffering *either* as wholly gratuitous *or* as ultimately good – or at least offset by good – is simply impossible. For Chrétien, we are left in the phenomenological middle in which good and evil comingle, a world in which evil often masquerades as good and good is often less good than we take it to be. But it is likewise a world in which evil is not always quite as evil as guessed or feared. Chrétien is no wide-eyed optimist, but he is too nuanced as a phenomenologist to reduce the phenomena to any simple categories. The result is that the reader is left with a certain unease, for there is no real resolution or clear conclusion, just a meditation on the phenomena that leaves them in all of their complexity and paradox.

Yet Chrétien *does* envision a kind of *parousia*. In much the same way that he affirms a kind of memory beyond that remembered, so he speaks of a future that cannot be anticipated, one that "exceeds all expectation, and thereby founds anticipation."[103] Here Chrétien's "anticipation" and a future exceeding expectation sounds like Derrida's messianic and *l'avenir*. Chrétien himself says that "the *unhoped for* is what transcends all our expectations." Yet, unlike Derrida, Chrétien sets this within a decidedly Christian context. As he goes on to say, "at the point where Revelation permits hope to become hope in God and confidence in God's promise, the unhoped for is charged with a new meaning."[104]

---

101. Jean-Louis Chrétien, "Retrospection," in *The Unforgettable and the Unhoped For*, 122.
102. *Ibid.*, 126.
103. Jean-Louis Chrétien, *L'Antiphonaire de la nuit* (Paris: Éditions de L'Herne, 1989), 75.
104. Chrétien, *The Unforgettable and the Unhoped For*, 105, 107.

VIII. CONCLUSION

With Levinas, Henry, Marion, Chrétien – and even Derrida – phenomenology both goes in a distinctly theological direction and undergoes a startling phenomenological reversal. These moves have had a number of significant consequences. First, the Kantian move of "making room for faith" is put into question. Is it reason making room for faith or – as with these first four philosophers – faith being kind enough to make room for reason? Second, given this uncertainty of who is making room for whom, the very assumption of the superiority of reason over faith is put into question. No longer is it clear which truly has the upper hand. And it is Derrida, the one who "rightly passes for an atheist" – who particularly points this out. Third, whether violence is simply gratuitous and so should be minimized at all costs may be the conclusion of Derrida, but it is not that of either Henry or Chrétien. Although hardly champions of violence or suffering, they conclude that the picture is considerably more complicated. Fourth, whatever one makes of them, the challenges to phenomenology posed by Levinas, Henry, Marion, and Chrétien cannot be simply ignored. They are rigorous, substantial, and made precisely in the name of phenomenology. Fifth, all four of these thinkers provide helpful ways for moving philosophy of religion beyond its Babylonian captivity to onto-theology.

Of course, the debate is hardly over. Since 1995, there have been plenty of new works, topics, and voices. Yet one thing is clear: while once somewhat moribund, continental philosophy of religion has come back to health in a vigorous way and shows no signs of abating.

MAJOR WORKS

Jean-Louis Chrétien

La Voix nue: Phénoménologie de la promesse. Paris: Éditions de Minuit, 1990.

L'Inoubliable et l'inespéré. Paris: Desclée de Brouwer, 1991. Published in English as *The Unforgettable and the Unhoped For*, translated by Jeffrey Bloechl. New York: Fordham University Press, 2002.

L'Appel et la réponse. Paris: Éditions de Minuit, 1992. Published in English as *The Call and the Response*, translated by Anne A. Davenport. New York: Fordham University Press, 2004.

Corps à corps: À l'écoute de l'œuvre d'art. Paris: Éditions de Minuit, 1997. Published in English as *Hand to Hand. Listening to the Work of Art*, translated by Stephen E. Lewis. New York: Fordham University Press, 2002.

La Joie spacieuse: Essai sur la dilatation. Paris: Éditions de Minuit, 2006.

Jacques Derrida

De l'esprit. Paris: Éditions Galilée, 1987. Published in English as *Of Spirit: Heidegger and the Question*, translated by Geoffrey Bennington and Rachel Bowlby. Chicago, IL: University of Chicago Press, 1989.

Donner la mort. In *L'Éthique du don: Jacques Derrida et la pensée du don*, 11–108. Paris: Métailié-Transition, 1992. Published in English as *The Gift of Death*, translated by David Wills. Chicago, IL: University of Chicago Press, 1995.

Sauf le nom. Paris: Éditions Galilée, 1993. Published in English as "*Sauf le nom (Post-Scriptum*," in *On the Name*, edited by Thomas Dutoit, translated by David Wood, John P. Leavey, and Ian McLeod, 35–85. Stanford, CA: Stanford University Press, 1995.

Force de loi: Le "Fondement mystique de l'autorité." Paris: Éditions Galilée, 1994. Published in English as "Force of Law: The 'Mystical Foundation' of Authority," translated by Mary Quaintance, in *Acts of Religion*, edited by Gil Anidjar, 230–98. New York: Routledge, 2002.

Foi et Savoir. In *La Religion*, edited by Jacques Derrida and Gianni Vattimo. Paris: Éditions du Seuil, 1996/2000. Published in English as "Faith and Knowledge: The Two Sources of 'Religion' at the Limits of Reason Alone," translated by Samuel Weber, in *Acts of Religion*, edited by Gil Anidjar, 42–101. New York: Routledge, 2002.

Michel Henry

L'Essence de la manifestation. Paris: Presses Universitaires de France, 1963. Published in English as *The Essence of Manifestation*, translated by Girard Etzkorn. The Hague: Martinus Nijhoff, 1973.

Marx: I. Une philosophie de la réalité. II. Une philosophie de l'économie. Paris: Gallimard, 1976. Abridged in English as *Marx: A Philosophy of Human Reality*, translated by Kathleen McLaughlin. Bloomington, IN: Indiana University Press, 1983.

L'Amour les yeux fermés. Paris: Gallimard, 1976.

Phénoménologie matérielle. Paris: Presses Universitaires de France, 1990.

C'est moi la Vérité: Pour une philosophie du christianisme. Paris: Éditions du Seuil, 1996. Published in English as *I am the Truth: Toward a Philosophy of Christianity*, translated by Susan Emanuel. Stanford, CA: Stanford University Press, 2003.

Incarnation: Une Philosophie de la chair. Paris: Éditions du Seuil, 2000.

Paroles du Christ. Paris: Éditions du Seuil, 2002.

Emmanuel Levinas

De l'existence à l'existant. Paris: Vrin, 1947. Published in English as *Existence and Existents*, translated by Alphonso Lingis. The Hague: Martinus Nijhoff, 1978.

Totalité et infini: Essai sur l'extériorité. The Hague: Martinus Nijhoff, 1961. Published in English as *Totality and Infinity: An Essay on Exteriority*, translated by Alphonso Lingis. Pittsburgh, PA: Duquesne University Press, 1969.

Difficile liberté: Essais sur le judaïsme. Paris: Albin Michel, 1963. Published in English as *Difficult Freedom: Essays on Judaism*, translated by Seán Hand. Baltimore, MD: Johns Hopkins University Press, 1990.

Autrement qu'être ou au-delà de l'essence. The Hague: Martinus Nijhoff, 1974. Published in English as *Otherwise than Being, or, Beyond Essence*, translated by Alphonso Lingis. The Hague: Martinus Nijhoff, 1981.

De Dieu qui vient à l'idée. Paris: Vrin, 1982. Published in English as *Of God Who Comes to Mind*, translated by Bettina Bergo. Stanford, CA: Stanford University Press, 1998.

Entre nous: Essais sur le penser-à-l'autre. Paris: B. Grasset, 1991. Published in English as *Entre Nous: On Thinking-of-the-Other*, translated by Michael B. Smith and Barbara Harshav. New York: Columbia University Press, 1998.

Jean-Luc Marion

L'Idole et la distance. Paris: B. Grasset, 1977. Published in English as *The Idol and Distance*, translated by Thomas A. Carlson. New York: Fordham University Press, 2001.

Dieu sans l'être: Hors-texte. Paris: Fayard, 1982. Published in English as *God Without Being: Hors-Texte*, translated by Thomas A. Carlson. Chicago, IL: University of Chicago Press, 1991.

Prolégomènes à la charité. Paris: Éditions de la Différence, 1986. Published in English as *Prolegomena to Charity*, translated by Stephen E. Lewis. New York: Fordham University Press, 2002.

Reduction et donation: Recherches sur Husserl, Heidegger et la phénoménologie. Paris: Presses Universitaires de France, 1989. Published in English as *Reduction and Givenness: Investigations of Husserl, Heidegger, and Phenomenology*, translated by Thomas A. Carlson. Evanston, IL: Northwestern University Press, 1998.

Etant donné: Essai d'une phénoménologie de la donation. Paris: Presses Universitaires de France, 1997. Published in English as *Being Given: Toward a Phenomenology of Givenness*, translated by Jeffrey L. Kosky. Stanford, CA: Stanford University Press, 2002.

De Surcroît: Études sur les phénomènes saturés. Paris: Presses Universitaires de France, 2001. Published in English as *In Excess: Studies of Saturated Phenomena*, translated by Robyn Horner and Vincent Berraud. New York: Fordham University Press, 2002.

Paul Ricoeur

Philosophie de la volonté, I: Le Volontaire et l'involontaire. Paris: Éditions Montaigne, 1950. Published in English as *Freedom and Nature: The Voluntary and the Involuntary*, translated by Erazim V. Kohák. Evanston, IL: Northwestern University Press, 1966.

Philosophie de la volonté, II: Finitude et culpabilité. I. L'Homme fallible. II. La Symbolique du mal. Paris: Éditions Montaigne, 1960. Published in English as *Fallible Man*, translated by Walter J. Lowe. Chicago, IL: Regnery, 1965; and *The Symbolism of Evil*, translated by Emerson Buchanan. New York: Harper and Row, 1967.

La Révélation. Brussels: Facultés Universitaires Saint-Louis, 1977.

Le Mal: Un défi à la philosophie et à la théologie. Genève: Labor et Fides, 1986. Published in English as *Evil: A Challenge to Philosophy and Theology*, translated by John Bowden. London: Continuum, 2007.

Figuring the Sacred: Religion, Narrative, and Imagination. Edited by Mark I. Wallace. Translated by David Pellauer. Minneapolis, MN: Fortress, 1995.

The Religious Significance of Atheism (with Alasdair MacIntyre). New York: Columbia University Press, 1969.

Essays on Biblical Interpretation (with Lewis S. Mudge). Philadelphia, PA: Fortress, 1980.

Penser la Bible (with André LaCocque). Paris: Éditions du Seuil, 1998. Published in English as *Thinking Biblically*, translated by David Pellauer. Chicago, IL: University of Chicago Press, 1998.

13

THE PERFORMATIVE TURN AND THE EMERGENCE OF POST-ANALYTIC PHILOSOPHY

José Medina

Although the linguistic turn has been praised as the major philosophical achievement of contemporary philosophy, there is also another important "turn" that – I will argue – has been in fact more epochal and philosophically significant if considered in terms of its long-term impact across traditions and in its influence in shaping the contemporary philosophical agenda. For while the linguistic turn has been pivotal in the emergence of some trends and schools of thought within analytic and continental philosophy, the performative turn has not only created trends and schools within these traditions but has in fact challenged their boundaries, leading to the emergence of perspectives that live across traditions or in the interstices between them. Not only has the turn to performance resulted in the development of philosophical perspectives that are hard to classify and impossible to pigeonhole, but their proponents and followers have engaged in multifaceted and multilayered debates that span across traditions and even across disciplines, reshaping theoretical landscapes and challenging their most basic assumptions. In a broad range of philosophical issues concerning identity, knowledge, and values, performative approaches have flourished, transforming and enriching philosophical research and calling for interdisciplinary collaborations that reach beyond the boundaries of philosophy (especially in feminist theory, race theory, social epistemology, political philosophy, and aesthetics). But what exactly am I calling "the performative turn"? In this introduction I will briefly sketch what the philosophical turn to performance entails, setting the stage for my account of its occurrence across philosophical traditions and for my exploration of the consequences and implications of its legacy in the philosophical movements of the twentieth century and in the philosophical agenda of the twenty-first century.

The performative turn can be said to have taken place in different ways in different places: different philosophical traditions have put performance at the center of philosophical debates and have called attention to the crucial connection between philosophical problems and human actions and practices. Many would argue that in the continental tradition this turn had been in the making for centuries, culminating with the Romantic movement of the nineteenth century establishing a deep and intimate connection between subjectivity and its expressions in action. Charles Taylor, for example, has traced the development of an expressive tradition in European philosophy of language from Hamann, Herder, and Humboldt to Husserl, Heidegger, and Habermas.[1] Others have also emphasized the performative aspects of Romantic expressivism, with its emphasis on cultural practices as constituting (as well as expressing) human values, human taste, human reality, and human knowledge. In this sense Hegel himself can be seen as a major contributor to the performative turn.[2] But I am more interested here in highlighting how the turn to action and performance took place at the threshold of the twentieth century, reconceptualizing philosophical problems within continental thought during that century. In this sense, although we can trace its historical roots much further, the performative turn in twentieth-century continental philosophy is closely linked to the refocusing of interpretative questions in practical terms: by focusing on action and performance, traditional epistemic issues concerning human understanding became social, political, and historical issues.

We can identify three philosophical movements that made crucial contributions to the performative turn in European thought: Marxism, with its reversal of the traditional relationship of theory to practice; phenomenology, with its analysis of the *lifeworld*; and hermeneutics, with its dynamic and immanent approach to understanding grounded in historically situated practices of interpretation. The Marxist philosophy of praxis brought to the fore the social and political aspects of traditional epistemic questions, presenting a new methodological approach to interpretation with the critique of ideology. Interestingly enough, in the early twentieth century even phenomenological theories of subjectivity were reoriented toward the practical and the social, with Husserl himself moving the focus of his philosophy from intentional meaning-conferring acts to the *lifeworld* – an intersubjectively shared background that supports meaning and

---

1. See Charles Taylor, *Human Agency and Language* (Cambridge: Cambridge University Press, 1985).
2. See John McCumber, *Poetic Interaction* (Chicago, IL: University of Chicago Press, 1989), and *The Company of Words* (Evanston, IL: Northwestern University Press, 1993). If the latter book argues for an interpretation of Hegel as one of the creators of the linguistic turn, the former can be said to show Hegel's crucial contributions to the performative turn.

communication. In this way phenomenology moved from an intentionalistic semantics to a social pragmatics that re-cognizes socialization into a form of life as a prerequisite for meaning and understanding. It is this priority of the practical and the social that grounded the convergence between phenomenology and Marxist philosophy – otherwise quite different schools of thought – that we see, for example, in the early Marcuse or the later Sartre.[3] On the other hand, hermeneutics also brought the epistemology of interpretation to the realm of concrete sociohistorical practices. From Dilthey to Gadamer and Ricoeur,[4] the rethinking of interpretative methodologies in the human sciences resulted in the rich situating of reason in society and history and in the provocative reconceptualization of interpretative subjectivities as embodied in language and action.[5]

The performative turn was produced rather differently in the analytic and pragmatic schools of thought within Anglo-American philosophy. I will be teasing out some parts (or threads) of this complex story in the next two sections, so here I will simply lay out the two criteria I have used to compose the story I will tell about the development and impact of the performative turn. In the first place, I want to explore the intersection between the performative turn and the linguistic turn. Therefore, I will focus on those performative theories that are also at the same time theories of language and communication. In the second place, since I want to identify those performative insights that have had an important impact across philosophical traditions, the protagonists of my story will be those philosophers whose performative approaches have influenced and shaped discussions in a wide range of philosophical schools. For this reason, I will give priority to authors such as Wittgenstein and Austin over others such as Ryle and Grice. For, although Ryle's logical behaviorism and Grice's pragmatics have been highly influential performative theories, they have been comparatively less pivotal in generating philosophical discussions of performance across traditions.[6]

---

3. See Jürgen Habermas, *Postmetaphysical Thinking: Philosophical Essays* (Cambridge, MA: MIT Press, 1992), 8.

*4. For discussions of the hermeneutic theories of Dilthey, Gadamer, and Ricoeur, see the essays by Eric Sean Nelson in *The History of Continental Philosophy: Volume 2*, Daniel L. Tate in *The History of Continental Philosophy: Volume 4*, and Wayne J. Froman in *The History of Continental Philosophy: Volume 6*.

5. I am here calling attention to the contribution of hermeneutics to the performative turn, but perhaps this should be qualified, for, although there are performative strands in this school of thought, not all hermeneutic approaches are performative and there are indeed some idealistic tendencies within hermeneutics.

6. See Paul Grice, "Logic and Conversation," in *The Philosophy of Language*, A. P. Martinich (ed.) (Oxford: Oxford University Press, 2006); and Gilbert Ryle, *The Concept of Mind* (New York: Barnes & Noble, 1949). For a discussion of Gricean and Rylean pragmatic perspectives,

I will articulate a two-part story about the performative turn in analytic and pragmatist philosophy. In the first part of my story I will focus on some central figures in Anglo-American philosophy (Austin, Dewey, and Wittgenstein in particular), tracing the impact of their central ideas not only among their followers but also, and more importantly, among theorists of different philosophical traditions (Butler, Cavarero, and Habermas, among others). This section will already highlight the beginnings of a process of hybridization between philosophical traditions, a productive *mestizaje* that makes one hopeful about new generations of theorists who are problem-oriented and are willing to use conceptual tools from a variety of sources, without letting their allegiances to particular traditions become obstacles to their reflections or to the philosophical dialogues in which they engage. In the second part of my story I will sketch my own account of the emergence of *post-analytic philosophy* as a result of the linguistic and performative turns. I will highlight the strength of this new school of thought in reconceptualizing fundamental questions concerning normativity in performative terms. By focusing on the interrelations between language and action, problems concerning knowledge, values, and reality appear in a new light. My analysis will underscore the generative potential of the American performative turn in reconceptualizing traditional philosophical problems and creating new ones.

I will also highlight an important weakness in post-analytic philosophy: what I call *the evasion of identity*. Until recently the authors in this school of thought for the most part neglected issues of identity and thereby disregarded some of the most important ideas and cultural developments of the twentieth century. We can add to W. E. B. Du Bois's claim that the problem of the twentieth century was the problem of the color line, that it was also the problem of the gender and sexual lines. But most post-analytic American philosophers – from Quine and Sellars to Davidson and Putnam – missed an opportunity to incorporate in their theorizing some of the most important sociopolitical and cultural movements of modern times: the civil rights movement, the women's liberation movement, and the sexual liberation (and GLBT) movement. This suggests not only an intellectual oversight, but also an important disconnect with (and possibly a lack of concern for) some of the most central problems of the contemporary world. How can one philosophize about knowledge without taking into account issues of gender and race when women and racial minorities were being excluded from the institutions in charge of producing and disseminating knowledge? How can one theorize about human relations and disregard race, gender, sexual orientation, and class in a society in which racism, sexism, and homophobia are rampant, and economic oppression everywhere?

---

see Marcelo Dascal, *Pragmaticism and the Philosophy of Mind* (Amsterdam: John Benjamins, 1984).

These criticisms against analytic philosophy have been forcefully voiced by many.[7] But they still apply to an important degree even to post-analytic philosophy. And this lacuna becomes all the more dramatic in a school of thought that is oriented toward action and performance. But there have been some important exceptions in this respect (Stanley Cavell being perhaps the most notable) and glimpses of concern for identity issues have appeared here and there in post-analytic philosophy, especially in the late 1980s and 1990s. I will discuss how the evasion of identity in post-analytic philosophy is being addressed by some and I will argue that repairing this evasion requires a dialogue among philosophical traditions that is critical and challenging – in identifying and contesting gaps and exclusions – as well as mutually enriching – in sharing existing theoretical resources and strategies and creating new ones. There is reason for hope, I will contend, and it lies in the recently developed and ongoing collaborations across philosophical traditions and across disciplines. I will conclude with a brief note on the philosophical agenda for the twenty-first century, which must be pluralistic, interdisciplinary, and cross-cultural in order to address the needs and concerns of the multicultural and globalized communities of today.

I. THE PERFORMATIVE LEGACY

I will start developing my account of the performative turn in analytic and pragmatist philosophy by calling attention to the similarities of the views of communication and action of two central figures in these philosophical traditions: Wittgenstein[8] and Dewey. I focus on these two authors because of their unparalleled influence and their converging contributions to the performative and linguistic (or better yet, communicative) turns of early-twentieth-century philosophy. As I have argued elsewhere,[9] Wittgenstein and Dewey share a similar contextualist view that underscores that words are inextricably interwoven with actions. The intimate bond between words and actions is precisely what the Wittgensteinian notion of a language-game is supposed to highlight: "I shall … call the whole, consisting of language and the actions into which it is woven, the 'language-game'";[10] "the term 'language-*game*' is meant to bring into promi-

---

7. See, for example, Charles Mills's critique of Rawls in *The Racial Contract* (Ithaca, NY: Cornell University Press, 1999). See also John McCumber, *Time in the Ditch: American Philosophy and the McCarthy Era* (Evanston, IL: Northwestern University Press, 2001).

*8. For an extended discussion of Wittgenstein, see the essay by John Fennell and Bob Plant in *The History of Continental Philosophy: Volume 3*.

9. See my *Speaking from Elsewhere: A New Contextualist Perspective on Meaning, Identity, and Discursive Agency* (Albany, NY: SUNY Press, 2006), ch. 1.

10. Ludwig Wittgenstein, *Philosophical Investigations* (Oxford: Blackwell, 1985), §7.

nence the fact that the *speaking* of language is part of an activity, or of a form of life.”[11] In a similar vein, Dewey understands language as a form of *agency*: “language is primarily a mode of action”;[12] and the inseparability of words and actions is at the core of his “naturalistic” account of language as “the tool of tools.”[13] In short, the *performativity* of language is the centerpiece of Dewey’s and Wittgenstein’s contextualism. As Wittgenstein puts it, “words are deeds.”[14]

Wittgenstein and Dewey call our attention to the *pragmatic contexts of communication*; they stress that language and its contexts of use are action-oriented. As I have argued in detail elsewhere,[15] both Wittgenstein and Dewey explain the contextual formation and transformation of meaning in a strikingly similar way. They both argue that the meaning of words and sentences becomes contextually determinate through the *tacit agreement in action* of the participants in communicative practices. This suggests that the meaning or interpretation of a speech act is not in the hands of anyone in particular, but in the hands of all speakers/writers taken collectively, that is, in the hands of the linguistic community. But this can be understood in different ways: as emphasizing the fixity of meaning established by social and pragmatic means; or as underscoring the instability of meaning that is always scattered and dispersed in a multiplicity of communicative encounters in heterogeneous pragmatic contexts. The former understanding of the semantic role of communal agreement is the one suggested by *a consensus view of meaning* such as Kripke’s community interpretation of Wittgenstein on meaning and rule-following.[16] A nonrelativistic and nonskeptical version of the consensus view of meaning can be found in Peirce’s semiotics and in Habermas’s account of communicative action.[17] On this transcendental view, what fixes meaning is not the *de facto* (and perhaps arbitrary) consensus of a contingent community but, rather, the rational consensus of an idealized

---

11. *Ibid.*, §23.

12. John Dewey, *Experience and Nature*, in *John Dewey: The Later Works, 1925–1953, Vol. 1: 1925* (Carbondale, IL: Southern Illinois University Press, 1988), 160; see also 137 and 139.

13. *Ibid.*, 134.

14. Ludwig Wittgenstein, *Culture and Value* (Chicago, IL: University of Chicago Press, 1980), 46.

15. See my *Speaking from Elsewhere*, ch. 1.

16. On Kripke’s skeptical reading of Wittgenstein in *Wittgenstein on Rules and Private Language*, the lack of semantic foundations is compensated by the arbitrary decisions of the community and thus, on this decisionistic view, what the community decides is the new foundation of language, the be-all and end-all of meaning and communication. It is worth noting that the Kripkean reading of Wittgenstein has been very influential although it has also come under heavy attack in recent years.

17. See Jürgen Habermas, *The Theory of Communicative Action, Vol. 1* (Boston, MA: Beacon Press, 1985) and *Postmetaphysical Thinking*, and Charles Sanders Peirce, *Peirce on Signs: Writings on Semiotic by Charles Sanders Peirce* (Chapel Hill, NC: University of North Carolina Press, 1991). [*] For a discussion of Jürgen Habermas, see the essay by Christopher F. Zurn in *The History of Continental Philosophy: Volume 6*.

community. Semantic foundations are here found in transcendental idealizations that operate as regulative ideals: Habermas's Ideal Speech Situation and the idealized community of all possible participants in communication; or the Peircean notion of the End of Inquiry, invoked by Hilary Putnam in *Reason, Truth, and History*. According to these transcendental views, our communicative practices are grounded in and guided by idealizations that are always implicitly presupposed and make our communicative interactions possible; and the determinacy and stability of our meanings are to be measured by their asymptotic approximation to the full determinacy and permanent fixity that would be achieved under idealized conditions. But appeals to idealizations are notoriously problematic, among other things because they are always formulated from a situated and partial perspective, and it is unclear how these appeals can overcome the contextualized relativity from which the transcendental views try to escape.[18] Also problematic is the fact that, according to these transcendentally idealized views, semantic determinacy requires a background agreement not only in *action* (in ways of doing things), but also in *content* (in ways of representing things) and, therefore, a strong semantic *uniformity* across speakers and linguistic communities. But it is not at all clear that, for the meanings that circulate in our communicative practices, this strong semantic uniformity should be conceived as possible, required, or desirable, even as an idealization.

There is an alternative way of understanding the semantic role of practical agreement and how semantic determinacy is communally achieved in our communicative practices. This is what I have termed – in my interpretation of Wittgenstein's and Dewey's semantic views – the idea of *contextual determinacy*, according to which meanings acquire transitory and imperfect determinacy when contextualized, that is, when situated in pragmatic contexts of communication. Even when they become sufficiently determinate for the purposes of communication, meanings remain *unstable and heterogeneous*: that is, they remain open to contestation, rather than fixed once and for all; and they become constituted by different perspectives and voices within them, without necessarily becoming uniform and suppressing disparities and dissent.

The instability and heterogeneity of meaning have been emphasized by a variety of contemporary perspectives on communication in analytic and continental philosophy, by theories as different as those of Donald Davidson and Judith Butler.[19] For Davidson, all we need to share for successful communication is a *passing* theory (not a *prior* theory) of interpretation. The meanings

---

18. See my critique of semantic transcendental idealizations in *The Unity of Wittgenstein's Philosophy* (Albany, NY: SUNY Press, 2002), and *Speaking from Elsewhere*.

*19. Davidson and Butler are addressed in detail by, respectively, John Fennell and Gayle Salamon in essays in *The History of Continental Philosophy: Volume 8*.

that we share in successful communicative encounters are simply the result of a transitory convergence of perspectives. These meanings can be entirely *ad hoc*; there is no need for shared meanings to be previously *prepared* or ready-made. Davidson's argument tries to establish that the interpretative task that interlocutors face is the task of *adjusting* their theories of interpretation until they *converge*. On Davidson's view, communication is a matter of *mutual adjustment* of theories of interpretation, a process of interpretative negotiation or give and take between speakers who are constantly reinterpreting each other. For Davidson, the meanings that come first in the order of interpretation are *transient meanings*: first meanings are transitory meanings constructed for the purpose of a particular communicative exchange and there is no reason to think that they will survive that exchange. According to this view, the meanings that matter for the purpose of communication have no semantic stability whatsoever. They are the *ad hoc* constructs of *converging passing theories*.[20] Davidson's account of meaning and communication in terms of converging passing theories leads to a radical redescription of the traditional notions of language and linguistic competence. As Davidson puts it, his account gives new content to "the idea of two people 'having the same language' by saying that they tend to converge on passing theories."[21] But this seems to relativize and ultimately dissolve *the very notion of a language*, for "any theory on which a speaker and an interpreter converge is a language" and "then there would be *a new language for every unexpected turn in the conversation*."[22] Thus, on Davidson's view, the notion of a shared language becomes *philosophically irrelevant*; it is simply not needed for a philosophical theory of communication and communicative competence. Thus, on this view, the notion of a shared language is replaced with that of an *idiolect*, and communication is understood as the intersection in passing of the individualistic perspective of particular interlocutors who come into contact.

The instability and heterogeneity of meaning are understood and explained in a very different way in social accounts of language and communicative interaction. It is a mistake to assume (as Davidsonians often do) that a social perspective will necessarily conceive of language as a set of stable conventions that

---

20. The core of Davidson's controversial argument is that we can always bring prior theories closer and closer together until they ultimately converge in passing theories that fit one another: no matter how far apart the prior theories of two interlocutors may be, it is always *in principle* possible to tinker with them – to adjust them and transform them – in a process of self-correction, until they converge (so that the speaker intends the hearer to interpret her utterance in a particular way, and the hearer uses a passing theory that interprets the utterance in just that way).

21. Donald Davidson, "A Nice Derangement of Epitaphs," in *Philosophical Grounds of Rationality*, Richard E. Grandy and Richard Warner (eds) (Oxford: Oxford University Press, 1986), 173.

22. *Ibid.*, emphasis added.

turn meanings into reified, ready-made products that are homogenized across speakers and fixed once and for all. This is not true of all social accounts that depict language as a shared social practice. In particular, it is not true of those social accounts that conceptualize language from a performative perspective, for the focus here is language in action, that is, language as a living practice (*parole*) and not as an inert system of signs or code (*langue*). On these social and performative views, meanings emerge from the *clashing and meshing of perspectives* that are shared in communication through the use of signs. And given that meanings are continually tied to this interactive process of relating communicative perspectives, they display an intrinsic semantic instability and heterogeneity that cannot be fully eliminated; for, no matter how much commonality of perspective we find, no matter how successful processes of semantic homogenization and stabilization happen to be, there is always the possibility of diverse (even diverging) perspectives appearing and disrupting the semantic life of our signs.[23] In this sense, meanings are always in the making; the process of meaning formation (and re-formation) always remains open to new perspectives; and, therefore, there is always a residual semantic heterogeneity and instability that cannot be eliminated. Different articulations of this social-performative account of the openness, fragility, and fragmentary nature of meanings can be found in the pragmatist tradition and in contemporary continental philosophy.

In the pragmatist tradition, we find a highly influential social-performative account of meaning in George Herbert Mead's *Mind, Self, and Society*. For Mead, meanings go beyond the purely "psychical"; they belong to *the interactional*, that is, to intersubjective processes of communicative interaction. Mead's interactionism yields a *relational* view of meaning. On this view, meaning is a relation among certain phases of social interaction: a communicative action, a reaction to it, and the resulting act that completes the interaction. As Mead explains his interactional semantic view, "the logical structure of meaning" consists in "a threefold or triadic relation between gesture, adjustive response, and resultant of the social act which the gesture initiates."[24] Mead emphasizes that the specifically human forms of communication that require meanings involve a very peculiar kind of cooperation. What characterizes the kind of cooperation made possible by human language, what defines communicative interaction with symbols, is that it requires *reflexivity*: that is, the capacity to take the attitude of the other toward oneself. All gestures are tools for the coordination of action. But what distinguishes gestures with meaning is that they carry with them an attitude that

---

23. In *Speaking from Elsewhere,* I have tried to offer a full account of this point, drawing on the diverse but curiously converging perspectives of Bourdieu, Butler, Dewey, Mead, and Wittgenstein.
24. George H. Mead, *Mind, Self, and Society* (Chicago, IL: University of Chicago Press, 1934), 80.

is *mutually recognized* by sender and recipient. For Mead, symbolic interaction involves the reversibility of roles or communicative perspectives. He develops his distinctive symbolic interactionism through his theory of role-taking. The claim about the mutual recognition of communicative attitudes involved in the thesis of reflexivity or reversibility seems fairly intuitive and uncontroversial. What is far more problematic, though, is the claim about similarity of response in speaker and hearer that Mead also includes in his account of reflexivity. It seems wrong to say that meaningful gestures have the *same* effect on issuer and addressee. If I issue a verbal threat, my threatening noises do not scare me and I do not feel threatened. For, indeed, to *recognize* is not to be similarly affected. One can reply that the claim about similarity of response that Mead's reversibility thesis makes only involves that the speaker must know (or have some sense of) what it is like to be the recipient of the address – for example, what it is like to be the object of a threat, even if she does not feel threatened. This is indeed more plausible, but still problematic in some cases: For example, must the harasser know what it is like to be harassed? Must the abuser know what it feels like to be mistreated? Do slave-holders really have an inkling of what it feels like to be dominated? Mead seems to go too far when he claims that meaningful symbolic interaction requires "an arousal in the individual himself of the response which he is calling out in the other individual, a taking of the role of the other, a tendency to act as the other person acts."[25]

Similar issues appear in the social-performative accounts of contemporary continental philosophy, although the emphasis here is not on mutual recognition, but on misrecognition or lack of recognition; and on the incongruity of communicative perspectives, rather than on the meshing and coordination of perspectives. In these accounts the notion of communicative interaction is articulated through the notion of *a voice* and, thus, the themes of semantic instability and heterogeneity are developed in terms of *the plurivocity of meaning*. A good example of this can be found in the work of Adriana Cavarero.[26] By calling attention to the voice, Cavarero brings to the fore three crucial aspects of symbolic performance: its embodiment, its singularity, and its relationality. The sound of the voice is always something unique, a concrete particular. But the material particularity of a voice, its concreteness and uniqueness, can be produced and recognized only in relation to other voices. In other words, the peculiar embodied singularity of a voice can be achieved only relationally. As Diane Perpich puts it, "voices are inherently plural and relational," for to speak is to address another, and therefore, it "presupposes the other (and still other

---

25. *Ibid.*, 73.
26. See Adriana Cavarero, *Relating Narratives: Storytelling and Selfhood* (New York: Routledge, 2000).

others) by virtue of the plurivocity of language."[27] This plurivocity of language is contained and maintained in each particular voice, in which the voices of past and future speakers resonate: "In speaking, I speak a language that was already given to me by others, a language that contains already a plurality of voices and a consequent plurality of shades of meaning."[28] A voice always *echoes* other voices; and with this reverberation through chains of voices, each voice becomes performatively entangled in a network of voices.[29] As Butler puts it, combining the performative views of Austin and Althusser, the voice of an I "is an inherited set of voices, *an echo of others* who speaks as the 'I.'"[30] I will come back to Butler's influential account of plurivocity and symbolic agency, but first let us move from meaning to illocution, that is, from semantic issues about the content of our speech acts to pragmatic issues about their performative force. For we need to elucidate the role of our consensus of action not only in the formation and circulation of meanings, but also in the configuration of illocutionary forces. That is, we need to interrogate also the role of practical agreement in establishing the force of our speech acts, and ask whether there is also heterogeneity and instability in the things that we do with words, and not only in the things we say; in other words, whether performative fixity and homogeneity (either socially or individualistically achieved) are to be expected in our communicative practices. I will start by calling attention to J. L. Austin's celebrated ideas and how his insights and distinctions have been read and used in the speech act theories developed in different philosophical traditions.

Austin famously formulated the notion of *performative utterances*, emphasizing that our verbal pronouncements are not only sayings, but also doings, that is, they not only convey certain contents but also perform certain acts. Austin proposed a threefold distinction for the analysis of speech acts: *locutionary* content, that is, the representational information conveyed by the utterance; *illocutionary* force, that is, the kind of strength that our words have and makes our utterances the kinds of acts that they are (e.g. promising, threatening, prohibiting, etc.); and *perlocutionary* effects, that is, pragmatic consequences that are not specifically linguistic or semantic but are achieved through our locutions (e.g. amusing, charming, scarring, etc.), although their achievement is not guaranteed by the locution itself – that is, by the very act of enunciation

---

27. Diane Perpich, "Subjectivity and Sexual Difference: New Figures of the Feminine in Irigaray and Cavarero," *Continental Philosophical Review* 36 (2003), 412.

28. *Ibid.*

29. Bringing together continental and pragmatist perspectives, in *Speaking from Elsewhere* I have analyzed this phenomenon of reverberation as the *echoing* that maintains meanings alive, being both the source of semantic stability and the source of semantic innovation.

30. Judith Butler, *Excitable Speech: A Politics of the Performative* (New York: Routledge, 1997), 25, emphasis added.

– but is dependent on the reception of the words enunciated by the audience or addressees. Austin focused on the first two elements for the evaluation of speech acts. He emphasized that while the correctness of its representational content depended on the *truth conditions* of the utterance, the appropriateness of its illocutionary force was to be assessed in terms of its *felicity conditions*, that is, those conditions under which the kind of act the utterance tries to produce is felicitously achieved. Austin remarked that the kinds of acts we can perform in and through language depend on the linguistic practices and social institutions available to us. So, for example, it is because we have the particular institution of marriage that we have that under certain conditions the words "I hereby pronounce you husband and wife" produce an act of marriage felicitously, while under other conditions they do not; and it is because we have the particular linguistic practices that we have, codifying certain illocutionary forces and not others, that saying "I promise you so-and-so" is, under normal conditions, the issuing of a promise. Austin also suggested that, although they emerged socially, illocutionary forces are inscribed in the speech acts themselves, so that our utterances reflexively call attention to the kind of act they try to perform, that is, sometimes they do this explicitly ("I hereby promise you X" or "I hereby warn you about Y") and sometimes implicitly ("I will do X" or "Beware of Y").

This suggestion has been taken up and elaborated by some speech act theorists. It is what Habermas has termed the *self-referentiality* of speech acts. Habermas emphasizes that this is in fact the fundamental feature of linguistic performativity that distinguishes linguistic acts from nonlinguistic acts:

> An observer can only understand a nonlinguistic action when he knows the intention that is supposed to be satisfied through it. *Speech acts, on the other hand, identify themselves.* Because in carrying out an illocutionary act a speaker simultaneously *says* what he is *doing*, a hearer who understands the meaning of what is said can, without further ado, identify the performed act as some specific action. ... The acts carried out in a natural language are always self-referential.[31]

But of course not every speech act theorist agrees with the thesis of self-referentiality, and contemporary speech act theory is in fact divided over the question of whether illocutionary forces are implicitly and internally present in the act, in its underlying structure; or whether, alternatively, they are a matter of interpretation or negotiation in which external factors also play a role. I want to call attention to two very different readings and uses of Austinian ideas in this

---

31. Habermas, *Postmetaphysical Thinking*, 64, some emphasis added.

respect: those of Searle and Habermas, on the one hand; and those of Cavell and Butler, on the other hand. The authors in the first group underscore the reflexivity of linguistic performativity and they argue that illocutionary forces are implicit in the very structure of the speech act, whereas authors in the second group reject the idea that illocutionary forces are self-contained within the act, arguing that the force of any given speech act is always interpretable and negotiable, that it depends on its reception and on the consequences it effects, on its social uptake and its productivity within a performative chain. From this disagreement there emerge two very different kinds of speech act theories. The Searlian and Habermasian variety tries to systematize speech acts through their internal analysis, arguing that, at any given time, we can fix and catalogue the kinds of linguistic actions and illocutionary forces available to us. By contrast, the alternative formulation of speech act theory calls into question the alleged fixity and systematicity of linguistic performativity, rejecting the idea that illocutionary forces can be systematically classified, that is, that we can come up with a systematic catalogue of the speech acts that can be performed in our communicative interactions. The Cavellian and Butlerian variety of speech act theory thus underscores the *instability* and *uncontrollability* of illocutionary force.

Can speech acts and their illocutionary forces be fixed and controlled? According to the sociological reading of Austin, the answer is yes: linguistic conventions and standardized procedures and rituals fix and maintain the illocutionary force of our speech acts. But this reading (often assumed by speech act theorists) was challenged by interpreters of Austin such as Cavell and Shoshana Felman.[32] These authors emphasized the *excessive* nature of linguistic performativity, that is, the fact that our performances always exceed the norms and expectations contained in established practices and institutions. On this view, while previous practice and established procedure do constrain what we can do with our words, they do not determine, fix, or fully control our linguistic performances, which are carried out through our embodied voices and writing styles in such a way that not every aspect of what is done can be anticipated and normatively domesticated. Our linguistic performativity is always producing according to established expectation, but always *failing* to produce as expected. And this constant failing and exceeding are directly related to the *embodied* nature of performativity. As Felman puts it, embodiment is "the blindspot of speech," the point at which speaking necessarily fails to recognize itself and what it does: "language is inhabited by the *act of failing* through which the body is

---

32. Stanley Cavell, *Must We Mean What We Say?* (Cambridge: Cambridge University Press, 1976), and *The Claim of Reason* (Oxford: Oxford University Press, 1979); Shoshana Felman, *The Literary Speech Act: Don Juan with J. L. Austin, or Seduction in Two Languages* (Ithaca, NY: Cornell University Press, 1983).

lacking to itself: the act of failing through which the body's *doing* always fails to speak itself, whereas the *speaking* never fails to *do*."[33] On Felman's view, speakers are *blind* because their speaking bodies are always ignorant about what they perform and always say something they do not intend. Following Felman, Butler explains this blindness or ignorance of the speaking body as follows: "the body is the blindspot of speech, that which acts in excess of what is said, but which also acts in and through what is said."[34]

Feminist theorists such as Butler and Felman have called our attention to the corporeal dimension of performativity: it is not an inner subjectivity, but a body that speaks. And this corporeal dimension of speech affects crucially our discursive agency: which body speaks (a male or female body, a racial body, an ethnic body, etc.) has a tremendous impact on the illocutionary – that is, on the kind of speech act it is and the force attached to it; on the perlocutionary – that is, on the effects or consequences of the speech act; and on the semantic and interpretative – that is, on the content of the speech act as a whole and the meanings ascribed to its components. This emphasis on the body that is characteristic of performative views informed by phenomenological perspectives is lost in analytic and post-analytic performative theories; and this is an important reason (perhaps the most important reason) why those theories have failed to address fundamental philosophical issues concerning identity that are bound up with the philosophical questions concerning the normativity of language and action. I will develop this diagnosis in the next section.

II. THE EMERGENCE OF POST-ANALYTIC PHILOSOPHY AND THE EVASION OF IDENTITY

In the story I am developing here, I am emphasizing the crucial significance that the convergence of the performative turn and the linguistic turn had for the development of post-analytic approaches. But of course this is not the only factor that played an important role in the emergence of post-analytic philosophy. For example, *naturalism* has had an enormous impact on the reconceptualization of philosophical problems, and another (not necessarily competing, but perhaps supplemental) story about the emergence of post-analytic philosophy could be told with naturalism as its main protagonist.[35] Not surprisingly the emergence of a philosophical movement often has many facets and

---

33. *Ibid.*, 78.
34. Butler, *Excitable Speech,* 11.
*35. For a part of this story of the impact of naturalism on post-analytic philosophy, see the essay by John Fennell in *The History of Continental Philosophy: Volume 8.*

it involves many components in complex interaction with one another; and all this complexity perhaps can only be captured in the composite image offered by multiple accounts of that historical development. So the account presented here hopes to be a contribution to such a complex story.

As discussed in the previous section, by focusing attention on the relation between language and performance, the performative turn raises a broad spectrum of issues concerning content and force, bringing together in a rich way a host of epistemic and sociopolitical issues concerning representation and action. More specifically, I want to emphasize as a major consequence of the legacy of the performative turn in the last part of the twentieth century the *rethinking of normativity*, that is, the reconceptualization of normativity in performative terms from the engaged perspective of the speaker and agent participating in communicative practices. This was done in different ways in continental philosophy by, for example, Habermas and Lyotard. But it was also done in a very particular and powerful way in the 1980s and 1990s by a group of philosophers who were drawing on two philosophical traditions: the analytic tradition informed by the performative turn and the pragmatist tradition from Peirce and Dewey to Quine and Sellars. The philosophers who contributed to the formation of a post-analytic school of thought include, among others, Stanley Cavell, Robert Brandom, John McDowell, the later Hilary Putnam, and Richard Rorty. These philosophers draw on classical American pragmatists as well as on rebellious analytic philosophers such as Davidson, Evans, Quine, and Wittgenstein. In what follows I will briefly highlight some of the crucial contributions of these authors to the reconceptualization of normativity in performative terms. I will also emphasize the shortcomings of these post-analytic views of normativity, in particular, the neglect of issues concerning embodied identity that, I will argue, result in an evasion of the political in philosophical reflections of normativity. I will give a separate treatment to Cavell, whose work (unlike that of other post-analytic philosophers) brought together the normative and the sociopolitical in a way that is highly sensitive to philosophical questions concerning embodied identities.

It is important to note that Wilfrid Sellars (1912–89) laid the groundwork of American post-analytic philosophy with his critical rethinking of central questions in the analytic tradition. Incorporating important insights from the pragmatist tradition, the Sellarsian rethinking of analytic philosophy involved the critique and rejection of central tenets or assumptions concerning "immediacy" and the empirically "given." Sellars taught and deeply influenced some of the major contributors to post-analytic philosophy, especially Rorty and Brandom. His critique of "the Myth of the Given" in the landmark essay "Empiricism and the Philosophy of Mind" (1956) had an influence in the US (although not in Europe) comparable to that of Quine's "Two Dogmas of Empiricism" (1951) and Wittgenstein's *Philosophical Investigations*. Sellars shared Quine's and Wittgenstein's hostility to immediacy, but the role of his critique of sense-data empiricism in challenging and revolutionizing analytic philosophy has not been recognized by historians of Anglo-American philosophy until recently. Mainly motivated by the work of his disciples, the 1990s saw a revival of Sellarsian ideas and an exploration of their implications. Sellars described his own philosophical project as an attempt to usher analytic philosophy out of its Humean and into its Kantian stage. Using as a motto the Kantian dictum that "intuitions without concepts are blind," Sellars argued against the empiricist foundationalism that was pervasive in analytic philosophy. His critique of "the Myth of the Given" tried to show the impossibility of finding empirical foundations, that is, objects of direct acquaintance that appear "immediately before the mind." Sellars proposed a "psychological nominalism" according to which "*all* awareness of *sorts, resemblances, facts*, etc., in short all awareness of abstract entities – indeed, all awareness even of particulars – is a linguistic affair."[36] According to Sellars, as soon as our mental states or episodes enter in the realm of the meaningful and knowable, they are in "the logical space of reasons," that is, in the normative space created by our sociolinguistic practices of justification. As he puts it, "in characterizing an episode or a state as that of *knowing*, ... we are placing it in the logical space of reasons, of justifying and being able to justify what one says."[37] For Sellars, our mental and cognitive lives are inseparable from our social justificatory practices; they are subject to the norms implicit in these practices. Insofar as it is intelligible, everything we think, say, and do is answerable to the reasons that can be mobilized by the fellow speakers and agents we encounter in our practices. The conclusion of Sellars's critique of "the Myth of the Given" is that we cannot get outside language, that we cannot "break out of discourse," that our rational lives are bound up with our discursive practices. Intelligibility and rationality are not governed by norms that are somehow given prior to our discursive practices; they are, rather, discursively regulated by the practices we develop and the norms underlying these practices. This immanent view of the norms of intelligibility and rationality inspired new and provocative reflections on normativity in the 1990s.

A systematic internalist account of normativity as immanent in our discursive practices was articulated by Brandom in *Making it Explicit*. This account elaborates some of the central insights of Sellars's immanentism concerning normativity while at the same time going beyond it. As Rorty puts it, Brandom's book "offers the first systematic and comprehensive attempt to follow up on

---

36. Wilfrid Sellars, *Empiricism and the Philosophy of Mind* (Cambridge, MA: Harvard University Press, 1997), §28.

37. *Ibid.*, §36.

Sellars's thought," "an attempt to usher analytic philosophy from its Kantian to its Hegelian stage."[38] The starting-point of Brandom's view of normativity is the fundamental Kantian and Sellarsian insight that our "judgments and actions are to be understood to begin with in terms of the special way in which we are *responsible* for them."[39] According to Brandom, our discursive responsibility or answerability as thinkers and agents is not to formal norms of thought and action that exist independently of our practices, but rather, to the practical norms implicit in the *inferential connections* among judgments and actions that are forged in our discursive practices. Thus he proposes a *material inferentialism* that derives conceptual contents and conceptual norms from the normative assessments that we make in our actual discursive practices, rather than the other way round, that is, rather than our normative appraisals being derived from and grounded in conceptual norms and contents that are somehow given prior to and independently of our practices. Brandom rejects the formalist idea that every inference is based on the logical form of the propositions involved and hence on content-independent rules of logical syntax. Instead, his inferentialism focuses on relations of *material* inference that are based on the *content* of the propositions involved. On this view, semantic content derives from what we actually say and do in our discursive practices; more specifically, the content of a proposition derives from its "circumstances of application" and its "consequences of application."[40] Brandom's inferentialism offers an alternative to *representationalism*,[41] that is, to the view that contents are somehow given prior to and independent of the inferential relations in which they enter in our discursive practices. Brandom describes the justificatory practices that create the normative space of reasons as the practices in which we "keep score" of the normative correctness of our actions and utterances. On his view, these "score-keeping" practices have to be harmonized following the normative desiderata and principles that emerge from the practices themselves and from the normative orientations of their agents toward the world and toward each other. Brandom concludes his material-inferentialist account of normativity with the "social self-consciousness" that a community of "score-keepers" can reach through the expressive practices of making things explicit, a "social self-consciousness" that involves "the complete and explicit interpretive equilibrium exhibited by a community whose members adopt the explicit discursive stance

---

38. Richard Rorty, "Introduction," in Wilfrid Sellars, *Empiricism and the Philosophy of Mind* (Cambridge, MA: Harvard University Press, 1997), 8–9.
39. Robert Brandom, *Making it Explicit* (Cambridge, MA: Harvard University Press, 1994), 8.
40. *Ibid.*, 116–32.
41. Brandom divides philosophers into "representationalists" (such as Descartes and Locke) and "inferentialists" (such as Leibniz, Kant, Frege, the later Wittgenstein, and Sellars).

toward each other."[42] In this way Brandom returns to and substantiates a possibility that he sketched in the introduction of his book, namely, the possibility that all language-users could form "one great Community comprising members of all particular communities."[43]

Brandom's unified and Hegelian picture of normativity contrasts with the fractured view of normativity that seems to emerge from Davidson's account of interpretation.[44] On the Davidsonian view, language is inevitably splintered into idiolects and the only unification of semantic and normative assessments we can have is local and ephemeral, achieved through mutual adjustments of our theories of interpretation in fragile and transient encounters in discursive practices. Building on this Davidsonian account, Rorty has elaborated a thoroughly pluralistic and relativistic view of normativity based on a deflationary theory of truth.[45] In a number of essays published in the 1980s and 1990s,[46] Rorty interprets Davidson's view as a radical deflationism about truth that explains agreement with the world in terms of agreement with each other, thus reducing objectivity to solidarity. With this problematic interpretation,[47] Rorty wants to assimilate Davidson's view to the *social-practice approach to truth* inaugurated by Dewey, Heidegger, Sellars, and Wittgenstein. Against the representationalist paradigm that views truth as correspondence with a language- and mind-independent

---

42. Brandom, *Making it Explicit*, 643.

43. *Ibid.*, 4.

44. Among contemporary analytic philosophers, Davidson is perhaps the one who has had the deepest impact on post-analytic philosophy of the 1980s and 1990s, either by inspiring his followers – such as Rorty – to develop the normative implications of his views, or by inspiring his critics – such as Putnam – to develop alternatives.

45. In such a theory, truth is deflated of philosophical content, that is, it is not given any metaphysical or epistemic content. Instead, it is taken as something simple and indefinable that cannot be reduced to something more basic (such as the epistemic property of coherence or the metaphysical property of correspondence). Deflationary theories typically treat the notion of truth as unproblematic and intuitively understood, and they elucidate it as it operates in the assertoric attitudes of speakers, that is, in their attitude of holding something to be true (which is taken to be the most basic semantic attitude in communicative interaction).

46. See Robert Brandom, *Rorty and his Critics* (Oxford: Blackwell, 2000), and Richard Rorty, *Objectivity, Relativism, and Truth* (Cambridge: Cambridge University Press, 1991). [*] For a detailed discussion of Rorty, see the essay by David R. Hiley in *The History of Continental Philosophy: Volume 6.*

47. Rorty's interpretation of Davidson is problematic for a number of reasons. To begin with, Davidson himself has emphasized that his account of interpretation in terms of Tarskian theories of truth for particular languages takes truth as the most primitive semantic notion and does not provide a *theory* of truth – deflationary or otherwise – being in fact quite antithetical to any such theory. On the other hand, many have read Davidson's view of interpretation and his methodological maxims (including the principle of charity) as showing that agreement with the world and with each other are inextricably interwoven but cannot be reduced to one another, so that objectivity and intersubjective agreement should be thought of as interrelated but irreducible notions.

world, the social-practice paradigm contends that the normativity of truth can be fully captured by elucidating the normative structure of the communicative practices in which truth claims are raised, challenged, and settled. Rorty emphasizes that there is always the danger of falling back into the representationalist paradigm by thinking of truth as going beyond the limits of our practices and the consensus of their participants. We are tempted to think this way when we look for an external or transcendent dimension of truth that can explain the limitations and imperfections of our current practices and the fact that they are always open to change and improvement. Any appeal to an extra dimension of validity that relates our practices to something beyond themselves is, according to Rorty, "an unfortunate slide back into representationalism."[48] Rorty argues that both Heidegger and Sellars are "backsliding" social-practice theorists because the external or transcendent dimension of correctness is retained in the former's notion of "disclosedness" and in the latter's notion of "picturing." Rorty praises Brandom for rejecting Sellars's attempts to revive the "picturing" relationship between language and world that Wittgenstein formulated in the *Tractatus*, thus bringing post-analytic philosophy to a new stage.[49] Arguing against this tempting but regressive "backsliding," Rorty proposes a thoroughgoing internalism and deflationism that eradicates the illusion of transcendence once and for all. Following Davidson, he argues that holding something to be true should not be understood as the ascription of a property that ties statements to a conceptual scheme or a set of assertibility criteria or semantic rules, but rather as the mere expression of assent and agreement, that is, the expression of harmony between our assertoric attitude and that of others with respect to particular claims.[50] Rorty acknowledges that there is a gap between truth and assertibility, but he argues that this gap does not take truth outside our assertoric practices, but simply reflects the fallibilist attitude in our orientation toward truth, that is, our openness to be proved wrong. Rorty emphasizes that, far from being incompatible with the social-practice strategy of explaining objectivity in terms of solidarity, fallibilism actually strengthens it, for it is indicative of our predisposition to extend agreement beyond our community, to seek more

---

48. Rorty, *Objectivity, Relativism, and Truth*, 152.

49. As Rorty puts it, "Brandom stands to 'Empiricism and the Philosophy of Mind' as Davidson … stands to 'Two Dogmas.' Both men cultivate their respective teacher's central insight by stripping it of accidental accretions" (Rorty, "Introduction," 8).

50. This is explained through an elucidation of the *disquotational* use of the truth predicate. As suggested by Tarski's Convention T, in disquotational contexts what the use of the truth predicate does is to express commitment to the assertion quoted and, therefore, it is equivalent to its repetition (hence the redundancy property of truth): "'p' is true = p." This exemplifies the Sellarsian and Davidsonian strategy of explaining truth in terms of one's own language, "idiolect," or web of belief.

solidarity, rather than to transcend agreement. But this consensus view, Rorty insists, should not be assimilated to a rule-conforming view of normativity, for it is based on the Wittgensteinian insight that normativity is not a matter of obedience to codifiable standards, but rather, a matter of "give-and-take participation in a cooperative social project."[51]

Rorty's neopragmatism and his consensus theory of truth have been criticized by many contemporary figures, such as Jürgen Habermas in European philosophy and John McDowell within the post-analytic movement. Both Habermas and McDowell have replied to Rorty's relativistic approach to truth and normativity in a similar vein, arguing that Rorty's view fails to accommodate the normative attitudes and the realist intuitions of participants in communicative practices.[52] But while Habermas's argument focuses on the *unconditionality* of truth, McDowell develops his objection through an argument about the *objectivity* of truth. Habermas argues that Rorty's radical "epistemization" of truth reduces validity to coherence with current standards and therefore neglects what was right about the correspondence theory of truth, namely, the notion of *unconditional* validity. For Habermas, unconditionality is rooted in the *everyday realism* of our communicative practices: it is a formal presupposition of the participants in communication in the lifeworld that extends itself into the discourses in which their problematized claims are vindicated or "redeemed." Habermas maintains that what Rorty's relativistic pragmatism misses is precisely this everyday realism that provides the "normative reference point" for our truth claims and their discursive "redemption."[53]

McDowell, on the other hand, argues that Rorty's relativistic pragmatism lacks realism and misses the *objectivity* of truth, that is, the *answerability to the world* of our truth-seeking practices of inquiry. McDowell warns that Rorty and other relativists try to impose a false dichotomy on us: either inquiry is thought to be answerable to a language- and mind-independent reality, or, alternatively, it is thought to be answerable to nothing but the norms of current practice. McDowell agrees with Rorty that we should reject the illusory transcendence of a language- and mind-independent reality, but he insists that we should understand the *internality* of truth differently. On his view, that truth is internal to our practices of inquiry does not mean that it is reducible to agreement within those practices, but, rather, that it involves an orientation to the world that is embedded in the normative standpoint of our practices. McDowell contends

---

51. Rorty, "Introduction," 6.

52. The rest of this paragraph has been adapted from an introduction I wrote for José Medina and David Wood (eds), *Truth: Philosophical Engagements across Traditions* (New York: Blackwell, 2005), 96–7.

53. See Jürgen Habermas, "Richard Rorty's Pragmatic Turn," in *Truth: Philosophical Engagements across Traditions*, Medina and Wood (eds).

that the norms of inquiry transcend consensus: they demand of truth-seekers that they have *the world in view*. Having *the world in view*, he argues, constitutes an "innocuous transcendence" – a harmless appearance/reality distinction – which does not require any metaphysical picture, for it is fully explicable in terms of the norms of objectivity immanent in our practices. According to these norms, inquiry is normatively beholden both to our practices and to its subject matter.[54]

A similar *minimal* (or *commonsense*) *realism* can be found in the work of Putnam in the 1990s.[55] Moving away from the metaphysical realism he defended in the 1960s and 1970s and from his "internal realism" of 1980s,[56] Putnam argues that we need to dissolve the false dilemma between metaphysical realism and antirealism or deflationism about truth. On the one hand, Putnam rejects the metaphysical realist conception of truth as correspondence with a language- and mind-independent reality, which makes truth inaccessible and skepticism inescapable. But, on the other hand, Putnam argues that antirealists and deflationists go too far in the opposite direction and mistakenly deny the claim that truth can be recognition-transcendent in any sense. Against the deflationary views of truth inspired by Ramsey, Tarski, and Davidson, Putnam contends that being true cannot be identified with being verified or with being assertible. Through his interpretation of Wittgenstein, Putnam develops an alternative view of truth that supports a commonsense realism ("a second naiveté") that avoids the metaphysical and epistemic idealizations of his earlier realist views. This view preserves the core semantic insights of deflationary views; namely, that truth is internal to language and that the face of our cognitive relation to the world is the face of meaning. However, *pace* deflationists and antirealists, Putnam argues that the *new face of cognition* must make room for the concepts of representation and correspondence with reality. Putnam rejects the idea of representation as an "interface" between two independent relata, language and

---

54. See John McDowell, "Towards Rehabilitating Objectivity," in *Truth: Philosophical Engagements across Traditions*, Medina and Wood (eds). A full discussion of the metaphysics and epistemology behind McDowell's *realism* can be found in his *Mind and World*.

55. See Hilary Putnam, *The Threefold Cord: Mind, Body, and World* (New York: Columbia University Press, 1999), and "The Face of Cognition," in *Truth: Philosophical Engagements across Traditions*, Medina and Wood (eds).

56. This is the *realism* that Putnam defended in *Reason, Truth, and History*. Trying to overcome the omniscient perspective or God's-eye view presupposed by his former metaphysical realist view, what Putnam's internal realism did was to internalize this ideal observer within our practices so that, instead of being judged according to an external perspective, truth was to be determined according to ideal standards of justification that can be derived from our practices (although our actual practices never reach ideal epistemic conditions). This internal realist view identifies truth with idealized consensus and is in line with Peirce's and (the early) Habermas's epistemic view of truth.

the world. He suggests that the notions of representation and correspondence should be internalized, that is, that they should be understood in terms of the representational activities that take place in everyday linguistic practices. This view depicts the recognition-transcendence of truth as well entrenched in the normative presuppositions of ordinary practices. According to Putnam, what this shows is that we have a symbolic access to the world, a linguistic contact with reality, which goes beyond our powers of recognition. With this neopragmatist internalism, Putnam claims to have rescued realist intuitions without metaphysical or epistemic idealizations.

Being caught up in the metaphysical and epistemic disputes of the realism–antirealism debates, the post-analytic rethinking of normativity in pragmatic terms has a very abstract flavor, which contrasts with the more historicized and politicized texture of reconceptualizations of normativity in pragmatic terms in continental philosophy: for example, in Jean-François Lyotard's *The Postmodern Condition* or *The Differend*, or in Pierre Bourdieu's *Language and Symbolic Power*. In European philosophy, the social and the political take center stage in the pragmatic rethinking of normative concepts – even in the most universalist and analytically minded of continental philosophers, Habermas. By contrast, although post-analytic and neopragmatist philosophers appeal to a situated speaker and agent, they still invoke or presuppose an abstract subject, namely, the speaker and agent who can become situated in *any* practice, without paying special attention to the historical and cultural specificity of that practice or to the particularity of subjects in it. By leaving the performative processes of differentiation unspecified, these neopragmatist views treat differences as empirical details that add nothing of substance to our philosophical elucidations of normativity; and by relegating differences to a secondary level of analysis that is extraneous to the structure of normativity, the subject presupposed by these views becomes (even if unintentionally and inadvertently) a homogenous and universal subject that remains uniform across all practices and agential positions within those practices.

This is what I call *the evasion of identity* (and diversity, we could add) in post-analytic philosophy, which occurs when subjectivities are not socially differentiated and do not become corporealized in historically concrete identities that are culturally specific and have been genderized, sexualized, ethnicized, and racialized. As we will see, this evasion is not *equally* present in *all* post-analytic philosophers, but it is a very common phenomenon in this school of thought, and one that often goes unrecognized or unacknowledged. This is all the more surprising given the fact that most of post-analytic philosophy is produced and discussed in the identity-obsessed culture of the US. By contrast, identity issues become unavoidable in the performative theorizing that takes place in the contemporary European context. And even thinkers who are not themselves drawn to these issues are forced to address them. Thus, for example, although issues of identity and diversity did not take center stage in Habermas's theory, his followers and critics have forced him to include issues of gender, race, and multiculturalism in his theorizing.

By contrast, the pressures of the intellectual milieu in post-analytic philosophy are rather different, discouraging the theorization of differences and making it difficult to address issues of identity and diversity as an integral part of the philosophical elucidation of normativity. Normative reflections on identity and diversity in this context are typically categorized as empirical discussions within social and political philosophy, without there being a presumption of a deep and intimate connection between these discussions and those of normativity in epistemology, metaphysics, philosophy of language, and philosophy of mind, whereas there seems to be such a presumption in continental philosophy. Even the arguably most political of post-analytic thinkers, Rorty, does not seem to be capable of developing a full theoretical engagement with identity questions because his views are developed within the framework of liberalism and a difference-blind conception of justice. Many of Rorty's readers are likely to have a different impression: a picture of Rorty as a thinker preoccupied with identity and diversity. But this is in fact a false impression, or at least a superficial one, for it is clear that Rorty's prolific production does not contain robust discussions of race, ethnicity, and sexual difference. The appeals to identity in Rorty's work are often appeals to formal notions of nationality, for example a difference-blind and culturally neutral notion of American identity, to vague notions of cultural identity ("we Westerners"), or to ideological notions (such as political identity or socioeconomic class – "we bourgeois liberals"), which are informed by a liberalism that claims to be above the internal differences of a multicultural society.[57]

The evasion of identity rests on – and at the same time reinforces and hardens – a *double evasion*: the evasion of the body and the evasion of the political. As discussed in the previous section, with the notable exception of Cavell and some other neo-Wittgensteinians (more on this later), post-analytic performative theories have often treated speech acts as disembodied – despite there being numerous influential arguments to the contrary within the performative legacy (from James and Wittgenstein, for example). On the other hand, post-analytic theories of normativity often exhibit a peculiar inability to put the normative aspects of language or communication in a political perspective, paying attention to power dynamics. In this way the evasion of identity brings up a more general problem: the evasion of politics. Despite having a wealth of political

---

57. See Richard Rorty, *Achieving Our Country: Leftist Thought in Twentieth-Century America* (Cambridge, MA: Harvard University Press, 1999), and *Take Care of Freedom and Truth Will Take Care of Itself*, interviews conducted by Eduardo Mendieta (Stanford, CA: Stanford University Press, 2005).

thought to draw on in the American pragmatist tradition (in Dewey and his followers, for example), the kind of neopragmatism that has become most visible and influential in post-analytic philosophy seems to be less politically sensitive than contemporary European pragmatism. It is important to notice how certain normative issues that are immediately put in the context of power structures and power dynamics and are regarded as political problems concerning justice are treated rather differently when power relations and power differentials are taken out of the equation. Take for example the issue of the normative significance of *style*, of situated and embodied uses of language. Depending on how this issue is conceptualized, it may or may not appear as a crucial sociopolitical issue about the normativity of language and communication. In this respect, William James offered an interesting insight into the power dynamics of language use at the beginning of the twentieth century. In "The Social Value of the College Bred" (1907), James argues that democracy requires for its survival the normative elucidation and critique of the issue of "tone," which is at the core of an entire machinery of social reproduction. It is the question of "tone" that is at the basis of the creation and maintenance of prestige and sociocultural power, of the power of one's voice, that is, of one's capacity to speak effectively and to be listened to. James calls attention to our sensibility to what counts as the "proper tone" and to the social imperative that "we ourselves must use the proper tone, which we, in turn, must have caught from our own teachers." Linking democracy and education, he goes on to say:

> It all reverts in the end to the action of innumerable imitative individuals upon each other and to the question of whose tone has the highest spreading power. As a class, we college graduates should look to it that ours has spreading power. It ought to have the highest spreading power.[58]

The mechanics of this "spreading power" – how it is acquired, used, and reproduced – is what Pierre Bourdieu[59] explained with his notions of "linguistic capital" and "cultural capital," and with his account of how they are accrued in "linguistic markets" and how they operate through social distinctions and the creation of "a field" in which a habitus can flourish. There is no comparable treatment of the normativity of style in post-analytic philosophy. Thus, while this Jamesian insight about "tone" has been fully elaborated in European philos-

---

58. William James, "The Social Value of the College-Bred," www.des.emory.edu/mfp/jaCollegeBred.html (accessed May 2010). I am grateful to Jeffrey Edmonds, who called my attention to this text.

*59. Bourdieu is the focus of an essay by Derek Robbins in *The History of Continental Philosophy: Volume 6*.

ophy (especially by Bourdieu and his followers), it has received little attention by contemporary mainstream neopragmatists in the American establishment.

But of course the normative and political significance of issues of identity and diversity are not *always* disregarded or minimized in post-analytic philosophy. In fact, it has been receiving increasing attention in recent years, as references to these issues in their reflections on normativity have become more frequent. Robert Brandom, for example, illustrates his account of material inference with a discussion of derogatory terms such as "*Boche.*" The goal of inferential analysis, Brandom argues, is to *make explicit* the circumstances and consequences of the application of a term, thus bringing to the fore the material-inferentialist commitments underlying its use. The problem with a value-laden term such as "*Boche*" is that it involves descriptive circumstances of application (concerning nationality: being German) and evaluative consequences of application (i.e. being deemed cruel). Thus Brandom argues: "If one does not believe that the inference from German nationality to cruelty is a good one, one must eschew the concept *Boche*. ... One can only refuse to employ the concept, on the grounds that it embodies an inference one does not endorse."[60] Brandom remarks that highly charged words such as "nigger" and "whore" present a similar problem: "they couple 'descriptive' circumstances of application with 'evaluative' consequences."[61] By making explicit the normative presuppositions and implications of the use of our terms (what we are committing ourselves to with their use),[62] we can bring our concepts under rational control. In this way Brandom defends his expressive inferentialism as a version of the Socratic method, that is, as "a way of bringing our practices under rational control, by expressing them explicitly in a form in which they can be confronted with objections and alternatives."[63] It is certainly praiseworthy that Brandom illustrates his expressive inferentialism and Socratic intellectualism with a discussion of derogatory terms, thus addressing normative issues concerning identity and politics. This indeed enriches the applications of the normative apparatus of his expressive theory. But we should not conclude that the issues of prejudice, hate speech, and stigmatized identities have taken center stage. Discussions of the sociopolitical aspects of normativity and their relation to differentiated identities remain incidental. These discussions take the form of mere allusions or illustrations, without being knitted into the core of the philosophical elucidations of normativity being developed. Thus, although normative issues concerning identity are acknowledged and used in recent post-analytic philosophy, this school

---

60. Brandom, *Making it Explicit*, 126.
61. *Ibid.*
62. For Brandom, "thinking clearly is a matter of knowing what one is committing oneself to by a certain claim, and what would entitle one to that commitment" (*Making it Explicit*, 120).
63. *Ibid.*, 106.

of thought seems to be still under the sway of what I have called the evasion of identity, even if it is slowly breaking out of it.

Stanley Cavell, however, has been the most prominent exception within the post-analytic movement in this respect. From early on, his elucidations of normative concepts that regulate our speech and action ("truth," "knowledge," "justice," "authenticity," etc.) included discussions of differentiated identities; and more importantly, these discussions were a constitutive and integral part of his neo-Wittgensteinian and Emersonian framework. This is not entirely surprising since Cavell has been one of the few thinkers in this school who has given special attention to the embodied nature of speech and to the social and cultural conditions that sustain the force and content of our speech acts. Cavell's skepticism and perfectionism call for a constant evaluation and critique of our speech and action, which require an examination of the sociopolitical structures and institutions that shape our lives. In his normative elucidations, speakers and agents do not remain abstract subjects; they have differentiated and embodied identities. This has become particularly perspicuous in Cavell's work on film in the last two decades, which is motivated by and structured around normative issues concerning gender (and, to a lesser extent, race[64]). In *Pursuits of Happiness*, Cavell analyzes the genre of remarriage comedy in Hollywood films from the 1930s and 1940s. This analysis offers a critical commentary on the gender norms underlying the contemporary institution of marriage and on the available social scripts for gender dynamics. According to Cavell, remarriage comedies contain the normative depiction of an aspiration: a partnership between equals who are mutually appreciative as an ideal we should aspire to. These films, Cavell argues, envision a relation of equality between human beings that we may characterize in Emersonian terms as a relation of rightful attraction, of expressiveness, and of joy – a relation that is presented as rare to find, but as exemplary of the possibilities of our society. But although in these films gender relations are informed by the ideal of a conversation between equals, remarriage comedies implicitly convey the problematic privileging of the male within an apparent atmosphere of equality, for marriage and remarriage function as the vehicle for the creation and

64. Cavell has addressed normative issues concerning race and racial relations in a couple of places: in his reading of *Othello* in *Disowning Knowledge: Six Plays of Shakespeare*, in which he examines the racial dynamics underlying erotic and skeptical attitudes (the racial dimensions of desire and suspicion); and in his 1996 presidential address to the American Philosophical Association ("Something Out of the Ordinary," *Proceedings and Addresses of the American Philosophical Association*), and his 1998 Spinoza lectures (see Stanley Cavell, *Philosophy the Day after Tomorrow* [Cambridge, MA: Harvard University Press, 2005], esp. ch. 3, 61–82), in which he develops an analysis of Fred Astaire's dance routines in the Hollywood film *The Band Wagon*, an analysis that is at the service of his rethinking of the Kantian notion of subjectivity in Emersonian terms.

re-creation of "the new woman" through her education by the man. In *Contesting Tears*, Cavell expands his critique of cultural depictions of gender dynamics with an analysis of another Hollywood genre: what he calls "the melodrama of the unknown woman." These melodramas negate marriage as the route to creation, to a new and original integrity; and they explore an alternative route: metamorphosis, the radical and melodramatic change of a woman's identity. In these films the re-making or re-structuration of identity is presented as a process of self-creation that often has tragic consequences. This process takes place outside the institution of marriage and outside the idealized conversation with men as equals. As Cavell puts it, women's "integrity or metamorphosis happens elsewhere, in the abandoning of that *shared* wit and intelligence and exclusive appreciation. This elsewhere is a function of something within the melodrama genre that I will call the world of women."[65] Especially intended for female audiences, these "women's films" or "tear-jerkers" theorize our desire and "have designs upon our tears"; they provide powerful gender scripts. As Cavell explains in Emersonian language, the melodramas problematize and call into question the relation of equality idealized by remarriage comedies, while gesturing toward *self-reliance* insofar as they demand that expressiveness and joy be sought first in relation to oneself. Although strongly criticized by some feminist theorists,[66] Cavell's film analyses have offered influential ways of theorizing and reflecting on the normativity of desire, education, and the process of identity formation in our society and culture. His work has certainly helped to bring discussions of normativity to a concrete level of differentiation and thus to escape the evasion of identity and difference.

III. PERFORMATIVITY IN THE PHILOSOPHICAL AGENDA OF THE TWENTY-FIRST CENTURY

Following Cavell's lead, other Wittgenstein scholars have broadened contemporary discussions of normativity by addressing issues of identity and diversity. The recent post-analytic literature contains Wittgensteinian analyses of gender and sexuality[67] as well as of race, ethnicity, class, and nationality.[68] Among these

---

65. Stanley Cavell, *Contesting Tears: The Hollywood Melodrama of the Unknown Woman* (Chicago, IL: University of Chicago Press, 1996), 6–7.

66. See especially Tania Modleski, *Feminism without Women: Culture and Criticism in a "Post-Feminist" Age* (New York: Routledge, 1991).

67. See especially Naomi Scheman and Peg O'Connor (eds), *Feminist Interpretations of Ludwig Wittgenstein* (University Park, PA: Penn State University Press, 2002).

68. See especially Jorge J. E. Gracia, *Hispanic/Latino Identity* (Oxford: Blackwell, 2000); and my "Identity Trouble: Disidentification and the Problem of Difference," *Philosophy and Social*

scholars, it is important to mention the pioneering work of Naomi Scheman. Drawing on feminist theory and queer theory, Scheman's Wittgensteinian analyses have addressed normative issues concerning intelligibility and agency. Her work on silence and nonsense has thematized relations of oppression in our discursive practices, focusing on the speech and action of marginalized and disempowered subjects. Scheman's notions of "intelligible nonsense" and "'meaning' in spite of senselessness" suggest that certain possibilities, experiences, and actions are rendered unintelligible by the discursive norms of our linguistic practices, but that nevertheless it is conceivable and in principle *possible* that we will be able to find or create new discursive contexts or new practices in which those possibilities, experiences, and actions become intelligible. As many feminist, queer, and race theorists have emphasized, it is often the case that what the normative structure of our practices renders unintelligible is not simply particular experiences and actions, but entire identities and the lives they lead. Scheman, for example, shows how the identity and life of the transsexual are rendered unintelligible by heteronormativity, and how the identity and life of the secular Jew are rendered unintelligible by Christianormativity. As a result, she contends, transsexuals and secular Jews are forced to "live as impossible beings."[69] As Scheman explains, "placement at the intelligible center is always a matter of history, of the playing out of privilege and power, and is always contestable."[70] These normative and political contestations have been explored by a new generation of Wittgensteinians influenced by Scheman, working on gender and sexuality as well as on race and ethnicity.[71] This literature emphasizes that we have to take *responsibility* for marginalized or excluded possibilities,[72] which can become critical and transformative possibilities. More generally, we have to take responsibility for the relations of inclusion and exclusion that constitute our practices and normatively shape the lives of those within them.

Criticism 29(6) (2003), and "Pragmatism and Ethnicity: Critique, Reconstruction, and the New Hispanic," *Metaphilosophy* 35(1/2) (2004).

69. Naomi Scheman, "Queering the Center by Centering the Queer," in *Feminists Rethink the Self*, Diana T. Meyers (ed.) (Boulder, CO: Westview Press, 1997), 152.

70. *Ibid.*, 132.

71. On gender and sexuality see Alice Crary, "A Question of Silence: Feminist Theory and Women's Voices," *Philosophy* 76 (2001); Peg O'Connor, "Moving to New Boroughs: Transforming the World by Inventing Language Games," in *Feminist Interpretations of Ludwig Wittgenstein*, Scheman and O'Connor (eds), and "Identity Trouble and the Politics of Privilege: Commentary on Medina's 'Identity Trouble,'" *Symposia on Gender, Race, and Philosophy* II (2005), http://web.mit.edu/sgrp/2005/no1/O%27Connor0505.pdf (accessed May 2010). On race and ethnicity see Medina, "Identity Trouble," and "Pragmatism and Ethnicity."

72. Bringing together Deweyan, Wittgensteinian, and Bourdieuean perspectives and developing a thoroughly pluralistic view of discursive practices, I have also explored the possibilities for thought, speech, and action that lie *elsewhere*, outside the normative centers of what is considered mainstream or normal. See my *Speaking from Elsewhere*.

Indeed, the rethinking of agency and responsibility – I contend – constitutes the core of the philosophical agenda for performative theories in the twenty-first century.

Judith Butler has articulated better than anyone the philosophical challenges posed for our notions of agency and responsibility by the emerging, post-sovereign views of identity and subjectivity:

> Untethering the speech act from the sovereign subject founds an *alternative notion of agency and, ultimately, of responsibility*, one that more fully acknowledges the way in which the subject is constituted in language, how what it creates is also what it derives *from else-where*. Whereas some critics mistake the critique of sovereignty for the demolition of agency, I propose that agency begins where sovereignty wanes. The one who acts (who is not the same as the sovereign subject) acts precisely to the extent that he or she is constituted as an actor and, hence, operating within a linguistic field of enabling constraints from the outset.[73]

We need a conception of discursive agency and discursive responsibility that transcends traditional conceptions of sovereign subjectivity. After overcoming abstract conceptions of subjectivity that take subjects outside the rough ground of power relations and sociocultural conditions and constraints, we need to rethink the notions of agency and responsibility in a new way.

In *Speaking from Elsewhere*, I have tried to contribute to this reconceptualization with my contextualist view of discursive agency and my notion of *echoing responsibility*: the responsibility we have to take as discursive agents for echoing voices and their speech acts (including utterances and silences). Echoing responsibility is a more robust notion than it may seem at first sight, for it concerns crucial normative issues and the mobilization of our discursive powers to tackle these issues. The issues we are confronted with as speakers are whether a legacy of use is worth maintaining and in what way, whether the received use should be modified and how. In any performative chain in which we participate, we should ask ourselves: What are the transformations that are needed in this chain, if any? And how can they be produced? These normative questions involved in the echoing responsibility of speakers reveal that although our discursive agency is not absolute or autonomous, it contains nonetheless tremendous transformative powers that often go unrecognized and unexploited. Our echoing responsibility refers to the negotiations that are constantly taking place in our communicative exchanges and discursive responsiveness to one another. Although we are

---

73. Butler, *Excitable Speech*, 15–16, emphasis added.

typically not aware of these ongoing discursive negotiations, our speech acts are nonetheless situated in them; and given the position our speech acts come to occupy in performative sequences, they make particular contributions to the implicit negotiations that animate the performative chains.

On my view, discursive agency should be conceived first and foremost as a process of negotiation. When we speak we are *implicitly negotiating* legacies of use with our interlocutors as well as with possible communication partners from the past and from the future. The negotiation processes through which the meaning and force of our speech acts are manufactured and reproduced, made and remade, are processes of *re-signification*. Whether they result in the maintenance of a legacy of use or in its transformation, our speech acts always *re-signify*. In any performative chain there is always a continuum of cases of possible re-signification ranging from the closest fidelity available to us (which always involves differences in the speech situation that are regarded as negligible) to radical reversals of meaning and force. As Butler puts it: "There is no possibility of *not* repeating. The only question that remains is: How will that repetition occur, at what site, juridical or nonjuridical, and with what pain and promise?"[74] In other words, we are doomed to repeat, but how we repeat is up to us. My notion of echoing tries to broaden this notion of repetition or citation by including silences among the speech acts that re-signify in performative chains (without explicitly repeating or citing). With the proper support of the discursive context in which speakers find themselves, a legacy of use can be echoed in a silence and critical demands can be imposed on this legacy by silent speakers. When properly contextualized, certain silences can be construed as the refusal to repeat, as a kind of *negative echoing*; and therefore, they constitute critical interventions in our performative chains.

The reconceptualization of the notions of agency and responsibility constitutes a point of convergence in the contemporary philosophical debates across traditions, and a cornerstone of new performative theories in the twenty-first century. In a recent book, *Giving an Account of Oneself*, Butler has developed a powerful exploration of the intersections among identity, agency, and responsibility. Other explorations of these intersections have also been developed by contemporary authors who bring together in their approaches phenomenological, hermeneutic, and post-analytic theories.[75] There are many contemporary problem-oriented approaches that resist and undermine traditional classifications. I take this to be good news and reason for hope in a future philosophical community that is not bogged down by inflexible frontiers and oppositions,

---

74. *Ibid.*, 102.
75. See, for example, Linda M. Alcoff, *Visible Identities: Race, Gender, and the Self* (Oxford: Oxford University Press, 2006); and my *Speaking from Elsewhere*.

a community whose members can enjoy a new flow of ideas and freedom of movements across traditions and disciplines, tapping into theoretical resources wherever they may fall – although not without taking into account their history and the background in which they are rooted.

As a postscript to my account of the performative turn and its legacy, I hope to have shown in this brief, concluding section that the philosophical agenda of the twenty-first century calls for collaborations across philosophical traditions and across disciplines. To end on an optimistic note, I have also called attention to a promising process of hybridization in contemporary post-analytic philosophy, with the emergence of authors who use theoretical resources elaborated on both sides of the Atlantic and are repairing the philosophical evasion of identity, diversity, and the political that has afflicted the Anglo-American tradition. Progress in facing the theoretical challenges of performative approaches in this century are likely to come from the dialogue between these neo-Wittgensteinians and neopragmatists who have incorporated identity issues in their theorizing and performative theorists working within continental philosophy. This dialogue has the potential of being mutually corrective and enriching, for their participants can identity and challenge each other's theoretical presuppositions as well as sharing and complementing their theoretical strategies and conceptual tools.

14

OUT OF BOUNDS: PHILOSOPHY IN AN AGE OF TRANSITION

Judith Butler and Rosi Braidotti

This essay is a joint venture between two thinkers who address philosophy's multiple lives in the period 1980–95, that is to say, the time span covered by this volume, which roughly coincides with the period from which our graduate training came to an end to our mid-career. The authors, trained in philosophy, built quite a philosophical curriculum and full academic careers while always being housed outside the disciplinary quarters – one employed in rhetoric and comparative literature departments and the other in gender studies. From these relatively marginal positions, we will attempt to account for the many shifts in philosophy's excursions towards multiple outsides, by stressing their experimental, transgressive, but also systematic and engaged character.

The essay has accordingly a triple aim. First, we aim to focus on the growth of several kinds of new philosophical practice in the period under scrutiny, by providing a synoptic overview of the most relevant developments. Second, we want to map our continuing involvement with a discipline that institutionally did not welcome the critical theories and theorists of the 1970s and 1980s, but rather tended to exclude or marginalize us. To achieve this goal, we will rely on autobiographical accounts and personal information in order to document the specific shifts of location and contextual conditions that affected the practice of philosophy in this period. As a result, this chapter will mix personal voices and individual accounts with the more standard academic tone. The sections related to the former appear in italics.

Third, we argue that the emergence of new experimental modes and venues of thinking combine to form both creative tensions and contradictions that have left a problematic legacy for future generations of philosophers. Writing about them is a way of making ourselves accountable for this legacy.

I. THE GROWTH OF NEW KINDS OF PHILOSOPHICAL PRACTICE

Throughout the 1980s, in response to both external prompts and internal dynamics, the practice of philosophy expanded toward activities that were outside the established institutions of the discipline. We will call these extramural or real-life trajectories "philosophy outside its bounds." Concretely, this way of designating an operation of thought means that throughout the 1980s philosophical concepts burst out of their formal academic setting in modes of concrete engagement with the world, continuing in a new way the activist dispositions of the 1960s and 1970s, but also reflecting the changing conditions of culture, in ways that are both informed by, and informing, the arts and media culture.

The experience of the intense political activism of the 1970s had demonstrated not only that philosophy is capable of taking on a different role in public venues than the one traditionally accorded it within the university, but also that it could find renewed energy and inspiration in doing so. What happens through the 1980s, therefore, is not only a quantitative change in philosophy's expansion toward the outside, but also a qualitative shift. Philosophical practice grows into and out of locations and activities that were not traditionally associated with it, and it does not remain confined to the historical venues and actors linked to political "engagement" and activist social movements. Domains into which this new kind of expansion took place include the media, the corporate world of business management, medical ethics, and popular culture. As a result, philosophy "takes place" in different times and venues, functioning as part of humanitarian efforts, as modes of popular and public culture, and as art practices. It engenders not only informed scholars, but also engaged citizens and discerning consumers.

French philosophers have a long established tradition of intervention in social, cultural, and political life, as public intellectuals, social critics, and activists. The figures of Jean-Paul Sartre and Simone de Beauvoir stand high in this tradition, lending their support to a variety of crucial causes such as decolonization, socialism and antiracism (Fanon and Césaire), feminism and pacifism. They also founded new journals and publication venues, such as *Les Temps modernes, Libération,* and *Questions féministes.* There is, however, a difference in the scale and mode of engagements of the philosophers who come after them. They intervene on questions of justice, human suffering, responsibility, economic and social sustainability, and global belonging, making use of visual culture and media and reflecting on its meaning, and they do so not in the name of an engagement with Marxist or any other ideology, but rather as an end in itself. They prioritize the critical analysis of power relations at both the macro and the micro levels as the main task for philosophers.

Michel Foucault and Gilles Deleuze[1] captured both the spirit of the times and its profound ambivalence when they posited the emergence of a new type of function for the philosopher as public intellectual. If the contrast with the received Hegelian model of the universalistic philosopher as rational guardian of the moral development of mankind (the gender is not a coincidence) is easily drawn, the difference from the engaged or "organic" intellectual of the previous generation of Marxist and existential thinkers requires more cautious phrasing. As Foucault and Deleuze put it:

> At one time, practice was considered an application of theory, a consequence; at other times, it had an opposite sense and it was thought to inspire theory … In any event, their relationship was understood in terms of a process of totalization. For us, however, the question is seen in a different light. The relationships between theory and practice are far more partial and fragmentary. … The relationship which holds in the application of a theory is never one of resemblance. … Practice is a set of relays from one theoretical point to another and theory is a relay from one practice to another. … A theorizing intellectual, for us, is no longer a subject, a representing or representative consciousness. … Representation no longer exists; there's only action – theoretical action and practical action which serve as relays and form networks.[2]

The main legacy of "high poststructuralist" thought, therefore, is that the political and conceptual contestation of the totalizing power of the discipline of philosophy does not inaugurate a "crisis" for its own sake. It is rather an encouragement to pursue philosophy by all possible means and hence it is a sign of great theoretical vitality. Coherent in their practice, the poststructuralists conjugate philosophy in the plural and move it toward social, political, and ethical concerns. They see themselves as "specific" intellectuals, providers of critical services, analysts of the conditions of possibility of discourse, working with ideas that are also programs for action rather than dogmatic stockpiles of beliefs. This style is "problematizing" in its radical empiricism, or antiuniversalism, and in the awareness of the partiality of all philosophical statements. As a result, the kind of philosophy that emerged in the late 1980s was on the edge of institutionalization, embodying what Foucault called "permanent critique." Because

---

*1. Foucault and Deleuze are discussed in essays by, respectively, Timothy O'Leary and Daniel W. Smith, in *The History of Continental Philosophy: Volume 6*.

2. See Michel Foucault and Gilles Deleuze, "Intellectuals and Power," in *Language, Counter-Memory and Practice*, Donald F. Bouchard (ed.), Donald F. Bouchard and Sherry Simon (trans.) (Ithaca, NY: Cornell University Press, 1977), 205–7.

of this radical commitment to philosophy and its outsides, training as philosophers while being activists at that point in time actually meant having to ask fundamental questions such as: Why think? How can we connect the practice of thinking to larger social and ethical concerns? How can we resist the negative and oppressive aspects of the present? What is philosophy all about and how can it help us lead politically useful, socially productive, and morally adequate lives?[3] These questions were also our entry-point into the discipline.

What attracted us both to poststructuralism is that it was one of the answers to the decline of modernist utopias, mostly Marxism and various brands of post-Marxist master narratives of politics. It was an attempt to rearticulate a radical sense of materialism, embodiment, and accountability and to redefine the question of praxis in terms of ethical agency. Last but not least it made it not only possible, but also necessary, to connect the task of philosophy to the challenges coming from the new social movements – mostly those associated with feminists, gay and lesbian rights, environmentalists and peace activists, racial and ethnic minorities in the context of postcoloniality. Critical philosophical theory challenges the dominant representation of the subject of knowledge and develops it into a critique of the hidden assumptions about who is entitled to do philosophy and to what ends.

Early formations

JB: *The period of 1980–1995 was one in which I became trained officially as a PhD in philosophy but entered into teaching environments in which I taught the humanities more generally, including social theory. Because I was at Yale University for both my undergraduate and graduate training, and there were some very pronounced tensions between literary studies and philosophy as well as acute conflicts between traditions and styles of philosophical reflection, I was constantly aware of a number of boundaries that had to be negotiated, especially if I was somehow to "succeed" in getting a PhD and a position of employment.[4] It is important to add to this autobiographical sketch my own involvement at the time with the Women's Center in the city of New Haven, where most of the feminists were not involved with the university at all, and my engagement with an emergent movement of lesbian and gay activists, many of whom were in New York. So I did not have a single "track" that I followed, and I was aware at every turn that I would*

---

3. For an important introduction to the spirit of this philosophical age, see François Laruelle, *Les Philosophies de la différence: Introduction critique* (Paris: Presses Universitaires de France, 1986); published in English as *Philosophies of Difference: A Critical Introduction to Non-Philosophy*, Rocco Gangle (trans.) (New York: Continuum 2010).

4. For an earlier consideration of this period, see my "Can the 'Other' of Philosophy Speak?," in *Undoing Gender* (New York: Routledge, 2004).

have to negotiate certain boundaries and limits if I were to "survive" within the institutional forms that were available to me. Of course, I was in an enormously privileged position as a US academic at one of the most elite schools, but my life did not center there, and I believe that when my name was called out at the graduate ceremonies for my undergraduate degree, no one there knew who I was. So I was constantly escaping: in my apartment, reading; on the train to New York; in the bars, pursuing conversations and political actions outside the academy on sexuality, rights, representation, power, coalitions, social norms, psychic life. These were sites of enormous intellectual intensity, and in many ways they prompted and informed the kinds of questions that I brought into my own academic work, especially my philosophical work.

RB: *Philosophy has always been part of my life and culture. Growing up in Italy in a socialist family committed to anti-fascism, I got accustomed early on to ideas like freedom, justice, and responsibility. Besides, in Italian high schools, just like in France, philosophy was a compulsory subject of study; I delighted in it. When I migrated to Australia at the age of fifteen, I hated having to give up philosophy to embrace whatever the syllabus was in Melbourne inner city high school in the early 1970s – the period just prior to the emergence of Australian multiculturalism. Philosophy came to represent a sort of surrogate home and a vulnerable but resilient feature of my intellectual genealogy.[5] I had taken a few of my philosophy books with me; more were sent to me by my maternal uncle, a Catholic priest who worked with Italian migrants in Switzerland. Some were his own, from his school days, and I turned those thin yellowed pages with respect and relish. They were in Italian, of course, and signified some sort of safety and a safeguard of my own cultural identity. In between attending "remedial English" classes for new migrants and doing the normal homework, I made sure to complete the Italian philosophy curriculum. This consisted essentially of the history of philosophy in chronological order, with emphasis on the great classics; Plato, Aristotle, Saint Augustine, Seneca, Marcus Aurelius were among the favorites. So many of them were foreigners, exiles, displaced people – like Spinoza for instance – I felt we all shared in a radical form of non-belonging. With Pascal I confronted my adolescent self-doubts; from Voltaire I learned the powers of a relentless wit. My diaries of those days are full of references to them. It was years before I got upset by the fact that there was not a woman in sight in this philosophical canon. Because of the intimate relationship to those texts, philosophy became both a permanent feature of my mental landscapes and a private site marked by the oscillation between loss and belonging. It*

---

5. For an earlier account of this period, see my "Introduction," in *Nomadic Subjects: Embodiment and Sexual Difference in Contemporary Feminist Theory* (New York: Columbia University Press, 1994).

both confirmed and challenged my sense of identity, of being a European migrant and an Italian-French-speaker. It was a rather classical and old-fashioned idea of European culture, modeled on an Enlightenment-based idea of human progress through the deployment of reason, truth, and justice. Later on I ended up questioning all this, of course, but for many years those philosophy texts were my most trusted friends and loyal companions. I felt we shared a secret.

JB: *In the early 1970s, I discovered philosophy through reading some key texts that I found in the basement of my home – books that my parents had bought for their college education and had shelved there with the expectation that they would never be read again. It was paradoxical that I would go to the basement, lock the door behind me, to secure some distance from my parents only to find myself engrossed by their books. I would put on music, and write some in a diary, but I would also comb those shelves looking for texts that might help me to think about how to live. So as I reached for some of those books – Spinoza's* Ethics *and Kierkegaard's* Either/ Or *in particular – I was quite literally reaching for philosophy as a kind of guide, a source of wisdom, as a book that might accompany me in my confused despair and longing in order to find a way. I certainly had not had a course in philosophy, and yet I understood that these books were about the search for wisdom – and I wanted some. I had had some exposure to philosophical thinking at my synagogue, but it wasn't until I took the books down and started reading that I had the experience of needing these books, quite literally, in order to survive. Of course, it was in Plato that one found an explicit set of definitions for philosophy, ones that had to do with learning how to live and, more specifically, how to live or lead the good life. I wanted to be able to survive, and it seemed to me that survival was not possible unless I could secure meaning for life. I also knew that survival was not quite enough, that one had to live well, that one had to somehow identify and pursue a good life. If there was no good life to have, then why live at all?*

  I was operating out of a certain adolescent darkness, to be sure, but I was also quite passionate about reading. I read because I was passionate, and did not know what to make of my passions. I also read about the passions, thinking I might finally understand conceptually something about human nature or the human life that would make my own predicaments less singular and personal. So reading about passion made me a passionate reader of philosophy. And both Spinoza and Kierkegaard were nothing without the former's emphasis on desire, and the latter's notion of passion and faith.

First institutional encounters

RB: *In 1973 I enrolled at university and read for a joint degree in literature and philosophy. It was what they called "continental" philosophy, which was marginal in Australia, in relation to the dominant British analytic tradition. To me, this was the heart of the matter. I took to phenomenology with great enthusiasm: Merleau-Ponty's insight into embodiment and memory resonated with my experience. I was also fascinated by Freud's psychoanalysis with the emphasis on the instability, but also the stubborn, repetitive structure of identity formations. I will never forget reading Juliet Mitchell's introduction to Lacan: a true revelation! This was the high 1970s in all their impetuous intensity, of course, and I was working on Althusser just as the fast-growing women's movement and the anti-Vietnam moratorium contributed to politicize issues of identity, political subjectivity, and resistance. The Australian scene was dominated by figures of the caliber of Germaine Greer, whose passionate politics shaped both my thinking and the way I wanted to live my life. All of a sudden philosophy was all around me, literally in the streets. It provided both alternative social values and new mental spaces. With my friends the discussions centered on issues of social justice, anticolonialism, women's rights, and nonviolence. I expected philosophy to teach me about responsibility, justice, community, and how to combine theory and practice with coherence and dignity.*

I was very fortunate in having as my BA supervisor a great and important teacher, whose influence will continue throughout my adult life: Genevieve Lloyd. She was just getting started then on her landmark volume The Man of Reason *as she taught me the history of philosophy. With a PhD from Oxford, Genny Lloyd was completely acceptable to the analytic philosophers, while her heart was in continental philosophy. A most remarkable intellect, she transmitted her passion for Spinoza while she taught Foucault as part of the basic curriculum. That's how I came to choose to move to Paris in the late 1970s, to study philosophy at the Sorbonne. I did not even wait for the BA graduation ceremony.*

Paris at the time was, philosophically, the most exciting place on earth. While I enrolled for my postgraduate degree in what they called "history of systems of thought," which was related to Foucault's Chair at the Collège de France, I savored everything the city had to offer intellectually. Foucault's magisterial courses on bio-power are forever engraved in my mind, while Irigaray held seminars in makeshift locations after Lacan threw her out of his "École freudienne" for excessive independence of mind. It was not until I started attending Deleuze's seminars at Vincennes that I discovered what great philosophy in the making was all about. Cixous and Lyotard were also teaching there: it was like a whirlpool of activity that took my breath away.[6] I became more and more intrigued by the collective character of philosophical thoughts in general and more particularly of so many utterances and knowledge claims that I had learned to call my own. Thinking seemed to happen in groups, in the company of others. Although it was formatted and framed by reason,

---

6. See also my "The Way We Were: Some Post-Structuralist Memoirs," *Women's Studies International Forum* 23(6) (November–December 2000).

thinking was an outward-bound, external, and often reactive activity, driven by forces and affects which acted independently of the rational will. I experienced this insight with almost joyful relief and grew suspicious of both claims to liberal individualism from the Right and also of the identity politics that was so central to the Left theories of the time. I was increasingly critical of rigid claims to steady identities and rooted subject positions. I re-routed myself towards more fluid and multilayered understandings of what makes a subject.

JB: *As I grew older, I found out that I could take a college class in this subject called "philosophy," something that I approached with great enthusiasm. I had prepared myself in high school by reading parts of Plato and Aristotle, the tradition of classical political liberalism (some Locke and Montesquieu), and a rather large swath from the legacies of existentialism, including existential theology. At the same time, I was reading texts from the antipsychiatry movement, and starting to read feminism and texts from the Black Power movement (Eldridge Cleaver, especially). I understood myself to be a radical, even a revolutionary, although my thoughts on these subjects were somewhat confused. When I did arrive at my first university course, I could not really understand what kind of philosophy this was. The term "philosophy" became something of a category in crisis. We were reading Plato's* Republic *and John Rawls's early essays on justice, and we were asked to focus on certain kinds of semantic problems and argumentative forms in both texts. Although I learned to do this with some difficulty, I could not see at all how any of this "philosophy" was related to the question of how best to live a life, how to find and know the good life, how to secure those kinds of meanings that might make life seem livable and worthwhile.*

Where was the investment, the sense of quest, the sense of existential urgency? It was one thing to ask "How do I know what the good life is, and how do I go about living it?" That question presumes that the "I" in the sentence is an existing person who has an investment in pursuing the answer to the question posed. That "person" dropped out of the picture in my first encounter with institutionalized philosophy. Instead, we thought about the meaning of the word "good." Now, of course, one cannot simply ask what the good life is without having some sense of what the word "good" is doing in the question. There are several ways in which "good" can be used, and it seems obligatory to parse these various meanings and to offer a justification for the particular usage at issue in the question posed. And there were epistemological problems that compounded the semantic ones: Even if there is a life that we might reasonably call "good," how might we come to know it? And do we have the appropriate cognitive capacity to know it at all? In this context, philosophy turned out to be a reflection on the confused meaning of words (ordinary people use language in a confused way, but philosophers seek to alleviate language of its confusion or to show that the confusions make impossible any substantive progress on a particular problem). Or philosophy turned out to be a reflection on the limits of what we can know. If we could gain a clear picture ("clear pictures" were very important) of the limits of what we can know, then we would cease to ask certain kinds of highly speculative questions and reconcile ourselves to matters that were decidedly more narrow and workable.

I was, of course, driven into a sense of embarrassment about my own philosophical passions, especially since the questions that I most wanted to ask and pursue were for the most part discredited as worth pursuing in that form. I felt that my own questions were too passionate and too large. I remember learning how to do the kind of analysis that those philosophers required of their students, and I am sure that it helped me to formulate arguments with greater clarity than I otherwise would have. But I did, from the outset of my encounter with the institution of philosophy, understand that I would have to go underground in order to pursue what I meant by "philosophy." It was only later that I came to understand that this is an institutional feature of philosophy: it helps to produce a certain underground even as it discredits the underground that it produces. In addition, it also spends a fair amount of its time showing how the kinds of questions and the modes of thinking that take place in "ordinary" life are in need of an idiomatic reduction, reformulation, simplification, and amplification.

Of course, the question of whether certain modes of philosophy have an idiom is an important one. I made the mistake, for instance, of thinking in my first philosophy course that it made a difference that Plato's Republic was written in dialogue form. What was the importance of counterposing voices within the text? Of interruptions? Of silences? Of the places where the text breaks off? Did the occasional belching of the interlocutor "say" something in the text? Did it draw attention to the body in the dialogue or to a dimension of language that was articulate in ways that could not be reduced to semantic content? What about the status of fables or stories in philosophical works? Were they simply ways of "illustrating" a set of philosophical points that could just as easily be offered in propositional form? Or were they important ways of sustaining "arguments" in nonpropositional modalities? Were they also ways of calling into question the centrality of argument to philosophy itself? How were we to understand irony, narrative, and voice as philosophical features of the text? Did it really not matter who was talking, and to whom, and whether or not something true was constituted and conveyed in that exchange?

RB: *The core of my philosophical interest was by now set on questions of identity, responsibility, becoming a subject of both knowledge and transformative politics or praxis.*

The main questions I kept asking were: How can we do justice to experiences that have no recognition in the language and practice of conventional wisdom, common sense, reasonableness? What is the appropriate language in which to express silences and missing voices? The politics of discourse and the limits of representation became crucial concerns. So much of our collective embodied experience – as women, gays, pacifists, leftists – seemed somehow pitched against what was discursively acceptable or even sayable. Philosophy was as much part of the problem as part of a possible solution; deconstructing it seemed imperative. The existential component of my philosophical work was boosted at this time by another major event: I undertook a long personal psychoanalysis in French, with a brilliant nonaligned psychoanalyst. This was not uncommon at the time: a "slice" (as they called it then) of psychoanalytic treatment was considered an integral part of a philosophical education. Lacan's influence on this generation was immense, of course, and I think beneficial in the long run: he recommended not working with psychoanalytic concepts unless one had actually undergone at least some practice. Lacanian psychoanalysis clearly aspires to gain philosophical credentials by highlighting the structural function of desire and inventing a suitable method to deal with it. Seven years later, I simultaneously chose to stay on in Europe, although not in Paris, and to accept a job in the margins of academia, namely in an interdisciplinary women's studies department, which I had the fortune of founding and directing when I moved to Utrecht in 1988.

The amazing opportunity to be able to start up an entirely new program is a typically Dutch phenomenon: here I was, a relative youngster and a foreigner, and Utrecht put me in charge of creating a new academic program from scratch. In the USA, in the few places where women's studies programs were being created at the time, it was usually senior women scholars who were appointed in virtue of their having "earned" the right to opt out of their disciplines. The reason for this comes down to two main factors: the first is the impetus and the political power of the Dutch Left throughout the 1970s and 1980s. The grass-roots movement was huge and it shared in the spirit of May '68 that declared that we should not trust the older generation (or anybody much over thirty). This made it imperative to appoint a younger person to the job. The second reason was more pragmatic: giving a temporary (tenure came many years afterwards) albeit senior job to a relatively unknown foreign entity bypassed all the local quarrels and made it easier for the institution to assess my work on strictly objective grounds. Thus, everything was indexed on producing results quickly and efficiently. When it became clear that this was the case, the Utrecht women's studies program received wide recognition and I earned my tenure. But that took about ten years.

Working in a feminist academic environment, which means an interdisciplinary, intellectually experimental, and politically progressive – if not downright transgressive – context, had its advantages. It made it possible to combine my feminist political passions with academic work and life, which had not happened until now. The price to pay, however, was to accept my distance from the institutional practice of philosophy. This focus allowed me to liberate my own philosophical thought from a number of institutional habits. Not the least of these was the respect for the authority of the history of philosophy, and hence also the deferential implementation of ways of thinking that had much more to do with the past than with the actual present: for instance, the idea that philosophy should be self-referential and do justice to its own history, before it even attempts or claims to make a significant impact on that history. That's the first habit I swapped for a renewed sense of social relevance: gender, feminist, and women's studies theories became my favorite location. They functioned like navigational tools between academic practice and its "outsides" and provided much-needed theoretical focus. More importantly even, they kept me motivated to go on thinking, doing philosophy even though I had no authority, nor anybody recognizing my work as of philosophical importance. I was simultaneously on my own in the margins and stunned to see how crowded and theoretically vibrant the margins actually were.

JB: *Because of my oldest interests and my newest questions, my own teaching and writing became interdisciplinary with time. But this did not mean that I "left" philosophy behind. My works engaged feminism, psychoanalysis, anthropology, law, politics, performance studies, sociology, social theory, literature, and literary theory. This range has been very important for me in my adult career; it not only produces all kinds of conversations, but it imposes the task of translating from one domain of thought into another. It also allows one to develop a critical position that belongs to no discipline, but which is quite essential to understanding the task of the university more generally. I would point to these two features of intellectual work – translation and critique – as central to my own current practices. It means that I need to draw on all kinds of work if I am to pursue some of the questions that focus my work: How do unlivable lives become more livable? How do we analyze and transform the situation in which a nation such as my own becomes wildly righteous when it openly murders some populations and madly outraged with horror when it sees other populations being destroyed, or sees itself as vulnerable to injury? The good life: Who defines it? Who controls it? Who has access to it, and what terms do we need in order to enfranchise those who are not recognized as having anything to say or claim?*

Perhaps the issue here has to do with whether we understand philosophy as an enclosed and self-regulating institution that defines itself over and against other forms of knowledge, or whether we actually understand the obligation of philosophy to be open precisely to a wide domain of intellectual activities in order to engage in a knowing way with the world whose truth it claims to know. This would mean that philosophy, to be responsive to its world, has to be a decentered undertaking.

II. A CHANGING CONTEXT

Philosophy meetings in cafes, in conferences, in feminist collectives, gay and lesbian political meetings, antiwar rallies and demonstrations, editorial boards, bars, and film festivals, in transnational contexts, all move beyond the specific "sites" of legitimate institutionalization to produce the possibility of thinking philosophy in the world. This was important to us both as philosophers and feminists and gay and lesbian activists. We form an "intermediary generation"[7] that witnessed some key moments in the history of feminism: respectively the "sex wars" in the USA[8] and the rise of the "feminism of difference" in Paris. We may be the first generation of philosophers who did have the chance to study with great feminist thinkers such as Genevieve Lloyd, Seyla Benhabib, and Luce Irigaray. But this first-hand experience also taught us bitter lessons from the start: some feminist philosophers were traditionally not well received in philosophy departments and had to find other venues for seminar activity and collective discussions. These interrelations were only occasionally supported by institutional "sites": most of the interesting discussions took place elsewhere. And even today, the university sites where philosophy takes place often include interdisciplinary programs outside departments of philosophy: "women's studies," "feminist studies," "media studies," "cultural studies," as well as centers and institutes for "humanities" or "critical theory." As these interdisciplinary programs are more developed in the USA than in Europe, this leaves many European radical philosophers as homeless as before.

The media and the publishing world, of course, have helped. The period 1980–95 saw a real explosion of alternative publication venues often within existing publishers such as Routledge in the US/UK, Suhrkamp in Germany, Éditions de Minuit in France, and Editori Riuniti in Italy.[9] Academic publishing reflected this shift in the institutional settings of philosophy, recognizing the desire to make philosophy popular, and the demand to produce texts that travel in nonphilosophical quarters. Thus, the genre of do-it-yourself or self-help manuals in the teaching of philosophy emerged as a fast-selling sector. These new cultural forms for philosophical engagement go beyond the essay and the book, establishing broader sites of textuality and practical engagements at the same time that they continue certain modes of philosophical inquiry. It is

---

*7. See Rosi Braidotti's chapter on feminism in this volume.

8. See Jane Gallop, *Feminist Accused of Sexual Harassment* (Durham, NC: Duke University Press, 1997).

9. In particular, the Routledge series "Thinking Gender," started by philosophy editor Maureen MacGrogan and the cultural studies series supported by Bill Germano should be noted. And Suhrkamp was without question the leading publishing house for philosophical books in Germany in the period 1980–95.

remarkable, as we go through our CVs, to see how many experimental journals we published in and how many brand new – and sometimes very short-lived – publications we actually took the risk of publishing in. We are very aware, however, that taking this sort of risk by publishing in marginal journals and with nonacademic publishers may have directly contributed to many members of our generation actually not getting tenure in "first tier" philosophy departments. Considering how the political climate has changed, it may still constitute a risk today.

RB: *Most of my mid-career in philosophy was built by reading and publishing in challenging and thought-provoking journals such as* Radical Philosophy, L'Autre Journal, *where Deleuze and Lyotard published regularly, and the Italian* MicroMega *and* Aut-Aut.[10] *We were surrounded by brand new journals, magazines and printed material of all kinds:* Questions féministes *(1981),* Sorcières *(1976),* La femme d'en face *(1979). My very first academic publication was in* Hecate *(founded in 1976), the Australian radical feminist journal, where I published a critical review of the anthology* New French Feminism; *the second was in* Penelope, *the feminist history journal founded in 1979 by the Paris VII-Jussieu collective of Michelle Perrot. For years my monthly articles in the feminist magazines* Histoires d'Elles *(1978) and the Italian* Noi Donne *(1948) mattered far more than anything that may have helped me gain academic credibility. If I can name my favorites from those days, they would be the UK-based* M/F *(1978),* Feminist Studies *(1979) and* Women's Studies International Forum *(1978); the newly founded* Signs *(1975) directed by my mentor Kate Stimpson, and the*

---

10. *Radical Philosophy* is a journal of socialist and feminist philosophy. It was founded in 1972 in response to the widely felt discontent with the sterility of academic philosophy at the time (in Britain completely dominated by the narrowest sort of "ordinary-language" philosophy), with the purpose of providing a forum for the theoretical work that was emerging in the wake of the radical movements of the 1960s, in philosophy and other fields.

    L'Autre Journal is a theory and culture magazine that started publication in December 1984 with Michel Butel as general editor. It quickly acquired cult status among philosophers because of the original and clever manner in which it addressed the main philosophical questions of the day. A second series started up again in May 1990. The title exists now as a blog linked to the website of *Le Monde*.

    MicroMega is a political, cultural, social, and economic magazine, published bimonthly in Italy. Founded in March 1986 by the editors Giorgio Ruffolo and Paolo Flores d'Arcais, it is an elite journal publishing long essays and reports by leading philosophers, scientists, and other personalities.

    Aut-Aut is a leading Italian philosophy journal founded by Enzo Paci in 1951 with a strong phenomenological orientation. Between 1974 and 1976, the philosopher Pier Aldo Rovatti took a leading role in the editorial board and turned the journal into a crucial forum for discussion of Marxism, poststructuralism, and related political and ethical issues. The journal is published today as an independent critical journal.

Belgian-based Cahiers du Grif *(1973), where I worked for many years alongside Françoise Collin. The first acknowledgment of my work came in an interview with Hazel Rowley in another Australian radical feminist magazine:* Refractory Girl *(1972). But I was not alone in this: all around me, everybody was starting up journals, magazines, and alternative publications. This was before the internet multiplied these efforts – we were still very Gutenberg Galaxy then. For instance, Paul Patton and Meaghan Morris produced the first English translations of Foucault, Deleuze, and Irigaray for the Sydney-based* Working Papers *in general philosophy. Colin Gordon, at the same time, was building up* Ideology & Consciousness *to greater heights than ever. Of course, I could not resist the temptation of starting something on my own as well, so together with my friend Alice Jardine we made a brilliant start to what would become a one-issue only hit:* Copyright *was the perfect manifestation of the adventurous interdisciplinary spirit of the time: smart, cutting-edge, highly theoretical, and totally broke! Almost everyone who contributed to that issue went on to an incredible academic career, but the journal did not make it past the first issue.*

JB: *In the US, intellectual excitement revolved around the journal* differences, *established by Elizabeth Weed and Naomi Schor in 1989, but also the galvanizing work of Gayatri Chakravorty Spivak and Joan Wallach Scott. It seemed as if philosophical questions of materialism, experience, identity, and the subject were now being taken up by literary critics and radical historians, and that these philosophical concepts were being probed in order to sharpen a set of critical modes within politics. There were debates happening at the conferences for women historians (the "Berkshire" conference), the Socialist Scholars conference, the Barnard College "Scholar and Feminist" conferences, the Rethinking Marxism conferences, and very often the debates were fierce between those who saw potential in continental theory and those who did not. Rarely did anyone stop to ask whether Marx himself was a continental philosopher. Debates broke out as well in* The New York Times *and the* Nation, *and although the animus was strong against certain modes of "deconstruction," it was also clear that such modes of thought had pervaded not only the academy, but Left intelligentsia. People worried about the end to foundations, the loss of disciplinary boundaries, and the lack of clear norms. But, in fact, all of these concepts were being rethought in light of new historical formations, and the process of change was not easy for many to accept. The experience in the US was that the explosion of new cultural venues for reflection that were contaminated by poststructuralist and other philosophies went hand in hand with a higher degree of specification of the practice of philosophy, which struck a distinctly interdisciplinary note of its own. Some early journals in this vein are:* Critical Inquiry *(started in 1974),* Diacritics *(1977),* boundary 2 *(1970),* Glyph *(1977), and others. A new generation of interdisciplinary journals also comes into being. I am thinking for instance of media, film and art theory, and the creation of highly theoretical journals in these fields, such as* Camera Obscura *(1976),* October *(1976),* Feminist Review *(1979); sexuality and cultural studies also grew at an explosive rate, with journals such as* Semiotext(e) *(1974),* SubStance *(1971), and* Hypatia *(1986).*

The extent to which the institutional practice of philosophy recognized and accepted interaction with this parallel universe of highly scientific, but transgressive, publications needs to be mapped more carefully than we can do here. Suffice it to say that, whereas the US remained more open to these boundary-breakers, the European university system, traditionally dominated by the disciplines, proved more resistant. The emergence of philosophers within mainstream culture, the arts, and the media is important to read therefore in light of this rejection, as well as a sign of the engagement of philosophers in public politics. Although the figure of the philosopher as public intellectual has deep roots in European culture, it became a more global phenomenon as the US and Australia succumbed to the "theory wars" in the late 1980s and throughout the 1990s. Think, for instance, of the role that philosophers play in human rights struggles, in nongovernmental organizations such as Médecins sans Frontières, in Amnesty International, Human Rights Watch, and Greenpeace. Consider how many poststructuralist thinkers have made significant contributions to human rights discourse in recent years.[11] By extension this means that law has become a site for the reflection on key philosophical categories such as justice, force, futurity, and the imaginary. Legal discourse also gets positively contaminated and a school of critical legal theory emerges with conferences on law, culture, and the humanities as well as journals with the same focus.[12]

The transdisciplinary philosophical impetus is so intense and stimulating that a new classification emerges under the rubric of "critical theory."[13] Bookstores start to make separate sections to accommodate the proliferations of publications in a counter-philosophical philosophy. This counter-philosophy continues certain modes of philosophical inquiry, but in cultural venues and through media that establish philosophy as impure, hybrid, crossing genres and media. Although philosophical films have claims to a certain status in experimental

---

11. See, for instance, the proceedings from "The Humanities in Human Rights: Critique, Language, and Politics" conference, October 21–2, 2005, published in *PMLA* 121(5) (2006). See also papers published in *South Atlantic Quarterly* 103 (2004).

12. A case in point is the conference at the Benjamin N. Cardozo School of Law at Yeshiva University in New York on "Deconstruction and the Possibility of Justice" in October 1989, at which Jacques Derrida presented "Force of Law: The 'Mystical Foundations of Authority.'" Following that conference, Derrida returned to Cardozo on an annual basis.

13. "Critical Theory" here has a broader extension than writings associated with Frankfurt School critical theory, whose "third generation" is discussed by Amy Allen in her essay in this volume.

media (e.g. Jarman on Wittgenstein;[14] the recent film on Iris Murdoch, *Iris*; Cornell West appearing in *The Matrix*; Derrida in *Ghost Dance*; and more recently, Astra Taylor's *Examined Life*, with extended discussions with eight major philosophers), the evolution of the media presence of philosophers and philosophical talk shows and programs in the period 1980–95 is quite striking. Again, the change is in scale and quality, supported also by the restructuring and transformation of the old medium of television in this period. There are some important precedents of mediated philosophy,[15] of course, but the pace definitely picks up in the period we are discussing. This is evidenced by the creation of new televisions channels that carry the French-German ARTE in 1992,[16] the French "Apostrophes" (which ran from 1975 to 1990), and many French radio programs, including "France Culture" (which has at least three ongoing philosophy shows), "RAI Radio Fahrenheit" in Italy, and "Kulturzeit" in Germany.

The undisputed media stars of the period in France are the philosophically undertitillating group known as the "Nouveaux Philosophes," who created the phenomenon of philosopher-writer/TV producer and film-maker Bernard-Henri Lévy. Regularly featured nowadays in the pages of glossy magazines such as *Vanity Fair*, Lévy built a brilliant and controversial career by striking a conservative tone politically, while targeting the previous generation of poststructuralist thinkers for systematic attack.

The situation was no less lively in Germany,[17] where the philosophical media star is Peter Sloterdijk, who has been running his successful talk show since 2002 on a range of interdisciplinary topics.[18] From 1988 to 2000, the German television station Westdeutscher Rundfunk ran a very high quality and ambitious series of features on philosophical topics: "Philosophie heute" (Philosophy

---

14. Derek Jarman's film *Wittgenstein* (BFI, 1993). See also Derek Jarman and Terry Eagleton, *"Wittgenstein": The Terry Eagleton Script and the Derek Jarman Film* (London: BFI Publishing, 1993).

15. Tamara Chaplin's *Turning on the Mind: French Philosophers on Television* argues that already in the 1950s French television featured regular discussions of philosophy and philosophers. See for instance the program *Lectures pour tous* (1953–58), in which Bachelard and Foucault appeared, and Sartre and Camus were often discussed.

16. ARTE (Association Relative à la Télévision Européenne) is a Franco-German television network started in 1992. It describes itself as a European culture channel and aims to promote quality programming especially in areas of culture and the arts. ARTE is also available in Belgium, the Netherlands, and Canada via cable, and the Australian Special Broadcasting Service translates many ARTE programs into English for broadcast on its own television network.

17. With sincere thanks to Dieter Thomä for this targeted information.

18. Since 2002, Peter Sloterdijk and Rüdiger Safranski have been presenting on the German public television channel Zweites Deutsches Fernsehen a philosophical talk show, similar to "Apostrophes," called "Philosophisches Quartett," which deals with a broad range of social questions.

today).[19] In the US, there are now philosophy talk radio shows and popular venues in which large questions in philosophy and religion are pursued. More recently, both Pierre Bourdieu and Jacques Derrida have been the "stars" of feature-length documentaries: Pierre Carles's *La Sociologie est un sport de combat* (2001) and Kirk Dick and Amy Z. Kofman's *Derrida* (2002). The authors of this article, however, are neither immune from nor external to television, video and new media coverage and appearances, and thus the question of assessing the general impact of these mediated forms of philosophical inquiry is more topical than ever. As a generation we watched the rise of this new, alternative media culture and also saw how negatively the university reacted to it – to be a media star was equated then with shallowness and lack of scientific rigor. Thus we have to raise an issue that we find still relevant today: Are philosophers commodified cultural "spectacles" in such instances, or do they appeal to intellectual need through a popular medium? Is it the case that philosophy turns into a fundamentally different activity when it becomes a media event?

III. THE INSTITUTIONAL DIMENSION

At the same time, however, philosophy as a discipline and a formal institutional space was concerned not to lose its core identity in the midst of such hybridization processes. There were clearly struggles, increasingly sectarian, over what "counts" as philosophy or, minimally, "good philosophy." And institutions house these battles with the presumption that the walls they build will continue to stand.

From 1980 to 1995, the public debate around the critical legacy of the 1970s grew more bitter and contested. The rise of Reagonomics and Thatcherite authoritarianism installed a climate of right-wing political backlash, which could not fail to attack the credibility of European and especially French poststructuralist theories. These were dismissed by the political Right as being both relativistic and a sign of wishy-washy liberalism. The debate was *even more* acrimonious among French philosophers, many of whom turned their backs on their youthful radicalism, especially after François Mitterrand's election to the French presidency. It was disconcerting to say the least, although somehow predictable, to watch the oedipal struggle between the philosophers of the 1960s and the generation that followed. The media-driven *nouveaux philosophes*, mentioned above, turned vehemently against the very home-grown philosophical theories

---

19. More than a hundred features were produced, including portraits of leading philosophers and documentaries on controversial topics, many of which can be found via the website www.wdr. de. The program producer edited a volume with some of the interviews; see Ulrich Boehm (ed.), *Philosophie heute* (Frankfurt: Campus, 1997).

of their teachers and older poststructuralist brothers that we, the foreigners and outsiders, were both reading and drawing such inspiration from. Among a relatively older generation, born in the 1940s, philosophical revisionism set in, offering at best a reappraisal of decent neohumanism[20] or a single-minded critique of the allegedly murderous character of communism,[21] and at worst media-savvy glamour.[22] On the other hand, among people of our generation, born in the 1950s, the reaction was ferocious: Alain Finkielkraut, and Luc Ferry and Alain Renaut indicted without appeal the events of 1968 as a symbol of left-wing authoritarianism and revolutionary violence.[23] Adding insult to injury, they accused all poststructuralist philosophies of complicity with terror and mass murder. This coincided with the media revolution we discussed above and with the new media-cracy turning against both the spirit and the philosophical and political agenda of 1968. The key insights of poststructuralist philosophy survived in exile along the transatlantic axis.

Deleuze was one of the first to comment on this hasty and fallacious historical dismissal of critical radicalism in both politics and philosophy. Targeting the fame-seeking narcissism of the *nouveaux philosophes*, Deleuze stressed the political conservatism that results in the reassertion of the banality of individualistic self-interest.[24] This is constitutive of the neoconservative political liberalism of our era and of the arrogance with which it proclaimed the "end of history."[25] Deleuze stressed instead how critical philosophers have tried to avoid the arrogance of the universalizing posture. Other leading figures of philosophical poststructuralism, such as Lyotard, Dominique Lecourt, and the gay activist Guy Hocquenghem, also took a clear stand against the trivialization and self-serving dismissal of the spirit of radical philosophy.[26]

---

20. See Tzvetan Todorov, *Imperfect Garden: The Legacy of Humanism* (Princeton, NJ: Princeton University Press, 2002).

21. See André Glucksmann, *La Cuisinière et le mangeur d'hommes: Essai sur l'État, le marxisme, les camps de concentration* (Paris: Éditions du Seuil, 1976).

22. Bernard-Henri Lévy, *La Barbarie à visage humain* (Paris: Grasset, 1977); published in English as *Barbarism with a Human Face*, George Holoch (trans.) (New York: Harper & Row, 1979).

23. Alain Finkielkraut, *La Défaite de la pensée* (Paris: Gallimard, 1987); published in English as *The Defeat of the Mind*, Judith Friedlander (trans.) (New York: Columbia University Press, 1995); Luc Ferry and Alain Renaut, *La Pensée 68: Essai sur l'anti-humanisme contemporain* (Paris: Gallimard, 1985); published in English as *French Philosophy of the Sixties: An Essay on Antihumanism*, Mary Schnackenberg Cattani (trans.) (Amherst, MA: University of Massachusetts Press, 1990).

24. Gilles Deleuze, "On the New Philosophers (Plus a More General Problem)" and "May '68 Didn't Happen," in *Two Regimes of Madness: Texts and Interviews 1975–1995* (New York: Semiotext(e), 2006).

25. Francis Fukuyama, *The End of History and the Last Man* (New York: Simon & Schuster, 1992).

26. See Jean-François Lyotard and Jacob Rogozinski, "La Police de la pensée," *L'Autre Journal* 10 (1985); Dominique Lecourt, *Les Piètres penseurs* (Paris: Flammarion, 1999); published

On the other hand, some modes of institutionalization have sought to take into account the subversive and transformative reach of new philosophical movements. Thus, at the same time as the backlash set in, new forms of creative institutionalization also started up. These were ways in which the corporate discipline itself both reconfirmed its traditional institutional settings and went on to occupy new and powerful institutional grounds. Examples are firstly the Vincennes University experiment with new structures of thought and scientific investigation, with high degrees of social accountability and a healthy distance from the canonical tradition of the disciplines. This radical pedagogy was supported by and central to the work of Gilles Deleuze.[27] Second, the foundation of the Collège International de Philosophie in 1983 in France.[28] Both authors participated in the Collège activities: one the very year of its foundation and the other in recent years. Organizations such as the International Association of Philosophy and Literature[29] and the Society for Phenomenology and Existential Philosophy (SPEP, founded in 1962)[30] are at once outside disci-

---

in English as *The Mediocracy: French Philosophy Since the Mid-1970s*, Gregory Elliot (trans.) (London: Verso, 2001); Guy Hocquenghem, *Lettre ouverte à ceux qui sont passés du col Mao au Rotary* (Marseille: Agone, 1986).

27. See Gilles Deleuze, "Sur la philosophie," in *Pourparlers* (Paris: Éditions de Minuit, 1990); published in English as "On Philosophy," in *Negotiations: 1972–1990*, Martin Joughin (trans.) (New York: Columbia University Press, 1995).

28. The Collège International de Philosophie (Ciph), located in Paris, was cofounded in 1983 by Jacques Derrida, François Châtelet, Jean-Pierre Faye, and Dominique Lecourt in an attempt to rethink the teaching of philosophy in France, and to liberate it from any institutional authority (most of all from the university). The Collège recognizes that philosophy is better served by being located at "intersections" such as philosophy/science or philosophy/law. Attendance in seminars is open and free, just as in the Collège de France.

29. The International Association for Philosophy and Literature, founded in 1976 and directed since its inception by Hugh Silverman, is, according to its website (www.iapl.info), "dedicated to the exchange of ideas and scholarly research within the humanities. Founded to provide a context for the interplay of Philosophy, Literary Theory, and Cultural/Aesthetic/Textual Studies, the IAPL brings together scholars from the full range of disciplines concerned with philosophical, historical, critical, and theoretical issues."

30. SPEP has its origins as an idea of Harvard University professor John Wild (1902–72) for a new professional society devoted to the examination of recent continental philosophy, and in particular the works of Heidegger, Husserl, Merleau-Ponty, and Sartre. After Wild left Harvard in 1961 to become Chairperson of the Department of Philosophy at Northwestern University, he and an organizational committee including his two Northwestern colleagues, William Earle and James Edie, George Schrader of Yale University, and Calvin Schrag, a former student of Wild's at Harvard, who had recently accepted an appointment at Purdue University, founded SPEP. According to its website (www.spep.org), "SPEP is the Society for Phenomenology and Existential Philosophy, a professional organization, founded in 1962 and devoted to supporting philosophy inspired by continental European traditions. With a membership of over 2500 people, it is one of the largest American philosophical societies, and strives to encourage work not only in the philosophical traditions of phenomenology and existentialism, but also in all those areas commonly associated with 'continental

plinary settings, but also help to define the discipline on new grounds. Similar organizations formed in Canada (Canadian Society for Hermeneutics and Postmodern Thought, which later became the Canadian Society for Continental Philosophy[31]); in Australia (Australasian Society for Continental Philosophy[32]) and in the UK (Society for European Philosophy and Forum for European Philosophy[33]). The emergence of a strong feminist presence in these societies

philosophy,' such as animal studies, critical theory, cultural studies, deconstruction, environmental philosophy, feminism, German idealism, hermeneutics, philosophy of the Americas, post-colonialism, post-structuralism, psychoanalysis, queer theory and race theory. We foster discussion on all philosophical topics, from art and nature to politics and science, and in the classic philosophical disciplines of metaphysics, epistemology, ethics, and aesthetics. SPEP is actively committed to philosophical pluralism and to the support of historically under-represented groups in the philosophical profession."

31. According to its website (www.c-scp.org) "The Canadian Society for Continental Philosophy" was founded in 1984 under the name "Canadian Society for Hermeneutics and Postmodern Thought." Its broad purpose is to promote scholarship in several traditions of continental philosophy by means of an annual conference and other activities. Current members include scholars and graduate students working in such fields as German idealism, existentialism, phenomenology, hermeneutics, critical theory, feminism, postmodernism, poststructuralism, and deconstruction, from various disciplinary approaches within the humanities, social sciences, and fine arts.

32. According to its website (www.ascp.org.au) "The Australasian Society for Continental Philosophy" was established in 1995 as the revamped "Australasian Society for Phenomenology and Social Philosophy," with the aim of becoming the region's premier reference point for people working with continental philosophy. The Society endeavors to promote the inter-disciplinary exchange of ideas inspired by the diverse traditions of European thought (such as phenomenology, existentialism, critical theory, hermeneutics, feminism, deconstruction, poststructuralism, and so on), and to develop productive links with other international societies and associations that share similar goals and views.

33. Since 2004, the Society for European Philosophy (SEP) and the Forum for European Philosophy (FEP) have held a joint annual meeting. Originating as an idea of Andrew Benjamin, then at the University of Warwick, in response to the unjustly poor performance of nonanalytic departments in the UK Research Assessment Exercise, the SEP held its first meeting in 1998 at Birkbeck College, establishing a venue for philosophers in the UK to present their work in the various traditions of modern European philosophy. Among its principal organizers, in addition to Benjamin (who served as Chair from 1997 to 2001), were Christine Battersby, Andrew Bowie, Howard Caygill, Simon Critchley, Peter Dews, Joanna Hodge, Peter Osborne, and Jonathan Rée. The FEP began in the spring of 1996 out of a desire to promote wider dialogue and exchange between philosophers working within and out of the different European traditions in philosophy. For its first year, the FEP was guided by an *ad hoc* and entirely provisional executive committee chaired by Alan Montefiore and including Lilian Alweiss, Catherine Audard, Nick Bunnin, Simon Critchley, Marian Hobson, Anthony O'Hear, and Jonathan Rée. According to its website (www.lse.ac.uk/collections/forumForEuropeanPhilosophy), the FEP, currently located at the London School of Economics, is an educational charity that organizes and runs a full and varied program of philosophy and interdisciplinary events in the UK. These include seminars, reading groups, public lectures on a range of themes and socially relevant topics, book discussions, public debates on the idea of European philosophy and an annual conference.

has changed the focus of public discourse in recent years, but feminists were also coming together in the 1970s and 1980s in organizations like the International Association of Women Philosophers.[34] And the Radical Philosophy Association[35] and the Society for Women in Philosophy[36] became important venues for philosophers who were thinking and working at the juncture of new social movements and philosophical reflection. Further input came from associations that had specialized in high-profile philosophical events and took a radical turn in this period: for instance, the Cerisy Colloquia,[37] and the critical theory meetings in Dubrovnik and later in Prague.[38]

---

34. According to its website (www.iaph.org), the International Association of Women Philosophers is a professional association that aims at counteracting the under-representation of women in philosophy everywhere. It provides a forum for interaction and cooperation among women engaged in teaching and research in all aspects of philosophy, with a particular emphasis on feminist philosophy. Founded in 1974 in Würzburg (Germany) the IAPh has gradually grown into an international organization with 380 members from thirty-five different countries.

35. The Radical Philosophy Association (www.radicalphilosophy.org) was founded in 1982. They define themselves in the following way: "RPA members struggle against capitalism, racism, sexism, homophobia, disability discrimination, environmental ruin, and all other forms of domination. We also oppose substituting new forms of authoritarianism for the ones we are now fighting. Our efforts are guided by the vision of a society founded on cooperation instead of competition, in which all areas of society are, as far as possible, governed by democratic decision-making. We believe that fundamental change requires broad social upheavals but also opposition to intellectual support for exploitative and dehumanizing social structures. Our members are from many nations and continue a variety of radical traditions including (but not limited to) feminism, phenomenology, Marxism, anarchism, post-structuralism, post-colonial theory and environmentalism."

36. The Society for Women in Philosophy (www.uh.edu/~cfreelan/SWIP) was founded in 1972. Although clearly not an organization devoted to continental feminism, it has nevertheless sponsored important debates and discussions in that area.

37. According to its website (www.ccic-cerisy.asso.fr) The International Cultural Centre of Cerisy-la-Salle was founded as far back as 1952 by the association of the Friends of Pontigny-Cerisy with the aim to support and organize exchanges among intellectuals, scholars, artists and concerned well-read individuals the world over. The centre organizes every year, from June to September, a number of important international conferences. Most of the significant French philosophers have attended events at Cerisy.

38. According to its website (http://www.iuc.hr/#), the Inter-University Centre Dubrovnik (IUC) was founded in 1971 at the height of the Cold War and became one of the most important venues for the exchange of ideas by scholars from both the East and West. The IUC is currently an independent international institution for advanced studies. It is a meeting ground for learning and scholarship and is cosponsored by some two hundred member universities and institutions of higher learning around the world. It is maintaining high standards of independent scholarship, but at the same time, it is looking for opportunities in bridge-building in a region of the world that must continue to rededicate itself to pluralism. Its agenda focuses on the social sciences and the humanities, with special emphasis on issues of postcommunism and European integration. The academic programme offers a full curriculum of open postgraduate courses, conferences and symposia, and residencies.

Thus, the practice of philosophy was enriched and innovated by this prolif-eration of new initiatives, structures and venues that ran and still run alongside the institutional academic practice of professional philosophers. The result is that two almost parallel universes emerged and contacts and cross-references between them became controlled and restricted. Our generation of philoso-phers and critical thinkers zigzagged in between these separate spheres, trying to connect them, translate from each other and recompose both an agenda and a community across their borders. We had to learn to cultivate and negotiate with complex and internally contradictory modes of multiple belonging.

IV. WHAT IS EUROPEAN ABOUT CONTINENTAL PHILOSOPHY?

The two authors stood on the opposite shores of what has become known as the great "Trans-Atlantic dis-connection."[39] The 1980–95 period saw the restruc-turing of the privileged relationship that connects the US to the French cultural and philosophical elites. The landmark date of 1989 stands as a point of reference in this context. This produced two simultaneous effects, which shaped the philo-sophical debates in the period. First, in the general American academic debate of the day, the discursive equation between "Europe" and "French theory" was challenged by broader, more Europe-wide perspectives. Second, as we argued before, French philosophy came under violent attack from the mainstream of the philosophical profession and the political Right, for being obscure, self-referential, radical, and, in any case, foreign.[40] The late 1980s in Europe was a period of political hope built on the collapse of the Berlin Wall and the rise of great – albeit short-lived – expectations about the future of the European Union. In terms of philosophy, however, the backlash against the critical theories of the 1960s and 1970s gained extra momentum and was no less strong and reductive in Europe than in the US. Considering the relatively higher degree of acceptance of interdisciplinary methods in the North American universities, however, a genuine dissemination of poststructuralist and critical theories did occur there. This took place less through philosophy than comparative literature and English departments, as well as gender, cultural and postcolonial studies. If anything, considering the growth of parallel organizations and associations, more English-speaking philosophers adopted the terminology and the philosophical agenda

---

39. That expression was coined by Domna Stanton in "Language and Revolution: The Franco-American Dis-connection," in *The Future of Difference*, Hester Eisenstein and Alice Jardine (eds) (Boston, MA: G. K. Hall, 1980). It was subsequently replaced by the idea of "travelling theories," launched by Edward Said in *Orientalism* (New York: Vintage, 1978).

40. See Jeffrey Williams (ed.), *PC Wars: Politics and Theory in the Academy* (New York: Routledge, 1994).

of poststructuralism than their European counterparts. Paradoxically enough, most of the leading French thinkers of the poststructuralist generation were awarded honorary and prestigious Chairs at leading American universities,[41] while their work was either criticized or ignored at home.[42]

The Franco-German philosophical relationship was also restructured significantly in this period. While analytic philosophers continued to make jokes about "the Nothing" – considered to be among the most preposterous of Heideggerian inheritances – some left-wing critics came to associate the difficulty and ostensible obscurantism of German and French philosophy with suspect or weak political positions.[43] Especially vehement was also the criticism and political rejection of the French philosophers on the part of the Frankfurt School and especially by Habermas, who was no less critical of the French than the analytic camp. This Franco-German hostility is also significant because at the same time Habermas's critical theory is engaging and being engaged by Rawls and other analytic political and social theorists. This movement stood in stark contrast to the politically animating force of phenomenology and poststructuralism, including its Nietzschean variants, for feminist theory and radical philosophy in the US. Representative of this anti-poststructuralist trend is also the Institute for Human Sciences,[44] based in Vienna and Boston, which acts as a significant relay-point toward Eastern Europe and strikes a distinctly conservative note both on moral issues and on the idea of Europe.

It was precisely the effort to get beyond certain entrenched identitarian ways of thinking that intellectuals on the Left, especially the feminist Left, turned to poststructuralism. Whereas a dominant trend in US left politics was to stake one's claim in identity and experience, the countertrend sought recourse to

---

41. Kristeva has been a recurring visitor at Columbia University for years; Derrida and Lyotard held positions at Irvine; and Foucault visited California regularly. Among those who never entered this transatlantic institutional connection, Irigaray and Deleuze stand out.

42. For instance, the feminism of difference was largely ignored as irrelevant in France and sent into exile, as exemplified by the difficult career of Luce Irigaray. For a detailed account of this feminist controversy, see Claire Duchen, *Feminism in France: From May '68 to Mitterrand* (London: Routledge, 1986).

43. The case of Paul de Man is emblematic of this approach, as is the "Heidegger affair," initiated by the publication of Victor Farias's *Heidegger et la nazisme* in 1987.

44. According to its own website (www.iwm.at), the Institute for Human Sciences (IWM) is an independent institute for advanced study in the humanities and social sciences, founded in 1982. Seeking to bring together academics and intellectuals from Eastern and Western Europe, the IWM is linked to its North American affiliate, the Institute for Human Sciences at Boston University, and it contributes to policy and cultural dialogue between Europe and the US and Canada. Research at the institute is currently focused on five fields: "Sources of Inequality/ Social Solidarity"; "Religion and Secularism"; "United Europe – Divided Memory"; Cultures and Institutions: Central and Eastern Europe in a Global Context"; and "The Philosophical Work of Jan Patočka."

poststructuralism to ask how identity categories are constructed, how difference is effaced, and how we might think more critically about how the field of intelligible politics is established and regulated. In this way, poststructuralism offered a way out of identitarian forms of pluralism and toward the possibility of making new political subjectivities.

This transgressive but productive aspect of poststructuralism was felt strongly in Germany, where, after reunification in 1989, new philosophical initiatives flourished. Under the influence of Foucault especially, there was a turn away from sociology and back to philosophy, based on the premise that thinking is not so much about institutions or external constraints, but about interpreting everyday life and being involved as an individual.[45] It renewed possible forms of "engagement" but in a less abstract sense. Since 1981 there has also been a rise of the so-called "Philosophical Praxis"[46] in Germany and Switzerland, which aims at overcoming academic philosophy and turning thinking into "practice" in the social, corporate, and ethical sense of the term. Very significant was also the relaunch of the East German journal *Deutsche Zeitschrift für Philosophie*, which became the most important philosophical journal in the German-speaking world, with Axel Honneth as the *primus inter pares* of the editorial board. The journals *Texte zur Kunst* and *Kunstforum International* also have considerable philosophical ambitions, mainly in the area of postmodern thought.

The shifting philosophical landscape in the aftermath of 1989 allows for the emergence of cross-European perspectives, which alter the terms of the historical Franco-American privileged relationship. Europe emerged as a contested but highly productive forum for discussions.[47] New collaborative initiatives were undertaken, often with the financial backing of the European Commission. Most notable among them are the already mentioned ARTE television, the *European Journal of Women's Studies* (1994), the *European Journal of Cultural Studies* (1998), and the journal *Lettre International*, which is as pan-European as any publication could be.[48]

---

*45. See the chapter by Dieter Thomä in this volume.

46. The leading figures of this movement are Gerd Achenbach (www.achenbach-pp.de) and Wilhelm Schmid (www.wilhelm-schmid.de). Achenbach was involved in the founding of the "Internationale Gesellschaft für philosophische Praxis" in 1982 (www.igpp.org). Schmid has been highly successful with books on the "art of living" and is a popular public lecturer.

*47. For further discussion of this issue, see the essay by Rosi Braidotti in *The History of Continental Philosophy: Volume 8*.

48. According to its website (www.lettre.de/english), *Lettre International* is an international and interdisciplinary publication that was started in France in 1984 and in Germany in 1988. It has a unique format that connects several editorial boards in Europe, rests on a transcultural worldwide network of contributors and contacts, and is published in many languages. It is a high-quality magazine that aims to promote the advancement of world consciousness by bringing together the diverse approaches of economics, politics, art, philosophy, and literature.

Emergent critique, wider worlds

RB: *On the issue of Europe, my existential and the philosophical lines of questioning converged and became almost synchronized. As I said, my first encounter by becoming a migrant was with Europe in exile, Europe in migration. And this was in some way a formative moment, where I became aware not only of the contingent nature of identity, but also the extreme complexity of something that we could call Europe subject positions. I think I became aware of my Europeanness in this moment of distance, of dis-identification, of loss, of taking my departure from the self-evidence of that location. Philosophically, as my work focused more on the project of decentering the subject and the practice of critical theory, I learned a great deal from race and postcolonial philosophical studies. The critique of Eurocentrism evolved as the counterpart of the rejection of the universalizing powers of self-reflexive reason. The self-aggrandizing gesture that positions "Europe" as a concept that mobilizes and enhances the higher human mental faculties has to be deflated, regrounded and held accountable. More specifically it has to be read alongside the devastating historical phenomena that have been central to the alleged civilizing mission of the European "mind": colonialism, racism, fascist denial of Otherness. It was clear to me that recognizing this corrupt historical legacy, while also acknowledging the great aspects and qualities of our culture, was the beginning of wisdom and also of historical lucidity. As Glissant and Balibar argue, it is also the end of a self-replicating sense of ignorance about those "others" who constitute such an integral part of European culture, including philosophy. The early awareness that so many of my favorite philosophers were foreigners, migrants, exiles, grew into the project of returning European critical theory to its specific location. Another Europe is possible, one that rejects the imperial posture and its arrogant pretensions and accepts its new historical role as a significant peripheral. So, becoming accountable for my Europeanness coincided with my becoming aware of the impossibility of being one, in the unitary sense of the term. Becoming nomadic seemed the most appropriate option for an antinationalist, antiracist, non-Eurocentric and Europe-based feminist philosopher. French philosophy remained an existential and cognitive travel companion in this trajectory.*

JB: *It seems clear that we cannot take into account our formations in European philosophy without thinking about the sense of "Europe" we were inheriting and how, politically, it becomes a certain obligation to contest and redefine Europe right now. It wasn't until I started studying philosophy at Yale that I came to understand how conflicted the question of philosophy could become. At that time, the division was between "analytic" and "continental," but that did not really explain very much about why people were so angry, why they wanted other people to lose their jobs, why they were angry enough to move to the other side of the country to get away from those with whom they disagreed. But it was then that I also became involved in other sorts of activities, including the reading of literature (which I loved) and certain political activities outside the academy. In literature classes, I could think about all kinds of dimensions of language, including address, ellipsis, metonymy – many of the important contributions of structuralism and poststructuralism. These kinds of readings were difficult and demanding, and they clearly had their own rigor as well; they very often took aim at those philosophical texts that regularly dismissed the ways in which language figured so centrally to their claims of truth. Accordingly, they were dismissed as "nonsense" by some faculty in philosophy. So I also learned quickly that one could not take that kind of analysis into a philosophy course, and I learned to divide myself for the purposes of getting through those programs. Because of my political engagements and an emerging political way of thinking about the world, I had to figure out whether the kinds of questions that were raised in those political contexts could "translate" into a philosophical idiom. And sometimes my concerns made me have to break with the idioms altogether.*

If we go back to the heartfelt question I posed in the basement of my parents home (my own version of Plato's cave) – "How do I lead a good life?" – then I would say that the question has not really changed for me, although it has taken on new dimensions that are quite important. The "I" who poses the question – how are we to think about this subject, a subject who can pose a question to itself, capable of reflexivity? And this life? What do we make of Adorno's important supplement to Socrates: how does one lead a good life in a bad life? In other words, if this life is pervaded by forms of power and domination that demean the value of life, and if only certain lives are regarded as valuable, and others not, then how do we rethink in political ways how the "goodness" of life is distributed unequally? How do I live, or how do we live in a context in which "life" itself has been brutally appropriated by reactionary forces ("pro-life") or where certain lives, such as those my government kills in war, are not considered worthy of the name of "life"? This suggests to me that there can be no pursuit of the moral question "How do I live?" without an engagement with a social and political question: what has been made of life, and how do we understand those forms of power that differentiate between lives worth living and sheltering and lives worth neglecting and destroying?

The question of the "I" who would live, or seek to live well, became a permanent problem for my academic work. It seemed that the "I" who could speak, who could query life, could only become audible and only gain standing to the extent that the speaking subject conformed to certain gender norms, and that "the speaking I" was already a profoundly complex matter – politically saturated and textually consequential. The "I" who would speak and pose its question has to be "recognized" within those norms that make the speaking subject visible and audible. But if those norms constrain who may speak by masculinizing the position of the speaking subject, for instance, then we have to be able to ask political questions about how established enunciatory positions depend on constitutive exclusions. Through what methods and means do we open up the sites of articulation to contest these hegemonic claims? In my early work on gender, I wondered whether there could be an "I" who was not already supported by established gender norms, but this meant only that new formations of subjectivity were crucial in order to disrupt disciplinary power in the domain of sexuality and gender.

V. PHILOSOPHY OUTSIDE ITS BOUNDS

Philosophical works are now varied in their form and argument, and they are part of a shifting landscape of unauthorized explorations that avoid blind loyalty to established institutional norms but also trace modes of belonging that are activated in the context of political and artistic engagement. Philosophy no longer belongs to a single site, but emerges as a mode of intervention that crosses time and space, forming global circuits of community as it goes. It is important to note, however, that these circuits of community are not based on sameness, but on persistent and animating differences. Indeed, "difference" is in some ways the rallying point for both a new and open mode of philosophizing and a form of political solidarity.

RB: *Speaking as a philosopher who defends a materialist theory of becoming, I see my task as the passionate search for alternatives in our ideas and representations of human subjectivity. I believe that philosophy and critical theory have to be something else and possibly more than the protocol of critiques and other rules of reason. Institutional philosophy gets so technical: often little more than an elaborate mechanism of interpreting and footnoting canonical texts, it reduces intellectuals to the status of guardians of the great dead white men of Western culture. I think critical theory can be much more than that. I'm a feminist, I am a philosopher, and this double allegiance makes it imperative to go on looking for new ways of thinking about the kind of subjects we have become: not for the sake of narcissistic self-glorification, but rather for the contrary reason – in order to develop adequate cartographic accounts of the sort of subjects-in-process, in transition and in mutation, that we have already become. There is no question that we are in serious trouble understanding the world we're living in. The deficit of representation is gigantic and it is not due to the fact that we are lazy and fundamentally stupid, but because advanced capitalism is moving so fast, and in such a schizoid manner, as to defy simple interpretations. It is a nonlinear, and fundamentally irrational, system. To make sense of this insanity and of its structural injustice and violence is something that is beyond the forces of one, single individual; therefore theory should be a collective endeavor aiming to draw adequate cartographies of the world we're living in. We need to compare notes on how we see these forces moving, make mappings of ideas that can be points of resistance, compare notes on these maps in a very humble, situated, and partial manner. To be aware of the power that we have as Europeans, as Americans, or Westerners, by a world plagued by the "clash of civilizations." Critical theory is about this type of accountability that lends us the courage to go beyond the established habits and the institutional conventions. We should see mental habits even when they're traditions of thought, as forms of legalized addictions that we need to grow out of. We have to cultivate the humble recognition of the collective nature of our utterances, that is to say, of how much we owe, theoretically and existentially, to others.*

JB: *My belief is that philosophy takes place any time and every time that a set of assumptions are called into question. And this is central to what we both understand as "critical" philosophy. When we go to the "root" of a problem, we exercise radicalism, which is why philosophy is only doing its job when it is radical. The exercise of critique is not a positive philosophical position, but it is a practice or, indeed, an "attitude," to cite Foucault, that asks after the means by which truth becomes established, and the terms through which truth becomes justified. If disciplinary hermeticism is one means through which a certain regime of truth gets established, then it would only be by opening up the borders that the radical vocation of philosophy might be pursued. This means affirming the necessarily interdisciplinary context for contemporary knowledge, but also maintaining a reference to the world – to life, to lives in the plural – as they are lived and as they die. We can only ask how to live the good life if we understand that that life is shared and if we have the means for translating that complex commonality of living beings (human and nonhuman). And we can only call into question entrenched modes of living and dying (such as those that are most intensely and consequentially executed in war), if we become critical of the very ways in which our knowledge is delimited in advance. This does not mean that anything and everything is permitted as knowledge, but only that we do not take institutional prohibitions as the intrinsically wise. If we ask about how disciplines are made and enforced, we pose a set of critical questions, drawing from a philosophical tradition of critique, but subjecting the institution of philosophy to such critical questions. It is in this sense that critique is the term that calls into question whether philosophy can, or ought to be, fully identified with its institutionalized forms. This suggests as well that the "underground" to philosophy, the "philosophy" that lives and thrives outside philosophy is crucial to making sure that the critical tradition of philosophy remains contemporary and alive.*

RB: *The strength of philosophy as a discipline of thought is that it has codified not only its own discursive rules of argumentative reason, but also forms of profound disagreement. Philosophy is proud of both acknowledging and even rewarding the systematic practice of theoretical disobedience and textual disrespect. Rather, this discipline encourages us to conjure up the best way to respect traditions while innovating on it, even by betraying it. Critical theory since Erasmus of Rotterdam has formulated both the rhetorical schemes and the propositional content required to sustain this balancing act. Too much of contemporary philosophy is unable to question the authority of the past and is ever so willing to comply with it. It is as if this discipline has accepted with resignation a sort of archival function, to become a mausoleum of past ideas, a contemplation of inspiration lost.*

It is crucial to combine critique with creativity, thinking with affectivity and passion, theory with active social engagement in the world we inhabit. All this is connected to the ethical impulse to really try to make a contribution in a historical time when the sense of the collective community is collapsing. I see the task of philosophy as that of being worthy of our times by accepting complexity and contradiction in a creative mode, so as to insert some positive energy into the public debate. We can do this with Spinoza and Deleuze: invigorate this passion for doing and making it into a collective enterprise. We can also do it with the feminist Emma Goldman, who famously stated that, if it did not make her want to dance, this was no revolution that she cared to be a part of. In this world in which everything is privatized and commodified, and where individualism rules supreme, we need to put the "active" back into activism. This is the sort of affirmative theory that can't be disconnected from the collective task of constructing social horizons of hope. Which I consider as fundamental enough to make me want to take a few chances – for the hell of it, that is to say, for the love of it.

CHRONOLOGY

	PHILOSOPHICAL EVENTS	CULTURAL EVENTS	POLITICAL EVENTS
1620	Bacon, *Novum organum*		
1633		Condemnation of "Galileo	
1634		Establishment of the Academie Française	
1637	Descartes, *Discourse on Method*		
1641	Descartes, *Meditations on First Philosophy*		
1642		Rembrandt, *Nightwatch*	English Civil War begins
1651	Hobbes, *Leviathan*		
1662	*Logique du Port-Royal*		
1665		Newton discovers calculus	
1667		John Milton, *Paradise Lost*	
1670	Spinoza, *Tractatus theologico-politicus*		
1675		Leibniz discovers calculus	
1677	Spinoza, *Ethics*		
1687		Newton, *Philosophiae naturalis principia mathematica*	
1689	Locke, *A Letter Concerning Toleration* (–1690) Locke, *An Essay Concerning Human Understanding* and *Two Treatises of Civil Government*		
1695		Bayle, *Dictionnaire historique et critique, vol. I*	

PHILOSOPHICAL EVENTS	CULTURAL EVENTS	POLITICAL EVENTS
1739 Hume, *A Treatise of Human Nature*		
1748 Hume, *An Enquiry Concerning Human Understanding*		
1751 Diderot and D'Alembert, *Encyclopédie, vols 1 & 2*		
1755 Rousseau, *Discours sur l'origine et les fondements de l'inégalité parmi les hommes*		
1759	Voltaire, *Candide*	
1762 Rousseau, *Du contrat social* and *Émile ou de l'éducation*		
1774	Goethe, *Sorrows of Young Werther*	
1776 Death of Hume	Adam Smith, *Wealth of Nations*	American Declaration of Independence
1781 Kant, *Kritik der reinen Vernunft*		
1783 Kant, *Prolegomena zu einer jeden künftigen Metaphysik*		
1784 Kant, "Beantwortung der Frage: Was ist Aufklärung?"		
1785 Kant, *Grundlegung zur Metaphysik der Sitten*		
1787		US Constitution
1788 Birth of Arthur Schopenhauer Kant, *Kritik der praktischen Vernunft*	Gibbon, *The Decline and Fall of the Roman Empire*	
1789 Death of d'Holbach	Adoption of *La Déclaration des droits de l'Homme et du citoyen*	French Revolution and the establishment of the First Republic
1790 Kant, *Kritik der Urteilskraft*	Edmund Burke, *Reflections on the Revolution in France*	
1791	Tom Paine, *The Rights of Man*	
1792 Mary Wollstonecraft, *Vindication of the Rights of Woman*		
1794	Creation of the École Normale Supérieure	Death of Robespierre
1795 Schiller, *Briefe über die ästhetische Erziehung des Menschen*		
1797 Schelling, *Ideen zu einer Philosophie der Natur als Einleitung in das Studium dieser Wissenschaft*	Hölderlin, *Hyperion, vol. 1*	

	PHILOSOPHICAL EVENTS	CULTURAL EVENTS	POLITICAL EVENTS
1798	Birth of Auguste Comte	Thomas Malthus, *Essay on the Principle of Population*	
1800	Fichte, *Die Bestimmung des Menschen* Schelling, *System des transcendentalen Idealismus*	Beethoven's First Symphony	
1804	Death of Kant		Napoleon Bonaparte proclaims the First Empire
1805		Publication of Diderot, *Le Neveu de Rameau*	
1806	Birth of John Stuart Mill	Goethe, *Faust, Part One* Reinstatement of the Sorbonne by Napoleon as a secular university	Napoleon brings the Holy Roman Empire to an end
1807	Hegel, *Die Phänomenologie des Geistes*		
1812	(–1816) Hegel, *Wissenschaft der Logik*		
1815		Jane Austen, *Emma*	Battle of Waterloo; final defeat of Napoleon
1817	Hegel, *Encyclopedia*	Ricardo, *Principles of Political Economy*	
1818	Birth of Karl Marx	Mary Shelley, *Frankenstein, or, The Modern Prometheus*	
1819	Schleiermacher, *Hermeneutik* Schopenhauer, *Die Welt als Wille und Vorstellung*	Byron, *Don Juan*	
1821	Hegel, *Grundlinien der Philosophie des Rechts*		Death of Napoleon
1830	(–1842) Auguste Comte, *Cours de philosophie positive* in six volumes	Stendhal, *The Red and the Black*	
1831	Death of Hegel	Victor Hugo, *The Hunchback of Notre Dame*	
1832	Death of Bentham	Clausewitz, *Vom Kriege*	
1833	Birth of Wilhelm Dilthey	Pushkin, *Eugene Onegin*	Abolition of slavery in the British Empire
1835		The first volume of Alexis de Tocqueville's *Democracy in America* is published in French	
1837		Louis Daguerre invents the daguerreotype, the first successful photographic process	
1841	Feuerbach, *Das Wesen des Christentums*		

	PHILOSOPHICAL EVENTS	CULTURAL EVENTS	POLITICAL EVENTS
1841	Kierkegaard, *On the Concept of Irony with Constant Reference to Socrates*	R. W. Emerson, *Essays: First Series*	
1842		Death of Stendhal (Marie-Henri Beyle)	
1843	Kierkegaard, *Either/Or* and *Fear and Trembling* Mill, *A System of Logic*		
1844	Marx writes *Economic-Philosophic Manuscripts*	Alexandre Dumas, *The Count of Monte Cristo*	
1846	Kierkegaard, *Concluding Unscientific Postscript*		
1847	Boole, *The Mathematical Analysis of Logic*	Helmholtz, *On the Conservation of Force*	
1848		Publication of the *Communist Manifesto*	Beginning of the French Second Republic
1851		Herman Melville, *Moby Dick* Herbert Spencer, *Social Statics* The Great Exhibition is staged at the Crystal Palace, London	
1852			Napoleon III declares the Second Empire
1853			(–1856) Crimean War
1854		H. D. Thoreau, *Walden*	
1855		Walt Whitman, *Leaves of Grass*	
1856	Birth of Sigmund Freud		
1857	Birth of Ferdinand de Saussure Death of Comte	Charles Baudelaire, *The Flowers of Evil* Gustav Flaubert, *Madame Bovary*	
1859	Birth of Henri Bergson, John Dewey, and Edmund Husserl Mill, *On Liberty*	Charles Darwin, *Origin of Species*	(–1860) Italian Unification, except Venice (1866) and Rome (1870)
1861		Johann Jakob Bachofen, *Das Mutterrecht*	Tsar Alexander II abolishes serfdom in Russia
1863	Mill, *Utilitarianism*	Édouard Manet, *Olympia*	Abraham Lincoln issues the *Emancipation Proclamation*
1865		(–1869) Leo Tolstoy, *War and Peace*	The surrender of General Robert E. Lee signals the conclusion of the American Civil War
1866		Fyodor Dostoevsky, *Crime and Punishment*	
1867	Marx, *Das Kapital, vol. I*		
1868	Birth of Émile Chartier ("Alain")	Birth of W. E. B. Du Bois	

	PHILOSOPHICAL EVENTS	CULTURAL EVENTS	POLITICAL EVENTS
1868		Creation of the École Pratique des Hautes Études (EPHE)	
1869	Mill, *The Subjection of Women*	(–1870) Jules Verne, *Twenty Thousand Leagues Under the Sea*	Completion of the Suez Canal
1870			(–1871) Franco-Prussian War Establishment of the Third Republic
1871	Lachelier, *Du fondement de l'induction*	Darwin, *The Descent of Man* Eliot, *Middlemarch*	Unification of Germany: Prussian King William I becomes emperor of Germany and Otto von Bismarck becomes Chancellor
1872	Nietzsche, *Die Geburt der Tragödie*		
1873	Death of Mill	(–1877) Tolstoy, *Anna Karenina*	End of German Occupation following France's defeat in the Franco-Prussian War
1874	Birth of Max Scheler Émile Boutroux, *La Contingence des lois de la nature* Brentano, *Psychologie vom empirischen Standpunkt*	First Impressionist Exhibition staged by the Société anonyme des peintres, sculpteurs et graveurs (Pissarro, Monet, Sisley, Degas, Renoir, Cézanne, Guillaumin and Berthe Morisot)	
1877		Henry Morton Stanley completes his navigation of the Congo River	
1878			King Leopold II of Belgium engages explorer Henry Morton Stanley to establish a colony in the Congo
1879	Frege, *Begriffsschrift*	Georg Cantor (1845–1918) becomes Professor of Mathematics at Halle Henrik Ibsen, *A Doll's House* Thomas Edison exhibits his incandescent light bulb	
1883	Birth of Karl Jaspers and José Ortega y Gasset Death of Marx Dilthey, *Einleitung in die Geisteswissenschaften* (–1885) Nietzsche, *Also Sprach Zarathustra*	Cantor, "Foundations of a General Theory of Aggregates"	
1884	Frege, *Die Grundlagen der Arithmetik*	Mark Twain, *Adventures of Huckleberry Finn*	

	PHILOSOPHICAL EVENTS	CULTURAL EVENTS	POLITICAL EVENTS
1886	Nietzsche, *Jenseits von Gut und Böse*		
1887	Nietzsche, *Zur Genealogie der Moral*		
1888	Birth of Jean Wahl		
1889	Birth of Martin Heidegger, Gabriel Marcel, and Ludwig Wittgenstein, Bergson, *Essai sur les données immédiates de la conscience*		
1890	William James, *Principles of Psychology*		
1892	Frege, "Über Sinn und Bedeutung"		
1893	Xavier Léon and Élie Halévy cofound the *Revue de métaphysique et de morale*		
1894			Captain Alfred Dreyfus (1859–1935), a Jewish-French army officer, is arrested and charged with spying for Germany
1895	Birth of Max Horkheimer	The Lumière brothers hold the first public screening of projected motion pictures; Wilhelm Conrad Röntgen discovers X-rays	
1896		Athens hosts the first Olympic Games of the modern era	
1897	Birth of Georges Bataille		
1898	Birth of Herbert Marcuse		
1899			Start of the Second Boer War
1900	Birth of Hans-Georg Gadamer; Death of Nietzsche and Félix Ravaisson; (–1901) Husserl, *Logische Untersuchungen*	Freud, *Interpretation of Dreams*; Planck formulates quantum theory	
1901	Birth of Jacques Lacan		
1903	Birth of Theodor W. Adorno and Jean Cavaillès	Du Bois, *The Souls of Black Folk*	
1904	(–1905) Weber, *Die protestantische Ethik und der Geist des Kapitalismus*		
1905	Birth of Raymond Aron and Jean-Paul Sartre	Einstein formulates the special theory of relativity	Law of separation of church and state in France

	PHILOSOPHICAL EVENTS	CULTURAL EVENTS	POLITICAL EVENTS
1906	Birth of Hannah Arendt and Emmanuel Levinas	Birth of Léopold Sédar Senghor	The Dreyfus Affair ends when the French Court of Appeals exonerates Dreyfus of all charges
1907	Birth of Jean Hyppolite Bergson, *L'Evolution créatrice*	Pablo Picasso completes *Les Demoiselles d'Avignon*	
1908	Birth of Simone de Beauvoir, Claude Lévi-Strauss, Maurice Merleau-Ponty, and W. V. O. Quine		
1911	Victor Delbos publishes the first French journal article on Husserl: "Husserl: Sa critique du psychologisme et sa conception d'une Logique pure" in *Revue de métaphysique et de morale*	The Blaue Reiter (Blue Rider) group of avant-garde artists is founded in Munich	
1913	Birth of Albert Camus, Aimé Césaire, and Paul Ricoeur Husserl, *Ideen*	Marcel Proust (1871–1922), *Swann's Way*, the first volume of *Remembrance of Things Past* First performance of Stravinsky's *Rite of Spring*	
1914			Germany invades France
1915	Birth of Roland Barthes	Franz Kafka, *Metamorphosis*	
1916	Publication of Saussure's *Cours de linguistique générale*		
1917	Death of Durkheim		Russian Revolution
1918	Birth of Louis Althusser Death of Georg Cantor and Lachelier		World War One ends
1920			Ratification of the 19th amendment to the US Constitution extends suffrage to women
1922	Wittgenstein, *Tractatus Logico-Philosophicus* Bataille begins his twenty-year career at the Bibliothèque Nationale	T. S. Eliot, *The Waste Land* Herman Hesse, *Siddhartha* James Joyce, *Ulysses*	
1924	Birth of Jean-François Lyotard Raymond Aron, Georges Canguilhem, Daniel Lagache, Paul Nizan, and Sartre enter the École Normale Supérieure	André Breton, *Le Manifeste du surréalisme* Thomas Mann, *The Magic Mountain*	Death of Vladimir Lenin
1925	Birth of Zygmunt Bauman, Gilles Deleuze, and Frantz Fanon	Franz Kafka, *The Trial* First Surrealist Exhibition at the Galerie Pierre, Paris	

343

PHILOSOPHICAL EVENTS	CULTURAL EVENTS	POLITICAL EVENTS
1926 Birth of Michel Foucault Jean Hering publishes the first French text to address Husserl's phenomenology: *Phénoménologie et philosophie religieuse*	The film *Metropolis* by German director Fritz Lang (1890–1976) premieres in Berlin The Bauhaus school building, designed by Walter Gropius (1883–1969), is completed in Dessau, Germany	
1927 Heidegger, *Sein und Zeit* Marcel, *Journal métaphysique*	Virginia Woolf, *To the Lighthouse*	
1928 Birth of Noam Chomsky The first work of German phenomenology appears in French translation: Scheler's *Nature et formes de la sympathie: Contribution à l'étude des lois de la vie émotionnelle*	Bertolt Brecht (1898–1956) writes *The Threepenny Opera* with composer Kurt Weill (1900–1950) The first television station begins broadcasting in Schenectady, New York	
1929 Heidegger, *Kant und das Problem der Metaphysik* and *Was ist Metaphysik?* Husserl, *Formale und transzendentale Logik* Wahl, *Le malheur de la conscience dans la philosophie de Hegel* Husserl lectures at the Sorbonne		
1930 Birth of Pierre Bourdieu, Jacques Derrida, Félix Guattari, Luce Irigaray, and Michel Serres Levinas, *La Théorie de l'intuition dans la phénoménologie de Husserl*	(–1942) Robert Musil, *The Man Without Qualities*	
1931 Heidegger's first works appear in French translation: "Was ist Metaphysik?" in *Bifur*, and "Vom Wesen des Grundes" in *Recherches philosophiques* Levinas and Gabrielle Peiffer publish a French translation of Husserl's *Cartesian Meditations*	Gödel publishes his two incompleteness theorems	
1932 Birth of Stuart Hall Bergson, *Les Deux sources de la morale et de la religion*	Aldous Huxley, *Brave New World* BBC starts a regular public television broadcasting service in the UK	
1933 (–1939) Alexandre Kojève lectures on Hegel at the École Pratique des Hautes Études		Hitler becomes Chancellor of Germany

	PHILOSOPHICAL EVENTS	CULTURAL EVENTS	POLITICAL EVENTS
1936	Husserl, *Krisis der europäischen Wissenschaften und die transzendentale Phänomenologie* Sartre, "La Transcendance de l'égo" in *Recherches philosophiques*	Benjamin, "The Work of Art in the Age of Mechanical Reproduction"	
1937	Birth of Alain Badiou, Hélène Cixous, Françoise Laruelle	Picasso, *Guernica*	
1938	Death of Husserl	Sartre, *La Nausée*	
1939	Establishment of Husserl Archives in Louvain, Belgium (–1941) Hyppolite publishes his translation into French of Hegel's *Phenomenology of Spirit*	Joyce, *Finnegans Wake*	Nazi Germany invades Poland (September 1) and France and Britain declare war on Germany (September 3)
1940	Birth of Jaen-Luc Nancy and Jacques Rancière	Richard Wright, *Native Son*	
1941	Death of Bergson	Arthur Koestler, *Darkness at Noon*	Japan attacks Pearl Harbor, and US enters the Second World War
1942	Birth of Étienne Balibar Camus, *L'Étranger* and *Le Mythe de Sisyphe: Essai sur l'absurde* Merleau-Ponty, *La Structure du comportement* Lévi-Strauss meets Roman Jakobson at the École Libre des Hautes Études in New York		
1943	Death of Simone Weil Sartre, *L'Être et le néant*		
1944		Jorge Luis Borges, *Ficciones*	Bretton Woods Conference and establishment of the International Monetary Fund (IMF) Paris is liberated by Allied forces (August 25)
1945	Merleau-Ponty, *Phénoménologie de la perception*	George Orwell, *Animal Farm* Sartre, Beauvoir, and Merleau-Ponty begin as founding editors of *Les Temps modernes*	Atom bombs dropped on Hiroshima and Nagasaki Establishment of the United Nations
1946	Birth of Jean-Luc Marion Hyppolite, *Genèse et structure de la "Phénoménologie de l'esprit" de Hegel* Sartre, *L'Existentialisme est un humanisme*	Bataille founds the journal *Critique*	Beginning of the French Indochina War Establishment of the Fourth Republic

	PHILOSOPHICAL EVENTS	CULTURAL EVENTS	POLITICAL EVENTS
1947	Adorno and Horkheimer, *Dialektik der Aufklärung*	Camus, *The Plague*	(–1951) Marshall Plan
1947	Beauvoir, *Pour une morale de l'ambiguïté* Heidegger, "Brief über den Humanismus"	Thomas Mann, *Doctor Faustus*	Creation of General Agreement on Tariffs and Trade (GATT)
1948	(–1951) Gramsci, *Prison Notebooks* Althusser appointed *agrégé-répétiteur* ("caïman") at the École Normale Supérieure, a position he holds until 1980	Debut of *The Ed Sullivan Show*	
1949	Beauvoir, *Le Deuxième sexe* Lévi-Strauss, *Les Structures élémentaires de la parenté*	Cornelius Castoriadis and Claude Lefort found the revolutionary group and journal *Socialisme ou Barbarie*	Foundation of NATO
1950	Ricoeur publishes his translation into French of Husserl's *Ideas I*		Beginning of the Korean War
1951	Death of Alain and Wittgenstein Arendt, *The Origins of Totalitarianism* Quine, "Two Dogmas of Empiricism"	Marguerite Yourcenar, *Memoirs of Hadrian*	
1952	Birth of Bernard Stiegler Death of Dewey and Santayana Merleau-Ponty is elected to the Chair in Philosophy at the Collège de France	Samuel Beckett, *Waiting for Godot* Ralph Ellison, *Invisible Man*	
1953	Wittgenstein, *Philosophical Investigations* (posthumous) Lacan begins his public seminars	Lacan, together with Daniel Lagache and Françoise Dolto, founds the Société française de psychanalyse Crick and Watson construct the first model of DNA	Death of Joseph Stalin Ceasefire agreement (July 27) ends the Korean War
1954	Lyotard, *La Phénoménologie*		Following the fall of Dien Bien Phu (May 7), France pledges to withdraw from Indochina (July 20) Beginning of the Algerian revolt against French rule
1955	Marcuse, *Eros and Civilization* Cerisy Colloquium *Qu'est-ce que la philosophie? Autour de Martin Heidegger*, organized by Jean Beaufret	Vladimir Nabokov, *Lolita*	

	PHILOSOPHICAL EVENTS	CULTURAL EVENTS	POLITICAL EVENTS
1956			Hungarian Revolution and Soviet invasion
			The French colonies of Morocco and Tunisia gain independence
1957	Chomsky, *Syntactic Structures*	Jack Kerouac, *On the Road*	Rome Treaty signed by France, Germany, Belgium, Italy, the Netherlands, and Luxembourg establishes the European Economic Community
		Camus receives the Nobel Prize for Literature	
			The Soviet Union launches *Sputnik 1*, the first man-made object to orbit the Earth
1958	Lévi-Strauss, *Anthropologie structurale*	Chinua Achebe, *Things Fall Apart*	Charles de Gaulle is elected president after a new constitution establishes the Fifth Republic
		William S. Burroughs, *Naked Lunch*	
		(–1960) The first feature films by directors associated with the French "New Wave" cinema, including, in 1959, *Les Quatre Cent Coups* (*The 400 Blows*) by François Truffaut (1932–84) and, in 1960, *A bout de souffle* (*Breathless*) by Jean-Luc Godard (1930–)	
		The Sorbonne's "Faculté des Lettres" is officially renamed the "Faculté des Lettres et Sciences Humaines"	
1959	Birth of Catherine Malabou	Günter Grass, *The Tin Drum*	
	Lévi-Strauss is elected to the Chair in Social Anthropology at the Collège de France	Gillo Pentecorvo, *The Battle of Algiers*	
1960	Death of Camus	First issue of the journal *Tel Quel* is published	
	Gadamer, *Wahrheit und Methode*	The birth control pill is made available to married women	
	Sartre, *Critique de la raison dialectique*		
1961	Death of Fanon and Merleau-Ponty	Joseph Heller, *Catch 22*	Erection of the Berlin Wall
	Fanon, *Les Damnés de la terre*, with a preface by Sartre		Bay of Pigs failed invasion of Cuba
	Foucault, *Histoire de la folie à l'âge classique*		
	Heidegger, *Nietzsche*		
	Levinas, *Totalité et infini: Essai sur l'extériorite*		

PHILOSOPHICAL EVENTS	CULTURAL EVENTS	POLITICAL EVENTS
1962 Deleuze, *Nietzsche et la philosophie* Lévi-Strauss, *La Pensée sauvage* Thomas Kuhn, *The Structure of Scientific Revolutions*	Rachel Carson, *Silent Spring* Ken Kesey, *One Flew Over the Cuckoo's Nest*	France grants independence to Algeria Cuban Missile Crisis
1962 First meeting of SPEP at Northwestern University		
1963 Arendt, *Eichmann in Jerusalem*	Betty Friedan, *The Feminine Mystique* The first artificial heart is implanted	Assassination of John F. Kennedy Imprisonment of Nelson Mandela
1964 Barthes, *Eléments de sémiologie* Marcuse, *One-Dimensional Man* Merleau-Ponty, *Le Visible et l'invisible* (posthumous)	Lacan founds L'École Freudienne de Paris The Beatles appear on *The Ed Sullivan Show*	Gulf of Tonkin Incident US Civil Rights Act outlaws discrimination on the basis of race, color, religion, sex, or national origin
1965 Death of Buber Althusser, *Pour Marx*	Truman Capote, *In Cold Blood*	Assassination of Malcolm X
1966 Adorno, *Negative Dialektik* Deleuze, *Le Bergsonisme* Foucault, *Les Mots et les choses: Une archéologie des sciences humaines* Lacan, *Écrits*	Alain Resnais, *Hiroshima Mon Amour* Jacques-Alain Miller founds *Cahiers pour l'analyse* Johns Hopkins Symposium "The Languages of Criticism and the Sciences of Man" introduces French theory to the American academic community *Star Trek* premieres on US television	Foundation of the Black Panther Party for Self-Defense by Huey P. Newton and Bobby Seale (–1976) Chinese Cultural Revolution
1967 Derrida, *De la grammatologie, La Voix et le phénomène,* and *L'Écriture et la différence*	Gabriel Garcia Marquez, *One Hundred Years of Solitude*	Confirmation of Thurgood Marshall to the US Supreme Court
1968 Deleuze, *Différence et répétition, Spinoza et le problème de l'expression* Habermas, *Erkenntnis und Interesse*	The Beatles release the White Album Stanley Kubrick, *2001: A Space Odyssey*	Events of May '68, including closure of the University of Nanterre (May 2), police invasion of the Sorbonne (May 3), student demonstrations and strikes, and workers' occupation of factories and general strike Prague Spring Assassination of Martin Luther King Tet Offensive
1969 Death of Jaspers and Adorno	Woodstock Music and Art Fair	Stonewall riots launch the Gay Liberation Movement

348

	PHILOSOPHICAL EVENTS	CULTURAL EVENTS	POLITICAL EVENTS
1969	Death of Jaspers and Adorno Deleuze, *Logique du sens* Paulo Freire, *Pedagogy of the Oppressed*	Woodstock Music and Art Fair Neil Armstrong is the first person to set foot on the moon	Stonewall riots launch the Gay Liberation Movement
1970	Death of Carnap Adorno, *Ästhetische Theorie* Foucault elected to the Chair of the History of Systems of Thought at the Collège de France	Millett, *Sexual Politics* First Earth Day	Salvador Allende becomes the first Marxist head of state to be freely elected in a Western nation Shootings at Kent State University
1971	Lyotard, *Discours, figure*	Reorganization of the University of Paris	End of the gold standard for US dollar
1972	Bourdieu, *Esquisse d'une théorie de la pratique* Deleuze and Guattari, *Capitalisme et schizophrénie. 1. L'Anti-Oedipe* Derrida, *La Dissémination, Marges de la philosophie*, and *Positions* Colloquium on Nietzsche at Cerisy		Watergate break-in President Richard Nixon visits China, beginning the normalization of relations between the US and PRC
1973	Death of Horkheimer Lacan publishes the first volume of his *Séminaire*	Thomas Pynchon, *Gravity's Rainbow* (–1978) Aleksandr Solzhenitsyn, *The Gulag Archipelago* Roe *v.* Wade legalizes abortion	Chilean military coup ousts and kills President Salvador Allende
1974	Irigaray, *Speculum: De l'autre femme* Kristeva, *La Révolution du langage poétique*	Creation of the first doctoral program in women's studies in Europe, the Centre de Recherches en Études Féminines, at the University of Paris VIII–Vincennes, directed by Hélène Cixous	Resignation of Nixon
1975	Death of Arendt Foucault, *Surveiller et punir: Naissance de la prison* Irigaray, *Ce sexe qui n'en est pas un* Foundation of GREPH, the Groupe de Recherches sur l'Enseignement Philosophique	The Sixth Section of the EPHE is renamed the École des Hautes Études en Sciences Sociales	Death of Francisco Franco Andrei Sakharov wins Nobel Peace Prize Fall of Saigon, ending the Vietnam War First US–USSR joint space mission
1976	Death of Bultmann and Heidegger Foucault, *Histoire de la sexualité. 1. La Volonté de savoir*	Bertolucci, *1900*	Death of Mao Zedong Uprising in Soweto

PHILOSOPHICAL EVENTS	CULTURAL EVENTS	POLITICAL EVENTS
1976 Barthes is elected to the Chair of Literary Semiology at the Collège de France		
1977 Death of Ernst Bloch	240 Czech intellectuals sign Charter 77 The Centre Georges Pompidou, designed by architects Renzo Piano (1937–) and Richard Rogers (1933–), opens in Paris	Egyptian president Anwar al-Sadat becomes the first Arab head of state to visit Israel
1978 Death of Kurt Gödel Arendt, *Life of the Mind* Derrida, *La Vérité en peinture*	Edward Said, *Orientalism* Birmingham School: Centre for Contemporary Culture releases *Policing the Crisis* Louise Brown becomes the first test-tube baby	Camp David Accords
1979 Death of Marcuse Bourdieu, *La Distinction: Critique sociale du jugement* Lyotard, *La Condition postmoderne: Rapport sur le savoir* Prigogine and Stengers, *La Nouvelle alliance* Rorty, *Philosophy and the Mirror of Nature*	Edgar Morin, *La Vie de La Vie* Francis Ford Coppola, *Apocalypse Now* Monty Python, *Life of Brian* The first cognitive sciences department is established at MIT Jerry Falwell founds Moral Majority	Iranian Revolution Iran Hostage Crisis begins Margaret Thatcher becomes British Prime Minister (first woman to be a European head of state) Nicaraguan Revolution
1980 Death of Barthes and Sartre Deleuze and Guattari, *Capitalisme et schizophrénie. 2. Mille plateaux*	Lacan officially dissolves the École Freudienne de Paris Murder of John Lennon Cable News Network (CNN) becomes the first television station to provide twenty-four-hour news coverage	Death of Yugoslav president Josip Broz Tito Election of Ronald Reagan Solidarity movement begins in Poland
1981 Death of Lacan Habermas, *Theorie des kommunikativen Handelns* Bourdieu is elected to the Chair in Sociology at the Collège de France	The first cases of AIDS are discovered among gay men in the US Debut of MTV Madonna's first album becomes the highest selling recording by a female artist in UK singles-chart history	Release of American hostages in Iran François Mitterrand is elected as the first socialist president of France's Fifth Republic
1982 Badiou, *Théorie du sujet* Marion, *Dieu sans l'être* Foundation of the Collège International de Philosophie by François Châtelet, Jacques Derrida, Jean-Pierre Faye, and Dominique Lecourt	Michael Jackson releases *Thriller*, the world's best-selling album Debut of the Weather Channel	Falklands War

	PHILOSOPHICAL EVENTS	CULTURAL EVENTS	POLITICAL EVENTS
1983	Death of Aron Lyotard, *Le Différend* Sloterdijk, *Kritik der zynischen Vernunft*	Alice Walker, *The Color Purple*	
1984	Death of Foucault Lloyd, *The Man of Reason*	Marguerite Duras, *The Lover* William Gibson, *Neuromancer*	Year-long strike of the National Union of Mineworkers in the UK Assassination of Indira Gandhi
1985	Habermas, *Der philosophische Diskurs der Moderne* First complete translation into French of Heidegger's *Sein und Zeit*	Don Delillo, *White Noise* Donna Haraway, *Cyborg Manifesto*	Mikhail Gorbachev is named General Secretary of the Communist Party of the Soviet Union
1986	Death of Beauvoir Establishment of the Archives Husserl de Paris at the École Normale Supérieure	Art Spiegelman, *Maus I: A Survivor's Tale* The Oprah Winfrey Show debuts	Chernobyl nuclear accident in USSR Election of Corazon Aquino ends Marcos regime in Philippines
1987	David Held, *Models of Democracy* Gayatri Spivak, *In Other Worlds*	Toni Morrison, *Beloved* Discovery of Paul de Man's wartime journalism damages the popularity of deconstruction in America	In June Gorbachev inaugurates the perestroika (restructuring) that led to the end of the USSR The First Intifada begins in the Gaza Strip and West Bank
1988	Badiou, *L'Être et l'événement*	Salman Rushdie, *The Satanic Verses*	Benazir Bhutto becomes the first woman to head an Islamic nation Pan Am Flight 103, en route from London to New York, is destroyed by a bomb over Lockerbie, Scotland
1989	Heidegger, *Beiträge zur Philosophie (Vom Ereignis)* Marion, *Réduction et donation* Žižek, *The Sublime Object of Ideology*	*Exxon Valdez* oil spill in Alaska Tim Berners-Lee submits a proposal for an information management system, later called the World Wide Web	Fall of the Berlin Wall Students protest in Tiananmen Square, Beijing
1990	Death of Althusser Butler, *Gender Trouble* Glissant, *Poétique de la relation*	The World Health Organization removes homosexuality from its list of diseases Beginning of the Human Genome Project, headed by James D. Watson	Nelson Mandela is released from prison Reunification of Germany Break-up of the former Yugoslavia and beginning of the Yugoslav Wars Lech Walesa is elected president of Poland
1991	Deleuze and Guattari, *Qu'est-ce que la philosophie?* Laruelle, *En tant qu'un*	Fredric Jameson, *Postmodernism, or, The Cultural Logic of Late Capitalism*	First Gulf War

	PHILOSOPHICAL EVENTS	CULTURAL EVENTS	POLITICAL EVENTS
1991		The World Wide Web becomes the first publicly available service on the internet	
1992	Death of Guattari Guattari, *Chaosmose*	Rebecca Walker, *Third Wave Feminism*	Maastricht Treaty is signed, creating the European Union Dissolution of the Soviet Union
1993	Gilroy, *Black Atlantic* Nancy, *Le Sens du monde*		Dissolution of Czechoslovakia; Vaclav Havel is named the first president of the Czech Republic
1994	Death of Karl Popper Braidotti, *Nomadic Subjects* Grosz, *Volatile Bodies* Lingis, *The Community of Those Who Have Nothing in Common* Stiegler, *La technique et le temps I.* Publication of Foucault's *Dits et écrits*	The Channel Tunnel opens, connecting England and France	Genocide in Rwanda End of apartheid in South Africa; Nelson Mandela is sworn in as president North American Free Trade Agreement (NAFTA), signed in 1992, goes into effect
1995	Death of Deleuze		End of Bosnian War World Trade Organization (WTO) comes into being, replacing GATT
1996	Gatens, *Imaginary Bodies* Laruelle, *Principes de la non-philosophie* Nancy, *Être singulier pluriel*	Cloning of Dolly the sheep (died 2003)	Death of Mitterrand
1997	Marion, *Étant donné: essai d'une phénoménologie de la donation*	Vandana Shiva, *BioPiracy*	
1998	Death of Lyotard		
1999	Badiou leaves Vincennes to become Professor and Head of the Philosophy Department at the École Normale Supérieure		Introduction of the Euro Antiglobalization forces disrupt the WTO meeting in Seattle
2000	Death of Quine Negri and Hardt, *Empire* Rancière, *La Partage du sensible: esthétique et politique*		The Second Intifada
2001	Balibar, *Nous, citoyens d'Europe? Les Frontières, l'État, le peuple*		Terrorist attack destroys the World Trade Center
2002	Death of Bourdieu and Gadamer		

	PHILOSOPHICAL EVENTS	CULTURAL EVENTS	POLITICAL EVENTS
2003	Death of Davidson	Completion of the Human Genome Project	Beginning of conflict in Darfur
2004	Death of Derrida and Leopoldo Zea Malabou, *Que faire de notre cerveau?*	Asian tsunami	Madrid train bombings
2005	Death of Ricoeur	Hurricane Katrina	Start of the Second Gulf War Bombings of the London public transport system
2006	Badiou, *Logiques des mondes. L'Être et l'événement, 2.* Quentin Meillassoux, *Après la finitude. Essai sur la nécessité de la contingence*		Bombings of the Mumbai train system
2007	Death of Jean Baudrillard and Rorty		
2008	Publication of first of Derrida's Seminars: *La Bête et le souverain*	Death of Robbe-Grillet, Aimé Césaire, and Aleksandr Solzhenitsyn	Election of Barack Obama, the first African American president of the US International banking collapse
2009	Death of Lévi-Strauss, Leszek Kolakowski, Marjorie Grene	Death of Frank McCourt and John Updike	
2010	Death of Pierre Hadot and Claude Lefort	Death of Tony Judt and J. D. Salinger Mario Vargas Llosa wins Noble Prize in Literature	Arab Spring uprisings begin in Tunisia BP oil spill in Gulf of Mexico
2011	Death of Michael Dummett and Elizabeth Young-Bruehl SPEP celebrates 50th anniversary	Death of Friedrich Kittler and Christa Wolf	Death of Václav Havel US special forces kill Osama Bin Laden Capture and assassination of Muammar Gaddafi Occupy movement
2012		Death of Eric Hobsbawm and Adrienne Rich	

BIBLIOGRAPHY

Major works of some philosophers are collected at the end of the relevant essay in the text.

Abel, Günter. *Interpretationswelten*. Frankfurt: Suhrkamp, 1993.

Abel, Günter. *Nietzsche: Die Dynamik der Willen zur Macht und die ewige Wiederkehr*. Berlin: De Gruyter, 1984.

Adorno, Theodor. *Metaphysics: Concepts and Problems*. Edited by Rolf Tiedemann. Translated by Edmund Jephcott. Cambridge: Polity, 2000.

Agamben, Giorgio. *Homo sacer: Il potere sovrano e la nuda vita*. Turin: Einaudi, 1998. Published in English as *Homo Sacer: Sovereign Power and Bare Life*, translated by Daniel Heller-Roazen. Stanford, CA: Stanford University Press, 1998.

Agamben, Giorgio. *Potentialities: Collected Essays in Philosophy*. Edited and translated by Daniel Heller-Roazen. Stanford, CA: Stanford University Press, 1999.

Alcoff, Linda M. "Cultural Feminism versus Post-Structuralism: The Identity Crisis in Feminist Theory." *Signs: Journal of Women in Culture and Society* 13(3) (1988): 405–36.

Alcoff, Linda M. "Philosophy Matters: A Review of Recent Work in Feminist Philosophy." *Signs: Journal of Women in Culture and Society* 25(3) (2000): 841–82.

Alcoff, Linda M. *Visible Identities: Race, Gender, and the Self*. Oxford: Oxford University Press, 2006.

Alcoff, Linda M., and Elizabeth Potter, eds. *Feminist Epistemologies*. New York: Routledge, 1993.

Allen, Amy. *The Politics of Our Selves: Power, Autonomy, and Gender in Contemporary Critical Theory*. New York: Columbia University Press, 2008.

Althusser, Louis. "Ideology and Ideological State Apparatuses." In *Lenin and Philosophy and Other Essays*, translated by Ben Brewster, 127–86. London: New Left Books, 1971. Published in French as "Idéologies et appareils idéologiques d'État," in *Positions*, 67–125. Paris: François Maspéro, 1976.

Althusser, Louis, and Étienne Balibar. *Essays in Self-Criticism*. Translated by Grahame Lock. New York: New Left Books, 1976.

Althusser, Louis, and Étienne Balibar. *Reading Capital*. Translated by Ben Brewster. New York: Pantheon, 1970.

Amorós, Celia. *Feminismo: Igualdad y Differencia*. Mexico City: Universidad Nacional Autonoma de Mexico, 1994.

Amorós, Celia. *Hacia una crítica de la razón patriarchal.* Barcelona: Anthropos, 1985.

Anderson, Benedict. *Imagined Communities.* London: Verso, 1983.

Anderson, Joel. "The 'Third Generation' of the Frankfurt School." *Intellectual History Newsletter* 22 (2000). Available online at: www.phil.uu.nl/~joel/research/publications/3rdGeneration.htm (accessed May 2010).

Appadurai, Arjun. *Modernity at Large: Cultural Dimensions of Globalization.* Minneapolis, MN: University of Minnesota Press, 1996.

Arden McHugh, Nancy, ed. *Feminist Philosophies A–Z.* Edinburgh: Edinburgh University Press, 2007.

Arendt, Hannah. *The Origins of Totalitarianism.* London: Harcourt Brace, 1973.

Atkinson, Ti-Grace. *Amazon Odyssey.* New York: Link Books, 1974.

Austin, J. L. *How to Do Things with Words.* Cambridge, MA: Harvard University Press, 1975.

Bachelard, Gaston. *Le Rationalisme appliqué.* Paris: Presses Universitaires de France, 1949.

Badiou, Alain. *Being and Event.* Translated by Oliver Feltham. London: Continuum, 2005. Originally published as *L'Être et l'événement.* Paris: Éditions du Seuil, 1988.

Badiou, Alain. *Ethics.* Translated by Peter Hallward. London: Verso, 2001.

Badiou, Alain. *Logics of Worlds: Being and Event, Volume 2.* Translated by Alberto Toscano. London: Continuum, 2008. Originally published as *Logiques des mondes: L'Être et l'événement, 2.* Paris: Éditions du Seuil, 2006.

Badiou, Alain. "Marque et manque: À propos du zéro." *Cahiers pour l'analyse* 10 (1969): 150–73.

Badiou, Alain. *Theory of the Subject.* Translated by Bruno Bosteels. London: Continuum, 2009. Originally published as *Théorie du sujet.* Paris: Éditions du Seuil, 1982.

Bair, Deirdre. *Simone de Beauvoir: A Biography.* New York: Summit Books, 1990.

Balibar, Étienne. *Écrits pour Althusser.* Paris: La Découverte, 1991.

Balibar, Étienne. *Lieux et noms de la vérité.* La Tour-d'Aigues: Édition de l'Aube, 1994.

Balibar, Étienne. "Structuralism: A Destitution of the Subject." *Differences: A Journal of Feminist Cultural Studies* 14(1) (Spring 2003): 1–21.

Balsamo, Anne. *Technologies of the Gendered Body: Reading Cyborg Women.* Durham, NC: Duke University Press, 1996.

Barad, Karen. *Meeting the Universe Half Way.* Durham, NC: Duke University Press, 2007.

Barbaras, Renaud. *Le Désir et la distance.* Paris: Vrin, 1998.

Barbaras, Renaud. *Le Mouvement de l´existence.* Paris: Éditions de la transparence, 2007.

Barrotta, Luigi. "Contemporary Philosophy of Science in Italy: An Overview." *Journal for General Philosophy of Science* 29 (1998): 327–45.

Bartlett, Katharina T., and Rosanne Kennedy, eds. *Feminist Legal Theory: Readings in Law and Gender.* Boulder, CO: Westview Press, 1991.

Battersby, Christine. *The Phenomenal Woman: Feminist Metaphysics and the Patterns of Identity.* Cambridge: Polity, 1998.

Baudrillard, Jean. *The Consumer Society: Myths and Structures.* Translated by Chris Turner. London: Sage, 1998.

Baudrillard, Jean. *The Gulf War Did Not Take Place.* Translated by Paul Patton. Bloomington, IN: Indiana University Press, 1995.

Baudrillard, Jean. *The Mirror of Production.* Translated by Mark Poster. St. Louis, MO: Telos, 1975.

Baudrillard, Jean. *The Perfect Crime.* Translated by Chris Turner. London: Verso, 1996.

Baudrillard, Jean. *Seduction.* Translated by Brian Singer. London: Macmillan, 1990.

Baudrillard, Jean. *Simulacra and Simulations.* Translated by Sheila Faria Glaser. Ann Arbor, MI: University of Michigan Press, 1991. Originally published as *Simulacre et simulation.* Paris: Éditions Galilée, 1985.

Baudrillard, Jean. *Simulations*. Translated by Paul Foss, Paul Patton, and Philip Beitchman. New York: Semiotext(e), 1983.

Bausola, Adriano, Giuseppe Bedeschi, Mario Dal Pra, Eugenio Garin, Marcello Pera, and Valerio Verra, eds. *La filosofia italiana dal dopoguerra a oggi*. Rome-Bari: Laterza, 1985.

Bělohradský, Václav. *Přirozený svět jako politický problém* [The natural world as a political problem]. Prague: Československý spisovatel, 1991.

Benhabib, Seyla. "Sexual Difference and Collective Identities: The New Global Constellation," *Signs: Journal of Women in Culture and Society* 24(2) (1999): 353–61.

Benjamin, Jessica. *The Bonds of Love*. New York: Pantheon, 1988.

Bennington, Geoffrey, and Jacques Derrida. "*Circumfession.*" In *Jacques Derrida*, translated by Geoffrey Bennington, 3–315. Chicago, IL: University of Chicago Press, 1993.

Benso, Silvia. "On Luigi Pareyson: A Master of Italian Hermeneutics." *Philosophy Today* 49(4–5) (2005): 381–90.

Benso, Silvia, and Brian Schroeder, eds. *Contemporary Italian Philosophy: Crossing the Borders of Ethics, Politics, and Religion*. Albany, NY: SUNY Press, 2007.

Bernasconi, Robert. "Deconstruction and the Possibility of Ethics." In *Deconstruction and Philosophy*, edited by John Sallis, 122–39. Chicago, IL: University of Chicago Press, 1987.

Berti, Enrico. *Analitica e dialettica nel pensiero antico*. Naples: Edizioni Scientifiche Italiane, 1989.

Berti, Enrico. *Contraddizione e dialettica negli antichi e nei moderni*. Palermo: L'Epos, 1987.

Berti, Enrico. *Soggetti di responsabilità: Questioni di filosofia pratica*. Reggio Emilia: Diabasis, 1993.

Bhabha, Homi K. "'Foreword' to Frantz Fanon." In *The Wretched of the Earth*, translated by Richard Philcox, vii–xli. New York: Grove Press, 2004.

Bhabha, Homi K. *The Location of Culture*. New York: Routledge, 1994.

Bhabha, Homi K., ed. *Nation and Narration*. New York: Routledge, 1990.

Bieri, Peter. ed. *Analytische Philosophie der Erkenntnis*. Frankfurt: Athenäum, 1987.

Bieri, Peter. ed. *Analytische Philosophie des Geistes*. Königstein: Hain, 1981.

Bieri, Peter. *Das Handwerk der Freiheit: Über die Entdeckung des eigenen Willens*. Munich: Hanser, 2001.

Bieri, Peter. "Was bleibt von der analytischen Philosophie?" *Deutsche Zeitschrift für Philosophie* 55 (2007): 333–44.

Blanchot, Maurice. *The Blanchot Reader*. Edited by Michael Holland. Oxford: Blackwell, 1995.

Blanchot, Maurice. *The Writing of the Disaster*. Translated by Ann Smock. Lincoln, NE: University of Nebraska Press, 1986.

Blumenberg, Hans. *Lebenszeit und Weltzeit*. Frankfurt: Suhrkamp, 1986.

Blumenberg, Hans. *The Legitimacy of the Modern Age*. Translated by Robert M. Wallace. Cambridge, MA: MIT Press, 1983.

Blumenberg, Hans. *Paradigmen zu einer Metaphorologie*. Frankfurt: Suhrkamp, 1998.

Blumenberg, Hans. *Wirklichkeiten, in denen wir leben*. Stuttgart: Reclam, 1981.

Bodei, Remo. *Le forme del bello*. Bologna: Il Mulino, 1995.

Bodei, Remo. *Geometria delle passioni: Paura, speranza e felicità: filosofia e uso politico*. Milan: Feltrinelli, 1991.

Bodei, Remo. *Logics of Delusion*. Translated by Giacomo Donis. Aurora, CO: The Davies Group Publishers, 2007. Originally published as *Le logiche del delirion: Ragione, affetti, follia*. Rome-Bari: Laterza, 2002.

Bodei, Remo. *Multiversum: Tempo e storia in Ernst Bloch*. Naples: Bibliopolis, 1979.

Bodei, Remo. *Ordo amoris: Conflitti terreni e felicità celeste*. Bologna: Il Mulino, 1991.

Bodei, Remo. *Scomposizioni: Forme dell'individuo moderno*. Turin: Einaudi, 1987.

Bodei, Remo. *Sistema ed epoca in Hegel*. Bologna: Il Mulino, 1975.

Bodei, Remo. *We, the Divided: Ethos, Politics and Culture in Post-War Italy, 1943–2006*. Translated by Jeremy Parzen and Aaron Thomas. New York: Agincourt Press, 2006. Originally published as *Il noi diviso: Ethos e idee dell'Italia repubblicana*. Turin: Einaudi, 1988.

Boehm, Ulrich, ed. *Philosophie heute*. Frankfurt: Campus, 1997.

Bohrer, Karl Heinz. *Ästhetische Negativität*. Munich: Hanser, 2002.

Bohrer, Karl Heinz. *Suddenness: On the Moment of Aesthetic Appearance*. Translated by Ruth Crowley. New York: Columbia University Press, 1994.

Borges, Jorge Luis. "On Exactitude in Science." In *Collected Fictions*, translated by Andrew Hurley. Harmondsworth: Penguin, 1998.

Borradori, Giovanna. *Philosophy in a Time of Terror: Dialogues with Jürgen Habermas and Jacques Derrida*. Chicago, IL: University of Chicago Press, 2003.

Borradori, Giovanna, ed. *Recoding Metaphysics: The New Italian Philosophy*. Evanston, IL: Northwestern University Press, 1988.

Bosteels, Bruno. "Alain Badiou's Theory of the Subject: Part I. The Recommencement of Dialectical Materialism." *Pli* 12 (2001): 200–29.

Bourdieu, Pierre. *Language and Symbolic Power*. Cambridge, MA: Harvard University Press, 1991.

Bové, Paul A., ed. *Edward Said and the Work of the Critic: Speaking Truth to Power*. Durham, NC: Duke University Press, 2000.

Braidotti, Rosi. "A Critical Cartography of Feminist Post-postmodernism." *Australian Feminist Studies* 20(47) (2005): 169–80.

Braidotti, Rosi. *Metamorphoses: Towards a Materialist Theory of Becoming*. Cambridge: Polity, 2002.

Braidotti, Rosi. *Patterns of Dissonance: A Study of Women in Contemporary Philosophy*. Cambridge: Polity, 1991.

Braidotti, Rosi. "Sexual Difference Theory." In *A Companion to Feminist Philosophy*, edited by Alison M. Jaggar and Iris M. Young, 128–36. Oxford: Blackwell, 1998.

Braidotti, Rosi. "In Spite of the Times: The Postsecular Turn in Feminism." *Theory, Culture & Society* 25 (2008): 1–24.

Braidotti, Rosi. *Transpositions: On Nomadic Ethics*. Cambridge: Polity, 2006.

Braidotti, Rosi. "The Uses and Abuses of the Sex/Gender Distinction in European Feminist Practices." In *Thinking Differently: A Reader in European Women's Studies*, edited by Gabriele Griffin and Rosi Braidotti, 285–310. London: Zed Books, 2002.

Braidotti, Rosi. "The Way We Were: Some Post-Structuralist Memoirs." *Women's Studies International Forum* 23(6) (November–December 2000): 715–28.

Braidotti, Rosi, and Jane Weinstock. "Herstory as Recourse." *Hecate* 2 (1980): 25–8.

Brandom, Robert. *Making it Explicit*. Cambridge, MA: Harvard University Press, 1994.

Brandom, Robert. *Rorty and his Critics*. Oxford: Blackwell, 2000.

Brennan, Teresa. *History after Lacan*. New York: Routledge, 1993.

Buchanan, Ian, and Claire Colebrook, eds. *Deleuze and Feminist Theory*. Edinburgh: Edinburgh University Press, 2000.

Burke, Carolyn L., Naomi Schor, and Margaret Whitford, eds. *Engaging with Irigaray: Feminist Philosophy and Modern European Thought*. New York: Columbia University Press, 1994.

Butler, Judith. *Antigone's Claim: Kinship between Life and Death*. New York: Columbia University Press, 2000.

Butler, Judith. *Bodies that Matter: On the Discursive Limits of "Sex."* New York: Routledge, 1993.

Butler, Judith. *Excitable Speech: A Politics of the Performative*. New York: Routledge, 1997.

Butler, Judith. *Giving an Account of Oneself*. New York: Fordham University Press, 2008.

Butler, Judith. *Precarious Life: The Power of Mourning and Violence*. London: Verso, 2004.

Butler, Judith. *The Psychic Life of Power: Theories in Subjection*. Stanford, CA: Stanford University Press, 1997.

Butler, Judith. *Subjects of Desire: Hegelian Reflections in Twentieth-Century France.* New York: Columbia University Press, 1987.

Butler, Judith. *Undoing Gender.* New York: Routledge, 2004.

Butler, Judith, and Ernesto Laclau. "The Uses of Equality." *Diacritics* 27(1) (1997): 3–15.

Butler, Judith, Ernesto Laclau, and Slavoj Žižek. *Contingency, Hegemony, Universality: Contemporary Dialogues on the Left.* London: Verso, 2000.

Butler, Rex. *Jean Baudrillard: The Defence of the Real.* London: Sage, 1999.

Cacciari, Massimo. *L'arcipelago.* Milan: Adelphi, 1997.

Cacciari, Massimo. *Dell'inizio.* Milan: Adelphi, 1990.

Cacciari, Massimo. *Geo-filosofia dell'Europa.* Milan: Adelphi, 1994.

Cacciari, Massimo. *Icone della legge.* Milan: Adelphi, 1985.

Cacciari, Massimo. *Krisis: Saggio sulla crisi del pensiero negativo da Nietzsche a Wittgenstein.* Milan: Feltrinelli, 1976.

Cacciari, Massimo. *The Necessary Angel.* Translated by Miquel E. Vatter. Albany, NY: SUNY Press, 1994. Originally published as *L'Angelo necessario.* Milan: Adelphi, 1986.

Cacciari, Massimo. *Pensiero negativo e razionalizzazione.* Venice: Marsilio, 1977.

Caine, Barbara, Elizabeth A. Grosz, and Marie de Lepervanche, eds. *Crossing Boundaries: Feminisms and the Critique of Knowledges.* Sydney: Allen & Unwin, 1988.

Campbell, David, and Morton Schoolman, eds. *The New Pluralism: William Connolly and the Contemporary Global Condition.* Durham, NC: Duke University Press, 2008.

Canguilhem, Georges. "Dialectique et philosophie du non chez Gaston Bachelard." In *Etudes d'histoire et de philosophie des sciences*, 204—16. Paris: Vrin, 1970.

Canguilhem, Georges. *Ideology and Rationality in the History of Life Sciences.* Translated by Arthur Goldhammer. Cambridge: Cambridge University Press, 1988.

Canguilhem, Georges. "Qu'est-ce qu'une idéologie scientifique?" In *Idéologie et rationalité dans l'histoire des sciences de la vie*, 33–45. Paris: Vrin, 1977.

Caponigri, Robert. "Italian Philosophy, 1943–1950." *Philosophy and Phenomenological Research* 11 (1951): 489–509.

Cassirer, Ernst. *An Essay on Man.* New York: Doubleday, 1956.

Castelli Gattinara, Enrico. *Les Inquiétudes de la raison: Épistémologie et histoire en France dans l'entre-deux-guerres.* Paris: Vrin, 1998.

Cavarero, Adriana. *In Spite of Plato: A Feminist Writing of Ancient Philosophy.* Cambridge: Polity, 1995.

Cavarero, Adriana. *Relating Narratives: Storytelling and Selfhood.* New York: Routledge, 2000.

Cavell, Stanley. *The Claim of Reason.* Oxford: Oxford University Press, 1979.

Cavell, Stanley. *Contesting Tears: The Hollywood Melodrama of the Unknown Woman.* Chicago, IL: University of Chicago Press, 1996.

Cavell, Stanley. *Disowning Knowledge: Six Plays of Shakespeare.* Cambridge: Cambridge University Press, 1987.

Cavell, Stanley. *Must We Mean What We Say?* Cambridge: Cambridge University Press, 1976.

Cavell, Stanley. *Philosophy the Day after Tomorrow.* Cambridge, MA: Harvard University Press, 2005.

Cavell, Stanley. *Pursuits of Happiness: The Hollywood Comedy of Remarriage.* Cambridge, MA: Harvard University Press, 1981.

Cavell, Stanley. "Something Out of the Ordinary." *Proceedings and Addresses of the American Philosophical Association* 71(2) (1997): 23–37.

Caygill, Howard. *Levinas and the Political.* London: Routledge, 2002.

Červenka, Miroslav. *Styl a význam.* Prague: Československý spisovatel, 1991.

Césaire, Aimé. *Discourse on Colonialism.* Translated by Joan Pinkham. New York: Monthly Review Press, 2001. Originally published as *Discours sur le colonialisme.* Paris: Éditions Réclame, 1950.

Chalier, Cathérine. *Figures du féminin: Lecture d'Emmanuel Levinas.* Paris: La nuit surveillée, 1982.

Chanter, Tina. *Ethics of Eros. Irigaray's Re-writing of the Philosophers.* New York: Routledge, 1995.

Chomsky, Noam. *Current Issues in Linguistic Theory.* The Hague: Mouton, 1964.

Chomsky, Noam. *Some Concepts and Consequences of the Theory of Government and Binding.* Cambridge, MA: MIT Press, 1982.

Chomsky, Noam. *Syntactic Structures.* New York: de Gruyter, 2002.

Chrétien, Jean-Louis. *L'Antiphonaire de la nuit.* Paris: Éditions de L'Herne, 1989.

Chrétien, Jean-Louis. "Retrospection." In *The Unforgettable and the Unhoped For*, translated by Jeffrey Bloechl, 119–29. New York: Fordham University Press, 2002.

Chrétien, Jean-Louis. "The Wounded Word." Translated by Jeffrey L. Kosky. In Dominique Janicaud *et al. Phenomenology and the "Theological Turn": The French Debate*, 147–75. Originally published as "La Parole Blessée," in *Phénoménologie et théologie*, edited by Jean-François Courtine, 41–78. Paris: Criterion, 1992.

Chvatík, Květoslav. *Mensch und Struktur.* Frankfurt: Suhrkamp, 1987.

Chvatík, Květoslav. *Tchekoslowakischer Strukturalismus.* Munich: Wilhelm Fink, 1981.

Chvatík, Ivan, Pavel Kouba, and Miroslav Petříček. "Struktura 'Sebraných spisů' Jana Patočky jako problém interpretace." *Filosofický časopis* [The philosophical review] 3 (1991): 400–405.

Cixous, Hélène. *The Book of Promethea.* Translated by Betsy Wing. Lincoln, NE: Nebraska University Press, 1991.

Cixous, Hélène. *The Helene Cixous Reader.* London: Routledge, 1994.

Cixous, Hélène. "The Laugh of the Medusa." Translated by Keith Cohen and Paula Cohen. *Signs: Journal of Women in Culture and Society* 1(4) (1976): 875–93.

Code, Lorraine. *Epistemic Responsibility.* Hanover, NH: University Press of New England for Brown University Press, 1987.

Code, Lorraine. *What Can She Know? Feminist Theory and the Constitution of Knowledge.* Ithaca, NY: Cornell University Press, 1991.

Colebrook, Claire. "Postmodernism is a Humanism: Deleuze and Equivocity." *Women: A Cultural Review* 15 (2004): 283–307.

Colletti, Lucio. *Tramonto dell'ideologia.* Rome-Bari: Laterza, 1980.

Collin, Françoise. *Maurice Blanchot et la question de l'écriture.* Paris: Gallimard, 1971.

Collin, Françoise, Evelyne Pisier, and Eleni Varikas, eds. *Les Femmes de Platon à Derrida: Anthologie critique.* Paris: Plon, 2000.

Connolly, William E. *Capitalism and Christianity, American Style.* Durham, NC: Duke University Press, 2008.

Connolly, William E. *The Ethos of Pluralization.* Minneapolis, MN: University of Minnesota Press, 1995.

Connolly, William E. "The Evangelical-Capitalist Resonance Machine." *Political Theory* 33(6) (2006): 869–86.

Connolly, William E. *Identity/Difference: Democratic Negotiations of Political Paradox.* Ithaca, NY: Cornell University Press, 1991.

Connolly, William E. "Immanence, Abundance, Democracy." In *Radical Democracy: Politics between Abundance and Lack*, edited by Lars Tønder and Lasse Thomassen, 239–55. Manchester: Manchester University Press, 2005.

Connolly, William E. "The Twilight of Idols." *Philosophy and Social Criticism* 21(3) (1995): 127–37.

Connolly, William E. *Why I Am Not a Secularist.* Minneapolis, MN: University of Minnesota Press, 1999.

Cornell, Drucilla. *The Imaginary Domain: Abortion, Pornography and Sexual Difference.* New York: Routledge, 1995.

Costantini, Dino. *Una malattia europea.* Pisa: Edizioni Plus, 2006.

Crary, Alice. "A Question of Silence: Feminist Theory and Women's Voices." *Philosophy* 76 (2001): 371–95.

Crenshaw, Kimberle W. "Demarginalizing the Intersections of Race and Sex: A Black Feminist Critique of Antidiscrimination Doctrine, Feminist Theory and Antiracist Politics." *The University of Chicago Legal Forum* (1989): 139–67.

Critchley, Simon. *Infinitely Demanding: Ethics of Commitment, Politics of Resistance*. London: Verso, 2007.

Critchley, Simon, and Oliver Marchart, eds. *Laclau: A Critical Reader*. London: Routledge, 2004.

Croce, Benedetto. *The Aesthetic as the Science of Expression and of the Linguistic in General*. Translated by Colin Lyas. Cambridge: Cambridge University Press, 1992. Originally published as *Estetica come scienza dell'espressione e linguistica generale*. Milan: Remo Sandron, 1902.

Croce, Benedetto. *Historical Materialism and the Economics of Karl Marx*. New York: Evergreen Review, 2008. Published in Italian as *Materialismo storico ed economia marxista*. Rome-Bari: Laterza, [1900] 1978.

Croce, Benedetto. *History as the Story of Liberty*. Translated by Sylvia Sprigge. New York: Norton, 1941. Reprinted, Indianapolis: Liberty Fund, 2000. Originally published as *La storia come pensiero e come azione*. Bari: Laterza, 1938.

Croce, Benedetto. *Philosophy of the Practical: Economic and Ethic*. Translated by Douglas Ainslie. Whitefish, MT: Kessinger, 2004. Originally published as *Filosofia della practica: Economica ed etica*. Milan: Remo Sandron, 1909.

Daly, Mary. *Gyn/Ecology: The Meta-Ethics of Radical Feminism*. Boston, MA: Beacon Press, 1978.

Dascal, Marcelo. *Pragmatics and the Philosophy of Mind*. Amsterdam: John Benjamins, 1984.

Davidson, Donald. *Inquiries into Truth and Interpretation*. Oxford: Clarendon, 1984.

Davidson, Donald. "A Nice Derangement of Epitaphs." In *Philosophical Grounds of Rationality*, edited by Richard E. Grandy and Richard Warner, 157–74. Oxford: Oxford University Press, 1986.

Davis, Angela. *Women, Race, Class*. London: Women's Press, 1981.

Davis, Bret W., Brian Schroeder, and Jason Wirth, eds. *Japanese and Continental Philosophy: Conversations with the Kyoto School*. Bloomington, IN: University of Indiana Press, 2010.

Debord, Guy. *The Society of the Spectacle*. Translated by Donald Nicholson-Smith. New York: Zone Books, 2002.

De Lauretis, Teresa. *Technologies of Gender: Essays on Theory, Film, and Fiction*. Bloomington, IN: Indiana University Press, 1987.

Deleuze, Gilles. "Gueroult's General Method for Spinoza." In *Desert Islands and Other Texts (1953–1974)*, edited by David Lapoujade, translated by Mike Taormina, 146–55. New York: Semiotext(e), 2004.

Deleuze, Gilles. "How do we Recognize Structuralism?" In *Desert Island and Other Texts (1953–1974)*, edited by David Lapoujade, translated by Mike Taormina, 170–92. New York: Semiotext(e), 2004.

Deleuze, Gilles. *Negotiations: 1972–1990*. Translated by Martin Joughin. New York: Columbia University Press, 1995. Originally published as *Pourparlers*. Paris: Éditions de Minuit, 1990.

Deleuze, Gilles. *Two Regimes of Madness: Texts and Interviews 1975–1995*. New York: Semiotext(e), 2006.

Delphy, Christine. *Close to Home: A Materialist Analysis of Women's Oppression*. Amherst, MA: University of Massachusetts Press, 1984.

Derrida, Jacques. *Adieu to Emmanuel Levinas*. Translated by Pascale-Anne Brault and Michael Naas. Stanford, CA: Stanford University Press, 1999.

Derrida, Jacques. "Différance." In *Margins of Philosophy*, translated by Alan Bass, 1–27. Chicago,

IL: University of Chicago Press, 1982. Originally published as "La Différance," in *Théorie d'ensemble. Coll. Tel Quel*, 41–66. Paris: Éditions du Seuil, 1968.

Derrida, Jacques. *Donner la mort*. Paris: Éditions Galilée, 1999.

Derrida, Jacques. *Given Time I: Counterfeit Money*. Translated by Peggy Kamuf. Chicago, IL: University of Chicago Press, 1992. Originally published as *Donner le temps: La Fausse monnaie*. Paris: Éditions Galilée, 1991.

Derrida, Jacques. "How to Avoid Speaking: Denials." Translated by Ken Frieden. In *Derrida and Negative Theology*, edited by Harold Coward and Toby Foshay, 73–142. Albany, NY: SUNY Press, 1992. Originally published as "Comment ne pas parler: Dénégations," in *Psyché: Inventions de l'autre*, 535–95. Paris: Éditions Galilée, 1987.

Derrida, Jacques. *Monolingualism of the Other; or, The Prosthesis of Origin*. Translated by Patrick Mensah. Stanford, CA: University of Stanford Press, 1998. Originally published as *Le Monolinguisme de l'autre, ou, La prothèse d'origine*. Paris: Éditions Galilée, 1996.

Derrida, Jacques. *Of Grammatology*. Translated by Gayatri Chakravorty Spivak. 2nd ed. Baltimore, MD: Johns Hopkins Press, 1997.

Derrida, Jacques. "Some Statements and Truisms about Neologisms, Newisms, Postisms, Parasitisms, and Other Small Seismisms." In *The States of "Theory": History, Art, and Critical Discourse*, edited by David Carroll, 63–94. New York: Columbia University Press, 1990.

Derrida, Jacques. *Specters of Marx: The State of the Debt, the Work of Mourning, & the New International*. Translated by Peggy Kamuf. London: Routledge, 1994.

Derrida, Jacques. "Tajemství, kacířství a odpovědnost u Jana Patočky." Translated by Miroslav Petříček. *Filosofický časopis* [The philosophical review] 4 (1992): 551–73 and 5 (1992): 857–67.

Derrida, Jacques. *Texty k dekonstrukci* [On deconstruction]. Translated by Miroslav Patříček. Bratislava: Archa, 1993.

Derrida, Jacques. "Violence and Metaphysics: An Essay on the Thought of Emmanuel Levinas." In *Writing and Difference*, translated by Alan Bass, 79–153. Chicago, IL: University of Chicago Press, 1978.

Derrida, Jacques. *Writing and Difference*. Translated by Alan Bass. Chicago, IL: University of Chicago Press, 1978. Originally published as *L'Écriture et la différence*. Paris: Éditions du Seuil, 1967.

Derrida, Jacques and Maurizio Ferraris. *A Taste for the Secret*. Edited by Giacomo Donis and David Webb. Translated by Giacomo Donis. Cambridge: Polity, 2001.

Derrida, Jacques, Jean-Luc Marion, and Richard Kearney. "On the Gift: A Discussion Between Jacques Derrida and Jean-Luc Marion." In *God, the Gift, and Postmodernism*, edited by John D. Caputo and Michael J. Scanlon (eds), 54–78. Bloomington, IN: Indiana University Press, 1999.

Descombes, Vincent. *Modern French Philosophy*. Translated by L. Scott-Fox and J. M. Harding. New York: Cambridge University Press, 1980. Originally published as *Le Même et l'autre*. Paris: Éditions de Minuit, 1979.

Deudon, Eric Hollingsworth. *Nietzsche en France: L'Antichristianisme et la critique, 1891–1915*. Washington, DC: University Press of America, 1982.

Dewey, John. *Experience and Nature*. In *John Dewey: The Later Works, 1925–1953, Vol. 1: 1925* Carbondale, IL: Southern Illinois University Press, 1988.

Diamond, Irene, and Lee Quinby, eds. *Feminism and Foucault: Reflections on Resistance*. Boston, MA: Northeastern University Press, 1988.

Djebar, Assia. *Women of Algiers in their Apartments*. Translated by Marjolina de Jager. Charlottesville, VA: University Press of Virginia, 1992. Originally published as *Femmes d'Alger dans leur appartement*. Paris: Albin Michel, 1980.

Dubský, Ivan. *Filosof Jan Patočka* [Jan Patočka, philosopher]. Prague: OIKOYMENH, 1997.

Duchen, Claire. *Feminism in France: From May '68 to Mitterrand*. London: Routledge, 1986.

Duffy, Simon. "The Differential Point of View of the Infinitesimal Calculus in Spinoza, Leibniz and Deleuze." *Journal of the British Society for Phenomenology* 37(3) (2006): 286–307.

Duffy, Simon. *The Logic of Expression: Quality, Quantity and Intensity in Spinoza, Hegel and Deleuze.* Aldershot: Ashgate, 2006.

Dufrenne, Mikel. "Pour une philosophie non-théologique" [In defense of a nontheological philosophy]. In *Le Poétique*, 7–57. 2nd ed. Paris: Presses Universitaires de France, 1973.

Duhacek, Dasa. "Eastern Europe." In *A Companion to Feminist Philosophy*, edited by Alison M. Jaggar and Iris M. Young, 128–36. Oxford: Blackwell, 1998.

Duhacek, Dasa. "Women's Time in Former Yugoslavia." In *Gender Politics and Post-Communism: Reflections from Eastern Europe and the Former Soviet Union*, edited by Nanette Funk and Magda Mueller, 131–7. New York: Routledge, 1993.

Eco, Umberto. *Interpretation and Overinterpretation.* Cambridge: Cambridge University Press, 1992. Published in Italy as *Interpretazione e sovrainterpretazione*. Milan: Bompiani, 1995.

Eco, Umberto. *The Limits of Interpretation.* Bloomington, IN: Indiana University Press, 1990. Originally published as *Ilimiti dell'interpretazione*. Milan: Bompiani, 1990.

Eco, Umberto. *The Role of the Reader: Explorations in the Semiotics of Texts.* Bloomington, IN: Indiana University Press, 1979.

Eco, Umberto. *A Theory of Semiotics.* Bloomington, IN: Indiana University Press, 1976. Originally published as *Trattato di semiotica generale*. Milan: Bompiani, 1975.

Eisenstein, Hester. *Contemporary Feminist Thought.* Boston, MA: G.K. Hall, 1983.

Eisenstein, Hester, and Alice Jardine, eds. *The Future of Difference.* Boston, MA: G. K. Hall, 1980.

Elshtain, Jean B. *Public Man, Private Woman: Women in Social and Political Thought.* Princeton, NJ: Princeton University Press, 1981.

Enloe, Cynthia. *The Morning After: Sexual Politics at the End of the Cold War.* Berkeley, CA: University of California Press, 1993.

Fabian, Johannes. *Time and the Other: How Anthropology Makes its Object.* New York: Columbia University Press, 1983.

Fanon, Frantz. *Black Skin, White Masks.* Translated by Charles Lam Markmann. London: Pluto, 1986. Originally published as *Peau noire, masques blancs*. Paris: Éditions de Seuil, 1952.

Fanon, Frantz. *A Dying Colonialism.* Translated by Haakon Chevalier. New York: Grove Press, 1965. Originally published as *L'An V de la révolution algérienne*. Paris: Maspero, 1959.

Fanon, Frantz. *Towards the African Revolution.* Translated by Haakon Chevalier. New York: Grove Press, 1969. Originally published as *Pour la révolution africaine*. Paris: Maspero, 1964.

Fanon, Frantz. *The Wretched of the Earth*, translated by Richard Philcox. New York: Grove Press, 2004. Originally published as *Les Damnés de la terre*. Paris: Maspero, 1961.

Felman, Shoshana. *The Literary Speech Act: Don Juan with J. L. Austin, or Seduction in Two Languages.* Ithaca, NY: Cornell University Press, 1983. Second ed. 2002.

Felman, Shoshana. *What Does a Woman Want? Reading and Sexual Difference.* Baltimore, MD: Johns Hopkins University Press, 1993.

Ferguson, Ann. "Twenty Years of Feminist Philosophy." *Hypatia* 9(3) (1994): 197–215.

Ferry, Luc, and Alain Renaut. *French Philosophy of the Sixties: An Essay on Antihumanism*, translated by Mary Schnackenberg Cattani. Amherst, MA: University of Massachusetts Press, 1990. Published in French as *La Pensée 68: Essai sur l'anti-humanisme contemporain*. Paris: Gallimard, 1985.

Fink, Bruce. *The Lacanian Subject: Between Language and Jouissance.* Princeton, NJ: Princeton University Press, 1995.

Finkielkraut, Alain. *The Defeat of the Mind*, translated by Judith Friedlander. New York: Columbia University Press, 1995. Published in French as *La Défaite de la pensée*. Paris: Gallimard, 1987.

Fisher, Linda, and Lester Embree, eds. *Feminism and Phenomenology.* Dordrecht: Kluwer, 1996.

Flax, Jane. "Postmodernism and Gender Relations in Feminist Theory." *Signs: Journal of Women in Culture and Society* 12(4) (1987): 621–43.

Fontenay, Elisabeth de. *Diderot ou le matérialisme enchanté*. Paris: Grasset, 1981.

Fontenay, Elisabeth de. *Le Silence des bêtes: La Philosophie à l'épreuve de l'animalité*. Paris: Fayard, 1999.

Foucault, Michel. *The Archaeology of Knowledge*. Translated by A. M. Sheridan Smith. New York: Pantheon Books, 1972. Originally published as *L'Archéologie du savoir*. Paris: Gallimard, 1969.

Foucault, Michel. "Critical Theory/Intellectual History." Translated by Jeremy Harding. In *Politics, Philosophy, Culture: Interviews and Other Writings, 1977–1984*, edited by Lawrence D. Kritzman, 17–46. New York: Routledge, 1988.

Foucault, Michel. *Les Mots et les choses: Une archéologie des sciences humaines*. Paris: Gallimard, 1966.

Foucault, Michel, and Gilles Deleuze. "Intellectuals and Power." In *Language, Counter-Memory and Practice*, edited by Donald F. Bouchard, translated by Donald F. Bouchard and Sherry Simon, 205–14. Ithaca, NY: Cornell University Press, 1977. Originally published as "Les Intellectuels et le pouvoir," *L'Arc* 49 (1972): 3–10.

Fox Keller, Evelyn. *A Feeling for the Organism*. New York: Freeman, 1985.

Fox Keller, Evelyn. *Reflections on Gender and Science*. New Haven, CT: Yale University Press, 1985.

Frank, Manfred. *Die Unhintergehbarkeit von Individualität*. Frankfurt: Suhrkamp, 1986.

Frank, Manfred. *What Is Neostructuralism?* Translated by Sabine Wilke and Richard Gray. Minneapolis, MN: University of Minnesota Press, 1989.

Franklin, Sarah, Celia Lury, and Jackie Stacey. *Off-centre: Feminism and Cultural Studies*. London: HarperCollins, 1991.

Fraser, Mariam, Sarah Kember, and Celia Lury. *Inventive Life: Approaches to the New Vitalism*. London: Sage, 2005.

Fricker, Miranda and Jennifer Hornsby, eds. *The Cambridge Companion to Feminism in Philosophy*. Cambridge: Cambridge University Press, 2000.

Frye, Marilyn. "The Necessity of Differences: Constructing a Positive Category of Women." *Signs: Journal of Women in Culture & Society* 21(4) (1996): 991–1011.

Frye, Marilyn. *The Politics of Reality: Essays in Feminist Theory*. Trumansberg, NY: Crossing Press, 1983.

Fukuyama, Francis. *The End of History and the Last Man*. New York: Simon & Schuster, 1992.

Fuss, Diane. *Essentially Speaking: Feminism, Nature and Difference*. New York: Routledge, 1989.

Gallop, Jane. *Around 1981: Academic Feminist Literary Theory*. New York: Routledge, 1992.

Gallop, Jane. *Feminist Accused of Sexual Harassment*. Durham, NC: Duke University Press, 1997.

Garavaso, Pieranna, and Nicla Vassallo. *Filosofie delle Donne*. Laterza: Bari, 2007.

Garber, Marjorie. *Vested Interests: Cross-dressing and Cultural Anxiety*. New York: Routledge, 1992.

Gargani, Aldo. *L'altra storia*. Milan: Il Saggiatori, 1990.

Gargani, Aldo. "L'attrito del pensiero." In *Filosofia '86*, edited by Gianni Vattimo, 5–22. Rome-Bari: Laterza, 1987.

Gargani, Aldo. *Il coraggio di essere: Saggio sulla cultura mitteleuropea*. Rome-Bari: Laterza, 1992.

Gargani, Aldo, ed. *Crisi della ragione: Nuovi modelli nel rapporto tra sapere e attività umane*. Turin: Einaudi, 1979.

Gargani, Aldo. *Il sapere senza fondamenti*. Turin: Einaudi, 1975.

Gargani, Aldo. *Sguardo e destino*. Rome-Bari: Laterza, 1988.

Gargani, Aldo. *Lo stupore e il caso*. Rome-Bari: Laterza, 1986.

Gargani, Aldo. "La verità come immagine influente." In *Il destino dell'uomo nella società post-industriale*, edited by Aldo Gargani, 5–18. Rome-Bari: Laterza, 1987.

Gatens, Moira. *Feminism and Philosophy: Perspectives on Difference and Equality.* Bloomington, IN: Indiana University Press, 1991.

Gatens, Moira, and Genevieve Lloyd. *Collective Imaginings: Spinoza, Past and Present.* London: Routledge, 1999.

Gehlen, Arnold. *Man: His Nature and Place in the World.* Translated by Clare McMillan and Karl Pillemer. New York: Columbia University Press, 1988. Originally published as *Der Mensch: Seine Natur und seine Stellung in der Welt.* Berlin: Junker & Dünnhaupt, 1940. Reprinted, Bonn: Athenäum-Verlag, 1950.

Gentile, Giovanni. *Origins and Doctrine of Fascism: With Selections from Other Works.* Edited and translated by A. James Gregor. Edison, NJ: Transaction Publishers, 2004. Originally published as *Origini e dottrina del fascismo.* Florence: Sansoni, 1929. Reprinted, New York: Ams Press, 1979.

Gentile, Giovanni. *The Reform of Education.* Translated by Dino Bigongiari. Whitefish, MT: Kessinger Publishing, 2007. Originally published as *La riforma dell'educazione.* Florence: Le Lettere, [1920] 2003.

Gentile, Giovanni. *La riforma della dialettica hegeliana.* Florence: Sansoni, [1913] 1975.

Gentile, Giovanni. *The Theory of Mind as Pure Act.* Translated by H. Wildon Carr. Whitefish, MT: Kessinger Publishing, 2007. Originally published as *La teoria generale dello spirito come atto puro.* Florence: Le Lettere, [1916] 2004.

Gibson-Graham, J. K. *The End of Capitalism (as We Knew It): A Feminist Critique of Political Economy.* 2nd ed. Minneapolis, MN: University of Minnesota Press, 2006.

Giddens, Anthony. *The Consequences of Modernity.* Stanford, CA: Stanford University Press, 1990.

Gilligan, Carol. *In a Different Voice: Psychological Theory and Women's Development.* Cambridge, MA: Harvard University Press, 1982.

Gilroy, Paul. *The Black Atlantic: Modernity and Double Consciousness.* Cambridge, MA: Harvard University Press, 1992.

Givone, Sergio. *Disincanto del mondo e pensiero tragico.* Milan: Il Saggiatore, 1988.

Givone, Sergio. *Ermeneutica e romanticismo.* Milan: Mursia, 1983.

Givone, Sergio. *Storia del nulla.* Rome-Bari: Laterza, 1996.

Glissant, Édouard. *Caribbean Discourse: Selected Essays.* Translated by J. Michael Dash. Charlottesville, VA: University Press of Virginia, 1989.

Glissant, Édouard. *Poetics of Relation.* Translated by Betsy Wing. Ann Arbor, MI: University of Michigan Press, 1997.

Glucksmann, André. *La Cuisinière et le mangeur d'hommes: Essai sur l'État, le marxisme, les camps de concentration.* Paris: Éditions du Seuil, 1976.

Gould, Carol C., and Marx W. Wartofsky, eds. *Women and Philosophy: Towards a Theory of Liberation.* New York: Putnam, 1976.

Gracia, Jorge J. E. *Hispanic/Latino Identity.* Oxford: Blackwell, 2000.

Gramsci, Antonio. *Gli intellettuali e l'organizzazione della cultura.* Turin: Einaudi, 1949.

Gramsci, Antonio. *Prison Notebooks.* 3 vols. Edited and translated by Joseph A. Buttigieg. Cambridge: Harvard University Press, 1991, 1996, 2007. Published in Italian as *Quaderni dal carcere,* 4 vols. Turin: Einaudi, [1948–51] 2001.

Grandy, Richard E., and Richard Warner. *Philosophical Grounds of Rationality.* Oxford: Oxford University Press, 1986.

Grewal, Inderpal, and Caren Kaplan, eds. *Scattered Hegemonies: Postmodernity and Transnational Feminist Practices.* Minneapolis, MN: University of Minnesota Press, 1994.

Grice, Paul. "Logic and Conversation." In *The Philosophy of Language,* edited by A. P. Martinich, 156–67. Oxford: Oxford University Press, 2006.

Griffin, Gabriele, and Rosi Braidotti, eds. *Thinking Differently: A Reader in European Women's Studies.* London: Zed Books, 2002.

Griffiths, Morwenna, and Margaret Whitford, eds. *Feminist Perspectives in Philosophy*. London: Macmillan, 1989.

Grimshaw, Jean. *Philosophy and Feminist Thinking*. Minneapolis, MN: University of Minnesota Press, 1986.

Grosz, Elizabeth A. *Becomings: Explorations in Time, Memory and Futures*. Ithaca, NY: Cornell University Press, 1999.

Grosz, Elizabeth A. *Sexual Subversions: Three French Feminists*. Sydney: Allen & Unwin, 1989.

Guattari, Félix. *Chaosmosis. An Ethico-aesthetic Paradigm*. Sydney: Power Publications, 1995.

Guattari, Félix. *The Three Ecologies*. London: Athlone, 2002.

Habermas, Jürgen. "Individuation through Socialization: On George Herbert Mead's Theory of Subjectivity." In *Postmetaphysical Thinking: Philosophical Essays*. Translated by William Mark Hohengarten, 149–204. Cambridge, MA: MIT Press, 1992.

Habermas, Jürgen. *Justification and Application: Remarks on Discourse Ethics*. Translated by Ciaran Cronin. Cambridge, MA: MIT Press, 1993.

Habermas, Jürgen. *Moral Consciousness and Communicative Action*. Translated by Christian Lenhardt and Shierry Weber Nicholsen. Cambridge, MA: MIT Press, 1990.

Habermas, Jürgen. *The Philosophical Discourse of Modernity: Twelve Lectures*. Translated by Frederick G. Lawrence. Cambridge, MA: MIT Press, 1987.

Habermas, Jürgen. *Postmetaphysical Thinking: Philosophical Essays*. Cambridge, MA: MIT Press, 1992. Published in German as *Nachmetaphysisches Denken*. Frankfurt: Suhrkamp, 1988.

Habermas, Jürgen. "Richard Rorty's Pragmatic Turn." In *Truth: Philosophical Engagements across Traditions*, edited by Medina and Wood, 109–29.

Habermas, Jürgen. "Struggles for Recognition in the Democratic Constitutional State." Translated by Shierry Weber Nicholsen. In *Multiculturalism: Examining the Politics of Recognition*, edited by Amy Gutmann, 107–48. Princeton, NJ: Princeton University Press, 1994.

Habermas, Jürgen. *The Theory of Communicative Action, Vol. 1*. Boston, MA: Beacon Press, 1985.

Habermas, Jürgen. *Truth and Justification*. Translated by Barbara Fultner. Cambridge, MA: MIT Press, 2003.

Habermas, Jürgen, and Niklas Luhmann. *Theorie der Gesellschaft oder Sozialtechnologie*. Frankfurt: Suhrkamp, 1971.

Hacke, Jens. *Philosophie der Bürgerlichkeit*. Göttingen: Vandenhoeck & Ruprecht, 2006.

Halberstam, Judith, and Ira Livingston. *Posthuman Bodies*. Bloomington, IN: Indiana University Press, 1995.

Hall, Stuart. *Encoding and Decoding in the Television Discourse*. CCCS Stenciled Paper 7, 1973.

Hall, Stuart. *The Hard Road to Renewal: Thatcherism and the Crisis of the Left*. London: Verso, 1988.

Hall, Stuart. "New Ethnicities." In *Stuart Hall: Critical Dialogues in Cultural Studies*, edited by David Morley and Kuan-Hsing Chen, 441–51. London: Routledge, 1996.

Hall, Stuart. *The Popular Arts*. London: Hutchinson, 1964.

Hall, Stuart, ed. *Representation: Cultural Representations and Signifying Practices*. London: Sage, 1997.

Hall, Stuart. "What is This 'Black' in Black Popular Culture?" In *Black Popular Culture*, edited by Gina Dent, 21–33. Seattle, WA: Boy Press, 1992.

Hall, Stuart, and Paul du Gay, eds. *Questions of Cultural Identity*. London: Sage, 1996.

Hall, Stuart, and Tony Jefferson, ed. *Resistance Through Rituals: Youth Subcultures in Postwar Britain*. London: Hutchinson, 1976.

Hall, Stuart, Bob Lumley, and Greg McLennan, eds. *On Ideology*. London: Hutchinson, 1978.

Hall, Stuart, Charles Critcher, Tony Jefferson, and John Clarke. *Policing the Crisis*. London: Macmillan, 1978.

Hallward, Peter. *Badiou: A Subject to Truth*. Minneapolis, MN: University of Minnesota Press, 2003.

Han, Béatrice. *Foucault's Critical Project: Between the Transcendental and the Historical*. Translated by Edward Pile. Stanford, CA: Stanford University Press, 2002.

Haraway, Donna. *Modest_Witness@Second_Millennium. FemaleMan©_Meets_Oncomouse™: Feminism and Technoscience*. New York: Routledge, 1997.

Haraway, Donna. *Primate Visions: Gender, Race, and Nature in the World of Modern Science*. New York: Routledge, 1990.

Haraway, Donna. "Situated Knowledges: The Science Question in Feminism and the Privilege of Partial Perspective." *Feminist Studies* 14(3) (1988): 575–99.

Harding, Sandra. *The "Racial" Economy of Science*. Bloomington, IN: Indiana University Press, 1983.

Harding, Sandra. *Whose Science? Whose Knowledge?* Ithaca, NY: Cornell University Press, 1991.

Harding, Sandra, and Merrill B. Hintikka, eds. *Discovering Reality: Feminist Perspectives on Epistemology, Metaphysics, Methodology and Philosophy of Science*. Boston, MA: Reidel, 1983.

Hardt, Michael, and Antonio Negri. *Empire*. Cambridge, MA: Harvard University Press, 2000.

Hartsock, Nancy C. M. "The Feminist Standpoint: Developing the Ground for a Specifically Feminist Historical Materialism." In *Discovering Reality*, edited by Sandra Harding and Merrill B. Hintikka, 283–310. Dordrecht: Reidel, 1983.

Hawksworth, Mary. "Knowers, Knowing, Known: Feminist Theory and Claims to Truth." *Signs: Journal of Women in Culture and Society* 14(3) (1989): 533–57.

Hayles, Katherine N. *How we Became Posthuman: Virtual Bodies in Cybernetics, Literature, and Informatics*. Chicago, IL: University of Chicago Press, 1999.

Hegel, G. W. F. *Hegel's Lectures on the History of Philosophy*. Translated by Elizabeth S. Haldane and Francis Simson. 3 vols. London: Routledge & Kegan Paul, 1955.

Hegel, G. W. F. *Hegel's Science of Logic*. Translated by A. V. Miller. London: George Allen & Unwin, 1969.

Heidegger, Martin. *Basic Writings*. Edited by David Farrell Krell. New York: Harper & Row, 1977.

Heidegger, Martin. *Being and Time*. Translated by John Macquarrie and Edward Robinson. New York: Harper & Row, 1962. Originally published as *Sein und Zeit*. Halle: Niemeyer, 1927.

Heidegger, Martin. "Introduction to 'What is Metaphysics?'" Translated by Walter Kaufmann. In *Pathmarks*, edited by William McNeill, 277–90. Cambridge: Cambridge University Press, 1998. Originally published as *Was ist Metaphysik?* Frankfurt: V. Klostermann, 1949.

Heidegger, Martin. "Letter on Humanism." (i) Translated by Frank A. Capuzzi. In *Pathmarks*, edited by William McNeill, 239–76. Cambridge: Cambridge University Press, 1998. (ii) Translated by David F. Krell. In *Basic Writings*, edited by David Farrell Krell, 193–242. New York: Harper & Row, 1977. Originally published in *Platons Lehre von der Wahrheit: Mit einem Brief über den Humanismus*, 53–119. Bern: Francke, 1947. Reprinted in *Wegmarken*, 145–94. Frankfurt: V. Klostermann, 1967.

Heidegger, Martin. *Nietzsche*, 2 vols. Pfullingen: Neske, 1961.

Heidegger, Martin. "Nietzsche's Word: 'God is Dead.'" In *Off the Beaten Track*, edited and translated by Julian Young and Kenneth Haynes, 157–99. Cambridge: Cambridge University Press, 2002. Originally published as "Nietzsches Wort 'Gott ist tot,'" in *Holzwege*, 193–247. Frankfurt: V. Klostermann, 1950.

Heidegger, Martin. "The Onto-theo-logical Constitution of Metaphysics." In *Identity and Difference*, translated by Joan Stambaugh, 42–74. Chicago, IL: University of Chicago Press, 2002. Originally published as "Die Onto-Theo-Logische Verfassung der Metaphysik," in *Identität und Differenz*, 35–74. Pfullingen: Neske, 1957.

Heidegger, Martin. "The Origin of the Work of Art." In *Poetry, Language, Thought*, translated by Albert Hofstadter, 15–86. New York: Harper & Row, 1971.

Hejdánek, Ladislav. *Filosofie a víra*. Prague: OIKOYMENH, 1990.

Hejdánek, Ladislav. *Nepředmětnost v myšlení a ve skutečnosti* [Nonobjectiveness in thought and in reality]. Prague: ΟΙΚΟΥΜΕΝΗ, 1997.

Hejdánek, Ladislav. "Nicota a odpovědnost: problém negativního platonismu v Patočkově filosofii" [Nothingness and responsibility: the problem of negative Platonism in Patočka's philosophy] *Filosofický časopis* [The philosophical review] 39(1) (1991): 32–7.

Hekman, Susan J. *Gender and Knowledge: Elements of a Postmodern Feminism*. Boston, MA: Northeastern University Press, 1990.

Held, Virginia. *Justice and Care: Essential Readings in Feminist Ethics*. Boulder, CO: Westview Press, 1995.

Henrich, Dieter. *Bewußtes Leben*. Stuttgart: Reclam, 1999.

Henrich, Dieter. *Denken und Selbstsein*. Frankfurt: Suhrkamp, 2007.

Henrich, Dieter. "Die Einheit der Subjektivität." *Philosophische Rundschau* 3 (1955): 28–69.

Henrich, Dieter. "Die Grundstruktur der modernen Philosophie." In *Subjektivität und Selbsterhaltung*, edited by Hans Ebeling, 97–143. Frankfurt: Suhrkamp, 1976.

Henrich, Dieter. "Selbstbewußtsein, kritische Einleitung in eine Theorie." In *Hermeneutik und Dialektik*, edited by Rüdiger Bubner, Konrad Cramer, Reiner Wiehl *et al.*, 257–84. Tübingen: Mohr/Siebeck, 1970.

Henrich, Dieter. "Selbsterhaltung und Geschichtlichkeit." In *Subjektivität und Selbsterhaltung*, edited by Hans Ebeling, 303–13. Frankfurt: Suhrkamp, 1976.

Henry, Astrid. *Not My Mother's Sister: Generational Conflict and Third-Wave Feminism*. Bloomington, IN: Indiana University Press, 2004.

Herbert, Thomas. "Pour une théorie générale des idéologies." *Cahiers pour l'analyse* 9 (Summer 1968): 74–92.

Herbert, Thomas. "Réflexions sur la situation théorique des sciences sociales et, spécialement, de la psychologie sociale." *Cahiers pour l'analyse* 2 (February 1966): 139–65.

Hocquenghem, Guy. *Lettre ouverte à ceux qui sont passés du col Mao au Rotary*. Marseille: Agone, 1986.

Höffe, Otfried. *Democracy in an Age of Globalisation*. Translated by Dirk Haubrich and Michael Ludwig. Dordrecht: Springer, 2007.

Honneth, Axel. "The Other of Justice: Habermas and the Ethical Challenge of Postmodernism." In *The Cambridge Companion to Habermas*, edited by Stephen White, 289–324. Cambridge: Cambridge University Press, 1995.

hooks, bell. *Yearning*. Toronto: Between the Lines, 1990.

Horkheimer, Max, and Theodor W. Adorno. *Dialectic of Enlightenment*. (i) Translated by John Cumming. New York: Herder & Herder, 1972. (ii) Translated by Edmund Jephcott. Stanford, CA: Stanford University Press, 2002. Originally published as *Philosophische Fragmente*. New York: Social Studies Association, 1944. Rev. ed., *Dialektik der Aufklärung. Philosophische Fragmente*. Amsterdam: Querido, 1947.

Howarth, David, Aletta J. Norval, and Yannis Stavrakakis, eds. *Discourse Theory and Political Analysis: Identities, Hegemonies and Social Change*. Manchester: Manchester University Press, 2000.

Hoy, David, and Thomas McCarthy. *Critical Theory*. London: Blackwell, 1994.

Husserl, Edmund. *Cartesian Meditations*. Translated by Dorian Cairns. 5th ed. The Hague: Martinus Nijhoff, 1974. Originally published as *Méditations cartésiennes: Introduction á la phénoménologie*, translated by Gabrielle Peiffer and Emmanuel Levinas. Paris: A. Colin, 1931.

Husserl, Edmund. *The Crisis of European Sciences and Transcendental Phenomenology: An Introduction to Phenomenological Philosophy*. Translated by David Carr. Evanston, IL: Northwestern University Press, 1970. Originally published as *Die Krisis der europäischen Wissenschaften und die Transzendentale Phänomenologie: Eine Einleitung in die phänomenologische Philosophie*, edited by Walter Biemel. The Hague: Martinus Nijhoff, 1954.

Husserl, Edmund. *Ideas Pertaining to a Pure Phenomenology and a Phenomenological Philosophy. Book I: General Introduction to a Pure Phenomenology*. Translated by Fred Kersten. The Hague: Martinus Nijhoff, 1982. Originally published as *Ideen zu einer reinen Phänomenologie und phänomenologischen Philosophie*, in *Jahrbuch für Philosophie und phänomenologische Forschung*. Halle: M. Niemeyer, 1913.

Hyppolite, Jean. *Genesis and Structure of Hegel's Phenomenology of Spirit*, translated by Samuel Cherniak and John Heckman. Evanston, IL: Northwestern University Press, 1974. Published in French as *Genèse et structure de la "Phénoménologie de l'esprit" de Hegel*. Paris: Aubier, 1946.

Irigaray, Luce. "Equal to Whom?" *Differences. A Journal of Feminist Cultural Studies* 1(2) (1988): 59–76. Published in French as "Egales à qui?" *Critique: Revue générale des publications Françaises et étrangères* 43(480) (1987): 420–37.

Irigaray, Luce. *An Ethics of Sexual Difference*. Translated by Carolyn Burke and Gillian Gill. Ithaca, NY: Cornell University Press, 1993. Originally published as *L'Éthique de la différence sexuelle*. Paris: Éditions de Minuit, 1984.

Irigaray, Luce. *The Forgetting of Air in Martin Heidegger*. Translated by Mary Beth Mader. Austin, TX: University of Texas Press, 1999. Originally published as *L'Oubli de l'air chez Martin Heidegger*. Paris: Éditions de Minuit, 1983.

Irigaray, Luce. *Marine Lover of Friedrich. Nietzsche*. Translated by Gillian Gill. New York: Columbia University Press, 1991. Originally published as *Amante marine: De Friedrich Nietzsche*. Paris: Éditions de Minuit, 1980.

Irigaray, Luce. *The Sex Which Is Not One*. Translated by Catherine Porter. Ithaca, NY: Cornell University Press, 1985. Originally published as *Ce sexe qui n'en est pas un*. Paris: Éditions de Minuit, 1977.

Irigaray, Luce. *Speculum of the Other Woman*. Translated by Gillian Gill. Ithaca, NY: Cornell University Press, 1985. Originally published as *Spéculum: De l'autre femme*. Paris: Éditions de Minuit, 1974.

Ivekovic, Rada. *Orients: Critique de la raison postmoderne*. Paris: Blandin, 1992.

Ivekovic, Rada. *Le Sexe de la philosophie*. Paris: L'Harmattan, 1997.

Jaggar, Alison M. *Feminist Politics and Human Nature*. Totowa, NJ: Rowman & Allanheld, 1983.

Jaggar, Alison M. and Susan Bordo, eds. *Gender/Body/Knowledge: Feminist Reconstructions of Being and Knowing*. New Brunswick, NJ: Rutgers University Press, 1989.

Jaggar, Alison M., and Iris M. Young, eds. *A Companion to Feminist Philosophy*. Oxford: Blackwell, 1998.

Jameson, Fredric. *Postmodernism, or, the Cultural Logic of Late Capitalism*. Durham, NC: Duke University Press, 1991.

Janicaud, Dominique. *Phenomenology "Wide Open": After the French Debate*. Translated by Charles N. Cabral. New York: Fordham University Press, 2005. Originally published as *La Phénoménologie éclatée*. Paris: Éditions de L'éclat, 1998.

Janicaud, Dominique. *The Theological Turn of French Phenomenology*. Translated by Bernard G. Prusak. In Dominique Janicaud *et al.*, *Phenomenology and the "Theological Turn": The French Debate*, 3–106. New York: Fordham University Press. Originally published as *Le Tournant théologique de la phénoménologie française*. Paris: Éditions de L'éclat, 1991.

Janicaud, Dominique, Jean-François Courtine, Jean-Louis Chrétien *et al*. *Phenomenology and the "Theological Turn": The French Debate*. New York: Fordham University Press, 2000.

Jankélévitch, Vladimir. "Should We Pardon Them?" Translated by Ann Hobart. *Critical Inquiry* 22 (Spring 1996): 557–72.

Janković, Milan. "Dílo jako dění smyslu" [The work as a process of meaning]. In *Cesty za smyslem literárního díla* [Pathways toward the meaning of literary work], 9–100. Prague: Karolinum, 2005.

Jardine, Alice. *Gynesis.* Ithaca, NY: Cornell University Press, 1985.

Jarman, Derek, and Terry Eagleton. *"Wittgenstein": The Terry Eagleton Script and the Derek Jarman Film.* London: BFI Publishing, 1993.

Joas, Hans. *The Genesis of Values.* Translated by Gregory Moore. Chicago, IL: University of Chicago Press, 2001.

Joas, Hans. *The Imperative of Responsibility: Towards an Ethics of the Technological Age.* Translated by Hans Joas and David Herr. Chicago, IL: University of Chicago Press, 1984.

Johnson, Barbara. *The Critical Difference.* Baltimore, MD: Johns Hopkins University Press, 1980.

Johnson, Barbara. *The Feminist Difference: Literature, Psychoanalysis, Race and Gender.* Cambridge, MA: Harvard University Press, 1998.

Kalivoda, Jan. *Moderní duchovní skutečnost a marxismus* [Modern spiritual reality and Marxism]. Prague: Československý spisovatel, 1968.

Kant, Immanuel. *Critique of Pure Reason.* Edited and translated by Paul Guyer and Allen W. Wood. Cambridge: Cambridge University Press, 1998. Originally published as *Kritik der reinen Vernunft.* Riga: Hartknoch, 1781.

Kant, Immanuel. *Religion Within the Boundaries of Mere Reason.* In *Religion and Rational Theology*, edited and translated by Allen W. Wood and George Di Giovanni, 57–215. Cambridge: Cambridge University Press, 1996. Originally published as *Die Religion innerhalb der Grenzen der blossen Vernunft.* Königsberg: Friedrich Nicolovius, 1793.

Kant, Immanuel. "What is Enlightenment?" In *Practical Philosophy*, edited and translated by Mary J. Gregory, 17–22. Cambridge: Cambridge University Press, 1996. Originally published as "Beantwortung der Frage: Was ist Aufklärung?" In *Berlinische Monatschrift* 4 (1784): 481–94.

Karatani, Kojin. *Transcritique: On Kant and Marx.* Translated by Sabu Kohso. Cambridge, MA: MIT Press, 2003.

Karfíková, Lenka. "Továrna na budoucno." *Reflexe* 32 (2007): 127–33.

Kearney, Richard. *Dialogues with Contemporary Continental Thinkers: The Phenomenological Heritage.* Manchester: Manchester University Press, 1984.

Keenan, Alan. *Democracy in Question: Democratic Openness in a Time of Political Closure.* Stanford, CA: Stanford University Press, 2003.

Kelly, Joan. "The Double-edged Vision of Feminist Theory." *Feminist Studies* 5(1) (1979): 216–27.

Kennedy, Ellen, and Susan Mendus, eds. *Women in Western Political Philosophy: Kant to Nietzsche.* New York: St. Martin's Press, 1987.

Keohane, Nannerl O., Michelle Z. Rosaldo, and Barbara C. Gelpi, eds. *Feminist Theory. A Critique of Ideology.* Chicago, IL: University of Chicago Press, 1982.

Kersting, Wolfgang. *Theorien der sozialen Gerechtigkeit.* Stuttgart: Metzler, 2000.

Kittay, Eva Feder, and Diana T. Meyers, eds. *Women and Moral Theory.* Totowa, NJ: Rowman and Littlefield, 1987.

Knops, Andrew. "Agonism as Deliberation – On Mouffe's Theory of Democracy." *Journal of Political Philosophy* 15(1) (2007): 115–26.

Kohák, Erazim. "Jan Patočka: A Philosophical Biography." In *Jan Patočka: Philosophy and Selected Writings*, edited by E. Kohák, 3–135. Chicago, IL: University of Chicago Press, 1989.

Kofman, Sarah. *Le Respect des femmes.* Paris: Éditions Galilée, 1982.

Kouba, Pavel. *Nietzsche: Filosofická interpretace* [Nietzsche: A philosophical interpretation]. Prague: OIKOYMENH, 2006.

Kouba, Pavel. "Nietzsche dnes." *Česká mysl* [Czech mind] 1–2 (1992): 61–9.

Kripke, Saul. *Wittgenstein on Rules and Private Language.* Cambridge, MA: Harvard University Press, 1982.

Kristeva, Julia. *About Chinese Women.* New York: Marion Boyars, 1977.

Kristeva, Julia. *Colette.* Translated by Jane Marie Todd. New York: Columbia University Press, 2004.

Originally published as *La Genié féminin: La Vie, la folie, les mots, III: Colette*. Paris: Gallimard, 2002.

Kristeva, Julia. *Desire in Language: A Semiotic Approach to Literature and Art*. Translated by Leon S. Roudiez. New York: Columbia University, 1980.

Kristeva, Julia. *Hannah Arendt*. Translated by Ross Guberman. New York: Columbia University Press, 2001. Originally published as *La Genié féminin: La Vie, la folie, les mots, I: Hannah Arendt*. Paris: Gallimard, 1999.

Kristeva, Julia. *The Kristeva Reader*. New York: Columbia University Press, 1986.

Kristeva, Julia. *Melanie Klein*. Translated by Ross Guberman. New York: Columbia University Press, 2002. Originally published as *La Genié féminin: La Vie, la folie, les mots, II: Mélanie Klein*. Paris: Gallimard, 2000.

Kristeva, Julia. *Powers of Horror*. Translated by Leon S. Roudiez. New York: Columbia University Press, 1982. Originally published as *Pouvoirs de l'horreur*. Paris: Éditions du Seuil, 1980.

Kristeva, Julia. *Strangers to Ourselves*. Translated by Leon S. Roudiez. New York: Columbia University Press, 1994. Originally published as *Étrangers à nous-mêmes*. Paris. Flammarion, 1991.

Kristeva, Julia. "Women's Time." Translated by Alice Jardine and Harry Blake. *Signs: Journal of Women in Culture and Society* 7(1) (1981): 13–35.

Krüger, Hans-Peter. *Zwischen Lachen und Weinen, Vol. 1: Das Spektrum menschlicher Phänomene*. Berlin: Akademie, 1999.

Krüger, Hans-Peter. *Zwischen Lachen und Weinen, Vol. 2: Der dritte Weg Philosophischer Anthropologie und die Geschlechterfrage*. Berlin: Akademie, 2001.

Lacan, Jacques. *Écrits: The First Complete Edition in English*. Translated by Bruce Fink. New York: Norton, 2006. Published in French as *Écrits*. Paris: Éditions du Seuil, 1966.

Laclau, Ernesto. *Emancipation(s)*. London: Verso, 1996.

Laclau, Ernesto. *New Reflections on the Revolution of Our Time*. London: Verso, 1990.

Laclau, Ernesto. *On Populist Reason*. London: Verso, 2005.

Laclau, Ernesto. "Why Constructing a People is the Main Task of Radical Politics." *Critical Inquiry* 32 (2006): 646–80.

Laclau, Ernesto, and Chantal Mouffe. *Hegemony and Socialist Strategy: Towards a Radical Democratic Politics*. 2nd ed. London: Verso, 2001.

Laks, Bernard. *Langage et cognition: L'Approche connexionniste*. Paris: Hermès, 1996.

Langacker, Ronald W. *Foundations of Cognitive Grammar, Vol. I: Theoretical Prerequisites*. Stanford, CA: Stanford University Press, 1987.

Laruelle, François. *Philosophies of Difference: A Critical Introduction to Non-Philosophy*. Translated by Rocco Gangle. New York: Continuum 2010. Published in French as *Les Philosophies de la différence: Introduction critique*. Paris: Presses Universitaires de France, 1986.

Lecourt, Dominique. *Déclarer la philosophie*. Paris: Presses Universitaires de France, 1997.

Lecourt, Dominique. *Marxism and Epistemology: Bachelard, Canguilhem and Foucault*. Translated by Ben Brewster. London: New Left Books, 1975. Originally published as *Pour une critique de l'épistémologie (Bachelard, Canguilhem, Foucault)*. Paris: François Maspéro, 1972.

Lecourt, Dominique. *The Mediocracy: French Philosophy Since the Mid-1970s*. Translated by Gregory Elliot. London: Verso, 2001. Published in French as *Les Piètres penseurs*. Paris: Flammarion, 1999.

Lecourt, Dominique. *Proletarian Science? The Case of Lysenko*. Translated by Ben Brewster. New York: Humanities Press, 1978. Published in French as *Lyssenko: Histoire réelle d'une "science prolétarienne."* Paris: François Maspéro, 1976.

Lecourt, Dominique. *Prométhée, Faust, Frankenstein: Fondements imaginaires de l'éthique*. Le Plessis-Robinson: Institut Synthélabo, 1996.

Le Doeuff, Michèle. *Hipparchia's Choice: An Essay Concerning Women, Philosophy etc.* Translated by Trista Selous. Oxford: Blackwell, 1991.

Le Doeuff, Michèle. *The Philosophical Imaginary.* Translated by Colin Gordon. Stanford, CA: Stanford University Press, 1989.

Lennon, Kathleen, and Margaret Whitford, eds. *Knowing the Difference: Feminist Perspectives in Epistemology.* New York: Routledge, 1994.

Levinas, Emmanuel. "As If Consenting to Horror." Translated by Paula Wissing. *Critical Inquiry* 15 (Winter 1989): 485–8.

Levinas, Emmanuel. *Basic Philosophical Writings.* Edited by Adriaan T. Peperzak, Simon Critchley, and Robert Bernasconi. Bloomington, IN: Indiana University Press, 1996.

Levinas, Emmanuel. *Collected Philosophical Papers.* Translated by Alphonso Lingis. Dordrecht: Kluwer, 1987.

Levinas, Emmanuel. *Ethics and Infinity: Conversations with Philippe Nemo.* Translated by Richard A. Cohen. Pittsburgh, PA: Duquesne University Press, 1985.

Levinas, Emmanuel. *God, Death and Time.* Translated by Bettina Bergo. Stanford, CA Stanford University Press, 2000.

Levinas, Emmanuel. "God and Philosophy." Translated by Alphonso Lingis, Richard Cohen, Robert Bernasconi, and Simon Critchley. In *Basic Philosophical Writings*, edited by Adriaan T. Peperzak, Simon Critchley, and Robert Bernasconi, 129–48. Bloomington, IN: Indiana University Press, 1996. Originally published as "Dieu et la Philosophie," *Le Nouveau Commerce* 30–31 (1975): 97–128.

Levinas, Emmanuel. "Interview with François Poirié." In *Is It Righteous to Be? Interviews with Emmanuel Lévinas*, edited by Jill Robbins, 23–83. Stanford, CA: Stanford University Press, 2001.

Levinas, Emmanuel. "Philosophy and Awakening." Translated by Mary Quaintance. In *Who Comes after the Subject?*, edited by Eduardo Cadava, Peter Connor, and Jean-Luc Nancy, 206–16. New York: Routledge, 1991.

Levinas, Emmanuel. *The Theory of Intuition in Husserl's Phenomenology.* Translated by André Orianne. Evanston, IL: Northwestern University Press, 1973. Originally published as *Théorie de l'intuition dans la phénoménologie de Husserl* (1930).

Levinas, Emmanuel. "The Trace of the Other." Translated by Alphonso Lingis. In *Deconstruction in Context: Literature and Philosophy*, edited by Mark C. Taylor, 345–59. Chicago, IL: University of Chicago Press, 1986. Originally published as "La Trace de L'Autre." *Tijdschrift voor Filosofie* 3 (1963): 605–23.

Lévi-Strauss, Claude. *Introduction to the Work of Marcel Mauss.* Translated by Felicity Baker. London: Routledge & Kegan Paul, 1987. Originally published as *Introduction à l'œuvre de Marcel Mauss.* Paris: Presses Universitaires de France, 1950.

Lévy, Bernard-Henri. *Barbarism with a Human Face.* Translated by George Holoch. New York: Harper & Row, 1979. Published in French as *La Barbarie à visage humain.* Paris: Grasset, 1977.

Little, Adrian. "Between Disagreement and Consensus: Unraveling the Democratic Paradox." *Australian Journal of Political Science* 42(1) (2007): 143–59.

Little, Adrian. "Community and Radical Democracy." *Journal of Political Ideologies* 7(3) (2002): 369–83.

Lloyd, Genevieve. *Part of Nature: Self-knowledge in Spinoza's Ethic.* Ithaca, NY: Cornell University Press, 1994.

Lloyd, Genevieve. *Spinoza and the Ethics.* New York: Routledge, 1996.

Lübbe, Hermann, Robert Spaemann, Hans Bausch, Golo Mann, Wilhelm Hahn, Nikolaus Lobkowitz. "Erklärung." In *Mut zur Erziehung*, edited by Wilhelm Hahn, Hans Bausch, Nikolaus Lobkowicz *et al.*, 163–5. Stuttgart: Klett-Cotta, 1979.

Luhmann, Niklas. *Soziale Systeme*. Frankfurt: Suhrkamp, 1984.

Lyotard, Jean-François. "Answering the Question: What is Postmodernism?" Translated by Regis Durand. In *The Postmodern Condition: A Report on Knowledge*, edited by Geoff Bennington and Brian Massumi, 71–82. Minneapolis, MN: University of Minnesota Press, 1984.

Lyotard, Jean-François. *The Confession of Augustine*. Translated by Richard Beardsworth. Stanford, CA: Stanford University Press, 2000.

Lyotard, Jean-François. *The Differend: Phrases in Dispute*. Translated by Georges Van Den Abeele. Minneapolis, MN: University of Minnesota Press, 1988.

Lyotard, Jean-François. *Duchamp's TRANS/formers*. Translated by Ian McLeod. Venice, CA: Lapis, 1990.

Lyotard, Jean-François. *The Inhuman: Reflections on Time*. Translated by Geoffrey Bennington and Rachel Bowlby. Cambridge: Polity, 1993.

Lyotard, Jean-François. *Libidinal Economy*. Translated by Iain Hamilton Grant. London: Athlone, 1993.

Lyotard, Jean-François. *Peregrinations: Law, Form, Event*. New York: Columbia University Press, 1988.

Lyotard, Jean-François. *The Postmodern Condition: A Report on Knowledge*. Translated by Geoff Bennington and Brian Massumi. Minneapolis, MN: University of Minnesota Press, 1984.

Lyotard, Jean-François. *Postmodern Fables*. Translated by Georges Van Den Abeele. Minneapolis, MN: University of Minnesota Press, 1997.

Lyotard, Jean-François. "Rewriting Modernity." In *The Inhuman*, 24–35.

Lyotard, Jean-François. "The Sublime and the Avant-Garde." In *The Inhuman*, 89–107.

Lyotard, Jean-François, and Jacob Rogozinski. "La Police de la pensée." *L'Autre Journal* 10 (1985): 27–34.

MacCormack, Patricia. *Cinesexuality*. Aldershot: Ashgate, 2008.

Maihofer, Andrea. "Ansätze zur Kritik des moralischen Universalismus: Zur moraltheoretischen Diskussion um Gilligans Thesen zu einer 'weiblichen' Moralauffassung." *Feministische Studien* 6(1) (1988): 32–53.

Maihofer, Andrea. *Geschlecht als Existenzweise: Macht, Moral, Recht und Geschlechterdifferenz*. Frankfurt: Helmer, 1995.

Maniglier, Patrice. *La Vie énigmatique des signes: Saussure et la naissance du structuralisme*. Paris: Léo Scheer, 2006.

Maniglier, Patrice, and Rabouin, David. "A quoi bon l'ontologie? Les Mondes selon Badiou." *Critique* 719 (April 2007): 279–94.

Mannoni, Octave. *Prospero and Caliban: The Psychology of Colonization*. Translated by Pamela Powesland. New York: Praeger, 1956.

Marcelli, Miroslav. *Michal Foucault alebo stať sa iným*. Bratislava: Archa, 1995.

Margulis, Lynn, and Dorion Sagan. *What is Life?* Berkeley, CA: University of California Press, 1995.

Mari, Giovanni, ed. *Moderno Postmoderno*. Milan: Feltrinelli, 1987.

Marion, Jean-Luc. "The Saturated Phenomenon." Translated by Thomas A. Carlson. In Dominique Janicaud *et al*. *Phenomenology and the "Theological Turn": The French Debate*, 176–216. Originally published as "La Phénomène saturé," in *Phénoménologie et théologie*, edited by Jean-François Courtine, 79–128. Paris: Criterion, 1992.

Marquard, Odo. "Kompensation: Überlegungen zu einer Verlaufsfigur geschichtlicher Prozesse." In *Aesthetica und Anaesthetica*, edited by Odo Marquard, 64–81. Paderborn: Schöningh, 1989.

Marquard, Odo. *Schwierigkeiten mit der Geschichtsphilosophie*. Frankfurt: Suhrkamp, 1973.

Marquard, Odo. *Skepsis und Zustimmung*. Stuttgart: Reclam, 1994.

Marten, Rainer. *Der menschliche Mensch*. Paderborn: Schöningh, 1988.

Masullo, Aldo. *Antimetafisica del fondamento*. Naples: Guida, 1971.

Masullo, Aldo. *Filosofie del soggetto e diritto del senso*. Genoa: Marietti, 1990.

Masullo, Aldo. *Il senso del fondamento*. Naples: Libreria Scientifica Editrice, 1967.

Matheron, Alexandre. "*L'Anomalie sauvage* d'Antonio Negri." *Cahiers Spinoza* 4 (1982–83): 39–60.

Matheron, Alexandre. "A propos de Spinoza: Entretien réalisé par Laurent Bove et Pierre-François Moreau." *Multitudes* (2000). Interview of June–November 1997. http://multitudes.samizdat.net/A-propos-de-Spinoza.html (accessed May 2010).

Maturana, Humberto, and Francisco Varela. *Autopoesis and Cognition: The Realization of the Living*. Dordrecht: Reidel, 1972.

McCarthy, Thomas. *Ideals and Illusions: On Deconstruction and Reconstruction in Contemporary Critical Theory*. Cambridge, MA: MIT Press, 1991.

McCarthy, Thomas. Review of *Redistribution or Recognition? A Political-Philosophical Exchange*. *Ethics: An International Journal of Social, Political and Legal Philosophy* 113(2) (January 2005): 397–402.

McCumber, John. *The Company of Words*. Evanston, IL: Northwestern University Press, 1993.

McCumber, John. *Poetic Interaction*. Chicago, IL: University of Chicago Press, 1989.

McCumber, John. *Time in the Ditch: American Philosophy and the McCarthy Era*. Evanston, IL: Northwestern University Press, 2001.

McDowell, John. *Mind and World*. Cambridge, MA: Harvard University Press, 1996.

McDowell, John. "Towards Rehabilitating Objectivity." In *Truth: Philosophical Engagements across Traditions*, edited by Medina and Wood, 130–45.

McNay, Lois. *Foucault and Feminism: Power, Gender and the Self*. Cambridge: Polity, 1992.

Mead, George H. *Mind, Self, and Society*. Chicago, IL: University of Chicago Press, 1934.

Medina, José. "Identity Trouble: Disidentification and the Problem of Difference." *Philosophy and Social Criticism* 29(6) (2003): 657–82.

Medina, José. *Language: Key Concepts in Philosophy*. London: Continuum, 2005.

Medina, José. "Pragmatism and Ethnicity: Critique, Reconstruction, and the New Hispanic." *Metaphilosophy* 35(1/2) (2004): 115–46.

Medina, José. *Speaking from Elsewhere: A New Contextualist Perspective on Meaning, Identity, and Discursive Agency*. Albany, NY: SUNY Press, 2006.

Medina, José. *The Unity of Wittgenstein's Philosophy*. Albany, NY: SUNY Press, 2002.

Medina, José, and David Wood, eds. *Truth: Philosophical Engagements across Traditions*. New York: Blackwell, 2005.

Meehan, Johanna, ed. *Feminists read Habermas: Gendering the Subject of Discourse*. New York: Routledge, 1995.

Melchiorre, Virgilio. *Corpo e persona*. Genoa: Marietti, 1987.

Melchiorre, Virgilio. *Essere e parola: Idee per una antropologia metafisica*. Milan: Vita e Pensiero, 1982.

Melchiorre, Virgilio. *La via analogica*. Milan: Vita e Pensiero, 1996.

Memmi, Albert. *The Colonizer and the Colonized*. Translated by Howard Greenfield. New York: Orion, 1965. Published in French as *Portrait du colonisé: Portrait du colonisateur*. Paris: Buchet-Chastel, 1957.

Ménage, Gilles. *Histoire des Femmes Philosophes*. Paris: Arlea, 2003.

Menke, Christoph. *Reflections of Equality*. Translated by Howard Rouse and Andrei Denejkine. Stanford, CA: Stanford University Press, 2006.

Menke, Christoph. *The Sovereignty of Art: Aesthetic Negativity in Adorno and Derrida*. Translated by Neil Solomon. Cambridge, MA: MIT Press, 1998.

Mercer, Kobena. *Welcome to the Jungle: New Positions in Black Cultural Studies*. New York: Routledge, 1994.

374

Mernissi, Fatima. *Beyond the Veil: Male–Female Dynamics in Modern Muslim Society*. London: AlSaqi Books, 1985.

Michálek, Jiří. *Co je filosofie?* Prague: Institut pro středoevropskou kulturu a politiku, 1992.

Milan Women's Bookstore Collective. *Sexual Difference: A Theory of Social-Symbolic Practice*. Bloomington, IN: Indiana University Press, 1990.

Miller, Jacques-Alain. "Action de la Structure." *Cahiers pour l'analyse* 9 (Summer 1968): 93–105. Republished in *Un début dans la vie*, 57–82.

Miller, Jacques-Alain. *Un début dans la vie*. Paris: Gallimard, 2002.

Miller, Jacques-Alain. "Matrice." *Ornicar?* 4 (1975): 3–8. Republished in *Un début dans la vie*, 135–44.

Miller, Jacques-Alain. "*Suture* (Elements of the Logic of the Signifier)." Translated by Jacqueline Rose. *Screen* 18 (Winter 1978): 23–34. Originally published as "La Suture: Éléments de la logique du signifiant." *Cahiers pour l'analyse* 1 (1966): 37–49. Republished in *Un début dans la vie*, 94–115.

Miller, Nancy. *The Poetics of Gender*. New York: Columbia University Press, 1987.

Mills, Charles. *The Racial Contract*. Ithaca, NY: Cornell University Press, 1999.

Milner, Jean-Claude. *For the Love of Language*. Translated by Ann Banfield. Basingstoke: Macmillan, 1990. Published in French as *L'Amour de la langue*. Paris: Éditions du Seuil, 1978.

Milner, Jean-Claude. *Introduction à une science du langage*. Paris: Éditions du Seuil, 1989.

Milner, Jean-Claude. *L'Œuvre claire: Lacan, la science, la philosophie*. Paris: Éditions du Seuil, 1995.

Milner, Jean-Claude. *Le Périple structural: Figures et paradigmes*. Paris: Éditions du Seuil, 2002.

Mitchell, Juliet. *Psychoanalysis and Feminism: Freud, Reich, Laing and Women*. New York: Pantheon Press, 1974.

Modleski, Tania. *Feminism without Women: Culture and Criticism in a "Post-Feminist" Age*. New York: Routledge, 1991.

Mohanty, Chandra. "Under Western Eyes: Feminist Scholarship and Colonial Discourse." *Boundary 2* 12(3)/13(1) (1984): 333–58.

Mohanty, Chandra, Ann Russo, and Lourdes Torres, eds. *Third World Women and the Politics of Feminism*. Bloomington, IN: Indiana University Press, 1991.

Moi, Toril. *Feminist Theory and Simone de Beauvoir*. Oxford: Blackwell, 1990.

Montag, Warren. *Bodies, Masses, Power: Spinoza and his Contemporaries*. New York: Verso, 1999.

Morley, David, and Kuan-Hsing Chen, eds. *Stuart Hall: Critical Dialogues in Cultural Studies*. London: Routledge, 1996.

Mouffe, Chantal. *The Democratic Paradox*. London: Verso, 2000.

Mouffe, Chantal, ed. *Dimensions of Radical Democracy: Pluralism and Citizenship*. London: Verso, 1992.

Mouffe, Chantal. "For an Agonistic Public Sphere." In *Radical Democracy: Politics between Abundance and Lack*, edited by Lars Tønder and Lasse Thomassen, 123–32. Manchester: Manchester University Press, 2005.

Mouffe, Chantal. *The Return of the Political*. London: Verso, 1993.

Mudimbe, Valentin Y. *The Invention of Africa: Gnosis, Philosophy and the Order of Knowledge*. Bloomington, IN: Indiana University Press, 1988.

Mukařovský, Jan. *Aesthetic Function, Norm, and Value as Social Facts*. Translated by M. E. Suino. Ann Arbor, MI: University of Michigan Press, 1970. Published in Czech as "Estetická funkce, norma a hodnota jako sociální fakty." In *Studie z estetiky* [Studies in aesthetics], 17–54. Prague: Odeon, 1966.

Müller-Lauter, Wolfgang. *Nietzsche-Interpretationen I–III*. Berlin: De Gruyter, 1999–2000.

Nagl-Docekal, Herta. *Feminist Philosophy*. Translated by Katharina Vester. Boulder, CO: Westview Press, 2004.

Nagl-Docekal, Herta, and Herlinde Pauer-Studer, eds. *Denken der Geschlechterdifferenz: Neue Fragen und Perspektiven der feministischen Philosophie*. Vol. 14. Vienna: Wiener Frauenverlag, 1990.

Nancy, Jean-Luc. *The Inoperative Community*. Edited by Peter Connor. Translated by Peter Connor, Lisa Garbus, Michael Holland, and Simon Sawhney. Minneapolis, MN: University of Minnesota Press, 1991.

Narayan, Uma. "The Project of Feminist Epistemology: Perspectives from a Non-Western Feminist." In *Gender/Body/Knowledge: Feminist Reconstructions of Being and Knowing*, edited by Alison M. Jaggar and Susan Bordo, 256–69. New Brunswick, NJ: Rutgers University Press, 1989.

Natoli, Salvatore. *L'esperienza del dolore: Le forme del patire nella cultura occidentale*. Milan: Feltrinelli, 1995.

Natoli, Salvatore. *Soggetto e fondamento: Il sapere dell'origine e la scientificità della filosofia*. Milan: Bruno Mondadori, 1996.

Natoli, Salvatore. *Vita buona, vita felice: Scritti di etica e di politica*. Milan: Feltrinelli, 1990.

Negri, Antonio. *Marx Beyond Marx: Lessons on the* Grundrisse. Translated by Michael Hardt. New York: Autonomedia, 1991. Originally published as *Marx oltre Marx: Quaderno di lavoro sui Grundrisse*. Milan: Feltrinelli, 1979. Reprinted, Rome: Manifestolibri, 2003.

Negri, Antonio. *Stato e politica*. Milan: Feltrinelli, 1970.

Negri, Antonio, and Michael Hardt. *Labor of Dionysus: A Critique of the State-Form*. Minneapolis, MN: University of Minnesota Press, 1994. Published in Italian as *Il lavoro di Dioniso: Per la critica dello stato postmoderno*, translated by G. Ballarino and V. Marchi. Rome: Manifestolibri, 1995.

Nelson, Lynn H. *Who Knows: From Quine to a Feminist Empiricism*. Philadelphia, PA: Temple University Press, 1990.

Neubauer, Zdeněk. *Smysl a svět* [Sense and world]. Prague: Moravia Press, 2001.

Newman, Saul. *Unstable Universalities: Poststructuralism and Radical Politics*. Manchester: Manchester University Press, 2007.

Nietzsche, Friedrich. *Basic Writings*. Translated by Walter Kaufmann. New York: Modern Library, 1968.

Nietzsche, Friedrich. "On Truth and Lying in a Non-Moral Sense." In *The Birth of Tragedy and Other Writings*, edited by Raymond Geuss and Ronald Speirs, translated by Ronald Speirs, 141–53. Cambridge: Cambridge University Press, 1999.

Nietzsche, Friedrich. *Twilight of the Idols*. Translated by Richard Polt. Indianapolis, IN: Hackett, 1997.

Norris, Christopher. *Uncritical Theory: Postmodernism, Intellectuals and the Gulf War*. London: Lawrence & Wishart, 1992.

Norval, Aletta J. "Radical Democracy." In *Encyclopedia of Democratic Thought*, edited by P. Barry Clarke and Joe Foweraker, 587–94. London: Routledge, 2001.

Nowicki, Andrzej. "Marxism and Phenomenology in Contemporary Italian Philosophy." *Dialectics and Humanism* 2 (1975): 157–75.

Noys, Benjamin. "The End of the Monarchy of Sex: Sexuality and Contemporary Nihilism." *Theory, Culture & Society* 25(5) (2008): 104–22.

Nussbaum, Martha. "Aristotelian Social Democracy." In *Liberalism and the Good*, edited by R. Bruce Douglass, Gerald M. Mara, and Henry S. Richardson, 203–52. New York: Routledge, 1990.

Nussbaum, Martha. *Cultivating Humanity: A Classical Defense of Reform in Liberal Education*. Cambridge, MA: Harvard University Press, 1999.

Nuzzo, Angelica. "An Outline of Italian Hegelianism (1832–1998)." *Owl of Minerva* 29(2) (1998): 165–205.

Nye, Andrea. *Feminist Theory and the Philosophies of Man*. New York: Routledge, 1988.

O'Connor, Peg. "Identity Trouble and the Politics of Privilege: Commentary on Medina's 'Identity Trouble.'" *Symposia on Gender, Race, and Philosophy* II (2005). http://web.mit.edu/sgrp/2005/no1/O%27Connor0505.pdf (accessed May 2010).

O'Connor, Peg. "Moving to New Boroughs: Transforming the World by Inventing Language Games." In *Feminist Interpretations of Ludwig Wittgenstein*, edited by Naomi Scheman and Peg O'Connor, 432–49. University Park, PA: Penn State University Press, 2002.

Okin, Susan M. *Women in Western Political Thought*. London: Virago Press, 1979.

Olkowski, Dorothea. *Gilles Deleuze and the Ruin of Representation*, Berkeley, CA: University of California Press, 1999.

Pagano, Maurizio. "Contemporary Italian Philosophy: The Confrontation between Religious and Secular Thought." In *Contemporary Italian Philosophy: Crossing the Borders of Ethics, Politics, and Religion*, edited by Silvia Benso and Brian Schroeder, translated by Silvia Benso, 1–13. Albany, NY: SUNY Press, 2007.

Palek, Karel. *Jazyk a moc* [Langauge and power]. Munich: K. Jadrný, 1983. Published in French as *L'Esprit post-totalitaire*, translated by Erica Abrams. Paris: B. Grasset, 1986.

Panizza, Francisco, ed. *Populism and the Mirror of Democracy*. London: Verso, 2005.

Papic, Zarana. "Europe after 1989: Ethnic Wars, the Fascistization of Civil Society and Body Politics in Serbia." In *Thinking Differently: A Reader in European Women's Studies*, edited by Gabriele Griffin and Rosi Braidotti, 127–44. London: Zed Books, 2002.

Papic, Zarana. "Nationalismus, Patriarchat und Krieg." In *Frauen zwischen Grenzen. Rassismus und Nationalismus in der feministischen Diskussion*, edited by Olga Uremović and Gundula Oerfer, 107–17. Frankfurt: Campus, 1988.

Pareyson, Luigi. *Dostoevskij: Filosofia, romanzo ed esperienza religiosa*. Turin: Einaudi, 1993.

Pareyson, Luigi. *Esistenza e persona*. Turin: Taylor, 1950. Reprinted, Genoa: Il Melangolo, 1985.

Pareyson, Luigi. *Essere libertà ambiguità*. Milan: Mursia, 1998.

Pareyson, Luigi. *Estetica: Teoria della formatività*. Turin: Edizioni di Filosofia, 1954.

Pareyson, Luigi. *Ontologia della libertà: Il male e la sofferenza*. Turin: Einaudi, 1995.

Pareyson, Luigi. *Verità e interpretazione*. Milan: Mursia, 1971.

Parisi, Luciana. *Abstract Sex: Philosophy, Bio-Technology and the Mutations of Desire*. London: Continuum, 2004.

Parkes, Graham. *Heidegger and Asian Philosophy*. Honolulu, HI: University of Hawaii Press, 1990.

Parrini, Paolo. "Neo-Positivism and Italian Philosophy." *Vienna Circle Institute Yearbook* 6 (1998): 275–94.

Passerini, Luisa, Enrica Capussotti, Dawn Lyon, and Ioanna Laliotou, eds. *Women Migrants from East to West: Gender, Mobility, and Belonging in Contemporary Europe*. New York: Berghahn Books, 2007.

Pateman, Carole. *The Sexual Contract*. Cambridge: Polity, 1988.

Patočka, Jan. *Body, Community, Language, World*. Translated by Erazim Kohák. La Salle, IL: Open Court, 1998. Originally published as *Tělo, společenství, jazyk, svět*. Prague: OIKOYMENH, 1995.

Patočka, Jan. "Epoché und Reduktion: Einige Bemerkungen." In *Bewußt Sein: Gerhard Funke zu eigen*, edited by A. J. Bucher, H. Drüe, and T. M. Seebohm, 76–85. Bonn: Bonnier Verlag H. Grundmann, 1975.

Patočka, Jan. *Heretical Essays in the Philosophy of History*. Translated by Erazim Kohák. La Salle, IL: Open Court, 1996. Published in Czech as *Kacířské eseje o filosofii dějin*. Prague: Academia, 1990.

Patočka, Jan. *Negativní platonismus*. Prague: OIKOYMENH, 2007.

Patočka, Jan. *Přirozený svět jako filosofický problém* [The natural world as a philosophical problem]. Prague: Československý spisovatel, 1992.

Patočka, Jan. "Der Subjektivismus der Husserlschen und die Forderung einer asubjektive Phänomenologie." *Sborník prací filosofické fakulty brněnské univerzity* [The yearbook of the Faculty of Arts of Brno University] 19–20 (1971): 11–26.

Patočka, Jan. "Der Subjektivismus der Husserlschen und die Möglichkeit einer asubjektive Phänomenologie." In *Philosophische Perspektiven, ein Jahrbuch*, vol. 2, edited by R. Berlinger and E. Fink, 317–34. Frankfurt: V. Klostermann, 1970.

Pechar, Jiří. *Prostor imaginace* [The space of imagination]. Prague: Psychoanalytické nakladatelství, 1992.

Pêcheux, Michel. *Analyse automatique du discours*. Paris: Dunod, 1969.

Pêcheux, Michel. *L'Inquiétude du discours*. Paris: Éditions des Cendres, 1990.

Pêcheux, Michel. *Language, Semantics and Ideology*. Translated by Harbans Nagpal. Basingstoke: Macmillan, 1982. Originally published as *Les Vérités de la palice: Linguistique, sémantique, philosophie*. Paris: Maspéro, 1975.

Peirce, Charles Sanders. *Peirce on Signs: Writings on Semiotic by Charles Sanders Peirce*. Chapel Hill, NC: University of North Carolina Press, 1991.

Perniola, Mario. *Art and Its Shadow*. Translated by Massimo Verdicchio. London: Continuum, 2004. Originally published as *L'arte e la sua ombra*. Turin: Einaudi, 2000.

Perniola, Mario. *Ritual Thinking: Sexuality, Death, World*. Translated by Massimo Verdicchio. Amherst, NY: Humanity Books, 2000. Originally published as *La società dei simulacra*, Bologna, Cappelli, 1980, and *Transiti: Come si va dallo stesso allo stesso*, Bologna, Cappelli, 1985.

Perniola, Mario. *The Sex Appeal of the Inorganic: Philosophies of Desire in the Modern World*. Translated by Massimo Verdicchio. London: Continuum, 2004. Originally published as *Il sex appeal dell'inorganico*. Turin: Einaudi, 1994.

Perniola, Mario. *La società dei simulacra*. Bologna: Cappelli, 1980.

Perniola, Mario. *Transiti. Come si va dallo stesso allo stesso*. Bologna: Cappelli, 1985.

Perpich, Diane. "Subjectivity and Sexual Difference: New Figures of the Feminine in Irigaray and Cavarero." *Continental Philosophical Review* 36 (2003): 391–413.

Pešek, Jiří. *Dialektika dělby práce*. Prague: Univerzita Karlova, 1966.

Petitot, Jean. *Morphogenesis of Meaning*. Berne: Peter Lang, 2003. Originally published as *Morphogenèse du sens, I*. Paris: Presses Universitaires de France, 1985.

Petitot, Jean. "Structure." In *Encyclopedic Dictionary of Semiotics, Vol. 2*, edited by Thomas A. Sebeok, 991–1022. New York: de Gruyter, 1986.

Petitot, Jean. "Why Connectionism is such a Good Thing: A Criticism of Fodor's and Pylyshyn's Criticism of Smolensky." *Philosophica* 47(1) (1991): 49–79.

Petříček, Miroslav. "Derrida a Lévinas" [Derrida and Levinas]. *Česká mysl* [Czech mind] 1–2 (1992): 61–9.

Petříček, Miroslav. "Jan Patočka a myšlenka přirozeného světa" [Jan Patočka and the idea of the natural world]. *Filosofický časopis* [The philosophical review] 38(1–2) (1990): 22–44.

Petříček, Miroslav. *Majestát zákona*. Prague: Herrmann a synové, 2000.

Petříček, Miroslav. "Mukařovský a dekonstrukce." *Kritický sborník* 11 (1991): 1–5.

Petříček, Miroslav. "Mýtus v Patočkově filosofii" [Myth in Patočka's philosophy]. *Reflexe* 5–6 (1992): 1–16.

Petříček, Miroslav. "Patočkův filosofický projekt" [Patočka's philosophical project]. In Jan Patočka, *Přirozený svět jako filosofický problém* [The natural world as a philosophical problem], 269–80. Prague: Československý spisovatel, 1992.

Petříček, Miroslav. "Předmluva, která nechce být návodem ke čtení" [A preface that is not supposed to be a reader's guide]. In Jacques Derrida, *Texty k dekonstrukci* [On deconstruction], translated by Miroslav Petříček, 7–30. Bratislava: Archa, 1993.

Petříček, Miroslav. *Úvod do (současné) filosofie*. Prague: Herrmann a synové, 1991.

Phillips, Anne. *Democracy and Difference*. Cambridge: Polity, 1993.

Plumwood, Val. *Feminism and the Mastery of Nature*. New York: Routledge, 1993.

Politzer, Georges. *Critique of the Foundations of Psychology: The Psychology of Psychoanalysis*. Translated by Maurice Apprey. Pittsburgh, PA: Duquesne University Press, [1928] 1994.

Prusak, Bernard G. "The Science of Laughter: Helmuth Plessner's Laughing and Crying Revisited." *Continental Philosophy Review* 38(1–2) (2005): 41–69.

Putnam, Hilary. "The Face of Cognition." In *Truth: Philosophical Engagements across Traditions*, edited by Medina and Wood, 80–92.

Putnam, Hilary. *Reason, Truth, and History*. Cambridge: Cambridge University Press, 1981.

Putnam, Hilary. *The Threefold Cord: Mind, Body, and World*. New York: Columbia University Press, 1999.

Radcliffe Richards, Janet. *The Sceptical Feminist: A Philosophical Enquiry*. London: Routledge & Kegan Paul, 1980.

Reagan, Charles E. *Paul Ricoeur: His Life and His Work*. Chicago, IL: University of Chicago Press, 1998.

Rentsch, Thomas. *Heidegger und Wittgenstein*. Frankfurt: Suhrkamp, 1990.

Rezek, Petr. *Fenomenologická psychologie*. Prague: Ztichlá klika, 2008.

Rezek, Petr. *Filosofie a politika kýče*. Prague: OIKOYMENH, 1991.

Rezek, Petr. *Jan Patočka a věc fenomenologie*. Prague: OIKOYMENH, 1993.

Rezek, Petr. *Tělo, věc a skutečnost v současném umění*. Prague: Jazzová sekce, 1982.

Rich, Adrienne. *Blood, Bread and Poetry*. New York: Norton, 1985.

Rich, Adrienne. *On Lies, Secrets and Silence*. New York: Norton, 1979.

Ricoeur, Paul. *The Conflict of Interpretation: Essays on Hermeneutics*. Translated by Don Ihde. Evanston, IL: Northwestern University Press, 1974.

Ricoeur, Paul. "Intellectual Autobiography." In *The Philosophy of Paul Ricoeur*, edited by Lewis Edwin Hahn, 1–53. Library of Living Philosophers. La Salle, IL: Open Court, 1995.

Ricoeur, Paul. *Oneself as Another*. Translated by Kathleen Blamey. Chicago, IL: University of Chicago Press, 1992. Published in French as *Soi-même comme un autre*. Paris: Éditions de Seuil, 1990.

Ricoeur, Paul. "Pocta Janu Patočkovi." Translated by Marcela Sedláčková. *Filosofický časopis* [The philosophical review] 39(1) (1991): 5–12.

Ritter, Joachim. *Hegel and the French Revolution*. Translated by Richard Dien Winfield. Cambridge, MA: MIT Press 1984.

Ritter, Joachim. *Metaphysik und Politik*. Frankfurt: Suhrkamp, 1969.

Ritter, Joachim. *Subjektivität*. Frankfurt: Suhrkamp, 1974.

Rorty, Richard. *Achieving Our Country: Leftist Thought in Twentieth-Century America*. Cambridge, MA: Harvard University Press, 1999.

Rorty, Richard. "Introduction." In Wilfrid Sellars, *Empiricism and the Philosophy of Mind*, 1–12. Cambridge, MA: Harvard University Press, 1997.

Rorty, Richard. *Objectivity, Relativism, and Truth*. Cambridge: Cambridge University Press, 1991.

Rorty, Richard. *Take Care of Freedom and Truth Will Take Care of Itself*. Interviews conducted by Eduardo Mendieta. Stanford, CA: Stanford University Press, 2005.

Rose, Gillian. *Judaism and Modernity*. Oxford: Blackwell, 1993.

Rossi, Paolo. *Paragone degli ingegni moderni e postmoderni*. Bologna: Il Mulino, 1989.

Rossi, Pietro, and Carlo A.Viano, eds. *Filosofia italiana e filosofie straniere neldopoguerra*. Bologna: Il Mulino, 1991.

Rovatti, Pier A. *Abitare la distanza: Per un'etica del linguaggio*. Milan: Feltrinelli, 1994.

Rovatti, Pier A. *L'esercizio del silenzio*. Milan: Cortina, 1992.

Rovatti, Pier A. *La posta in gioco*. Milan: Bompiani, 1987.

Rovatti, Pier A. *Le trasformazioni del soggetto: Un itinerario filosofico*. Padua: Il Poligrafo, 1992.

Rovatti, Pier A., with Alessandro Dal Lago. *L'elogio del pudore: Per un pensiero debole*. Milan: Feltrinelli, 1989.

Ruggenini, Mario. *Il discorso dell'altro: Ermeneutica della differenza*. Milan: Il Saggiatore, 1996.

Ruggenini, Mario. *I fenomeni e le parole: La verità finita dell'ermeneutica*. Genoa: Marietti, 1991.

Ruggenini, Mario. *Volontà e interpretazione: Le forme della fine della filosofia*. Milan: Franco Angeli, 1984.

Ryle, Gilbert. 1949. *The Concept of Mind*. New York: Barnes & Noble.

Said, Edward. *Covering Islam: How the Media and the Experts Determine How We See the Rest of the World*. New York: Vintage, 1981.

Said, Edward. *Culture and Imperialism*. New York: Vintage, 1993.

Said, Edward. *Musical Elaborations*. New York: Columbia University Press, 1991.

Said, Edward. *Orientalism*. New York: Vintage, 1978.

Said, Edward. *Reflections on Exile*. London: Granta, 2000.

Santa Cruz, Maria I., Marie-Luisa Femenias, and Anna-Maria Bach. *Mujeres y Filosofia (I, II) Teoría Filosófica del Género*. Buenos Aires: Centro Editor de América Latina, 1994.

Santambrogio, Marco. *Forma e oggetto*. Milan: Il Saggiatore, 1992.

Santambrogio, Marco., ed. *Introduzione alla filosofia analitica del linguaggio*. Rome-Bari: Laterza, 1992.

Sartre, Jean-Paul. *Being and Nothingness: An Essay on Phenomenological Ontology*. Translated by Hazel E. Barnes. London: Routledge, 1956. Published in French as *L'Être et le néant: Essai d'ontologie phénoménologique*. Paris: Gallimard, 1943.

Saussure, Ferdinand de. *Writings in General Linguistics*. Translated by Carol Sanders and Matthew Pires. Oxford: Oxford University Press, 2006. Originally published as *Écrits de Linguistique Générale*. Paris: Gallimard, 2002.

Scheman, Naomi. "Queering the Center by Centering the Queer." In *Feminists Rethink the Self*, edited by Diana T. Meyers, 124–62. Boulder, CO: Westview Press, 1997.

Scheman, Naomi, and Peg O'Connor, eds. *Feminist Interpretations of Ludwig Wittgenstein*. University Park, PA: Penn State University Press, 2002.

Schnädelbach, Herbert. "Die Verteidigung der Republik." *Deutsche Zeitschrift für Philosophie* 55 (2007): 649–60.

Schor, Naomi. "Dreaming Dissymetry: Barthes, Foucault, and Sexual Difference." In *Men in Feminism*, edited by Alice Jardine and Paul Smith, 98–110. New York: Methuen, 1987.

Schott, Robin M. *Cognition and Eros: A Critique of the Kantian Paradigm*. Boston, MA: Beacon Press, 1988.

Schott, Robin M. *Feminist Interpretations of Immanuel Kant*. University Park, PA: Penn State University Press, 1997.

Schroeder, Brian. "Theological Nihilism and Italian Philosophy." *Philosophy Today* 49(4–5) (Winter 2005): 355–61.

Sciacca, Michele F. "Chronicle I: Present-Day Italian Philosophy." *New Scholasticism* 39 (1965): 69–83.

Seel, Martin. *Aesthetics of Appearing*. Translated by John Farrell. Stanford, CA: Stanford University Press, 2004.

Seel, Martin. *Versuch über die Form des Glücks*. Frankfurt: Suhrkamp, 1995.

Sellars, Wilfrid. *Empiricism and the Philosophy of Mind*. Cambridge, MA: Harvard University Press, 1997.

Šerý, Ladislav. *První knížka o tom, že řád je chaos*. Prague: Dharmagaia, 1997.

Severino, Emanuele. *L'anello del ritorno*. Milan: Adelphi, 1999.

Severino, Emanuele. *Destino della necessità*. Milan: Adelphi, 1980.

Severino, Emanuele. *Essenza del nichilismo*. Milan: Adelphi, 1972.

Severino, Emanuele. *Techne: Le radici della violenza*. Milan: Rusconi, 1979.

Shiva, Vandana. *Bio-piracy: The Plunder of Nature and Knowledge*. Boston, MA: South End Press, 1997.

Silverman, Hugh. "Postmodernism and Contemporary Italian Philosophy." *Man and World* 27(4) (1994): 343–8.

Simon, Josef. *Philosophy of the Sign*. Translated by George Heffernan. Albany, NY: SUNY Press, 1995.

Simons, Margaret A., ed. *Feminist Interpretations of Simone de Beauvoir*. University Park, PA: Pennsylvania State University Press, 1995.

Sini, Carlo. *Ethics of Writing*. Translated by Silvia Benso with Brian Schroeder. Albany, NY: SUNY Press, 2009. Originally published as *Etica della scrittura*. Milan: Il Saggiatore, 1992.

Sini, Carlo. *Passare il segno*. Milan: Il Saggiatore, 1981.

Sini, Carlo. *Il silenzio e la parola: Luoghi e confine del sapere per un uomo planetario*. Genoa: Marietti, 1989.

Sloterdijk, Peter. *Critique of Cynical Reason*. Translated by Michael Eldred. Minneapolis, MN: University of Minnesota Press, 1987. Published in German as *Kritik der zynischen Vernunft*. Frankfurt: Suhrkamp, 1983.

Sloterdijk, Peter. "Regeln für den Menschenpark: Ein Antwortschreiben zu Heideggers Brief über den Humanismus." In *Nicht gerettet: Versuche nach Heidegger*, edited by Peter Sloterdijk, 302–37. Frankfurt: Suhrkamp, 2001.

Sloterdijk, Peter. *Sphären I/II/III: Blasen/Globen/Schäume*. Frankfurt: Suhrkamp, 1998–2004.

Sobotka, Milan. *Člověk a práce v německé klasické filosofii*. Prague: Nakladatelství politické literatury, 1964.

Sobotka, Milan. *Člověk, práce a sebevědomí*. Prague: Svoboda, 1969.

Sobotka, Milan. *Stati k Hegelově Fenomenologii a filosofii práva*. Prague: Karolinum, 1993.

Sobotka, Milan, and Ladislav Major. *G. W. F. Hegel, život a dílo*. Prague: Mladá fronta, 1979.

Spaemann, Robert. "Niklas Luhmanns Herausforderung der Philosophie: Laudatio anläßlich der Verleihung des Hegel-Preises 1989 an Niklas Luhmann." In Niklas Luhmann and Robert Spaemann, *Paradigm lost: Über die ethische Reflexion der Moral*, 51–73. Frankfurt: Suhrkamp, 1990.

Spaemann, Robert. *Personen: Versuche über den Unterschied zwischen "etwas" und "jemand."* Stuttgart: Klett-Cotta, 1996.

Spelman, Elizabeth. *Inessential Woman: Problems of Exclusion in Feminist Thought*. Boston, MA: Beacon Press, 1988.

Spengler, Oswald. *The Decline of the West*. Translated by Charles Francis Atkinson. New York: Knopf, 1996.

Spinoza, Benedict. *Ethics*. In *The Collected Works of Spinoza, Volume I*, translated by Edwin M. Curley. Princeton, NJ: Princeton University Press, 1985.

Spinoza, Benedict. *Tractatus Politicus*. In *Spinoza: Complete Works*, edited by Michael L. Morgan, translated by Samuel Shirley, 676–754. Indianapolis, IN: Hackett, 2002.

Spinoza, Benedict. *Tractatus Theologico-Politicus*. In *Spinoza: Complete Works*, edited by Michael L. Morgan, translated by Samuel Shirley, 383–583. Indianapolis, IN: Hackett, 2002.

Spivak, Gayatri C. *A Critique of Postcolonial Reason: Towards a History of the Vanishing Present*. Cambridge, MA: Harvard University Press, 1999.

Spivak, Gayatri C. *Death of a Discipline*. New York: Columbia University Press, 2003.

Spivak, Gayatri C. *Outside in the Teaching Machine*. New York: Routledge, 1993.

Spivak, Gayatri C. *The Post-Colonial Critic*. New York: Routledge, 1990.

Spivak, Gayatri C. "Translator's Preface." In Jacques Derrida, *Of Grammatology*, ix–lxxxvii. Baltimore, MD: Johns Hopkins University Press, 1976.

Spivak, Gayatri C., and Ranajit Guha, eds. *Selected Subaltern Studies*. New York: Oxford University Press, 1988.

Stanton, Domna C. *The Female Autograph: Theory and Practice of Autobiography from the Tenth to the Twentieth Century*. Chicago, IL: University of Chicago, 1987.

Stanton, Domna. "Language and Revolution: The Franco-American Dis-connection." In *The Future of Difference*, edited by Hester Eisenstein and Alice Jardine, 73–87. Boston, MA: G. K. Hall, 1980.

Stavrakakis, Yannis. *The Lacanian Left*. Edinburgh: Edinburgh University Press, 2007.

Stegmaier, Werner. *Nietzsches "Genealogie der Moral."* Darmstadt: WBG, 1994.

Stengers, Isabelle. *D'une science à l'autre: Des concepts nomades*. Paris: Éditions du Seuil, 1987.

Stengers, Isabelle. *Power and Invention: Situating Science*. Translated by Paul Bains. Minneapolis, MN: University of Minnesota Press, 1997.

Stimpson, Catharine. *Where the Meanings Are*. New York: Methuen, 1988.

Taussig, Michael. *Shamanism, Colonialism and the Wild Man: A Study in Terror and Healing*. Chicago, IL: University of Chicago Press, 1991.

Taylor, Charles. *Human Agency and Language*. Cambridge: Cambridge University Press, 1985.

Taylor, Charles. "The Politics of Recognition." In *Multiculturalism: Examining the Politics of Recognition*, edited by Amy Gutmann, 25–73. Princeton, NJ: Princeton University Press, 1994.

Thomassen, Lasse. "Discourse Analytical Strategies: Antagonism, Hegemony and Ideology after Heterogeneity." *Journal of Political Ideologies* 10(3) (2005): 289–309.

Theunissen, Michael. *Der Andere: Studien zur Sozialontologie der Gegenwart*. Berlin: De Gruyter, 1965.

Theunissen, Michael. *Negative Theologie der Zeit*. Frankfurt: Suhrkamp, 1991.

Theunissen, Michael. *Selbstverwirklichung und Allgemeinheit*. Berlin: De Gruyter, 1982.

Thomä, Dieter. "Verhältnis zur Ontologie: Adornos Denken des Unbegrifflichen." In *Theodor W. Adorno, Negative Dialektik*, edited by Axel Honneth and Christoph Menke, 29–48. Berlin: Akademie, 2006.

Todorov, Tzvetan. *Imperfect Garden: The Legacy of Humanism*. Princeton, NJ: Princeton University Press, 2002.

Tønder, Lars, and Lasse Thomassen, eds. *Radical Democracy: Politics between Abundance and Lack*. Manchester: Manchester University Press, 2005.

Trend, David, ed. *Radical Democracy: Identity, Citizenship and the State*. London: Routledge, 1996.

Tronti, Mario. *Hegel politico*. Rome: Istituto dell'Enciclopedia italiana, 1975.

Tronti, Mario. *Operai e capitale*. Turin: Einaudi, 1966.

Tronti, Mario. *La politica al tramonto*. Turin: Einaudi, 1998.

Tronti, Mario. *Sull'autonomia del politico*. Milan: Feltrinelli, 1977.

Tronto, Joan C. *Moral Boundaries: A Political Argument for an Ethic of Care*. New York: Routledge, 1993.

Tuana, Nancy, ed. *Feminism and Science*. Bloomington, IN: Indiana University Press, 1989.

Tuana, Nancy, ed. *Re-Reading the Canon: Feminist Interpretations of Plato*. University Park, PA: Penn State University Press, 1994.

Tuana, Nancy. *Woman and the History of Philosophy*. New York: Paragon House, 1992.

Tugendhat, Ernst. *Anthropologie statt Metaphysik*. Munich: Beck, 2007.

Tugendhat, Ernst. *Egozentrizität und Mystik*. Munich: Beck, 2003.

Tugendhat, Ernst. *Ethik und Politik*. Frankfurt: Suhrkamp, 1992.

Tugendhat, Ernst. *Self-Consciousness and Self-Determination*. Translated by Paul Stern. Cambridge, MA: MIT Press, 1986. Published in German as *Selbstbewußtsein und Selbstbestimmung*. Frankfurt: Suhrkamp, 1979.

Vance, Carol. *Pleasure and Danger: Exploring Female Sexuality*. London: Routledge & Kegan Paul, 1984.

Vattimo, Gianni. *The Adventure of Difference: Philosophy after Nietzsche and Heidegger*. Translated by Cyprian Blamires and Thomas Harrison. Baltimore, MD: Johns Hopkins University Press, 1993. Originally published as *Le aventure della differenza*, Milan: Garzanti, 1980.

Vattimo, Gianni. *Al di là del soggetto*. Milan: Feltrinelli, 1981.

Vattimo, Gianni. *Beyond Interpretation: The Meaning of Hermeneutics for Philosophy*. Translated by David Webb. Stanford, CA: Stanford University Press: 1997. Originally published as *Oltre l'interpretazione: Il significato dell'ermeneutica per la filosofia*. Rome-Bari: Laterza, 1994.

Vattimo, Gianni. *The End of Modernity: Nihilism and Hermeneutics in Postmodern Culture*. Translated by Jon R. Snyder. Baltimore, MD: Johns Hopkins University Press, 1991. Originally published as *La fine della modernità*. Milan: Garzanti, 1985.

Vattimo, Gianni. *Il soggetto e la maschera: Nietzsche e il problema della liberazione*. Milan: Bompiani, 1974.

Vattimo, Gianni. *The Transparent Society*. Translated by David Webb. Cambridge: Polity, 1992. Originally published as *La società trasparente*. Milan: Garzanti, 1989.

Vattimo, Gianni, and Pier A. Rovatti, eds. *Weak Thought*. Translated by Peter Carravetta. New York: Columbia University Press. Originally published as *Il pensiero debole*. Milan: Feltrinelli, 1983.

Veca, Salvatore. *Cittadinanza: Riflessioni filosofiche sull'idea di emancipazione*. Milan: Feltrinelli, 1990.

Veca, Salvatore. *La filosofia politica*. Rome-Bari: Laterza, 1998.

Veca, Salvatore. *Fondazione e modalità in Kant*. Milan: Il Saggiatore, 1969.

Veca, Salvatore. *La società giusta*. Milan: Il Saggiatore, 1982.

Veca, Salvatore, and Francesco Alberoni. *L'altruismo e la morale*. Milan: Garzanti, 1988.

Veca, Salvatore, Alberto Martinelli, and Michele Salvati. *Progetto Ottantanove*. Milan: Il Saggiatore, 1989.

Vergès, Françoise. *Monsters and Revolutionaries: Colonial Family Romance and Métissage*. Durham, NC: Duke University Press, 1999.

Vetterling-Braggin, Mary, Frederick A. Elliston, and Jane English, eds. *Feminism and Philosophy*. Totowa, NJ: Rowman & Littlefield, 1977.

Viano, Carlo Augusto. *Va' pensiero: Il carattere della filosofia italiana contemporanea*. Turin: Einaudi, 1985.

Vintges, Karen. *Philosophy as Passion: The Thinking of Simone de Beauvoir*. Bloomington, IN: Indiana University Press, 1996.

Virno, Paolo. *Convenzione e materialismo*. Rome: Theoria, 1986.

Virno, Paolo. *Parole con parole: Poteri e limiti del linguaggio*. Rome: Donzelli, 1995.

Virno, Paolo. *Il ricordo del presente: Saggio sul tempo storico*. Turin: Bollati Boringhieri, 1999.

Vitiello, Vincenzo. *Cristianesimo senza redenzione*. Rome-Bari: Laterza, 1995.

Vitiello, Vincenzo. *Topologia del moderno*. Genoa: Marietti, 1992.

Vitiello, Vincenzo. *Utopia del nichilismo*. Naples: Guida, 1983.

Viveiros de Castro, Eduardo. "Intensive Filiation and Demonic Alliance." In *Deleuzian Intersections in Science, Technology, and Anthropology*, edited by Casper Bruun Jensen and Kjetil Rödje, 219–54. Oxford: Berghan Books, 2009.

Walcott, Derek. *Collected Poems, 1948–1984*. New York: Farrar, Straus & Giroux, 1987.

Waldenfels, Bernhard. *Order in the Twilight*. Translated by David J. Parent. Athens, OH: Ohio University Press, 1996.

Waldenfels, Bernhard. *The Question of the Other*. Albany, NY: SUNY Press, 2007.

Waldenfels, Bernhard. *Der Stachel des Fremden*. Frankfurt: Suhrkamp, 1990.

Walzer, Michael. *Spheres of Justice*. New York: Basic Books, 1983.

Ware, Vron. *Beyond the Pale: White Women, Racism and History*. London: Verso, 1992.

Weil, Simone. *La Pésenteur et la grâce*. Paris: Gallimard, 1947.

Wellmer, Albrecht. *Ethik und Dialog*. Frankfurt: Suhrkamp, 1986.

Welsch, Wolfgang. *Aisthesis*. Stuttgart: Klett-Cotta, 1987.

Welsch, Wolfgang. *Undoing Aesthetics*. Translated by Andrew Inkpin. Thousand Oaks, CA: Sage, 1997.

Wenman, Mark A. "Agonistic Pluralism and Three Archetypal Forms of Politics." *Contemporary Political Theory* 2(2) (2003): 165–86.

Wenman, Mark A. "Laclau or Mouffe? Splitting the Difference." *Philosophy & Social Criticism* 29(5) (2003): 581–606.

Williams, Jeffrey, ed. *PC Wars: Politics and Theory in the Academy*. New York: Routledge, 1994.

Wittgenstein, Ludwig. *Culture and Value*. Chicago, IL: University of Chicago Press, 1980.

Wittgenstein, Ludwig. *Philosophical Investigations*. Oxford: Blackwell, 1985.

Wittig, Monique. *The Straight Mind and Other Essays*. Boston, MA: Beacon Press, 1992.

Wolf, Ursula. *Das Tier in der Moral*. Frankfurt: Klostermann, 1990.

Wyschogrod, Edith. *Emmanuel Levinas: The Problem of Ethical Metaphysics*. The Hague: Martinus Nijhoff, 1974.

Young, Iris M. *Justice and the Politics of Difference*. Princeton, NJ: Princeton University Press, 1990.

Young, Robert. *White Mythologies: Writing History and the West*. London: Routledge, 1990.

Zabala, Santiago, ed. *Weakening Philosophy: Essays in Honour of Gianni Vattimo*. Montreal: McGill-Queen's University Press, 2007.

Zerilli, Linda M. G. *Signifying Women: Culture and Chaos in Rousseau, Burke, and Mill*. Ithaca, NY: Cornell University Press, 1994.

Žižek, Slavoj. "Against the Populist Temptation." *Critical Inquiry* 32 (2006): 551–74.

Žižek, Slavoj. "*Schlagend, aber nicht Treffend!*" *Critical Inquiry* 33 (2006): 185–211.

Zourabichvili, François. *Le Conservatisme paradoxal de Spinoza: Enfance et royauté*. Paris: Presses Universitaires de France, 2002.

Zourabichvili, François. "Deleuze et Spinoza." In *Spinoza au XXe siècle*, edited by Olivier Bloch, 237–45. Paris: Presses Universitaires de France, 1993.

Zourabichvili, François. *Spinoza, une physique de la pensée*. Paris: Presses Universitaires de France, 2002.

Zurn, Christopher. "Anthropology and Normativity: A Critique of Axel Honneth's 'Formal Conception of Ethical Life.'" *Philosophy and Social Criticism* 26(1) (2000): 115–24.

Zurn, Christopher. "Identity or Status? Struggles over 'Recognition' in Fraser, Honneth, and Taylor." *Constellations* 10(4) (2003): 519–37.

INDEX

Abbagnano, Nicola 85
Abel, Günter, *Interpretationswelten* 45
Abraham 266–7
Absolute 85, 99
actuality, ontology of 106
l'adonné 264
Adorno, Theodor W. 35, 38, 46, 88, 119, 203–4, 332
   Dialectic of Enlightenment 38
aesthetics 26, 121–3
affectivity 98
Agamben, Giorgio 180, 185, 199
Agazzi, Evandro 94
agonistic democracy 175, 179, 182–4
Alcoff, Linda 222, 228, 238
Algerian War 189
Aliotta, Antonio 98
Allen, Amy 10
   The Politics of Our Selves 132n
Alquié, Ferdinand 150–51
   Le Rationalisme de Spinoza 150
alterity 107, 120, 125
Althusser, Louis 8, 55, 59, 62, 71, 86, 88, 151, 189, 285
   Essays in Self-Criticism 151
analytic philosophy 93–4, 204, 277–9
Anderson, Joel, "The 'Third Generation' of the Frankfurt School" 130n, 131n, 136
anthropology 39, 49–54, 198
Antisera, Dario 94
Apel, Karl-Otto 88, 133

Aquinas, Thomas 84–6
Arata, Carlo 85
Arendt, Hannah 117n, 120, 129n, 141, 232n, 237
   The Origins of Totalitarianism 217
Aristotle 27, 41, 84, 86, 99
art 17–18, 46–8, 116–17, 200, 211, 321
   as "blank pastiche" 17
Aschenbach, Gerd 330
atheism 105, 149, 267, 272
attributes 159, 162
Augustine 27, 97, 267
Austin, J. L. 277, 285–6
Australasian Society for Continental Philosophy 326n
Australia 227–8n, 311–13, 321, 326
author, death of 126
autonomy 47, 133, 136, 177

Bachelard, Gaston 62, 71
Badaloni, Nicola 86
Badiou, Alain 8, 56, 67–70, 76, 185, 207, 216
   Being and Event 67–8
   Logic of Worlds 72n
   "Marque et Manque" 66
Balibar, Étienne 8, 10, 56, 71–3, 112, 331
   Écrits pour Althusser 71
   Lieux et noms de la vérité 71
   on Spinoza 151–2, 163–5
Barad, Karen 242
Barbaras, Renaud 118, 121

Barone, Francesco 94
Barthes, Roland 124, 126
  La Chambre claire 119
  Sade, Fourier, Loyola 123
  S/Z 123
Bataille, Georges 114, 126
Battersby, Christine 222, 326n
Baudrillard, Jean 7, 15, 19–24, 27, 93n
  The Consumer Society 23
  The Mirror of Production 22
  Simulations 22
beauty 27, 97
Beauvoir, Simone de 222, 230, 237, 308
becoming 102–3
Being 105, 262–3, 265
being-in-the-world 36, 114
belief
  fixation of 48
  and religious identity 256–7
Bělohradský, Václav 120
Benhabib, Seyla 46, 129, 131–4, 141, 146–7,
    222, 318
  The Claims of Culture 141
  Critique, Norm and Utopia 132, 134
  debate with Butler 138–41
  Situating the Self 133, 134
  on subjectivity 141–2
Benyovszky, Ladislav 128
Bergson, Henri 9n, 119, 212
Berlin Wall 1–2, 8, 14, 91, 226, 328
Berti, Enrico 99
  Le vie della ragione 101
Bhabha, Homi K. 187, 200
Bieri, Peter 43–4
  Das Handwerk der Freiheit 43
Biswas, Sutapa 201
black arts movement 201
Black Power movement 314
black subjectivity 187
black women 231
Blanchot, Maurice 211–13, 247n
  The Infinite Conversation 212
  The Writing of the Disaster 212
Bloch, Ernst 88, 97n
Blumenberg, Hans 37, 44, 52–3
Bobbio, Norberto 85, 89–90, 93
Bodei, Remo 93, 98
  Geometria dell passioni 97
  Logics of Delusion 97
  Ordo amoris 97
  Scomposizioni 97

We The Divided 92n
bodies 268
  and language 287–8
  postcolonial 188
  and power 238–9
  and writing 110
Bohrer, Karl Heinz 46
Bonomi, Andrea 93
Bontadini, Gustavo 84, 102
Borges, Jorge Luis, "On Exactitude in Science"
    21
Bourdieu, Pierre 298, 323
  Language and Symbolic Power 296
Braidotti, Rosi 221, 226
  life and career 311–17, 319, 331
  Thinking Differently 237
Brandom, Robert 38, 289–92, 299
  Making it Explicit 290
Butler, Judith 81, 176, 219–21, 239, 303–4
  debate with Benhabib 138–41
  Gender Trouble 240
  Giving an Account of Oneself 304
  influence of Foucault 137, 240
  interdisciplinarity 11, 228, 317
  life and career 310–17, 320–21, 331–3
  on language and communication 199, 281,
    285, 287, 303

Cacciari, Massimo 93n, 100
  L'arcipelago 96
  Dell'inizio 96
  Geo-filosofia dell'Europa 96
  Icone della legge 96
  Krisis 95–6
  The Necessary Angel 96
  Pensiero negativo e rezionalizzazione 95
Les Cahiers du Grif 232n, 320
Cahiers pour l'analyse 8, 56, 59–61, 66, 73, 76
Canadian Society for Continental Philosophy
    326n
Canguilhem, Georges 61–2, 71
capitalism 2, 26, 86, 102, 130, 333
  and colonialism 197
  and democracy 185–6
  global 16, 22–3
Caracciolo, Alberto 87
Carbonara, Cleto 98
care 41, 43, 223
Carles, Pierre, *La Sociologie est un sport de
    combat* 323
Carlini, Armando 85

Carnap, Rudolf vii
Cassirer, Ernst 35n, 53
catastrophe theory 78
Catholicism 8, 50, 83, 261
causality, structural 62
Cavarero, Adriana 100, 284
Cavell, Stanley 278, 287, 289, 297, 300–301
    Contesting Tears 301
    Disowning Knowledge 300n
    Pursuits of Happiness 300
Caygill, Howard 218, 326n
Cerisy Colloquia 327
Červenka, Miroslav
    Styl a význam 122
Césaire, Aimé 187, 193
Chaplin, Tamara, Turning on the Mind 322n
Charter 77 111, 115
Chomsky, Noam 60n, 66, 76–8
Chrétien, Jean-Louis 247, 260, 268–72
Christian Democratic Party (Italy) 83, 89
Christianity 2, 84, 87, 99, 105, 107–8, 236,
    255–6, 259–61, 266
    end of 249
    and politics 225
Chvatík, Ivan 112, 120
Chvatík, Květoslav
    Mensch und Struktur 122
    Tschekoslowakischer Strukturalismus 122
citizenship 146, 171, 176, 200, 223
civil rights movement 278
Cixous, Hélène 224, 232, 313
class 174, 186, 197, 278, 301
    struggle 91, 173
Cleaver, Eldridge 314
cloning 5, 242
Code, Lorraine 227
co-evolution 48
cognitivism 55, 80
Cohen, Paul 68
Cold War 2–3, 8, 219
Colebrook, Claire 228n, 242
Collège International de Philosophie (Ciph)
    325n
Colletti, Lucio 88n, 91n, 101
Collin, François 232, 320
Collins, Patricia Hill 229
    Black Feminist Thought 235
colonialism 3, 187, 189–91, 193
commitment 43, 48
commodification 18–19, 25
communication 135, 269, 276, 283

technology 22, 30–31
communicative action 46, 140, 280–81
communism 1, 143, 219
Communist Party (Italy) 83, 85, 89n
communitarianism 47, 136, 180
community 134, 135–6, 165, 215
compensation 49–50, 53
computerization 16, 22
consumption 18–19
concentration camps 194
concepts 63–4
    derogatory 299
confidence 136, 142
Connolly, William E. 10, 175, 179, 183–4
consciousness 30, 40–42, 62, 84n, 103, 120,
    172, 205, 250–51, 263–5
consensus 179, 181, 200
contextual determinacy 281
continental philosophy
    definition vii
    as European 328–33
    in North America 328
    Trans-Atlantic dis-connection 328
contractualism 109
contrapuntal reading (Said) 191
Cornell, Drucilla 222, 228, 236
corporeality 99, 123
correspondence theory of truth 249, 294–6
corruption 91–2
cosmopolitanism 131, 139, 146–7
creation, from nothingness (creatio ex nihilo)
    107
creolization 200
Critchley, Simon, The Ethics of Deconstruction
    219–20
critical distance, end of 19–21
critical theory 36, 87, 222, 318, 321, 333–4
    first generation 135
    second generation 129
    social and cultural context 130, 133
    third generation 129–48
Croce, Benedetto 84–5, 87, 98
cross, symbolism of 108
cultural identity 7, 297
Cultural Revolution 206
cultural studies 187–201, 318, 321, 328
culture 56n, 146, 190
    schizophrenic 18–19
Czech Republic/Czechoslovakia 8, 9,
    111–28, 174
    availability of translated philosophy 127

influence of French thought 126
after 1989 127–8
samizdat/underground publications 111, 113
"underground university" 112–13
visits from "Western" philosophers 112

Dal Lago, Alessandro 105, 106
Dal Pra, Mario 85, 101
Daly, Mary 236
Dasein 209–10, 215
Davidson, Donald 278, 292–3
on meaning 281–2
Debord, Guy, *The Society of the Spectacle* 21
decline, ontology of 105
deconstruction 109, 119, 206
development of 215
and ethics 219
as justice 266
and transgression 124
del Noce, Augusto 88
Deleuze, Gilles 5, 10, 55, 196, 199, 224, 229, 247n, 309, 313, 319, 324–5
Expressionism in Philosophy/Spinoza et la problème de l'expression 152, 155–8
"How do we Recognize Structuralism?" 77
influence on feminist philosophy 240–41, 243
on Spinoza 151–3, 155–8
Della Volpe, Galvano 86, 90n
democracy x, 165, 298
agonistic 184
deliberative 178
free-market 14
and media 92
radical 169–86
social 51
democratic legitimacy 146
Derrida, Jacques 8, 36, 55, 92, 123, 126, 189, 224, 229, 240, 329n
arrest in Prague 112
on democracy 146, 169–70, 172, 184
on ethics 206–7, 219
"The Force of Law" 321n
The Gift of Death 266–7
"How to Avoid Speaking: Denials" 265
influence 88, 109, 146
on Levinas 214–15, 255
Margins of Philosophy 118
as a media "star" 322–3
not a postmodernist 15

on Patočka 121
Positions 118
on religion 10, 247n, 264–72
Speech and Phenomena 118
"Violence and Metaphysics" 214–15, 218
Writing and Difference 118
Descartes, René 97, 112, 153, 156
Foucault on 126
desire 196–7
ontological 118
deterritorialization 196
Deutsche Zeitschrift für Philosophie 330
Deutscher, Penelope 228n
Dewey, John 88, 278–81, 289, 292
dialectics 62, 155, 159
Dick, Kirk, *Derrida* 323
différance 119, 125, 265–6
difference 7, 119, 124, 228–9, 297
feminism of 100, 318
differends, as events 29–30
diminution, ethics of 107
Diotima 99–100
diremption (*Entzweiung*) 39
discourse theory 75, 79–80, 129, 132, 237
Djebar, Assia 197
Dolly the Sheep 5, 242
Dostoevsky, Fyodor 105
Du Bois, W. E. B. 278
Dubský, Ivan 120
Dufrenne, Mikel 247n
Duhacek, Dasa 226
Duns Scotus, John 96, 156–7
Duras, Marguerite, *The Summer of 1980* 1
Dutch Republic 163
Dworkin, Andrea 224n

eccentric positionality 51
Eckhardt, Meister 96, 259
Eco, Umberto 100, 105, 107, 109
École freudienne 313
École Normale Israélite Orientale 207, 253n
École Normale Supérieure 56, 90n
economics 14, 86, 185
education 231, 298
Elliston, Frederick, *Feminism and Philosophy* 234
emancipation 52, 176
embodiment, feminist theories of 238–9
empiricism, radical 243
English, Jane, *Feminism and Philosophy* 234
Enlightenment 7, 14, 38

environmentalism 205, 327n
epistemological breaks 86
epistemology, feminist 231, 237–8
equality 184, 300
essentialism
  biological 7
  black 10
eternal recurrence 102
ethical turn 203–20
ethics
  applied 94
  of care 223
  communicative 132–4
  discourse 46, 132–3
  and feminism 223
  meta- 210
  and politics 218–19
  and religion 215–16, 266
  Spinoza on 156–7
  virtue 214
ethnicity 296, 301
  and identity 296
Europe 3, 193–4, 197, 331–3
European Commission 330
European Union (EU) 3, 226, 328
evil 253, 271
existentialism ix, 86, 103
experience 85, 116, 165
  embodied 316

Fabro, Cornelio 84
faith 267
  dogmatic 267
  and reason 84, 248–9, 272
Falcone, Giovanni 91–2
Fanon, Frantz 187–8, 190n, 192, 197
  The Wretched of the Earth 190–91
fascism 3, 331
Felman, Shoshana 224n, 287–8
feminism/feminist theory 10, 99–100, 134,
    190, 205, 278, 308
  American 224
  analytic influences 223–4
  cyborg-feminism 242
  and difference 229, 318
  ecofeminism 236
  and epistemology 237–8
  "Franco-American disconnection" 221
  and genealogy 231
  "intermediate generation" 227–30
  and legal theory 235–6

and materialism 241–2
and meaning 288
and moral philosophy 223
Muslim feminism 236
organizations 327
and philosophy 221–46, 310–11, 316–18,
    326–7, 333–5
and postmodernism 138–9
and poststructuralism 221, 223–7, 235,
    243
and psychoanalysis 236–7
radical 224–5n
second wave 221, 227, 232
spirituality 236
standpoint 234
and technologies 241–2
utopian 138
influence of Wittgenstein 302
see also gender; sexuality
Ferry, Luc 324
Feyerabend, Paul 231
Fichte, Johann 40, 104, 128
film 22, 300–301, 322
film theory 236, 321
Filosofický časopis 115, 127–8
finitude, ethics of 98–9
Fink, Eugen 97n
Finkielkraut, Alain 324
First World 194, 196
Flax, Jane 233, 236
Florence 85, 87, 101
forgiveness 212
forms, emerging 80
Foucault, Michel 5, 55, 92, 97, 98, 119, 124,
    189, 196, 309, 313
  The Archaeology of Knowledge 70n, 198
  on democracy 169, 184
  influence on third generation critical
      theorists 136–40
  Madness and Civilization 125n
  influence on feminist theory 224, 231, 240
  influence of Marx 88
  influence of Nietzsche 44
  not a postmodernist 15
  The Order of Things 125n
foundationalism 178, 290
Frank, Manfred 41–3
Frankfurt, Harry 43, 50
Frankfurt School 35–9, 87, 129, 321n, 329
Franklin, Sarah, *Off-Centre: Feminism and
    Cultural Studies* 235

Fraser, Nancy   46, 129, 131, 137, 140n, 143–7, 222, 228
  "From Discipline to Flexibilization"   138n
  on Foucault   138
  Redistribution or Recognition?   143–5
  Unruly Practices   130, 137
free will, and neuroscience   43
freedom   50, 105, 154
  ontology of   102
  spiritual   98
Frege, Gottlob   vii, 74
  Foundations of Arithmetic   63, 66
Freire, Paulo   230
Freud, Sigmund   33–4, 57, 96, 313
Fukuyama, Francis   2, 14
  The End of History and the Last Man   20
fundamentalism   184

Gadamer, Hans-Georg   35, 44, 88, 92, 277
Giacon, Carlo   84
Gallop, Jane   221, 225
Garber, Marjorie   224n
Gargani, Aldo   98, 100
  Crisi della ragione   94
  Il sapere senza fondamenti   95
Gatens, Moira   167, 228n, 239
Gehlen, Arnold   49–50, 51, 53
Geist   261
Gemelli, Agostino   84
gender   133, 190, 205, 278, 300, 316–17, 328, 333
  and identity   296
  Wittgensteinian analysis   301–2
  see also feminism
General Will   171
genetics   49
genocide   194, 205, 212
Gentile, Giovanni   84–5, 87, 98
Gentile, Marino   84, 99n
German philosophy
  classical   111
  as "continental" philosophy   33–54
Gerratana, Valentina   86
Gestalt psychology   97, 118
gesture, semantic   122–3
Geymonat, Ludovico   85–8
gift   266–7, 269
Gilligan, Carol   141, 223
Gilroy, Paul   10, 187
Gilson, Étienne   252
Giorello, Giulio   94

Given, Myth of the   289–90
givenness   263–4, 268
Givone, Sergio   95n, 97n
Glissant, Édouard   187, 197, 331
globalization   5, 16, 130, 174, 201, 205, 226n, 278
God   105, 108, 156, 248, 254, 259–60, 262, 267
  death of   99, 105, 106, 249, 261
  existence of   153
  and Good   256, 265
  Jewish   256
  and metaphysics   251–2
  as the Other   216
  and prayer   270
  as a signifier   251
  as trace   254–5
Goldman, Emma   335
good   255, 265, 314
good life   50–51, 136, 271, 332
Gordon, Colin   320
Gould, Carol   234
grammar
  generative   66, 77
  judgments of   76
Gramsci, Antonio   89, 181, 190
  Prison Notebooks   85
Grice, Paul   277
Griffin, Gabriele, *Thinking Differently*   237
Grimshaw, Jean   233
Grosz, Elisabeth   228, 239
Guattari, Félix   197, 243
Guéroult, Martial   152–3, 157n, 167
  Spinoza I and *Spinoza II*   150–51
Guha, Ranajit   187, 190
  History at the Limit of World-History   191
Gulf War   15, 23–4, 226
Guzzo, Augusto   85, 104

Habermas, Jürgen   8, 10, 88, 112, 289, 294, 296–7
  on democracy   178–9
  and the Frankfurt School   35–6, 329
  influence on third generation critical theorists   129, 131–7
  on language   276, 286–7
  The Philosophical Discourse of Modernity   137n
  on social philosophy   48
  on subjectivity   42
Hall, Stuart   10, 187–8, 190, 200

"New Ethnicities" 187
happiness 23, 52, 99
Haraway, Donna 236, 238, 242
   "A Cyborg Manifesto" 5
   "Situated Knowledges" 238
Harding, Sandra 233, 238
Hardt, Michael 180–81, 185, 199
Hecate 319
Hegel, G. W. F. 33, 88, 97, 129n, 132, 151
   on history 155–6
   The History of Philosophy 158
   influence on Honneth 135
   influence on Lyotard 25
   Phenomenology of Spirit 249–50
   The Philosophy of Right 20
   The Science of Logic 155, 158–9
   on Spinoza 158–9
   on subjectivity 58
hegemony 181–2
Heidegger, Martin 33, 88, 92, 96, 98, 109,
      111, 205, 276, 292
   Being and Time 37–8, 113, 209, 251
   influence 35, 41–2
   Kant and the Problem of Metaphysics 40
   "Letter on Humanism" 251, 262
   on modernity 36–7
   Nazism 209
   influence of Nietzsche 44
   "The Onto-theo-logical Constitution of
      Metaphysics" 251
   "The Origin of the Work of Art" 18
   on subjectivity 58
   on technology 102
   on truth and meaning 293
Hejdánek, Ladislav 112–13, 115–16
Held, Virginia 223
Heloïse complex 232
Henrich, Dieter 37, 40–44, 97n
   Denken und Selbstsein 42
Henry, Astrid 244n
Henry, Michel 10, 247, 258–60, 270–72
   The Essence of Manifestation 259–60
Herbert, Thomas *see* Pêcheux, Michel
hermeneutics 103, 104, 253
   Gadamer on 44
   influence on Italian philosophy 107–8
   and performance 276
Histoires d'Elles 319
historiography 88n, 101
history 20, 189, 198
   and colonialism 191, 193

as a metamorphosis 97
   philosophy of 114
Hobbes, Thomas 52, 90n, 97, 101
Hocquenghem, Guy 324
Höffe, Otfried 47
Hollywood films 300–301
Holocaust 205, 207–8, 212
Honneth, Axel 8, 36, 46, 129, 130n, 148, 330
   The Critique of Power 139
   on Habermas 134–7, 139–40
   on recognition 47
   Redistribution or Recognition? 143–5
   The Struggle for Recognition 135–6, 140
   on subjectivity 141–2
Horkheimer, Max 35, 88, 129n
   Dialectic of Enlightenment 38
human rights 47, 321
humanism 3, 5, 85, 137, 230
Hungarian Revolution 86
Hungary 174
Husserl, Edmund vii, 33, 88, 110–11, 119,
      205, 252, 257–60, 276–7
   Cartesian Meditations 250–51
   The Idea of Phenomenology 263
Hypatia 233
hyperreality 20, 22–3, 27
hyperstructuralism 60, 67, 79–80
Hyppolite, Jean 249

Ideal Speech Situation (Habermas) 281
idealism viii, 85, 88, 111
ideality 113–14
identity 141, 174–6, 278, 302, 315
   communal 182–3
   countersexual 241
   cultural 191
   and diversity 298–9
   evasion of 278, 296, 300
   gendered 296
   and lack 182–3
   and politics 34, 183, 225, 241
   and postcolonialism 198
   sexualized 296
ideology 2, 69–75, 80, 297
   and science 66, 71
Ideology and Consciousness 320
idolatry 261–4
imagination 71, 157
immanence 250, 260, 290
immediacy 289
imperialism 196

inadequation 265
individualism 93, 229
individuality 156–7
inferential analysis 299
inferential connections 291
inferentialism
  expressive 299
  material 291
ingenium 166
Inquiry, End of 281
institutions 222
  compensatory 53
intelligence, skeptical 15
intentionality 250
interdisciplinarity 4, 191, 236
interlocution, webs of 141, 142
interloqué 263
International Association for Philosophy and
    Literature (IAPL) 325n
interpellation, theory of 73
interpretation 109, 277, 292
  passing theory 281–2
intersubjectivity 39, 58, 98, 269
Iranian revolution 2
Irigaray, Luce 100, 224, 228–9, 232, 236, 243,
    313, 318
is–ought distinction 51
Italy 8, 83–110, 311
iterability 146
Iveković, Rada 226

Jaggar, Alison 233–4
Jaja, Donato 84n
Jakobson, Roman 121–2
James, William 298
Jameson, Frederic 15–18
  *Postmodernism, or, the Cultural Logic of Late
    Capitalism* 4, 16
Janicaud, Dominique 257–9, 268
  The Theological Turn of French Philosophy
    247, 253
Jankélévitch, Vladimir 212
Janković, Milan, *Dilo jako deni smyslu* 122–3
Japan 8, 9n
Jardine, Alice 224n, 320
Jewishness 207–8
Joas, Hans, *The Genesis of Values* 47
John Paul II, Pope 213
Johnson, Barbara 224n
Jonas, Hans 48, 51n, 52
  The Imperative of Responsibility 51

journals 233, 330
  experimental or marginal 319–21
Judaism 208, 213, 255–6
justice 47, 94, 136, 297, 308, 321
  communal 217
  cosmopolitan 146
  deconstruction as 266
  global 93, 131, 146–7
  subjects of 146

Kalivoda, Robert 122
Kant, Immanuel 195–6, 254, 262
  Critique of Judgment 26–7
  Critique of Pure Reason 248
  influence vii, 40, 56
  moral theory 132
  *Religion Within the Boundaries of Mere
    Reason* 248
  on subjectivity 57–8
  "What is Enlightenment?" 249
Karásek, Jindřich 128
Karfík, Filip 128
Karfíková, Lenka 128
Keller, Evelyn Fox 238
Kelly, Joan 237
Kersting, Wolfgang 47
Khomeini, Ayatollah 2
Kierkegaard, Søren 84, 266
  on subjectivity 58
Klíma, Ladislav 122
knowledge 190, 251
  as a commodity 14
  of the self 40
  situated 278
Kofman, Amy Z., *Derrida* 323
Kofman, Sarah 224
Kohák, Erazim 121
  *Jan Patočka: Philosophy and Selected
    Writings* 121
Kohlberg, Lawrence 141
Kojève, Alexandre 249
Korea 8
Kouba, Pavel 120, 127
  Nietzsche: Filosofická interpretace 124–5
Kripke, Saul 280
  Wittgenstein on Rules and Private Language
    280n
Krisis 95
Kristeva, Julia 189, 224, 226–7, 232, 236,
    329n
Krüger, Hans-Peter 51

Kuhn, Thomas 231
Kuki Shūzō 9n
Kunstforum International 330

La femme d'en face 319
Labriola, Antonio 84n
Lacan, Jacques 1, 8, 55, 57, 170, 184, 224,
 230, 313, 316
lack 175, 185
 causality of 63–5
 filled by hegemony 182
Laclau, Ernesto 10, 75, 81, 172, 176, 181–3,
 185–6
laicism 83, 85
language vii, 129, 165, 174, 277, 283, 332
 and action 279–80
 aesthetic and expressive qualities 46
 analytic philosophy of 93–4
 derogatory 299
 ethical 204
 and God 262
 Heidegger on 37
 and hermeneutics 44
 as performative 281–3
 plurivocity of 284–5
 as relative 281–2
 self-referential 286
 and subjectivity 41
 truth conditions of 286
 unstable 287
 unstable state 29
 violence of 198
language-game 279
langue 59, 76, 123, 283
Lauretis, Teresa de, *Technologies of Gender*
 235
L'Autre Journal 319
law, discourse theory of 129
Le Doeuff, Michèle 232
Leavis, F. R. 191
Lebenswelt 114, 116–17
Lecaldano, Eugenio 94
Lecourt, Dominique 8, 56, 70–71, 324
legal theory, feminist 235
lesbian continuum 236
lesbian theory 236
lesbianism 225
 "third sex" view 236
 see also sexual orientation
Levinas, Emmanuel 8, 36, 113, 120
 on Derrida 255

on ethics 207–20, 254–5
Existence and Existents 208
"God and Philosophy" 255
on Heidegger 208–9
influence 10, 124, 204
life 207
Otherwise than Being 208, 210, 213,
 216–17
Outside the Subject 212
on philosophy of religion 247, 250, 253–8,
 270–73
Totality and Infinity 119, 208, 211, 213–14,
 216–17, 253, 257
Lévi-Strauss, Claude 8, 55, 79–80, 189
 The Savage Mind 64
Lévy, Bernard-Henri 322
liberalism 169, 177, 219, 297, 323
Libération 308
life-worlds 46, 132, 276–7
linguistics 59–61, 109, 175, 198
literature 95, 211, 332
Lloyd, Genevieve 167, 227, 318
 The Man of Reason 227–8n, 234, 313
location, politics of 231
logic 63–4
logical behaviorism 277
logocentrism 37, 236
logos 218, 251
love 135–6, 142
Luhmann, Niklas, *Social Systems* 48
Lukács, Georg 88
Luporini, Cesare 86
Lury, Celia, *Off-Centre: Feminism and
 Cultural Studies* 235
Luxemburg, Rosa 88, 237
Lyotard, Jean-François 7, 176, 289, 313, 319,
 329n
 "Answering the Question: What is
 Postmodernism?" 25–6, 29
 critique of Marxism 25–6
 Des dispositifs pulsionnels 119
 The Differend: Phrases in Dispute 29–30,
 213, 296
 The Inhuman 119
 Libidinal Economy 25–6
 The Postmodern Condition 4, 13–14, 25,
 126, 296
 Postmodern Fables 27, 119
 on postmodernism 24–31

MacCormack, Patricia 243

Macherey, Pierre   10, 151–2
    Hegel ou Spinoza   158–9
    on Spinoza   158–60
MacIntyre, Alasdair   214
Maffettone, Sebastiano   94
Mafia   91–2, 92n
Major, Ladislav   111
    *Stati k Hegelově Fenomenologii a filosofii
        práva*   111
Majority subject   229
man
    death of   229
    dissolving of   189
Mancini, Italo   87
Mannoni, Octave   194
Marcel, Gabriel   252
Marcelli, Miroslav, *Michal Foucault alebo stat'
        ds iným*   125–6
Marconi, Diego   93, 105
Marcuse, Herbert   1, 88, 277
Margulis, Lynn   243
Mari, Giovanni, *Moderno Postmoderno*   101
Marion, Jean-Luc   10, 115, 213, 247, 250, 252,
        260–64, 268, 270, 272, 274
    Being Given   263–4
    God without Being   261, 263
    The Idol and Distance   261
Marquard, Odo   49–50
marriage, in film   300–301
Marten, Rainer   48
Martin, Fernando Fernàndez-Savater   8
Marxism   33, 88, 101–2, 111, 189–90, 220
    decline/failure of   1, 206
    and democracy   172, 176, 185
    influence on feminist philosophy   233
    influence on Italian philosophy   85–6
    influence on Lyotard   25–6
    influence of Spinoza   151, 153
    Italian   83, 85, 88–9
    and performance   276–7
    and psychoanalysis   62
master–slave dialectic   249
Masullo, Aldo   93n, 98
material phases, transitions between   78
materialism   ix, 85–6, 88
    bodily   238
    and feminism   241–2
mathematics   75, 77, 80
Matheron, Alexandre   151–5
    Individu et communauté chez Spinoza
        152–3

matter, as a self-organizing principle   242
matter-realism   241–3
May 1968   130, 206, 324
McCarthy, Thomas, *Ideals and Illusions*   132n
McDowell, John   289, 294
McKinnon, Catharine   224n
Mead, George Herbert   135
    Mind, Self and Society   283–4
meaning   100
    consensus view   280, 293–4
    and contexts   281
    Frege on   66
    hermeneutical account   44–5
    materialist theory   73
    performative account   280–83
    plurivocity of   284–5
    and reality   45
    relational view   283
    shared   281–2
    unstable   281–2, 287
mechanics   71
media   14, 22–3, 92, 200, 308, 321
Medina, José   11, 303–4
    Speaking from Elsewhere   283n, 285n, 302n,
        303
Meillassoux, Quentin, *After Finitude*   216
Melchiorre, Virgilio   103
melodrama   301
Memmi, Albert   194–5
Menke, Christoph   46
Mercer, Kobena   188
Merleau-Ponty, Maurice   45, 313
    Le Visible et l'invisible   119
Mernissi, Fatima   236
messianic   264–8
metaphysics   297
    classical   103
    history of   37, 96
    nostalgic   106
    overcoming   37
    of presence   172
metastructure   68
Metropoli   91n
Michálek, Jiří   120
MicroMega   319
Milan Women's Bookstore Collective,
        Sexual Difference   223n
Miller, Jacques-Alain   56, 68–9, 76, 78–9
    "Action de la structure"   59–62
    "Matrice"   64–5
    "La Suture"   63–4

Mills, Charles, *The Racial Contract* 279n
Milner, Jean-Claude 56, 60n, 68–9, 76
 Le Périple structural 60, 61n, 65
Mitchell, Juliet 236
Mitsein 210, 215
Mitterand, François 2, 225, 323
modernism 27–8
modernity 36, 50, 100, 193
 crisis of x, 38
 defense of 101–3
 and postmodernity 100–103
modesty 106–7
Mohanty, Chandra 235
Montaigne, Michel de 27, 53, 119
Montefiore, Alan 112, 326n
morality, discourse theory of 129
Moravia, Sergio 94
Moreau, Pierre-François 152, 165–6
 Spinoza: L'Expérience et l'éternité 165–6
Mori, Maurizio 94
Moro, Aldo 89–90
morphology 49, 80
Mouffe, Chantal 10, 172, 179, 182–6
movement 114, 117
Mudimbe, V. Y. 198
Mukařovský, Jan 121–3
Müller-Lauter, Wolfgang 44
Muraro, Luisa 100
murder 211
Myth of the Given 289–90

Nancy, Jean-Luc 215
narrative 141, 176
Natoli, Salvatore 98–9
naturalism 288
Nazism 35, 205, 207, 209, 212, 217
 as colonialism 193–4
necessity, ontology of 102
negative theology 247n, 262, 264–5
negative thought 96, 106, 113–14
Negri, Antonio 10, 90–91, 151–2, 164, 185,
 199
 on democracy 180–81
 The Savage Anomaly 160, 162
 on Spinoza 160–62
Němec, Jiří 120
neopaganism 99
neo-Parmenideanism 102
Neoplatonism 108
neopositivism 87, 94n
neorationalism 76

Neubauer, Zdeněk 112, 116
Newton, Isaac 71
Nicholson, Linda, *Feminism/Postmodernism*
 235
Nietzsche, Friedrich 33, 88, 92, 96, 98, 102,
 120, 125, 184, 249–50
 influence on Foucault 44
 influence on German philosophy 43
 Untimely Meditations 113
nihilism 96, 102, 107, 205
Nishida Kitaro 9n
Nishitani Keiji 9n
Nobel Peace Prize 1–3
Noi Donne 319
nonobjectivity 115
normativity 289, 300–301
Norris, Christopher, *Uncritical Theory* 24
nothingness 107–8
Nouveaux Philosophes 322–4
Novotný, Karel 128
Nussbaum, Martha 51, 223

objectivity 95, 115–16
object-relations theory 237
Occhetto, Achille 91n
OIKOYMENH 113, 127
Olgiati, Francesco 84
ontology 57, 76, 102, 105–6
organic intellectual 89
otherness 190–92, 198, 206, 254–5
 denial of 331
 and ethics 210–11
 and God 216
 non-human 242, 244

Paci, Enzo 85, 87–8
Padovani, Umberto 84, 90n
Padua tradition 86
Palek, Karel 113
pantheism 149, 161
Papic, Zarana 226
parenting 51
Pareyson, Luigi 87, 96n, 97n, 109
 Essere libertà ambiguità 105
 Verità e interpretazione 104
Parisi, Luciana 243
Parrini, Paolo 94
participation, parity of 144–6, 179
Partito Democratico della Sinistra (PDS)
 91n
passion 97, 99

Pateman, Carol   228n
Patočka, Jan   111, 127, 266
    archive   120–21
    Heretical Essays in the Philosophy of History
        114, 117
    on phenomenology   113–21
    Přirozený svet jako filosofický problém   120
    Přirozený svět jako politický problém   120
    tradition of seminars   112
    translations   120
    "Wars of the Twentieth Century and the
        Twentieth Century as War"   114
Pechar, Jiří   126
Pêcheux, Michel   56, 73–5
Peirce, Charles Sanders   48, 88, 109, 280–81,
    289
Penelope   319
pensiero debole   103–5
Il pensiero debole (Vattimo and Rovatti)   105
Pera, Marcello   94
perception   251
performative turn   275–305
performative utterances   285
performativity, and the body   288
Perniola, Mario   92–3
Perone, Ugo   93n
Perpich, Diane   284
perspectivism   44–6, 124
Pešek, Jiří   111–12, 127
Petitot, Jean   56, 76–81
    Morphogénèse due Sens   76
Petříček, Miroslav   116, 118–19, 127
    The Majesty of Law   119
    "Mukařovský and Deconstruction"   123–4
    as a translator   126
    Úvod do (současné) filosofie   119
phallo-logocentrism   229–30, 242–3
phenomenology   85
    accused of fideism   216
    asubjective   114, 119
    Czech   113
    influence of religion   247–59, 268–71
    Italian   86
    and performance   276–7
    responsive   45
philosopher-kings   93
philosophy
    history of   44, 209
    in the media   322–3
    new kinds of practice   307–23
    organizations   325–7

outside its bounds   308
    purpose and role of   308–10, 314–18,
        322–3, 332–5
    self-taught   318
    traditions   311–13
    trivializing of   324
    underground   113, 115
    under-representation of women   234
phonemes   77–8
phonetic spaces   78
Pinc, Zdeněk   127
Plato   37, 265, 314
    Republic   315
Platonism, negative   113–14, 115n
Plessner, Helmuth   51
Plumwood, Val   236
pluralism   93, 175
poetics   71, 122
poetry   121–2
political activism   91–2, 308, 310–11, 324
political systems, self-regulating   154
political theory   129, 218
Politzer, Georges, *Critique des fondements de
    la psychologie*   57
Popper, Karl   94, 113
post-analytic philosophy   278–9, 288–301
post-Christianity   99
postcolonial studies   187–201, 328
postcolonialism   3–4, 205, 229, 234–5, 244
postmodernism   7, 100, 206
    Baudrillard on   19–24
    essence of   31
    and feminism   138–9
    opponents of   101–3
    origins   14–15
poststructuralism   x, 80
    critiques of   137–9
    critiques of Stalinism   2
    and democracy   169–77
    as European   328–33
    and feminism   221, 223–7, 235, 243
    and language   174
    legacy   9, 309–10
    and political activism   323–4
postwar period   35
power   196–7
    Foucault on   137–40
    Habermas on   131–2
    spreading   298
pragmatism   47–8, 85, 87–8, 298
    and performance   277–8, 283

Prague Linguistic Circle 121–2
praxis 276, 330
prayer 265, 269–70
premodern traditions 49
Preti, Giulio 85, 88
production, aesthetics of 17
proletariat 16, 135
psychoanalysis 316
  and feminism 236–7
  and Marxism 62
  and structuralism 56–7
publishing 127–8, 318
  underground 113
Putnam, Hilary 278, 289
  Reason, Truth, and History 281, 295n
  on truth and meaning 295–6

queer theory 236, 240, 302
questioning 212
Questions féministes 308, 319
Quine, W. V. O. 34, 278, 289–90
  "Two Dogmas of Empiricism" 289

race 187–201, 205, 222, 228, 230, 234–5, 244,
    278, 296, 301
racism 7, 190, 193, 278, 308
Radcliffe Richards, Janet, *The Skeptical
    Feminist* 223n
Radical Philosophy 319
Radical Philosophy Association 327n
radicalism 170, 175
radio 322–3
rationality 95, 97, 99, 165, 177
  discursive conception of 133
  postmodern abandonment of 101
  scientific 7
Rawls, John 47, 177, 314
Reagan, Ronald 2, 14, 173, 206, 225, 323
reality, "murder of" 20
reason 277
  classical 95, 101
  crisis of 96
  dialectical 91n
  and faith 84
  and reality 21
  transcendent 138
recognition 47, 143–5, 284
Red Brigades 89–91
redistribution 144–5
reflexivity 283
Refractory Girl 320

religion 83, 141, 208, 213, 247–74
Renaut, Alain 324
representation 188, 291, 293, 296
  political 146
responsibility 92, 210, 291, 302, 308
  echoing 303–4
Rezek, Petr 112, 116–17, 127
  Filosofie a politika kýče 116
  Jan Patočka a věc fenomenologie 116
  Tělo, věc a skutečnost v současném umění
    116–17
Rich, Adrienne 231
  Blood, Bread and Poetry 236
  Of Lies, Secrets and Silence 236
  Of Woman Born 236
Ricoeur, Paul 10, 59, 88, 103, 112, 189,
    213–14, 274, 277
  Fallible Man 253
  Freedom and Nature 253
  Oneself as Another 214
  on philosophy of religion 251–3
  "Pocta Janu Patočkovi" 117n
  The Symbolism of Evil 253
  Time and Narrative 119, 252
rights 135, 142, 172, 176, 178, 278
Risorgimento 83, 88
Ritter, Joachim 35, 35n, 39
Ritter School 35, 39
  second generation 49–51
Rivista di Filosofia 101
Romanticism 104, 149, 276
Rorty, Richard 92, 112, 289–93, 297
Rose, Gillian 216
Rossi, Paulo 85, 100
  *Paragone degli ingegni moderni e
    postmoderni* 101
Rousseau, Jean-Jacques 126
  on democracy 171–2, 185
Rovatti, Pier Aldo 199
  Il pensiero debole 105
  L'elogio del pudore 106
  L'esercizio del silenzio 106–7
Rovighi, Sofia Vanni 87
Ruggenini, Mario 107
Ryle, Gilbert 277

sacrifice 266–7
Sagnier, Eugenio Trías 8
Said, Edward 191, 224
salvation, ethics of 98
samizdat publications 113

Santambrogio, Marco 93
Sartre, Jean-Paul 1, 58, 88, 190, 277, 308
  Morts sans sépulture 203–4
saturated phenomenon 115, 261
Saussure, Ferdinand de 56, 58–9, 61, 64–5,
  75
Schelling, Friedrich 96, 105, 119
Scheman, Naomi 302
Schmid, Wilhelm 330
Schmitt, Carl 90n, 183
Sciacca, Michele Federico 85, 92n
science 56, 62, 66, 70–71, 85, 231, 238
sculpture 117–18
Second World War 83, 85, 87, 205
secularization 52
Seel, Martin 46, 47
self-acquaintance 52
self-awareness 40–41
self-determination 38
self-esteem 136, 142
self-presentation 29
self-preservation 52–3
self-regulation 154
self-respect 136, 142
Sellars, Wilfrid 278, 289–93
  "Empiricism and the Philosophy of Mind"
    289
semantic gesture 122–3
semantics 109, 281
semiology 123
semiotics 75, 109, 280–83
Šerý, Ladislav 126
Severino, Emanuele 88, 98, 102, 107
sex wars 224n, 318
sexual orientation 228, 278
sexuality 100, 205, 240, 243, 321
  and feminist theory 240–42
  and identity 296
  Wittgensteinian analysis 301–2
shadow zone 107
Shoah 194, 208, 212
signifier 174, 182
  autonomy of 125
  logic of 63–4, 66, 69, 75, 80
signs 23, 61, 73, 109–10, 283
  differential nature of 65
  ontology of 80
Signs: A Journal of Women in Culture and
  Society 237, 319
Simon, Josef 45
simulacra 93

simulation, postmodern 21
Sini, Carlo 107, 109–10
Sloterdijk, Peter 48–9, 322
Sobotka, Milan 111, 127
  Man and Work in German Philosophy
    111–12
social constructivism 231, 240
social contract 141, 153–5
social philosophy 46–9
social spheres 47
socialism 173, 308
Socialisme ou Barbarie 25–6
Socialist Party (Italy) 83
Society for European Philosophy 326n
Society for Phenomenology and Existential
  Philosophy (SPEP) 325–6n
sociology ix, 189, 198
Sokol, Jan 127
solidarity 136–7, 142
Solzhenitsyn, Alexander, *Gulag Archipelago*
  2
Sorcières 319
Soviet Union, end of 1, 130, 173–4
Spaemann, Robert 49–50, 52
speech 59, 280–81
  embodied 287–8
  self-referentiality 286
Spelman, Elizabeth 238
Spengler, Oswald, *The Decline of the West*
  49
Spinoza, Benedict de (Baruch) 97, 239
  Ethics 150, 156–63, 165
  influence 149–68
  Tractatus Politicus 151, 153–5, 164–5
  Tractatus Theologico-Politicus 151, 153,
    156–7, 160–64, 166
Spirit 84n
Spivak, Gayatri 10, 187, 195, 199, 224n,
  225, 320
  "Can the Subaltern Speak?" 241
  A Critique of Postcolonial Reason 195–7
  Death of a Discipline 3, 242
  In Other Worlds 235
Stacey, Jackie, *Off-Centre: Feminism and
  Cultural Studies* 235
Stalin, Josef 2, 206
Stanton, Domna 221n, 224n, 328n
state, as a collective individual 164
status 143
Stegmaier, Werner 45
Stengers, Isabelle 238

Stimpson, Katharina   224n, 319
structuralism
   Czech   113, 121–5
   legacy   55–81
   and Marxism   122
   problems of   79
   and psychoanalysis   56–7
   on subjectivity   56–63
structure   81
   action of   78–9
subaltern   189–92, 196–9
Subaltern Studies Group   190
subject
   death of (death of man)   16, 138
   loss of   115
subjectivity   64–81, 99, 116, 175–6, 229, 303
   Adorno on   38
   and autonomy   96
   and domination   38
   embodied in language and action   277
   gendered   138
   genesis of   97
   Heidegger on   37–8
   and language   199
   linguistic theory   41
   materialist theory   73
   paradox of   75
   and passivity   98
   postmodern   21
   and race   187
   and rights   178
   Ritter School on   40–44
   self-centered   95
   as socially constructed   231
   structuralist account   56–63
   in third generation critical theory   141–3
   women's   100
subject–object relations   115
suffering   260, 270–71, 308
   and joy   270
suicide   266–7
Sus, Oleg   122
symbolic performance   284
syntagms   79
systems, self-referential   48

Talmud   208
Tanabe Hajime   9n
Tanner Lectures   146
Tarski, Alfred   293n, 295
Taussig, Michael   193

Taylor, Astra   322
Taylor, Charles   38, 136, 142, 276
technologies   19–21, 92, 102, 205, 241
   and feminism   241–2
television   200, 322–3
temporality, female   227
Les Temps modernes   308
terrorism   15, 89, 91–2
   and poststructuralism   324
text, "nothing outside"   124
Texte zur Kunst   330
Thatcher, Margaret   2, 5, 14, 173, 200, 206,
      323
Thein, Karel   128
theology   96, 115, 247
   negative   247n
theories, and practices   110
"theory wars"   321
Theunissen, Michael   48, 52
thinking   251
Third World   194, 196
Thom, René   78
Thomä, Dieter   8
Thomassen, Lasse   10
threats   284
time, scientific   212
Tito, General   1
Togliatti, Palmiro   86
topology   108
Tosaka Jun   9n
Touraine, Alain   2
trace   65n
tradition   101
Trakl, Georg   96
Trans-Atlantic dis-connection   328
transcendence   123, 181, 243
transgression   123–4, 126
transition phases   78–9
traveling theories   224
Tronti, Mario   90–91
Tronto, Joan   223
truth   14, 96, 106, 259, 292n
   absolute   72n
   deflationary theory   292–3
   and interpretation   104
   as multiple   108
   objective   106, 294
   as a process   72
   realist view   295
   social practice approach   292–3
   theory of   249, 294–6

truth claims 332
Tuana, Nancy 234
Tugendhat, Ernst 37, 112
   Egozentriztät und Mystik 42
   Self-Consciousness and Self-Determination 34
   on subjectivity 41–3
Turin School 90n, 101
Turing Machine 80

Überwindung 106
unconscious, subject of 64
United Nations 91–2
United States, migration to xi
universalism 132–4
Università del Sacro Cuore, Milan 86, 87, 102
Università Statale, Milan 86
University of Paris VIII–Vincennes 90n, 313, 325
utility 154

Van Gogh, Vincent 18
Vattimo, Gianni 89, 93n, 100, 199
   The Adventure of Difference 100
   Al di là del soggetto 105
   The End of Modernity 100, 105
   Il pensiero debole 105
Veca, Salvatore 93
Verges, François 194–5
Verona, University of 99–100
Vetterling-Braggin, Mary, *Feminism and Philosophy* 234
Viano, Carlo Augusto 85, 100–101
   Va' pensiero 101
Vico, Giovanni Battista 87, 97, 101
Vietnam War 173
violence 89, 249, 260, 270–71
   of colonialism 192–3
Virno, Paulo 91
Vitiello, Vincenzo 107–8
Vodička, Felix 122
Volpi, Franco 99

Vries, Simon de 165

Walcott, Derek 188
Waldenfels, Bernhard 45, 48
wars 226; *see also* Second World War
Wartofsky, Marx, *Women and Philosophy* 234
Weed, Elizabeth 320
Weil, Simone 236
Welsch, Wolfgang 46
West, Cornel 322
white mythologies 189
will to power 37, 44, 102, 107
Winfrey, Oprah 4
Winnicott, Donald 142
witnessing 212
Wittgenstein (film) 322
Wittgenstein, Ludwig 37, 88, 92, 96, 277, 278–81, 289, 292–5
   influence on theories gender and sexuality 301–2
   Philosophical Investigations 126, 290
Wittig, Monique 236
Wolf, Ursula 47
Wollstonecraft, Mary 237
woman-centered approaches 231–2
women's movements 99n, 100, 278
women's studies 99n, 226, 237, 316–18
Woolf, Virginia 231
workers' organizations 91
writing 110

xenophobia 174

Yale School 224n, 310–11
Young, Iris Marion 222, 234
Yugoslav War 226

Zamboni, Chiara 100
zero 64–7
Žižek, Slavoj 10, 81, 185–6, 217
Znoj, Milan 112, 128
Zumr, Josef 122

DH

190
AFT